CRIMINOLOGY

Eighth Edition

Freda Adler

University of Pennsylvania

Gerhard O. W. Mueller

Rutgers University

William S. Laufer

University of Pennsylvania

CRIMINOLOGY, EIGHTH EDITION

Published by McGraw-Hill, a business unit of The McGraw-Hill Companies, Inc., 1221 Avenue of the Americas, New York, NY, 10020. Copyright © 2013 by The McGraw-Hill Companies, Inc. All rights reserved. Printed in the United States of America. Previous editions © 2010, 2007, and 2004. No part of this publication may be reproduced or distributed in any form or by any means, or stored in a database or retrieval system, without the prior written consent of The McGraw-Hill Companies, Inc., including, but not limited to, in any network or other electronic storage or transmission, or broadcast for distance learning.

Some ancillaries, including electronic and print components, may not be available to customers outside the United States.

This book is printed on acid-free paper.

1 2 3 4 5 6 7 8 9 0 QDB/QDB 1 0 9 8 7 6 5 4 3 2

ISBN 978-0-07-8026423
MHID 0-07-8026423

Senior Vice President, Products & Markets: *Kurt L. Strand*
Vice President, General Manager, Products & Markets: *Michael Ryan*
Vice President, Content Production & Technology Services: *Kimberly Meriwether David*
Managing Director: *Gina Boedecker*
Executive Director of Development: *Lisa Pinto*
Senior Sponsoring Editor: *William Minick*
Developmental Editor: *Amy Mittelman*
Editorial Coordinator: *Adina Lonn*
Marketing Specialist: *Alexandra Schultz*
Director, Content Production: *Terri Schiesl*
Lead Project Manager: *Jane Mohr*
Buyer: *Sandy Ludovissy*
Cover Designer: *Studio Montage, St. Louis, MO.*
Cover Image: *©Jasper James*
Media Project Manager: *Sridevi Palani*
Typeface: *9.5/11 Palatino LT STD Roman*
Compositor: *Laserwords Private Limited*
Printer: *Quad/Graphics*

All credits appearing on page or at the end of the book are considered to be an extension of the copyright page.

Library of Congress Cataloging-in-Publication Data

Adler, Freda.
   Criminology / Freda Adler, Gerhard O.W. Mueller, William S. Laufer. —
8th ed.
     p. cm.
   ISBN 978-0-07-802642-3 (alk. paper)
   1. Criminology. I. Mueller, Gerhard O. W. II. Laufer, William S. III. Title.
   HV6025.A35 2013
   364—dc23

                                                           2012021845

The Internet addresses listed in the text were accurate at the time of publication. The inclusion of a website does not indicate an endorsement by the authors or McGraw-Hill, and McGraw-Hill does not guarantee the accuracy of the information presented at these sites.

About the Authors

FREDA ADLER is Visiting Professor, and Director, Master of Science Program in Criminology, University of Pennsylvania, and Emeritus Distinguished Professor of Criminal Justice at Rutgers University, School of Criminal Justice. She received her B.A. in sociology, her M.A. in criminology, and her Ph.D. in sociology from the University of Pennsylvania. Dr. Adler began her career in criminal justice as an evaluator of drug and alcohol treatment programs for federal and state governments. She has been teaching since 1968; her subjects include criminal justice, criminology, comparative criminal justice systems, statistics, and research methods. She has served as criminal justice advisor to the United Nations, as well as to federal, state, and foreign governments. Dr. Adler's published works include 15 books as author or coauthor, 10 books as editor or coeditor, and over 80 journal articles. She has served on the editorial boards of the *Journal of Criminal Justice, Criminology,* and the *Journal of Research on Crime and Delinquency.* Dr. Adler is editorial consultant to the *Journal of Criminal Law and Criminology* and is coeditor of *Advances in Criminological Theory.* She has also served as president of the American Society of Criminology (1994–1995).

GERHARD O. W. MUELLER is the late Distinguished Professor of Criminal Justice at Rutgers University, School of Criminal Justice. After earning his J.D. degree from the University of Chicago, he went on to receive a master of laws degree from Columbia University. He was awarded the degree of Dr. Jur. h. c. by the University of Uppsala, Sweden. His career in criminal justice began in 1945, when he served as a chief petty officer in the British Military government Water Police, where he commanded a Coast Guard cutter. His teaching in criminal justice, begun in l953, was partially interrupted between 1974 and l982 when, as Chief of the United Nations Crime Prevention and Criminal Justice Branch, he was responsible for all of the United Nations' programs dealing with problems of crime and justice worldwide. He continued his service to the United Nations as chair ad interim of the Board of the International Scientific and Professional Advisory Council of the United Nations Crime Prevention and Criminal Justice Programme. Professor Mueller was a member of the faculties of law at the University of Washington, West Virginia University, New York University, and the National Judicial College, with visiting appointments and lectureships at universities and institutes in the Americas, western and eastern Europe, Africa, Asia, and Australia. He was the author of some 50 authored or edited books and 270 scholarly articles.

WILLIAM S. LAUFER is the Julian Aresty Professor at the Wharton School of the University of Pennsylvania, where he is Professor of Legal Studies and Business Ethics, Sociology, and Criminology. Dr. Laufer, former chair of the Department of Criminology at Penn, received his B.A. in social and behavioral sciences at Johns Hopkins University, his J.D. at Northeastern University School of Law, and his Ph.D. at Rutgers University, School of Criminal Justice. Dr. Laufer's research has appeared in law reviews and a wide range of criminal justice, legal, and psychology journals, including *Journal of Research in Crime and Delinquency, American Journal of Criminal Law, Law and Human Behavior, Journal of Personality and Social Psychology,* and *Business Ethics Quarterly.* His most recent book is *Corporate Bodies and Guilty Minds: The Failure of Corporate Criminal Liability* (University of Chicago Press). Dr. Laufer is coeditor of the *Handbook of Psychology and Law; Personality, Moral Development and Criminal Behavior;* and *Crime, Values and Religion.* He is series coeditor with Freda Adler of *Advances in Criminological Theory.*

To: *David S., Daniel A., Julia A., Noah A., Zoe A., Hannah M., Nicolai A., John J., Lauren E., Stephen W., Anna L., Erik D., Johann D., Sasha K., Misha K.*

Brief Contents

*Part 4, Chapters 15–18, are available only at the Instructor Edition of the Online Learning Center: **www.mhhe.com/adlercrim8e.**

Contents

3   Schools of Thought throughout History   57

*Part 4, Chapters 15–18, are available only at the Instructor Edition of the Online Learning Center: **www.mhhe.com/adlercrim8e**.

List of Boxes

Preface

Criminology is a young discipline. In fact, the term "criminology" is only a little more than a century old. But in this brief time, criminology has emerged as an important social and behavioral science devoted to the study of crime and criminal behavior, and the society's response to both. Criminology fosters theoretical debates, contributes ideas and constructs, develops and explores new research methodologies, and suggests policies and solutions to a wide range of crime problems that dramatically affect the lives of countless people in the United States and around the world. Problems as vital and urgent as those addressed in this book are challenging, exciting, and, at the same time, disturbing and tragic. Moreover, these problems are immediately relevant to all of our lives. This is especially true today, when crimes here and abroad touch so many lives, in so many ways.

Our goal with this book has been, and remains, to discuss these problems, their origins, and their possible solutions in a clear, practical, straightforward fashion that brings the material to life for students. We invite faculty and students alike to join the authors' in traveling along criminology's path, exploring its expanding boundaries, and mapping out its future.

THE EIGHTH EDITION

In the seven preceding editions of this text, we sought to prepare students of criminology to appreciate the contemporary problems with which criminology is concerned and to anticipate those problems society would have to face as we progress in the twenty-first century. It is now time to face the new century's crime problems as we simultaneously continue to work on solutions to old problems. Because of the forward-looking orientation of previous editions of *Criminology* and the respect and acceptance those editions have enjoyed, we maintain the book's established structure and approach with modest but significant changes.

In prior editions we spent considerable time with the emergence of the crime of terrorism in the field of criminology, highlighting the threat of domestic terrorism as a catalyst of change in the criminal justice system. No single crime was ever poised to share and reshape the field of criminology like the crime of terrorism. It remains unclear that this has happened or should happen. There is no doubt, however, that terrorism will continue to be studied intensely by criminologists around the world, and that such research will result in theoretically-rich and policy-relevant work. To that end, we continue to incorporate the latest findings from criminological research into terrorism.

The continued spate of corporate malfeasance represents another potential challenge to our field. We continue to expand our coverage of white-collar and corporate crimes, including significant coverage of some of the criminological antecedents of the credit crisis in the United States. Like crimes of terrorism, white-collar and corporate offenses have been on the periphery of the field of criminology—but no longer.

As in prior revisions, we have vigorously researched, refined, and updated every chapter of the text—not only to maintain this edition's scholarly integrity, but also to ensure its relevance. In addition to updating the research presented in every chapter, we expanded coverage of the most critical issues facing the field, and how advances in sister disciplines, including the neurosciences, inform our research.

Inasmuch as developments in criminology influence and are influenced by media reports of national and local significance, students will find discussion and analysis of recent major current events.

As in previous editions, we have endeavored not only to reflect developments and changes, but also anticipate them on the basis of the latest criminological data. After all, those who study criminology with the eighth edition must be ready to address and resolve new criminological problems of tomorrow, when they are decision makers, researchers, faculty, and policy analysts. The aim with this edition, however, remains the same as it was with the first edition more than twenty years ago: to arrive at a future as free from crime as possible.

ORGANIZATION

The eighth edition of Criminology continues with the revised format of our book. The printed book contains Chapters 1–14, covering criminology. The remaining criminal justice chapters (Chapters 15–18) are available solely at the instructor edition of our book-specific Online Learning Center (**www.mhhe.rnm/adlercrim8e**). For schools that retain the traditional criminology course, which includes criminological coverage of criminal justice, our text and the online chapters provide the ideal resource.

Part 1, "Understanding Criminology," presents an overview of criminology—now made more exciting with integrated coverage of terrorism and related crimes—and describes the vast horizon of this science. It explains what crime is and techniques for measuring the amount and characteristics of crime and criminals. It also traces the history of criminological thought through the era that witnessed the formation of the major schools of criminology: classicism and positivism (eighteenth and nineteenth centuries).

Part 2, "Explanations of Crime and Criminal Behavior," includes explanations of crime and criminal behavior based on the various theories developed in the twentieth century. Among the subjects covered are theories that offer biological, neurocriminological, psychological, sociological, sociopolitical, and integrated explanations. Coverage of research by radical, socialist, and feminist criminologists has been updated. Theories that discuss why offenders choose to commit one offense rather than another at a given time and place are also covered in Part 2.

Part 3, "Types of Crimes," covers the various types of crimes from a legal and sociological perspective. The familiar street crimes, such as homicide and robbery, are assessed, as are criminal activities such as white-collar and corporate crime—so much in the spotlight these days—as well as technology-dependent crimes that have been highlighted by researchers only in recent years.

Part 4, "A Criminological Approach to the Criminal Justice System" (available only online), includes an explanation of the component parts and functioning of the system. It explains contemporary criminological research on how the people who run the criminal justice system operate it, the decision-making processes of all participants, and the interaction of all the system components.

PEDAGOGICAL AIDS

Working together, the authors and the editors developed a format for the text that supports the goal of achieving a readable, practical, and attractive text. In addition to the changes already mentioned, we include plentiful, current photographs to make the book even more approachable. Redesigned and carefully updated tables and figures highlight and amplify the text. Chapter outlines, lists of key terms, chapter review sections, and a comprehensive end-of-book glossary all help students master the material. Always striving to help students see the relevance of criminology in

their lives, we also updated a number of the features to this edition:

- **New *Theory Connects* marginal inserts.** These notes in the text margins correlate the intensely applied material in Part 3 of the text ("Types of Crimes") with the heavily theoretical material in Part 2 ("Explanations of Crime"), giving students much-needed cross-reference material and posing critical-thinking questions that will help them truly process what they are reading.

- **New *Criminology & Public Policy* exercises.** These end-of-chapter activities challenge students to explore policy issues related to criminology.

- *Crime Surfing.* These particularly interesting web addresses accompanied by mini-exercises allow students to explore chapter topics further.

- *Did You Know?* These surprising factual realities provide eye-opening information about chapter topics.

- *Theory Informs Policy.* These brief sections in theory chapters demonstrate how problems identified by criminologists have led to practical solutions.

Our "box" program continues to be updated and improved. In the boxes, we highlight significant criminological issues that deserve special attention. All chapters have a number of boxes that enhance and highlight the text—including boxes that raise debatable issues, criminological concerns, and reveal just how the field of criminological touches every part of the world.

SUPPLEMENTS PACKAGE

Visit our Online Learning Center at **www.mhhe .com/adlercrim8e** for robust student and instructor resources.

For the Student

Our book-specific Online Learning Center features unique Interactive Modules that allow students to explore some of the hottest topics in criminal justice today, including terrorism, white-collar crime, and the drug trade. Multiple-choice quizzes and Internet exercises allow students to delve deeper into topics within each chapter.

For the Instructor

The password-protected instructor portion of the Online Learning Center includes Chapters 15–18 on the criminal justice system. These chapters can be distributed to your students. The site also includes the instructor's manual, a comprehensive computerized test bank, and PowerPoint lecture slides. Other dynamic instructor resources include the following:

 With the CourseSmart eTextbook version of this title, students can save up to 50% off the cost of a print book, reduce their impact on the environment, and access powerful web tools for learning. Faculty can also review and compare the full text online without having to wait for a print desk copy. CourseSmart is an online eTextbook, which means users need to be connected to the Internet in order to access it. Students can also print sections of the book for maximum portability. For further details contact your sales representative or go to **www.coursesmart.com**.

Tegrity Campus is a service that makes class time available all the time by automatically capturing every lecture in a searchable format for students to review when they study and complete assignments. With a simple one-click start-and-stop process, you can capture all computer screens and corresponding audio. Students can replay any part of any class with easy-to-use browser-based viewing on a PC or Mac.

Educators know that the more students can see, hear, and experience class resources, the better they learn. With Tegrity Campus, students quickly recall key moments by using Tegrity Campus's unique search feature, which helps students efficiently find what they need when they need it across an entire semester of class recordings. Help turn all your students' study time into learning moments immediately supported by your lectures.

To learn more about Tegrity Campus, watch a 2-minute Flash demo at **http://tegritycampus.mhhe.com**.

- McGraw-Hill's online courses provide interactive digital content and activities aligned with learning objectives that work with most learning management systems. Designed to be used in conjunction with a textbook, McGraw-Hill's online course tools combine visual, auditory, and interactive elements to encourage all types of learners to connect with and retain knowledge. Course content includes animation, graphics, streaming video, and interactive activities to enliven the content and motivate the learner. Specifically, for the area of criminal justice, the McGraw-Hill online course content tools were developed around content areas that have been established by the Academy of Criminal Justice Sciences' Minimum Standards of Criminal Justice Education. Preview the criminal justice course content and more at **www.OnlineLearning.com**.

- *NBC News Lecture Launcher DVD.* This unique video features several brief clips from *NBC News* that can be used to jumpstart lectures in the most exciting, relevant ways.

- *Full-Length Videotapes.* A wide variety of videotapes from the Films for the Humanities and Social Sciences series is available to adopters of the text.

- *Course Management Systems.* Whether you use WebCT, Blackboard, e-College, or another course management system, McGraw-Hill will provide you with a *Criminology* cartridge that enables you either to conduct your course entirely online or to supplement your lectures with online material.

- *Primis Online.* This unique database publishing system allows instructors to create their own custom text from material in *Criminology* or elsewhere and deliver that text to students electronically as an e-book or in print format via the bookstore.

Please contact your local McGraw-Hill representative for more information on any of the above supplements.

IN APPRECIATION

We greatly acknowledge the assistance and support of a number of dedicated professionals. At Rutgers University, the librarian of the N.C.C.D. Criminal Justice Collection, Phyllis Schultze, has been most helpful in patiently tracking and tracing sources. We thank Professor Sesha Kethineni (Illinois State University) for her tireless assistance on the first edition, Deborah Leiter-Walker for her help on the second, Kerry Dalip and Nhung Tran (University of Pennsylvania) for their assistance on the fourth, Reagan Daly and Ashish Jatia (University of Pennsylvania) for their work on the sixth edition, and Melissa Meltzer (University of Pennsylvania) for her work on the seventh edition. Gratitude is also owed to the many former and current Rutgers University students who have valiantly contributed their labors to all editions. They include Susanna Cornett, Dory Dickman, Lisa Maher, Susan Plant, Mangai Natarajan, Dana Nurge, Sharon Chamard, Marina Myhre, Diane Cicchetti, Emmanuel Barthe, Illya Lichtenberg, Peter Heidt, Vanja Steniius, Christine Tartaro, Megan McNally, Danielle Gunther, Jennifer Lanterman, Smita Jain, and Kim Roberts. Thanks also to Maria Shields for revising the supplements to accompany the seventh edition of this text.

Many academic reviewers offered invaluable help in planning and drafting chapters. We thank them for their time and thoughtfulness and for the experience they brought from their teaching and research:

Jay Albanese, *Virginia Commonwealth University*

Thomas E. Allen, Jr., *University of South Dakota*

W. Azul La Luz, *University of New Mexico*

Tony A. Barringer, *Florida Gulf Coast University*

Stephen Brodt, *Ball State University*

Daniel Burgel, *Vincennes University*

Alison Burke, *Southern Oregon University*

David A. Camp, *Culver-Stockton College*

Daniel D. Cervi, *University of New Hampshire*

Bernard Cohen, *Queens College, New York*

Ellen Cohn, *Florida International University*

Cavit Cooley, *Truman State University*

Roger Cunningham, *Eastern Illinois University*

Richard P. Davin, *Riverside Community College*

Julius Debro, *University of Hartford*

Albert Dichiara, *Eastern Illinois University*

Sandra Emory, *University of New Mexico*

Edna Erez, *Kent State University*

Raymond A. Eve, *University of Texas, Arlington*

The late Franco Ferracuti, *University of Rome, Italy*

Edith Flynn, *Northeastern University*

Harold A. Frossard, *Moraine Valley Community College*

Karen Gilbert, *University of Georgia*

Ronald J. Graham, *Fresno City College*

Clayton Hartjen, *Rutgers University*

Marie Henry, *Sullivan County Community College*

John Hill, *Salt Lake Community College*

Matrice Hurrah, *Southwest Tennessee Community College*

Randy Jacobs, *Baylor University*

Joseph Jacoby, *Bowling Green State University*

Debra L. Johnson, *Lindenwood University*

Kareen Jordan, *University of Central Florida*

Deborah Kelly, *Longwood College*

Dennis Kenney, *John Jay College of Criminal Justice*

James Kenny, *Fairleigh Dickinson University*

Nicholas Kittrie, *American University*

Kathryn Noe Kozey, *University of Maryland*

James J. Lauria, *Pittsburgh Technical Institute*

Matthew T. Lee, *University of Akron*

Anna C. Leggett, *Miami Dade Community College*

Linda Lengyel, *The College of New Jersey*

Michael A. Long, *Colorado State University*

Joel Maatman, *Lansing Community College*

Coramae Mann, *Indiana University, Bloomington*

Harry L. Marsh, *Indiana State University*

Robert McCormack, *The College of New Jersey*

P. J. McGann, *University of Michigan*

Jean Marie McGloin, *University of Maryland*

Sharon S. Oselin, *University of California, Irvine*

Jesenia Pizarro, *Michigan State University*

Lydia Rosner, *John Jay College of Criminal Justice*

Lee E. Ross, *University of Wisconsin*

Harjit Sandhu, *Oklahoma State University*

Jennifer L. Schulenberg, *Sam Houston State University*

Clayton Steenberg, *Arkansas State University*

Richard Steinhaus, *New Mexico Junior College*

Melvina Sumter, *Old Dominion University*

Austin T. Turk, *University of California, Riverside*

Prabha Unnithan, *Colorado State University*

James Vrettos, *John Jay College of Criminal Justice*

Charles Wellford, *University of Maryland at College Park*

Frank Williams, *California State University, San Bernardino*

The late Marvin E. Wolfgang, *University of Pennsylvania*

We thank our colleagues overseas who have prepared translations of *Criminology* to help familiarize students of foreign cultures with criminological problems that are now global, with our theories, and with efforts to deal with the persistent problem of crime in the future:

The Arabic translation:
Dr. Mohammed Zeid, Cairo, Egypt, and Rome, Italy

The Japanese translation:
Dr. Toyoji Saito, Kobe, Japan, and his colleagues

The Hungarian translation:
Dr. Miklos *Levai, Miskolc, Hungary, and his colleagues*

The Georgian translation:
Dr. Georgi Glonti, Tbilisi, Georgia

Finally, we owe a special debt to the team at McGraw-Hill: Thank you for the leadership, encouragement, support, and timeless editorial work.

A combined total of over a hundred years of teaching criminology and related subjects provides the basis for the writing of *Criminology,* Eighth Edition. We hope the result is a text that is intellectually provocative, factually rigorous, and scientifically sound and that offers a stimulating learning experience for the student.

Freda Adler
William S. Laufer

A Guided Tour

Up-to-the-Minute Coverage

The expansion of white-collar and corporate crime, the effects of the current global economic downturn, and a new look at the connection between biology and criminology are among the cutting-edge topics discussed in this Eighth Edition.

■ Fired Arthur Andersen auditor David Duncan, right, listens to his attorney, Robert Giuffra, on Capitol Hill on Thursday, January 24, 2002, before a House Energy subcommittee hearing on the destruction of Enron-related documents. Duncan cited his Fifth Amendment rights, declining to testify to Congress about anything he knows or anything he did in the destruction of Enron documents.

Chapter Openers

Each chapter opens with an outline of key topics, followed by a lively excerpt highlighting concepts from the field of criminology.

NEW! World News Boxes

Part of our acclaimed thematic box program, World News boxes feature current issues and problems reported from across the globe.

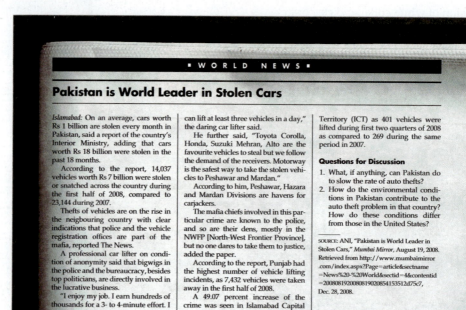

▪ WORLD NEWS ▪

Pakistan is World Leader in Stolen Cars

Islamabad: On an average, cars worth Rs 1 billion are stolen every month in Pakistan, said a report of the country's Interior Ministry, adding that cars worth Rs 18 billion were stolen in the past 18 months.

According to the report, 14,037 vehicles worth Rs 7 billion were stolen or snatched across the country during the first half of 2008, compared to 23,144 during 2007.

Thefts of vehicles are on the rise in the neigbouring country with clear indications that police and the vehicle registration offices are part of the mafia, reported The News.

A professional car lifter on condition of anonymity said that bigwigs in the police and the bureaucracy, besides top politicians, are directly involved in the lucrative business.

"I enjoy my job. I earn hundreds of thousands for a 3- to 4-minute effort. I can lift at least three vehicles in a day," the daring car lifter said.

He further said, "Toyota Corolla, Honda, Suzuki Mehran, Alto are the favourite vehicles to steal but we follow the demand of the receivers. Motorway is the safest way to take the stolen vehicles to Peshawar and Mardan."

According to him, Peshawar, Hazara and Mardan Divisions are havens for carjackers.

The mafia chiefs involved in this particular crime are known to the police, and so are their dens, mostly in the NWFP [North-West Frontier Province], but no one dares to take them to justice, added the paper.

According to the report, Punjab had the highest number of vehicle lifting incidents, as 7,432 vehicles were taken away in the first half of 2008.

A 49.07 percent increase of the crime was seen in Islamabad Capital Territory (ICT) as 401 vehicles were lifted during first two quarters of 2008 as compared to 269 during the same period in 2007.

Questions for Discussion

1. What, if anything, can Pakistan do to slow the rate of auto thefts?
2. How do the environmental conditions in Pakistan contribute to the auto theft problem in that country? How do these conditions differ from those in the United States?

SOURCE: ANI, "Pakistan is World Leader in Stolen Cars," *Mumbai Mirror,* August 19, 2008. Retrieved from http://www.mumbaimirror .com/index.aspx?Page=article&sectname =News%20-%20World&sectid=4&contentid =200808192008080819020854153512d75c7, Dec. 28, 2008.

Window to the World Boxes

Drawing on criminology's increased emphasis on global factors, Window to the World boxes examine developments abroad that affect America's crime situation.

WINDOW TO THE WORLD

Nations with Low Crime Rates

Most criminologists devote their efforts to learning why people commit crime and why there is so much crime. A few have looked at the question from the opposite perspective: In places with little crime, what accounts for the low crime rate? Using the United Nations' first World Crime Survey (1970–1975), Freda Adler studied the two countries with the lowest crime rates in each of five general cultural regions of the world:[1]

Western Europe: Switzerland and the Republic of Ireland

Eastern Europe: the former German Democratic Republic (East Germany) and Bulgaria

Arab countries: Saudi Arabia and Algeria

Asia: Japan and Nepal

Latin America: Costa Rica and Peru(2)

▪ Workers in Japan showing solidarity in an early morning exercise ritual.

This is an odd assortment of countries. They seem to have little in common. Some are democratic, others authoritarian. Some are republics, others monarchies. Some are ruled by dictators, others by communal councils. Some are rural, others highly urbanized. Some are remote and isolated; others are in the political mainstream. Some are highly religious, some largely atheistic. Some have a very high standard of living, others a very low one. What explains their common characteristic of low crime rates?

Investigations slowly revealed a common factor in all 10 countries: Each appeared to have an intact social control system, quite apart from whatever formal control system (law enforcement) it had. Here are brief descriptions of the types of social control systems identified:

Western Europe: Switzerland fostered a strong sense of belonging to and participating in the local community.[3] The family was still strong in the Republic of Ireland, and it was strengthened by shared religious values.

Eastern Europe: The former German Democratic Republic involved all youths in communal activities, organized by groups and aimed at having young people excel at having young people excel for the glory of self and country. In Bulgaria, industrialization focused on regional industry centers so that the workers would not be dislodged from their hometowns, which served as continuing social centers.

Arab countries: Islam continued to be strong as a way of life and exercised a powerful influence on daily activities, especially in Saudi Arabia. Algeria had, in addition, a powerful commitment to socialism in its postindependence era, involving the citizens in all kinds of commonly shared development activities.

Asia: Nepal retained its strong family and clan ties, augmented by councils of elders that oversaw the community and resolved problems. Highly industrialized Japan had lost some of the social controls of family and kinship, but it found a substitute family in the industrial community, to which most Japanese belonged: Mitsubishi might now be the family that guides one's every step.

Latin America: Costa Rica spent all the funds that other governments devoted to the military on social services and social development, caring for and strengthening its families. Peru went through a process of urbanization in stages: Village and family cohesion marked the lives of people in the countryside, and this cohesion remained with the people as they migrated from Andean villages to smaller towns and then to the big city, where they were received by and lived surrounded by others from their own hometowns.

The study concluded that **synnomie**, a term derived from the Greek *syn* meaning "with" and *nomos* meaning "norms," marked societies with low crime rates.

In an update of Adler's original low-crime-rate study, Janet Stamatel wrote:

The capacity for societies to maintain social control can change over time in response to other changes in social conditions. This means that countries labeled as either "low crime" or "high crime" at one point in time may experience changes in their crime status as social control mechanisms change over time. For example, in a study examining low crime rates in the ten countries that Adler identified as low crime in the late 1970s have changed.as of 2000, Stamatel analyzed crime statistics from the United Nations and the World Health Organization to find that several of these countries (e.g., Algeria, Japan, Nepal, Saudi Arabia, and Switzerland) have remarkably been able to maintain low crimes rates for several decades. In contrast, a couple of these countries, namely Bulgaria and Peru, were not able to maintain their "low crime" status as dramatic political and economic changes severely disrupted their social control systems.

Not only can we learn a lot about how to control crime from countries with consistently low crime rates, but we can also learn much about what happens to crime rates when social control mechanisms are no longer able to function as intended by studying changing crime rates over time.[4]

Sources

1. United Nations, *Report of the Secretary General on Crime Prevention and Control,* A/32/199 (popularly known as the First U.N. World Crime Survey) (New York: United Nations, 1977).
2. Freda Adler, *Nations Not Obsessed with Crime* (Littleton, Colo.: Fred B. Rothman, 1983).
3. Marshall B. Clinard, *Cities with Little Crime: The Case of Switzerland* (Cambridge, Mass.: Cambridge University Press, 1978).
4. Janet P. Stamatel, "Revisiting Nations Not Obsessed with Crime" (working paper, December 2008).

Questions for Discussion

1. People in the United States work in factories, live in family groups, go to church, and join youth groups. Why do these institutions not function effectively as forms of social control to keep the crime rate low?
2. How could government or community decision makers use the information presented by this study to help solve crime problems in the United States?

Debatable Issues Boxes

These boxes highlight controversies requiring real-world resolutions.

Maximum-Security Schools?

The 2005 *Indicators of School Crime and Safety* report places the problem of school violence in some perspective:

In the 2002–03 school year, an estimated 54.2 million students in prekindergarten through grade 12 were enrolled in about 125,000 U.S. elementary or secondary schools. Preliminary data on fatal victimizations show youth ages 5–19 were victims of 22 school-associated violent deaths from July 1, 2001, through June 30, 2002 (17 homicides and 5 suicides) (*Indicator 1*). In 2003, students ages 12–18 were victims of about 1.9 million nonfatal crimes at school, including about 1.2 million thefts and 740,000 violent crimes (simple assault and serious violent crime)—150,000 of which were serious violent crimes (rape, sexual assault, robbery, and aggravated assault) (*Indicator 2*). These figures represent victimization rates of 45 thefts and 28 violent crimes, including 6 serious violent crimes, per 1,000 students at school in 2003. Students were more likely to be victims of serious violence or a homicide away from school. In 2003, students ages 12–18 reported being victims of serious violence at a rate of 12 crimes per 1,000 students away from school and 6 crimes per 1,000 students at school. Similarly, in each school year from July 1, 1992, through June 30, 2002, youth ages 5–19 were over 70 times more likely to be murdered away from school than at school.

For several measures, data show trends in student victimization decreasing over the last decade. The nonfatal victimization rate for students

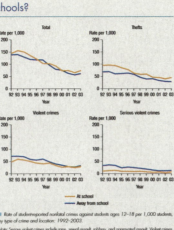

▤ Rate of student-reported nonfatal crimes against students ages 12–18 per 1,000 students, by type of crime and location: 1992–2003.

Note: Serious violent crimes include rape, sexual assault, robbery, and aggravated assault. Violent crimes include serious violent crimes and simple assault. Total crimes include violent crimes and theft. "At school" includes inside the school building, on school property, or on the way to or from school.

Source: U.S. Department of Justice, Bureau of Justice Statistics, National Crime Victimization Survey (NCVS), 1992–2003.

serious violent crimes (*Indicator 2*). However, when looking at the most recent years, no differences were detected between 2002 and 2003 in the rates of total victimization, violent victimization, or theft at school. For fatal victimization, between July

the 1998–99 and 1999–2000 school years, the number of homicides of school-age youth at school declined from 33 to 14 homicides. Since then, there have been between 12 and 17 homicides in each school year through 2001–

▤ In some inner-city schools, security measures rival those used in prison: metal detectors, drug-sniffing dogs, frequent searches for weapons, and surveillance cameras that monitor the movement of students in and out of classrooms.

well as experts' premonitions of doom and gloom, we are actually in the midst of a decline in violent crime in American schools.

Target hardening and situational crime prevention in schools are taken quite seriously. Schools in certain parts of some cities have had metal detectors, doors with alarms, and locker searches for years. Then there are the other schools in towns few have heard of: places like Paducah, Conyers, and Littleton. The image of these suburban schools as safe havens has been shattered. Although the likelihood of a shooting in any particular school is small, officials are not taking any chances. Interestingly, the prevention measures listed below fall squarely into Clarke and Homel's situational-crime-prevention model (see Table 9.3).

Access control
• Intercom systems are being used at locked doors to buzz in visitors.[2]

• Students have to flash or swipe computerized identification cards to get into school buildings.
• Perimeter fences delineate school property and secure cars after hours.

Controlling facilitators
• Students in Deltona, Florida, get an extra set of books to leave at home. The schools have banned backpacks and dismantled lockers to eliminate places to stash weapons. Other school districts are encouraging see-through lockers and backpacks.
• After the Littleton, Colorado, incident, school boards across the country banned trench coats and other oversize garments, apparently to prevent students from hiding weapons on their bodies or in their clothing.

Entry/exit screening
• Handheld and walk-through metal detectors keep anyone with a weapon from entering schools.

Formal surveillance
• Uniformed police officers and private security guards, some of them armed, patrol school halls.
• Schools are installing surveillance cameras in hallways and on school buses.

Surveillance by employees (or, in this case, students)
• Students are carrying small notebooks so that they can log and then report overheard threats.

Identifying property
• Tiny microfilm is hidden inside expensive school property so that it can be identified if stolen.

On the face of it, these measures seem to make good sense. They can prevent people from bringing weapons into schools and keep unauthorized people out. They increase the ability of school officials to detect crime, identify evildoers, and prevent criminal incidents from happening. But have school officials and others gone too far? Diana Philip is the director of the

American Civil Liberties Union of Texas for the northern region, which has filed several lawsuits against schools. She observes that "over the summer, we have had school boards putting together the most restrictive policies we have ever seen. A lot of them are in clear violation of the Fourth Amendment, which guarantees freedom from unreasonable searches."[3]

Chicago Tribune columnist Steve Chapman argues that schools treat students as "dangerous, incorrigible, undeserving of respect" or privacy. He asks, "What's the difference between school and prison? At school, you don't get cable TV."[4]

Sources
1. J. F. DeVoe, K. Peter, M. Noonan, T. D. Snyder, and K. Baum, *Indicators of School Crime and Safety: 2005* (Washington, D.C.: Department of Justice, 2005).
2. Jacques Steinberg, "Barricading the School Door," *New York Times*, Aug. 22, 1999, New York section, p. 5.
3. S. C. Gwynne, "Is Anyplace Safe?" *Time*, Aug. 23, 1999.
4. Walter Olson, "Dial 'O' for Outrage: The Sequel—Tales from an Overlawyered America," *Reason*, Nov. 1999, pp. 54–56.

Questions for Discussion
1. Do you think there would be as much concern over school violence if these shooting incidents had happened in urban schools? Why are people more upset when crime happens in places they perceive to be safe (such as in the suburbs)?
2. Does your high school or college campus have any security measures in place? If so, how do they fit into Clarke and Homel's 16 techniques of situational prevention?
3. Is there a point at which security measures in schools become so extreme that they can no longer be justified? Have we reached that point yet?

Criminological Concerns Boxes

These boxes focus on problems that challenge us to come up with effective responses right now.

The Girls in the Gang

Psychologist Anne Campbell studied female gangs in New York City and published her findings in her 1984 book, *The Girls in the Gang*. She summarizes some of her observations here:

All the girls in the gang come from families that are poor. Many have never known their fathers. Most are immigrants from Puerto Rico. As children the girls moved from apartment to apartment as they were evicted or burned out by arsonists. Unable to keep any friends they managed to make and alienated from their mothers, whose lack of English restricted their ability to control or understand their daughters' lives, the girls dropped out of school early and grew up on the streets. In the company of older kids and street-corner men, they graduated early into the adult world. They began to use drugs and by puberty had been initiated into sexual activity. By fifteen many were pregnant. Shocked, their mothers tried to

▤ A portrait of Hispanic teen female members of the Pico Rivera gang, with one member holding her child.

in Puerto Rico while they had their babies. Abortion was out of the question in this Catholic world. Those who stayed had "spoiled their identity" as good girls. Their reputations were marred before they ...

the girls found a convenient identity in the female gang. Often they had friends or distant relatives who introduced them as "prospects." After a trial period, they could undertake the initiation rite: they ...

What was at issue was not winning or losing but demonstrating "heart," or courage. Gangs do not welcome members who join only to gain protection. The loyalty of other gang members has to be won by a clear demonstration of willingness to "get down," or fight. Paradoxically, the female gang goes to considerable lengths to control the sexual behavior of its members. Although the neighborhood may believe they are fast women, the girls themselves do not tolerate members who sleep around. A promiscuous girl is a threat to the other members' relationships with their boyfriends. Members can take a boyfriend from among the male gang members (indeed, they are forbidden to take one from any other gang) but they are required to be monogamous. A shout of "Whore!" is the most frequent cause of fistfights among the female members.

On the positive side, the gang provides a strong sense of belonging and sisterhood. After the terrible isolation of their lives, the girls acquire a ready-made circle of friends who have shared many of their experiences and who are

against hostile words or deeds by outsiders. Fighting together generates a strong sense of camaraderie and as a bonus earns them the reputation of being "crazy." This reputation is extremely useful in the tough neighborhoods where they live. Their reputation for carrying knives and for solidarity effectively deters outsiders from challenging them. They work hard at fostering their tough "rep" not only in their deeds but in their social talk. They spend hours recounting and embroidering stories of fights they have been in. Behind all this bravado it is easy to sense the fear they work so hard to deny. Terrified of being victims (as many of them have already been in their families and as newcomers in their schools), they make much of their own "craziness"—the violent unpredictability that frightens away anyone who might try to harm them.[1]

Campbell demonstrates the commonality of violence in the lives of female gang members in the early 1980s. There is growing concern over the increasing prevalence and severity of violence in some areas of the

members and the extent of changes in the use of violence are, however, still debated among researchers.[3]

Sources
1. Written by Anne Campbell. Adapted from Anne Campbell, *The Girls in the Gang* (New York: Basil Blackwell, 1984).
2. John M. Hagedorn, "Gang Violence in the Postindustrial Era," in *Youth Violence, Crime and Justice: A Review of Research*, vol. 24, eds. Michael Tonry and Mark H. Moore (Chicago: University of Chicago Press, 1998), pp. 365–419.
3. Margaret O'Brien, "At Least 16,000 Girls in Chicago's Gangs More Violent than Some Believe, Report Says," *Chicago Tribune*, September 17, 1999, p. 5.

Questions for Discussion
1. How similar are Campbell's female gangs to the male gangs described in this chapter? Are there any significant differences?
2. Would you expect female gangs to become as involved in criminal activity as male gangs? Why or why not?

cal processes as any other behavior. Behavior is learned when it is reinforced or rewarded; it is not learned when it is not reinforced. We learn behavior in various ways: observation, direct experience, and differential reinforcement.

Observational Learning

Albert Bandura, a leading proponent of social learning theory, argues that individuals learn violence and aggression through **behavioral modeling:** Children learn how to behave by fashioning their behavior after that of others. Behavior is socially transmitted through examples, which come primarily from the family, the subculture, and the mass media.[82]

Psychologists have been studying the effects of family violence (Chapter 10) on children. They have found that parents who try to resolve family controversies by violence teach their children to use similar tactics. Thus, a cycle of violence may be perpetuated through generations. Observing a healthy and happy family environment tends to result in constructive and positive modeling.

To understand the influence of the social environment outside the home, social learning theorists have studied gangs, which often provide excellent models of observational learning of violence and aggression. They have found, in fact, that violence is very much a norm shared by some people in a community or gang. The highest incidence of aggressive behavior occurs where aggressiveness is a desired characteristic, as it is in some subcultures.

Observational learning takes place in front of the television set and at the movies as well. Children who have seen others being rewarded for

---

Crime Surfing WWW

www.ncjrs.org

Maternal deprivation can be related to delinquent behavior. What happens to deprived (often abused and neglected) children? Is there a cycle of violence?

DID YOU KNOW?

... that, while evidence is lacking that deprivation directly causes delinquency, research on the impact of family-based crime prevention programs is promising? Programs that target family risk factors in multiple settings (ecological contexts) have achieved success (Table 4.2).

Crime Surfing Features

Internet references accompanied by mini-exercises allow students to further explore chapter topics.

Did You Know? Facts

Intriguing, little-known facts related to specific chapter topics engage students' natural curiosity about criminology.

Theory Connects Features

These marginal notes correlate the applied material in Part 3 of the text ("Types of Crimes") with the theoretical material in Part 2 ("Explanations of Crime"), giving students much needed cross-reference material and posing critical-thinking questions.

THEORY CONNECTS

Pornography

Psychologists have long studied the deleterious effect on children of violence on television (Chapter 4). Does cyber pornography pose similar threats to children? To what extent does violent pornography, freely available on the Internet, legitimize violence against girls and women?

---

ability of pornography and crime rates, the experience of sex offenders with pornography, and the relation between pornography and behavior. The commission concluded:

[E]mpirical research designed to clarify the question has found no evidence to date that exposure to explicit sexual materials plays a significant role in the causations of delinquent or criminal behavior among youth or adults. The Commission cannot conclude that exposure to erotic materials is a factor in the causation of sex crimes or sex delinquency.[80]

Between 1970 (when the National Commission reported its findings) and 1986 (when the Attorney General's Commission issued its report), hundreds of studies had been conducted on this question. For example:

• Researchers reported in 1977 that when male students were exposed to erotic stimuli, those stimuli neither inhibited nor had any effect on levels of aggression. When the same research team worked with female students, they found that mild erotic stimuli inhibited aggression and that stronger erotic stimuli increased it.[81]

• Researchers who exposed students to sexually explicit films during six consecutive weekly sessions in 1984 concluded that exposure to increasingly explicit erotic stimuli led to a decrease in both arousal responses and aggressive behavior. In short, these subjects became habituated to the pornography.[82]

After analyzing such studies, the Attorney General's Commission concluded that nonviolent and nondegrading pornography is not significantly associated with crime and aggression. It did conclude, however, that exposure to pornographic materials

(1) leads to a greater acceptance of rape myths and violence against women; (2) results in pronounced effects when the victim is shown enjoying the use of force or violence; (3) is arousing for rapists and for some males in the general

---

is acceptable behavior or an innocuous form of sex education.[84]

Hoff's definition also suggests that pornography, obscenity, and erotica may do far more than offend sensitivities. Such material may victimize not only the people who are depicted but all women (or men or children, if they are the people shown). Pornographers have been accused of promoting the exploitation, objectification, and degradation of women. Many people who call for the abolition of violent pornography argue that it also promotes violence toward women. Future state and federal legislation is likely to focus on violent and violence-producing pornography, not on pornography in general.

The Legal View: Supreme Court Rulings

Ultimately, defining pornographic acts subject to legal prohibition is a task for the U.S. Supreme Court. The First Amendment to the Constitution guarantees freedom of the press. In a series of decisions culminating in *Miller v. California* (1973), however, the Supreme Court articulated the view that obscenity, really meaning pornography, is outside the protection of the Constitution. Following the lead of the Model Penal Code and reinterpreting its own earlier decisions, the Court announced the following standard for judging a representation as obscene or pornographic:

• The average person, applying contemporary community standards, would find that the work, taken as a whole, appeals to prurient interests.

• The work depicts or describes, in a patently offensive way, sexual conduct specifically defined by the applicable state law.

• The work, taken as a whole, lacks serious literary, artistic, political, or scientific value.[85]

While this proposed standard is flexible enough to be expanded or contracted as standards change over time and from place to place, its terms are so vague that they give little guidance to local law

country like a corporation," and economic terms such as "accountability" are adopted by educators.

Messner and Rosenfeld contend that as long as there is a disproportionate emphasis on monetary rewards, the crime problem will increase. In fact, if economic opportunities increase, there may be an increase in the preoccupation with material success. Crime will decrease only when noneconomic institutions have the capacity to control behavior.[37]

Freda Adler's study of 10 countries with low crime rates supports this argument. She demonstrates that where economic concerns have not devalued informal social control institutions such as family, community, or religion, crime rates are relatively low and stable. This finding held for non-industrialized *and* highly industrialized societies.[38]

General Strain Theory

Sociologist Robert Agnew substantially revised Merton's theory in order to provide a broader explanation of criminal behavior.[39] The reformulation is called **general strain theory.** Agnew argues that failure to achieve material goals (the focal point of Merton's theory) is not the only reason for committing crime. Criminal behavior may also be related to the anger and frustration that result when an individual is treated in a way he or she does not want to be treated in a social relationship. General strain theory explains the range of strain-producing events:

• *Strain caused by failure to achieve positively valued goals.* This type of strain is based on Merton's view that lower-class individuals are often prevented from achieving monetary success goals through legitimate channels. When people do not have the money to get what they want, some of them turn to illegitimate means to get it.

• *Stress caused by the removal of positively valued stimuli from the individual.* This type of strain results from the actual or anticipated loss of something or someone important in one's life: death of a loved one, breakup with a boyfriend/girlfriend, divorce of parents, move to a new school. Criminal behavior results when individuals seek revenge against those responsible, try to prevent the loss, or escape through illicit drug use.

• *Strain caused by the presentation of negative stimuli.* The third major source of strain involves stressful life situations. Adverse situations and events may include child abuse, criminal victimization, bad experiences with peers, school problems, or verbal threats. Criminal behavior in these situations may result when an individual tries to run away from the situation, end the problem, or seek revenge.[40]

According to Agnew, each type of strain increases an individual's feelings of anger, fear, or depression. The most critical reaction for general strain theory is anger, an emotion that increases the desire for revenge, helps justify aggressive behavior, and stimulates individuals to act.

General strain theory acknowledges that not all persons who experience strain become criminals. Many are equipped to cope with their frustration and anger. Some come up with rationalizations ("don't really need it anyway"), others use techniques for physical relief (a good workout at the gym), and still others walk away from the condition causing stress (get out of the house). The capacity to deal with strain depends on personal experience throughout life. It involves the influence of peers, temperament, attitudes, and, in the case of pressing financial problems, economic resources. Recent empirical tests show preliminary support for general strain theory.[41] By broadening Merton's concepts, general strain theory has the potential to explain a wide range of criminal and delinquent behavior, including aggressive acts, drug abuse, and property offenses, among individuals from all social classes.

THEORY INFORMS POLICY

Strain theory has helped us develop a crime-prevention strategy. If, as the theory tells us, frustration builds up in people who have few means for reaching their goals, it makes sense to design programs that give lower-class people a bigger stake in society.

Head Start

It was in the 1960s that President Lyndon Johnson inaugurated the Head Start program as part of a major antipoverty campaign. The goal of Head Start is to make children of low-income families more socially competent, better able to deal with their present environment and their later responsibilities. The youngsters get a boost (or a head start) in a 1-year preschool developmental program that is intended to prevent them from dropping out of society. Program components include community and parental involvement, an 8-to-1 child–staff ratio, and daily evaluation and involvement of all the children in the planning of and responsibility for their own activities.

Because a 1-year program could not be expected to affect the remainder of a child's life, Project Follow Through was developed in an effort to provide the same opportunities for Head Start youngsters during eleme[...] began as a modest summer ex[...] million preschool children has [...] year-round program that prov[...] and social services to millions [...] and their families. Head Start [...] ple of a program intended to l[...] group most likely to develop c[...]

A 2005 evaluation of Head [...] sought evidence of the impac[...]

Theory Informs Policy

These brief sections in theory chapters demonstrate how problems identified by criminologists have led to practical solutions.

End-of-Chapter Features

Every chapter concludes with a Review, Criminology & Public Policy exercise, You Be the Criminologist exercise, and a listing of chapter-specific Key Terms. These tools help students reinforce and expand the chapter content.

CHAPTER 9

REVIEW

This chapter focuses on situational theories of crime. These theories, which assume that there are always people motivated to commit crime, try to explain why crimes are being committed by a particular offender against a particular target. They analyze opportunities and environmental factors that prompt a potential perpetrator to act.

We discussed the three most prominent situational approaches to crime: environmental criminology, the rational-choice perspective, and the routine-activity approach. We noted that they have merged somewhat, particularly insofar as all these approaches aim at preventing victimization by altering external conditions that are conducive to crime.

Theories of victimization view crime as the dynamic interaction of perpetrators and victims (at a given time and place). Here, too, the aim is to find ways for potential victims to protect themselves. Research into lifestyles, victim-offender interaction, repeat victimization, hot spots, and geography of crime has vast implications for crime control in entire cities or regions. Situational theories of crime and theories of victimization are interrelated. Most of the theories and perspectives in this chapter can be used to explain and possibly predict the decision making of criminal organizations, including terrorist organizations.

CRIMINOLOGY & PUBLIC POLICY

The kind of terrorism we are talking about is different in many respects from other crimes such as murder, rape, and robbery. The difference is that terrorism is generally more calculated, more premeditated, and more goal-oriented than impulsive crimes or crimes of passion. Criminal justice expert Philip Heymann has observed:

As a crime, terrorism is different. Most crimes are the product of greed, anger, jealousy, or the desire for domination, respect, or position in a group, and not of any desire to "improve" the state of the world or of a particular nation. Most crimes do not involve—as part of the plan for accomplishing their objectives—trying to change the occupants of government positions, their actions, or the basic structures and ideology of a nation. Some would argue that violence carried out for political purpose is more altruistic; others would vigorously deny that. But all would agree that political violence is different from ordinary crime, in that it is planned to force changes in government actions, people, structure, or even ideology as a means to whatever ends the perpetrators are seeking with whatever motivations drive them towards those ends. It is in that sense that the U.S. State Department definition says that the violence is usually "perpetrated for political reasons."

Terrorism—at least of the kind described by Heymann—is thus more, not less, subject to disincentive and deterrence techniques than most ordinary crimes. To be sure, some acts of terrorism are revenge-driven and impulsive, but most are carefully calculated to achieve a goal. Sometimes the goal will be specific and immediate, while other times it may be more general, long term, and apocalyptic. But whatever the object, if it becomes clear that it will be disserved by terrorism—that the cause will be worse off—then it will be only a matter of time until co-supporters of the cause turn against those who resort to terrorism. Without widespread support from within the cause they are seeking to promote, terrorists cannot long thrive. Certainly if there is widespread opposition to terrorism within the cause, it will soon dry up. (Source: Alan M. Dershowitz, *Why Terrorism Works* [New Haven, CT: Yale University Press, 2002].)

Questions for Discussion What do rational-choice theorists have to contribute to the ongoing "war" against terrorism? Is terrorism rational? In what ways? What counterterrorist strategies can you think of that would be effective against terrorism committed against targets in the United States?

YOU BE THE CRIMINOLOGIST

Imagine that you are a security consultant working for a major department store chain. Recently, one of the stores, located in the downtown area of a large city, has experienced very high levels of shoplifting and employee theft. You must design a comprehensive program to protect merchandise from theft by customers and by people who work at the store. First, identify some of the store's most vulnerable areas (it may help to visit a local department store to observe how it operates). Then, using the 16 techniques of situational crime prevention as a model, prepare a list of prevention strategies.

KEY TERMS

The numbers next to the terms refer to the pages on which the terms are defined.

displacement (224)

environmental criminology (207)

rational choice (208)

routine-activity (209)

target hardening (220)

theories of victimization (212)

Online Learning Center, Including Additional Chapters

Visit our Online Learning Center at **www.mhhe.com/adlercrim8e** for robust student and instructor resources. Also included on the password-protected instructor portion of the site are Chapters 15–18, covering the Criminal Justice system.

Understanding Criminology

Criminology is the scientific study of the making of laws, the breaking of laws, and society's reaction to the breaking of laws. Sometimes these laws are arrived at by the consensus of most members of a community; sometimes they are imposed by those in power. Communities have grown in size, from village to world, and the threats to communities have grown accordingly. World-level threats, or at least perceptions of threats, necessitated that criminological research and crime prevention strategies become globalized. Nationally and internationally, criminological research has become influential in policy making, and criminologists seek greater influence (Chapter 1).

Criminologists have adopted methods of study from all the social and behavioral sciences. Like all other scientists, criminologists measure. They assess crime over time and place, and they measure the characteristics of criminals and crimes. Like other social scientists, criminologists pose research questions, state hypotheses, and test the validity of these hypotheses. (Chapter 2).

Throughout history, thinkers and rulers have written about crime and criminals and the control of crime. Yet the term *criminology* is little more than a century old, and the subject has been of scientific interest for only two centuries. Two schools of thought contributed to modern criminology: the classical school, associated predominantly with Cesare Beccaria (eighteenth century), which focused on crime, and the positivist school, associated with Cesare Lombroso, Enrico Ferri, and Raffaele Garofalo (nineteenth and early twentieth centuries), which focused on criminals (Chapter 3). Contemporary American criminology owes much to these European roots.

The Changing Boundaries
of Criminology

■ *Search and rescue efforts after the 2011 earthquake and tsunami in Japan*

March 11, 2011. It's a Friday. At 2:26 P.M. The most powerful earthquake to hit Japan since records were kept, struck the northeast coast, about 250 miles from the heart of Tokyo. The tremor triggered a massive tsunami. Everything in its path of the massive wall of water was stripped from the land: Cars, ships and buildings were literally swept away.

Japan's ground self-defense forces were deployed, and the government asked the U.S. military based in the country for assistance. The scale of destruction was nearly unimaginable, with tens of thousands of deaths. In the aftermath of the earthquake and tsunami, residents of affected communities formed long, orderly lines outside grocery stores, where employees try to fairly distribute limited supplies of food and water. There was no civil unrest or looting. Civility and cooperation are everywhere to be found.

February 27, 2010. It's a Saturday, around 3:30 P.M. A massive 8.8 magnitude earthquake erupts right off of tne cost the Biobio Region of Chile with intense shaking lasting for about three minutes. It is the sixth largest earthquake ever to be recorded by a seismograph. Tremors from the earthquake are felt as far away as

Argentina, and southern Peru. Ninety-three percent of the country's population loses electricity. Chile's President declares a state of catastrophe and sends military troops to take control of the most affected areas. Images of people ransacking supermarkets in Concepción and Santiago capture great media attention. The Chilean government deploys more than 10,000 soldiers into the most affected areas to help keep order and distribute aid. It also imposes a temporary curfew for the worst-hit areas.

January 12, 2010. It's a Tuesday in the late afternoon. Without warning, a magnitude 7.0 earthquake hits the town of Léogâne, approximately 16 miles west of Port-au-Prince, Haiti's capital. Given the densely populated area in and around the epicenter of the earthquake, literally millions of Haitians were affected—approximately 316,000 people died, another 300,000 were injured and more than 1,000,000 made homeless. Close to 250,000 residences and 30,000 commercial buildings collapsed or were severely damaged. In less than two weeks after the earthquake, at least 52 aftershocks measuring 4.5 or greater are recorded. Without a discernable police presence in cities and towns, violence in the streets erupted, marked by looting and gang-related gunfire, making relief and humanitarian efforts that much more challenging.

August 26, 2005. It's a Friday. People all along America's Gulf Coast are going about their business and pleasure. Out in the Gulf of Mexico, a monstrous tropical storm is developing, dubbed Katrina. Its winds blow at category 5, the most severe storm. When Katrina makes landfall early in the morning of August 29, 80 percent of the city is under water, and thousands of residents huddle on rooftops waiting to be rescued. Looters take over some neighborhoods in the city, forcing the mayor to order 1,500 police officers on search-and-rescue duty to return to the streets to rein them in.

By now you may well be asking, What does this have to do with criminology? A great deal. Criminologists who study

natural disasters have found that different types of crimes (including looting, violence, and fraud) can be expected at each stage of a disaster.[1] Why, then, are officials in charge of emergencies so totally unprepared to deal with the crimes and their impact on communities, which cause losses of life, destruction of property, and exploitation of the population? One answer, both self-serving and apparently true, is that those most responsible for failed leadership before, during, and after a disaster are not as acquainted as they should be with criminological research.

The first lesson of this book, then, is that criminology is not simply an abstract, theoretical science. Rather, it is a science that has much to offer policy—specifically, policy aimed at protecting the community from the most significant of all harms, criminal harm. In the aftermath of the earthquake and tsunami that devastated Japan in 2011, there is also another lesson. In even the most affected communities along the coast of Japan, stores were not looted, and there were no robberies or gang-related violence. Why? The boundaries of Criminology are quite elastic. Criminologists consider individual differences in both prosocial and anti-social behavior, group differences, and the role of culture, sub-culture, and opportunities in offending (Chapters 4 through 9). Indeed, the boundaries of Criminology allow for a special consideration of the different types of offending, including the Criminology of terrorism (Chapter 1 and 14), and a Criminology of white collar and corporate offending (Chapter 12), among others. We readily acknowledge that there are many criminologies yet to be discovered. And this is where our story begins.

THE CHANGING BOUNDARIES OF CRIMINOLOGY

911 is the number Americans call when they need police protection from a criminal attack or similar emergency. In a very real sense, then, 911 starts the process of criminal justice and its inquiry about perpetrators and victims, causes and motivations, offenses and defenses. 911, therefore, is a

good symbol with which to start a course—or a book—dedicated to criminology. In 2001, 911 took on yet another meaning, not only to the worldwide public, in general, but to criminologists, in particular.

It was in the morning hours of September 11, 2001, that four airliners were diverted in flight by perpetrators who had subdued or killed the crews. Two of the jets crashed into the New York World Trade Center. A third plane smashed into the Pentagon, in Washington, D.C. The fourth plane, apparently headed toward Washington, D.C., crashed into a field in Pennsylvania, allegedly as a result of passengers trying to overpower the hijackers.

The World Trade Center collapsed within the hour; the Pentagon was in flames; all passengers and crews of the airplanes died in fiery crashes. The death toll was nearly three thousand. It was the worst criminally caused catastrophe in American history. To this day, even as the 9/11 Memorial and Museum regularly open their doors to the public, neither the American economy nor the American psyche has fully recovered from this act of terrorism. And some very successful attacks on al-Qaeda's leadership did little to help either. This includes killing Osama bin Laden in Pakistan by a Navy SEALs unit on May 2, 2011, and the September 30, 2011 drone attacks that killed Anwar al-Awlaki, the leader of external operations for al-Qaida in the Arabian Peninsula and Samir Khan, who ran an al-Qaida-linked website that called for attacks on the United States.

In this post-9/11 world, the threat of another domestic terrorist attack—no matter how inevitable or likely—is used to support legislation and criminal justice policies that affect our civil rights and liberties. Criminologists have been slow to respond to reforms justified by concerns over homeland security with systematic research, and even slower to tackle the criminology of terrorism. However, criminologists have much to say. After all, terrorism is a crime!

Terrorism

The federal and state penal codes contain a number of crimes referring to terrorism. The federal criminal code has listed several new crimes regarding terrorism, including "acts of terrorism transcending national boundaries," "use of certain weapons of mass destruction," and "financial transactions" to finance terrorism. Several states have adopted similar legislation, many of which are based on global United Nations conventions.[2] Few of these laws define terrorism as such. Most incorporate crimes that terrorists are likely to commit in furtherance of their objective, such as murder, arson, kidnapping, and so on. While there is no universally agreed-upon definition of the term "terrorism," Title 22 of the United States Code, Section 2656f(d), defines it as "premeditated, politically motivated violence perpetrated against noncombatant targets by subnational groups or clandestine agents, usually intended to influence an audience."[3] Most definitions imply the use of violence or other significant forms of criminality to achieve the perpetrators' purpose. We are proposing our own definition: "The use or threat of violence directed at people or governments to punish them for past action and/or to bring about a change of policy that is consistent with the terrorists' objectives." This concept incorporates many forms of criminal conduct and is therefore of prime significance to criminologists.

There is a second and equally important reason for criminologists to study terrorism: It is at the center of many forms of criminality that feed or are fed by terrorism. This can best be demonstrated by a wheel, the hub of which is terrorism. The seven spokes of the wheel are the seven forms of transnational criminality (see Chapter 14) that are directly relevant to terrorism, either because they support it or because they are a consequence or by-product of it. Let us continue our search for the reach of criminology by examining these seven categories (Figure 1.1).

Illicit Drug Trafficking

Terrorists need money for their operations. The drug trade provides easy access to large funds. The Taliban financed their terrorist activities from the vast opium production of Afghanistan. Terrorists in Colombia derive their funds from the coca trade of Latin America. And that holds true for just about every other terrorist group around the world. Globally, it has been estimated that approximately $1 trillion in "dirty money" is available for financing illegal activities, including terrorism. Approximately $500 billion comes into the West from transitional and emerging economies, much of it from the illegal drug trade. Others estimate that between two to five percent of the worldwide global economy involves laundered money. Most criminologists, while recognizing the significance of the problem, are hesitant to offer an estimate without more and better data. While the "war on drugs" had received widespread attention in the media and on the part of government officials and criminologists, the "war against terrorism" has virtually replaced the prior emphasis. This is particularly disturbing when it is becoming ever more clear that the drug trade nurtures terrorism and fosters the growth of international criminal organizations.[4]

Strong Words on Dirty Money

The globalizing era has produced an explosion in the volume of illegitimate commercial and financial transactions. North American and European banking and investment institutions have been

FIGURE 1.1 Wheel of terrorism.

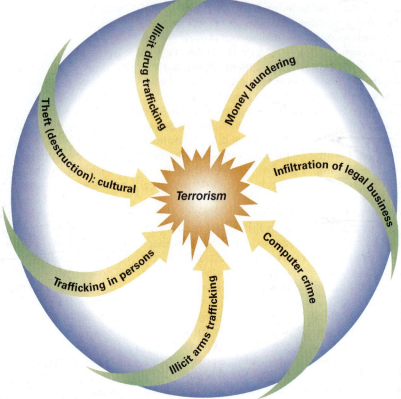

flooded with laundered and ill-gotten gains. Amounting to trillions of dollars, most of these sums are generated through secretive arrangements between cooperating but distant private-sector entities.

Lagging legal codes have proven inadequate to deal with the situation. Much of this subject is taboo in business and government circles, yet this torrent of stolen, disguised, and hidden resources poses a major risk to state security, corporate stability, democracy, free enterprise, the effectiveness of international aid programs and the lives and well-being of billions across the world.

For more than a 100 years, North America and Europe solicited, transferred, and managed illicit proceeds seeking exit from other countries and residence in western accounts. In recent years, no nation received more such criminal, corrupt, and commercial dirty money than the United States. Our reasons are straightforward: we like the arriving billions of dollars and assume the inflows are good for our economy. And it is this equation that now demands searching reevaluation.

America cannot wage a successful war against drugs, crime, terrorism, global poverty, and state collapse, while simultaneously seeking and harboring ill-gotten gains from across our borders. To think we can is folly.

Those who favor the status quo—facilitating the inflow of all or some of the dirty money still legal—must make the argument that the benefits outweigh the costs to our society. In the absence of such a credible argument, logic dictates an alternative conclusion: We don't want it.

The remaining question is then narrowed and simplified: How do we curtail the billions of illegal, unwanted dollars arriving at our doorstep? The answer begins with a willingness to put all three forms of dirty money—criminal, corrupt, and commercial—squarely on the political-economy table for determined action.

The notion that we can build the kind of orderly, globalizing world we want while feeding our appetite for dirty money is unsustainable. This process, a relic of an earlier age, needs to be promptly changed. America will be stronger, not weaker, as a result. Political will is the missing ingredient.

Source: Excerpt from Raymond Baker, Dirty Money and its Global Effects, International Policy Report (Washington, D.C.: Center for International Policy, 2003) (available at: http://www.ciponline.org/dirtymoney.pdf)

Money Laundering

"Dirty" (illegally obtained) money cannot be spent freely. While there is evidence that terrorist weapons have been obtained by direct ex-change for drugs, or for dirty money, most expenditures by terrorists are for goods or services obtained on the free market, which demands clean cash. Hence, much of the dirty money must be laundered in a vast criminal enterprise called "money laundering." Of course, it is not just drug money that requires laundering. All illegally obtained funds (for example, from bribery, black-market activities, corruption, extortion, and embezzlement) require laundering. Thus, money laundering is an activity aimed at making illegally obtained and, therefore, untaxed funds appear legitimate. Usually this is done by depositing such funds in numbered but unnamed (secret) accounts in banks of a number of countries where that is still possible. From there the funds are rapidly transferred elsewhere, and yet again, until it becomes impossible to trace them to the criminal activity that created them.[5] Despite increased international cooperation to curb money laundering, it appears that terrorism has benefited greatly from this criminal activity.

Money laundering allows crime to pay by permitting criminals to hide and legitimize proceeds derived from illegal activities. According to one recent estimate, worldwide money-laundering activity amounts to roughly $1 trillion a year.

Infiltration of Legal Business

Dirty money, once laundered, can be used freely (for example, to buy or establish a legitimate business). By way of example, police in Ham-burg, Germany, discovered that the innocent-looking import-export firms Tatari Design and Tatex Trading GmbH were not so innocent at all. They had been established as fronts for terrorist operatives to smuggle money, agents, and supplies.[6] Of course, it is often the case that laundered funds, rather than directly financing terrorist enterprises, will be invested in businesses controlled by organized crime, such as trash hauling, construction, seafood, or investment banking.[7]

Computer Crime

Cyberspace is there for everyone to use—or to abuse. And the abuses are increasingly being discovered and, indeed, legislated as crime. Above all, there is the abuse of cyberspace for money laundering, ultimately to support terrorist groups.[8] Beyond that, there is the potential of cyberattacks on the national security and technology infrastructure of the United States. The security community generally expects terrorists to launch major strikes through networks in the intermediate, if not immediate, future.[9] Al Qaeda is deemed to possess the capacity for these major cyber-attacks.[10]

Illicit Arms Trafficking

The wars of the past have provided terrorists of the past—and the present—with surplus and remnant arms and munitions to fight for their causes. The market in small arms is vast and mostly clandestine. What is new, however, is the market for weapons of mass destruction: nuclear, biological, and chemical. There is considerable evidence that nuclear materials have been diverted from now-defunct former Soviet installations. During both the Clinton and the Bush administrations, fears were expressed that rogue states that have traditionally supported terrorism sought these materials for the creation of weapons of mass destruction. The United States finds itself at war with this justification as its premise. One of the pretexts for the U.S.-Iraq war was the issue of United Nations inspections of suspected Iraqi nuclear arms facilities. As history has demonstrated, no weapons of mass destruction were found by UN inspectors or U.S. military personnel.

Trafficking in Persons

Smuggling would-be illegal migrants from less-desirable homelands to more promising lands of opportunity has become a huge criminal enterprise involving millions of human beings, billions in funds paid to smugglers, and the loss of a great number of innocent lives. Many of the countries of destination fear the growth of immigrant communities that might be terrorist havens, like the refugee camps of Palestine. Even greater is the fear that terrorist organizations deliberately infiltrate their members into immigrant populations. To their dismay, for example, Italian law enforcement authorities have learned that among the waves of illegal immigrants washing ashore in Sicily are increasing numbers of persons linked to terrorist organizations.[11] There are also masses of

In the Words of Al Qaeda: What Else Is There to Say about September 11?

AKHU MAN TA`A ALLAH

Since September 11 America has been spending billions of dollars to protect its infrastructure and interests around the world.

The attacker determines the timing of the strike. He will carryout a concentrated strike one time at a weak point and then sit in ambush again. So the enemy will look for a gap and close it, this is not necessarily where he was hit but all other similar targets. So striking the American embassies in Kenya and Tanzania means protecting every American embassy in the world. Striking the [U.S.S.] Cole at sea means protecting all American assets in the seas. Diversifying targets means protecting all American things in every land that may have terrorists!

So if the strategic goal is defense, this does not mean that the tactic should also be defense, the best method of defense is offense. Here we choose guerilla warfare that relies on the principle of defense strategy in an offensive tactic in which you withdraw from every position of defense and take an offensive posture everywhere and strike the enemy where he does not expect it.

If the enemy is situated within the [Muslim] nation, then he should be struck everywhere he is present to show the [Muslim] population, and to have the Muslim nation participate in fighting its enemy. If the enemy possesses agents and collaborators, then we should strike the enemy by targeting these agents and collaborators, to expose to the people his agents who will find it necessary to declare their collaboration and defend their master to the death.

If the enemy places his armies away from his soil to get internal peace of mind for the attacks on the military will occur away from home, then we should sneak deep into enemy territory and strike him in the heart. This is what we mean by using guerrilla warfare in urban areas which is also named city warfare. It is when you are close to the enemy and you strike him so he does not recover, with God's permission.

If the enemy used his economy to rule the world and hire collaborators, then we need to strike this economy with harsh attacks to bring it down on the heads of its owners.

If the enemy has built his economy on the basis of open markets and free trade by getting the monies of investors, then we have to prove to these investors that the enemy's land is not safe for them, that his economy is not capable of guarding their monies, so they would abandon him to suffer alone the fall of his economy.

If the enemy like everyone else has points of strength and points of weakness, we should surpass his points of strength and attack his points of weakness to collapse his strength.

illegal aliens who have moved from Iran, Iraq, and Turkey—across the Aegean Sea—into Northern Africa, where they become vulnerable recruits for terrorist activities. The problem of illegal immigration is now a major political issue in the United States, raising concerns about border security, civil liberties, and the rights of citizenship.

■ *The perils of illegal immigration are vast. Many risk not only arrest and deportation but their lives for the hope of a better life in the United States.*

If the enemy terrorizes us by killing civilians, then we should strike at his civilians which god allows us to kill, and to not decrease our strikes on the military which the enemy accepts their deaths, for this is the nature of military.

If the enemy has build his country on the principles of institutions and democracy where people rule, then we should make the people take our side not the side of the enemy, by proving to the people that the policies of their government bring forth more and more attacks against them. This is what we saw in the attacks in Spain which in turn fired its dictator (Aznar).

This is about Jihad against the crusader enemy, so what about the September 11 operation?

Hijacking planes is a well known tactic, which was used by various fighters and freedom fighters, so what's new about this operation?

People used to hijack planes and consider them a target, but those who are willing to put in the extra effort turned these planes into a method only, a projectile shot into the heart of the enemy.

The hijackers used to pressure the pilot to do what they wish, but would the pilot be receptive if you order him to kill himself and his passengers and destroy his infidel country with his plane? Of course not. So the planes are going to be flown by young men you surrendered their lives to god, this is what happened when the hijackers became pilots who mastered flying.

The enemy used to protect his external interests and has spent exuberant sums for this protection, so he was surprised when he was struck inside his borders. The enemy used to protect a thousand interests outside his county, now he has to protect a million interests inside his country that need continuing protection!!

The attack on the [World] Trade Center forced America since that day to spend billions to protect the huge economic infrastructure that runs the American economy.

Using planes in this attack has forced America to spend billions to protect the planes and airports in all possible ways. This protection is not limited to the hundreds of American airports but also to every airport in the world. Anyone related to the aviation industry is spending excessive amounts to guard air travel; the matter has reached protecting the skies.

Has anyone throughout history ever heard of protecting the skies?

America is conducting patrols, not with cars like Ford and Lumina, but rather patrols with F-16s that circle the skies of New York since September 11th and up to today. Now they are debating reducing these patrols.

This is how America was transformed after one strike, protecting all that can be struck, as they guard all that can be used to strike with!! This is related to armed protection. As for surveillance, now America monitors everything, it even needed to change its laws and to give up on what it used to pride itself of civil rights and personal freedoms. It has violated all previous taboos searching for terrorists.

Questions for Discussion

1. Some scholars arque that Al Qaeda is a "rational" organization. After reading this excerpt, do you agree?
2. Based on this excerpt alone, how significant a threat is Al Qaeda?

SOURCE: Akhu Man Ta`a Allah, "What Else Is There to Say about September 11?" *Sawt al-Jihad* (*Voice of Jihad* magazine—Al Qaeda's official publication in Saudi Arabia), vol. 26, pp. 35–42.

Destruction of Cultural Property

Lenin's terrorists became infamous for their efforts to destroy the evidence of a culture past: Christian churches were destroyed. Hitler's terrorists burned down the synagogues of Germany and every other cultural symbol, especially literature, art, and music, deemed inconsistent with the new "culture" they wanted to impose. The Taliban took delight in firing artillery shells into two ancient statues of Buddha—the largest in the world—reducing them to rubble. And when the 9/11 terrorists destroyed the World Trade Center, they not only eradicated a symbol of American trade leadership, but also destroyed a beautiful, unique structure of American architecture. Terrorists, especially those with millennial goals or of religious or political extremism, seek to destroy past cultures and to impose their own vision of culture.

The Reach of Criminology

We have completed our examination of the hub and the seven spokes of our criminological wheel. These represent terrorism and seven other forms of criminality that support or are the product of terrorism. These eight forms of criminality are part of a group of 18 that the United Nations has defined as "transnational criminality." Not crimes by themselves but rather a mixture of other crimes, they all have in common the fact that they transcend national boundaries and affect several nations and therefore are hard for just one nation to deal with. (We shall return to transnational criminality in Chapter 14, where we discuss the remaining 10 forms.)

Our effort to demonstrate the reach of criminology is not yet complete. As any exposure to today's media will tell you, there is a competition for attention among those who deem terrorism to be the principal national problem and those who point to our lagging economy. Why? Democrats and Republicans might give you different answers, but all agree that the compromise of our credit markets by a wide range of lending and financial institutions (known generally as the "subprime crisis") lies at the root of the

■ A gaping hole in the mountain is all that is left of Buddhism's most prized religious symbols—the colossal Buddhas of Afghanistan—purposefully destroyed by Taliban artillery.

■ Sailors of a Spanish naval vessel—part of an international armada—boarding an unflagged ship, the Sosan, 600 miles off the coast of East Africa, after the captain refused to identify the vessel. Initially, the North Korean master of the vessel claimed she was carrying cement. The Spanish search revealed 15 missiles and other sophisticated weaponry.

markets' most recent decline. There is now little doubt, though, that other reasons explain market weakness and the wild swings up and down. Economists discuss the effects of rising government deficits and debt levels in the United States and across the globe and how they have combined, in disturbing ways, with a wave of downgrading of government debt.

Criminologists continue to focus on fraud, mismanagement, failed regulation, and failures of self-regulation as explanations for the kinds of market failures that have brought down some of the most powerful financial institutions, from the investment bank Lehman Brothers to the insurance giant, AIG (Chapter 12). Nearly a decade later, however, it remains to be seen just how much criminal fraud was involved in lending practices and whether criminal prosecutions will follow the government's bailout of some key lending institutions (e.g., Fannie Mae). Frustrations with the failure of the Securities and Exchange Commission and the Department of Justice to bring targeted cases against at least some of key financial institutions continue to rise. You will find out more about this in Chapter 12.

By this time, you may be asking, Is there no limit to the reach of criminological inquiry? There is not, because every human activity is capable of deviance that produces significant harm, thus requiring criminological scrutiny. Not even the ocean is the limit. It is the oceans, covering nearly three-quarters of the world's surface, that make life on Earth possible. Yet the oceans are being threatened by many types of criminality, of which the most deadly is pollution. In earlier editions of this book, we discussed the case of the supertanker *Exxon Valdez*, which negligently had ruptured her hull in Alaska waters, spilling 11 million gallons of crude oil. This caused the greatest environmental disaster North America had yet known. At the time we expressed our hope that this criminally caused disaster would lead to greater efforts to prevent recurrences. But no. Oil spill disasters that should have been prevented have occurred with heightening regularity off the coasts of China, South Africa, the Galápagos Islands, American Samoa, Denmark, Thailand, Brazil, Finland, Germany, the Netherlands, and Vietnam, among other areas.[12] This criminality, destroying the environment, is called "ecocide." It presents yet another task for criminologists. And this task is not limited to environmental disasters that are prosecuted or labeled "criminal." Criminologists followed British Petroleum's (BP) Deepwater Horizon explosion and resulting oil spill that occurred April 20, 2010, in the Gulf of Mexico with great interest. The scale of this disaster, the costs, and the lessons learned (and apparently not learned) fall well within the boundaries of Criminology.

As far as the reach of criminology is concerned, do not be deceived by the media and their symbiotic relationship with legislatures. Today's focus of the media on a given crime problem is no indication of the extent of criminology's tasks. In the 1960s, the emphasis was on juvenile delinquency; in the 1970s, attention turned to street crime in general and drugs in particular, which led, in the 1980s, to a focus on prison overcrowding, on one hand, and target hardening, on the other. Then, in the 1990s, more attention was being paid to foreign influences on our crime rates, in the wake of globalization. Domestic (school shootings) and foreign violence, along with terrorism, dictated the market for ideas, with competing attention focused on computer, white-collar, and corporate criminality. Today, in the second decade of the twenty-first century, it is clear that these problems demand more of criminology than it is capable of delivering as yet. The principal crime problems of today are totally globalized. Criminology has to become equally globalized. This remains the principal challenge of criminology.

Seemingly we have neglected street crimes and delinquency in this survey of the reach of criminology. These topics are, and will remain, a major focus of criminologists—in competition with all the other forms of criminality to which we have alluded. Now that you are acquainted with the changing and elastic boundaries of criminology, we next introduce you to what this discipline is all about.

WHAT IS CRIMINOLOGY?

In the Middle Ages, human learning was commonly divided into four areas: law, medicine, theology, and philosophy. Universities typically had four faculties, one for each of these fields. Imagine a young person in the year 1392—100 years before Columbus came ashore in America—knocking at the portal of a great university with this request: "I would like to study criminology. Where do I sign up?" A stare of disbelief would have greeted the student, because the word had not yet been coined. Cautiously the student would explain: "Well, I'm interested in what crime is, and how the law deals with criminals." The university official might smile and say, "The right place for you to go is the law faculty. They will teach you everything there is to know about the law."

The student might feel discouraged. "That's a lot more than I want to know about the law. I really don't care about inheritance laws and the law of contracts. I just want to study all about crime and criminality. For example, why are certain actions considered wrong or evil in the first place, and—" The official would interrupt: "Then you must go to the faculty of theology. They know all there is to know about good and evil, heaven and hell." The student might persist: "But could they teach me what it is about the human body and mind that could cause some people and not others to commit crime?" "Oh, I see," the official would say. "You really should study medicine." "But, sir, medicine probably is only part of what I need to know, and really only part of medicine seems relevant. I want to know all there is to know about—" And then would come the official's last attempt to steer the student in the right direction: "Go and study philosophy. They'll teach you all there is to know!"

For centuries, all the knowledge the universities recognized continued to be taught in these four faculties. It was not until the eighteenth and nineteenth centuries that the natural and social sciences became full-fledged disciplines. In fact, the science of criminology has been known as such for only a little more than a century.

In 1885, the Italian law professor Raffaele Garofalo coined the term "criminology" (in Italian, *criminologia*).[13] The French anthropologist Paul Topinard used it for the first time in French (*criminologie*) in 1887.[14] "Criminology" aptly described and encompassed the scientific concern with the phenomenon of crime. The term immediately gained acceptance all over the world, and criminology became a subject taught at universities. Unlike their predecessors in 1392—or even in 1892—today's entering students will find that teaching and learning are distributed among 20 or 30 disciplines and departments. And criminology or criminal justice is likely to be one of them.

Criminology is a science, an empirical science. More particularly, it is one of the social, or behavioral, sciences. It has been defined in various ways by its scholars. The definition provided in 1934 by Edwin H. Sutherland, one of the founding scholars of American criminology, is widely accepted:

Criminology is the body of knowledge regarding crime as a social phenomenon. It includes within its scope the process of making laws, of breaking laws, and of reacting toward the breaking of laws. . . . The objective of criminology is the development of a body of general and verified principles and of other types of knowledge regarding this process of law, crime, and treatment or prevention.[15]

This definition suggests that the field of criminology is narrowly focused on crime yet broad in scope. By stating as the objective of criminology the "development of a body of general and verified principles," Sutherland mandates that **criminologists,** like all other scientists, collect information for study and analysis in accordance with the research methods of modern science. As we shall see in Chapter 3, it was in the eighteenth century that serious investigations into criminal behavior were first conducted. The investigators, however, were not engaged in empirical research, although they based their conclusions on factual information. Only in the nineteenth century did criminologists begin to systematically gather facts about crime and criminals and evaluate their data in a scientific manner.

Among the first researchers to analyze empirical data (facts, statistics, and other observable information) in a search for the causes of crime was Cesare Lombroso (1835–1909) of Italy (Chapter 3). His biologically oriented theories influenced American criminology at the turn of the twentieth century. At that time, the causes of crime were thought to rest within the individual: Criminal behavior was attributed to feeblemindedness and "moral insanity." From then on, psychologists and psychiatrists played an important role in the study of crime and criminals.

By the 1920s, other scholars attributed the cause of crime to the influx of immigrants and their alien behaviors. The search then moved on to cultural and social interpretations. Crime was explained not only in terms of the offender but also in terms of social, political, and economic problems.

In increasing numbers, sociologists, political scientists, legal scholars, and economists have entered the arena of criminology. Architects, too, have joined the ranks of criminologists in an effort to design housing units that will be relatively free from crime. Engineers are working to design cars that are virtually theft-proof. Pharmacologists play a role in alleviating the problem of drug addiction. Satellites put into space by astrophysicists can help

control the drug trade. Specialists in public administration work to improve the functioning of the criminal justice system. Educators have been enlisted to prepare children for a life as free from delinquency as possible. Economists and social workers are needed to help break the cycle of poverty and crime. Biologists, neuroscientists, and endocrinologists have expanded our understanding of the relationship between biology, the brain, and deviant behavior. Clearly, criminology is a discipline composed of the accumulated knowledge of many other disciplines. Criminologists acknowledge their indebtedness to all contributing disciplines and concede that the most powerful explanations of crime and criminality likely will come from interdisciplinary scholarship.

In explaining what is meant by Sutherland's definition—"making laws," "breaking laws," and "reacting toward the breaking of laws"—we will use a contemporary as well as a historical perspective on these processes, and a global as well as a local focus.

THE MAKING OF LAWS

Conjure up a picture of a crowded supermarket just after working hours, when most people are eager to get home after a busy day. The checkout counters have long lines of carts overflowing with groceries. One counter—an express line—takes 10 items only. You have 15, but you get in line anyway. People behind you in the line stare. Your behavior is not acceptable. You are a nonconformist, a deviant.

Deviance

Criminologists use the term **deviance** to describe behavior that violates **social norms,** including laws. The customary ways of doing everyday things (like not exceeding the posted limit of items at supermarket express lines) are governed by norms other than laws. More serious deviant behavior, like taking someone else's property, is governed by laws. Criminologists are interested in all social norms and in how society reacts to success or failure of compliance.[16] They are interested in what society does when customary ways of doing things no longer prove effective in controlling conduct perceived as undesirable. New Yorkers concerned over the problem of dog droppings provide an example.

Disciplined city dwellers had always observed the custom of curbing their dogs. Street signs warned them to do this. But as more and more dog owners failed to comply, New Yorkers decided that the cleanliness of the sidewalks was an important issue. Laws were enacted making it an offense not to clean up after one's dog. The need for law, or the most formal of social controls,

A sign that says "Stop Massacre" at a rally against the new one dog policy outside the entrance of the Beijing Zoo (China).

is often determined by social norms and practices. In Beijing, China, for example, all dogs were once banned from the city. Today, there are 900,000 registered dogs in Beijing (and many more unregistered), even though there remain restrictions on the number of dogs that may be owned and their height.

The difference between crime and other forms of deviance is subject to constant change and may vary from one state or country to another and from one time to another. What yesterday was only distasteful or morally repugnant may today be illegal. Criminologists are therefore interested in all norms that regulate conduct. Making something that is distasteful into a crime may be counter productive and detrimental to the social order. If everything deviant (inconsistent with the majority's norms) were to be made criminal, society would become very rigid. The more rigid a society, the more that behavior defined as violating social norms is prohibited by law.

Jack D. Douglas and Frances C. Waksler have presented the continuum of deviance as a funnel (Figure 1.2). This funnel consists of definitions ranging from the broadest (a "feeling that something is vaguely wrong, strange, peculiar") to the narrowest (a "judgment that something is absolutely evil"). Somewhere between these two extremes, deviant behavior becomes criminal behavior. The criminologist's interest in understanding the process begins at the earliest point—when a behavior is first labeled "deviant."[17]

Although criminologists are interested in all deviant behavior—even that of no interest to the law—their primary interest is in criminal behavior, behavior that violates the law.

The Concept of Crime

A **crime** is any human conduct that violates a criminal law and is subject to punishment. What leads a society to designate some deviant

Most inclusive

I. Feeling that something is vaguely wrong, strange, peculiar
II. Feelings of dislike, repugnance
III. Feeling that something violates values or rules
IV. Feeling that something violates moral values or moral rules
V. Judgment that something violates values or rules
VI. Judgment that something violates moral values or moral rules
VII. Judgment that something violates morally legitimate misdemeanor laws
VIII. Judgment that something violates morally legitimate felony laws
IX. Judgment that something violates moral human nature
X. Judgment that something is absolutely evil

Least inclusive

FIGURE 1.2 The funnel of deviance.

Source: Adapted from Jack D. Douglas and Frances Chaput Waksler, *The Sociology of Deviance* (Boston: Little, Brown, 1982), Figure 1.1, p. 11. Copyright © 1982 by Jack D. Douglas and Frances Chaput Waksler. Reprinted by permission of the authors.

Terrorism and the Fear of Terrorism

Since it opened in 1903, the Taj Mahal Palace & Tower, Mumbai, has created its own unique history. From maharajas and princes to various kings, presidents, CEOs and entertainers, the Taj has played the perfect host, supportive of their every need.

Built in 1903, the hotel is an architectural marvel and brings together Moorish, Oriental, and Florentine styles. Offering panoramic views of the Arabian Sea and the Gateway of India, the hotel is a gracious landmark of the city of Mumbai, showcasing contemporary Indian influences along with beautiful vaulted alabaster ceilings, onyx columns, graceful archways, handwoven silk carpets, crystal chandeliers, a magnificent art collection, an eclectic collection of furniture, and a dramatic cantilever stairway.

Over the past century, the Taj Mahal Palace & Tower, Mumbai, has amassed a diverse collection of paintings and works of art and is a veritable showcase of artifacts and art of the era. From Belgian chandeliers to Goan Christian artifacts, the hotel incorporates a myriad of artistic styles and tastes.(1)

■ *The Taj Mahal Palace & Tower, Mumbai.*

Voted "The World's Best Overseas Business Hotel" by readers of *Condé Nast Traveller UK* in 2008, the Taj Mahal Palace & Tower is nothing short of a hotel icon. It stands as India's most famous and most luxurious hotel. In November 2008, it was also the primary site of an extremely well-coordinated terror plot that, along with separate attacks in nine other locations in this capital city of India, resulted in the death of more than 180 people.(2) More than 240 people were injured.

behavior a crime and leave other wrongs to be settled by private or civil remedies? For centuries, natural-law philosophers, believing in the universal rightness and wrongness of certain human behavior, held the view that some forms of behavior are innately criminal and that all societies condemn them equally. Homicide and theft were thought to be among these.

This notion is no longer supported. Raffaele Garofalo, who gave our discipline its name, defended the concept of natural crime, by which he meant behavior that offends basic moral sentiments, such as respect for the property of others and revulsion against the infliction of suffering. Nevertheless, he admitted that although we might think such crimes as murder and robbery would be recognized by all existing legal systems, "a slight investigation seems to dispel this idea."[18]

Garofalo was right. The earliest codes, including the Babylonian Code of Hammurabi (about 1750 B.C.) and the Roman Law of the Twelve Tables (451–450 B.C.), do not list homicide or ordinary theft as crimes. Problems like these were settled without resorting to punishment. But all early societies imposed punishment for acts detrimental to their own existence: acts of treason. Other crimes depended on socioeconomic needs (destroying a bridge was a crime among the Incas; stealing a beehive was a crime among the ancient Germanic tribes; stealing a horse or a blanket was a crime among American Plains Indians).

The question arises: Who in a society decides—and when and under what circumstances—which acts that are already considered deviant in that society should be elevated to the level of gross deviance or crime, subject to punishment?

The Consensus and Conflict Views of Law and Crime

In the traditional interpretation of the historical development of legal systems, and of criminal justice in particular, lawmaking is an accommodation of interests in a society, whether that

The hotel had prior warning that an attack might take place. Staff heeded the warning, but to no avail. Even with additional security, the attack was not easily prevented. According to Ratan Tata, chairman of the Tata Group that owns the hotel, "[The terrorists] knew what they were doing, and they did not go through the front. All of our [security] arrangements are in the front," he said. "They planned everything. I believe the first thing they did, they shot a sniffer dog and his handler. They went through the kitchen." To make matters worse, according to Tata, Mumbai's emergency response infrastructure was inadequate.

There is an emerging consensus about the lessons learned from this attack, lessons that complement Ratan Tata's critical view:

■ Bloodshed in Mumbai: Tourists and police targeted in 10 attacks.

- *The public expects and deserves competent law enforcement responses.* Law enforcement's response in Mumbai was underwhelming.
- *Low-tech, highly synchronized attacks can exact a significant toll.* The only weapons it takes for a successful terrorist attack are automatic rifles and hand grenades.
- *Terrorists can influence elections.* Major terrorist incidents tend to congregate around election time.

Madrid, Iraq, and Pakistan are far from coincidences.
- *Despite promises of prompt reform, don't expect much.* In the past year, India has experienced a dramatic upsurge in terrorism, even though such attacks are far from new.

As you read this book, consider how a criminologist might best be deployed in order to strengthen homeland security for all the obvious and less-than-obvious targets.

Sources

1. www.tajhotels.com/Palace/The%20 Taj%20Mahal%20Palace%20 &%20Tower,MUMBAI/default.htm.
2. "Bloodshed in Mumbai: Tourists and Police Targeted in 10 Attacks," Associated Press, Nov. 28, 2008.

Questions for Discussion

1. What are the most likely targets of terrorist groups?
2. How would you go about developing a counterterrorist strategy?

society is composed of equals (as in a democracy) or of rulers and ruled (as in absolute monarchies), so as to produce a system of law and enforcement to which everybody basically subscribes. This is the **consensus model.** According to this view, certain acts are deemed so threatening to the society's survival that they are designated crimes. If the vast majority of a group shares this view, we can say the group has acted by consensus.

The model assumes that members of a society by and large agree on what is right and wrong and that codification of social values becomes law, with a mechanism of control that settles disputes that arise when some individuals stray too far from what is considered acceptable behavior. In the words of the French sociologist Émile Durkheim, "we can . . . say that an act is criminal when it offends strong and defined states of the collective conscience."[19] Consensus theorists view society as a stable entity in which laws are created for the general good. Laws function to reconcile and to harmonize most of the interests that most of us accept, with the least amount of sacrifice.

Some criminologists view the making of laws in a society from a different theoretical perspective. In their interpretation, known as the **conflict model,** the criminal law expresses the values of the ruling class in a society, and the criminal justice system is a means of controlling the classes that have no power. Conflict theorists claim that a struggle for power is a far more basic feature of human existence than is consensus. It is through power struggles that various interest groups manage to control lawmaking and law enforcement. Accordingly, the appropriate object of criminological investigation is not the violation of laws but the conflicts within society.

Traditional historians of crime and criminal justice do not deny that throughout history there have been conflicts that needed resolution. Traditionalists claim that differences have been resolved by consensus, while conflict theorists claim that the dominant group has ended the

■ The Code of Hammurabi, king of ancient Babylonia, is the oldest complete legal code in existence (about 1750 B.C.). The 8.2-foot carving, found in Iraq in 1902, is now on display in the Louvre in Paris. The only exact replica is at the United Nations building in New York.

conflicts by imposing its will. This difference in perspective marks one of the major criminological debates today, as we shall see in Chapter 8. It also permeates criminological discussion of who breaks the criminal laws and why.

Fairy Tales and Crime

Have you ever wondered about the wolf who accosts Little Red Riding Hood as she makes her way through the forest to her grandmother's house? Later he devours both Grandma and Little Red Riding Hood. Who is that wolf who speaks like a man?

The Wolf-Outlaw

Scholarly research suggests that he is a wolf of the two-legged variety—a convicted criminal banished to the woods. Fairy tales embody ancient folk wisdom and law. Before there were written legal codes, law was transmitted orally from generation to generation. The Red Riding Hood fairy tale reflects a time when the punishment for the most serious crimes was to be treated like a wolf. Like the four-legged variety, the offender was

banished from human society and condemned to the forest, there to live or die among the four-legged wolves, shunned or hunted like one of them.

The ancient European tribes, ever on the move, could not rely on prisons as punishment for offenders. Outlawry seemed to be the perfect solution, and the wolf provided a model.

Imprisonment as a punishment for crime does not appear in any of the Grimms' fairy tales, another accurate reflection of historical fact: German principalities began to use imprisonment only in the fourteenth century, and the tales collected by the Grimm brothers generally predated that period.

Catalogs of Crime and Punishment

Fairy tales are rich in criminological lore. Every category of crime and the punishments that were in vogue in the early Middle Ages appear in the Grimms' tales. Death by fire was the punishment of choice for witchcraft, as in "Hansel and Gretel," where the witch is incinerated in her own stove. Murderers were drowned, burned, or banished to the forest, and grand larceny was punished by hanging, as in the fairy tale "The Master-Thief" (although the ruler commuted the sentence). Petty larceny was punished corporally, and impersonation and involuntary servitude, as in "Cinderella," were punished by blinding, a penalty German tribes regarded as very severe. Tarring also appeared as a punishment for serious crimes, both in the fairy tales and in law documents from the period.

In the fairy tale "The Twelve Brothers," perverting justice and attempting to cause an innocent person to be executed was punished by being boiled in oil into which vipers were thrown, the most unusual penalty that appears in the Grimms' collection. But it, too, reflects historical fact; a similar punishment is recorded in early Roman law.

Psychological Treatises

These tales can tell us about more than just types of crimes and punishments. The author of a research report entitled "The Criminal Element in German Folk Tales," published in 1910, used a criminological psychology approach to analyze the Grimms' tales and those collected by others. This report uncovered "every conceivable criminal motivation, from base greed to the grossest form of psychopathology." Perhaps fairytales would be useful "required reading" for students of criminology.

Source: Gerhard O. W. Mueller, "The Criminological Significance of the Grimms' Fairy Tales," in *Fairy Tales and Society: Illusion, Allusion, and Paradigm,* ed. Ruth B. Bottigheimer (Philadelphia: University of Pennsylvania Press, 1986), pp. 217–227.

THE BREAKING OF LAWS

Sutherland's definition of criminology includes within its scope investigating and explaining the process of breaking laws. This may seem simple if viewed from a purely legal perspective. A prosecutor is not interested in the fact that hundreds of people are walking on Main Street. But if one of those hundreds grabs a woman's purse and runs away with it, the prosecutor is interested, provided the police have brought the incident to the prosecutor's attention. What alerts the prosecutor is the fact that a law has been broken, that one of those hundreds of people on Main Street has turned from a law-abiding citizen into a law-breaker. This event, if detected, sets in motion a legal process that ultimately will determine whether someone is indeed a law-breaker.

Sutherland, in saying that criminologists have to study the process of lawbreaking, had much more in mind than determining whether someone has violated the criminal law. He was referring to the process of breaking laws. That process encompasses a series of events, perhaps starting at birth or even earlier, that results in the commission of crime by some individuals and not by others.

Let us analyze the following rather typical scenario: In the maximum-security unit of a midwestern penitentiary is an inmate we will call Jeff. He is one of three robbers who held up a check-cashing establishment. During the robbery, another of the robbers killed the clerk. Jeff has been sentenced to life imprisonment.

Born in an inner-city ghetto, Jeff was the third child of an unwed mother. He had a succession of temporary "fathers." By age 12, he had run away from home for the first time, only to be brought back to his mother, who really did not care much whether he returned. He rarely went to school because, he said, "all the guys were bigger." At age 16, after failing two grades, Jeff dropped out of school completely and hung around the streets of his deteriorated, crime-ridden neighborhood. He had no job. He had no reason to go home, because usually no one was there.

One night he was beaten up by members of a local gang. He joined a rival gang for protection and soon began to feel proud of his membership in one of the toughest gangs in the neighborhood. Caught on one occasion tampering with parking meters and on another trying to steal a car navigation system, he was sentenced to two months in a county correctional institution for boys. By the age of 18, he had moved from petty theft to armed robbery.

Many people reading the story of Jeff would conclude that he deserves what is coming to him and that his fate should serve as a warning to others. Other people would say that with his background, Jeff did not have a chance. Some may even marvel at Jeff's ability to survive at all in a very tough world.

To the criminologist, popular interpretations of Jeff's story do not explain the process of breaking laws in Sutherland's terms. Nor do these interpretations explain why people in general break a certain law. Sutherland demanded scientific rigor in researching and explaining the process of breaking laws. As we will see later in the book (Parts 2 and 3), scientists have thoroughly explored Jeff's story and the stories of other lawbreakers. They ask, Why are some people prone to commit crime and others are not? There is no agreement on the answer as yet. Researchers have approached the question from different perspectives. Some have examined delinquents (juvenile offenders) and criminals from a biological perspective in order to determine whether some human beings are constitutionally more prone to yield to opportunities to commit criminal acts. Are genes to blame? Hormones? Diet? Neuroanatomical differences? Others have explored the role played by moral development and personality. Is there a criminal personality? (These questions are discussed in Chapter 4.)

Most contemporary criminologists look to factors such as economic and social conditions, which can produce strain among social groups and lead to lawbreaking (Chapter 5). Others point to subcultures committed to violent or illegal activities (Chapter 6). Yet another argument is that the motivation to commit crime is simply part of human nature. So some criminologists examine the ability of social groups and institutions to make their rules effective (Chapter 7).

The findings of other scholars tend to show that lawbreaking depends less on what the

Fame and Crime

- Lindsay Lohan was arrested on December 11, 2006, on DUI charges after witnesses saw her driving the wrong way on the Burbank freeway in her black Mercedes-Benz sport utility vehicle. In a deal with prosecutors, Lohan pleaded guilty to a misdemeanor DUI charge, to avoid a longer jail term since it was her second DUI conviction.

  On November 15, 2007, Lohan reported to the Los Angeles County women's detention center in Lynwood where she was searched and fingerprinted, then stayed in a holding cell and released in just 84 minutes.

- Wesley Snipes was convicted and sentenced in April 2008 on three counts of failing to file his income tax returns. Snipes was sentenced to three years in prison, which his lawyers fought vigorously to have dismissed. In November 2010, Snipes lost his appeals and the following month he reported to the federal correctional institution McKean near Lewis Run, Pennsylvania. Snipes is expected to be released in July 2013. Wesley Snipes is best known for his role as Blade in the "Blade" trilogy.

- On June 27, 1995, Hugh Grant was arrested for engaging in oral copulation with a prostitute, Divine Brown, while parked in his BMW. He was fined $1,180 and received two-year's probation.

- On October 9th, 2007, Kiefer Sutherland pled no contest to a DUI charge and received a 48-day jail sentence. This mug shot was taken on December 6, 2007, when he surrendered to the Glendale Police Department to begin his jail term.

- On July 28, 2006, actor, director, and producer Mel Gibson was arrested on suspicion of driving under the influence while speeding (87 miles per hour in a 45-mph zone) in Malibu, California.

  The intoxicated Gibson became belligerent with police during his arrest and according to L.A. County Sheriff's Deputy James Mee's report, Gibson used bad language, threatened the arresting officer, repeatedly banged himself against the police car interior, and made anti-Semitic statements, including telling the policeman that, "The Jews are responsible for all the wars in the world."

  On August 18, Gibson pleaded no contest to one count of driving with blood alcohol content above .08%. The other charges were dropped, and he was sentenced to three years probation, a 90-day alcohol-abuse program, 12 months of Alcoholics Anonymous meetings and fined $1,300 with a 90-day meetings, fined $1,300, and given license restriction. Gibson volunteered to do public-service announcements on the hazards of drinking and driving, and to enter rehab.

- In July 1994, O.J. Simpson was arrested in Los Angeles, and charged with the murder of his wife, Nicole Simpson, and her friend Ron Goldman. He was found not guilty in a highly publicized trial. He was later found liable for damages in the murders during a civil trial.

  Five years before the murder of Nicole and Goldman, Simpson was arrested for beating his wife, paid a fine, and did 200 hours of community service.

  Nicole and Goldman were viciously attacked and butchered outside of Nicole's home. No one else was ever charged for the murders.

- R. Kelly was charged with 14 counts of child pornography and illegally engaging in sexual acts with a minor occurring sometime between November 1997 and February 2002.[1]

The stories never seem to end. One star after another faces arrest. The mug shots of famous musicians, sports heroes, actors, comedians, business tycoons, and public officials make their way to tabloid websites, magazines, and newspapers. Their dramatic fall from grace is amazing, exciting, and tragic all at the same time.

Criminologists look at these arrests and think about a wide range of explanations, from failures of self-control offender does than on what society, including the criminal justice system, does to the offender (Chapter 8). This is the perspective of the labeling, conflict, and radical theorists, who have had great influence on criminological thinking since the 1970s.

Scholars have also researched the question of why people who are inclined to break laws engage in particular acts at particular times. They have demonstrated that opportunity plays a large role in the decision to commit a crime. Opportunities are suitable targets inadequately protected. In these circumstances, all that is required for a crime to be committed is a person motivated to offend. These claims are made by criminologists who explain crime in terms of two perspectives: routine activities and rational choice (Chapter 9).

SOCIETY'S REACTION TO THE BREAKING OF LAWS

Criminologists' interest in understanding the process of breaking a law (or any other social norm) is tied to understanding society's reaction to deviance. The study of reactions to lawbreaking demonstrates that society has always tried to control or prevent norm-breaking.

In the Middle Ages, the wayfarer entering a city had to pass the gallows, on which the bodies of criminals swung in the wind. Wayfarers had to enter through gates in thick walls, and the drawbridges were lowered only during the daylight hours; at nightfall the gates were closed. In front of the town hall, stocks and pillory warned dishonest vendors and

and social control (Chapter 7) to the strain of celebrity (Chapter 5), from drug abuse and dependence (Chapter 13) to rational-choice and routine-activity theories (Chapter 9). Criminologists think about how representative these cases are relative to the street crimes of inner-city youth. They wonder how the criminal justice system accommodates privilege, wealth, celebrity, and fame. Do police, prosecutors, and judges deal differently with such cases? Should they?

To a large extent, the images of Lindsay Lohan, Wesley Snipes, Hugh Grant, Kiefer Sutherland, Mel Gibson, O.J. Simpson, and R. Kelly frame our perceptions about deviance. Their arrests are remarkable for so many fascinating and disturbing reasons. They have wealth and fame. They are at the top of their game and have so much to lose. We idolize them, admire their talent and boundless success, and think about what life might be like as a world famous rapper, actor, or sports star.

■ Lindsay Lohan

■ Wesley Snipes

■ Hugh Grant

■ Kiefer Sutherland

■ Mel Gibson

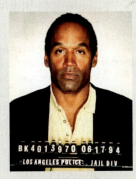
■ O. J. Simpson

■ R. Kelly

Source

1. Charles Montaldo, "Celebrity Mug Shots: Celebrities at Their Worst," at http://crime.about.com/od/famousdiduno/ig/celebrity_mugshots.

Questions for Discussion

1. What can we learn from the celebrities' arrests about why people, in general, commit crime, about who commits crime, and about how society should respond to crime?

2. To what extent are celebrities victimized by their own fame and thus less blameworthy for acts of deviance? (See, e.g., Ruth Penfold, "The Star's Image, Victimization and Celebrity Culture," *Punishment & Society*, 6, [**3**], [2004]: 289–302.)

pickpockets. Times have changed, but perhaps less than we think. Today penitentiaries and jails dot the countryside. Teams of work-release convicts work along highways under guard. Signs proclaim "Drug-Free School Zone," and decals on doors announce "Neighborhood Crime Watch." Police patrol cars are as visible as they are audible.

These overt signs of concern about crime provide us with only a surface view of the apparatus society has created to deal with lawbreaking; they tell us little of the research and policy making that have gone into the creation of the apparatus. Criminologists have done much of the research on society's reaction to the breaking of laws, and the results have influenced policy making and legislation aimed at crime control.

The research has also revealed that society's reaction to lawbreaking has often been irrational, arbitrary, emotional, politically motivated, and counterproductive.

Research on society's reaction to the breaking of laws is more recent than research on the causes of crime. It is also more controversial. For some criminologists, the function of their research is to assist government in the prevention or repression of crime. Others insist that such a use of science only supports existing power structures that may be corrupt. The position of most criminologists is somewhere in between. Researchers often discover inhumane and arbitrary practices and provide the database and the ideas for a humane, effective, and efficient **criminal justice system.**

Criminology and the Criminal Justice System

The term "criminal justice system" is relatively new. It became popular only in 1967, with the publication of the report of the President's Commission on Law Enforcement and Administration of Justice, *The Challenge of Crime in a Free Society*. The discovery that various ways of dealing with lawbreaking form a system was itself the result of criminological research. Research into the functioning of the system and its component parts, as well as into the work of functionaries within the system, has provided many insights over the last few decades.

Scientists who study the criminal justice system are frequently referred to as "criminal justice specialists." This term suggests a separation between criminology and criminal justice. In fact, the two fields are closely interwoven. Scholars of both disciplines use the same scientific research methods. They have received the same rigorous education, and they pursue the same goals. Both fields rely on the cooperation of many other disciplines, including sociology, psychology, political science, law, economics, management, and education. Their origins, however, differ. Criminology has its roots in European scholarship, although it has undergone refinements, largely under the influence of American sociology. Criminal justice is a recent American innovation.

The two fields are also distinguished by a difference in focus. Criminology generally focuses on scientific studies of crime and criminality, whereas criminal justice focuses on scientific studies of decision-making processes, operations, and justice-related concerns such as the efficiency of police, courts, and corrections systems; the just treatment of offenders; the needs of victims; and the effects of changes in sentencing philosophy.

The United States has well over 50 criminal justice systems—those of the 50 states and of the federal government, the District of Columbia, Puerto Rico, Guam, the U.S. Virgin Islands, American Samoa, the Commonwealth of the Northern Mariana Islands, Palau, and the military. They are very similar: All are based on constitutional principles and on the heritage of the common law, and all were designed to cope with the problem of crime within their territories on the assumption that crime is basically a local event calling for a local response. Crimes that have an interstate or international aspect are under the jurisdiction of federal authorities, and such offenses are prosecuted under the federal criminal code.

The Global Approach to the Breaking of Laws

Until fairly recently, there was rarely any need to cooperate with foreign governments, because crime had few international connections. This situation has changed drastically. Crime, like life itself, has become globalized, and responses to lawbreaking have inevitably extended beyond local and national borders. In the first three and a half decades after World War II, from 1945 until the late 1970s, the countries of the world gradually became more interdependent. Commercial relations among countries increased. Modern commercial aviation (the "jet age") brought a huge increase in international travel and transport. Satellite communications facilitated intense and continuous public and private relationships. The Internet added the final touch to globalization.

Beginning in the 1980s, the internationalization of national economies accelerated sharply, and with the collapse of Marxism in Eastern Europe in the 1990s, a global economy is being created. These developments, which turned the world into what has been called a "global village,"

In Placentia, California, residents clamor for protection of children from convicted and released child molesters. Public protests have led to a flood of local laws regarding the identification of where these ex-offenders are residing.

TABLE 1.1 The Relationship between Determinants of Human Insecurity, Violent Conflict, and Climate Change

Factors affecting violent conflict	Processes which climate change could affect/exacerbate
Vulnerable livelihoods	Climate change is likely to cause widespread impacts on water availability, coastal regions, agriculture, extreme events, and diseases. The impacts on livelihoods will be more significant in sectors of the population with high resource-dependency, and in more environmentally and socially marginalised areas. Some of these climate-driven outcomes are long term and chronic (such as declining productivity of agricultural land), while others are episodic (such as floods). These impacts on livelihoods will be widespread both in developing and developed countries.
Poverty (relative/chronic/transitory)	Poverty (and particularly relative deprivation) is affected by the spatial differentiation of climate impacts and the sensitivity of places to them. Climate change may directly increase absolute, relative, and transient poverty by undermining access to natural capital. It may indirectly increase poverty through its effects on resource sectors and the ability of governments to provide social safety nets. Stresses from climate change will differentially affect those made vulnerable by political-economic processes such as liberalization of markets for agricultural commodities.
Weak states	The impacts of climate change are likely to increase the costs of providing public infrastructure such as water resources, and services such as education, and may decrease government revenues. So climate change may decrease the ability of states to create opportunities and provide important freedoms for citizens as well as decrease the capacity of government agencies to adapt and respond to climate change itself.
Migration	Migration may be one response of people whose livelihoods are undermined by climate change. However, climate is unlikely to be the sole, or even the most important "push" factor in migration decisions. Yet large-scale movements of people may increase the risk of conflict in host communities.

have also had considerable negative consequences. As everything else in life became globalized, so did crime. Transnational crimes, with which we began this chapter, suddenly boomed. Then there are the truly international crimes—those that are proscribed by international law—such as crimes against the peace and security of mankind, genocide, and war crimes. But even many apparently purely local crimes, whether local drug crime or handgun violence, now have international dimensions. In view of the rapid globalization of crime, we devote an entire chapter (Chapter 14) to the international dimensions of criminology. In addition, "Window to the World" boxes explore the international implications of crime and criminology.

The importance of a global approach to criminology is beyond controversy. However, developing the cross-national dialogue and collaboration necessary to build a robust field remains a challenge. This challenge will gain significance as the effects of globalization reveal just how connected we are to the economic and social development of emerging and transitional countries. It will be affected as well by global threats not typically considered by criminologists, such as climate change. Even the most conservative scenarios by leading nongovernmental organizations (for example, the Intergovernmental Panel on Climate Change) suggest massive displacement and shifts in population in some of the poorest of the poor nations. The consequences of these movements, along with the changing landscape of countries already experiencing dramatic social and economic crises, will likely keep criminologists busy for many years to come (See Table 1.1).

RESEARCH INFORMS POLICY

Skeptics often ask: With so many criminologists at work in the United States, and so many studies conducted over the last half century, why do we have so much crime, why is some of it increasing, and why do new forms of crime emerge constantly? There are several answers. Crime rates go up and down. Through the 1990s crime decreased, and then in the first decade of the new century it increased. The perception that the crime problem is increasing or decreasing rests on a fear of crime that is fueled by media portrayals. Sensational reports often sell newspapers and TV programs. Politicians, in turn, seek security in office by catering to public perceptions of crime rather than to its reality. They therefore propose and enact measures that respond to popular demands and that often are more symbolic than result-oriented. At the moment, this means ever harsher and more punitive measures for dealing with the crime problem.

Few criminologists believe that enough research exists at present to justify such an approach. In fact, some criminological research demonstrates the futility of escalating punishments and often points to measures of quite a different nature as more promising, more humane, and more cost-beneficial. So why do criminologists not make

themselves heard? The answer is that criminologists are social scientists, not politicians. Criminologists are not voted into Congress or to the presidency or a governorship. Criminologists have served on virtually every federal and state commission dealing with problems of crime or criminal justice, but just as the Pentagon cannot declare war, criminologists cannot dictate national or state crime-control policies. They can, however, provide pertinent research findings that inform national policy making.[20] In the past, the attorney general of the United States asked criminologists to formulate policy recommendations based on their research findings in areas such as delinquency prevention, drug control, global crime, youth violence, and violence against women.[21] More collaboration is being sought in order to bring the field of criminology to those responsible for setting criminal justice policy.

CHAPTER 1

REVIEW

Very little happens on Earth that does not concern criminology. Yet criminology as a science is only a century old. Edwin H. Sutherland provided the most widely accepted definition: "The body of knowledge regarding crime as a social phenomenon. It includes within its scope the process of making laws, of breaking laws, and of reacting toward the breaking of laws."

Criminologists study behavior that violates all social norms, including laws. They distinguish between two conflicting views of the history of criminal law: the consensus view, which regards lawmaking as the result of communal agreement about what is to be prohibited, and the conflict view, according to which laws are imposed by those with power over those without power.

The breaking of laws (the subject to which much of this book is devoted) is not merely a formal act that may lead to arrest and prosecution, but an intricate process by which some people violate some laws under some circumstances. Many disciplines contribute to understanding the process of breaking laws or other norms, but as yet there is no consensus on why people become criminals. Society has always reacted to lawbreaking, although the scientific study of lawbreaking is of very recent origin. Today criminologists

analyze the methods and procedures society uses in reacting to crime; they evaluate the success or failure of such methods; and on the basis of their research, they propose more effective and humane ways of controlling crime.

Criminologists have discovered that the various agencies society has created to deal with lawbreaking constitute a system that, like any other system, can be made more efficient. Research on the system depends on the availability of a variety of data, especially statistics. The gathering and analysis of statistics on crime and criminal justice are among the primary tasks of criminologists. The effectiveness of their work depends on reliable data.

The province of criminology today is the entire world: Every aspect of life, including crime, has become increasingly globalized in recent years as a result of both rapid advances in technology and economic integration.

Criminology is a politically sensitive discipline. Its findings inform public policy. While criminologists cannot dictate what the branches of government—the legislative, the judicial, and the executive—should do about crime, their research findings are being used increasingly in making governmental decisions.

CRIMINOLOGY & PUBLIC POLICY

Crime waves always carry with them calls for more law enforcement authority. What happened on September 11, 2001, was, among other things, a crime wave—that one day caused the number of homicides in America in 2001 to be 20 percent higher than the year before. It is no surprise, then, that even before the fires in the rubble that was

the World Trade Center burned themselves out, some politicians were calling for broader powers for law enforcement and greater restrictions on citizens, all in the effort to fight this particular crime wave.

That is not a bad thing. Law enforcement authority naturally varies with the nature and size of the crime problems police must combat. A glance at the recent history of criminal procedure shows as much. Most legal restrictions on policing date from the criminal procedure revolution of the 1960s, which itself can be seen as a consequence of the low-crime 1950s. Higher crime rates led to cutbacks in those legal protections in the 1970s and 1980s, just as lower crime rates have led to some expansion in the past few years. In short, Fourth and Fifth Amendment rights have varied with crime before, and they will probably do so in the future, as they must if the law is to reflect a sensible balance between the social need for order and individuals' desire for privacy and liberty. The terrorist attacks on New York and Washington raised the demands on law enforcement. Those increased demands have already led to some increases in law enforcers' legal authority, and that trend will—and probably should—continue, at least for a while. (Source: William J. Stuntz, "Local Policing after Terror." Reprinted by permission of The Yale Law Journal Company, Inc., from *The Yale Law Journal*, vol. 111, p. 2137 [2002]).

Questions for Discussion Sutherland's broad definition of criminology (see p. 22) includes a critical examination of the criminal justice response to crimes. Following the spirit of his definition, how should we fashion and refashion our criminal justice system in response to the threat of terrorism in the United States? Should we increasingly delegate the responsibility for investigating and combating terrorism to local law enforcement agencies? How, then, do we control the flow of intelligence data?

One of the most significant questions concerns the extent to which our response to 9/11 will jeopardize the constitutional rights of U.S. citizens. How much freedom are you willing to give up in the name of law enforcement?

YOU BE THE CRIMINOLOGIST

How would you teach the ideal course on criminology? (Don't answer until you have completed the course!)

KEY TERMS

The numbers next to the terms refer to the pages on which the terms are defined.

conflict model (15)
consensus model (15)
crime (13)
criminal justice system (19)
criminologists (12)
criminology (12)
deviance (12)
social norms (12)

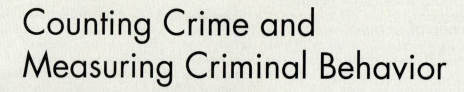

2

Counting Crime and Measuring Criminal Behavior

■ *Many large police departments conduct weekly crime-control strategy sessions or COMPSTAT (Computerized Statistics) meetings to increase the flow of information between police executives and the commanders of operational units.*

In 1978, inmates of Rahway maximum-security prison in New Jersey started a program for young "delinquent" teens called Scared Straight. The premise of the program was simple: Take juvenile delinquents into a rough prison environment, have inmates expose them to what it means to live a life of crime and to the horrors of incarceration, and literally scare them straight. If these at-risk teens understood the path they were on and the brutality of prison life, most if not all would reconsider their deviant ways. At least this was the hypothesis behind Scared Straight.

Early evidence of the success of Scared Straight was hyped in a 1979 documentary, in which viewers were told of a 94 percent success rate for juveniles over a 3-month period; that is, only 6 percent of those "scared straight" were arrested. The program now had both intuitive appeal and some (apparent) empirical evidence of its success in deterring youth from a life of adult crime. Moreover, at times when the public urges politicians to get tough on crime, programs such as Scared Straight fit the bill—literally. The cost of Scared Straight was estimated to be no more than $1 per participant.

Three years after the start of the program, Jim Finckenauer conducted a simple experiment to test, far more rigorously, just how successful Scared Straight was.[1] Using a randomized controlled trial—much in the same way drug companies ensure the efficacy of a new pain reliever—Finckenauer compared the arrest rates of the participants of Scared Straight (treatment group) with a no-treatment control group of at-risk juveniles.

Finckenauer's results were remarkable, for a host of reasons. First, the Scared Straight program was not deterring at-risk youth. Second, arrest rates were actually higher in the treatment group than in the controls. Perhaps as important, Finckenauer's work suggested the importance of moving beyond politically expedient, ideologically consistent, and intuitively pleasing juvenile justice programs to those shown by empirical (experimental) evidence to work. In other words, programs designed to deter juveniles must be evidenced-based. A systematic review of randomized experimental research on Scared Straight programs over the past 25 years recently concluded, as Finckenauer did, that Scared Straight was actually more harmful to juveniles than doing nothing at all.[2]

The field of criminology has increasingly embraced systematic, empirically rigorous tests of criminal justice programs and initiatives. The trend in recent years is to subject our evaluation of such programs and initiatives to randomized controlled trials, a trend captured by the emergence of an evidence-based approach to criminology called "experimental criminology."

Questions about how crime is measured and what those measurements reveal about the nature and extent of crime are among the most important issues in contemporary criminology. Researchers, theorists, and practitioners need information in order to explain and prevent crime, to evaluate the success of programs like Scared Straight, and to operate agencies that deal with problems of crime and justice.

And there is good reason to believe that experimental criminology influences criminal justice policy. Perhaps the best

FIGURE 2.1 Can you see all seven requirements? When is a crime committed?

Source: © 1962 *The Saturday Evening Post.* Reprinted by permission of *The Saturday Evening Post.*

evidence of this influence comes from Lawrence Sherman and Richard Berk's work on the importance of arrest in domestic violence calls to police. Under a grant from the National Institute of Justice, the Minneapolis Police Department, and the Police Foundation, these researchers conducted an experiment from early 1981 to mid-1982 testing police responses to domestic violence. The data demonstrated the power of arrest over police attempting to counsel parties or sending assailants away from home for several hours (see Figure 2.1). The study strongly influenced police departments around the United States to make mandatory arrests, encouraging a sea change in the way in which law enforcement conceives of these crimes.

We begin this chapter with an explanation of the ingredients that all crimes share. We then look at the objectives and methods of collecting information on specific types of crimes. Next, we consider the limitations of the information sources criminologists most frequently use to estimate the nature and extent of crime in the United States. We then explore measurement of the characteristics of crimes and criminals.

THE INGREDIENTS OF CRIME

Before we begin to measure specific crimes, we will examine the part of criminal law that deals with the common legal ingredients, or elements, found in all crimes. Generally speaking, if any one of these elements is not present, no crime has been committed. All the defenses available to a person charged with a crime allege that at least one of these elements is not present.

American criminal law scholar Jerome Hall has developed the theory that a human event, in order to qualify as a crime, must meet seven basic requirements:[3]

1. The act requirement

2. The legality requirement

3. The harm requirement

4. The causation requirement

5. The mens rea requirement

6. The concurrence requirement

7. The punishment requirement[4]

The Act Requirement

Legal scholars have long agreed that one fundamental ingredient of every crime is a human act. In this context, what is an "act"? Suppose a sleepwalker, in a trance, grabs a stone and hurls it at a passerby, subsequently killing him. The law does not consider this event to be an act. Before any human behavior can qualify as an act, there must be a conscious interaction between mind and body, a physical movement that results from the determination or effort of the actor. Thus, a reflex or convulsion, a bodily movement that occurs during unconsciousness or sleep, conduct that occurs during hypnosis or results from hypnotic suggestion, or a bodily movement that is not determined by the actor—as when somebody is pushed by another person—is a behavior that is not considered a voluntary act.[5] It is only when choices are overpoweringly influenced by forces beyond our control that the law will consider behavior irrational and beyond its reach.

Act versus Status

The criminal law, in principle, does not penalize anyone for a status or condition. Suppose the law made it a crime to be more than 6 feet tall or to have red hair. Or suppose the law made it a crime to be a member of the family of an army deserter or to be of a given religion or ethnic background. That was exactly the situation in the Soviet Union under Stalin's penal code, which made it a crime to be related to a deserter from the Red Army.[6]

There is thus more to the act requirement than the issue of a behavior's being voluntary and rational: There is the problem of distinguishing between act and status. A California law made it a criminal offense, subject to a jail term, to be a drug addict. In *Robinson v. California*, the U.S. Supreme Court held that statute to be unconstitutional. By making a status or condition a crime, the statute violated the Eighth Amendment to the U.S. Constitution, which prohibits "cruel and unusual punishments." Addiction, the Court noted, is a condition, an illness, much like leprosy or venereal disease.[7]

Failure to Act

The act requirement has yet another aspect. An act requires the interaction of mind and body. If only the mind is active and the body does not move, we do not have an act: Simply thinking about punching someone in the nose is not a crime (Figure 2.1). We are free to think. But if we carry a thought into physical action, we commit an act, which may be a crime.

Then there is the problem of omission, or failure to act. If the law requires that convicted sex offenders register with the police, and such a person decides not to fill out the registration form, that person is guilty of a crime by omission. But he has acted! He told his hand not to pick up that pen, not to fill out the form. Inaction may be action when the law clearly spells out what one has to do and one decides not to do it.

The law in most U.S. states imposes no duty to be a Good Samaritan, to offer help to another person in distress. The law requires action only if one has a legal duty to act. Lifeguards, for example, are contractually obligated to save bathers from drowning; parents are obligated by law to protect their children; law enforcement officers and firefighters are required to rescue people in distress.

The Legality Requirement

Marion Palendrano was charged with, among other things, being a "common scold" because she disturbed "the peace of the neighborhood and of all good and quiet people of this State."[8] Mrs. Palendrano moved that the charge be dismissed, and the Superior Court of New Jersey agreed with her, reasoning:

1. Such a crime cannot be found anywhere in the New Jersey statute books. Hence there is no such crime, although, long ago, the common law of England may have recognized such a crime.

2. "Being a common scold" is so vague a concept that to punish somebody for it would violate constitutional due process: "We insist

that laws give the person of ordinary intelligence a reasonable opportunity to know what is prohibited, so that he may act accordingly," ruled the court.[9]

If we want a person to adhere to a standard, the person has to know what that standard is. Thus, we have the ancient proposition that only conduct that has been made criminal by law before an act is committed can be a crime. Police, prosecutors, and courts are not interested in the billions of acts human beings engage in unless such acts have previously been defined by law as criminal. The law is interested only in an act (*actus*) that is guilty, evil, and prohibited (*reus*).

The Harm Requirement

Every crime has been created to prevent something bad (a given harm) from happening. Murder is prohibited because we don't want people to be killed. This detrimental consequence that we are trying to avoid is called "harm." If the specified harm has not been created by the defendant's act, the crime is not complete. Just think of would-be assassin John W. Hinckley Jr., who tried to kill President Reagan. He shot Reagan, but the president did not die. The harm envisioned by the law against murder had not been accomplished. (Hinckley could have been found guilty of attempted murder, but he was acquitted by reason of insanity; see Chapter 4.)

From a criminological perspective, most crimes are grouped by the harm that each entails. Offenses against the person involve harm to an individual, and offenses against property involve damage to property or loss of its possession.

The Causation Requirement

What is the act of hitting a home run? Of course, it is a hit that allows a batter to run to first, second, and third base, and then back to home plate. Actually, it is much more complicated than that. It starts with the decision to swing a bat, at a certain angle, with a particular intensity, in a specific direction, in order to cause a home run. Suppose that at a San Diego Padres home game, the batter hits a ball unusually high into the air. A passing pelican picks it up, flies off with it, and then drops it into the bleachers. Has the batter hit a home run? We doubt it.

It's the same in crime. Causation requires that the actor achieve the result (the harm) through his or her own effort. Suppose that A, in an effort to kill B, wounds him and that B actually dies when the ambulance carrying him to the hospital collides with another vehicle. Despite B's death, A did not succeed in her personal attempt to kill B. Thus, the act of murder is incomplete, although A

The posting of "pooper-scooper" regulations has had its effect. Most inner-city residents consider the failure to "pick up" to be a sign of disrespect and a violation of custom.

may be guilty of an attempt to kill. The causation requirement, then, holds that a crime is not complete unless the actor's conduct necessarily caused the harm without interference by somebody else and that it is the proximate cause of the act.[10]

Mens Rea: The "Guilty Mind" Requirement

Every crime, according to tradition, requires **mens rea,** a "guilty mind." Let us examine the case of Ms. Lambert. She was convicted in Los Angeles of an offense created by city ordinance: having lived in the city without registering with the police as a person previously convicted of a crime. Ms. Lambert had no idea that Los Angeles had such a registration requirement. Nor could she possibly have known that she was required to register. She appealed all the way to the U.S. Supreme Court, and she won. Said the Court: "Where a person did not know [of the prohibition] (s)he may not be convicted consistent with due process."[11]

■ *Amanda Knox arrives in court before the start of her appeal in Italy. She served four years of a twenty-six year murder sentence before the court ordered her conviction overturned in October 2011. An appeal against the acquittal was filed on February 14, 2012, by Italian prosecutors.*

which the actors consciously risk causing a prohibited harm (for example, the driver who races down a rain-slicked highway or the employer who sends his employees to work without safety equipment, knowing full well that lives are thereby being endangered).

Strict liability is an exception to the mens rea requirement. There is a class of offenses for which legislatures or courts require no showing of criminal intent or mens rea. For these offenses, the fact that the actor makes an innocent mistake and proceeds in good faith does not affect criminal liability. Strict-liability offenses range all the way from possessing a firearm to distributing adulterated food to running a red light. Typically, these offenses are subject to small penalties only, but in a few cases substantial punishments can be and have been imposed.

The Concurrence Requirement

The concurrence requirement states that the criminal act must be accompanied by an equally criminal mind. Suppose a striker throws a stone at an office window in order to shatter it, and a broken piece of glass pierces the throat of a secretary, who bleeds to death. Wanting to damage property deserves condemnation, but of a far lesser degree than wanting to kill. Act and intent did not concur in this case, and the striker should not be found guilty of murder. The law has created many exceptions to the concurrence requirement, one of which, the felony murder rule, we discuss in Chapter 10.

The Punishment Requirement

The last ingredient needed to constitute a crime is that of punishment. An illegal act coupled with an evil mind (criminal intent or mens rea) still does not constitute a crime unless the law subjects it to a punishment. If a sign posted in the park states "Do not step on the grass" and you do it anyway, have you committed a criminal offense? Not unless there is a law that subjects that act to punishment. Otherwise it is simply an improper or inconsiderate act.

The punishment requirement, more than any of the others, helps us differentiate between crimes (which are subject to punishments) and **torts**, civil wrongs for which the law does not prescribe punishment but merely grants the injured party the right to recover damages.

The nature and severity of punishments also help us differentiate between grades of crime. Most penal codes recognize three degrees of severity: **Felonies** are severe crimes, subject to punishments of a year or more in prison or to capital punishment. **Misdemeanors** are less-severe crimes, subject to a maximum of 1 year in jail. (For crimes of both grades, fines can also be imposed as punishments.) **Violations** are minor offenses, normally subject only to fines.

Of course, to blame Ms. Lambert for violating the Los Angeles city ordinance would make no sense. Ms. Lambert had no notion that she was doing something wrong by living in Los Angeles and not registering herself as a convicted person. With Ms. Lambert's case, we have reached a fundamental point: No one can be guilty of a crime unless he or she acted with the knowledge of doing something wrong. This principle always has existed. It is implicit in the concept of crime that the perpetrator know the wrongfulness of the act. It is not required that the perpetrator know the penal code or have personal feelings of guilt. It is enough that the perpetrator knows that he or she had no right to do what he or she did and decided to do it anyway.[12]

Anyone who violently attacks another person, takes another's property, invades another's home, forces intercourse, or forges a signature on someone else's check knows rather well that he or she is doing something wrong. All these examples of mens rea entail an intention to achieve harm or a knowledge that the prohibited harm will result. For some crimes, however, less than a definite intention suffices: reckless actions by

THE DEFENSES

You will soon see that we measure the amount of crime at various stages of the criminal process. For example: How many crimes are reported to the police? For how many of these crimes have convictions been obtained? There is a huge discrepancy. Far fewer convictions have been obtained than crimes reported or even prosecuted. There are several reasons for this discrepancy. One of the principal reasons is that not all elements of the crime charged could be proved in court. Why not? Because frequently the defendant has offered one of a number of defenses to the offense charged. Each of these defenses simply negates the existence of one (or more) of the elements of the offense charged.

Let us take the insanity defense as an example. When the defendant pleads the existence of a mental disease or defect (a psychiatric question), he claims that he could not have acted (did not appreciate the nature and quality of the act—consequently, no *actus reus*) or he could not form the requisite mens rea (did not appreciate the wrongfulness of the act).[13]

The defense of infancy could have been worked out similarly. But instead, it was decided at common law that nobody under age 7 should be deemed capable of acting rationally or to have the requisite mens rea. At age 14, all youngsters are deemed to have that capacity. The defense of infancy varies widely among the states.

Let us look at the defense of mistake of fact. Here the defendant claims that by reason of a factual error (e.g., taking someone else's coat believing it to be one's own), she did not, and could not, realize that she did something wrong. Hence, there was no mens rea (or sometimes not even the requisite *actus reus*).

In some situations, the defendant's defense is that the element of wrongfulness was lacking (the legality requirement). Normally, touching another person without consent amounts to assault and battery. The police officer's defense is that the law requires that he touch others without consent. Therefore, what is normally illegal has become legal (the defense of public duty). Other defenses, such as duress, necessity, self-defense, and defense of property, all work pretty much on the same principle—they negate an essential element of the offense charged.

TYPOLOGIES OF CRIME

The general term "crimes" covers a wide variety of types of crimes, with their own distinct features. Murder and arson, for example, both are crimes. They have the same seven general elements, including a criminal intent (mens rea) and a harm element. But these elements take different forms in different crimes. In murder, the criminal intent takes the form of intending to kill another human being wrongfully, while in arson the intent is that of wrongfully burning the property of another. Lawyers and criminologists have searched for a system of grouping the many types of crimes into coherent, rational categories, for ease of understanding, of learning, and of finding them in the law books and for purposes of studying them from both a legal and a criminological perspective. Such categorizations are called "typologies."

Here are some examples: The ancient Romans classified their crimes as those against the gods and those against other human beings. As late as the eighteenth century, some English lawyers simply listed crimes alphabetically. The French of the early nineteenth century created a typology with three categories: serious crimes (which we would call "felonies"), medium-serious crimes (which we would call "misdemeanors"), and crimes of a petty character (which we would call "violations"). The more serious crimes were grouped into categories based on the harm those crimes entailed, such as harm against life, against physical integrity, against honor, against property, and so on.

Nowadays the French categorization is generally accepted worldwide, although lawyers and criminologists may differ on the desirability of lumping various crime types together into categories. Lawyers, after all, may be much more interested in the procedural consequences that flow from the categorizations, while criminologists may be much more concerned with criminological implications for studying different types of perpetrators and devising schemes of crime prevention.

There are also political considerations in devising a typology. For example, the criminal codes of the former communist countries had large categories of political crimes, which were given the most prominent place in those codes. They included many crimes that in Western democracies are grouped in other categories, such as property crimes or crimes against the person, or that may have no counterpart at all.

The typology we have chosen for this book seeks to accommodate both the established legal typology—for example, that used in the Model Penal Code—and the criminological objectives that are so important for the study of crime from a sociological and behavioral perspective. These categories are:

- Violent crimes
- Crimes against property
- White-collar and corporate crime
- Drug-, alcohol-, and sex-related crimes

We discuss these categories in Part III.

MEASURING CRIME

There are three major reasons for measuring characteristics of crimes and criminals. First, researchers need to collect and analyze information in order to test theories about why people commit crime. One criminologist might record the kinds of offenses committed by people of different ages; another might count the number of crimes committed at different times of the year. But without ordering these observations in some purposeful way, without a **theory**, a systematic set of principles that explain how two or more phenomena are related, scientists would be limited in their ability to make predictions from the data they collect.

The types of data that are collected and the way they are collected are crucial to the research process. Criminologists analyze these data and use their findings to support or refute theories. In Part II, we examine several theories (including the one outlined briefly here) that explain why people commit crime, and we will see how these theories have been tested.

One theory of crime causation, for example, is that high crime rates result from the wide disparity between people's goals and the means available to them for reaching those goals. Those who lack legitimate opportunities to achieve their goals (primarily, people in the lower class) try to reach them through criminal means. To test this theory, researchers might begin with the **hypothesis** (a testable proposition that describes how two or more factors are related) that lower-class individuals engage in more serious crimes and do so more frequently than middle-class individuals. (See "Social Class and Crime" later in this chapter.) Next they would collect facts, observations, and other pertinent information—called **data**—on the criminal behavior of both lower-class and middle-class individuals. A finding that lower-class persons commit more crimes would support the theory that people commit crimes because they do not have legitimate means to reach their goals.

The second objective of measurement is to enhance our knowledge of the characteristics of various types of offenses. Why are some offenses more likely to be committed than others? What situational factors, such as time of day or type of place, influence the commission of crime? Experts have argued that this information is needed if we are to prevent crime and develop strategies to control it (Chapter 9 deals with this subject).

Measurement has a third major objective: Criminal justice agencies depend on certain kinds of information to facilitate daily operations and to anticipate future needs. How many persons flow through county jails? How many will receive prison sentences? Besides the questions that deal with the day-to-day functioning of the system

(number of beds, distribution and hiring of personnel), other questions affect legislative and policy decisions. For instance, what effect does a change in law have on the amount of crime committed? Consider legislation on the death penalty. Some people claim that homicides decrease when a death penalty is instituted. Others claim that capital punishment laws make no difference. Does fear of crime go down if we put more police officers in a neighborhood? Does drug smuggling move to another entry point if old access routes are cut off? These and other potential changes need to be evaluated—and evaluations require measurement.

Methods of Collecting Data

Given the importance of data for research, policy making, and the daily operation and planning of the criminal justice system, criminologists have continued to refine data-collection techniques. Through the years, these methods have become increasingly sophisticated.

Depending on what questions they are asking, criminologists collect their data in a variety of ways: through survey research, experiments, observation, and case studies. One of the most widely used methods is survey research, which is a cost-effective method of measuring characteristics of groups. Experimental studies are difficult and costly to conduct, and for that reason they are used infrequently. But they have been, and still are, an important means of collecting data on crime. Participant observation involves the direct participation of the researcher in the activities of the people who are the subjects of the research. A variation of this technique is nonparticipant observation, in which the researcher collects data without joining in the activity. Another way to collect information about crime, and especially about criminal careers, is to examine biographical and autobiographical accounts of individual offenders (the case study method).

Data can be found in a wide variety of sources, but the most frequently used sources are statistics compiled by government agencies, private foundations, and businesses. Familiarity with the sources of data and the methods used to gather data will help in understanding the studies we discuss throughout this book. The facts and observations researchers gather for the purpose of a particular study are called **primary data.** Those they find in government sources, or data that were previously collected for a different investigation, are called **secondary data.**

Surveys

Most of us are familiar with surveys—in public-opinion polls, marketing research, and election-prediction studies. Criminologists use surveys to obtain quantitative data. A **survey** is the systematic collection of respondents' answers to questions asked in questionnaires or interviews; interviews may be conducted face-to-face or by telephone. Generally, surveys are used to gather information about the attitudes, characteristics, or behavior of a large group of persons, who are called the **population** of the survey. Surveys conducted by criminologists measure, for example, the amount of crime, attitudes toward police or toward the sentencing of dangerous offenders, assessment of drug abuse, and fear of crime.

Instead of interviewing the total population under study, most researchers interview a representative subset of that population—a **sample.** If a sample is carefully drawn, researchers can generalize the results from the sample to the population. A sample determined by random selection, whereby each person in the population to be studied has an equal chance of being selected, is called a **random sample.**

Surveys are a cost-effective method, but they have limitations. If a study of drug use by high school students were done one time only, the finding of a relationship between drug use and poor grades would not tell us whether drug use caused bad grades, whether students with bad grades turned to drugs, or whether bad grades and drug taking resulted from some other factor, such as lack of a stable family. Panel studies, which repeatedly survey the same sample at various points in time, address this problem. Not surprisingly, they are more costly than cross-sectional studies.

Experiments

The **experiment** is a technique used in the physical, biological, and social sciences. An investigator introduces a change into a process and makes measurements or observations in order to evaluate the effects of the change. Through experimentation, scientists test hypotheses about how two or more **variables** (factors that may change) are related. The basic model for an experiment involves changing one variable, keeping all other factors the same (controlling them, or holding them constant), and observing the effect of that change on another variable. If you change one variable while keeping all other factors constant and then find that another variable changes as well, you may safely assume that the change in the second variable was caused by the change in the first.

Most experiments are done in laboratories, but it is possible to do them in real-world, or field, settings (hence the name **field experiment**), as we see with the Scared Straight program evaluation and the Minneapolis Domestic Violence Experiment.

Evidence that criminologists are embracing experimental methods is seen in the creation of the Academy of Experimental Criminology (AEC). The AEC seeks to promote the use of randomized trials in crime and justice research and to recognize criminologists who have successfully led

■ *The year 2000 census started when Harold Johnson visited the Eskimo village of Unalkleet, Alaska, on January 19, 2000. The U.S. Census provides information on all Americans and their lifestyles and problems, including, through random survey done in cooperation with the Bureau of Justice Statistics, data on crime victimization.*

randomized field experiments. David Weisburd and his colleagues explain, in simple terms, why such research is important:

> Random allocation thus allows the researcher to assume that the only logical explanation for any systematic differences between the treatment and comparison groups are due to the treatments or interventions applied. When the study is complete, the researcher can argue with confidence that if a difference has been observed between treatment and comparison groups, it is likely the result of the treatment itself (since randomization has isolated the treatment effect from other possible causes). In nonrandomized studies, it is much more difficult to make this claim because of the difficulty of controlling for both measured and unmeasured factors or influences. For this reason, randomized experiments have often been described as the "gold standard" for evaluation research.[14]

The requirements for experiments using randomized controlled trials (RCT) are threefold:

1. Program participants and nonparticipants can be randomly assigned to two or more groups large enough to comprise a statistically valid sample.

DID YOU KNOW?

. . . that some treatment programs for offenders are based on cognitive behavioral therapy work? See "Experiments in Criminology" later in this chapter.

■ Despite experimental evidence that the Scared Straight experience may be counterproductive, the program (now called the Juvenile Awareness Program) continues at East Jersey State Prison (formerly Rahway State Prison). Here, a member of the Lifer's group appears in a 1999 Scared Straight! video. The film is an update of the original Scared Straight! video that shows how inmates give young people in trouble a taste of prison life.

2. Each group can be administered a distinct intervention (or nonintervention, which would be the control condition).

3. For each group, the program can measure the outcomes that the intervention is designed to improve.[15]

Experiments employing RCT have been used to test the effectiveness of substance-abuse treatment, child-care and preschool interventions, police strategies in inner-city high-crime areas, prosecutorial and sentencing strategies, prison reentry programs, and sales tax compliance strategies.[16] According to Lawrence Sherman, its application to critically important questions in criminology cannot be underestimated. We can now ask and answer, with definitive evidence, questions such as these: How much crime does prison prevent—or cause—for different kinds of offenders? Does visible police patrol prevent crime everywhere or just in certain locations? What is the best way for societies to prevent crime from an early age? How can murder be prevented among high-risk groups of young men?

Research employing RCT has some limitations, however. The Coalition for Evidence-Based Policy noted some general characteristics of research that lends itself to experiments using RCT:

• There must be a possibility of selecting randomized intervention and control groups.

• There must be sufficient discretion in the administration of the program to permit random assignment of groups that will receive a program intervention and groups that will not (or that will receive a different intervention).

• Subjects should not be excluded from an intervention that provides a public good (for example, clean air or homeland security), as this would likely raise ethical—if not legal—issues.[17]

The coalition also offered some concrete examples of research that defies the use of RCTs:

• One cannot carry out an RCT to evaluate whether reducing carbon emissions will prevent global warming, because there is only one planet Earth. (However, it may be possible to randomize industrial sites in order to evaluate the effectiveness and cost of various methods of reducing carbon emissions.)

• One cannot carry out an RCT to evaluate the effectiveness of manned space flight, because we can only afford to carry out one such program.

• One cannot carry out an RCT to evaluate military assistance to NATO countries because of the political impossibility of randomizing countries as well as the lack of sufficient numbers of countries to allow valid statistical groupings.

• One cannot choose a random sample of military operations in which to use particular operational strategies, because once a particular operation is approved, any tool or strategy that might help under changing conditions must be available for use.[18]

Experiments in Criminology: The Importance of Evidence-Based Crime and Justice Policy

1. **Do certain community-based treatment programs work? Yes.** J. McGuire and colleagues report the outcome of a 17-month follow-up of three different community-based, offense-focused intervention programs in England created to decrease the rate of reconviction of offenders receiving probation supervision. The study included three treatment groups (215 male offenders who had completed programs, 181 male offenders who had not completed programs, and 339 male offenders who had not started programs) compared to a control group of 339 male offenders who were not assigned to treatment programs. The authors first evaluated the groups by comparing the three experimental groups to the comparison (control) group and found that individuals in the comparison group were not more likely to be reconvicted. McGuire and colleagues also compared all four groups separately. They found that those offenders who had completed programs were significantly less likely to be reconvicted than were offenders in the other three groups.[19]

2. **Do "closed-circuit television" monitoring efforts decrease crime rates? Yes.** D. S. Farrington and his colleagues conducted an analysis of 14 closed-circuit television (CCTV) projects in several different areas in England, including city and town centers, a hospital, parking areas, and residential areas. The question they asked was, What are the effects of CCTV on crime? They reviewed CCTV police and victimization data in the above-noted areas before and after CCTV was installed. They found that CCTV was useful in decreasing crime in parking areas of train stations and also seemed to be effective in decreasing vehicle crimes but was not effective in city or town centers. CCTV intervention was most effective when coverage was high and when other interventions, such as improved lighting, were included.[20]

3. **Do written warnings threatening an investigation for insurance fraud deter fraud claims? Yes.** E. Blais and J. L. Bacher designed a randomized field experiment to evaluate the effects of a written threat in the form of a deterrent letter, which reminded the insured individual of punishment for insurance fraud. They wanted to evaluate if there would be a difference between those receiving the written warning and those subject to the usual standard of practice in the insurance company (control) with regard to claim-padding behaviors for individuals filing claims for residential theft. They performed this experiment at four insurance companies. The authors found that individuals in the experimental group (those receiving a written warning) were less likely to pad their claims than those in the control group, independent of how the letter was delivered. The authors concluded that having a written threat at the time of this criminal opportunity seems to be effective in preventing this type of economic crime.[21]

4. **Do boot camps decrease recidivism? Not sure.** D. L. MacKenzie and colleagues' study evaluated 234 adult male inmates entering prison who were randomly assigned to a program in a correctional boot camp or a large, traditional prison in the Maryland state correctional system. They wanted to look at the impact of boot camp on recidivism. They had three main areas of focus: comparing the recidivism between the two groups, the impact of the two programs on participants' criminogenic attitudes and impulses, and whether changes in these attitudes and impulses could explain the differences in recidivism. The authors found that participation in boot camp was associated with a marginally significant lower recidivism compared to those who entered the traditional correctional facility. The boot camp program had little effect on criminogenic characteristics noted by pre- and posttest self-report surveys, except for a lowering of self-control. On the other hand, inmates in the traditional correctional facility became more antisocial, had lower self-control, were worse at anger management, and self-reported more criminal tendencies by the end of their prison stay. The authors noted that these findings suggested that differences in criminal behavior were due to negative changes in the controls, rather than to changes in the boot camp participants.[22]

Participant and Nonparticipant Observation

Researchers who engage in participant and nonparticipant observation use methods that provide detailed descriptions of life as it actually is lived—in prisons, gangs, and other settings.

Observation is the most direct means of studying behavior. Investigators may play a variety of roles in observing social situations. When they engage in **nonparticipant observation,** they do not join in the activities of the groups they are studying; they simply observe the activities in everyday settings and record what they see. Investigators who engage in **participant observation** take part in many of the activities of the groups in order to gain acceptance, but they generally make clear the purpose of their participation. Anne Campbell, a criminologist who spent 2 years as a participant observer of the lifestyles of girl gang members, explains:

> My efforts to meet female gang members began with an introduction through the New York City Police Department's Gang Crimes Unit. Through one of their plainclothes gang liaison officers, John Galea, I was introduced first to the male gang members of a number of Brooklyn gangs. On being reassured that I "only" wanted to talk to the female members, the male leaders gave their OK and I made arrangements to meet with the girls' leaders or "godmothers." At first they were guarded in their disclosures to me. They asked a lot about my life, my background and my reasons for wanting to hang out with them. Like most of us, however, they enjoyed talking about themselves and over the period of six months that I spent with each of three female gangs they opened up a good deal—sitting in their kitchens, standing on the stoops in the evenings or socializing at parties with allied gangs.[23]

Observations of groups in their natural setting afford the researcher insights into behavior and attitudes that cannot be obtained through techniques such as surveys and experiments.

Case Studies

A **case study** is an analysis of all pertinent aspects of one unit of study, such as an individual, an institution, a group, or a community. The sources of information are documents such as life histories, biographies, diaries, journals, letters, and other records. A classic demonstration of criminologists' use of the case study method is found in Edwin Sutherland's *The Professional Thief*, which is based on interviews with a professional thief.

Sutherland learned about the relationship between amateur and professional thieves, how thieves communicate, how they determine whether to trust each other, and how they network. From discussions with the thief and an analysis of his writings on topics selected by the researcher, Sutherland was able to draw several conclusions that other techniques would not have yielded. For instance, a person is not a professional thief unless he is recognized as such by other professional thieves. Training by professional thieves is necessary for the development of the skills, attitudes, and connections required in the "profession."[24] One of the drawbacks of the case study method is that the information given by the subject may be biased or wrong and by its nature is limited. For these reasons it is difficult to generalize from one person's story—in this instance—to all professional thieves.

Using Available Data in Research

Besides collecting their own data, researchers often utilize secondary data collected by private and public organizations. The police, the courts, and corrections officials, for example, need to know the number of persons passing through the criminal justice system at various points in order to carry out day-to-day administrative tasks and to engage in long-range planning. It is not always feasible to collect new data for a research project, nor is it necessary to do so when such vast amounts of relevant information are already available.

To study the relationship between crime and variables such as average income or single-parent households, one might make use of the Uniform Crime Reports (see "Police Statistics" later in this chapter), together with information found in the reports of the Bureau of the Census. Various other agencies, among them the Federal Bureau of Prisons, the Drug Enforcement Agency, the Treasury Department, and the Labor Department, are also excellent sources of statistics useful to criminologists. At the international level, UN world crime surveys contain information on crime, criminals, and criminal justice systems in countries on all continents.

Researchers who use available data can save a great deal of time and expense. However, they have to exercise caution in fitting data not collected for the purpose of a particular study into their research. Many official records are incomplete, or the data have been collected in such a way as to make them inadequate for the research. It is also frequently difficult to gain permission to use agency data that are not available to the public because of a concern about confidentiality.

Ethics and the Researcher

In the course of their research, criminologists encounter many ethical issues. Chief among such issues is confidentiality. Consider the dilemma faced by a group of researchers in the late 1960s. In interviewing a sample of 9,945 boys born in 1945, the team collected extensive self-reported criminal histories of offenses the boys had committed before and after they turned 18. Among the findings were four unreported homicides and 75 rapes. The researchers were naturally excited about capturing such interesting data. More important, the researchers had feelings of grave concern. How should they handle their findings?

Should the results of these interviews be published?

Could the failure of the research staff to disclose names be considered the crime of obstructing justice?

Does an obligation to society as a whole to release the names of the offenders transcend a researcher's obligation to safeguard a subject's confidentiality?

What is the best response to a demand by the police, a district attorney, or a court for the researchers' files containing the subjects' names?

Should criminologists be immune to prosecution for their failure to disclose the names of their subjects?

Is it possible to develop a technique that can ensure against the identification of a subject in a research file?[25]

Such questions have few clear-cut answers. When researchers encounter these problems, however, they can rely on standards for ethical human experimentation. Institutional review boards (IRBs), also referred to as independent ethics committees (IECs) or ethical review boards (ERBs), exist in all government agencies and nearly all universities to ensure the protection of human subjects. The committee is responsible for approving the initial research proposal to certify that the project has scientific merit, the risks to subjects are balanced by the potential benefits to society, and, most important, informed consent is adequately addressed. Study participants must be fully notified about all the potential risks associated with the study, alternatives to participation, and the extent to which the researchers can protect participants' confidentiality. Researchers must obtain informed consent in writing for all study participants.

Because of heightened awareness of the ethical issues involved in human experimentation—particularly in correctional institutions, where coercion is difficult to avoid—the field of criminology and criminal justice is in the process of adopting formal codes of ethics. The guidelines include fully reporting experimental findings, honoring commitments made to respondents, not misleading respondents, and protecting respondents' confidentiality. Special provisions for what are called "vulnerable populations" (e.g., the illiterate, the mentally ill, children, those with low social status, and those under judicial or penal supervision) include taking appropriate steps to secure informed consent and to avoid invasions of privacy.[26] In the end, however, as Seth Bloomberg and Leslie Wilkins have noted, "the responsibility for safeguarding human subjects ultimately rests with the researcher. . . . A code of ethics may provide useful guidelines, but it will not relieve the scientist of moral choice."[27]

THE NATURE AND EXTENT OF CRIME

As we have seen, criminologists gather their information in many ways. The methods they choose depend on the questions they want answered. To estimate the nature and extent of crime in the United States, researchers rely primarily on the Uniform Crime Reports, data compiled by the police; on the National Crime Victimization Survey, which measures crime through reports by victims; and on various self-report surveys, which ask individuals about criminal acts they have committed, whether or not these acts have come to the attention of the authorities.

Official statistics gathered from law enforcement agencies provide information available on the crimes actually investigated and reported by these agencies. But not all crimes appear in police statistics. In order for a criminal act to be "known to the police," the act first must be *perceived* by an individual (the car is not in the garage where it was left). It must then be *defined*, or classified, as something that places it within the purview of the criminal justice system (a theft has taken place), and it must be *reported* to the police. Once the police are notified, they classify the act and often *redefine* what may have taken place before *recording* the act as a crime known to the police (Figure 2.2). Information about criminal acts may be lost at any point along this processing route, and many crimes are never discovered to begin with.

Police Statistics

In 1924, the director of the Bureau of Investigation, J. Edgar Hoover, initiated a campaign to make the bureau responsible for gathering national statistics. With support from the American Bar Association (ABA) and the International Association of Chiefs of Police (IACP), the House of Representatives in 1930 passed a bill authorizing the bureau (later renamed the Federal Bureau of Investigation, or FBI) to collect data on crimes known to the police. These data are compiled into reports called the Uniform Crime Reports (UCR). At present, approximately 17,000 city, county, and state law enforcement agencies, which cover 95 percent of the total population, voluntarily contribute information on crimes brought to their attention. These agencies represent over 254 million U.S. inhabitants, with higher representation in large urban areas (97 percent) than in smaller cities (90 percent) or rural areas (87 percent). If the police verify that a crime has been committed, that crime goes into the report, whether or not an arrest has been made. Each month, reporting agencies provide data on offenses in 29 categories.

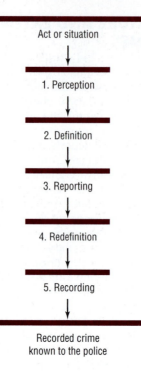

FIGURE 2.2 The process of bringing crime to the attention of police.

Source: R. F. Sparks, H. G. Genn, and D. J. Dodd, *Surveying Victims: A Study of the Measurement of Criminal Victimization, Perceptions of Crime, and Attitudes to Criminal Justice* (Chichester, Eng.: Wiley, 1977), p. 6. Copyright © 1977 by John Wiley & Sons Ltd. Reproduced with permission.

Part I and Part II Offenses

The UCR divide offenses into two major categories: Part I and Part II. Part I offenses include eight crimes, which are aggregated as **crimes against the person** (criminal homicide, forcible rape, robbery, and aggravated assault) and **crimes against property** (burglary, larceny-theft, motor vehicle theft, and arson). Collectively, Part I offenses are called **Index crimes.** Because they are serious, these crimes tend to be reported to the police more reliably than others and therefore can be used in combination as an index, or indicator, of changes over time. All other offenses, except traffic violations, are Part II crimes. These 21 crimes include fraud, embezzlement, weapons offenses, vandalism, and simple assaults.

Crime Rates

To analyze crime data, experts frequently present them as crime rates. Crime rates are computed by the following formula:

$$\text{Crime rate} = \frac{\text{number of reported crimes}}{\text{total population}} \times 100{,}000$$

Crime rates may be computed for groups of offenses (such as the Index crimes or crimes against the person) or for specific offenses (such as homicide). If we say, for example, that the homicide rate is 10.2, we mean that there were 10.2 homicides for every 100,000 persons in the population under consideration (total U.S. population, say, or all males in the United States). Expressing the amount of crime in terms of rates over time shows whether an increase or a decrease in crime results from a change in the population or a change in the amount of crime committed.

In addition to data on reported crimes, the UCR include the number of offenses cleared by arrest. Crimes may be cleared in one of two ways: by the arrest, charging, and turning over to the courts of at least one person for prosecution; or by disposition of a case when an arrest is not possible, as when the suspect has died or has fled the jurisdiction. Besides reported crimes and crimes cleared by arrest, the reports contain data on characteristics of crimes (such as geographical location, time, and place), characteristics of criminals (such as gender, age, and race), and distribution of law enforcement personnel. We shall look at what these statistics reveal about the characteristics of crime and criminals in more detail later, but first we must recognize their limitations.

Limitations of the Uniform Crime Reports

Despite the fact that the UCR are among the main sources of crime statistics, their research value has been questioned. The criticisms deal with methodological problems and reporting practices. Some scholars argue, for example, that figures on reported crime are of little use in categories such as larceny, in which a majority of crime is not reported. The statistics present the amount of crime known to law enforcement agencies, but they do not reveal how many crimes have actually been committed. Another serious limitation is the fact that when several crimes are committed in one event, only the most serious offense is included in the UCR; the others go unreported. At the same time, when certain other crimes are committed, each individual act is counted as a separate offense. If a person robs a group of six people, for example, the UCR list one robbery (Figure 2.3). But if a person assaults six people, the UCR list six assaults. UCR data are further obscured by the fact that they do not differentiate between completed acts and attempted acts.

Police reports to the FBI are voluntary and vary in accuracy. In a study conducted on behalf of the Police Foundation, Lawrence Sherman and Barry Glick found that while the UCR require

One offense   Six offenses

FIGURE 2.3 Counting crime in the Uniform Crime Reports.

that arrests be recorded even if a suspect is released without a formal charge, all 196 departments surveyed recorded an arrest only after a formal booking procedure.[28] In addition, police departments may want to improve their image by showing that their crime rate has either declined (meaning the streets are safer) or risen (justifying a crackdown on, say, prostitution).[29] New record-keeping procedures can also create significant changes (the New York robbery rate appeared to increase 400 percent in 1 year).[30] Many fluctuations in crime rates may therefore be attributable to events other than changes in the actual numbers of crimes committed.

Finally, the UCR data suffer from several omissions. Many arsons go unreported because not all fire departments report to the UCR.[31] Federal cases go unlisted. Most white-collar offenses are omitted because they are reported not to the police but to regulatory authorities, such as the Securities and Exchange Commission and the Federal Trade Commission.

In 1986, the International Association of Chiefs of Police, the National Sheriffs' Association, and state-level UCR programs joined forces with the FBI to develop an incident-based reporting system to address the limitations associated with the UCR data.[32] The National Incident-Based Reporting System (NIBRS) provides data on each single crime occurrence and arrest from local, state, and federal automated records systems.

Reporting to the NIBRS is voluntary and coexists with the UCR. The NIBRS is a major attempt to improve the collection of crime data. But it deals only with crimes that come to the attention of the police. What about crimes that remain unreported? For what is called the "dark figure of crime," we have to rely on victimization data and self-report studies.

Victimization Surveys

Victimization surveys measure the extent of crime by interviewing individuals about their experiences as victims. The Bureau of the Census, in cooperation with the Bureau of Justice Statistics, collects information annually about persons and households that have been victimized. The report is called the "National Crime Victimization Survey" (NCVS). Researchers for the NCVS estimate the total number of crimes committed by asking respondents from a national sample of approximately 43,000 households, representing 80,000 persons over the age of 12 (parental permission is needed for those under 14 years old), about their experiences as victims during a specific time period. Interviewers visit (or sometimes telephone) the homes selected for the sample. Each housing unit remains in the sample for 3 years. Every 6 months, 10,000 households are rotated out of the sample and replaced by a new group.

Statistics Watchdog Chief Accuses Home Office of Abusing Crime Statistics

RICHARD FORD

The Home Office is at the centre of another row over crime figures after the head of the UK Statistics Authority accused it of issuing "selective" statistics on knife offending.

Sir Michael Scholar, head of the Authority, said the release of details on an initiative to tackle knife attacks by both the Home Office and 10 Downing Street had been "premature."

The rebuke, which oversees the Office for National Statistics, is highly damaging, particularly as it follows disputes over the way the Home Office has dealt with release of crime and immigration and asylum figures.

Sir Michael said that the release of stabbing data was "premature, irregular and selective."

The figures were handed to the BBC which used them in its lead story during early morning bulletins on Radio 4.

Sir Michael wrote to Jeremy Heywood, permanent secretary at 10 Downing Street, and said that figures on hospital admissions for stabbing injuries had not been properly checked and putting them out early was "corrosive of public trust."

He said in his letter that he had been told that officials or advisors in Number 10 had "caused" the Home Office to issue the release.

The statisticians who produced the figures attempted to block their release on the grounds it was in breach of the National Statistics Code of Practice.

Sir Michael said: "These statistics were not due for publication for some time and had not therefore been through the regular process of checking and quality assurance."

"The statisticians who produced them, together with the National Statistician, tried unsuccessfully to prevent their premature, irregular and selective release."

"I hope you will agree that the publication of prematurely released and unchecked statistics is corrosive of public trust in official statistics and incompatible with the high standards which we are all seeking to establish."

The NCVS measures the extent of victimization by rape, robbery, assault, larceny, burglary, personal theft, and motor vehicle theft. Note that two of the UCR Part I offenses—criminal homicide and arson—are not included (Table 2.1, page 40).[33] Homicide is omitted because the NCVS covers only crimes whose victims can be interviewed. The designers of the survey also decided to omit arson, a relative newcomer to the UCR, because measuring it with some validity by means of a victimization survey was deemed to be too difficult. Part II offenses have been excluded altogether because many of them are considered victimless (prostitution, vagrancy, drug abuse, drunkenness) or because victims are willing participants (gambling, con games) or do not know they have been victimized (forgery, fraud).

The survey covers characteristics of crimes such as time and place of occurrence, number of offenders, use of weapons, economic loss, and time lost from work; characteristics of victims, such as gender, age, race, ethnicity, marital status, household composition, and educational attainment; perceived characteristics of offenders, such as age, gender, and race; circumstances surrounding the offenses and their effects, such as financial loss and injury; and patterns of police reporting, such as rates of reporting and reasons for reporting and for not reporting. Some questions also encourage interviewees to discuss family violence.

Limitations of Victimization Surveys

While victimization surveys give us information about crimes that are not reported to the police, these data, too, have significant limitations. The NCVS covers crimes in a more limited way than the UCR; the NCVS includes only 7 offenses, whereas there are 8 offenses in Part I of the UCR and an additional 21 in Part II. Although the NCVS is conducted by trained interviewers, some individual variations in interviewing and recording style are inevitable, and, as a result, the information recorded may vary as well.

Because the NCVS is based on personal reporting, it also suffers from the fact that memories may fade over time, so some facts are forgotten while others are exaggerated. Moreover, some interviewees may try to please the interviewer by fabricating crime incidents.[34] Respondents also have a tendency to telescope events—that is, to move events that took place in an earlier time period into the time period under study. Like the UCR, the NCVS records only the most serious

"I would be grateful for your comments and for your assurance that there will be no repetition of this breach of the National Statistics Code of Practice."

In the press release Jacqui Smith, the Home Secretary, said there had been an overall fall in the number of people caught carrying knives and claimed that those found guilty of possessing knives were receiving longer sentences.

But the Home Office was unable to provide the statistics to support the claims saying they were "interim findings."

A Home Office fact sheet claimed hospital admissions were down 27 percent since the crackdown on knife crime in ten areas began in July and stated there had been 18 percent fewer victims under 20 in London between April and September 2008 than in the same period in 2007.

Sources at the authority said Sir Michael was "furious" over the breach of the rules.

Sir Michael's intervention follows concern in the Office for National Statistics at the way in which the Home Office has dealt with figures in politically sensitive areas such as crime and asylum and immigration.

It is the second time in recent months that the Home Office has been criticised over its use of statistics.

Professor David Hand, head of the Royal Statistical Society, highlighted "serious" bad practices during the release of immigration figures in August.

The latest row over is damaging for the Government as it once again casts doubt on whether people can believe official statistics on crime—an area where ministers are struggling to convince the public that offending is falling.

In October the Home Office was forced to admit that serious violent crime is much worse than they had been claiming because police forces had been failing to record offences properly.

Dominic Grieve, the shadow Home Secretary, said: "The knife crime epidemic is a tragedy that has claimed too many young lives."

"If government ministers have sanctioned the selective and manipulative spinning of these statistics, it is reckless and irresponsible."

"Labour should immediately publish the full figures so that we can see the truth."

Questions for Discussion

1. How vulnerable are crime statistics to political pressure?
2. What are the limitations of "official" statistics, that is, those statistics issued by the government?

SOURCE: Richard Ford, "Statistics Watchdog Chief Accuses Home Office of Abusing Crime Statistics." © Richard Ford/NI Syndication Limited, December 12, 2008.

---

offense committed during an event in which several crimes are perpetrated.

Self-Report Surveys

Another way to determine the amount and types of crime actually committed is to ask people to report their own criminal acts in a confidential interview or, more commonly, on an anonymous questionnaire. These investigations are called **self-report surveys**.

Findings of Self-Report Surveys

Self-reports of delinquent and criminal behavior have produced several important findings since their development in the 1940s. For one thing, they quickly refuted the conventional wisdom that only a small percentage of the general population commits crimes. The use of these measures over the last several decades has demonstrated very high rates of law-violating behavior by seemingly law-abiding people. Almost everyone, at some point in time, has broken a law.

In 1947, James S. Wallerstein and Clement J. Wyle questioned a group of 1,698 individuals on whether they had committed any of 49 offenses that were serious enough to require a maximum sentence of not less than 1 year. They found that over 80 percent of the men reported committing malicious mischief, disorderly conduct, and larceny. More than 50 percent admitted a history of crimes, including reckless driving and driving while intoxicated, indecency, gambling, fraud, and tax evasion. The authors acknowledged the lack of scientific rigor of their study. No attempt was made to ensure a balanced or representative cross section of the individuals surveyed.[35] However, these findings do suggest that the distinction between criminals and noncriminals may be more apparent than real.

Studies conducted since the 1940s have provided a great deal more information. These studies suggest that a wide discrepancy exists between official and self-report data with regard to the age, race, and gender of offenders.[36] Unrecorded offenders commit a wide variety of offenses, rather than specializing in one type of offense.[37] It also appears that only one-quarter of all serious, chronic juvenile offenders are apprehended by the police. Moreover, an estimated 90 percent of all youths commit delinquent or criminal acts, primarily truancy, use of false identification, alcohol abuse, larceny, fighting, and marijuana use.[38]

TABLE 2.1 How Do the Uniform Crime Reports and the National Crime Victimization Survey Differ?

	Uniform Crime Reports	National Crime Victimization Survey
Offenses measured	Homicide	
	Rape	Rape
	Robbery (personal and commercial)	Robbery (personal)
	Assault (aggravated)	Assault (aggravated and simple)
	Burglary (commercial and household)	Household burglary
	Larceny (commercial and household)	Larceny
	Motor vehicle theft	Personal theft
	Arson	Motor vehicle theft
Scope	Crimes reported to the police in most jurisdictions; considerable flexibility in developing small-area data	Crimes both reported and not reported to police; all data are for the nation as a whole; some data are available for a few large geographical areas
Collection method	Police department reports to FBI	Survey interviews; periodically measures the total number of crimes committed by asking a national sample of 42,000* households representing 76,000* persons over the age of 12 about their experiences as victims of crime during a specified period
Kinds of information	In addition to offense counts, provides information on crime clearances, persons arrested, persons charged, law enforcement officers killed and assaulted, and characteristics of homicide victims	Provides details about victims (such as age, race, sex, education, and income, and whether the victim and offender were related to each other) and about crimes (such as time and place of occurrence, whether reported to police, use of weapons, occurrence of injury, and economic consequences)
Sponsor	Department of Justice, Federal Bureau of Investigation	Department of Justice, Bureau of Justice Statistics

*Figures have been updated.

SOURCES: Adapted from U.S. Department of Justice, Bureau of Justice Statistics, *Report to the Nation on Crime and Justice*, 2nd ed. (Washington, D.C.: U.S. Government Printing Office, 1988), p. 11; U.S. Department of Justice, Bureau of Justice Statistics, *Criminal Victimization 1997* (Washington, D.C.: U.S. Government Printing Office, December 1998), pp. 1–2.

From 1991 to 1993, the first International Self-Report Delinquency (ISRD) study was conducted in Finland, Great Britain, the Netherlands, Belgium, Germany, Switzerland, Portugal, Spain, Italy, Greece, the United States, and New Zealand. Each country used the same questionnaire, which had been translated into the respective languages. The studies used various sampling techniques, so the results from each country are not strictly comparable. Nonetheless, the findings support much of what is found in the self-report literature. Boys commit about twice as many offenses as girls. The peak age of offending in the participating countries is 16 to 17 years. Violence is strongly related to lower educational levels. No relationship was found between socioeconomic status and delinquency. Drug use seems related to truancy and unemployment. School failure is related to violent offenses.[39]

Limitations of Self-Report Surveys

Self-report surveys have taught us a great deal about criminality. But, like the other methods of data collection, they have drawbacks. The questionnaires are often limited to petty acts, such as truancy, and therefore do not represent the range of criminal acts that people may commit. Michael Hindelang, Travis Hirschi, and Joseph Weis argue that researchers who find discrepancies with respect to gender, race, and class between the results produced by official statistics and those collected by self-report methods are in fact measuring different kinds of behavior rather than different amounts of the same behavior. They suggest that if you take into account the fact that persons who are arrested tend to have committed more serious offenses and to have prior records (criteria that affect decisions to arrest), then the two types of statistics are quite comparable.[40]

Another drawback of self-reports is that most of them are administered to high school or college students, so the information they yield applies only to young people attending school. And who can say that respondents always tell the truth? The information obtained by repeated administration of the same questionnaire to the same individuals might yield different results. Many self-report measures lack validity; the data obtained do not correspond with some other criterion (such as school records) that measures the same behavior. Finally, samples may be biased. People who choose not to participate in the studies may have good reason for not wanting to discuss their criminal activities.

Each of the three commonly used sources of data—police reports, victim surveys, and self-report surveys—adds a different dimension to our knowledge of crime. All of them are useful in our search for the characteristics of crimes, criminals, and victims.

MEASURING CHARACTERISTICS OF CRIME

Streets in Charlotte, North Carolina, with tranquil names—Peaceful Glen, Soft Wind, Gentle Breeze—were killing lanes.[41] The city that had hoped to displace Atlanta as the "Queen City of the South" had 115 homicides in 1992, more than double the number it had had 6 years earlier. It seemed that the city was out of control. Experts pointed to drugs and to a growing number of swap shops and flea markets that served as unregulated outlets for buying guns as the reasons for the high number of homicides. Most of the killings took place in a 26-square-mile area inhabited primarily by low-income African-American families. Fortunately, within 8 years, the situation reversed itself. In 2009, the number of homicides in Charlotte was reduced to 58.[42] This information not only gives us general insights into the crime problem in Charlotte, but also enables us to examine the changes in the homicide rate over time, the high-risk areas, and the racial and economic composition of those areas in order to provide a full picture of the crime history.

Criminologists use these kinds of data about crimes in their research. Some investigators, for example, may want to compare drug use to crime in major cities. Others may want to explain a decrease or an increase in the crime rate in a single city (Charlotte), in a single neighborhood (the impoverished inner city), or perhaps in the nation as a whole.

Crime Trends

One of the most important characteristics of any crime is how often it is committed. From such data we can determine crime trends, the increases and decreases of crime over time. The UCR show that about 10.3 million Index crimes (excluding arson) were reported to the police in 2010 (Figure 2.4b). Of the total number of Index crimes, violent crimes make up a small portion with a murder rate of 4.8 per 100,000. Most Index crimes are property offenses, and two-thirds of property crimes were larceny thefts.[43]

The 2009 NCVS presents a somewhat different picture (Figure 2.4a). Although the data presented in the NCVS and the UCR are not entirely comparable because the categories differ, the number of crimes reported to the police and the number reported in the victimization survey clearly are far apart. According to the NCVS, there were slightly more than 20 million victimizations. Indeed, the NCVS reports more thefts than the total number of UCR Index offenses.[44]

According to UCR data, the crime rate increased slowly between 1930 and 1960. After 1960, it began to rise much more quickly. This trend continued until 1980 (Figure 2.5), when the crime rate rose to 5,950 per 100,000. From that peak, the rate steadily dropped until 1984, when there were 5,031.3 crimes per 100,000. After that year, the rate rose again until 1991. Since then, it has decreased every year, to 346.6 in 2009, the lowest rate since 1969.[45] The NCVS also shows that the victimization rate peaked from 1979 to 1981, but that in the 5-year span from 1993 to 1998, the victimization rates for all crimes dropped.[46] This trend continued through 2009.

The decline in the crime rate after 1980 is an important phenomenon that requires a bit more analysis. One important factor is the age distribution of the population. Given the fact that young people tend to have the highest crime rate, the age distribution of the population has a major effect on crime trends. After World War II, the birthrate increased sharply in what is known as the "baby boom." The baby-boom generation reached its crime-prone years in the 1960s, and the crime rate duly rose. As the generation grew older, the crime rate became more stable and in the 1980s began to decline. Some researchers claim that the children of the baby boomers may very well expand the ranks of the crime-prone ages once again and that crime will again increase.

During the period when the baby-boom generation outgrew criminal behavior, U.S. society was

Crime Surfing WWW

http://www.albany .edu/sourcebook

The "Sourcebook of Criminal Justice Statistics" is an excellent place to look for official data on all parts of the criminal justice system. Go to this website to find the most recent arrest data for the area in which you live. Which three offenses have the most arrests?

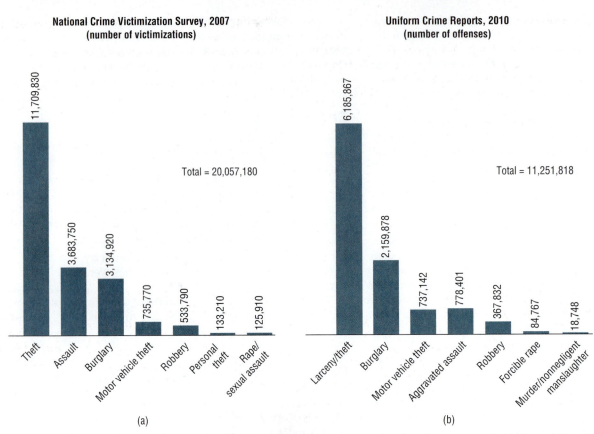

National Crime Victimization Survey, 2007
(number of victimizations)

11,709,830

Total = 20,057,180

3,683,750
3,134,920
735,770
533,790
133,210
125,910

Theft
Assault
Burglary
Motor vehicle theft
Robbery
Personal theft
Rape/ sexual assault

(a)

Uniform Crime Reports, 2010
(number of offenses)

6,185,867

Total = 11,251,818

2,159,878
737,142
778,401
367,832
84,767
18,748

Larceny/theft
Burglary
Motor vehicle theft
Aggravated assault
Robbery
Forcible rape
Murder/nonnegligent manslaughter

(b)

FIGURE 2.4 National Crime Victimization Survey and Uniform Crime Reports: a comparison of number of crimes reported. (a) National Crime Victimization Survey: total number of victimizations, 2007. (b) Uniform Crime Reports: Total number of Index offenses, 2007.

Sources: (a) Michael R. Rand, *National Crime Victimization Survey: Criminal Victimization, 2007* (Washington, D.C.: Bureau of Justice Statistics, 2008), p. 1. (b) Adapted from U.S. Department of Justice, Federal Bureau of Investigation, *Crime in the United States, 2007* (Washington, D.C.: Federal Bureau of Investigation, 2008). Retrieved February 1, 2009, from http://www.fbi.gov/ucr.

FIGURE 2.5 Uniform Crime Reports: rate of all Index crimes per 100,000 people, 1960–2007.

Sources: U.S. Department of Justice, Federal Bureau of Investigation, *Crime in the United States, 1975; 1980; 1992; 1994; 1997; 2000; 2003; 2004; 2005; 2006; 2007* (Washington D.C.: U.S. Government Printing Office, 1976, 1981, 1993, 1995, 1998, 2001, 2004, 2005, 2006, 2007, 2008).

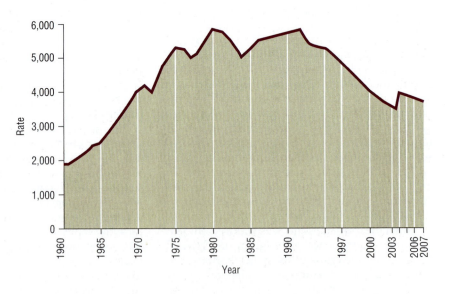

undergoing other changes. We adopted a get-tough crime-control policy, which may have deterred some people from committing crimes. Mandatory prison terms meant judges had less discretion in sentencing, and fewer convicted felons were paroled. In addition, crime prevention programs, such as Neighborhood Watch groups, became popular. These and other factors have been suggested to explain why the crime rate dropped, but we have no definitive answers.

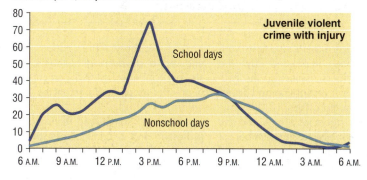

Offenders per 1,000 juvenile violent crime offenders

FIGURE 2.6 Serious juvenile violent crime with injury by time of day. On school days, violent crimes with injury cluster in the hours immediately after the close of school. On school days, violent crime with injury by juveniles peaks at 3:00 P.M., markedly decreasing in the evening hours. On nonschool days, the temporal pattern of juvenile violence with injury is similar to the overall pattern for adults: Juvenile violence occurs throughout the day and peaks between 7:00 P.M. and 9:00 P.M.

Note: Violent crimes include murder, violent sexual assault, robbery, aggravated assault, and simple assault.

Source: H. Snyder and M. Sickmund, *Juvenile Offenders and Victims: 2006 National Report* (Washington, D.C.: Office of Juvenile Justice and Delinquency Prevention, 2006), ch. 3. Retrieved June 4, 2008, from *OJJDP Statistical Briefing Book,* available at http://ojjdp.ncjrs.gov/ojstatbb/offenders/qa03304.asp?qaDate=2001.

Locations and Times of Criminal Acts

Statistics on the characteristics of crimes are important not only to criminologists who seek to know why crime occurs but also to those who want to know how to prevent it (Chapter 9). Two statistics of use in prevention efforts are those on *where* crimes are committed and *when* they are committed.

Most crimes are committed in large urban areas rather than in small cities, suburbs, or rural areas. This pattern can be attributed to a variety of factors that might include population, economic conditions, and the quality of law enforcement. The statistics for Charlotte, North Carolina, for example, show that most arrests took place in the poverty-ridden ghetto areas. The fact that the majority of those arrests were made in neighborhoods where drug dealers were visibly present on the streets fits the national picture.

According to NCVS data, the safest place to be is at home; however, we are most likely to be victimized when we are in familiar territory. In 2009, one-quarter of violent crimes took place at or near the victim's home, and nearly three-quarters of violent crimes occurred within 5 miles of the home. Common locations for violent crimes are streets other than those near the victim's home (15 percent), at school (14 percent), or at a commercial establishment (8 percent).[47]

NCVS data further reveal that more than half of violent crimes take place between 6:00 A.M. and 6:00 P.M., but nearly two-thirds of sexual assaults take place at night. Household crimes follow the same pattern: Of crimes committed within a known period, nearly 70 percent of household larcenies and 75 percent of motor vehicle thefts are committed at night. Most personal thefts, however, are committed during the day. For juveniles, 20 percent of violent crimes occur in the 4 hours (3:00 P.M. to 7:00 P.M.) immediately after the close of school (Figure 2.6).[48]

Nationwide crime rates also vary by season. Personal and household crimes are more likely to be committed during the warmer months of the year, perhaps because in summer people spend more time outdoors, where they are more vulnerable to crime.[49] People also often leave doors and windows open when they go out in warm weather.

Severity of Crime

We have seen that crime rates vary by time and place. They also vary in people's perception of their severity. To some extent, legislation sets a standard of severity by the punishments it attaches to various crimes. But let us take a critical look at such judgments.

Do you believe that skyjacking an airplane is a more serious offense than smuggling heroin? Is forcible rape more serious than kidnapping? Is breaking into a home and stealing $1,000 more serious than using force to rob a person of $10? A yes answer to all three questions conforms to the findings of the National Survey of Crime Severity, which in 1977 measured public perceptions of the seriousness of 204 events, from planting a bomb that killed 20 people to playing hooky from school.[50]

The survey, conducted by Marvin E. Wolfgang and his colleagues, found that individuals generally agree about the relative seriousness of specific crimes (Table 2.2). In ranking severity, people seem to base their decisions on such factors as the ability of victims to protect themselves, the amount of injury and loss suffered, the type of business or organization from which property is stolen, the relationship between offender and victim, and (for drug offenses) the types of drugs involved. Respondents generally agreed that violent crime is more serious than property crime. They also considered white-collar crimes, such as engaging in consumer fraud, cheating on income taxes, polluting, and accepting bribes, to be as serious as many violent and property crimes.

Steady Decline in Major Crime Baffles Experts

The number of violent crimes in the United States dropped significantly last year, to what appeared to be the lowest rate in nearly 40 years, a development that was considered puzzling partly because it ran counter to the prevailing expectation that crime would increase during a recession.

In all regions, the country appears to be safer. The odds of being murdered or robbed are now less than half of what they were in the early 1990s, when violent crime peaked in the United States. Small towns, especially, are seeing far fewer murders: In cities with populations under 10,000, the number plunged by more than 25 percent last year.

The news was not as positive in New York City, however. After leading a long decline in crime rates, the city saw increases in all four types of violent lawbreaking—murder, rape, robbery, and aggravated assault—including a nearly 14 percent rise in murders. But data from the past few months suggest the city's upward trend may have slowed or stopped.

Criminology experts said they were surprised and impressed by the national numbers, issued by the Federal Bureau of Investigation and based on data from more than 13,000 law-enforcement agencies. They said the decline nationally in the number of violent crimes, by 5.5 percent, raised the question, at least in some places, of to what extent crime could continue to fall—or at least fall at the same pace as the past two years. Violent crimes fell nearly the same amount in 2009.

"Remarkable," said James Alan Fox, a criminologist at Northeastern University. "Given the fact that we have had some healthy declines in recent years, I fully expected that the improvement would slow. There is only so much air you can squeeze out of a balloon."

There was no immediate consensus to explain the drop. But some experts said the figures collided with theories about correlations between crime, unemployment, and the number of people in prison.

Take robbery: The nation has endured a devastating economic crisis, but robberies fell 9.5 percent last year, after dropping 8 percent the year before.

"Striking," said Alfred Blumstein, a professor and a criminologist at the Heinz College at Carnegie Mellon University, because it came "at a time when everyone anticipated it could be going up because of the recession."

Nationally, murder fell 4.4 percent last year. Forcible rape—which excludes statutory rape and other sex offenses—fell 4.2 percent. Aggravated assault fell 3.6 percent. Property crimes—including burglary, larceny, motor vehicle theft, and arson—fell 2.8 percent, after a 4.6 percent drop the year before.

But the gains were uneven. New York City saw 536 murders in 2010—65 more than in 2009, which was the lowest since 1963.

The number of rapes in New York City jumped 24.5 percent, robberies, 5.4 percent, and aggravated assaults, 3.2 percent.

MEASURING CHARACTERISTICS OF CRIMINALS

Information on the characteristics of crimes is not the only sort of data analyzed by criminologists. They also want to know the characteristics of the people who commit those crimes.

Behind each crime is a criminal or several criminals. Criminals can be differentiated by age, ethnicity, gender, socioeconomic level, and other criteria. These characteristics enable researchers to group criminals into categories, and it is these categories that researchers find useful. They study the various offender groups to determine why some people are more likely than others to commit crimes or particular types of crimes. It has been estimated that 13.1 million arrests were made in 2010 for all criminal offenses except traffic violations. Figure 2.7 (page 47) shows how these arrests were distributed among the offenses.[51]

Age and Crime

Six armed men who have been called the "over-the-hill gang" were arrested trying to rob an elegant bridge and backgammon club in midtown New York City. The robbery began at 10:25 P.M. when the men, wearing rubber gloves and ski masks and armed with two revolvers, a shotgun, and a rifle, forced the customers and employees to lie down in a back room while they loaded a nylon bag with wallets, players' money, and the club's cash box. A club worker slipped out a side door to alert police, who arrived within minutes. They surprised and disarmed one member of the gang, a 48-year-old, whom they found clutching a .22-caliber revolver. They took a .38-caliber revolver from another gang member, 41 years old.

During the scuffle with the officers, one suspect tried to escape, fell, and broke his nose. The officers then found and arrested a 40-year-old man standing in the hallway with a 12-gauge Winchester shotgun. Meanwhile, the other gang members abandoned their gloves and masks and lay down among the people they had robbed. One of the suspects, age 72, who wore a back brace, complained of chest and back pain as police locked handcuffs on him. He was immediately hospitalized.[52]

New York was the only city with a population of more than a million people, besides San Antonio, that had an increase in the total number of violent crimes—a 4.6 percent jump, to 48,489—and the only city beside Philadelphia to see a rise in murders.

Some experts cautioned against reading too much into the city's numbers, noting that New York's drop in violent crime over the last two decades has far outpaced many places, some of which are only now catching up.

"It's been so huge, there's always been this lingering question, how low could it go?" said Michael Jacobson, director of the Vera Institute of Justice, and a former New York City correction and probation commissioner.

There were 2,245 murders in New York in 1990, but the total has been less than 600 for the past nine years.

"One murder is too many, but the 2010 spike has to be viewed in the context of the historic low the year before," said Paul J. Browne, the New York Police Department's chief spokesman. He said the department was doing more to encourage victims to report rapes.

Eli Silverman, a professor emeritus of criminal justice at John Jay College, said Mr. Browne's account might only be a "partial explanation"—the other part, he said, was increased scrutiny of the integrity of the department's crime statistics. When crime rates go up, the police say it is because they are encouraging more victims to come forward, Mr. Silverman said, "but when crime goes down, it's the work of the police."

Nationally, the drop in violent crime not only calls into question the theory that crime rates are closely correlated with economic hardship, but another argument as well, said Frank E. Zimring, a 'law professor at the University of California, Berkeley.

As the percentage of people behind bars has decreased in the past few years, violent crime rates have fallen as well. For those who believed that higher incarceration rates inevitably led to less crime, "this would also be the last time to expect a crime decline," he said.

"The last three years have been a contrarian's delight—just when you expect the bananas to hit the fan," said Mr. Zimring, the author of an upcoming book on the decline in the city's crime rate.

But Zimring said there was no way to know why a decline occurred—at least not yet.

"The only thing that is reassuring being in a room full of crime experts now is that they are as puzzled as I am," Mr. Zimring said.

Source

New York Times, "Steady Decline in Major Crime Baffles Experts," May 23, 2011 (available at: http://www.nytimes.com/2011/05/24/us/24crime.html).

Questions for Discussion

1. What is the best explanation for the drop in crime rates?
2. Should criminology theory (Chapters 4–8) offer a coherent explanation as to why crime rates increase or decrease?
3. Is the overall economy in the United States relevant in thinking about crime rate increases or decreases?

In another case, 94-year-old career criminal Wesley (Pop) Honeywood, from Jacksonville, Florida, was sentenced to 7 years after he pointed an unloaded gun at another man who warned him not to eat grapes growing in the man's yard. Mr. Honeywood was given the option of going to a nursing home instead of prison, but he resisted, saying, "If I go to jail, I may be out in a couple of years. If I go to a nursing home, I may be there the rest of my life."[53]

These cases are extraordinary for at least two reasons. First, in any given year, approximately half of all arrests are of individuals under age 25; second, gang membership is ordinarily confined to the young. Though juveniles (people under age 18) constitute about 8 percent of the population, they account for 15 percent of arrests for Index crimes in 2006. One-quarter of all larceny-theft offenses involved juveniles, and juveniles comprised half of all arson arrests.[54] While people age 65 and over constitute 12.4 percent of the population, they account for less than 1 percent of all arrests.[55] This **aging-out phenomenon**—or decline in criminal activities with age—has sparked a lively scientific debate. Michael Gottfredson

and Travis Hirschi contend there is a certain inclination to commit crimes that peaks in the middle or late teens and then declines throughout life. This relationship between crime and age does not change, "regardless of sex, race, country, time, or offense."[56]

Crime decreases with age, the researchers add, even among people who commit frequent offenses. Thus, differences in crime rates found among young people of various groups, such as males and females or lower class and middle class, will be maintained throughout the life cycle. If lower-class youths are three times more likely to commit crimes than middle-class youths, for instance, then 60-year-old lower-class persons will be three times more likely to commit crimes than 60-year-old middle-class persons, though crimes committed by both lower-class and middle-class groups will constantly decline.[57] According to this argument, all offenders commit fewer crimes as they grow older because they have less strength, less mobility, and so on.

James Q. Wilson and Richard Herrnstein support the view that the aging-out phenomenon is a natural part of the life cycle.[58] Teenagers may

TABLE 2.2　How Do People Rank the Severity of Crime?

Severity Score	Ten Most Serious Offenses	Severity Score	Ten Least Serious Offenses
72.1	Planting a bomb in a public building. The bomb explodes and 20 people are killed.	1.3	Two persons willingly engage in a homosexual act.
52.8	A man forcibly rapes a woman. As a result of physical injuries, she dies.	1.1	Disturbing the neighborhood with loud, noisy behavior.
43.2	Robbing a victim at gunpoint. The victim struggles and is shot to death.	1.1	Taking bets on the numbers.
39.2	A man stabs his wife. As a result, she dies.	1.1	A group continues to hang around a corner after being told to break up by a police officer.
35.7	Stabbing a victim to death.	0.9	A youngster under 16 years old runs away from home.
35.6	Intentionally injuring a victim. As a result, the victim dies.	0.8	Being drunk in public.
33.8	Running a narcotics ring.	0.7	A youngster under 16 years old breaks a curfew law by being out on the street after the hour permitted by law.
27.9	A woman stabs her husband. As a result, he dies.	0.6	Trespassing in the backyard of a private home.
26.3	An armed person skyjacks an airplane and demands to be flown to another country.	0.3	A person is a vagrant. That is, he has no home and no visible means of support.
25.8	A man forcibly rapes a woman. No other physical injury occurs.	0.2	A youngster under 16 years old plays hooky from school.

SOURCE: Adapted from Marvin E. Wolfgang, Robert Figlio, Paul E. Tracey, and Simon I. Singer, *National Survey of Crime Severity* (Washington, D.C.: U.S. Government Printing Office, 1985).

■ *Two very old inmates in the geriatric unit at Estelle Prison, Huntsville, Texas: an increasing burden for custodial care.*

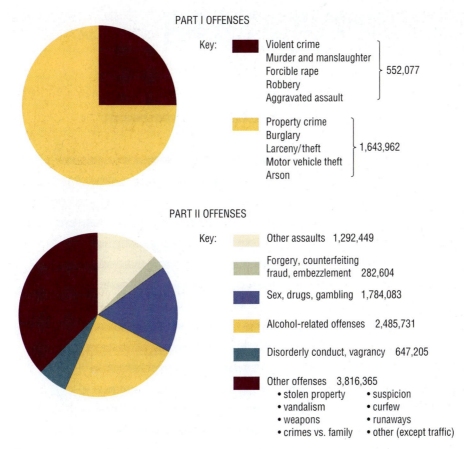

PART I OFFENSES

Key:
- ■ Violent crime
  Murder and manslaughter
  Forcible rape
  Robbery
  Aggravated assault } 552,077

- ■ Property crime
  Burglary
  Larceny/theft
  Motor vehicle theft
  Arson } 1,643,962

PART II OFFENSES

Key:
- Other assaults   1,292,449

- Forgery, counterfeiting
  fraud, embezzlement   282,604

- Sex, drugs, gambling   1,784,083

- Alcohol-related offenses   2,485,731

- Disorderly conduct, vagrancy   647,205

- Other offenses   3,816,365
  - stolen property   • suspicion
  - vandalism   • curfew
  - weapons   • runaways
  - crimes vs. family   • other (except traffic)

FIGURE 2.7   Distribution of total number of arrests, 2010 (estimated).

Source: U.S. Department of Justice, Federal Bureau of Investigation, *Crime in the United States, 2010.* Retrieved July 25, 2011, from http://www.fbi.gov/.

become increasingly independent of their parents yet lack the resources to support themselves; they band together with other young people who are equally frustrated in their search for legitimate ways to get money, sex, alcohol, and status. Together they find illegitimate sources. With adulthood, the small gains from criminal behavior no longer seem so attractive. Legitimate means open up. They marry. Their peers no longer endorse lawbreaking. They learn to delay gratification. Petty crime is no longer adventurous. It is at this time that the aging-out process begins for most individuals. Even those who continue to commit offenses will eventually slow down with increasing age.

The opposing side in this debate, sometimes called the "life-course perspective," argues that the decrease in crime rates after adolescence does not imply that the number of crimes committed by all individual offenders declines. In other words, the frequency of offending may go down for most offenders, but some chronic active offenders may continue to commit the same amount of crime over time. Why might this be so? Because the

factors that influence any individual's entrance into criminal activity vary, the number and types of offenses committed vary, and the factors that eventually induce the individual to give up criminal activity vary.[59]

According to this argument, the frequency of criminal involvement, then, depends on such social factors as economic situation, peer pressure, and lifestyle, and it is these social factors that explain the aging-out phenomenon. A teenager's unemployment, for example, may have very little to do with the onset of criminal activity because the youngster is not yet in the labor force and still lives at home. Unemployment may increase an adult's rate of offending, however, because an adult requires income to support various responsibilities. Thus, the relationship between age and crime is not the same for all offenders. Various conditions during the life cycle affect individuals' behavior in different ways.[60]

To learn how the causes of crime vary at different ages, Alfred Blumstein and his colleagues suggest that we study **criminal careers,** a concept that describes the onset of criminal activity, the types

Victims around the World

The International Crime Victim Survey (comparable to our National Crime Victimization Survey) became operational in 1989. The main object of ICVS is to advance international and comparative criminological research without the obvious limitations of officially recorded crime data.

ICVS surveys were administered in 1992, 1996, and 2000. The survey's fifth administration was in 2005. Within the past 15 years, a total of more than 300,000 people from 78 countries have been interviewed about their victimization.

As the graph in this box reveals, the top 15 countries by victimization rate include very affluent parts of the world. Some comparative criminologists, in response, ask whether there is still any truth to the conventional wisdom that poverty is the "dominant root cause of common crime."

Source

J. van Dijk, J. van Kerteren, and P. Smit, *Criminal Victimisation in International Perspective: Key Findings from the 2004–2005 ICVS and EU ICS* (The Hague: Boom Legal Publishers, 2007).

Questions for Discussion

1. Why are the victimization rates so high in affluent countries?
2. Are you surprised by how the United States ranks relative to other countries? Why or why not?

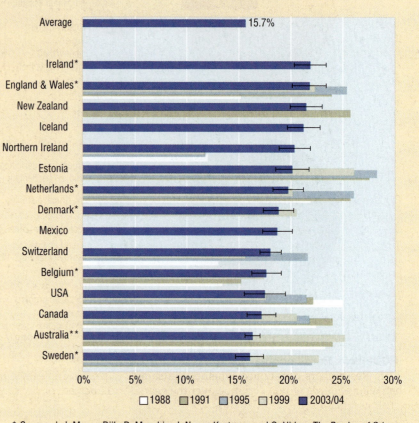

* Source: J. J. M. van Dijk, R. Manchin, J. N. van Kesteren, and G. Hideg, *The Burden of Crime in the EU. Research Report: A Comparative Analysis of the European Crime and Safety Survey (EU ICS)* 2005 (Brussels: Gallup Europe, 2007), p.19.

** The Australian victimization rate is based on nine crimes because the question about victimization by sexual offenses was omitted; if data on sexual victimization were included, the overall victimization rate would be a percentage point higher (est. 16.5 percent).

Overall victimization for 10 crimes; 1-year prevalence rates in 2003/04 of the top 15 countries and results from earlier surveys (1989–2005 ICVS and 2005 EU ICS).

and amount of crime committed, and the termination of such activity.[61] **Longitudinal studies** of a particular group of people over time should enable researchers to uncover the factors that distinguish criminals from noncriminals and those that differentiate criminals in regard to the number and kinds of offenses they commit.

Those involved in research on criminal careers assume that offenders who commit 10 crimes may differ from those who commit 1 or 15. They ask: Are the factors that cause the second offense the same ones that cause the fourth or the fifth? Do different factors move one offender from theft to rape or from assault to shoplifting? How many persons in a **birth cohort** (a group of people born in the same year) will become criminals? Of those, how many will become career criminals (chronic offenders)?

In the 1960s, researchers at the Sellin Center of the University of Pennsylvania began a search for answers. Their earliest publication, in 1972, detailed the criminal careers of 9,945 boys (a cohort) born in Philadelphia in 1945. Marvin Wolfgang, Robert Figlio, and Thorsten Sellin obtained their data from school records and official police reports. Their major findings were that 35 percent of the boys had had contact with the police before reaching their 18th birthday; of those boys, 46 percent were one-time offenders and 54 percent were repeat offenders. Of those with police contact, 18 percent had committed five or more offenses; they represented 6 percent of the total. The "chronic 6 percent," as they are now called, were responsible for more than half of all the offenses committed, including 71 percent of the homicides, 73 percent of the rapes, 82 percent of the robberies, and 69 percent of the assaults.[62]

Research continued on 10 percent of the boys in the original cohort until they reached the age of 30. This sample was divided into three groups: those who had records of offenses only as juveniles, those who had records only as adults, and those who were persistent offenders with both juvenile and adult records. Though they made up only 15 percent of the follow-up group, those who had been chronic juvenile offenders made up 74 percent of all the arrests. Thus, chronic juvenile offenders do indeed continue to break laws as adults.[63]

The boys in the original cohort were born in 1945. Researchers questioned whether the same behavior patterns would continue over the years. Criminologist Paul Tracy and his associates found the answer in a second study, which examined a cohort of 13,160 males born in 1958. The two studies show similar results. In the second cohort, 33 percent had had contact with the police before reaching their 18th birthday, 42 percent were one-time offenders, and 58 percent were repeat offenders. Chronic delinquents were found in both cohorts. The chronic delinquents in the second cohort, however, accounted for a greater percentage of the cohort—7.5 percent. They also were involved in more serious and injurious acts than the previous group.

The 1945 cohort study did not contain females, so no overall comparisons can be made over time. But comparing females and males in the 1958 cohort, we see significant gender differences. Of the 14,000 females in the cohort, 14 percent had had contact with the police before age 18. Among the female delinquents, 60 percent were one-time offenders, 33 percent were repeat offenders, and 7 percent were chronic offenders. Overall, female delinquency was less frequent and less likely to involve serious charges.[64]

In another longitudinal study, researchers followed about 4,000 youngsters in Denver, Pittsburgh, and Rochester, New York, for 5 years, 1988 through 1992. By age 16, over half the youngsters admitted to committing violent criminal acts. According to Terence P. Thornberry, the principal investigator in Rochester, chronic offenders also accounted for a high percentage of all violent offenses: 15 percent of the youths in the sample were responsible for 75 percent of the criminal acts.[65]

The policy implications of such findings are clear. If a very small group of offenders is committing a large percentage of all crime, the crime rate should go down if we incarcerate those offenders for long periods of time. Many jurisdictions around the country are developing sentencing policies to do just that, but such policies are quite controversial.

Gender and Crime

Except for such crimes as prostitution, shoplifting, and welfare fraud, males traditionally commit more crimes than females at all ages. According to the UCR for 2007, the arrest ratio is more than 3 male offenders to 1 female offender.[66] The NCVS reports a wider gap: For personal crimes of violence involving a single offender, 82 percent of victims perceived the gender of the offender as male.[67]

Since the 1960s, however, there have been some interesting developments in regard to gender and crime data. In 1960, females accounted for 11 percent of the total number of arrests across the country. They now account for about 23 percent. And while the female arrest rate is still much lower than that of males, the rate of increase for women has risen faster than the rate for men (Figure 2.8 shows juvenile rates).[68]

Self-report surveys, which show more similarities in male and female criminal activity than official reports do, find that males commit more offenses than females. However, several of these studies suggest that gender differences in crime may be narrowing. They demonstrate that the patterns and causes of male and female delinquent activity are becoming more alike.[69] John Hagan and his associates agree, but only with respect to girls raised in middle-class egalitarian families in which husband and wife share similar positions of power at home and in the workplace. They argue that girls raised in lower-class, father-dominated households grow up in a cult of domesticity that reduces their freedom and thus the likelihood of their delinquency.[70] Researchers Merry Morash and Meda Chesney-Lind disagree. In a study of 1,427 adolescents and their caretakers, they found gender differences in delinquency between girls and boys regardless of the type of family in which the youngsters were raised.[71]

FIGURE 2.8 Juvenile male and female arrest trends, 1980–2008.

Source: Charles Puzzanchera, Juvenile Arrests 2008 (Washington, D.C.: Department of Justice, 2009).

Robbery

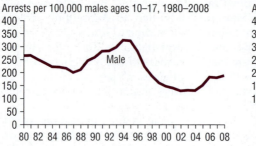

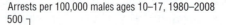

Aggravated assault

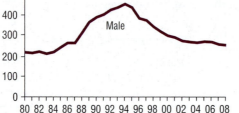

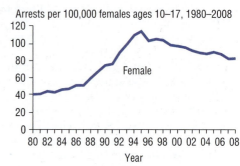

Other (simple) assault

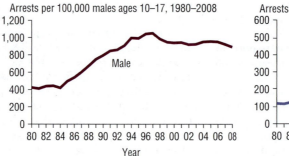

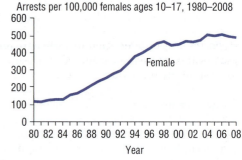

Drug abuse violations

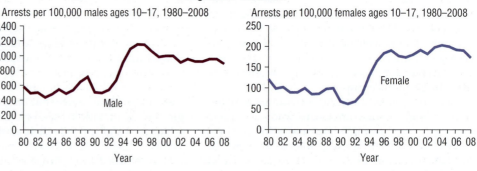

Because women traditionally have had such low crime rates, the scientific community and the mass media have generally ignored the subject of female criminality. Both have tended to view female offenders as misguided children who are an embarrassment rather than a threat to society. Only a handful of the world's criminologists have deemed the subject worthy of independent study. Foremost among them was Cesare Lombroso (whom we shall meet again in Chapter 3). His book *The Female Offender* (coauthored by William Ferrero), which appeared in 1895, detailed the physical abnormalities that would predestine some girls to be criminal from birth.[72] Lombroso's

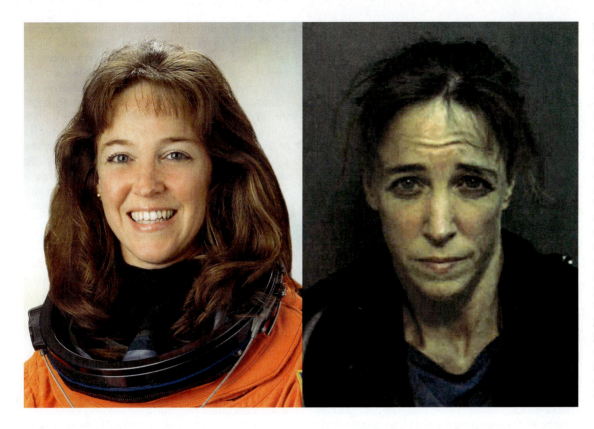

Lisa Marie Nowak, U.S. Naval Officer and former NASA astronaut (left), was charged in February 2007 with attempted kidnapping, burglary with assault, and misdemeanor battery (right). Nowak had a 2-year affair with fellow astronaut William Oefelein before he ended the relationship with Nowak to date U.S. Air Force Captain Colleen Shipman. Nowak drove from Houston to Orlando with latex gloves, a pistol and ammunition, pepper spray, a trench coat, a hammer drill, plastic bags, and an 8-inch knife to kidnap Shipman.

findings on male criminals, however, have not stood the test of later scientific research, and his portrayal of the female criminal has been found to be similarly inaccurate.

A little over a generation later, in the 1930s, Sheldon and Eleanor Glueck launched a massive research project on the biological and environmental causes of crime, with a separate inquiry into female offenders. Their conclusions were decidedly sociological. They said, in essence, that in order to change the incidence of female criminality, there would have to be a change in the social circumstances in which females grow up.[73]

Otto Pollack shared the Gluecks' views on sociological determinants. In 1952, he proposed that female crime has a "masked character" that keeps it from being properly recorded or otherwise noted in statistical reports. Protective attitudes toward women make police officers less willing to arrest them, victims less eager to report their offenses, district attorneys less enthusiastic about prosecuting them, and juries less likely to find them guilty. Moreover, Pollack noted that women's social roles as homemakers, child rearers, and shoppers furnish them with opportunities for concealed criminal activity and with victims who are the least likely to complain to and/or cooperate with the police. He also argued that female crime was limited by the various psychological and physiological characteristics inherent in the female anatomy.[74]

A quarter-century after Pollack's work, two researchers, working independently, took a fresh look at female crime in light of women's new roles in society. In 1975, Freda Adler posited that as social and economic roles of women changed in the legitimate world, their participation in crime would also change. According to this argument, the temptations, challenges, stresses, and strains to which women have been increasingly subjected in recent years cause them to act or react in the same manner in which men have consistently reacted to the same stimuli. In other words, equalization of social and economic roles leads to similar behavior patterns, both legal and illegal, on the part of both men and women. To steal a car, for example, one needs to know how to drive. To embezzle, one needs to be in a position of trust and in control of funds. To get into a bar fight, one needs to go to a bar. To be an inside trader on Wall Street, one needs to be on the inside.[75]

Rita Simon has taken a similar position. She, too, has argued that female criminality has undergone changes. But these changes, according to Simon, have occurred only in regard to certain property crimes, such as larceny/theft and fraud/embezzlement. Women are becoming more involved in these crimes because they have more opportunities to commit them. Simon hypothesizes that since the propensity of men and women to commit crime is not basically different, as more women enter the labor force and work in a much broader range of jobs, their property crime rate will continue to go up.[76]

Some criminologists have challenged the views of Adler and Simon. Many questions have been asked about the so-called new female criminal. Does she exist? If so, does she commit more crimes than the former female criminal did? What types of crimes? Is she still involved primarily in offenses against property, or has she turned to more violent offenses? Researchers differ on the answers. Some contend that the extent of female criminality has not changed through the years but that crimes committed by women are more often making their way into official statistics simply because they are more often reported and prosecuted. In other words, the days of chivalry in the criminal justice system are over.[77]

Others argue that female crime has indeed increased, but they attribute the increase to nonviolent, petty property offenses that continue to reflect traditional female gender roles.[78] Moreover, some investigators claim, the increased involvement in these petty property offenses suggests that women are still economically disadvantaged, still suffering sexism in the legitimate marketplace.[79] Other researchers support the contention of Adler and Simon that female roles have changed and that these changes have indeed led women to commit the same kinds of crimes as men—violent as well as property offenses.[80]

Though scholars disagree on the form and extent of female crime, they do seem to agree that the crimes women commit are closely associated with their socioeconomic position in society. The controversy has to do with whether that position has changed. In any case, the association between gender and crime has become a recognized area of concern in the growing body of research dealing with contemporary criminological issues.[81]

Social Class and Crime

Researchers agree on the importance of age and gender as factors related to crime, but they disagree strongly about whether social class is related to crime. First of all, the term "class" can have many meanings. If "lower class" is defined by income, then the category might include graduate students, unemployed stockbrokers, pensioners, welfare mothers, prison inmates, and many others who have little in common except low income. Furthermore, "lower class" is often defined by the low prestige associated with blue-collar occupations. Some delinquency studies determine the class of young people by the class of their fathers, even though the young people may have jobs quite different from those of their fathers.

Another dispute focuses on the source of statistics used by investigators. Many researchers attribute the relatively strong association between class and crime found in arrest statistics to class bias on the part of the police. If the police are more likely to arrest a lower-class suspect than a middle-class suspect, they say, arrest data will show more involvement of lower-class people in criminality whether or not they are actually committing more crimes. When Charles Tittle, Wayne Villemez, and Douglas Smith analyzed 35 studies of the relationship between social class and crime rates in 1978, they found little support for the claim that crime is primarily a lower-class phenomenon. An update of that work, which evaluates studies done between 1978 and 1990, again found no pervasive relationship.[82]

Many scholars have challenged such conclusions. They claim that when self-report studies are used for analysis, the results show few class differences because the studies ask only about trivial offenses. Delbert Elliott and Suzanne Ageton, for example, looked at serious crimes among a national sample of 1,726 young people ages 11 to 17. According to the youths' responses to a self-report questionnaire, lower-class young people were much more likely than middle-class young people to commit serious crimes such as burglary, robbery, assault, and sexual assault.[83] A follow-up study concluded that middle-class and lower-class youths differed significantly in both the nature and the number of serious crimes they committed.[84]

Controversies remain about the social class of people who commit crimes. There is no controversy, however, about the social class of people in prison. The probability that a person such as Martha Stewart—chief executive officer of Martha Stewart Omnimedia, who was convicted of lying to the government—would face prison time is usually extremely low. Stewart does not fit the typical profile of the hundreds of thousands of inmates of our nation's jails and prisons. She is educated. Only 28 percent of prison inmates have completed high school.[85] Her income is that of a high-ranking corporate officer. The average yearly income of jail inmates who work is $5,600. She has a white-collar job. Eighty-five percent of prison inmates are blue-collar workers. She committed a white-collar offense. Only 18 percent of those convicted of such offenses go to prison for more than 1 year, whereas 39 percent of the violent offenders and 26 percent of the property offenders go to prison.[86] Finally, Martha Stewart is white in a criminal justice system where blacks are disproportionately represented.

Strong Words from the Children's Defense Fund on the Cradle to Prison Pipeline Campaign February 19, 2009

A black boy born in 2001 has a one in three chance of going to prison in his lifetime; a Latino boy a one in six chance; and a white boy a one in 17 chance. A black girl born in 2001 has a one in 17 chance of going to prison in her lifetime; a Latino girl a one in 45 chance; and a white girl a one in 111 chance.

Pervasive Poverty

Poverty is the largest driving force behind the Pipeline crisis, exacerbated by race. Black children are more than three times as likely as white children to be born into poverty and to be poor, and are four times as likely to live in extreme poverty. One in three Latino babies and three in seven black babies are born into poverty. More than one in four Latino children and one in three black children are poor. Between 2000 and 2007, the number of poor Latino children increased by 960,000 (to 4.5 million) and the number of poor black children increased by 323,000 (to 3.9 million).

Inadequate Access to Health Coverage

One out of five Latino children and one out of eight black children are uninsured, compared to one out of 13 white children. A child is born uninsured every 39 seconds. More than 2,200 children are born uninsured every day. And about 800,000 pregnant women are uninsured, while each year, approximately 28,000 infants die in America before they reach their first birthday.

Gaps in Early Childhood Development

Studies have shown that children who do not get the early intervention, permanence, and stability they need are more likely to act out and fail in school because they lack the skills necessary to succeed. Researchers of early childhood emphasize the importance of early childhood nurturing and stimulation to help the brain grow, especially between birth and age seven, and even beyond, and thus help children to thrive and to be on a positive path toward successful adulthood. The importance of stimulation in the first years of life is dramatically underlined in the U.S. Department of Education's study of 22,000 kindergartners in the kindergarten class of 1998–99, which found that black and Hispanic children were substantially behind when they entered kindergarten.

Disparate Educational Opportunities

Children in the most economically depressed communities are at high risk of low achievement and attainment and are often stuck in underfunded, overcrowded schools. Poor urban schools have the highest numbers of teachers who are inexperienced or do not have degrees in the subjects they teach. Eighty-six percent of black, 83 percent of Latino, and 58 percent of white fourth graders cannot read at grade level; and 89 percent of black, 85 percent of Latino and 59 percent of white 8th graders cannot do math at grade level. Black students are more likely than any other students to be in special education programs for children with mental retardation or emotional disturbance. Black and American Indian children are almost twice as likely as white children to be retained in a grade. The public school suspension rate among black and American Indian students is almost three times that for whites. Black, Latino, and American Indian children are more than twice as likely as white children to drop out of school. According to the U.S. Department of Education, only 59 percent of black and 61 percent of Latino students graduated from high school on time with a regular diploma in 2006. When black children do graduate from high school, they have a greater chance of being unemployed and a lower chance of going to college full-time than white high school graduates. Only 48,000 black males earn a bachelor's degree each year, but an estimated one in three black men, ages 20–29, is under correctional supervision or control. Approximately 815,000 black males were incarcerated in state or federal prisons or local jails at midyear 2007.

Intolerable Abuse and Neglect

A child is abused or neglected every 35 seconds. Four in ten of the children who are abused or neglected get no help at all after their initial investigation. More than 800,000 children are in foster care each year, about 513,000 on a single day. Black children represent 32 percent of children in foster care but only 15 percent of all children.

Unmet Mental and Emotional Problems

A Congressional study found 15,000 children in juvenile detention facilities, some as young as seven years old, solely because community mental health services were unavailable. Studies have reported that as many as three-fourths of incarcerated youth have mental health disorders and about one in five has a severe disorder. Youths who age out of foster care are less likely to graduate from high school or college and experience more serious mental health problems, including posttraumatic stress disorder, than youths generally. They are less likely to receive adequate health and mental health care, and are more likely to experience homelessness, and to be involved in the criminal justice system.

Rampant Substance Abuse

Drugs, tobacco, and alcohol lead our children down the wrong path. Disconnected youth, lacking a decent education or high school degree, job training skills, and social support systems or mentors, often resort to self-destructive acts. Unfortunately, alcohol and other substance abuse treatment for youth and for parents and other adults is in too short supply. Only about 10 percent of youth with a substance use disorder receive treatment.

Overburdened, Ineffective Juvenile Justice System

One-size-fits-all zero tolerance school discipline policies are transforming schools into a major point of entry into the juvenile justice system as children are increasingly arrested on school grounds for subjectively and loosely defined behaviors. Black youth are about four times as likely as their white peers to be incarcerated. Black youth are almost five times as likely to be incarcerated as white youth for drug offenses. Of the 1.5 million children with an incarcerated parent in 1999, black children were nearly nine times as likely and Latino children were three times as likely to have an incarcerated parent as white children. Most juvenile correctional facility programs focus on punishment rather than treatment and rehabilitation, often creating environments that further harden youth. This makes it more difficult for them to productively reintegrate into their families and communities.

We must speak out against policies that contribute to criminalizing children at younger and younger ages, and fight for policies that help children thrive and put them on track to a productive adulthood.

We need to:

- End poverty by creating jobs that offer livable wages, increasing the minimum wage, expanding job training programs, making college affordable for every student, and expanding income supports such as the Child Tax Credit.

- Ensure all children and pregnant woman have access to affordable comprehensive health and mental health coverage and services.

- Make early childhood development programs accessible to every child by ensuring such programs are affordable, available, and of high quality.

- Help each child reach his/her full potential and succeed in work and life, by ensuring our schools have adequate resources to provide high quality education to every child.

- Expand prevention and specialized treatment services for children and their parents, connect children to caring permanent families, improve the quality of the child welfare workforce, and increase accountability for results for children.

- Reduce detention and incarceration by increasing investment in prevention and early intervention strategies, such as access to quality early childhood development and education services and to the health and mental health care children need for healthy development.

For those children who do get caught in the deeper end of the Pipeline, we must accelerate reforms of juvenile justice policy at the federal, state, and local level to ensure that troubled youth get the integrated services needed to put them on a sustained path to successful adulthood.

Source: http://www.childrensdefense.org/child-research-data-publications/data/cradle-prison-pipeline-summary-report.pdf

Race and Crime

Statistics on race and crime show that while African Americans constitute 13.6 percent of the population, they account for over 30 percent of all arrests for Index crimes.[87] Other statistics confirm their disproportionate representation in the criminal justice system. Fifty percent of black urban males are arrested for an Index crime at least once during their lives, compared with 14 percent of white males. The likelihood that any man will serve time in jail or prison is estimated to be 18 percent for blacks and 3 percent for whites. Moreover, the leading cause of death among young black men is murder.[88]

These statistics raise many questions. Do blacks actually commit more crimes, or are they simply arrested more often? Are black neighborhoods under more police surveillance than white neighborhoods? Do blacks receive differential treatment in the criminal justice system? If blacks commit more crimes than whites, why?

Some data support the argument that there are more African Americans in the criminal justice system because bias operates from the time of arrest through incarceration. Other data support the argument that racial disparities in official statistics reflect an actual difference in criminal behavior. Much of the evidence comes from the statistics of the NCVS, which are very similar to the statistics on race found in arrest data. When interviewers asked victims about the race of offenders in violent crimes, 21.3 percent identified the assailants as black.[89] Similarly, while self-report data demonstrate that less-serious juvenile offenses are about equally prevalent among black and white youngsters, more serious ones are not: Black youngsters report having committed many more Index crimes than do whites of comparable ages.[90]

If the disparity in criminal behavior suggested by official data, victimization studies, and self-reports actually exists, and if we are to explain it, we have to try to discover why people commit crimes. A history of hundreds of years of abuse, neglect, and discrimination against black Americans has left its mark in the form of high unemployment, residence in socially disorganized areas, one-parent households, and negative self-images.

In 1968, in the aftermath of the worst riots in modern American history, the National Advisory Commission on Civil Disorders alluded to the reasons blacks had not achieved the successes accomplished by other minority groups that at one time or another also were discriminated against. European immigrants provided unskilled labor needed by industry. By the time blacks migrated from rural areas to cities, the U.S. economy was changing and soon there was no longer much demand for unskilled labor. Immigrant groups had also received economic advantages by working for local political organizations. By the time blacks moved to the cities, the political machines no longer had the power to offer help in return for votes. Though both immigrants and blacks arrived in cities with little money, all but the very youngest members of the cohesive immigrant family contributed to the family's income. As slaves, however, black persons had been forbidden to marry, and the unions they formed were subject to disruption at the owner's convenience and therefore tended to be unstable. We will have more to say about the causal factors associated with high crime rates and race in Chapters 5 and 6.

Researchers have three main objectives in measuring crime and criminal behavior patterns. They need (1) to collect and analyze data to test theories about why people commit crime, (2) to learn the situational characteristics of crimes in order to develop prevention strategies, and (3) to determine the needs of the criminal justice system on a daily basis. Data are collected by surveys, experiments, nonparticipant and participant observation, and case studies. It is often cost-effective for researchers to use repositories of information gathered by public and private organizations for their own purposes. The three main sources of data for measuring crime are the Uniform Crime Reports, the National Crime Victimization Survey, and self-report questionnaires. Though each source is useful for some purposes, all three have limitations.

By measuring the characteristics of crime and criminals, we can identify crime trends, the places and times at which crimes are most likely to be committed, and the public's evaluation of the seriousness of offenses. Current controversies concerning offenders focus on the relationship between crime and age throughout the life cycle, the changing role of women in crime, and the effects of social class and race on the response of the criminal justice system. Crime is an activity disproportionately engaged in by young people, males, and minorities.

CRIMINOLOGY & PUBLIC POLICY

Police defend their racially disparate practices by saying that, generally, minorities commit more crimes than whites. They also hold that enforcement of criminal laws that are violated by whites and minorities in roughly even numbers (for example, narcotics violations) is disproportionate because the location and social impact of the same types of crimes justifies a more aggressive response in minority communities. They argue that current practices work: Aggressive policing and targeting of minority communities have led to significant seizures of contraband, weapons, and fugitives—and a reduction in crime.

In the wake of September 11 events, advocates of racial and ethnic profiling point to the need for heightened suspicion regarding the activities of young Arabic men. The arrests and detention of hundreds of people after the terrorist attacks has created considerable controversy—many of these people would not have been subject to this treatment were it not for ethnic characteristics, and the government fails to consistently provide evidence linking them to terrorist activities. Furthermore, it is not likely that ethnic profiling will be any more useful or constitutional than racial profiling. In the area in which racial profiling has been most controversial—narcotics enforcement—proponents' arguments do not withstand empirical and legal scrutiny. For example, the data do not indicate a minority-dominated drug trade. National drug abuse studies show that minorities possess and use drugs only slightly more frequently than whites do. "The typical cocaine user is white, male, a high school graduate employed full-time, and living in a small metropolitan area or suburb," former drug czar William Bennett has said.

Arrest statistics are also misleading. New Jersey's attorney general pointed out that these statistics are "a self-fulfilling prophecy where law enforcement agencies rely on arrest data that they themselves generated as a result of the discretionary allocation of resources and targeted drug

criminology. It is based on the assumption that individuals choose to commit crimes after weighing the consequences of their actions. According to classical criminologists, individuals have free will. They can choose legal or illegal means to get what they want, fear of punishment can deter them from committing crime, and society can control behavior by making the pain of punishment greater than the pleasure of the criminal gains.

The classical school did not remain unchallenged for long. In the early nineteenth century, great advances were made in the natural sciences and in medicine. Physicians in France, Germany, and England undertook systematic studies of crimes and criminals. Crime statistics became available in several European countries. There emerged an opposing school of criminology, the **positivist school.** This school posits that human behavior is determined by forces beyond individual control and that it is possible to measure those forces. Unlike classical criminologists, who claim that people rationally choose to commit crime, positivist criminologists view criminal behavior as stemming from biological, psychological, and social factors.

The earliest positivist theories centered on biological factors, and studies of those factors dominated criminology during the last half of the nineteenth century. In the twentieth century, biological explanations were ignored (and even targeted as racist after World War II). They did not surface again until the 1970s, when scientific advances in psychology shifted the emphasis from defects in criminals' bodies to defects in their minds. Throughout the twentieth century, psychologists and psychiatrists have played a major role in the study of crime causation. A third area of positivist criminology focuses on the relation of social factors to crime. Sociological theories, developed in the second half of the nineteenth century and advanced throughout the twentieth, continue to dominate the field of criminology today.

An understanding of the foundations of modern criminology helps us understand contemporary developments in the field. Let us begin with the developments that led to the emergence of the classical school.

CLASSICAL CRIMINOLOGY

In the late eighteenth to the mid-nineteenth centuries, during what is now called the "neoclassical period," the classical culture of the ancient Mediterranean was rediscovered. This was also a period of scientific discoveries and the founding of new scholarly disciplines. One of these disciplines was criminology, which developed as an attempt to apply rationality and the rule of law to brutal and arbitrary criminal justice processes. The work of criminology's founders—scholars like Cesare Beccaria and Jeremy Bentham—became known as "classical criminology."

The Historical Context

Classical criminology grew out of a reaction against the barbaric system of law, punishment, and justice that existed before the French Revolution of 1789. Until that time, there was no real

■ Public punishment: Painting depicts beheading of the French king's wife, Marie Antoinette, at the guillotine, October 16, 1793.

system of criminal justice in Europe. There were crimes against the state, against the church, and against the crown. Some of these crimes were specified; some were not. Judges had discretionary power to convict a person for an act not even legally defined as criminal.[2] Monarchs often issued what were called in French *lettres de cachet*, under which an individual could be imprisoned for almost any reason (disobedience to one's father, for example) or for no reason at all.

Many criminal laws were unwritten, and those that had been drafted, by and large, did not specify the kind or amount of punishment associated with various crimes. Arbitrary and often cruel sentences were imposed by judges who had unbounded discretion to decide questions of guilt and innocence and to mete out punishment. Due process in the modern sense did not exist. While there was some official consensus on what constituted crime, there was no real limit to the amount and type of legal sanction a court could command. Punishments included branding, burning, flogging, mutilating, drowning, banishing, and beheading.[3] In England, a person might receive the death penalty for any of more than 200 offenses, including what we today call "petty theft."

Public punishments were popular events. When Robert-François Damiens was scheduled to be executed on March 2, 1757, for the attempted murder of Louis XV, so many people wanted to attend the spectacle that window seats overlooking the execution site were rented for high prices. Torture to elicit confessions was common. A criminal defendant in France might be subjected to the *peine forte et dure,* which consisted of stretching him on his back and placing over him an iron weight as heavy as he could bear. He was left that way until he died or spoke. A man would suffer these torments and lose his life in order to avoid trial—and therefore conviction—so that his lands and goods would not be confiscated and would be preserved for his family. This proceeding was not abolished until 1772.[4]

Even as Europe grew increasingly modern, industrial, and urban in the eighteenth century, it still clung to its medieval penal practices. With prosperity came an increasing gulf between the haves and the have-nots. Just before the French Revolution, for example, a Parisian worker paid 97 percent of his daily earnings for a 4-pound loaf of bread.[5] Hordes of unemployed people begged by day and found shelter under bridges by night. One of the few ways in which the established upper class could protect itself was through ruthless oppression of those beneath it, but ruthless oppression created more problems. Social unrest grew. And as crime rates rose, so did the brutality of punishment. Both church and state became increasingly tyrannical, using violence to conquer violence.

The growing educated classes began to see the inconsistency in these policies. If terrible tortures

■ *Cesare Beccaria, the young Italian nobleman-dissident who became the father of modern criminology with his monograph* On Crimes and Punishment.

were designed to deter crime, why were people committing even more crimes? Something must be wrong with the underlying reasoning. By the mid-eighteenth century, social reformers were beginning to suggest a more rational approach to crime and punishment. One of them, Cesare Beccaria, laid the foundation for the first school of criminology—the classical school.

Cesare Beccaria

Cesare Bonesana, Marchese di Beccaria (1738–1794), was rather undistinguished as a student. After graduating with a law degree from the University of Pavia, he returned home to Milan and joined a group of articulate and radical intellectuals. Disenchanted with contemporary European society, they organized themselves into the Academy of Fists, one of many young men's clubs that flourished in Italy at the time. Their purpose was to discover what reforms would be needed to modernize Italian society.

In March 1763, Beccaria was assigned to prepare a report on the prison system. Pietro Verri, the head of the Academy of Fists, encouraged him to read the works of English and French philosophers—David Hume (1711–1776), John Locke (1632–1704), Claude Adrien Helvétius (1715–1771), Voltaire (1694–1778), Montesquieu (1689–1755), and Jean-Jacques Rousseau (1712–1778). Another member of the academy, the protector of prisons, revealed to him the inhumanities that were possible under the guise of social control. Beccaria learned well. He read, observed, and made notes on small scraps of paper. These notes, Harry Elmer Barnes has observed, were destined to "assure to its author immortality and would work a revolution in the moral world" upon their

Utilitarianism Gone Astray

Few people can be credited for their contribution to Anglo-American criminal law philosophy as much as Jeremy Bentham (1748–1832), the foremost spokesperson for the utilitarian approach to the management of people in general and criminals and potential criminals in particular. Above all, he is remembered for his proposition that the purpose of all legislation is to achieve "the greatest happiness of the greatest number." Punishments, he argued, should be no greater (or less) than necessary to achieve government's purpose to control crime.(1)

According to Princeton University professor Peter Singer, utilitarianism—the greatest good of the greatest number—implies that a child born with incurable birth defects should be killed, as its life would impose a far greater emotional and financial burden on its family and the community than its death.(2) Thus, Singer argues that "some infanticide is not even as important as, say, killing a happy cat."(3) Among his principal examples for justifiable infanticide are babies born with Down syndrome. Singer's argument fails to take into account the many adults with Down syndrome who take a bus to work every day, earn a salary, and pay taxes on their earnings.(2)

■ *Demonstrators picket Princeton University over its appointment of a controversial bioethics professor, Peter Singer, in Princeton, New Jersey, April 1999.*

Putting aside the difficulty of making a prognosis about a baby's chances of having a productive and content life, how would society determine where to put the limit on legalizing infanticide? Justice Holmes ruled in *Buck v. Bell* that "three generations of imbeciles are enough" in upholding a state statute

• *It is better to prevent crimes than to punish them.* "Would you prevent crimes? Let the laws be clear and simple, let the entire force of the nation be united in their defence, let them be intended rather to favour every individual than any particular classes.... Finally, the most certain method of preventing crime is to perfect the system of education."[7]

Perhaps no other book in the history of criminology has had so great an impact. Beccaria's ideas were so advanced that Voltaire, the great French philosopher of the time, who wrote the commentary for the French version, referred to Beccaria as "brother."[8] The English version appeared in 1767; by that time, 3 years after the book's publication, it had already gone through six Italian editions and several French editions.

After the French Revolution, Beccaria's basic tenets served as a guide for the drafting of the French penal code, which was adopted in 1791. In Russia, Empress Catherine II (the Great) convened a commission to prepare a new code and issued instructions, written in her own hand, to translate Beccaria's ideas into action. The Prussian King Friedrich II (the Great) devoted his reign to revising the Prussian laws according to Beccaria's principles. Emperor Joseph II had a new code drafted for Austria-Hungary in 1787—the first code to abolish capital punishment. The impact of Beccaria's treatise spread across the Atlantic as well: It influenced the first 10 amendments to the U.S. Constitution (the Bill of Rights).

Jeremy Bentham's Utilitarianism

Legal scholars and reformers throughout Europe proclaimed their indebtedness to Beccaria, but none owed more to him than the English legal

Crime Surfing

www.utm.edu/ research/iep/b/ beccaria.htm

If Beccaria were alive today, what arguments would he use in a debate on capital punishment?

that mandated the sterilization of "imbeciles" with a family record of imbecility.(4) By those utilitarian standards, killing *all* imbecile babies would be even more cost-beneficial. Should a similar mandate apply to three generations of criminals, as determined by convictions? And would society not be better off (in terms of cost-benefit calculations) if it were to get rid of *all* troublemakers? Would Professor Singer go that far?

Bentham had nothing of that sort in mind when he set forth his utilitarian principles. In fact, he was not even an advocate of capital punishment, considering it to be "unfrugal" and "irremissible."(1)

To demonstrate his utilitarianism, Jeremy Bentham decreed that upon his death (June 6, 1832) his body be dissected in the presence of his friends and the skeleton be reconstructed, supplied with a wax head to replace the original (to be mummified), dressed in his own clothes, and placed upright in a glass case so that he, himself, could be useful as a reminder of his principles. Until recently, once a year at meetings of the Bentham Society in London, Bentham's body was wheeled out and celebrated with a feast.

François de la Rochefoucauld once wrote, "Intellectual blemishes, like facial ones, grow more prominent with age." To refute this wonderful maxim with, albeit, a single case example,

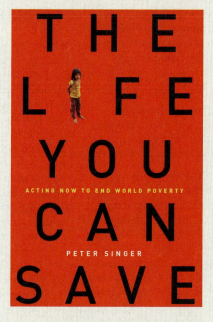

THE LIFE YOU CAN SAVE

ACTING NOW TO END WORLD POVERTY

PETER SINGER

Singer's most recent intellectual efforts stand in very sharp contrast to his earlier work on infanticide. He is now, apparently, both altruistic and strategically philanthropic. Evidence of this profound change may be found in one of Singer's most recent books, *The Life You Can Save: Acting Now to End World Poverty*.(5) This work suggests that we need to reconsider what it means to say that we are living an ethical life. Singer argues in favor of a life defined by personal philanthropy, local activism, and political awareness.

Sources

1. Jeremy Bentham, *An Introduction to the Principles of Morals and Legislation* (1789; New York: Haffner Library of Classics, 1948), esp. pp. 197, 200.
2. Peter Singer, *Rethinking Life and Death: The Collapse of Our Traditional Ethics* (New York: St. Martin's Press, 1996); *How Are We to Live? Ethics in an Age of Self-Interest* (New York: Prometheus Books, 1995).
3. George F. Will, "Life and Death at Princeton," *Newsweek*, Sept. 13, 1999, pp. 80–81.
4. *Buck v. Bell*, 274 U.S. 200, 207 (1927).
5. Peter Singer, *The Life You Can Save: Acting Now to End World Poverty* (New York: Random House, 2009)

Questions for Discussion

1. According to utilitarian principles, is capital punishment preferable to a life sentence?
2. Should abortion be legalized when a baby can be profiled (by family history) as at high risk for a life of crime?
3. Can you think of a way to use utilitarian principles to reduce the use and duration of imprisonment?

philosopher Jeremy Bentham (1748–1832). Bentham had a long and productive career. He inspired many of his contemporaries, as well as criminologists of future generations, with his approach to rational crime control.

Bentham devoted his life to developing a scientific approach to the making and breaking of laws. Like Beccaria, he was concerned with achieving "the greatest happiness of the greatest number."[9] His work was governed by utilitarian principles. **Utilitarianism** assumes that all human actions are calculated in accordance with their likelihood of bringing happiness (pleasure) or unhappiness (pain). People weigh the probabilities of present and future pleasures against those of present and future pain.

Bentham proposed a precise pseudomathematical formula for this process, which he called "felicific calculus." According to his reasoning, individuals are "human calculators" who put all the factors into an equation in order to decide whether a particular crime is worth committing. This notion may seem rather whimsical today, but at a time when there were over 200 capital offenses, it provided a rationale for reform of the legal system.[10] Bentham reasoned that if prevention was the purpose of punishment, and if punishment became too costly by creating more harm than good, then penalties needed to be set just a bit in excess of the pleasure one might derive from committing a crime, and no higher. The law exists in order to create happiness for the community. Because punishment creates unhappiness, it can be justified only if it prevents greater evil than it produces. Thus, Bentham suggested, if hanging a man's effigy produced the same preventive effect as hanging the man himself, there would be no reason to hang the man.

Sir Samuel Romilly, a member of Parliament, met Jeremy Bentham at the home of a mutual friend. He became interested in Bentham's idea that the certainty of punishment outweighs its severity as a deterrent against crime. On February 9, 1810, in a speech before Parliament, he advocated Benthamite ideas:

> So evident is the truth of that maxim that if it were possible that punishment, as the consequence of guilt, could be reduced to an absolute certainty, a very slight penalty would be sufficient to prevent almost every species of crime.[11]

Although conservatives prevented any major changes during Romilly's lifetime, the program of legislative pressure he began was continued by his followers and culminated in the complete reform of English criminal law between 1820 and 1861. During that period, the number of capital offenses was reduced from 222 to 3: murder, treason, and piracy. Gradually, from the ideals of the philosophers of the Age of Enlightenment and the principles outlined by the scholars of the classical school, a new social order was created, an order that affirmed a commitment to equal treatment of all people before the law.

The Classical School: An Evaluation

Classical criminology had an immediate and profound impact on jurisprudence and legislation. The rule of law spread rapidly through Europe and the United States. Of no less significance was the influence of the classical school on penal and correctional policy. The classical principle that punishment must be appropriate to the crime was universally accepted during the nineteenth and early twentieth centuries. Yet the classical approach had weaknesses. Critics attacked the simplicity of its argument: The responsibility of the criminal justice system was simply to enforce the law with swiftness and certainty and to treat all people in like fashion, whether the accused were paupers or nobles; government was to be run by the rule of law rather than at the discretion of its officials. In other words, the punishment was to fit the crime, not the criminal. The proposition that human beings had the capacity to choose freely between good and evil was accepted without question. There was no need to ask why people behave as they do, to seek a motive, or to ask about the specific circumstances surrounding criminal acts.

During the last half of the nineteenth century, scholars began to challenge these ideas. Influenced by the expanding search for scientific explanations of behavior in place of philosophical ones, criminologists shifted their attention from the act to the actor. They argued that people did not choose of their own free will to commit crime; rather, factors beyond their control were responsible for criminal behavior.

POSITIVIST CRIMINOLOGY

During the late eighteenth century, significant advances in knowledge of both the physical and the social world influenced thinking about crime. Auguste Comte (1798–1857), a French sociologist, applied the modern methods of the physical sciences to the social sciences in his six-volume *Cours de philosophie positive* (*Course in Positive Philosophy*), published between 1830 and 1842. He argued that there could be no real knowledge of social phenomena unless it was based on a positivist (scientific) approach. Positivism alone, however, was not sufficient to bring about a fundamental change in criminological thinking. Not until Charles Darwin (1809–1882) challenged the doctrine of creation with his theory of the evolution of species did the next generation of criminologists have the tools with which to challenge classicism.

The turning point was the publication in 1859 of Darwin's *Origin of Species*. Darwin's theory was that God did not make all the various species of animals in 2 days, as proclaimed in Genesis 1:20–26, but rather that the species had evolved through a process of adaptive mutation and natural selection. The process was based on the survival of the fittest in the struggle for existence. This radical theory seriously challenged traditional theological teaching. It was not until 1871, however, that Darwin publicly took the logical next step and traced human origins to an animal of the anthropoid group—the ape.[12] He thus posed an even more serious challenge to a religious tradition that maintained that God created the first human in his own image (Genesis 1:27).

The scientific world would never be the same again. The theory of evolution made it possible to ask new questions and to search in new ways for the answers to old ones. New biological theories replaced older ones. Old ideas that demons and animal spirits could explain human behavior were replaced by knowledge based on new scientific principles. The social sciences were born.

The nineteenth-century forces of positivism and evolution moved the field of criminology from a philosophical to a scientific perspective. But there were even earlier intellectual underpinnings of the scientific criminology that emerged in the second half of the nineteenth century.

BIOLOGICAL DETERMINISM: THE SEARCH FOR CRIMINAL TRAITS

Throughout history, a variety of physical characteristics and disfigurements have been said to characterize individuals of "evil" disposition. In the earliest pursuit of the relationship between

biological traits and behavior, a Greek scientist who examined Socrates found his skull and facial features to be those of a person inclined toward alcoholism and brutality.[13] The ancient Greeks and Romans so distrusted red hair that actors portraying evil persons wore red wigs. Through the ages, cripples, hunchbacks, people with long hair, and a multitude of others were viewed with suspicion. Indeed, in the Middle Ages, laws indicated that if two people were suspected of a crime, the uglier was the more likely to be guilty.[14]

The belief that criminals are born, not made, and that they can be identified by various physical irregularities is reflected not only in scientific writing but in literature as well. Shakespeare's Julius Caesar states:

Let me have men about me that are fat; Sleek-headed men, and such as sleep o' nights. Yond Cassius has a lean and hungry look; He thinks too much: such men are dangerous.

Although its roots can be traced to ancient times, it was not until the sixteenth century that Italian physician Giambattista della Porta (1535–1615) founded the school of human **physiognomy,** the study of facial features and their relation to human behavior. According to Porta, a thief had large lips and sharp vision. Two centuries later, Porta's efforts were revived by Swiss theologian Johann Kaspar Lavater (1741–1801).[15] They were elaborated on by the German physicians Franz Joseph Gall (1758–1828) and Johann Kaspar Spurzheim (1776–1832), whose science of **phrenology** posited that bumps on the head were indications of psychological propensities.[16] In the United States, these views were supported by physician Charles Caldwell (1772–1853), who searched for evidence that brain tissue and cells

regulate human action.[17] By the nineteenth century, the sciences of physiognomy and phrenology had introduced specific biological factors into the study of crime causation.

Lombroso, Ferri, Garofalo: The Italian School

Cesare Lombroso (1835–1909) integrated Comte's positivism, Darwin's evolutionism, and the many pioneering studies of the relation of crime to the body. In 1876, with the publication of *L'uomo delinquente* (*The Criminal Man*), criminology was permanently transformed from an abstract philosophy of crime control through legislation to a modern science of investigation into causes. Lombroso's work replaced the concept of free will, which had reigned for over a century as the principle that explained criminal behavior, with that of determinism. Together with his followers, the Italian legal scholars Enrico Ferri and Raffaele Garofalo, Lombroso developed a new orientation: the Italian, or positivist, school of criminology, which seeks explanations for criminal behavior through scientific experimentation and research.

Cesare Lombroso

After completing his medical studies, Cesare Lombroso served as an army physician, became a professor of psychiatry at the University of Turin, and later in life accepted an appointment as professor of criminal anthropology. His theory of the "born criminal" states that criminals are a lower form of life, nearer to their apelike ancestors than noncriminals in traits and dispositions. They are distinguishable from noncriminals by various

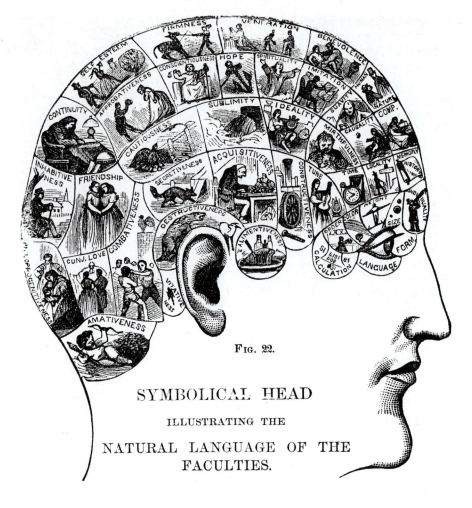

■ This depiction of the human brain appeared in an 1890s scientific book, How to Read Character: A New Illustrated Hand-Book of Physiology, Phrenology and Physiognomy for Students and Examiners.

FIG. 22.

SYMBOLICAL HEAD

ILLUSTRATING THE

NATURAL LANGUAGE OF THE FACULTIES.

atavistic stigmata—physical features of creatures at an earlier stage of development, before they became fully human.

He argued that criminals frequently have huge jaws and strong canine teeth, characteristics common to carnivores who tear and devour meat raw. The arm span of criminals is often greater than their height, just like that of apes, who use their forearms to propel themselves along the ground. An individual born with any five of the stigmata is a **born criminal.** This category accounts for about a third of all offenders.

The theory became clear to Lombroso "one cold grey November morning" while he pored over the bones of a notorious outlaw who had died in an Italian prison:

> This man possessed such extraordinary agility, that he had been known to scale steep mountain heights bearing a sheep on his shoulders. His cynical effrontery was such that he openly boasted of his crimes. On his death . . . I was deputed to make the postmortem, and on laying open the skull I found . . . a distinct depression . . . as in inferior animals.

Lombroso was delighted by his findings:

> This was not merely an idea, but a revelation. At the sight of that skull, I seemed to see all of a sudden, lighted up as a vast plain under a flaming sky the problem of the nature of the criminal—an atavistic being who reproduces in his person the ferocious instincts of primitive humanity.[18]

Criminal women, according to Lombroso, are different from criminal men. It is the prostitute who represents the born criminal among them:

> We also saw that women have many traits in common with children; that their moral sense is different; they are revengeful, jealous, inclined to vengeance of a refined cruelty. . . . When a morbid activity of the psychical centres intensifies the bad qualities of women . . . it is clear that the innocuous semi-criminal present in normal women must be transformed into a born criminal more terrible than any man. . . . The criminal woman is consequently a monster. Her normal sister is kept in the paths of virtue by many causes, such as maternity, piety, weakness, and when these

counter influences fail, and a woman commits a crime, we may conclude that her wickedness must have been enormous before it could triumph over so many obstacles.[19]

To the born criminal, Lombroso added two other categories: insane criminals and criminoloids. "Insane criminals" are not criminal from birth; they become criminal as a result of some change in their brains that interferes with their ability to distinguish between right and wrong.[20] "Criminoloids" make up an ambiguous group that includes habitual criminals, criminals by passion, and other diverse types.

Most scientists who followed Lombroso did not share his enthusiasm or his viewpoint. As happens so often in history, his work has been kept alive more by criticism than by agreement. The theory that criminals were lodged on the lower rungs of the evolutionary ladder did not stand up to scientific scrutiny. But the fact that Lombroso measured thousands of live and dead prisoners and compared these measurements with those obtained from control groups (however imperfectly derived) in his search for determinants of crime changed the nature of the questions asked by the generations of scholars who came after him.

His influence continues in contemporary European research; American scientists, as criminologist Marvin Wolfgang says, use him "as a straw man for attack on biological analyses of criminal behavior."[21] Thorsten Sellin has noted: "Any scholar who succeeds in driving hundreds of fellow-students to search for the truth, and whose ideas after half a century possess vitality, merits an honorable place in the history of thought."[22] At his death, true to his lifetime pursuits, Lombroso willed his body to the laboratory of legal medicine and his brain to the Institute of Anatomy at the University of Turin, where for so many years the father of empirical criminology had espoused biological determinism.[23]

Enrico Ferri

The best known of Lombroso's associates was Enrico Ferri (1856–1929). Member of Parliament, accomplished public lecturer, brilliant lawyer, editor of a newspaper, and esteemed scholar, Ferri had published his first major book by the time he was 21. By age 25, he was a university professor. Although Ferri agreed with Lombroso on the biological bases of criminal behavior, his interest in socialism led him to recognize the importance of social, economic, and political determinants.

Ferri was a prolific writer on a vast number of criminological topics. His greatest contribution was his attack on the classical doctrine of free will, which argued that criminals should be held morally responsible for their crimes because they must have made a rational decision to commit

■ *Dr. Cesare Lombroso (1835–1909), professor of criminal anthropology at Turin University and founder of the positivist school of criminology.*

these acts. Ferri believed criminals could not be held morally responsible because they did not choose to commit crimes but, rather, were driven to commit them by conditions in their lives. He did, however, stress that society needed protection against criminal acts and that it was the purpose of the criminal law and penal policy to provide that protection.

Although he advocated conventional punishments and even the death penalty for individuals he assumed would never be fit to live in society, he was more interested in controlling crime through preventive measures—state control of the manufacture of weapons, inexpensive housing, better street lighting, and so forth.

Ferri claimed that strict adherence to preventive measures based on scientific methods would eventually reduce crime and allow people to live together in society with less dependence on the penal system. Toward the end of his life, he proudly admitted that he was an idealist, a statement with which generations of scholars have agreed. Though his prescription for crime reduction was overly optimistic, Ferri's importance to the development of modern criminology is undisputed. "When Enrico Ferri died on April 12, 1929," wrote Thorsten Sellin, "one of the most colorful, influential figures in the history of criminology disappeared."[24]

Raffaele Garofalo

Another follower of Lombroso was the Italian nobleman, magistrate, senator, and professor of law Raffaele Garofalo (1851–1934). Like Lombroso and Ferri, Garofalo rejected the doctrine of free will and supported the position that the only way to understand crime was to study it by scientific methods. Influenced by Lombroso's theory of atavistic stigmata, in which he found many shortcomings, Garofalo traced the roots of criminal behavior not to physical features but to their psychological equivalents, which he called "moral anomalies." According to this theory, natural crimes are found in all human societies, regardless of the views of lawmakers, and no civilized society can afford to disregard them.[25]

Natural crimes, according to Garofalo, are those that offend the basic moral sentiments of probity (respect for the property of others) and piety (revulsion against the infliction of suffering on others). An individual who has an organic deficiency in these moral sentiments has no moral constraints against committing such crimes. Garofalo argued that these individuals could not be held responsible for their actions. But, like Ferri, he also emphasized that society needed protection and that penal policy should be designed to prevent criminals from inflicting harm.[26]

Influenced by Darwinian theory, Garofalo suggested that the death penalty could rid society of its maladapted members, just as the natural selection process eliminated maladapted organisms. For less-serious offenders, capable of adapting themselves to society in some measure, other types of punishments were preferable: transportation to remote lands, loss of privileges, institutionalization in farm colonies, or perhaps simply reparation. Clearly, Garofalo was much more interested in protecting society than in defending the individual rights of offenders.

Challenges to Lombrosian Theory

Although Lombroso, Ferri, and Garofalo did not always agree on the causes of criminal behavior or on the way society should respond to it, their combined efforts marked a turning point in the development of the scientific study of crime. These three were responsible for developing the positivist approach to criminality, which influences criminology to the present day. Nevertheless, they had their critics. By using the scientific method to explore crime causation, they paved the way for criminologists to support or refute the theories they had devised. The major challenge to Lombrosian theory came from the work of Charles Buckman Goring.

From 1901 until 1913, Charles Buckman Goring (1870–1919), a medical officer at Parkhurst Prison in England, collected data on 96 traits of more than 3,000 convicts and a large control group of Oxford and Cambridge university students, hospital patients, and soldiers. Among his research assistants was a famous statistician, Karl Pearson. When Goring had completed his examinations, he was armed with enough data to refute Lombroso's theory of the anthropological criminal type. Goring's report to the scientific community proclaimed:

> From a knowledge only of an undergraduate's cephalic [head] measurement, a better judgment could be given as to whether he

were studying at an English or Scottish university than a prediction could be made as to whether he would eventually become a university professor or a convicted felon.[27]

This evaluation still stands as the most cogent critical analysis of Lombroso's theory of the born criminal. Although Goring rejected the claim that specific stigmata identify the criminal, he was convinced that poor physical condition plus a defective state of mind were determining factors in the criminal personality.

A Return to Biological Determinism

After Goring's challenge, Lombrosian theory lost its academic popularity for about a quarter century. Then, in 1939, Ernest Hooten (1887–1954), a physical anthropologist, reawakened an interest in biologically determined criminality with the publication of a massive study comparing American prisoners with a noncriminal control group. He concluded:

> [I]n every population there are hereditary inferiors in mind and in body as well as physical and mental deficients. . . . Our information definitely proves that it is from the physically inferior element of the population that native born criminals from native parentage are mainly derived.[28]

Like his positivist predecessors, Hooten argued for the segregation of those he referred to as the "criminal stock," and he recommended their sterilization as well.[29]

The Somatotype School

In the search for the source of criminality, other scientists, too, looked for the elusive link between physical characteristics and crime. The **somatotype school** of criminology, which related body build to behavior, became popular during the first half of the twentieth century. It originated with the work of a German psychiatrist, Ernst Kretschmer (1888–1964), who distinguished three principal types of physiques: (1) the asthenic—lean, slightly built, narrow shoulders; (2) the athletic—medium to tall, strong, muscular, coarse bones; and (3) the pyknic—medium height, rounded figure, massive neck, broad face. He then related these physical types to various psychiatric disorders: pyknics to manic depression, asthenics and athletics to schizophrenia, and so on.[30]

Kretschmer's work was brought to the United States by William Sheldon (1898–1977), who formulated his own group of somatotypes: the "endomorph," the "mesomorph," and the "ectomorph." Sheldon's father was a dog breeder who used a point system to judge animals in competition, and Sheldon worked out a point system of his own for judging humans. Thus, one could actually measure on a scale from 1 to 7 the relative dominance of each body type in any given individual. People with predominantly mesomorph traits (physically powerful, aggressive, athletic physiques), he argued, tend more than others to be involved in illegal behavior.[31] This finding was later supported by Sheldon Glueck (1896–1980) and Eleanor Glueck (1898–1972), who based their studies of delinquents on William Sheldon's somatotypes.[32]

By and large, studies based on somatotyping have been sharply criticized for methodological flaws, including nonrepresentative selection of their samples (bias), failure to account for cultural stereotyping (our expectations of how muscular, physically active people should react), and poor statistical analyses. An anthropologist summed up the negative response of the scientific community by suggesting that somatotyping was "a New Phrenology in which the bumps on the buttocks take the place of the bumps on the skulls."[33] After World War II, somatotyping seemed too close to **eugenics** (the science of controlled reproduction to improve hereditary qualities), and the approach fell into disfavor. During the 1960s, however, the discovery of an extra sex chromosome in some criminal samples (see Chapter 4) revived interest in this theory.

Inherited Criminality

During the period when some researchers were measuring skulls and bodies of criminals in their search for the physical determinants of crime, others were arguing that criminality was an inherited trait passed on in the genes. To support this theory, they traced family histories. Richard Dugdale (1841–1883), for example, studied the lives of more than a thousand members of the family he called "Jukes." His interest in the family began when he found six related people in a jail in upstate New York. Following one branch of the family, the descendants of Ada Jukes, whom he referred to as the "mother of criminals," Dugdale found among the thousand of descendants 280 paupers, 60 thieves, 7 murderers, 40 other criminals, 40 persons with venereal disease, and 50 prostitutes.

His findings indicated, Dugdale claimed, that since some families produce generations of criminals, they must be transmitting a degenerate trait down the line.[34] A similar conclusion was reached by Henry Goddard (1866–1957). In a study of the family tree of a Revolutionary War soldier, Martin Kallikak, Goddard found many more criminals among the descendants of Kallikak's illegitimate son than among the descendants of his son by a later marriage with "a woman of his own quality."[35]

These early studies have been discredited primarily on the grounds that genetic and environmental influences could not be separated. But in the early twentieth century, they were taken quite seriously. On the assumption that crime could be controlled if criminals could be prevented from transmitting their traits to the next generation, some states permitted the sterilization of habitual offenders. Sterilization laws were held constitutional by the U.S. Supreme Court in a 1927 opinion written by Justice Oliver Wendell Holmes Jr., which included the following well-known pronouncement:

> It is better for all the world, if instead of waiting to execute degenerate offspring for crime, or to let them starve for their imbecility, society can prevent those who are manifestly unfit from continuing their kind. . . . Three generations of imbeciles are enough.[36]

Clearly, the early positivists, with their focus on physical characteristics, exerted great influence. They were destined to be overshadowed, though, by investigators who focused on psychological characteristics.

■ Dugdale and others identified the Jukes clan as determined by heredity to be criminals, imbeciles, and paupers. Research since then has shown that the methodology was flawed and many conclusions were fabricated.

Somatotyping: A Physique for Crime?

One afternoon in the late 1970s, deep in the labyrinthine interior of a massive Gothic tower in New Haven, an unsuspecting employee of Yale University opened a long-locked room in the Payne Whitney Gymnasium and stumbled upon something shocking and disturbing.

Shocking, because what he found was an enormous cache of nude photographs, thousands and thousands of photographs of young men in front, rear, and side poses. Disturbing, because on closer inspection the photos looked like the record of a bizarre body-piercing ritual: sticking out from the spine of each and every body was a row of sharp metal pins.

Half a generation after the "bizarre body-piercing rituals," it was a *New York Times Magazine* journalist who was shocked and disturbed, particularly so because he also had been exposed to the ritual while at Yale, and the same ritual might have been imposed upon him had he been a student at Mount Holyoke, Vassar, Smith, Princeton, or Wellesley.[1]

The implications were mind-boggling: A routine freshman procedure, supposedly aimed at assessing and improving posture, had yielded a cache of nude photographs including such luminaries as George Pataki and George Bush. While most of the schools shredded the photographs 10 or more years ago, thousands are still being kept under lock and seal at the Smithsonian in Washington. And what does all that have to do with criminology?

In 1949 the physician William H. Sheldon reported that 200 boys living in Boston's Hayden Goodwill Inn had body builds significantly different from a control group of 4,000 college students. That control group came out of the Ivy League's posture photos in the buff. The metal pins had not been inserted into the skin, but had been attached by tape.

Sheldon's Body Types

Sheldon classified physiques into three categories: endomorphs, mesomorphs, and ectomorphs. An endomorph has a predominance of soft roundness throughout the body; a mesomorph tends to be muscular, strong, heavy-boned, and firm; an ectomorph is Sheldon used his classifications to show that body types were related to behavior, temperament, and even life expectancy.

Sheldon's 200 young males included alcoholics, mental defectives, and psychopaths, nondelinquents, and criminals. He found that the fragile, thin, and delicate criminal types were more mesomorphic.

A follow-up study of these 200 youths 30 years later identified 14 "primary criminals," individuals who had felony convictions as adults. These persistent criminals were relatively mesomorphic, compared with the others.

Somatotyping: Pro and Con

In *Crime and Human Nature* (1985), James Q. Wilson and Richard J. Herrnstein evaluated a number of studies relating physique to delinquency, including Sheldon's. They stated: "[T]he main conclusions have been confirmed wherever they have been tested, despite the initial skepticism of criminologists."[2]

Somatotyping is not without its critics. In an extensive review of Wilson and Herrnstein's conclusions, Leon J. Kamin ridicules their presentation

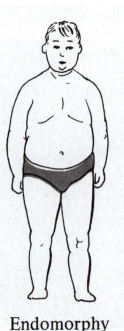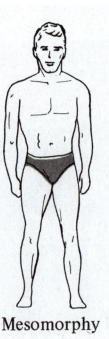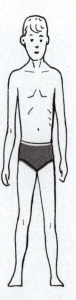

■ *Sheldon's body types: (a) endomorphic; (b) mesomorphic; (c) ectomorphic.*

Endomorphy   Mesomorphy   Ectomorphy

of the topic, claiming that they completely ignore a number of studies that have appeared since 1949.[3]

Wilson and Herrnstein themselves present information that raises questions about the value of somatotyping to criminology. They cite studies in which, while the tendency toward the mesomorphic was clear, "mesomorphs could be found among the nondelinquents and ectomorphs among the delinquents." And they emphasize the difference between correlation and causation, stating clearly, "Physique does not cause crime."

Sources

1. Ron Rosenbaum, "The Great Ivy League Nude Posture Photo Scandal," *New York Times Magazine,* January. 15, 1995, pp. 26–31, 40, 46, 55–56; quote from p. 26.
2. James Q. Wilson and Richard J. Herrnstein, *Crime and Human Nature* (New York: Simon & Schuster, 1985), p. 87.
3. Leon J. Kamin, "Crime and Human Nature," *Scientific American,* 254:22, February 1986.

PSYCHOLOGICAL DETERMINISM

On the whole, scholars who investigated criminal behavior in the nineteenth and early twentieth centuries were far more interested in the human body than in the human mind. During that period, however, several contributions were made in the area of psychological explanations of crime. Some of the earliest contributions came from physicians interested primarily in the legal responsibility of the criminally insane. Later, psychologists entered the field and applied their new testing techniques to the study of offenders (see Chapter 4).

Pioneers in Criminal Psychology

Isaac Ray (1807–1881), acknowledged as America's first forensic psychiatrist, was interested throughout his life in the application of psychiatric principles to the law. He is best known as the author of *The Medical Jurisprudence of Insanity,* a treatise on criminal responsibility that was widely quoted and influential.[37] In it he defended the concept of moral insanity, a disorder first described in 1806 by the French humanitarian and psychiatrist Philippe Pinel (1745–1826).[38] "Moral insanity" was a term used to describe persons who were normal in all respects except that something was wrong with the part of the brain that regulates affective responses. Ray questioned whether we could hold people legally responsible for their acts if they had such an impairment, because such people committed their crimes without an intent to do so.

Born in the same year as Lombroso, Henry Maudsley (1835–1918), a brilliant English medical professor, shared Ray's concerns about criminal responsibility. According to Maudsley, some people may be considered either "insane or criminal according to the standpoint from which they are looked at." He believed that for many persons, crime is an "outlet in which their unsound tendencies are discharged; they would go mad if they were not criminals."[39] Most of Maudsley's attention focused on the line between insanity and crime.

Psychological Studies of Criminals

Around the turn of the twentieth century, psychologists used their new measurement techniques to study offenders. The administering of intelligence tests to inmates of jails, prisons, and other public institutions was especially popular at that time, because it was a period of major controversy over the relation of mental deficiency to criminal behavior. The new technique seemed to provide an objective basis for differentiating criminals from noncriminals.

In 1914, Henry H. Goddard, research director of the Vineland, New Jersey, Training School for the Retarded, examined some intelligence tests that had been given to inmates and concluded that 25 to 50 percent of the people in prison had intellectual defects that made them incapable of managing their own affairs.[40] This idea remained dominant until it was challenged by the results of intelligence tests administered to World War I draftees, whose scores were found to be lower than those of prisoners in the federal penitentiary at Leavenworth. As a result of this study and others like it, intelligence quotient (IQ) measures largely disappeared as a basis for explaining criminal behavior.

SOCIOLOGICAL DETERMINISM

During the nineteenth and early twentieth centuries, some scholars began to search for the social determinants of criminal behavior. The approach had its roots in Europe in the 1830s, the time between Beccaria's *On Crimes and Punishment* and Lombroso's *The Criminal Man.*

Adolphe Quételet and André-Michel Guerry

Belgian mathematician Adolphe Quételet (1796–1874) and French lawyer André-Michel Guerry (1802–1866) were among the first scholars to repudiate the classicists' free-will doctrine. Working independently on the relation of crime statistics to factors such as poverty, age, sex, race, and climate, both scholars concluded that society, not the decisions of individual offenders, was responsible for criminal behavior.

The first modern criminal statistics were published in France in 1827. Guerry used those statistics to demonstrate that crime rates varied with social factors. He found, for example, that the wealthiest region of France had the highest rate of property crime but only half the national rate of violent crime. He concluded that the main factor in property crime was opportunity: There was much more to steal in the richer provinces.

Quételet did an elaborate analysis of crime in France, Belgium, and Holland. After analyzing criminal statistics, which he called "moral statistics," he concluded that if we look at overall patterns of behavior of groups across a whole society, we find a startling regularity of rates of various behaviors. According to Quételet:

> We can enumerate in advance how many individuals will soil their hands in the blood of their fellows, how many will be frauds, how many prisoners; almost as one can enumerate in advance the births and deaths that will take place.[41]

By focusing on groups rather than individuals, Quételet discovered that behavior is indeed predictable, regular, and understandable. Just as the physical world is governed by the laws of nature, human behavior is governed by forces external to the individual. The more we learn about those forces, the easier it becomes to predict behavior. A major goal of criminological research, according to Quételet, should be to identify factors related to crime and assign to them their "proper degree of influence."[42] Though neither he nor Guerry offered a theory of criminal behavior, the fact that both studied social factors scientifically, using quantitative research methods, made them key figures in the subsequent development of sociological theories of crime causation.

Gabriel Tarde

One of the earliest sociological theories of criminal behavior was formulated by Gabriel Tarde (1843–1904), who served 15 years as a provincial judge and then was placed in charge of France's national statistics. After an extensive analysis of these statistics, he came to the following conclusion:

> The majority of murderers and notorious thieves began as children who had been abandoned, and the true seminary of crime must be sought for upon each public square or each crossroad of our towns, whether they be small or large, in those flocks of pillaging street urchins who, like bands of sparrows, associate together, at first for marauding, and then for theft, because of a lack of education and food in their homes.[43]

Tarde rejected the Lombrosian theory of biological abnormality, which was popular in his time, arguing that criminals were normal people who learned crime just as others learned legitimate trades. He formulated his theory in terms of **laws of imitation**—principles that governed the process by which people became criminals. According to Tarde's thesis, individuals emulate behavior patterns in much the same way they copy styles of dress. Moreover, there is a pattern to the way such emulation takes place: (1) Individuals imitate others in proportion to the intensity and frequency of their contacts; (2) inferiors imitate superiors—that is, trends flow from town to country and from upper to lower classes; and (3) when two behavior patterns clash, one may take the place of the other, as when guns largely replaced knives as murder weapons.[44] Tarde's work served as the basis for Edwin Sutherland's theory of differential association, which we will examine in Chapter 5.

Émile Durkheim

Modern criminologists take two major approaches to the study of the social factors associated with crime. Tarde's approach asks how individuals become criminal. What is the process? How are behavior patterns learned and transmitted? The second major approach looks at the social structure and its institutions. It asks how crime arises in the first place and how it is related to the functioning of a society. For answers to these questions, scholars begin with the work of Émile Durkheim (1858–1917).

Of all nineteenth-century writers on the relationship between crime and social factors, none has more powerfully influenced contemporary criminology than Durkheim, who is universally acknowledged as one of the founders of sociology. On October 12, 1870, when Durkheim was 12 years old, the German army invaded and occupied his hometown, Epinal, in eastern France. Thus, at a very early age, he witnessed social chaos and the effects of rapid change, topics with which he remained preoccupied throughout his life. At the age of 24, he became a professor of philosophy, and at 29 he joined the faculty of the University of Bordeaux. There he taught the first course in sociology ever to be offered by a French university.

By 1902, he had moved to the University of Paris, where he completed his doctoral studies. His *Division of Labor* became a landmark work on the organization of societies. According to Durkheim, crime is as normal a part of society as birth and death. Theoretically, crime could disappear altogether only if all members of society had the same values, and such standardization is neither possible nor desirable. Furthermore, some crime is in fact necessary if a society is to progress:

> The opportunity for the genius to carry out his work affords the criminal his originality at a

lower level. . . . According to Athenian law, Socrates was a criminal, and his condemnation was no more than just. However, his crime, namely, the independence of his thought, rendered a service not only to humanity but to his country.[45]

Durkheim further pointed out that all societies have not only crime but also sanctions. The rationale for the sanctions varies in accordance with the structure of the society. In a strongly cohesive society, punishment of members who deviate is used to reinforce the value system—to remind people of what is right and what is wrong—thereby preserving the pool of common belief and the solidarity of the society. Punishment must be harsh to serve these ends. In a large, urbanized, heterogeneous society, on the other hand, punishment is used not to preserve solidarity but rather to right the wrong done to a victim. Punishment thus is evaluated in accordance with the harm done, with the goal of restitution and reinstatement of order as quickly as possible. The offense is not considered a threat to social cohesion, primarily because in a large, complex society, criminal events do not even come to the attention of most people.

The most important of Durkheim's many contributions to contemporary sociology is his concept of **anomie,** a breakdown of social order as a result of a loss of standards and values. In a society plagued by anomie (see Chapter 5), disintegration and chaos replace social cohesion.

Crime Surfing

http://durkheim.itgo .com/religion.html

According to Durkheim, what role does religion play in society?

■ *Émile Durkheim (1858–1917), one of the founders of sociology.*

HISTORICAL AND CONTEMPORARY CRIMINOLOGY: A TIME LINE

Classical criminologists thought the problem of crime might be solved through limitations on governmental power, the abolition of brutality, and the creation of a more equitable system of justice. They argued that the punishment should fit the crime. For over a century, this perspective dominated criminology. Later on, positivist criminologists influenced judges to give greater consideration to the offender than to the gravity of the crime when imposing sentences. The current era marks a return to the classical demand that the punishment correspond to the seriousness of the crime and the guilt of the offender. Table 3.1 presents a chronology of all the pioneers in criminology we have discussed.

As modern science discovered more and more about cause and effect in the physical and social universes, the theory that individuals commit crimes of their own free will began to lose favor. The positivists searched for determinants of crime in biological, psychological, and social factors. Biologically based theories were popular in the late nineteenth century, fell out of favor in the

early part of the twentieth century, and emerged again in the 1970s (see Chapter 4) with studies of hormone imbalances, diet, environmental contaminants, and so forth. Since the studies of criminal responsibility in the nineteenth century centering on the insanity defense and of intelligence levels in the twentieth century, psychiatrists and psychologists have continued to play a major role in the search for the causes of crime, especially after Sigmund Freud developed his well-known theory of human personality (Chapter 4). The sociological perspective became popular in the 1920s and has remained the predominant approach of criminological studies. (We will examine contemporary theories in Chapters 5 through 9.)

THE FUTURE OF OUR HISTORY

All the social sciences appear to follow alternating patterns of tradition-bound periods, such as periods of prevailing classical, deterministic, and neoclassical thought. Emerging ideas and paradigms that mark these periods often reflect the maturity of scientific growth—from preparadigmatic immature science, to normal science, and finally to a series of intellectual milestones that

TABLE 3.1 Pioneers in Criminology: A Chronology

Classical Criminology

FREE WILL

Cesare Beccaria (1738–1794). Devised the first design for a comprehensive, enlightened criminal justice system based on law

Jeremy Bentham (1748–1832). Developed utilitarian principles of punishment

Positivist Criminology

BIOLOGICAL DETERMINISM

Giambattista della Porta (1535–1615). Was the founder of the school of physiognomy, which is the study of facial features and their relation to human behaviors

Johann Kaspar Lavater (1741–1801). Espoused a biological approach to crime causation; developed phrenology

Franz Joseph Gall (1758–1828). Espoused a biological approach to crime causation; further developed phrenology

Charles Caldwell (1772–1853). Was a physician who searched for evidence that brain tissue and cells regulate human behavior

Johann Kaspar Spurzheim (1776–1832). Espoused a biological approach; continued studies of phrenology

Charles Darwin (1809–1882). Formulated theory of evolution, which changed explanations of human behavior

Cesare Lombroso (1835–1909). Saw determinism as explanatory factor in criminal behavior; posited the "born criminal"; father of modern criminology

Richard Dugdale (1841–1883). Related criminal behavior to inherited traits (Jukes family)

Raffaele Garofalo (1851–1934). Traced roots of criminal behavior to "moral anomalies" rather than physical characteristics

Enrico Ferri (1856–1929). Produced first penal code based on positivist principles; replaced moral responsibility with social accountability

Ernest Hooten (1887–1954). Related criminality to hereditary inferiority

Ernst Kretschmer (1888–1964). Introduced the somatotype school of criminology

William Sheldon (1898–1977). Related body types to illegal behavior

PSYCHOLOGICAL DETERMINISM

Isaac Ray (1807–1881). Questioned whether those who were "morally insane" could be held legally responsible for their acts

Henry Maudsley (1835–1918). Pioneered criteria for legal responsibility

Henry H. Goddard (1866–1957). Related criminal behavior to intelligence (Kallikak family)

SOCIOLOGICAL DETERMINISM

Adolphe Quételet (1796–1874). Was one of the first to repudiate classical free-will doctrine; studied social determinants of behavior

Auguste Comte (1798–1857). Brought modern scientific methods from physical to social sciences

André-Michel Guerry (1802–1866). Was one of the first to repudiate free-will doctrine; related crime statistics to social factors

Gabriel Tarde (1843–1904). Explained crime as learned behavior

Émile Durkheim (1858–1917). Was one of the founders of sociology; developed theory of anomie and idea that crime is normal in all societies

Charles Buckman Goring (1870–1919). Used empirical research to refute Lombroso's theory of criminal types

Sheldon Glueck (1896–1980) and Eleanor Glueck (1898–1972). Espoused primarily social causes of delinquency, but also psychological and biological explanations

effectively upset tradition, prompting the establishment of new paradigms. Prior generations of criminological thought discussed earlier in this chapter were, for much of the time, characteristically preparadigmatic. By the 1960s, however, the academic subject matter of criminology was bordering on what some have called "normal science" or "research firmly based upon one or more past scientific achievements, achievements that some particular community acknowledges for a time as supplying the foundation for its further practice."[46] By the late 1960s and early 1970s, a new generation of criminologists upset the accepted paradigms, repeatedly calling into question the value of "normal science."

To the extent that the history of criminology is fluid, it is only fair to ponder its future—the future of our history. First it is notable that some old but emergent themes are returning. For example, as we will see in Chapter 4, advances in the neurosciences are allowing a glimpse inside the neuroanatomy of the brain that reframes the old field of biological determinism and opens the door to new inquiry. A new specialty—neurocriminology—marks the progress of our field. Second, evidence-based research and the priority given to randomized controlled experiments encourage a new emphasis on criminology as a cutting-edge scientific discipline. As noted briefly in Chapter 2, the experimental method allows for definitive answers to some of the most important policy questions of our time. Finally, the somewhat provincial and often bounded view of American criminology is slowly giving way to the realization that research on crime and criminality outside the United States has much unrealized value.

In his 2006 presidential address to the American Society of Criminology (ASC), Gary LaFree argued in favor of expanding the domain of the field. This may be accomplished by exploring ways criminological research can nurture democratic, nonauthoritarian societies. "Although the most recent wave of democratization produced a record number of democratic regimes," LaFree writes, "we are observing ominous challenges to fundamental democratic rights from around the world. As criminologists, we have a vested interest in supporting the democratic, nonauthoritarian societies in which our craft has thrived."[47]

Richard Rosenfeld, in his 2010 presidential address to the ASC, suggests that this expansion will likely be constrained by the schools of thought emerging and also dominating the field: "Throughout its brief history, criminology has swung back and forth between an emphasis on explaining individual criminal behavior and explaining patterns and trends in crime rates. But the pendulum never swings too far, especially in American criminology, from a preoccupation with individual criminality and the microenvironments (families, schools, and neighborhoods) in which its putative causes are located. The current period, with its breakthrough studies of gene–environment interactions and individual development, epitomizes the dominance of microcriminology."[48]

In the history of criminology from ancient times to the early twentieth century, its many themes at times have clashed and at times have supported one another. There is no straight-line evolutionary track that we can follow from the inception of the first "criminological" thought to modern theories. Some scholars concentrated on criminal law and procedure, others on criminal behavior. Some took the biological route, others the psychological, and still others the sociological. And the work of some investigators has encompassed a combination of factors. Toward the end of the nineteenth century, a discipline began to emerge.

Tracing the major developments back in time helps us understand how criminology grew into the discipline we know today. Many of the issues that appear on the intellectual battlefields early in the twenty-first century are the same issues our academic ancestors grappled with for hundreds, indeed thousands, of years. With each new clash, some old concepts died, while others were incorporated within competing doctrinal boundaries, there to remain until the next challenge. The controversies of one era become the foundations of knowledge for the next. As societies develop and are subjected to new technologies, the crime problem becomes ever more complex. So do the questions it raises. In Part 2 we will see how twentieth-century theorists have dealt with those questions.

CRIMINOLOGY & PUBLIC POLICY

The execution methods debate is played out by legislative decision-makers, who oftentimes turn a blind eye to the concerns of those who actually have to kill. In turn, a considerable portion of doctors, nurses, and other medical personnel willingly participate in executions. Prison officials face the worst of both worlds: They have limited political clout by which to make their choices known and minimal guidance provided by those who make the choices

Biological and Psychological Perspectives

4

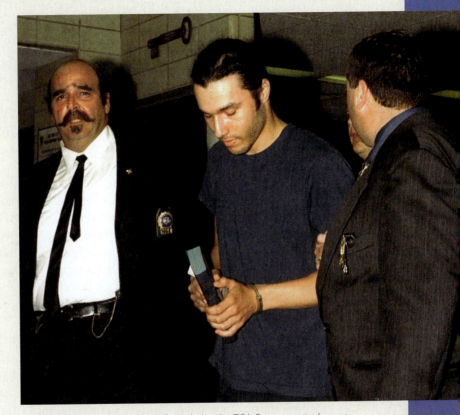

■ *Heriberto Seda, the Zodiac Killer, is led to the 75th Precinct stationhouse in Brooklyn, New York*

Heriberto Seda was a loner from birth. In a neighborhood overrun with crime, his mother tried to shield her only son from the dangers that lurked around every corner. She never let Heriberto have friends over or let him venture too far from home. Each day, Heriberto would return from school to his apartment where, in the solitude of his room, he watched television, looked at basketball trading cards, and developed a fascination with the concept of God.

In 1984, Heriberto was suspended for discharging a starter's pistol in class. A few months shy of graduation, Heriberto dropped out of Francis K. Lane High School and took to spreading the word of God on a full-time basis. He roamed the streets of his neighborhood to do "the will of God." Dressed in black, with his hair neatly restrained in a ponytail, Heriberto would emerge from his home after dark, and berate the drug dealers that conducted business in the hallways and on the streets. He preached by night and returned to the seclusion of his home by day. Here, his previously innocent hobbies had taken a sinister turn—basketball trading cards were replaced by those of serial murderers from the True Crime Series; the magazines now had a militaristic twist: *Soldier of Fortune* and mail-order catalogs for military

79

supplies; models of boats and ships were replaced by filed-down "zip guns" and homemade pipe bombs, with a generous sprinkling of gas masks, machetes, and hundreds of rounds of ammunition.

On March 8, 1990, Heriberto embarked on the first of many shootings in his crusade to eradicate evil—to dispose of the enemies of God. During the course of the next few years, Heriberto Seda shot eight people, killing three. All his victims were vulnerable: a homeless man asleep on a park bench, a crippled factory worker on his way home, a 78-year-old man who turned his back to get his murderer a glass of water.

After several of the shootings, cryptic messages with astrological underpinnings were found nearby, scrawled on pieces of paper. Similar letters were sent to *60 Minutes* and the *New York Post*, declaring him the Zodiac, all sealed with the same trademark signature: an encircled cross with three sevens. This signature would prove to be his downfall.

In 1994, Heriberto Seda was arrested for illegal possession of a firearm, but the charges were dropped a few days later when the weapon was deemed inoperable for safety reasons; in no time, Heriberto was back on the streets of New York. On June 18, 1996, Heriberto shot his 18-year-old sister in the back, after an alleged dispute over her promiscuity. A 3-hour standoff with the police ensued, ending in his capture and imprisonment.

Down at the police station, Heriberto Seda gave a signed statement sealed with his trademark: an encircled cross with three sevens. This evidence, in addition to expert fingerprint analysis linking him to four of the shootings in 1990, sealed the fate of the Zodiac Killer.

Richard Franklin Speck, 49, died of a heart attack on December 5, 1991, at Silver Cross Hospital in Illinois, near the prison that held him for a quarter century. In the summer of 1966, Speck had broken into a Chicago town house, where he gathered eight student nurses in one room and bound them with bed sheets. One by one he took them to another room. There he spent at least a half-hour alone with each

victim, brutally stabbed or strangled her, ritualistically washed his hands, and then went back for the next one. Speck was sentenced to death—a sentence that was eventually (by a Supreme Court ruling) changed to 400 to 1,200 years in the maximum-security Stateville Correctional Center in Joliet.

No one knows why Richard Speck committed these brutal murders. We know that this crime was not his first. Born in Kirkwood, Illinois, in 1941, he was one of eight children of Margaret and Benjamin Speck. Richard, who never went to high school, spent much of his time drinking excessively and reading comic books. By the spring of 1966 he had been arrested 37 times, on charges ranging from trespassing to burglary.

The murders prompted a massive hunt for the killer. Speck was arrested a few days later at the Cook County Hospital, where he went for treatment of a self-inflicted knife wound. Oddly enough, it was a tattoo on his left forearm (described to police by a sole survivor who had hidden under a bed) that led to his arrest. It read: "Born to Raise Hell."

On June 27, 2005, nearly three decades after his first killing, Dennis Rader, or the BTK killer as he is more commonly known, pleaded guilty in front of a Wichita, Kansas, courtroom to killing 10 people between 1974 and 1991. He described calmly and in great detail how he committed each murder.

Rader broke into the Otero home and tied up Julie, Joseph, and two of their children. He told them he just needed a car and food, and even put a pillow under Joseph's head so that he would be more comfortable. Then he realized that the family could identify him. "I didn't have a mask on or anything . . . [so] I made a decision to go ahead and put 'em down, I guess, or strangle them. . . . I had never strangled anyone before, so I really didn't know how much pressure you had to put on a person."[1]

Rader recounted how he selected several victims, or "projects," at a time and stalked them until one came to fruition. He chose them to fulfill sexual fantasies. He came to each crime with a "hit kit" and "hit clothes," which he later destroyed.

Rader often took pictures of his victims in lewd poses after he killed them.

Jeff Davis, whose mother, Dolores, was Rader's final victim in 1991, called the killer a "classic, textbook sociopath" with "no conscience, just a black hole inside the shell of a human being." He compared Rader's rendition of the killing to the reading of a recipe out of a cookbook.[2] Rader was sentenced to 10 consecutive life sentences and is serving these sentences in the Special Management Unit (solitary confinement) of the El Dorado Correctional Facility in El Dorado, Kansas. He remains in his cell for 23 hours a day, with an hour exercise time.

In the United States, explanations of criminal behavior have been dominated by sociological theories. These theories focus on lack of opportunity and the breakdown of the conventional value system in urban ghettos, the formation of subcultures whose norms deviate from those of the middle class, the disconnect between culturally prescribed goals and the means to attain those goals, and the increasing inability of social institutions to exercise control over behavior. Criminological texts treat biological and psychological theories as peripheral, perhaps because criminology's disciplinary allegiance is to sociology. Biological explanations have always raised a wide range of concerns, from intractable ethical questions to practical questions such as how data from genetic, biochemical, or neuroanatomical research might be used in the criminal justice system. When psychological theories were first advanced to explain criminal behavior, their emphasis was largely psychoanalytic, so they may have seemed not quantitative or scientific enough to some criminologists.[3] Others may have considered the early work of Lombroso, Goring, and Hooten too scientifically naive to be taken seriously. Over the past two decades, psychological research on crime and criminality has enjoyed a renaissance.

Sociological theories focus on crime rates of groups that experience frustration in their efforts to achieve accepted goals, not on the particular individual who remains law-abiding or becomes a criminal. Sociological theories cannot explain how one person can be born in a slum, be exposed to family discord and abuse, never attend school, have friends who are delinquents, and yet resist opportunities for crime, while another person can grow up in an affluent suburban neighborhood in a two-parent home, attend the finest schools, have every financial need met, and end up firing a gun at the president. In other words, sociologists do not address individual differences.[4] Instead, biologists and psychologists are interested in finding out what may account for individual differences.

It is clear that biological, psychological, and sociological explanations are not competing to answer the same specific questions. Rather, all three disciplines are searching for answers to different questions, even though they study the same act, status, or characteristic. We can understand crime in a society only if we view criminality from more than one level of analysis: why a certain individual commits a crime (biological and psychological explanations) and why some groups of individuals commit more or different criminal acts than other groups (sociological explanations).

Sociological theory and empirical research often ignore factors such as genetics and personality, almost as if they were irrelevant. And biological and psychological theories often focus on the individual, with little regard for the fact that while each one of us comes into the world with certain genetic predispositions, characteristics, and traits, from the moment we are born we interact with others in a complex social world that influences our behavior.

■ Serial killers stop murdering when they are caught or killed.

DID YOU KNOW?

... that a study published in the *Annals of Internal Medicine* concluded that there is a strong association between low cholesterol levels and violence?

BIOLOGY AND CRIMINALITY

Within the last three decades, biologists have followed in the tradition of Cesare Lombroso, Raffaele Garofalo, and Charles Goring in their search for answers to questions about human behavior. Geneticists, for example, have argued that the predisposition to act violently or aggressively in certain situations may be inherited. In other words, while criminals are not born criminal, the predisposition to be violent or to commit crime may be present at birth.

To demonstrate that certain traits are inherited, geneticists have studied children born of criminals but reared from birth by noncriminal adoptive parents. They have wanted to know whether the behavior of the adoptive children was more similar to that of their biological parents than to that of their adoptive parents. Their findings play an important role in the debate on heredity versus environment. Other biologists, sometimes called "biocriminologists" or "neurocriminologists," take a different approach. Some ask whether the brain's anatomy, brain damage, or inadequate nutrition results in criminal behavior. Others are interested in the influence of hormones, chromosomal abnormalities, and allergies. They investigate complex interactions between brain and behavior and between diet and behavior.

Modern Biocriminology

Biocriminology is the study of the physical aspects of psychological disorders.[5] It has been known for some time that adults who suffer from depression show abnormalities in brain waves during sleep, experience disturbed nervous system functioning, and display biochemical abnormalities. Research on depressed children reveals the same physical problems; furthermore, their adult relatives show high rates of depression as well. In fact, children whose parents suffer from depression are more than four times more likely than the average child to experience a similar illness.[6] Some researchers believe depression is an inherited condition that manifests itself in psychological and physical disturbances. The important point is that until only recently, physicians may have been missing the mark in their assessment and treatment of depressed children and adults by ignoring the physiological aspects.

Criminologists who study sociology and psychology to the exclusion of the biological sciences may also be missing the mark in their efforts to discover the causes of crime. Recent research has demonstrated that crime does indeed have psychobiological aspects similar to those found in studies of depression: biochemical abnormalities, abnormal brain waves, nervous system dysfunction. There is also evidence that strongly suggests a genetic predisposition to criminality.[7]

The resurgence of interest in integrating modern biological advances, theories, and principles into mainstream criminology began over three decades ago. The sociobiological work of Edward Wilson on the interrelationship of biology, genetics, and social behavior was pivotal.[8] So were the contributions of C. Ray Jeffery, who argued that a biosocial interdisciplinary model should become the major theoretical framework for studying criminal behavior.[9]

Criminologists once again began to consider the possibility that there are indeed traits that predispose a person to criminality and that these traits may be passed from parent to child through the genes. Other questions arose as well. Is it possible, for instance, that internal biochemical imbalances or deficiencies cause antisocial behavior? Could too much or too little sugar in the bloodstream increase the potential for aggression? Or could a vitamin deficiency or some hormonal problem be responsible? We will explore the evidence for a genetic predisposition to criminal behavior, the relationship between biochemical factors and criminality, and neurophysiological factors that result in criminal behavior. We will also briefly explore the emergence of a new specialty in criminology, neurocriminology. Advances in brain imaging allow some criminologists to make fascinating connections between the neuroanatomy of the brain and criminal behavior. The possibilities and boundaries of neurocriminology are still undefined, but the prospect for path-breaking research seems quite likely.

Genetics and Criminality

Today the proposition that human beings are products of an interaction between environmental and genetic factors is all but universally accepted.[10] We can stop asking, then, whether nature or nurture is more important in shaping us; we are the products of both. But what does the interaction between the two look like? And what concerns are raised by reliance on genetics to the exclusion of environmental factors? Consider the example of the XYY syndrome.

The XYY Syndrome

Chromosomes are the basic structures that contain our genes—the biological material that makes each of us unique. Each human being has 23 pairs of inherited chromosomes. One pair determines gender. A female receives an X chromosome from both mother and father; a male receives an X chromosome from his mother and a Y from his father. Sometimes a defect in the production of sperm or egg results in genetic abnormalities. One type of abnormality is the XYY chromosomal male. The XYY male receives two Y chromosomes from his father rather than one. Approximately 1 in 1,000 newborn males in the general population has this genetic composition.[11] Initial studies done in the 1960s found the frequency of XYY chromosomes to be about 20 times greater than normal XY chromosomes among inmates in maximum-security state hospitals.[12] The XYY inmates tended to be tall, physically aggressive, and, frequently, violent.

Supporters of these data claimed to have uncovered the mystery of violent criminality. Critics voiced concern over the fact that these studies were done on small and unrepresentative samples. The XYY syndrome, as this condition became known, received much public attention because of the case of Richard Speck. Speck, who in 1966 murdered eight nurses in Chicago, initially was diagnosed as an XYY chromosomal male. However, the diagnosis later turned out to be wrong. Nevertheless, public concern was aroused: Were all XYY males potential killers?

Studies undertaken since that time have discounted the relation between the extra Y chromosome and criminality.[13] Although convincing evidence in support of the XYY hypothesis appears to be slight, it is nevertheless possible that aggressive and violent behavior is at least partly determined by genetic factors. The problem is how to investigate this possibility. One difficulty is separating the external or environmental factors, such as family structure, culture, socioeconomic status, and peer influences, from the genetic predispositions with which they begin to interact at birth.

A particular individual may have a genetic predisposition to be violent but be born into a wealthy, well-educated, loving, and calm familial environment. He may never commit a violent act. Another person may have a genetic predisposition to be rule-abiding and nonaggressive yet be born into a poor, uneducated, physically abusive, and unloving family. He may commit violent criminal acts. How, then, can we determine the extent to which behavior is genetically influenced? Researchers have turned to twin studies and adoption studies in the quest for an answer.

Twin Studies

To discover whether crime is genetically predetermined, researchers have compared identical and fraternal twins. Identical twins, or **monozygotic (MZ) twins,** develop from a single fertilized egg that divides into two embryos. These twins share all their genes. Fraternal twins, or **dizygotic (DZ) twins,** develop from two separate eggs, both fertilized at the same time. They share about half their genes. Since the prenatal and postnatal family environments are, by and large, the same, greater behavioral similarity between identical twins than between fraternal twins would support an argument for genetic predisposition.

In the 1920s, a German physician, Johannes Lange, found 30 pairs of same-sex twins—13 identical and 17 fraternal pairs. One member of each pair was a known criminal. Lange found that in 10 of the 13 pairs of identical twins, both twins were criminal; in 2 of the 17 pairs of fraternal twins, both were criminal.[14] The research techniques of the time were limited, but Lange's results were nevertheless impressive.

Many similar studies have followed. The largest was a study by Karl Christiansen and Sarnoff A. Mednick that included all twins born between 1881 and 1910 in a region of Denmark, a total of 3,586 pairs. Reviewing serious offenses only, Christiansen and Mednick found that the chance of there being a criminal twin when the other twin was a criminal was 50 percent for identical twins and 20 percent for same-sex fraternal twins.[15] Such findings lend support to the hypothesis that some genetic influences increase the risk of criminality.[16] A more recent American study conducted by David C. Rowe and D. Wayne Osgood reached a similar conclusion.[17]

While the evidence from these and other twin studies looks persuasive, we should keep in mind the weakness of such research. It may not be valid to assume a common environment for all twins who grow up in the same house at the same time. If the upbringing of identical twins is much more similar than that of fraternal twins, as it well may be, that circumstance could help explain their different rates of criminality.

Adoption Studies

One way to separate the influence of inherited traits from that of environmental conditions would be to study infants separated at birth from their natural parents and placed randomly in foster homes. In such cases, we could determine whether the behavior of the adopted child resembled that of the natural parents or that of the adoptive parents, and by how much. Children, however, are adopted at various ages and are not placed randomly in foster homes. Most such children are matched to their foster or adoptive parents by racial and religious criteria. And couples who adopt children may differ in some important ways from other couples. Despite such shortcomings, adoption studies do help us expand our knowledge of genetic influences on human variation.

The largest adoption study conducted so far was based on a sample of 14,427 male and female adoptions in Denmark between 1924 and 1947. The hypothesis was that criminality in the biological parents would be associated with an increased risk of criminal behavior in the child. The parents were considered criminal if either the mother or the father had been convicted of a felony. The researchers had sufficient information on more than 4,000 of the male children to assess whether both the biological and the adoptive parents had criminal records. Mednick and his associates reported the following findings:

- Of boys whose adoptive and biological parents had no criminal record, 13.5 percent were convicted of crimes.
- Of boys who had criminal adoptive parents and noncriminal biological parents, 14.7 percent were convicted of crimes.
- Of boys who had noncriminal adoptive parents and criminal biological parents, 20 percent were convicted of crimes.
- Of boys who had both criminal adoptive parents and criminal biological parents, 24.5 percent were convicted of crimes.[18]

These findings support the claim that the criminality of the biological parents has more influence on the child than does that of the adoptive parents. Other research on adopted children has reached similar conclusions. A major Swedish study examined 862 adopted males and 913 adopted females. The researchers found a genetic predisposition to criminality in both sexes, but an even stronger one in females. An American study of children who were put up for adoption by a group of convicted mothers supports the Danish and Swedish findings on the significance of genetic factors.[19]

Results of adoption studies have been characterized as "highly suggestive" or "supportive" of a genetic link to criminality. But how solid is this link? There are significant problems with adoption studies. One is that little can be done to ensure the similarity of adopted children's environments. Of even greater concern to criminologists, however, is the distinct possibility of mistaking correlation for causation. In other words, there appears to be a significant correlation between the criminality of biological parents and adopted children in the research we have reviewed, but this correlation does not prove that the genetic legacy passed on by a criminal parent causes an offspring to commit a crime.

So far, research has failed to shed any light on the nature of the biological link that results in the association between the criminality of parents and that of their children. Furthermore, even if we could identify children with a higher-than-average probability of committing offenses as adults on the basis of their parents' behavior, it is unclear what we could do to prevent these children from following the parental model.

The Controversy over Violence and Genes

At the same time that advances in research on the biological bases of violence shed new light on crime, attacks on such research are calling its usefulness into question. Government-sponsored research plans have been called racist, a conference on genetics and crime was canceled after protests, and a session on violence and heredity at a recent American Association for the Advancement of Science meeting became "a politically correct critique of the research."[20]

Few involved in such research expect to find a "violence gene"; rather, researchers are looking for a biological basis for some of the behaviors associated with violence. As one explanation put it:

Scientists are . . . trying to find inborn personality traits that might make people more physically aggressive. The tendency to be a thrill seeker may be one such characteristic. So might "a restless impulsiveness, an inability to defer gratification." A high threshold for anxiety or fear may be another key trait. . . . Such people tend to have a "special biology," with lower-than-average heart rates and blood pressure.[21]

No one yet has found any direct link between genes and violence. In fact, Sarnoff Mednick, the psychologist who conducted adoption studies of criminal behavior in Denmark, found no evidence for the inheritance of violence. "If there were any genetic effect for violent crimes, we would have picked it up," says Mednick, whose study included 14,427 men.

The controversy over a genetic basis for violent behavior seems to deal less with actual research findings than with the implications of such findings. For example, Harvard psychologist Jerome Kagan predicts that in 25 years, biological and genetic tests will make it possible to identify the 15 children in every 1,000 who may have violent tendencies. Of those 15, only 1 will actually become violent. The ethical question, then, is what to do with this knowledge. "Do we tell the mothers of all 15 that their kids might be violent?" he asks. "How are the mothers then going to react to their children if we do that?"[22]

A National Academy of Science (NAS) report on violence recommended finding better ways to intervene in the development of children who could become violent, and it listed risk factors statistically linked to violence: hyperactivity, poor early grades, low IQ, fearlessness, and an inability to defer gratification, for example. A report released by the Office of Juvenile Justice and Delinquency Prevention's Study Group on Serious and Violent Juvenile Offenders identifies a number of behavioral precursors to juvenile violence, including difficult temperament, hyperactivity, impulsivity, aggression, lying, and risk-taking behavior.[23]

What frightens those opposed to biological and genetic research into the causes of violence is the thought of how such research could be used by policy makers. If a violent personality can be shown to be genetically determined, crime-prevention strategies might try to identify "potential criminals" and to intervene before their criminal careers begin and before anyone knows if they would ever have become criminals. "Should genetic markers one day be found for tendencies . . . that are loosely linked to crime," explains one researcher, "they would probably have little specificity, sensitivity or explanatory power: most people with the markers will not be criminals and most criminals will not have the markers."[24] On the other hand, when environment—poverty, broken homes, and other problems—is seen as the major cause of violence, crime prevention takes the shape of improving social conditions rather than labeling individuals.

A middle-of-the-road approach is proposed by those who see biological research as a key to helping criminals change their behavior. "Once you find a biological basis for a behavior, you can try to find out how to help people cope," says one such scholar. "Suppose the link is impulsivity, an inability to defer gratification. It might be you could design education programs to teach criminals to readjust their time horizon."[25]

The IQ Debate

A discussion of the association between genes and criminality would be incomplete without paying at least some attention to the debate over IQ and crime. Is an inferior intelligence inherited, and, if so, how do we account for the strong relationship between IQ and criminality?

The Research Background

Nearly a century ago, scientists began to search for measures to determine people's intelligence, which they believed to be genetically determined. The first test to gain acceptance was developed by a French psychologist, Alfred Binet. Binet's test measured the capacity of individual children to perform tasks or solve problems in relation to the average capacity of their peers.

Between 1888 and 1915, several researchers administered intelligence tests to incarcerated criminals and to boys in reform schools. Initial studies of the relationship between IQ and crime revealed some surprising results. Psychologist Hugo Munsterberg estimated that 68 percent of the criminals he tested were of low IQ. Using the Binet scale, Henry H. Goddard found that between 25 and 50 percent of criminals had low IQs.[26] What could account for such different results?

Edwin Sutherland observed that the tests were poor and there were too many variations among the many versions administered. He reasoned that social and environmental factors caused delinquency, not low IQ.[27] In the 1950s, psychologist Robert H. Gault added to Sutherland's criticism. He noted particularly that it was "strange that it did not occur immediately to the pioneers that they had examined only a small sample of caught and convicted offenders."[28]

For more than a generation, the question about the relationship between IQ and criminal behavior was not studied, and the early inconsistencies remained unresolved. Then, in the late 1970s, the debate resumed.[29] Supporters of the view that inheritance determines intelligence once again began to present their arguments. Psychologist Arthur Jensen suggested that race was a key factor in IQ differences; Richard J. Herrnstein, a geneticist, pointed to social class as a factor.[30] Both positions spurred a heated debate in which criminologists soon became involved. In 1977, Travis Hirschi and Michael Hindelang evaluated the existing literature on IQ and crime.[31] They cited the following three studies as especially important:

- Travis Hirschi, on the basis of a study of 3,600 California students, demonstrated that the effect of a low IQ on delinquent behavior is more significant than that of the father's education.[32]
- Marvin Wolfgang and associates, after studying 8,700 Philadelphia boys, found a strong relationship between low IQ and delinquency, independent of social class.[33]
- Albert Reiss and Albert L. Rhodes, after an examination of the juvenile court records of 9,200 white Tennessee schoolboys, found IQ to be more closely related to delinquency than is social class.[34]

Hirschi and Hindelang concluded that IQ is an even more important factor in predicting crime than is either race or social class. They found significant differences in intelligence between criminal and noncriminal populations within like racial and socioeconomic groups. A lower IQ increases the potential for crime within each group. Furthermore, they found that IQ is related to school performance. A low IQ ultimately results in a youngster's associating with similar nonperformers, dropping out of school, and committing delinquent acts. Hirschi and Hindelang's findings were confirmed by James Q. Wilson and Richard Herrnstein but rejected by criminologist Deborah Denno, who conducted a prospective investigation of 800 children from birth to age 17. Her results failed to confirm a direct relationship between IQ and delinquency. A recent review of research on IQ and delinquency suggests an indirect link as well, mediated by academic competence.[35]

The Debate: Genetics or Environment?

The debate over the relationship between IQ and crime has its roots in the controversy over whether intelligence is genetically or environmentally determined. IQ tests, many people believe, measure cultural factors rather than the innate biological makeup of an individual.[36] Studies by psychologists Sandra Scarr and Richard Weinberg of black and white adopted children confirmed that environment plays a significant role in IQ development. They found that both black and white children adopted by white parents had comparable IQs and performed similarly.[37] With evidence of cultural bias and environmental influence, why not abandon the use of intelligence tests? The answer is simple: They do predict performance in school and so have significant utility. It appears that this debate will be with us for a long time to come.

Biochemical Factors

Biocriminologists' primary focus has been on the relationship between criminality and biochemical and neurophysiological factors. Biochemical factors include food allergies, diet, hypoglycemia, and hormones. Neurophysiological factors include brain lesions, brain wave abnormalities, and minimal brain dysfunction.

Food Allergies

In 1993, by the time Rachel was 2 years old, she displayed a pattern of behavior that went way beyond the "terrible twos." Without warning, her eyes would glaze over, her speech would develop a lisp, and she'd kick and hit and thrash about wildly until her mother swaddled her tightly and she fell asleep, exhausted. She even developed a "kitty-cat" routine, complete with meowing, stalking, and growling, that often went on for hours.

When Rachel's sister Emma was born later that year, she nursed poorly and never slept through the night. After their mother introduced baby corn into her diet, Emma experienced severe intestinal distress, for which she was hospitalized. After a battery of medical tests proved inconclusive, she was sent home, but the symptoms continued intermittently, without apparent reason.

The following year, in desperation, their mother had Rachel and Emma, then 3 years and 15 months, tested for food allergies. Both showed marked sensitivity to corn, wheat, sugar, preservatives, and dairy products. After those foods were eliminated, Emma's health and well-being improved, and Rachel's perplexing and worrisome behavior all but disappeared.[38]

Over the last two decades, researchers have investigated the relation between food allergies and aggression and antisocial behavior. In fact, since 1908 there have been numerous medical reports indicating that various foods cause reactions such as irritability, hyperactivity, seizures, agitation, and behavior that is "out of character."[39] Investigators have identified the following food components as substances that may result in severe allergic reactions:

Phenylethylamine (found in chocolate)
Tyramine (found in aged cheese and wine)
Monosodium glutamate (used as a flavor enhancer in many foods)
Aspartame (found in artificial sweeteners)
Xanthines (found in caffeine)

Each of these food components has been associated with behavioral disorders, including criminality.

Diet

- Susan had been charged with 16 offenses, including criminal damage, solvent abuse, and vehicle theft, by the time she was 13. She had no friends, showed no affection toward her parents, and frequently hit her mother. Her schoolwork deteriorated, and she played truant most days. After 6 months on a changed diet, which excluded burgers, bananas, and chocolate, the number of her offenses dropped to zero. And for the first time since she was a young child, Susan gave her mother a hug.

- Craig, 15, vandalized his home several times and committed numerous petty crimes. He was a bully and was virtually impossible to teach. And his 8-year-old brother was beginning to follow in his footsteps. Both were put on a special diet, cutting out fizzy drinks and sweets and including more green vegetables and fresh fruit. Within months, says their mother, both were more pleasant and easier to deal with. But Craig has since quit the diet and has reoffended. The bullying and the violence have started again.

- Graham, an 11-year-old, turned from an uncontrollable delinquent into a normal, pleasant boy when pizzas, baked beans, and chocolate in his diet were replaced by fresh vegetables, coconut milk, and carrots. He became less aggressive and argumentative and, reportedly, was "happy" for the first time in his life. Graham's schoolwork improved, and he began to make friends.

Anecdotal reports, in addition to more scientific investigations, link criminality to diets high in sugar and carbohydrates, to vitamin deficiency or dependency, and to excessive food additives.

Criminologist Stephen Schoenthaler conducted a series of studies on the relation between sugar and the behavior of institutionalized offenders. In these investigations, inmates were placed on a modified diet that included very little sugar. They received fruit juice in place of soda and vegetables instead of candy. Schoenthaler found fewer disciplinary actions and a significant drop in aggressive behavior in the experimental group.[40] Some individuals charged with crimes have used this finding to build a defense like that of Dan White.

In 1979, San Francisco city supervisor Dan White was on trial for the murder of his fellow supervisor, Harvey Milk, and Mayor George Moscone—as depicted in the movie *Milk*. White defended himself with testimony on the impact of sugar on his behavior. The testimony showed that when White was depressed, he departed

from his normal, healthy diet and resorted to high-sugar junk food, including Twinkies, Coca-Cola, and chocolates. Thereafter, his behavior became less and less controllable. The jury found White guilty of manslaughter, rather than murder, due to diminished capacity. White served 5 years in prison and committed suicide after his release. His defense was promptly dubbed the "junk-food defense," "Dan White's defense," or the "Twinkie defense."

Most subsequent attempts to use the junk-food defense have failed. In a 1989 Ohio case, it was ruled that the defense may not be used to establish diminished capacity. In 1990, a Cape Cod man was unsuccessful when he defended himself on a charge of stealing (and eating) 300 candy bars. Nor did this defense (Twinkie and soda pop) succeed in a murder case in Ohio. But in a 1987 Florida case, a defendant was acquitted of drunk-driving charges on evidence that consumption of chocolate mousse after half a glass of sherry caused an unusual blood-sugar reaction.

Other researchers have looked for the causes of crime in vitamin deficiencies. One such study found that 70 percent of criminals charged with serious offenses in one Canadian jurisdiction had a greater-than-normal need for vitamin B$_6$.[41] Other studies have noted deficiencies of vitamins B$_3$ and B$_6$ in criminal population samples.

Some investigators have examined the effects of food additives and food dyes on behavior. Benjamin Feingold has argued that between 30 and 60 percent of all hyperactivity in children may be attributable to reactions to food coloring.[42] There is additional support for this hypothesis.[43] Some studies have suggested that a diet deficient in protein may be responsible for violent aggression.

Let us look at the association between the consumption of tryptophan, an amino acid (a protein building block), and crime rates. Tryptophan is a normal component of many foods. Low levels of it have been associated with aggression and, in criminal studies, an increased sensitivity to electric shock. Anthony R. Mawson and K. W. Jacobs reasoned that diets low in tryptophan would be likely to result in higher levels of violent crime, particularly violent offenses such as homicide.

They hypothesized that because corn-based diets are deficient in tryptophan, a cross-national comparison of countries should reveal a positive relationship between corn consumption and homicide rates. Mawson and Jacobs obtained homicide data from the United Nations and the mean per capita corn intake rates of 53 foreign countries from the U.S. Department of Agriculture. They discovered that countries whose per capita rates of corn consumption were above the median had significantly higher homicide rates than countries whose diets were based on wheat or rice.[44]

Hypoglycemia

What prompted an otherwise loving father to throw his 20-month-old daughter into a nearby lake? Neighbors knew that something was amiss when they noticed 22-year-old Joe Holt climb on the roof of his duplex in a quiet Orlando suburb. Joe then proceeded to dance, touching power lines in the course of his pantomime. No one sounded the alarm, however, until he disappeared into his lakeside apartment, returning momentarily with his daughter Ashley in his arms. The police arrived on the scene to find Joe in a state of agitation and Ashley facedown in Lake Apopka. Seated in the back of a squad car, handcuffed, the bewildered Joe had no recollection of the preceding events. When his blood was tested, he had a glucose level of 20 milligrams per deciliter of blood. The average is 80 to 120 milligrams. Joe was suffering from severe hypoglycemia. According to a sheriff's spokesman, "he had virtually no thought process."[45]

■ *Andrea Yates, convicted of drowning her children in a bathtub, was sentenced to life in prison in March 2002. Yates pleaded not guilty by reason of insanity—claiming postpartum psychosis and postpartum depression.*

Hypoglycemia is a condition that occurs when the level of sugar in the blood falls below an acceptable range. The brain is particularly vulnerable to hypoglycemia, and such a condition can impair its function. Symptoms of hypoglycemia include anxiety, headache, confusion, fatigue, and even aggressive behavior. As early as 1943, researchers linked the condition with violent crime, including murder, rape, and assault. Subsequent studies found that violent and impulsive male offenders had a higher rate of hypoglycemia than noncriminal controls.

Consider the work of Matti Virkkunen, who has conducted a series of studies of habitually violent and psychopathic offenders in Finland. In one such study done in the 1980s, he examined the results of a glucose tolerance test (used to determine whether hypoglycemia is present) administered to 37 habitually violent offenders with antisocial personalities, 31 habitually violent offenders with intermittent explosive disorders, and 20 controls. The offenders were found to be significantly more hypoglycemic than the controls.[46]

Hormones

Experiments have shown that male animals typically are more aggressive than females. Male aggression is directly linked to male hormones. If an aggressive male mouse is injected with female hormones, he will stop fighting.[47] Likewise, the administration of male hormones to pregnant monkeys results in female offspring who, even 3 years after birth, are more aggressive than the daughters of non-injected mothers.[48]

While it would be misleading to equate male hormones with aggression and female hormones with nonaggression, there is some evidence that abnormal levels of male hormones in humans may prompt criminal behavior. Several investigators have found higher levels of testosterone (the male hormone) in the blood of individuals who have committed violent offenses.[49] Some studies also relate premenstrual syndrome (PMS) to delinquency and conclude that women are at greater risk of aggressive and suicidal behavior before and during the menstrual period. After studying 156 newly admitted adult female prisoners, Katharina Dalton concluded that 49 percent of all their crimes were committed either in the premenstrual period or during menstruation.[50] More recently, however, critics have challenged the association between menstrual distress and female crime.[51]

Neurocriminology

In England in the mid-1950s, a father hit his son with a mallet and then threw him out of a window, killing him instantly. Instead of pleading insanity, as many people expected him to do, he presented evidence of a brain tumor, which, he argued, resulted in uncontrollable rage and violence. A jury acquitted him on the grounds that the brain tumor had deprived him of any control over and knowledge of the act he was committing.[52] Brain lesions or brain tumors have led to violent outbursts in many similar cases. Neurocriminological studies, however, have not focused exclusively on brain tumors; they have included a wide range of investigations: studies of cerebral structure, brain wave studies, clinical reports of minimal brain dysfunction, and theoretical explorations into the relationship between the limbic system and criminality.[53]

Advances in brain imaging made accessible by functional magnetic resonance imaging (fMRI) and other imaging technologies (for example, positron emission tomography, or PET scan) offer dramatic new insights into the brains of criminals. With well over a hundred brain imaging studies, evidence is steadily emerging that the brain functioning of murderers, psychopaths, and aggressive criminals simply is different.

In combination with the previously mentioned twin and adoption studies, Adrian Raine and others make the case that there are prefrontal structural and functional deficits strongly associated with delinquency. They maintain that empirical

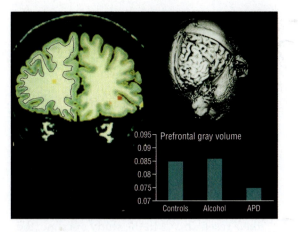

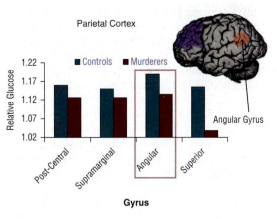

FIGURE 4.1 Differences in brain volume between alcoholic offenders and those with anti-personality disorder (APD).

Source: Adrian Raine, "Neurocriminology and Neuroethics: Brain Systems That Predispose to Violence, and Societal Implications" (lecture, National Taiwan University, Taiwan, October 12, 2007).

FIGURE 4.2 Differences in the volume of that part of the brain responsible for language and cognition between murderers and matched controls.

Source: A. Raine, M. S. Buchsbaum, and L. La Casse, "Brain Abnormalities in Murderers Indicated by Position Emission Tomography," *Biological Psychiatry,* **42** (1997): 495–508.

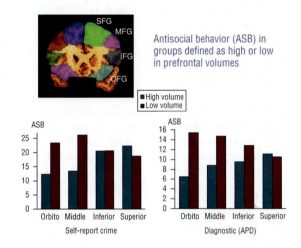

FIGURE 4.3 Differences in brain volume across a wide range of anatomies.

Source: A. Raine and Y. Yang, "The Neuroanatomical Bases of Psychopathy: A Review of Brain Imaging Findings," in *Handbook of Psychopathy,* ed. C. J. Patrick (New York: Guilford Press, 2006), pp. 278–295.

research and neurological case studies confirm the importance of the prefrontal and frontal lobes in a person's ability to organize, execute, and inhibit prosocial behavior. Thus, disruptions of these lobes are associated with antisocial and aggressive behavior.

Even more significant, the neuroanatomy of the brains of criminals seems to differ in prefrontal cortex volume. Overall, criminals appear to have an 11 percent reduction in gray matter relative to matched controls. Research reveals differences in the anatomy of mass murderers versus murderers and matched controls;[54] affective versus predatory murderers and matched controls;[55] and alcoholics versus offenders with anti-personality disorder[56] (Figure 4.1).

Additional research focuses on specific parts of the brain of criminals, identifying differences in cranial volume that are consistent, given our knowledge of brain function, with behavioral research. For example, Raine and his colleagues found significant differences in the volume of the angular and superior gyrus in murderers, parts of the brain responsible for language and cognition[57] (Figure 4.2). Most recently, Raine and his colleagues report brain volume differences in self-reported offenders across a wide range of anatomies[58] (Figure 4.3).

The implications of these studies are dramatic and, at the same time, concerning. What should be done if violent offenders have the anatomical capacity to regulate behavior? Assuming that subsequent studies confirm and add to this line of research, what policy ramifications flow from it? In what ways can this research assist in crime prevention efforts? Can you anticipate ethical concerns that may be raised? What, if anything, does this research tell us about the importance of the work discussed in later chapters, which links

concentrated poverty or the absence of social resources, for example, with the very same kind of behavior? As neurocriminological research continues, these questions remain largely unanswered.

In many ways, these are new questions. The neurophysiological factors criminologists once were exclusively concerned with—for example, EEG abnormalities and minimal brain dysfunction—raised fewer concerns.

EEG Abnormalities

Sam recalled that his wife, Janet, looked slightly different and that the house smelled funny, and he felt out of sorts. During an intimate moment in bed, Janet made a funny remark, after which Sam flew into a rage, choked her, and slashed her throat. When he came to his senses, he immediately went to the police and admitted to the crime, although he had little memory of his violent acts. Can EEG (electroencephalogram) tracings explain the behavior of this young U.S. Marine who had returned home on leave? Subsequent tracings were found to be abnormal—indicative of an "intermittent explosive disorder." After reviewing this evidence, the court reduced Sam's charges from first-degree murder to manslaughter.

The EEG is a tracing made by an instrument that measures cerebral functioning by recording brain wave activity with electrodes placed on the scalp. Numerous studies that have examined the brain activity of violent prisoners reveal significant differences between the EEGs of criminals and those of noncriminals. Other findings relate significantly slow brain wave activity to young offenders and adult murderers.[59] When Sarnoff A. Mednick and his colleagues examined the criminal records and EEGs of 265 children in a birth cohort in Denmark, they found that certain types of brain wave activity, as measured by the EEG, enabled investigators to predict whether convicted thieves would steal again.[60]

When Jan Volavka compared the EEGs of juvenile delinquents with those of comparable nondelinquents, he found a slowing of brain waves in the delinquent sample, most prominently in those children convicted of theft. He concluded that thievery "is more likely to develop in persons who have a slowing of alpha frequency than in persons who do not."[61]

Using positron emission tomography (PET) brain imaging, Adrian Raine, Monte Buchsbaum, and Lori LaCasse examined cortical and subcortical brain functioning in a matched sample of 41 murderers pleading not guilty by reason of insanity and 41 controls. Findings indicate that the murderers had abnormal brain functioning, including reduced glucose metabolism and abnormal asymmetries of activity.

Minimal Brain Dysfunction

Minimal brain dysfunction (MBD) is classified as "attention deficit hyperactivity disorder."[62] MBD produces asocial behavioral patterns such as impulsivity, hyperactivity, aggressiveness, low self-esteem, and temper outbursts. The syndrome is noteworthy for at least two reasons. First, MBD may explain criminality when social theories fail to do so—that is, when neighborhood, peer, and familial associations do not suggest a high risk of delinquency. Second, MBD is an easily overlooked diagnosis. Parents, teachers, and clinicians tend to focus more on the symptoms of a child's psychopathology than on the possibility

of brain dysfunction, even though investigators have repeatedly found high rates of brain dysfunction in samples of suicidal adolescents and youthful offenders.[63]

CRIME AND HUMAN NATURE

Criminologist Edward Sagarin has written:

In criminology, it appears that a number of views . . . have become increasingly delicate and sensitive, as if all those who espouse them were inherently evil, or at least stupidly insensitive to the consequences of their research. . . . In the study of crime, the examples of unpopular orientations are many. Foremost is the link of crime to the factors of genes, biology, race, ethnicity, and religion.[64]

Criticisms of Biocriminology

What is it about linking biology and criminality that makes the subject delicate and sensitive? Why is the concept so offensive to so many people? One reason is that biocriminologists often deny the existence of individual free will. The idea of predisposition to commit crimes fosters a sense of hopelessness. But this criticism seems to have little merit. As Diana H. Fishbein has aptly noted, the idea of a "conditioned free will" is frequently advocated.[65] This view suggests that individuals make choices in regard to a particular action within a range of possibilities that is "preset" yet flexible. When conditions permit rational thought, one is fully accountable and responsible for one's actions. It is only when conditions are somehow disturbed that free choice is constricted. The child of middle-class parents who has a low IQ might avoid delinquent behavior. But if that child's circumstances changed so that he lived in a lower-class, single-parent environment, he might find the delinquent lifestyle of the children in the new neighborhood too tempting to resist.

Critics have other concerns as well. Some see a racist undertone to biocriminological research. If there is a genetic predisposition to commit crime and if minorities account for a disproportionate share of criminal activity, are minorities then predisposed to commit crime? In Chapter 2, we learned that self-reports reveal that most people have engaged in delinquent or criminal behavior. How, then, do biocriminologists justify their claim that certain groups are more prone than others to criminal behavior? Could it be that the subjects of their investigations are only criminals who have been caught and incarcerated? And is the attention of the police disproportionately drawn to members of minority groups?

How do biocriminologists account for the fact that most criminologists see the structure of our society, the decay of our neighborhoods, and the subcultures of certain areas as determinants of criminality? Are biocriminologists unfairly deemphasizing social and economic factors? (In Chapters 5 through 9, we review theories that attribute criminality to group and environmental forces.)

These issues raise a further question that is at the core of all social and behavioral science: Is human behavior the product of nature (genetics) or nurture (environment)? The consensus among social and behavioral scientists today is that the interaction of nature and nurture is so pervasive that the two should not be viewed in isolation without appropriate caveats.

Supporters of biocriminology also maintain that recognizing a predisposition to crime is not inconsistent with considering environmental factors. In fact, some believe that predispositions are triggered by environmental factors. Even if we agree that some people are predisposed to commit crime, we know that the crime rate will be higher in areas that provide more triggers. In sum, while some people may be predisposed to certain kinds of behavior, most scientists agree that both psychological and environmental factors shape the final forms of those behaviors.

PSYCHOLOGY AND CRIMINALITY

Psychologists have considered a variety of possibilities to account for individual differences—defective conscience, emotional immaturity, inadequate childhood socialization, maternal deprivation, and poor moral development. They study how aggression is learned, which situations promote violent or delinquent reactions, how crime is related to personality factors, and how various mental disorders are associated with criminality.

Psychological Development

The **psychoanalytic theory** of criminality attributes delinquent and criminal behavior to at least three possible causes:

- A conscience so overbearing that it arouses feelings of guilt
- A conscience so weak that it cannot control the individual's impulses
- The need for immediate gratification

Consider the case of Richard. Richard was 6 when he committed his first delinquent act: He stole a comic book from the corner drugstore. Three months before the incident, his father, an alcoholic, had been killed in an automobile accident, and his mother, unable to care for the family, had abandoned the children.

For the next 10 years, the county welfare agency moved Richard in and out of foster homes. During this time, he actively pursued a life of crime, breaking into houses during daylight hours and stealing cars at night. By age 20, while serving a 10-year prison sentence for armed robbery, he had voluntarily entered psychoanalysis. After 2 years, Richard's analyst suggested three reasons for his criminality:

1. Being caught and punished for stealing made him feel less guilty about hating both his father for dying and thus abandoning him as well as his mother for deliberately abandoning him.

2. Stealing did not violate his moral and ethical principles.

3. Stealing resulted in immediate gratification and pleasure, both of which Richard had great difficulty resisting.

Sigmund Freud (1856–1939), the founder of psychoanalysis, suggested that an individual's psychological well-being is dependent on a healthy interaction among the id, ego, and superego—the three basic components of the human psyche. The **id** consists of powerful urges and drives for gratification and satisfaction. The **ego** is the executive of the personality, acting as a moderator between the superego and id. The **superego** acts as a moral code or conscience. Freud proposed that criminality may result from an overactive superego

■ *"The first human who hurled an insult instead of a stone was the founder of civilization."*

Sigmund Freud

or conscience. In treating patients, he noticed that those who were suffering from unbearable guilt committed crimes in order to be apprehended and punished.[66] Once they had been punished, their feelings of guilt were relieved. Richard's psychoanalyst suggested that Richard's anger over his father's death and his mother's abandonment created unconscious feelings of guilt, which he sought to relieve by committing a crime and being punished for it.

The psychoanalyst also offered an alternative explanation for Richard's persistent criminal activities: His conscience was perhaps not too strong, but too weak. The conscience, or superego, was so weak or defective that he was unable to control the impulses of the id. Because the superego is essentially an internalized parental image, developed when the child assumes the parents' attitudes and moral values, it follows that the absence of such an image may lead to an unrestrained id and thus to delinquency.[67]

Psychoanalytic theory suggests yet another explanation for Richard's behavior: an insatiable need for immediate reward and gratification. A defect in the character formation of delinquents drives them to satisfy their desires at once, regardless of the consequences.[68] This urge, which psychoanalysts attribute to the id, is so strong that relationships with people are important only so long as they help satisfy it. Most analysts view delinquents as children unable to give up their desires for instant pleasure.

The psychoanalytic approach is still one of the most prominent explanations for both normal and asocial functioning. Despite criticism,[69] three basic principles appeal to psychologists who study criminality:

1. The actions and behavior of an adult are understood in terms of childhood development.

2. Behavior and unconscious motives are intertwined, and their interaction must be unraveled if we are to understand criminality.

3. Criminality is essentially a representation of psychological conflict.

In spite of their appeal, psychoanalytic treatment techniques devised to address these principles have been controversial since their introduction by Freud and his disciples. The controversy has involved questions about improvement following treatment and, perhaps more important, the validity of the hypothetical conflicts the treatment presupposes.

Moral Development

Consider the following moral dilemma:

In Europe, a woman is near death from a special kind of cancer. There is one drug that the doctors think might save her. It is a form of radium that a druggist in the same town has recently discovered. The drug is expensive to make, and the druggist is charging ten times that cost. He paid $200 for the radium and is charging $2,000 for a small dose of the drug. The sick woman's husband, Heinz, goes to everyone he knows to borrow the money, but he can get together only $1,000. He tells the druggist that his wife is dying and asks him to sell the drug more cheaply or to let him pay later. The druggist says, "No, I discovered the drug and I'm going to make money from it." Heinz is desperate and considers breaking into the man's store to steal the drug for his wife.[70]

This classic dilemma sets up complex moral issues. While you may know that it is wrong to steal, you may believe that this is a situation in which the law should be circumvented. Or is it always wrong to steal, no matter what the circumstances? Regardless of what you decide, the way you reach the decision about whether to steal reveals much about your moral development.

Psychologist Lawrence Kohlberg, who pioneered moral developmental theory, has found that moral reasoning develops in three phases.[71] In the first, the preconventional level, children's moral rules and moral values consist of dos and don'ts to avoid punishment. A desire to avoid punishment and a belief in the superior power of authorities are the two central reasons for doing what is right. According to the theory, until the ages of 9 to 11, children usually reason at this level. They think, in effect, "If I steal, what are my chances of getting caught and being punished?"

Adolescents typically reason at the conventional level. Here individuals believe in and have adopted the values and rules of society. Moreover, they seek to uphold these rules. They think, in effect, "It is illegal to steal and therefore I should not steal, under any circumstances." Finally, at the postconventional level, individuals examine customs and social rules according to their own sense of universal human rights, moral principles, and duties. They think, in effect, "One must live within the law, but certain universal ethical principles, such as respect for human rights and for the dignity of human life, supersede the written law when the two conflict." This level of moral reasoning is generally seen in adults after the age of 20 (Table 4.1).

According to Kohlberg and his colleagues, most delinquents and criminals reason at the preconventional level. Low moral development or preconventional reasoning alone, however, does not result in criminality. Other factors, such as the presence or the absence of significant social bonds, may play a part. Kohlberg has argued that basic moral principles and social norms are learned through social interaction and

TABLE 4.1 Kohlberg's Sequence of Moral Reasoning

| | | Sample Moral Reasoning | |
Level	Stage	In Favor of Stealing	Against Stealing
Level 1: Preconventional morality. At this level, the concrete interests of the individual are considered in terms of rewards and punishments.	**Stage 1: Obedience and punishment orientation.** At this stage, people stick to rules in order to avoid punishment, and there is obedience for its own sake.	If you let your wife die, you will get in trouble. You'll be blamed for not spending the money to save her, and there'll be an investigation of you and the druggist for your wife's death.	You shouldn't steal the drug because you'll be caught and sent to jail if you do. If you do get away, your conscience will bother you, thinking how the police will catch up with you at any minute.
	Stage 2: Reward orientation. At this stage, rules are followed only for one's own benefit. Obedience occurs because of rewards that are received.	If you do happen to get caught, you could give the drug back and you wouldn't get much of a sentence. It wouldn't bother you much to serve a little jail term, if you have your wife when you get out.	You may not get much of a jail term if you steal the drug, but your wife will probably die before you get out, so it won't do much good. If your wife dies, you shouldn't blame yourself; it wasn't your fault she had cancer.
Level 2: Conventional morality. At this level, moral problems are approached by an individual as a member of society. People are interested in pleasing others by acting as good members of society.	**Stage 3: "Good boy" morality.** Individuals at this stage show an interest in maintaining the respect of others and doing what is expected of them.	No one will think you're bad if you steal the drug, but your family will think you're an inhuman husband if you don't. If you let your wife die, you'll never be able to look anybody in the face again.	It isn't just the druggist who will think you're a criminal; everyone else will too. After you steal it, you'll feel bad, thinking how you've brought dishonor on your family and yourself; you won't be able to face anyone again.
	Stage 4: Authority and social-order-maintaining morality. People at this stage conform to society's rules and consider that "right" is what society defines as right.	If you have any sense of honor, you won't let your wife die just because you're afraid to do the only thing that will save her. You'll always feel guilty that you caused her death if you don't do your duty to her.	You're desperate and you may not know you're doing wrong when you steal the drug. But you'll know you did wrong after you're sent to jail. You'll always feel guilty for your dishonesty and lawbreaking.
Level 3: Postconventional morality. People at this level use moral principles that are seen as broader than those of any particular society.	**Stage 5: Morality of contract, individual rights, and democratically accepted law.** People at this stage do what is right because of a sense of obligation to laws that are agreed upon within society. They perceive that laws can be modified as part of changes in an implicit social contract.	You'll lose other people's respect, not gain it, if you don't steal. If you let your wife die, it will be out of fear, not out of reasoning. So you'll just lose self-respect and probably the respect of others too.	You'll lose your standing and respect in the community and violate the law. You'll lose respect for yourself if you're carried away by emotion and forget the long-range point of view.
	Stage 6: Morality of individual principles and conscience. At this final stage, a person follows laws because they are based on universal ethical principles. Laws that violate the principles are disobeyed.	If you don't steal the drug, if you let your wife die, you'll always condemn yourself for it afterward. You won't be blamed and you'll have lived up to the outside rule of the law, but you won't have lived up to your own standards of conscience.	If you steal the drug, you won't be blamed by other people, but you'll condemn yourself because you won't have lived up to your own conscience and standards of honesty.

SOURCE: Adapted from Robert S. Feldman, *Understanding Psychology*, p. 378. Copyright © 1987 by The McGraw-Hill Companies, Inc. Reprinted by permission of The McGraw-Hill Companies, Inc.

TABLE 4.2 Family-Based Crime Prevention by Ecological Context

Ecological Context	Program	Prevention Agent
Home	Regular visits for emotional, informational, instrumental, and educational support for parents of preschool (or older) children	Nurses, teachers, paraprofessionals, preschool teachers
	Foster care outplacement for the prevention of physical and sexual abuse or neglect	Family services, social workers
	Family preservation of families at risk of outplacement of child	Private family-preservation teams
	Personal alarm for victims of serious domestic violence	Police
	In-home proactive counseling for domestic violence	Police, social workers
Preschool	Involvement of mothers in parent groups, job training, parent training	Preschool teachers
School	Parent training	Psychologists, teachers
	Simultaneous parent and child training	Psychologists, child-care workers, social workers
Clinics	Family therapy	Psychologists, psychiatrists, social workers
	Medication—psychostimulants for treatment of hyperactivity and other childhood conduct disorders	Psychiatrists, psychologists, pediatricians
Hospitals	Domestic violence counseling	Nurses, social workers
	Low-birthweight baby mothers' counseling and support	Nurses, social workers
Courts	Prosecution of batterers	Police, prosecutors
	Warrants for unarrested batterers	Police, prosecutors
	Restraining orders or "stay away" order of protection	Police, prosecutors, judges, victims' advocates
	Hotline notification of victim about release of incarcerated domestic batterer	Probation, victim's advocates
Battered-women's shelters	Safe refuge during high-risk 2 to 7 days' aftermath of domestic assault; counseling; hotlines	Volunteers, staff

the television programs he preferred when he was 8 years old."[84]

Results from the 3-year landmark *National Television Violence Study* initiated in 1994 suggest that the problem is one not only of violence, but also of the portrayal of violence—the absence of consequences for violent acts and the glamorization of violence.[85]

More recently, the Parents Television Council examined TV violence on the six major broadcast networks (ABC, CBS, NBC, Fox, UPN, and the WB) during prime time. With reference to earlier surveys conducted during the 1998, 2000, and 2002 television seasons, PTC examined trends over the past 8 years. PTC captured more than 1,180 programming hours combined.

Over the course of 8 years (from 1998 to 2006):

- Violence increased in every time slot:
  During the 8:00 P.M. Family Hour by 45 percent
  During the 9:00 P.M. hour by 92 percent
  During the 10:00 P.M. hour by 167 percent.

- ABC experienced the biggest increase in violent content overall. In 1998, ABC averaged 0.93 instance of violence per hour during prime time. By 2006, ABC was averaging 3.80 instances of violence per hour—an increase of 309 percent.

- Fox, the second-most-violent network in 1998, experienced the smallest increase. Fox averaged 3.43 instances of violence per hour in 1998 and 3.84 instances of violence per hour by 2006—an increase of only 12 percent.

- Violent scenes increasingly include a sexual element. Rapists, sexual predators, and fetishists are cropping up with increasing frequency on prime-time programs like *Law and Order: SVU, CSI, CSI: Miami, CSI: New York, Medium, Crossing Jordan, Prison Break, ER,* and *House.*

On an hour-by-hour basis:

- Every network experienced an increase in violence during the 9:00 P.M. and 10:00 P.M. hours between 1998 and the 2005–2006 television season.

- During the Family Hour, ABC experienced the biggest increase in violent content. In 1998, ABC was the least-violent network, averaging only 0.13 instance of violence per hour. By 2006, ABC was averaging 2.23 instances of violence per hour, an increase of 1,615.4 percent.

- UPN and Fox were the only networks to feature less violence during the Family Hour in 2005–2006 than in 1998: Violence decreased on Fox by 18 percent, and on UPN by 83 percent.

- During the 9:00 P.M. hour, ABC experienced the biggest increase in violent content, jumping from 0.31 instance per hour in 1998 to 5.71 instances per hour during the 2005–2006 season—an increase of 1,742 percent.

- During the 10:00 P.M. hour, NBC experienced the biggest increase in violent content—635 percent—from 2 instances of violence per hour in 1998 to nearly 15 instances of violence per hour in 2005–2006.[86]

Direct Experience

What we learn by observation is determined by the behavior of others. What we learn from direct experience is determined by what we ourselves do and what happens to us. We remember the past and use its lessons to avoid future mistakes. Thus, we learn through trial and error. According to social learning theorists, after engaging in a given behavior, most of us examine the responses to our actions and modify our behavior as necessary to obtain favorable responses. If we are praised or rewarded for a behavior, we are likely to repeat it. If we are subjected to verbal or physical punishment, we are likely to refrain from such behavior. Our behavior in the first instance and our restraint in the second are said to be "reinforced" by the rewards and punishments we receive.

Psychologist Gerald Patterson and his colleagues examined how aggression is learned by direct experience. They observed that some passive children at play were repeatedly victimized by other children but were occasionally successful in curbing the attacks by counteraggression. Over time, these children learned defensive fighting, and eventually they initiated fights. Other passive children, who were rarely observed to be victimized, remained submissive.[87] Thus, children, like adults, can learn to be aggressive and even violent by trial and error.

While violence and aggression are learned behaviors, they are not necessarily expressed until they are elicited in one of several ways. Albert Bandura describes the factors that elicit behavioral responses as "instigators." Thus, social learning theory describes not only how aggression is acquired but also how it is instigated. Consider the following instigators of aggression:

- *Aversive instigators.* Physical assaults, verbal threats, and insults; adverse reductions in conditions of life (such as impoverishment) and the thwarting of goal-directed behavior

- *Incentive instigators.* Rewards, such as money and praise

- *Modeling instigators.* Violent or aggressive behaviors observed in others

- *Instructional instigators.* Observations of people carrying out instructions to engage in violence or aggression

- *Delusional instigators.* Unfounded or bizarre beliefs that violence is necessary or justified[88]

Differential Reinforcement

In 1965, criminologist C. Ray Jeffery suggested that learning theory could be used to explain criminality.[89] Within one year, Ernest Burgess and Ronald Akers combined Bandura's psychologically based learning theory with Edwin Sutherland's sociologically based differential association theory (Chapter 5) to produce the theory of **differential association-reinforcement.** This theory suggests that (1) the persistence of criminal behavior depends on whether or not it is rewarded or punished and (2) the most meaningful rewards and punishments are those given by groups that are important in an individual's

streets. A woman crawling from a cardboard box. Men bathing at a fire hydrant. Men relieving themselves by the roadside. You stand on one side of the Hooghly River, a branch of the Ganges that runs through Kolkuta, and your friend tells you, "On the other bank millions of people live without a single sewer line."

On the other hand, the world's largest middle class, mostly lower-middle, but all the more admirable. The India of "Monsoon Wedding." Millionaires. Mercedes-Benzes and Audis. Traffic like Demo Derby. Luxury condos. Exploding education. A booming computer segment. A fountain of medical professionals. Some of the most exciting modern English literature. A Bollywood to rival Hollywood. "Slumdog Millionaire" bridges these two Indias by cutting between a world of poverty and the Indian version of "Who Wants to be a Millionaire." It tells the story of an orphan from the slums of Mumbai who is born into a brutal existence. A petty thief, impostor and survivor, mired in dire poverty, he improvises his way up through the world and remembers everything he has learned.

His name is Jamel (played as a teenager by Dev Patel). He is Oliver Twist. High-spirited and defiant in the worst of times, he survives. He scrapes out a living at the Taj Mahal, which he did not know about but discovers by being thrown off a train. He pretends to be a guide, invents "facts" out of thin air, advises tourists to remove their shoes and then steals them. He finds a bit part in the Mumbai underworld, and even falls in idealized romantic love, that most elusive of conditions for a slumdog.

His life until he's 20 is told in flashbacks intercut with his appearance as a quiz show contestant. Pitched as a slumdog, he supplies the correct answer to question after question and becomes a national hero. The flashbacks show why he knows the answers. He doesn't volunteer this information. It is beaten out of him by the show's security staff. They are sure he must be cheating.

The film uses dazzling cinematography, breathless editing, driving music and headlong momentum to explode with narrative force, stirring in a romance at the same time. For Danny Boyle, it is a personal triumph. He combines the suspense of a game show with the vision and energy of "City of God" and never stops sprinting.

When I saw "Slumdog Millionaire" at Toronto, I was witnessing a phenomenon: dramatic proof that a movie is about how it tells itself. I walked out of the theater and flatly predicted it would win the Audience Award. Seven days later, it did. And that it could land a best picture Oscar nomination. We will see. [In fact, it won not only a nomination, but also the Oscar.] It is one of those miraculous entertainments that achieves its immediate goals and keeps climbing toward a higher summit.[1] (Taken from the ROGER EBERT column by Roger Ebert © 2008 The Ebert Company. Dist. by UNIVERSAL UCLICK. Reprinted with permission. All rights reserved.)

Stories about the triumph of sheer will over class are more than stirring. They are truly inspiring. The scripts do everything to convince us that the impossible is possible, that aspiration and inspiration trump centuries of deeply encoded class differences that are apparent by appearance, speech, and one's last name. If only life were better at imitating art! If so, we would be nonplussed by the plot of Slumdog Millionaire. There would also be no need for a chapter that explores the effects of aspirations that meet frustration and strain where the means to obtain one's goals simply are not there. There would be no need for a chapter that considers theories of norms and values that, we are told, distinguish persons of different social and economic classes.

For all those who do not make it to a millionaire game show, who do not win the multistate lottery, or who do not grow up to be the next greatest sports hero, there are, of course, ways to adapt to the strain and frustration of not meeting aspirations. One way, as we shall see, is to reject the more conventional path to success when this path is unavailable or appears as if it is. And this takes us to the beginning of Chapter 5, to the early decades of the twentieth century that brought major changes to American society. One of the most significant was the change in the composition of the populations of cities. Between 1840 and 1924, 45 million people—Irish, Swedes, Germans, Italians, Poles, Armenians, Bohemians, Russians—left the Old World; two-thirds of them were bound for the United States.[2] At the same time, increased mechanization in this country deprived many American farmworkers of their jobs and forced them to join the ranks of the foreign-born and the black laborers who had migrated from the South to northern and midwestern industrial centers. During the 1920s, large U.S. cities swelled with 5 million new arrivals.[3]

Chicago's expansion was particularly remarkable: Its population doubled in 20 years. Many of the new arrivals brought nothing with them except what they could carry. The city offered them only meager wages, 12-hour working days in conditions that jeopardized their health, and tenement housing in deteriorating areas. Chicago had other problems as well. In the late 1920s and early 1930s, it was the home of major organized crime groups, which fought over the profits from the illegal production and sale of liquor during Prohibition (as we shall see in Chapter 10).

Teeming with newcomers looking for work, corrupt politicians trying to buy their votes, and bootleggers growing more influential through sheer firepower and the political strength they controlled, Chicago also had a rapidly rising crime rate. The city soon became an inviting urban laboratory for criminologists, who began to challenge the then-predominant theories of crime causation, which were based on biological and psychological factors. Many of these criminologists were associated with the University of Chicago, which has the oldest sociology program in the United States (begun in 1892). By the 1920s, these criminologists began to measure scientifically the amount of criminal behavior and its relation to the social turmoil Chicago was experiencing. Since that time, sociological theories have remained at the forefront of the scientific investigation of crime causation.

THE INTERCONNECTEDNESS OF SOCIOLOGICAL THEORIES

The biological and psychological theories of criminal behavior (Chapter 4) share the assumption that such behavior is caused by some underlying physical or mental condition that separates the criminal from the noncriminal. They seek to identify the kind of person who becomes a criminal and to find the factors that caused the person to engage in criminal behavior. Biological and psychological theories offer insight into individual cases, but they do not explain why crime rates vary from one neighborhood to the next, from group to group, within large urban areas, or within groups of individuals. Sociological theories seek the reasons for differences in crime rates in the social environment. These theories can be grouped into three general categories: strain, cultural deviance, and social control.[4]

The strain and cultural deviance theories formulated between 1925 and 1940 are still popular today and focus on the social forces that cause people to engage in criminal activity. These theories laid the foundation for the subcultural theories we discuss in Chapter 6. Social control theories (Chapter 7) take a different approach: They are based on the assumption that the motivation to commit crime is part of human nature. Consequently, social control theories seek to discover why people do not commit crime. They examine the ability of social groups and institutions to make their rules effective.

Strain and cultural deviance theories both assume that social class and criminal behavior are related, but they differ about the nature of the relationship. **Strain theory** argues that all members of society subscribe to one set of cultural values—that of the middle class. One of the most important middle-class values is economic success. Because lower-class persons do not have legitimate means to reach this goal, they turn to illegitimate means in desperation. **Cultural deviance theories** claim that lower-class people have a different set of values, which tend to conflict with the values of the middle class. Consequently, when lower-class persons conform to their own value system, they may be violating conventional or middle-class norms.

ANOMIE: ÉMILE DURKHEIM

Imagine a clock with all its parts finely synchronized. It functions with precision. It keeps perfect time. But if one tiny weight or small spring breaks down, the whole mechanism will not function properly. One way of studying a society is to look at its component parts in an effort to find out how they relate to one another. In other words, we look at the structure of a society to see how it functions. If the society is stable, its parts operating smoothly, the social arrangements are functional. Such a society is marked by cohesion, cooperation, and consensus. But if the component parts are arranged in such a way as to threaten the social order, the arrangements are said to be dysfunctional. In a class-oriented society, for example, the classes tend to be in conflict.

The Structural-Functionalist Perspective

The structural-functionalist perspective was developed by Émile Durkheim (1858–1917) before the end of the nineteenth century.[5] At the time, positivist biological theories, which relied on the search for individual differences between criminals and noncriminals, were dominant. So at a time when science was searching for the abnormality of the criminal, Durkheim was writing about the normality of crime in society. To him, the explanation of human conduct, and indeed human misconduct, lies not in the individual but in the group and the social organization. It is in this context that he introduced the term "anomie," the breakdown of social order as a result of the loss of standards and values.[6]

Throughout his career, Durkheim was preoccupied with the effects of social change. He believed that when a simple society develops into a modern, urbanized one, the intimacy needed to sustain a common set of norms declines. Groups become fragmented, and in the absence of a common set of rules, the actions and expectations of people in one sector may clash with those of people in another. As behavior becomes unpredictable, the system gradually breaks down, and the society is in a state of anomie.

Anomie and Suicide

Durkheim illustrated his concept of anomie in a discussion not of crime, but of suicide.[7] He suggested several reasons why suicide was more common in some groups than in others. For our purposes, we are interested in the particular form of suicide he called "anomic suicide." When he analyzed statistical data, he found that suicide rates increased during times of sudden economic change, whether that change was major depression or unexpected prosperity. In periods of rapid change, people are abruptly thrown into unfamiliar situations. Rules that once guided behavior no longer hold.

Consider the events of the 1920s. Wealth came easily to many people in those heady, prosperous years. Toward the end, through July, August, and September of 1929, the New York stock market soared to new heights. Enormous profits were made from speculation. But on October 24, 1929, a day history records as Black Thursday, the stock market crashed. Thirteen million shares of stock were sold. As more and more shares were offered for sale, their value plummeted. In the wake of the crash, a severe depression overtook the country and then the world. Banks failed. Mortgages were foreclosed. Businesses went bankrupt. People lost their jobs. Lifestyles changed overnight. Many people were driven to sell apples on street corners to survive, and they had to stand in mile-long breadlines to get food to feed their families. Suddenly the norms by which people lived were no longer relevant. People became disoriented and confused. Suicide rates rose.

It is not difficult to understand rising suicide rates in such circumstances, but why would rates also rise at a time of sudden prosperity? According to Durkheim, the same factors are at work in both situations. What causes the problems is not the amount of money available but the sudden change. Durkheim believed that human desires are boundless, an "insatiable and bottomless abyss."[8] Because nature does not set such strict biological limits on the capabilities of humans as it does on those of other animals, he argued, we have developed social rules that put a realistic cap on our aspirations. These regulations are incorporated into the individual conscience and thus make it possible for people to feel fulfilled.

But with a sudden burst of prosperity, expectations change. When the old rules no longer determine how rewards are distributed among members of society, there is no longer any restraint on what people want. Once again the system breaks down. Thus, whether sudden change causes great prosperity or great depression, the result is the same—anomie.

STRAIN THEORY

A few generations after Durkheim, American sociologist Robert Merton (1910–2003) also related the crime problem to anomie. But his conception differs somewhat from Durkheim's. The real problem, Merton argued, is created not by sudden social change but by a social structure that holds out the same goals to all its members without giving them equal means to achieve them. This lack of integration between what the culture calls for and what the structure permits, the former encouraging success and the latter preventing it, can cause norms to break down because they no longer are effective guides to behavior.

Merton borrowed the term "anomie" from Durkheim to describe this breakdown of the normative system. According to Merton,

> it is only when a system of cultural values extols, virtually above all else, certain common symbols of success for the population at large while its social structure rigorously restricts or completely eliminates access to approved modes of acquiring these symbols for a considerable part of the same population, that antisocial behavior ensues on a considerable scale.[9]

From this perspective, the social structure is the root of the crime problem (hence, the approach Merton takes is sometimes called a "structural explanation"). "Strain theory," the name given by contemporary criminologists to Merton's explanation of criminal behavior, assumes that people are law-abiding but when under great pressure will resort to crime. Disparity between goals and means provides that pressure.

Merton's Theory of Anomie

Merton argued that in a class-oriented society, opportunities to get to the top are not equally distributed. Very few members of the lower class ever get there. His anomie theory emphasizes the importance of two elements in any society: (1) cultural aspirations, or goals that people believe are worth striving for, and (2) institutionalized means or accepted ways to attain the desired ends. If a society is to be stable, these two elements must be reasonably well integrated; in other words, there should be means for individuals to reach the goals that are important to them. Disparity between goals and means fosters frustration, which leads to strain.

Merton's theory explains crime in the United States in terms of the wide disparities in income among the various classes. Statistics clearly demonstrate that such disparities exist.

- The official poverty rate in 2010 was 15.1 percent—up from 14.3 percent in 2009. This was the third consecutive annual increase in the poverty rate. Since 2007, the poverty rate has increased by 2.6 percentage points, from 12.5 percent to 15.1 percent.

- In 2010, 46.2 million people were in poverty, up from 43.6 million in 2009—the fourth consecutive annual increase in the number of people in poverty.

- Between 2009 and 2010, the poverty rate increased for non-Hispanic whites (from 9.4 percent to 9.9 percent), for blacks (from 25.8 percent to 27.4 percent), and for Hispanics (from 25.3 percent to 26.6 percent). For Asians, the 2010 poverty rate (12.1 percent) was not statistically different from the 2009 poverty rate.

- The poverty rate in 2010 (15.1 percent) was the highest poverty rate since 1993 but was 7.3 percentage points lower than the poverty rate in 1959, the first year for which poverty estimates are available.

- The number of people in poverty in 2010 (46.2 million) is the largest number in the 52 years for which poverty estimates have been published.

- Between 2009 and 2010, the poverty rate increased for children under age 18 (from 20.7 percent to 22.0 percent) and people aged 18 to 64 (from 12.9 percent to 13.7 percent), but was not statistically different for people aged 65 and older (9.0 percent).[10]

It is not, however, solely wealth or income that determines people's position on a social ladder that ranges from the homeless to the very, very rich who live on great estates. In 1966, Oscar Lewis described the "culture of poverty" that exists in inner-city slums. It is characterized by helplessness, apathy, cynicism, and distrust of social institutions such as schools and the police.[11] A few years later, Gunnar Myrdal argued that there is a worldwide "underclass, whose members lack the education and skills necessary to compete with the rest of society."[12] And in 1987, William Julius Wilson depicted the ranks of the underclass as the "truly disadvantaged." This group of urban inner-city dwellers is at the bottom of the ladder. Basic institutions such as the school and the family have deteriorated. There is little community cohesion. The people remain isolated—steeped in their own ghetto culture and the anger and aggression that accompany their marginal existence.[13]

In our society, opportunities to move up the social ladder exist, but they are not equally distributed. A child born to a single, uneducated, 13-year-old girl living in a slum has practically no chance to move up, whereas the child of a middle-class family has a better-than-average chance of reaching a professional or business position. Yet all people in our society share the same goals. And those goals are shaped by billions of advertising dollars spent each year to spread the message that everyone can tote around MacBook Air, drive an Aston Martin, and vacation in Santorini.

The mystique is reinforced by instant lottery millionaires, the earnings of superstar athletes, and rags-to-riches stories of people such as Ray Kroc. Kroc, a high school dropout, believed that a 15-cent hamburger with a 10-cent bag of French fries could make dining out affordable for

http://www.census.gov/hhes/www/poverty/about/overview/index.html

Institutional Imbalance and Crime

In their book *Crime and the American Dream*, Steven Messner and Richard Rosenfeld agree with Merton that the material success goal is pervasive in American culture. In essence, the American dream is quite clear—succeed by any means necessary, even if those means are illegitimate.[36] The American dream, then, encourages high crime rates. Messner and Rosenfeld expand on Merton's ideas on the relationships among culture, social structure, anomie, and crime rates (Figure 5.2). High crime rates, they contend, are more than a result of striving for monetary gains. They also result from the fact that our major social institutions do not have the capacity to control behavior. These institutions fail to counterbalance the ethos of the American dream. The dominance of economic institutions manifests itself in three ways: devaluation of other institutions, the accommodation of other institutions to economic needs, and the penetration of economic norms.

• *The devaluation of noneconomic roles and functions.* Performance in the economic world takes precedence over performance in other institutional settings: Noneconomic functions are devalued. Education is important, for example, only because it promises economic gains. Learning for its own sake is relatively unimportant. In the context of the family, the home owner is more important than the homemaker. In politics, too, there is a devaluation: If a citizen does not vote, there may be mild disapproval; if an adult citizen does not work, he or she loses status.

• *The accommodation of other institutions to economic needs.* In situations where institutions compete, noneconomic ones **accommodate.** Family life is generally dominated by work schedules. Individuals go to school primarily to get a "good" job. Once out of school, those who return usually do so to get a better job. In political accommodation, government strives to maintain an environment hospitable to business.

• *The penetration of economic norms.* Penetration of economic norms into those of other institutions is widespread. Spouses become partners in "managing" the home, businesspeople/politicians campaign for public office claiming they will "run the

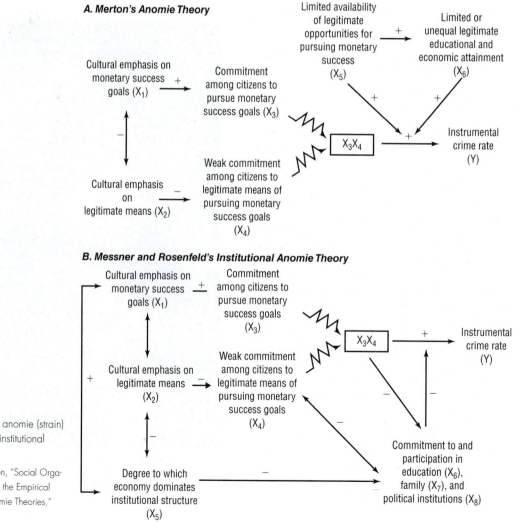

FIGURE 5.2 Comparing Merton's anomie (strain) theory with Messner and Rosenfeld's institutional anomie (strain) theory.

Source: Eric P. Baumer and Regan Gustafson, "Social Organization and Instrumental Crime: Assessing the Empirical Validity of Classic and Contemporary Anomie Theories," *Criminology,* **45** (2007): 617–663.

country like a corporation," and economic terms such as "accountability" are adopted by educators.

Messner and Rosenfeld contend that as long as there is a disproportionate emphasis on monetary rewards, the crime problem will increase. In fact, if economic opportunities increase, there may be an increase in the preoccupation with material success. Crime will decrease only when noneconomic institutions have the capacity to control behavior.[37]

Freda Adler's study of 10 countries with low crime rates supports this argument. She demonstrates that where economic concerns have not devalued informal social control institutions such as family, community, or religion, crime rates are relatively low and stable. This finding held for non-industrialized *and* highly industrialized societies.[38]

General Strain Theory

Sociologist Robert Agnew substantially revised Merton's theory in order to provide a broader explanation of criminal behavior.[39] The reformulation is called **general strain theory.** Agnew argues that failure to achieve material goals (the focal point of Merton's theory) is not the only reason for committing crime. Criminal behavior may also be related to the anger and frustration that result when an individual is treated in a way he or she does not want to be treated in a social relationship. General strain theory explains the range of strain-producing events:

• *Strain caused by failure to achieve positively valued goals.* This type of strain is based on Merton's view that lower-class individuals are often prevented from achieving monetary success goals through legitimate channels. When people do not have the money to get what they want, some of them turn to illegitimate means to get it.

• *Stress caused by the removal of positively valued stimuli from the individual.* This type of strain results from the actual or anticipated loss of something or someone important in one's life: death of a loved one, breakup with a boyfriend/girlfriend, divorce of parents, move to a new school. Criminal behavior results when individuals seek revenge against those responsible, try to prevent the loss, or escape through illicit drug use.

• *Strain caused by the presentation of negative stimuli.* The third major source of strain involves stressful life situations. Adverse situations and events may include child abuse, criminal victimization, bad experiences with peers, school problems, or verbal threats. Criminal behavior in these situations may result when an individual tries to run away from the situation, end the problem, or seek revenge.[40]

According to Agnew, each type of strain increases an individual's feelings of anger, fear, or depression. The most critical reaction for general strain theory is anger, an emotion that increases the desire for revenge, helps justify aggressive behavior, and stimulates individuals to act.

General strain theory acknowledges that not all persons who experience strain become criminals. Many are equipped to cope with their frustration and anger. Some come up with rationalizations ("don't really need it anyway"), others use techniques for physical relief (a good workout at the gym), and still others walk away from the condition causing stress (get out of the house). The capacity to deal with strain depends on personal experience throughout life. It involves the influence of peers, temperament, attitudes, and, in the case of pressing financial problems, economic resources. Recent empirical tests show preliminary support for general strain theory.[41] By broadening Merton's concepts, general strain theory has the potential to explain a wide range of criminal and delinquent behavior, including aggressive acts, drug abuse, and property offenses, among individuals from all social classes.

THEORY INFORMS POLICY

Strain theory has helped us develop a crime-prevention strategy. If, as the theory tells us, frustration builds up in people who have few means for reaching their goals, it makes sense to design programs that give lower-class people a bigger stake in society.

Head Start

It was in the 1960s that President Lyndon Johnson inaugurated the Head Start program as part of a major antipoverty campaign. The goal of Head Start is to make children of low-income families more socially competent, better able to deal with their present environment and their later responsibilities. The youngsters get a boost (or a head start) in a 1-year preschool developmental program that is intended to prevent them from dropping out of society. Program components include community and parental involvement, an 8-to-1 child–staff ratio, and daily evaluation and involvement of all the children in the planning of and responsibility for their own activities.

Because a 1-year program could not be expected to affect the remainder of a child's life, Project Follow Through was developed in an effort to provide the same opportunities for Head Start youngsters during elementary school. What began as a modest summer experience for half a million preschool children has expanded into a year-round program that provides educational and social services to millions of young people and their families. Head Start is a poignant example of a program intended to lower stress in the group most likely to develop criminal behavior.

A 2005 evaluation of Head Start programs sought evidence of the impact of Head Start on children's school readiness and on parental practices that support children's development. The study also examined the conditions under which Head Start achieves its greatest impact and for which children. Data from the four domains studied revealed, at best, small to moderate associations between the program objectives and results.[42]

- *Parenting practices domain.* The key findings in this domain, consisting of three constructs, are these:

  For children who entered the program as 3-year-olds, there are small statistically significant impacts in two of the three parenting constructs, including a higher use of educational activities and a lower use of physical discipline by parents of Head Start children. There were no significant impacts for safety practices.

  For children who entered the program as 4-year-olds, there are small statistically significant impacts on parents' use of educational activities. No significant impacts were found for discipline or safety practices.

- *Cognitive domain.* The cognitive domain consists of six constructs, each comprising one or more measures. The key findings in this domain are these:

  There are small to moderate statistically significant positive impacts for both 3- and 4-year-old children on several measures across four of the six cognitive constructs, including pre-reading, pre-writing, vocabulary, and parent reports of children's literacy skills.

  No significant impacts were found for the constructs oral comprehension and phonological awareness or early mathematics skills for either age group.

- *Social-emotional domain.* The social-emotional domain consists of three constructs, each comprising one or more parent-reported measures. The key findings in this domain are these:

  For children who entered the study as 3-year-olds, there is a small statistically significant impact in one of the three social–emotional constructs—problem behaviors.

  There were no statistically significant impacts on social skills and approaches to learning or on social competencies for 3-year-olds.

  No significant impacts were found for children entering the program as 4-year-olds.

- *Health domain.* The key findings in this domain, consisting of two constructs, are these:

  For 3-year-olds, there are small to moderate statistically significant impacts in both constructs: higher parent reports of children's access to health care and reportedly better health status for children enrolled in Head Start.

  For children who entered the program as 4-year-olds, there are moderate statistically significant impacts on access to health care, but no significant impacts on health status.

Perry Preschool Project

Another program that tried to ameliorate the disparity between goals and means in society was the Perry Preschool Project, begun in 1962 on the south side of Ypsilanti, Michigan. Its purpose was to develop skills that would give youngsters the means of getting ahead at school and in the workplace, thereby reducing the amount and seriousness of delinquent behavior. Overall, 123 black children 3 and 4 years old participated for 2 years, 5 days a week, 2½ hours a day. The program provided a teacher for every five children, weekly visits by a teacher to a child's home, and a follow-up of every child annually until age 11 and thereafter at ages 14, 15, and 19.

There is little doubt about the effectiveness of the project. The participants did better in several areas than a group that had not participated:

- Employment rates doubled.
- Rates of postsecondary education doubled.
- Teenage pregnancy was cut in half.
- The high school graduation rate was higher.
- Arrest rates were significantly lower (Figure 5.3).[43]

Job Corps

Yet another survivor of President Johnson's War on Poverty is the federal Job Corps program. It aims at "the worst of the worst," as Senator Orrin Hatch of Utah said.[44] The program enables neglected teenagers—otherwise headed for juvenile detention or jail—to master work habits that they did not learn at home. In 2007, 62,000 young people were serving in the Job Corps. Most of them had enlisted on the basis of recruitment posters, like those distributed by the armed forces. The average length of stay in the corps is just short of a year, at an annual cost of $18,831. That sounds expensive, but juvenile detention costs $29,600 a year—and residential drug-treatment centers cost $19,000. Since its inception in 1964, the program has served over 1.8 million people.[45]

Over two-thirds of former Job Corps members find jobs, and 17 percent go on to higher education. Research has shown that the Job Corps returns $1.46 for every dollar spent, because of increased tax revenue and decreased cost of welfare, crime, and incarceration. Over two-thirds of Job Corps members are members of minority groups; over 80 percent are high school dropouts. A recent advisory committee evaluation of Job Corps revealed some promising placement rates.

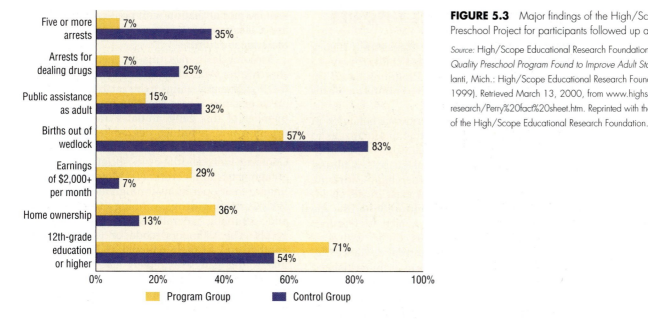

FIGURE 5.3 Major findings of the High/Scope Perry Preschool Project for participants followed up at age 27.

Source: High/Scope Educational Research Foundation, *High-Quality Preschool Program Found to Improve Adult Status* (Ypsilanti, Mich.: High/Scope Educational Research Foundation, 1999). Retrieved March 13, 2000, from www.highscope.org/research/Perry%20fact%20sheet.htm. Reprinted with the permission of the High/Scope Educational Research Foundation.

In a report to the U.S. Congress on which programs prevent crime, researchers at the University of Maryland classified the Job Corps program as "promising." Its potential for success includes the resocialization of youth through prosocial role models, a residential requirement that reduces contact with antisocial groups, and its vocational focus and attachment to the job market (Table 5.2).[46]

TABLE 5.2 Job Corps Common Measures—Performance and Results, Program Years 2004–2006*

Performance Goal 1.1B: Improve the educational achievements of Job Corps students and increase participation of Job Corps graduates in employment and education

Indicator	2004†		2005		2006	
	Target	Result	Target	Result	Target	Result
1. *Placement:* The percent of participants who will enter employment or enroll in postsecondary education or training/occupational skills training in the first quarter after exit	85%	84%	85%	80%	87%	75%
2. *Certificate Attainment:* The percent of students who will attain a GED, high school diploma, or certificate while enrolled in the program	64%	64%	64%	60%	65%	56%
3. *Literacy/Numeracy:* The percent of students who will achieve literacy or numeracy gains of one Adult Basic Education (ABE) level, equivalent to two grade levels	45%	47%	45%	58%	58%	56%

*2006 data through 3/31/07.

†Placement (for 2004 and 2005) was defined as the percent of Job Corps graduates (within one year of program exit) and former enrollees (within 90 days of program exit) who will enter employment or enroll in postsecondary education or advanced training/occupational skills training.

SOURCE: *Advisory Committee on Job Corps: Report and Recommendations to the Secretary of Labor.* Washington, DC: U.S. Department of Labor, April 2008, p. 34. Available at http://www.docstoc.com/docs/841778/Advisory-Committee-on-Job-Corps-Report.

CULTURAL DEVIANCE THEORIES

The programs that emanate from strain theory attempt to give underprivileged children ways to achieve middle-class goals. Programs based on cultural deviance theories concentrate on teaching middle-class values.

Strain theory attributes criminal behavior in the United States to the striving of all citizens to conform with the conventional values of the middle class, primarily financial success. Cultural deviance theories, on the other hand, attribute crime to a set of values that exist in disadvantaged neighborhoods. Conformity with the lower-class value system, which determines behavior in slum areas, causes conflict with society's laws. Both strain and cultural deviance theories locate the causes of crime in the marginalized position of those at the lowest stratum in a class-based society.

Scholars who view crime as resulting from cultural values that permit, or even demand, behavior in violation of the law are called "cultural deviance theorists." The three major cultural deviance theories are social disorganization, differential association, and culture conflict. **Social disorganization theory** focuses on the development of high-crime areas in which there is a disintegration of conventional values caused by rapid industrialization, increased immigration, and urbanization. **Differential association theory** maintains that people learn to commit crime as a result of contact with antisocial values, attitudes, and criminal behavior patterns. **Culture conflict theory** states that different groups learn different conduct norms (rules governing behavior) and that the conduct norms of some groups may clash with conventional middle-class rules.

All three theories contend that criminals and delinquents do in fact conform—but to norms that deviate from those of the dominant middle class. Before we examine the specific theories that share the cultural deviance perspective, we need to explore the nature of cultural deviance.

The Nature of Cultural Deviance

When you drive through rural Lancaster County in Pennsylvania or through Holmes County in Ohio or through Elkhart and Lagrange Counties in Indiana, in the midst of fertile fields and well-tended orchards, you will find isolated villages with prosperous and well-maintained farmhouses but no electricity. You will see the farmers and their families traveling in horse-drawn buggies, dressed in homespun clothes, and wearing brimmed hats. These people are Amish. Their ancestors came to this country from the German-speaking Rhineland region as early as 1683 to escape persecution for their fundamentalist Christian beliefs. Shunning motors, electricity,

jewelry, and affiliation with political parties, they are a *nonconformist* community within a highly materialistic culture.

Motorcycle gangs made their appearance shortly after World War II. The Hell's Angels was the first of many gangs to be established in slum areas of cities across the country. To become a member of this gang, initiates are subjected to grueling and revolting degradations. They are conditioned to have allegiance only to the gang. Contacts with middle-class society are usually antagonistic and criminal. Motorcycle gangs finance their operations through illegal activities, such as dealing drugs, running massage parlors and gambling operations, and selling stolen goods. The members' code of loyalty to one another and to their national and local groups makes the gangs extremely effective criminal organizations.

The normative systems of the Amish and the bikers are at odds with the conventional norms of the society in which they live. Both deviate from middle-class standards. Sociologists define **deviance** as any behavior that members of a social group define as violating their norms. As we can see, the concept of deviance can be

■ A man with a Hitler tattoo on his back sells white-power T-shirts at a Ku Klux Klan cross-burning rally in Hico, Texas. Deviant hate groups such as these exist throughout the United States and in many foreign countries.

FIGURE 5.4 Social disorganization.

Source: Donald J. Shoemaker, *Theories of Delinquency: An Examination of Explanations of Delinquent Behavior,* 4th ed. (2000), Figure 4 (p. 79). By permission of Oxford University Press, Inc. www.oup.com.

Rapid changes in industrialization or urbanization or increased immigration	→	Decline in the effectiveness of institutional and informal social control forces in communities or neighborhoods; that is, social disorganization	→	Development of delinquency areas, as exemplified by high rates of delinquency and the existence of delinquent traditions and values in specific geographical areas or neighborhoods

applied to noncriminal acts that members of a group view as peculiar or unusual (the lifestyle of the Amish) or to criminal acts (behavior that society has made illegal). The Hell's Angels fit the expected stereotype of deviance as negative; the Amish culture demonstrates that deviance is not necessarily bad, just different.

Cultural deviance theorists argue that our society is made up of various groups and subgroups, each with its own standards of right and wrong. Behavior considered normal in one group may be considered deviant by another. As a result, those who conform to the standards of cultures considered deviant are behaving in accordance with their own norms but may be breaking the law—the norms of the dominant culture.

You may wonder whether the Hell's Angels are outcasts in the slum neighborhoods where they live. They are not. They may even be looked up to by younger boys in places where toughness and violence are not only acceptable but also appropriate. Indeed, groups such as the Hell's Angels may meet the needs of youngsters who are looking for a way to be important in a disorganized ghetto that offers few opportunities to gain status.

Social Disorganization Theory

Scholars associated with the University of Chicago in the 1920s became interested in socially disorganized Chicago neighborhoods where criminal values and traditions replaced conventional values and were transmitted from one generation to the next. In their classic work *The Polish Peasant in Europe and America,* W. I. Thomas and Florian Znaniecki described the difficulties Polish peasants experienced when they left their rural life in Europe to settle in an industrialized city in America.[47] The scholars compared the conditions the immigrants had left in Poland with those they found in Chicago. They also investigated the immigrants' assimilation.

Older immigrants, they found, were not greatly affected by the move because they managed, even within the urban slums, to continue living as they had lived in Poland. But the second generation did not grow up on Polish farms; these people were city dwellers, and they were American. They had few of the old Polish traditions but were not

yet assimilated into the new ones. The norms of the stable, homogeneous folk society were not transferable to the anonymous, materially oriented urban settings. Rates of crime and delinquency rose. Thomas and Znaniecki attributed this result to *social disorganization*—the breakdown of effective social bonds, family and neighborhood associations, and social controls in neighborhoods and communities (Figure 5.4).

The Park and Burgess Model

Thomas and Znaniecki's study greatly influenced other scholars at the University of Chicago. Among them were Robert Park and Ernest Burgess, who advanced the study of social disorganization by introducing ecological analysis into the study of human society.[48] Ecology is the study of plants and animals in relation to each other and to their natural habitat, the place where they live and grow. Ecologists study these interrelationships, how the balance of nature continues, and how organisms survive. Much the same approach is used by social ecologists, scholars who study the interrelationships of people and their environment.

In their study of social disorganization, Park and Burgess examined area characteristics instead of criminals for explanations of high crime rates. They developed the idea of natural urban areas, consisting of concentric zones extending out from the downtown central business district to the commuter zone at the fringes of the city. Each zone had its own structure and organization, its own cultural characteristics and unique inhabitants (Figure 5.5). Zone I, at the center—called the "Loop" because the downtown business district of Chicago is demarcated by a loop of the elevated train system—was occupied by commercial headquarters, law offices, retail establishments, and some commercial recreation. Zone II was the zone in transition, where the city's poor, unskilled, and disadvantaged lived in dilapidated tenements next to old factories. Zone III housed the working class, people whose jobs enabled them to enjoy some of the comforts the city had to offer at its fringes. The middle class—professionals, small-business owners, and the managerial class—lived in Zone IV. Zone V was the commuter zone of satellite towns and suburbs.

Crime Surfing WWW

www.streetgangs.com/bibliography/gangbib.html

Learn more about gangs and street crimes.

investigation, researchers asked about the impact of Atlantic City casinos and the related increased crime rate on real estate in three southern New Jersey counties.[62] They found a sizable drop in house values. Those communities most accessible to Atlantic City suffered the worst economic consequences.

Middle- and working-class people tend to escape the urban ghetto, leaving behind the most disadvantaged. When you add to those disadvantaged the people moving in from outside who are also severely disadvantaged, over time these areas become places of concentrated poverty, isolated from the mainstream.

Some social ecologists argue that communities, like people, go through life cycles. Neighborhood deterioration precedes rising crime rates. When crime begins to rise, neighborhoods go from owner-occupied to renter-occupied housing, with a significant decline in the socioeconomic status of residents and an increase in population density. Later in the community life cycle, there is a renewed interest on the part of investors in buying up the cheap real estate with the idea of renovating it and making a profit (gentrification).[63]

Social Unrest in Los Angeles

On April 29, 1992, Los Angeles exploded in a firestorm of riots. It was the day of the announcement of the not-guilty verdicts in the trial of the four L.A. Police Department officers accused of beating black motorist Rodney King. While the variety of crimes that were committed during the week of rioting and looting might serve as case studies for many of the explanations of criminal behavior we consider in this section, the context in which the riots occurred provides a clear example of social disorganization. We shall let excerpts from the report of a special advisory committee that assessed the event tell the story, beginning with a description of the riots:

> Crowds began to congregate in South Central Los Angeles to protest the verdicts. As these street corner protests began to grow in number and size, they first became angry and then turned violent. . . . Over the course of the next six days, the reaction escalated into a terrifying reign of violence, widespread looting, and mass destruction of property in many communities across the City. . . . The perpetrators of this violence were not confined to any single racial or ethnic classification. . . . People of all ages and gender participated in the looting. . . .

A Context for Violence

The Rodney King incident did not occur in a vacuum but within the context of the entire social, economic, and political climate of the City. In the past decade,

Los Angeles has experienced rapid demographic and economic changes. The population of the City as a whole has grown by 17 percent during that period and now exceeds 3.5 million people. At the same time, the makeup of the population has shifted to 40 percent Hispanic, 37 percent Anglo, 13 percent African-American, 9 percent Asian-American, and 1 percent Native American. As the ethnic makeup of the City has changed fundamentally, so too has the economic stratification of its population. By 1990, more than 18.5 percent of Los Angeles residents were living below the poverty line.

Since its beginnings as a Spanish mission, the City has seen a steady immigration of diverse peoples. Today, the Los Angeles Unified School District consists of 700 schools with approximately 640,000 students who speak 100 different languages. This influx of people provides an enormous amount of creativity and energy . . . but the rapid growth also frustrates the development of a common civic culture. Indeed, the increasingly diverse population of Los Angeles is viewed as increasingly difficult to govern and . . . to police.

A Tinderbox Ready to Explode

The decade of the 1980s brought fewer jobs—but plenty of drugs, crime and violence—to many Los Angeles neighborhoods. Los Angeles street gangs now had crack cocaine. Like no other drug before it, crack had a devastating impact on families. . . . By early 1992, the problems of the inner city—gangs, crime, crack cocaine, poverty and homelessness, and racial and ethnic tension—had come to dominate daily fife for a great many residents of Los Angeles. The struggle to preserve a sense of community in the City had begun in earnest. The City of Los Angeles had become a tinderbox ready to explode at the striking of a single match.(l)

Source

1. *The City in Crisis: A Report by the Special Advisor to the Board of Police Commissioners on the Civil Disorder in Los Angeles,* October. 21, 1992, pp. 11, 13, 23, 34–35, 41–12.

Evaluation: Social Disorganization Theory

Although their work has had a significant impact, social ecologists have not been immune to challenges. Their work has been criticized for its focus on how crime patterns are transmitted, rather than on how they start in the first place. The approach has also been faulted for failing to explain why delinquents stop committing crime as they grow older, why most people in socially disorganized areas do not commit criminal acts, and why some bad neighborhoods seem to be insulated from crime. Finally, critics claim that this approach does not come to grips with middle-class delinquency.

Clearly, however, modern criminology owes a debt to social disorganization theorists, particularly to Shaw and McKay, who in the 1920s began to look at the characteristics of people and places and to relate both to crime. There is now a vast body of research for which they laid the groundwork.

Theorists of the Chicago School were the first social scientists to suggest that most crime is committed by normal people responding in expected ways to their immediate surroundings, rather than by abnormal individuals acting out individual pathologies. If social disorganization is at the root of the problem, crime control must involve social organization. The community, not individuals, needs treatment. Helping the community, then, should lower its crime rate.

The Chicago Area Project

Social disorganization theory was translated into practice in 1934 with the establishment of the Chicago Area Project (CAP), an experiment in neighborhood reorganization. The project was initiated by the Institute for Juvenile Research, at which Clifford Shaw and Henry McKay were working. It coordinated the existing community support groups—local schools, churches, labor unions, clubs, and merchants. Special efforts were made to control delinquency through recreational facilities, summer camps, better law enforcement, and the upgrading of neighborhood schools, sanitation, and general appearance.

In 1994, this first community-based delinquency-prevention program could boast 60 years of achievement. South Chicago remains an area of poverty and urban marginalization, dotted with boarded-up buildings and signs of urban decay, though the pollution from the nearby steel mills is under control. But the Chicago Area Project initiated by Shaw and McKay is as vibrant as ever, with its three-pronged attack on delinquency: direct service, advocacy, and community involvement. Residents, from clergy to gang members, are working with CAP to keep kids out of trouble, to help those in trouble, and to clean up the neighborhoods. "In fact, in those communities where area projects have been in operation for a number of years, incidents of crime and delinquency have decreased" (Figure 5.6).[64]

Operation Weed and Seed and Others

Operation Weed and Seed is a federal, state, and local effort to improve the quality of life in targeted high-crime urban areas across the country. The strategy is to "weed" out negative influences (drugs, crime) and to "seed" the neighborhoods with prevention and intervention.

When the program began in 1991, there were three target areas—Kansas City, Missouri; Trenton, New Jersey; and Omaha, Nebraska. By 1999, the number of target areas had increased to 200 sites.

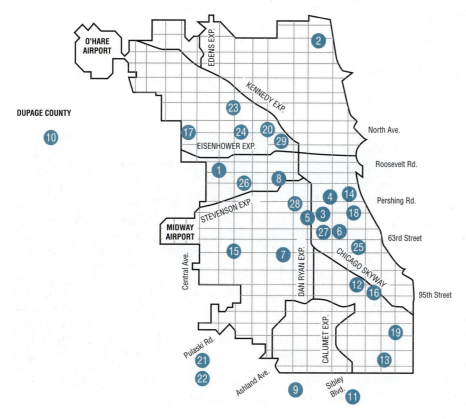

FIGURE 5.6 CAP affiliates now dot the Chicago landscape, from (1) Agape Youth Development/Family Services at 320 South Spaulding (East Garfield) and (2) Alternatives, Inc., at 1126 West Granville Avenue (Rogers Park—Uptown) to (28) Wentworth Residents United for Survival at 3752 South Wells (Wentworth Gardens) and (29) Youth Service Committee of the West Side at 1832 West Washington (Henry Horner Homes).

Source: www.chicagoareaproject.org/map.html.

An eight-state evaluation showed that the effectiveness of Operation Weed and Seed varied by the original severity of the crime problems, the strength of the established network of community organizations, early seeding with constant weeding, active leadership of key community members, and the formation of partnerships among local organizations.[65]

Another community action project has concentrated on revitalizing a Puerto Rican slum community. Sister Isolina Ferre worked for 10 years in the violent Navy Yard section of Brooklyn, New York. In 1969, she returned to Ponce Plaza, a poverty-stricken area in Ponce, Puerto Rico, infested with disease, crime, and unemployment. The area's 16,000 people had no doctors, nurses, dentists, or social agencies. The project began with a handful of missionaries, university professors, dedicated citizens, and community members who were willing to become advocates for their neighborhood. Among the programs begun were a large community health center, Big Brother/Big Sister programs for juveniles sent from the courts, volunteer tutoring, and recreational activities to take young people off the streets. Young photographers of Ponce Plaza, supplied with a few cameras donated by friends at Kodak, mounted an exhibit at the Metropolitan Museum of Art in New York. Regular fiestas have given community members a chance to celebrate their own achievements as well.[66]

Programs based on social disorganization theory attempt to bring conventional social values to disorganized communities. They provide an opportunity for young people to learn norms other than those of delinquent peer groups. Let us see how such learning takes place.

Differential Association Theory

What we eat, what we say, what we believe—in fact, the way we respond to any situation—depends on the culture in which we have been reared. In other words, to a very large extent, the social influences that people encounter determine their behavior. Whether a person becomes law-abiding or criminal, then, depends on contacts with criminal values, attitudes, definitions, and behavior patterns. This proposition underlies one of the most important theories of crime causation in American criminology—differential association.

Sutherland's Theory

In 1939, Edwin Sutherland introduced differential association theory in his textbook *Principles of Criminology*. Since then, scholars have read, tested, reexamined, and sometimes ridiculed this theory, which claimed to explain the development of all criminal behavior. The theory states that crime is learned through social interaction. People come into constant contact with "definitions favorable to violations of law" and "definitions unfavorable to violations of law." The ratio of these definitions—criminal to noncriminal—determines whether a person will engage in criminal behavior.[67] In formulating this theory, Sutherland relied heavily on Shaw and McKay's findings that delinquent values are transmitted within a community or group from one generation to the next.

Sutherland's Nine Propositions

Nine propositions explained the process by which this transmission of values takes place:

1. Criminal behavior is learned.

2. Criminal behavior is learned in interaction with other persons in a process of communication. A person does not become a criminal simply by living in a criminal environment. Crime is learned by participation with others in verbal and non-verbal communications.

A Latin Kings gang member teaches gang hand symbols to a child. Social interactions like these are learned and then transmitted from one generation to the next.

3. The principal part of the learning of criminal behavior occurs within intimate personal groups. Families and friends have the most influence on the learning of deviant behavior. Their communications far outweigh those of the mass media.

4. When criminal behavior is learned, the learning includes (a) techniques of committing the crime, which are sometimes very complicated, sometimes very simple and (b) the specific direction of motives, drives, rationalizations, and attitudes. Young delinquents learn not only how to shoplift, crack a safe, pick a lock, or roll a joint but also how to rationalize and defend their actions. One safecracker accompanied another safecracker for 1 year before he cracked his first safe.[68] In other words, criminals, too, learn skills and gain experience.

5. The specific direction of motives and drives is learned from definitions of the legal codes as favorable or unfavorable. In some societies, an individual is surrounded by persons who invariably define the legal codes as rules to be observed, while in others he or she is surrounded by persons whose definitions are favorable to the violation of the legal codes. Not everyone in our society agrees that the laws should be obeyed; some people define them as unimportant. In American society, where definitions are mixed, we have a culture conflict in relation to legal codes.

6. A person becomes delinquent because of an excess of definitions favorable to violation of law over definitions unfavorable to violation of law. This is the key principle of differential association. In other words, learning criminal behavior is not simply a matter of associating with bad companions. Rather, learning criminal behavior depends on how many definitions we learn that are favorable to law violation as opposed to those that are unfavorable to law violation.

7. Differential associations may vary in frequency, duration, priority, and intensity. The extent to which associations and definitions will result in criminality is related to the frequency of contacts, their duration, and their meaning to the individual.

8. The process of learning criminal behavior by association with criminal and anticriminal patterns involves all the mechanisms that are involved in any other learning. Learning criminal behavior patterns is very much like learning conventional behavior patterns and is not simply a matter of observation and imitation.

9. While criminal behavior is an expression of general needs and values, it is not explained by those general needs and values, since noncriminal behavior is an expression of the same needs and values. Shoplifters steal to get what they want.

Others work to get money to buy what they want. The motives—frustration, desire to accumulate goods or social status, low self-concept, and the like—cannot logically be the same because they explain both lawful and criminal behavior.

Tests of Differential Association Theory

Since Sutherland presented his theory 70 years ago, researchers have tried to determine whether his principles lend themselves to empirical measurement. James Short tested a sample of 126 boys and 50 girls at a training school and reported a consistent relationship between delinquent behavior and frequency, duration, priority, and intensity of interactions with delinquent peers.[69] Similarly, Travis Hirschi demonstrated that boys with delinquent friends are more likely to become delinquent.[70] Research on seventh- and eighth-grade students attending Rochester, New York, public schools in the late 1980s and early 1990s shows that gang membership is strongly associated with peer delinquency and the amount of delinquency and drug use.[71] Mark Warr demonstrated that while the duration of delinquent friendships over a long period of time has a greater effect than exposure over a short period, it is recent friendships rather than early friendships that have the greatest effect on delinquency.[72]

Adults have also been the subjects of differential association studies. Two thousand residents of New Jersey, Oregon, and Iowa were asked questions such as how many people they knew personally had engaged in deviant acts and how many were frequently in trouble. They were also asked how often they attended church (assumed to be related to definitions unfavorable to the violation of law). This differential association scale correlated significantly with crimes such as illegal gambling, income tax cheating, and theft.[73]

Evaluation: Differential Association Theory

Many researchers have attempted to validate Sutherland's differential association theory. Others have criticized it. Much of the criticism stems from errors in interpretation. Perhaps this type of error is best demonstrated by the critics who ask why it is that not everyone in heavy, prolonged contact with criminal behavior patterns becomes a criminal. Take, for argument's sake, corrections officers, who come into constant contact with more criminal associations than noncriminal ones. How do they escape learning to be law violators themselves?

The answer, of course, is that Sutherland does not tell us that individuals become criminal by associating with criminals or even by association with criminal behavior patterns. He tells us,

Cults—Culture Conflict—Crime

Warren Jeffs, president of the Fundamentalist Church of Jesus Christ of Latter-Day Saints (FLDS Church) gained international notoriety in May 2006 when he was placed on the FBI's Ten Most Wanted List for unlawful flight to avoid prosecution on Utah state charges related to his alleged arrangement of illegal marriages between his adult male followers and underage girls. Jeffs proclaimed himself a prophet of God and took as many as 70 wives. The 10,000-strong sect once dominated the towns of Colorado City (Arizona), Hildale (Utah), and Eldorado (Texas). Members believe a man must marry at least three wives in order to ascend to heaven. Women are taught that their path to heaven depends on being subservient to their husband.

In 2011, Jeffs was convicted of two felony counts of child sexual assault in Texas, and was sentenced to life in prison plus 20 years and a $10,000 fine, to be served consecutively, for sexual assault of both 12- and 15-year-old girls.

As the Hale-Bopp comet streaked through the sky over California on March 26, 1997, 39 members of the computer-related cult Heaven's Gate committed suicide at their luxurious Rancho Santa Fe, California, estate. The victims, males between 18 and 24 years old, fully expected to be conveyed to heaven by a waiting spacecraft.(1)

Heaven's Gate and the FLDS Church are but two of the many unusual cults that attract media coverage. In fact, in a ranking of the Top Ten cults, Heaven's Gate places only third. Consider the beliefs and practices of the following "cults":

10. *Raëlians:* If you believe UFOs spawned most religions, mind transfer is possible, and cloning can lead to reincarnation, then you might be a candidate for the Raëlian Church, started in France in the 1970s. A Raëlian follower made headlines in 2003 when she claimed to have conceived the first cloned human, but the event was later called a hoax.

9. *Cargo Cults:* If you're an island native isolated from modern society, encountering an AM/FM radio—or a boat full of symbol-clad soldiers—can be quite a shock. Many societies form a cult-like obsession with the technologically advanced "cargo." Some South Pacific islanders reportedly tote wooden guns and paint "USA" on their chests in rituals to attract more of the mysterious objects.

8. *Villa Baviera:* Also known as "Colonia Dignidad" (Dignidad Colony in English), Villa Baviera is a commune of German immigrants that was founded in 1961 by Paul Schäfer Schneider, a former Nazi party member. Human rights groups argue that Chile's secret police used the compound to torture and interrogate subjects, and former members have since issued apologies for molesting children.

7. *Order of the Solar Temple:* Luc Jouret, a Belgian religious leader and neo-Nazi, reportedly started the group in 1984 under Christian guises, namely the second coming of Christ and the Knights Templar. Jouret and other leaders in a Swiss village allegedly sacrificed a child they thought to be the Antichrist in 1994, days later committing suicide with dozens of followers. The French consider the organization to be criminal today.

6. *Bhagwan Shree Rajneesh's Communities:* Indian mystic Bhagwan Shree Rajneesh founded several cultist towns in Oregon through the 1980s—strangely, communities chock-full of Rolls Royce cars. Shree allegedly poisoned hundreds in The Dalles, Oregon, with salmonella bacteria in 1984 to rig local elections in his cult's favor. It's considered the first bioterrorist attack in the United States.

5. *Branch Davidians:* Considered to be a major split from the Seventh-Day Adventist Church, the Branch Davidians are famous for a 1993 FBI raid on their Waco, Texas, compound that left 76 dead. The event more or less resulted in the disappearance of what many consider to be a cult, whose members believed in an imminent apocalypse.

4. *Manson Family:* Charles Manson, who learned to play guitar in prison, formed his infamous "Family" of criminals in 1968. Manson thought an apocalyptic race war between whites and blacks would occur in 1969, after which the commune would rule the new world. When this didn't happen, he sent his followers on a string of murders.

3. *Heaven's Gate:* Followers of the Heaven's Gate cult, led primarily by Marshall Applewhite, thought Earth and everything on it were about to be "recycled" to a clean slate and believed that hitching a ride on comet Hale-Bopp in March 1997 could allow them to survive. Thirty-nine members (including Applewhite) poisoned themselves in shifts in a California mansion

rather, that a person becomes delinquent because of an "excess of definitions favorable to violation of law over definitions unfavorable to violation of law." The key word is "definitions." Furthermore, unfavorable definitions may be communicated by persons who are not robbers or murderers or tax evaders. They may, for example, be law-abiding parents who, over time, define certain situations in such a way that their children get verbal or nonverbal messages to the effect that antisocial behavior is acceptable.

Several scholars have asked whether the principles of differential association really explain all types of crime. They might explain theft, but what about homicide resulting from a jealous rage?[74] Why do some people who learn criminal

wearing Nike sneakers and armbands that read "Heaven's Gate Away Team."

2. *Aum Shinrikyo:* Founded some time in the mid-1980s, Aum Shinrikyo is famous for attacking Tokyo's subway system with Sarin gas in 1995, killing 12 and injuring more than 5,000. The cult's beliefs are often described as a hodgepodge of destructive aspects of various religions, and while many followers thought they would develop supernatural powers, others relished the chance to fight Japanese materialism.

1. *Peoples Temple:* Reverend Jim Jones started the Peoples Temple to help homeless, jobless, and sick people of all races, but former members claimed widespread abuse within the group. To remove his group from further scrutiny, Jones started a colony in the jungles of Guyana, where he hoped to build a tropical utopia. When a congressman visited the commune with three journalists to investigate the abuse claims, they were shot and killed when trying to leave. After the shootings, 913 commune members—including hundreds of children—drank poisoned Flavor Aid in a mass suicide.(2)

A cult is defined as "a great devotion to a person, idea, object, [or] movement; . . . a usually small group of people characterized by such devotion" (*Merriam Webster's Collegiate® Dictionary,* Tenth Edition). Most cults are marked by

- a dynamic leader;
- the willingness of members to surrender their worldly possessions;
- strict obedience to the leader;
- a communal social structure, with its own set of norms and values that

Shoko Asahara, leader of the Japanese cult Aum Shinrikyo.

are in conflict with those of conventional societies.

Experts estimate that there are 1,000 to 2,000 cults in America with as many as 4 to 6 million members.

Criminologists are interested primarily in destructive cults such as those in the Top Ten. There are other destructive cults of lesser rank. They exist worldwide. An Indian cult, for example, has its devotees "marry" their little daughters to a goddess. Upon reaching puberty, the little girls are sold into prostitution for about $200 each.(3)

A number of governments (China, Germany, and Russia) have outlawed cults. The Vatican has issued a strong report exhorting the church to fulfill the spiritual needs of the people to keep them from seeking salvation in cults.(4) The debate in America centers on First Amendment religious freedom. What governments, theologians, and criminologists have in common is their determination to bring alienated members of society into the mainstream to keep them out of destructive cults. But what is a destructive cult? Where should we draw the line between the freedom to exercise one's religious beliefs and the government's legitimate interest in protecting its citizens from coercive, destructive, and often violent religious groups?

Sources

1. Shirley Levung, "Deaths May Be Work of Religious Cult, Expert Says," *Boston Globe,* March. 27, 1997, p. A15.
2. LiveScience, Top 10 Crazy Cults, http://www.livescience.com/strangenews/top-10-crazy-cults-1.html. Reprinted by permission of Imaginova Corp.
3. "India Sex Cult's 'Handmaidens' Join Tribute to Hindu Goddess, Secret Society Forces Girls Who 'Marry' Yelamma into Prostitution," *Toronto Star,* January. 23, 1997, p. A16.
4. E. J. Dionne, "Vatican, Taking Some Blame, Cites Threat of Cults," *New York Times,* May 4, 1986, p. A10.

Questions for Discussion

1. Where and how can we draw the line between those cults that engage in violations of the criminal law (such as murder, arson, incitation to suicide, rape, child abuse, and prostitution) and those that have not (yet) committed any criminal act and therefore enjoy First Amendment privileges?
2. Both theologians and criminologists advocate narrowing the gap between conduct norms of deviant cultures (cults, sects) and the rules of mainstream society. How could either group practically accomplish that goal?

behavior patterns not engage in criminal acts? Why is no account taken of nonsocial variables, such as a desperate need for money? Furthermore, while the principles may explain how criminal behavior is transmitted, they do not account for the origin of criminal techniques and definitions. In other words, the theory does not tell us how the first criminal became a criminal.

Differential association theory suggests that there is an inevitability about the process of becoming a criminal. Once you reach the point where your definitions favorable to law violation exceed your definitions unfavorable to law violation, have you crossed an imaginary line into the criminal world? Even if we could add up the definitions encountered in a lifetime, could scientists measure the frequency, priority, duration, and intensity of differential associations?

Despite these criticisms, the theory has had a profound influence on criminology.[75] Generations of scholars have tested it empirically, modified it to incorporate psychologically based learning theory (see Chapter 4), and used it as a foundation for their own theorizing (Chapter 6). The theory has also had many policy implications.

If, according to differential association theory, a person can become criminal by learning definitions favorable to violating laws, it follows that programs that expose young people to definitions favorable to conventional behavior should reduce criminality. Educational efforts such as Head Start and the Perry Preschool Project have attempted to do just that. The same theory underlies many of the treatment programs for young school dropouts and pregnant teenagers.

An innovative Ohio program is trying to break the vicious cycle between poverty– welfare–school dropout–drugs–delinquency and teenage pregnancy. This program, LEAP (for learning, earning, and parenting), provides financial rewards for teenage single parents to stay in, or return to, school and deductions from the welfare checks of those who do not participate in education. A 1993 evaluation found that the program, which costs the state very little, has been moderately successful. Success appears to increase with increased counseling and aid services. Several states (for example, Virginia, Florida, Maryland, and Oklahoma) have instituted similar "learnfare" programs, while others are considering this option.[76]

Recently, schools in Chicago, New York, Boston, Los Angeles, Tucson, and Washington have introduced conflict resolution into the curriculum. These programs zero in on teaching youngsters to deal with problems nonviolently. For example, by role-playing situations, children practice how to respond when someone insults or challenges them. In the Chicago area alone, 5,000 students are going through this antiviolence program, which is supported by the National Institute of Mental Health.[77]

Culture Conflict Theory

Differential association theory is based on the learning of criminal (or deviant) norms or attitudes. Culture conflict theory focuses on the source of these criminal norms and attitudes. According to Thorsten Sellin, **conduct norms**—norms that regulate our daily lives—are rules that reflect the attitudes of the groups to which each of

■ MOVE members and neighbors watch their houses burn after aerial and ground attacks by the Philadelphia police, in May 1985. Over the next 11 years the city paid more than $30 million to rebuild homes and settle lawsuits filed by cult members and their families.

us belongs.[78] Their purpose is to define what is considered appropriate or normal behavior and what is inappropriate or abnormal behavior.

Sellin argues that different groups have different conduct norms and that the conduct norms of one group may conflict with those of another. Individuals may commit crimes by conforming to the norms of their own group if that group's norms conflict with those of the dominant society. According to this rationale, the main difference between a criminal and a noncriminal is that each is responding to different sets of conduct norms.

Examples of groups with values significantly deviating from those of the surrounding majority include MOVE, an African American group concerned with issues like police brutality, animal rights, and African heritage. MOVE, located in a house on Osage Street in Philadelphia, alienated its neighbors by broadcasting loud and profanity-laced loudspeaker messages. Mutual animosity escalated. Some MOVE members armed themselves. A police officer was killed. Ultimately, the police, armed with arrest warrants for some members, entered the area. The group did not surrender. The police attacked: 10,000 rounds of ammunition were fired, and a bomb was dropped from a police helicopter. All but two of the MOVE members died, and all the houses on the street went up in flames.

The last chapter in the MOVE drama was not written until February 1997, when the City of Philadelphia agreed to pay more than $500,000 each to the estates of MOVE founders John Africa and Frank James—after having spent over $30 million to rebuild the houses destroyed by the police bombing and to settle lawsuits filed by the estates of nine other MOVE members who had perished.

Another example—far more criminal—was the Solar Temple, founded by a former Gestapo officer, which flourished in Switzerland and Canada. This mystic cult attracted wealthy members who "donated" all their property to the cult, perhaps $93 million in all; much of it was spent for the personal benefit of two cult leaders. Cult members were heavily armed (and engaged in arms trading) in anticipation of the end of the world. Their end of the world came in the fall of 1994, when the two cult leaders murdered nearly all their followers and then committed suicide.

Sellin distinguishes between primary and secondary conflicts. "Primary conflict" occurs when norms of two cultures clash. A clash may occur at the border between neighboring cultural areas; a clash may occur when the law of one cultural group is extended to cover the territory of another; or it may occur when members of one group migrate to another culture. In a widening gap between cultural norms and generations, Southeast Asian immigrant children are running away from home in increasing numbers. They often run to an informal nationwide network of "safe houses." No one knows how many runaways there are, but it is estimated that at least one-third of all refugee families have had at least one child vanish for days, months, or even longer.

"Secondary conflict" arises when a single culture evolves into a variety of cultures, each with its own set of conduct norms. This type of conflict occurs when the homogeneous societies of simpler cultures become complex societies in which the number of social groupings multiplies constantly and norms are often at odds. Your college may make dormitory living mandatory for all freshmen, for example, but to follow the informal code of your peer group, you may seek the freedom of off-campus housing. Or you may have to choose whether to violate work rules by leaving your job half an hour early to make a mandatory class or to violate school rules by walking into class half an hour late. Life situations are frequently controlled by conflicting norms, so no matter how people act, they may be violating some rule, often without being aware that they are doing so.

In the next chapter, which deals with the formation and operation of subcultures, we will expand the discussion of the conflict of norms. We will also examine the empirical research that seeks to discover whether there is indeed a multitude of value systems in our society and, if so, whether and how they conflict.

REVIEW

Criminologists tend to divide the sociological explanation of crime into three categories: strain, cultural deviance, and social control. The strain and cultural deviance perspectives, described in this chapter, focus on the social forces that cause people to engage in deviant behavior. They assume that there is a relationship between social class and criminal behavior. Strain theorists argue that all people in society share one set of cultural values and that because lower-class persons often do not have legitimate means to attain society's goals, they may "innovate" by turning to illegitimate means instead. General strain theory, a revision of Merton's theory, relates criminal behavior to the anger that results when an individual is treated in a way he or she does not want to be treated in a social relationship. Cultural deviance theorists maintain that the lower class has a distinctive set of values and that these values often conflict with those of the middle class.

Cultural deviance theories—social disorganization, differential association, and culture conflict—relate criminal behavior to the learning of criminal values and norms. Social disorganization theory focuses on the breakdown of social institutions as a precondition for the establishment of criminal norms. Differential association theory concentrates on the processes by which criminal behavior is taught and learned. Culture conflict theory focuses on the specifics of how the conduct norms of some groups may clash with those of the dominant culture.

CRIMINOLOGY & PUBLIC POLICY

"In American society, personal worth tends to be evaluated on the basis of what people have achieved rather than who they are or how they relate to others in social networks. 'Success' is to a large extent the ultimate measure of social worth. Quite understandably, then, there are pervasive cultural pressures to achieve at any cost. A strong achievement orientation, at the level of basic cultural values, thus cultivates and sustains a mentality that "it's not how you play the game; it's

that while the threat posed by MS-13 to the United States as a whole is at the "medium" level, membership in parts of the country is so concentrated that we've labeled the threat level there "high."

Here are some other highlights from our threat assessment:

MS-13 operates in at least 42 states and the District of Columbia and has about 6,000–10,000 members nationwide. Currently, the threat is highest in the western and northeastern parts of the country, which coincides with elevated Salvadoran immigrant populations in those areas. In the southeast and central regions, the current threat is moderate to low, but recently, we've seen an influx of MS-13 members into the southeast, causing an increase in violent crimes there.

MS-13 members engage in a wide range of criminal activity, including drug distribution, murder, rape, prostitution, robbery, home invasions, immigration offenses, kidnapping, carjackings/ auto thefts, and vandalism. Most of these crimes, you'll notice, have one thing in common—they are exceedingly violent. And while most of the violence is directed toward other MS-13 members or rival street gangs, innocent citizens often get caught in the crossfire.

MS-13 is expanding its membership at a "moderate" rate through recruitment and migration. Some MS-13 members move to get jobs or to be near family members—currently, the southeast and the northeast are seeing the largest increases in membership. MS-13 often recruits new members by glorifying the gang lifestyle (often on the Internet, complete with pictures and videos) and by absorbing smaller gangs.

Speaking of employment, MS-13 members typically work for legitimate businesses by presenting false documentation. They primarily pick employers that don't scrutinize employment documents, especially in the construction, restaurant, delivery service, and landscaping industries.

Right now, MS-13 has no official national leadership structure. MS-13 originated in Los Angeles, but when members migrated eastward, they began forming cliques that for the most part operated independently. These cliques, though, often maintain regular contact with members in other regions to coordinate recruitment/ criminal activities and to prevent conflicts. We do believe that Los Angeles gang members have an elevated status among their MS-13 counterparts across the country, a system of respect that could potentially evolve into a more organized national leadership structure.

One final word about MS-13: The FBI, through its MS-13 National Joint Task Force and field investigations, remains committed to working with our local, state, national, and international partners to disrupt and dismantle this violent gang.[1]

There is a sense of urgency and concern underpinning this bulletin from the Federal Bureau of Investigation. Before dismissing both, it is worth considering these somber findings of the 2009 National Gang Threat Assessment from the United States Department of Justice:

- Approximately 1 million gang members belonging to more than 20,000 gangs were criminally activê within all 50 states and the District of Columbia as of September 2008.

- Local street gangs, or neighborhood-based street gangs, remain a significant threat because they continue to account for the largest number of gangs nationwide. Most engage in violence in conjunction with a variety of crimes, including retail-level drug distribution.

- According to NDTS data, 58 percent of state and local law enforcement agencies reported that criminal gangs were active in their jurisdictions in

2008 compared with 45 percent of state and local agencies in 2004.

- Gang members are migrating from urban areas to suburban and rural communities, expanding the gangs' influence in most regions; they are doing so for a variety of reasons, including expanding drug distribution territories, increasing illicit revenue, recruiting new members, hiding from law enforcement, and escaping other gangs. Many suburban and rural communities are experiencing increasing gang-related crime and violence because of expanding gang influence.

- Criminal gangs commit as much as 80 percent of the crime in many communities, according to law enforcement officials throughout the nation. Typical gang-related crimes include alien smuggling, armed robbery, assault, auto theft, drug trafficking, extortion, fraud, home invasions, identity theft, murder, and weapons trafficking.

- Gang members are the primary retail-level distributors of most illicit drugs. They also are increasingly distributing wholesale-level quantities of marijuana and cocaine in most urban and suburban communities.

- Some gangs traffic illicit drugs at the regional and national levels; several are capable of competing with U.S.-based Mexican Drug Trafficking Organizations.

- U.S.-based gang members illegally cross the U.S.–Mexico border for the express purpose of smuggling illicit drugs and illegal aliens from Mexico into the United States.

- Many gangs actively use the Internet to recruit new members and to communicate with members in other areas of the United States and in foreign countries.

- Street gangs and outlaw motorcycle gangs pose a growing threat to law enforcement along the U.S.–Canada border. They frequently associate with Canada-based gangs and criminal organizations to facilitate various criminal activities, including drug smuggling into the United States.[2]

How did gangs get started in American society? What keeps them going? And, just as important, how do criminological theories account for gang behavior?

THE FUNCTION OF SUBCULTURES

Strain theorists explain criminal behavior as a result of the frustrations suffered by lower-class individuals deprived of legitimate means to reach their goals. Cultural deviance theorists assume that individuals become criminal by learning the criminal values of the groups to which they belong. In conforming to their own group standards, these people break the laws of the dominant culture. These two perspectives are the foundation for subcultural theory, which emerged in the mid-1950s.

A **subculture** is a subdivision within the dominant culture that has its own norms, beliefs, and values. Subcultures typically emerge when people in similar circumstances find themselves isolated from the mainstream and band together for mutual support. Subcultures may form among members of racial and ethnic minorities, among prisoners, among occupational groups, and among ghetto dwellers. Subcultures exist within a larger society, not apart from it. They therefore share some of its values. Nevertheless, the lifestyles of their members are significantly different from those of individuals in the dominant culture.

SUBCULTURAL THEORIES OF DELINQUENCY AND CRIME

Subcultural theories in criminology were developed to account for delinquency among lower-class males, especially for one of its most important expressions—the teenage gang. According to subcultural theorists, delinquent subcultures, like all subcultures, emerge in response to special problems that members of the dominant culture do not face. Theories developed by Albert Cohen and by Richard Cloward and Lloyd Ohlin are extensions of the strain, social disorganization, and differential association theories. They explain why delinquent subcultures emerge in the first place (strain), why they take a particular form (social disorganization), and how they are passed on from one generation to the next (differential association).

The explanations of delinquency developed by Marvin Wolfgang and Franco Ferracuti and by Walter Miller are somewhat different from those previously mentioned. These theorists do not suggest that delinquency begins with failure to reach middle-class goals. Their explanations are rooted in culture conflict theory. The subculture of violence thesis argues that the value systems of some subcultures demand the use of violence in certain social situations. This norm, which affects daily behavior, conflicts with conventional middle-class norms. Along the same lines, Miller suggests that the characteristics of lower-class delinquency reflect the value system of the lower-class culture and that the lower-class values and norms conflict with those of the dominant culture.

Although Miller contends that the lower-class culture as a whole—not a subculture within it—is responsible for criminal behavior in urban slums, his theory is appropriate to our discussion because it demonstrates how the needs of young urban males are met by membership in a street gang. Miller's street gangs, like those of Cohen and of Cloward and Ohlin, condone violent criminal activity as one of the few means of attaining status in a slum.

The Middle-Class Measuring Rod

Albert Cohen was a student of Robert Merton and of Edwin Sutherland, both of whom had made convincing arguments about the causes of delinquency. Sutherland persuaded Cohen that differential association and the cultural transmission of criminal norms led to criminal behavior. From Merton he learned about structurally induced strain. Cohen combined and expanded these perspectives to explain how the delinquent subculture arises, where it is found within the social structure, and why it has the particular characteristics that it does.[3]

According to Cohen, delinquent subcultures emerge in the slum areas of large American cities. They are rooted in class differentials in parental aspirations, child-rearing practices, and classroom standards. The relative position of a youngster's family in the social structure determines the problems the child will have to face throughout life.

Lower-class families who have never known a middle-class lifestyle, for example, cannot socialize their children in a way that prepares them to enter the middle class. The children grow up with poor communication skills, a lack of commitment to education, and an inability to delay gratification. Schools present a particular problem. There lower-class children are evaluated by middle-class teachers on the basis of a middle-class measuring rod. The measures are based on middle-class values such as self-reliance, good manners, respect for property, and long-range planning. By such measures, lower-class children

fall far short of the standards they must meet if they are to compete successfully with middle-class children. Cohen argues that they experience status frustration and strain, to which they respond by adopting one of three roles: corner boy, college boy, or delinquent boy.

Corner Boy, College Boy, Delinquent Boy

"Corner boys" try to make the best of bad situations. The corner boy hangs out in the neighborhood with his peer group, spending the day in some group activity, such as gambling or athletic competition. He receives support from his peers and is very loyal to them. Most lower-class boys become corner boys. Eventually, they get menial jobs and live a conventional lifestyle.

There are very few "college boys." These boys continually strive to live up to middle-class standards, but their chances for success are limited because of academic and social hardships.

"Delinquent boys" band together to form a subculture in which they can define status in ways that to them seem attainable. Cohen claims that even though these lower-class youths set up their own norms, they have internalized the norms of the dominant class and feel anxious when they go against those norms. To deal with this conflict, they resort to **reaction formation,** a mechanism that relieves anxiety through the process of rejecting with abnormal intensity what one wants but cannot obtain. These boys turn the middle-class norms upside down, thereby making conduct right in their subculture precisely because it is wrong by the norms of the larger culture (Figure 6.1).

Consequently, their delinquent acts serve no useful purpose. They do not steal things to eat them, wear them, or sell them. In fact, they often discard or destroy what they have stolen. They appear to delight in the discomfort of others and in breaking taboos. Their acts are directed against people and property at random, unlike the goal-oriented activities of many adult criminal groups. The subculture typically is characterized by short-run hedonism, pure pleasure seeking, with no planning or deliberation about what to do or where or when to do it. The delinquents hang out on the street corner until someone gets an idea; then they act impulsively, without considering the consequences. The group's autonomy is all-important. Its members are loyal to each other and resist any attempts on the part of family, school, or community to restrain their behavior.

Tests of Cohen's Theory

Criminological researchers generally agree that Cohen's theory is responsible for major advances in research on delinquency.[4] Among them are researchers who have found a relationship

```
┌─────────────────┐     ┌─────────────────┐     ┌─────────────────┐
│ Working-class   │     │ Lower-class     │     │ Loss of self-   │
│ socialization   │ ──▶ │ failure         │ ──▶ │ esteem          │
│       +         │     │ in the school   │     │ and increased   │
│ Middle-class    │     │ system          │     │ feelings of     │
│ values          │     │ (among many)    │     │ rejection       │
│ of success      │     │                 │     │                 │
└─────────────────┘     └─────────────────┘     └─────────────────┘
                                                          │
┌─────────────────┐     ┌─────────────────┐     ┌─────────────────┐
│ School dropout  │     │ Increased       │     │ Improved self-  │
│ and             │     │ hostility       │     │ image           │
│ association with│ ──▶ │ and resentment  │ ──▶ │ in a gang       │
│ delinquent peers│     │ toward middle-  │     │ context         │
│ (among some)    │     │ class           │     │ and through     │
│                 │     │ standards and   │     │ negative and    │
│                 │     │ symbols, thus   │     │ malicious       │
│                 │     │ reaction        │     │ delinquent      │
│                 │     │ formation       │     │ behavior        │
└─────────────────┘     └─────────────────┘     └─────────────────┘
```

FIGURE 6.1 The process of reaction formation among delinquent boys.

Source: Donald J. Shoemaker, *Theories of Delinquency: An Examination of Explanations of Delinquent Behavior,* 4th ed. (2000), Figure 7 (p. 109). By permission of Oxford University Press, Inc. www.oup.com.

■ *Boredom in class, as demonstrated by this ninth-grade student, may lead to dropout and delinquency.*

between delinquency and social status in our society (Chapter 5). Much evidence also supports Cohen's assumption that lower-class children perform more poorly in school than middle-class children.[5] Teachers often expect them to perform less ably than their middle-class students, and this expectation is one of the components of poor performance.

Researchers have demonstrated that poor performance in school is related to delinquency. When Travis Hirschi studied more than 4,000 California schoolchildren, he found that youths who were academically incompetent and performed poorly in school came to dislike school. Disliking it, they rejected its authority; rejecting its authority, they committed delinquent acts (Chapter 7).[6] Delbert Elliott and Harwin Voss also investigated the relationship between school and delinquency. They analyzed annual school performance and delinquency records of 2,000 students in California from ninth grade to 1 year after the expected graduation date. Their findings indicated that those who dropped out of school had higher rates of delinquency than those who graduated. They also found that academic achievement and alienation from school were closely related to dropping out of school.[7]

From analysis of the dropout-delinquency relationship among over 5,000 persons nationwide, G. Roger Jarjoura concluded that while dropouts were more likely than graduates to engage in delinquent acts, the reason was not always simply the fact that they had dropped out. Dropping out because of a dislike for school, poor grades, or financial reasons was related to future involvement in delinquency; dropping out because of problems at home was not. Dropping out for personal reasons such as marriage or pregnancy was significantly related to subsequent violent offending.[8] All these findings support Cohen's theory. Other findings, however, do not.

In a study of 12,524 students in Davidson County, Tennessee, Albert Reiss and Albert Rhodes found only a slight relationship between delinquency and status deprivation.[9] This conclusion was supported by the research of Marvin Krohn and his associates.[10] Furthermore, several criminologists have challenged Cohen's claim that delinquent behavior is purposeless.[11] They contend that much delinquent behavior is serious and calculated and often engaged in for profit.[12] Others have also questioned the consistency of the theory: Cohen argues that the behavior of delinquent boys is a deliberate response to middle-class opinion, yet he also argues that the boys do not care about the opinions of middle-class people.[13]

Evaluation: Cohen's Theory

Researchers have both praised and criticized Cohen's work. Cohen's theory answers a number of questions left unresolved by the strain and cultural deviance theories. It explains the origin of delinquent behavior and why some youths raised in the same neighborhoods and attending the same schools do not become involved in delinquent subcultures. His concepts of status deprivation and the middle-class measuring rod have been useful to researchers. Yet his theory does not explain why most delinquents eventually become law-abiding even though their position in the class structure remains relatively fixed. Some criminologists also question whether youths are driven by some serious motivating force or are simply out on the streets looking for fun.[14] Moreover, if delinquent subcultures result from the practice of measuring lower-class boys by a middle-class measuring rod, how do we account for the growing number of middle-class gangs?

Other questions concern the difficulty of trying to test the concepts of reaction formation, internalization of middle-class values, and status deprivation, among others. To answer some of his critics, Cohen, with his colleague James Short, expanded the idea of delinquent subcultures to include not only lower-class delinquent behavior but also variants such as middle-class delinquent subcultures and female delinquents.[15] Cohen took Merton's strain theory a step further by elaborating on the development of delinquent behavior. He described how strain actually creates frustration and status deprivation, which in turn fosters the development of an alternative set of values that give lower-class boys a chance to achieve recognition. Since the mid-1950s, Cohen's theory has stimulated not only research but also the formulation of new theories.

DELINQUENCY AND OPPORTUNITY

Like Cohen's theory, the theory of differential opportunity developed by Richard Cloward and Lloyd Ohlin combines strain, differential association, and social disorganization concepts.[16] Both

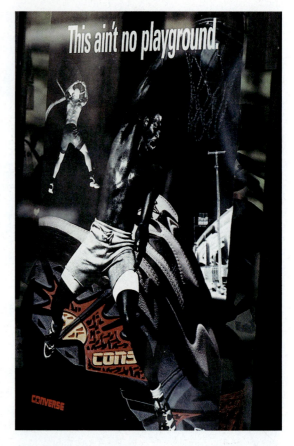

■ Multicultural advertisements appeal to young males concerned with showing toughness through masculinity. This billboard suggests that Converse sneakers are not for kids' playgrounds.

theories begin with the assumption that conventional means to conventional success are not equally distributed among the socioeconomic classes, that lack of means causes frustration for lower-class youths, and that criminal behavior is learned and culturally transmitted. Both theories also agree that the common solution to shared problems leads to the formation of delinquent subcultures. They disagree, however, on the content of these subcultures. As we have noted, norms in Cohen's delinquent subcultures are right precisely because they are wrong in the dominant culture. Delinquent acts are negative and nonutilitarian. Cloward and Ohlin disagree; they suggest that lower-class delinquents remain goal-oriented. The kind of delinquent behavior they engage in depends on the illegitimate opportunities available to them.

According to Cloward and Ohlin's **differential opportunity theory,** delinquent subcultures flourish in lower-class areas and take the particular forms they do because opportunities for illegitimate success are no more equitably distributed than those for conventional success. Just as means—opportunities—are unequally distributed in the conventional world, opportunities to reach

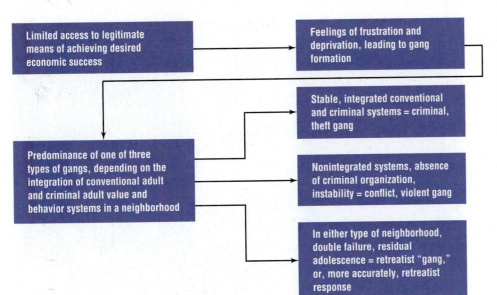

FIGURE 6.2 Factors leading to the development of three types of delinquent gangs.

Source: Donald J. Shoemaker, *Theories of Delinquency: An Examination of Explanations of Delinquent Behavior,* 4th ed. (2000), Figure 8 (p.117). By permission of Oxford University Press, Inc. www.oup.com.

one's goals are unequally distributed in the criminal world. A person cannot simply decide to join a theft-oriented gang or, for that matter, a violence-oriented one. Cloward and Ohlin maintain that the types of subcultures and the juvenile gangs that flourish within them depend on the types of neighborhoods in which they develop (Figure 6.2).

In areas where conventional and illegitimate values and behavior are integrated by a close connection of illegitimate and legitimate businesses, "criminal gangs" emerge. Older criminals serve as role models. They teach youngsters the kinds of people to exploit, the necessary criminal skills, the importance of loyal relationships with criminal associates, and the way to make the right connections with shady lawyers, bail bondsmen, crooked politicians, and corrupt police officers. Adolescent members of criminal gangs, like adult criminals in the neighborhood, are involved in extortion, fraud, theft, and other activities that yield illegal income.

This type of neighborhood was described by one of its members in a classic work published in 1930:

> Stealing in the neighborhood was a common practice among the children and approved by the parents. Whenever the boys got together they talked about robbing and made more plans for stealing. I hardly knew any boys who did not go robbing. The little fellows went in for petty stealing, breaking into freight cars, and stealing junk. The older guys did big jobs like stickups, burglary, and stealing autos. The little fellows admired the "big shots" and longed for the day when they could get into the big racket. Fellows who had "done time" were the big shots and looked up to and gave the little fellows tips on how to get by and pull off big jobs.[17]

Neighborhoods characterized by transience and instability, Cloward and Ohlin argue, offer few opportunities to get ahead in organized criminal activities. This world gives rise to "conflict gangs," whose goal is to gain a reputation for toughness and destructive violence. Thus "one particular biker would catch a bird and then bite off its head, allowing the blood to trickle from his mouth as he yelled 'all right!'"[18] It is the world of the warrior: Fight, show courage against all odds, defend and maintain the honor of the group. Above all, never show fear.

Violence is the means used to gain status in conflict gangs. Conventional society's recognition of the "worst" gangs becomes a mark of prestige, perpetuating the high standards of their members. Conflict gangs emerge in lower-class areas where neither criminal nor conventional adult role models exercise much control over youngsters.

A third subcultural response to differential opportunities is the formation of "retreatist gangs." Cloward and Ohlin describe members of retreatist gangs as double failures because they have not been successful in the legitimate world and have been equally unsuccessful in the illegitimate worlds of organized criminal activity and violence-oriented gangs. This subculture is characterized by a continuous search for getting high through alcohol, atypical sexual experiences, marijuana, hard drugs, or a combination of these.

The retreatist hides in a world of sensual adventure, borrowing, begging, or stealing to support his habit, whatever it may be. He may peddle drugs or work as a pimp or look for some other deviant income-producing activity. But the income is not a primary concern; he is interested only in the next high. Belonging to a retreatist gang offers a sense of superiority and well-being that is otherwise beyond the reach of these least-successful dropouts.

Three suspected members of the Crips, a gang reputed for its toughness and violence, hit the pavement after being chased by SAPD officers and deputies of the Bexar County (Texas) Gang Unit. The suspects' names were being checked through computers for any outstanding warrants. All three were arrested.

Not all lower-class youngsters who are unable to reach society's goals become members of criminal, conflict, or retreatist gangs. Many choose to accept their situation and to live within its constraints. These law-abiding youngsters are Cohen's corner boys.

Tests of Opportunity Theory

Cloward and Ohlin's differential opportunity theory presented many new ideas, and a variety of studies emerged to test it empirically.

The first of Cloward and Ohlin's assumptions—that blocked opportunities are related to delinquency—has had mixed support. Travis Hirschi, for example, demonstrated that "the greater one's acceptance of conventional (or even quasi-conventional) success goals, the less likely one is to be delinquent, regardless of the likelihood these goals will someday be attained."[19] In other words, the youngsters who stick to hard work and education to get ahead in society are the least likely to become delinquent, no matter what their real chances are of reaching their goals. John Hagedorn disagrees. In late 1992 and early 1993, he conducted interviews with 101 founding members of 18 gangs in Milwaukee. His conclusion: "Most of those we were trying to track appeared to be on an economic merry-go-round, with continual movement in and out of the secondary labor market. Although their average income from drug sales far surpassed their income from legal employment, most Milwaukee male gang members apparently kept trying to find licit work."[20] There is also evidence that both gang and nongang boys believe the middle-class values of hard work and scholastic achievement

to be important. Gang boys, however, are more ready to approve of a wide range of behaviors, including aggressive acts and drug use.[21]

The second assumption of differential opportunity theory—that the type of lower-class gang depends on the type of neighborhood in which it emerges—has also drawn the attention of criminologists. Empirical evidence suggests that gang behavior is more versatile and involves a wider range of criminal and noncriminal acts than the patterns outlined by Cloward and Ohlin. Ko-lin Chin's research on New York gangs in 1993 demonstrates that Chinese gangs are engaged in extortion, alien smuggling, heroin trafficking, and the running of gambling establishments and houses of prostitution.[22] A report from the Denver Youth Survey showed that while the most frequent form of illegal activity is fighting with other gangs, gang members are also involved in robberies, joyriding, assaults, stealing, and drug sales.[23]

Research does, however, support Cloward and Ohlin's argument that criminal gangs emerge in areas where conventional and illegitimate behavior have a close connection with illegitimate and legitimate businesses. Chinatowns in America, for example, are social, economic, political, and cultural units.[24] All types of organizations, including those that dominate illegal activities, play an important role in the maintenance of order in the community. The illegitimate social order has control of territorial rights, gambling places, heroin trafficking, alien smuggling, and loan-sharking. The illegal order defines who is in control of particular restaurants, retail shops, garment factories, and the like. Business owners pay a "membership fee" for protection. Adult criminals maintain control of youth gang members by threatening to

Source: Cartoon by Shaun Williams. www.CartoonStock.com.

exclude them from work that pays well. They also resolve conflicts, provide recreational facilities, lend money, and give the young gang members a chance to climb the illegitimate career ladder within the criminal organization. Gang activities are closely supervised by their leaders, who work with the adult crime groups. Elaborate initiation rites are conducted by an adult the youngsters call "uncle"—the link between the gang and the adult sponsoring organization.

Gang members (1,015) from California, Illinois, Iowa, Michigan, and Ohio also reported having a variety of legal and illegal income sources, collective gang "treasuries," and mostly adult leaders.[25] Their businesses included dance clubs; billiard halls; and stereo, liquor, jewelry, grocery, cellular phone/beeper, and auto repair shops. They also sold illegal goods: $268 for a 9-mm Glock semiautomatic pistol, $42 for a box of cartridges, $882 for 1 ounce of cocaine, and $155 for a stolen 12-gauge shotgun.[26] Such gangs operate somewhat like a union for the underground economy. Members attend meetings, pay dues, follow rules, have their own language, and make collective expenditures (for guns, funerals, attorneys).

Evaluation: Differential Opportunity Theory

For three decades, criminologists have reviewed, examined, and revised the work of Cloward and Ohlin.[27] One of the main criticisms is that their theory is class-oriented. If, as Cloward and Ohlin claim, delinquency is a response to blocked opportunities, how can we explain middle-class delinquency? Another question arises from contradictory statements. How can delinquent groups be nonutilitarian, negativistic, and malicious (Cohen)—and also goal-oriented and utilitarian? Despite its shortcomings, however, differential opportunity theory has identified some of the reasons lower-class youngsters may become alienated. Cloward and Ohlin's work has also challenged researchers to study the nature of the subcultures in our society. Marvin Wolfgang and Franco Ferracuti have concentrated on one of them—the subculture of violence.

THE SUBCULTURE OF VIOLENCE

Like Cohen, and like Cloward and Ohlin, Marvin Wolfgang and Franco Ferracuti turned to subcultural theory to explain criminal behavior among lower-class young urban males. All three theories developed by these five researchers assume the existence of subcultures made up of people who share a value system that differs from that of the dominant culture. And they assume that each subculture has its own rules or conduct norms that dictate how individuals should act under varying circumstances. The three theories also agree that these values and norms persist over time because they are learned by successive generations. The theories differ, however, in their focus.

Cohen and Cloward and Ohlin focus on the origin of the subculture, specifically, culturally induced strain. The thrust of Wolfgang and Ferracuti's work is culture conflict. Furthermore, the earlier theories encompass all types of delinquency and crime; Wolfgang and Ferracuti concentrate on violent crime. They argue that in some subcultures, behavior norms are dictated by a value system that demands the use of force or violence.[28] Subcultures that adhere to conduct norms conducive to violence are referred to as **subcultures of violence.**

Violence is not used in all situations, but it is frequently an expected response. The appearance of a weapon, a slight shove or push, a derogatory remark, or the opportunity to wield power undetected may very well evoke an aggressive reaction that seems uncalled for to middle-class people. Fists rather than words settle disputes. Knives or guns are readily available, so confrontations can quickly escalate. Violence is a pervasive part of everyday life. Childrearing practices (hitting), gang activities (street wars), domestic quarrels (battering), and social events (drunken brawls) are all permeated by violence.

Violence is not considered antisocial. Members of this subculture feel no guilt about their aggression. In fact, individuals who do not resort to violence may be reprimanded. The value system is transmitted from generation to generation, long after the original reason for the violence has disappeared. The pattern is very hard to eradicate.

When Wolfgang and Ferracuti described population groups that are likely to respond violently to stress, they posed a powerful question to the criminal justice system: How does one go about changing a subcultural norm? This question becomes increasingly significant with the merging of the drug subculture and the subculture of violence.

Tests of the Subculture of Violence

Howard Erlanger, using nationwide data collected for the President's Commission on the Causes and Prevention of Violence, found no major differences in attitudes toward violence by class or race. Erlanger concluded that though members of the lower class show no greater approval of violence than middle-class persons do, they lack the sophistication necessary to settle grievances by other means. Not all studies support this idea, however.

In *Code of the Street,* Elijah Anderson presents ethnographic evidence that violence is part of a complex street culture in impoverished communities that develops in response to structural obstacles. Other quantitative and review studies provide mixed evidence on the race/class/subculture of violence hypothesis.[29]

The subculture of violence thesis has also generated a line of empirical research that looks at regional differences in levels of violent crime.

The South (as you will see in Chapter 10) has the highest homicide rate in the country. Some researchers have attributed this high rate to subcultural values.[30] They argue that the Southern subculture of violence has its historical roots in an exaggerated defense of honor by Southern gentlemen, mob violence (especially lynching), a military tradition, the acceptance of personal vengeance, and the widespread availability and use of handguns.[31]

The problem with many of these studies is that it is difficult to separate the effects of economic and social factors from those of cultural values. Several researchers have sought to solve this problem. Colin Loftin and Robert Hill, for example, using a sophisticated measure of poverty, found that economic factors, not cultural ones, explained regional variation in homicide rates.[32] Similarly, others suggest that high homicide rates and gun ownership may have a great deal to do with socioeconomic conditions, especially racial inequality in the South.[33]

Researchers who support the subculture of violence thesis point to statistics on characteristics of homicide offenders and victims: Lower-class, inner-city black males are disproportionately represented in the FBI's Uniform Crime Reports.[34]

Furthermore, in a study of 556 males interviewed at age 26, 19 percent of the respondents, all inner-city males, reported having been shot or stabbed. These victimizations were found to be highly correlated with both self-reported offenses and official arrest statistics. In fact, the best single predictor of committing a violent act was found to be whether the individual had been a victim of

TABLE 6.1 Moderate and High Gang Involvement in Distribution (percent, by region)

Drug Type	Northeast	South	Midwest	West	Total
Powdered cocaine	52.9%	38.7%	37.5%	32.9%	38.2%
Crack cocaine	52.9	45.7	60.2	39.2	47.3
Heroin	45.1	17.9	25.0	35.7	27.9
Marijuana	56.9	54.3	67.0	79.0	64.8
Methamphetamine	17.6	24.9	23.9	73.4	39.1
MDMA	31.4	19.1	18.1	30.1	23.7

SOURCE: *The 2005 National Gang Threat Assessment* (Washington, D.C.: Bureau of Justice Assistance, 2006), p. vi; available at www.nagia.org/PDFs/2005_national_gang_threat_assessment.pdf.

a violent crime. Though most people in the dominant society who are shot or stabbed do not commit a criminal act in response, it appears that many inner-city males alternate the roles of victim and offender in a way that maintains the values and attitudes of a violent subculture.[35]

Evaluation: The Subculture of Violence Theory

Though empirical evidence remains inconclusive, the subculture of violence theory is supported by the distribution of violent crime in American society.[36] The number of gangs and the violence associated with their activities is growing.[37] Jeffrey Fagan noted that "drug use is widespread and normative" among gangs.[38] Gang warfare, which takes the lives of innocent bystanders in ghetto areas, is a part of life in most of the impoverished, densely populated neighborhoods in major cities such as Los Angeles, New York, Chicago, Miami, Washington, D.C., and Atlanta, as well as in smaller disintegrating urban centers. For example, over the 3 years between 1985 and 1988, Jamaican "posses"—gangs transplanted from Kingston, Jamaica, to the United States—were involved in 1,400 homicides.[39]

Though not all persons in these subcultures follow the norm of violence, it appears that a dismaying number of them attach less and less importance to the value of human life and turn increasingly to violence to resolve immediate problems and frustrations. (We return to this issue later in the chapter.)

FOCAL CONCERNS: MILLER'S THEORY

All the theorists we have examined thus far explain criminal and delinquent behavior in terms of subcultural values that emerge and are perpetuated from one generation to the next in lower-class urban slums. Walter Miller reasons differently. According to Miller,

> in the case of "gang" delinquency, the cultural system which exerts the most direct influence on behavior is that of the lower-class community itself—a long-established, distinctively patterned tradition with an integrity of its own—rather than a so-called "delinquent subculture" which has arisen through conflict with middle-class culture and is oriented to the deliberate violation of middle-class norms.[40]

To Miller, juvenile delinquency is not rooted in the rejection of middle-class values; rather, it stems from lower-class culture, which has its own value system. This value system has evolved as a response to living in disadvantaged neighborhoods characterized by single-parent households (Table 6.2). Gang norms are simply the adolescent

TABLE 6.2 Percentage of Children Living in Poverty or with No Working Parent

Many children live in poverty, often residing in single-parent households where the head of household does not have a job.

Living Arrangement	No Working Parent	Living in Poverty
Both parents	14%	10%
Single parent	34	43
Mother	37	47
Father	19	22

SOURCE: *Juvenile Offenders and Victims: 1999 National Report* (Washington, D.C.: Office of Juvenile Justice and Delinquency Prevention, 1999), pp. 6, 8.

■ *Rapper 50 Cent, pictured here in February 2003, expressed his values with his debut record, Get Rich or Die Tryin', which sold 892,000 copies in 4 days. His follow-up record, Massacre, sold 771,000 copies in its first full week of release.*

expression of the lower-class culture in which the boys have grown up. This lower-class culture exists apart from the middle-class culture, and it has done so for generations. The value system, not the gang norms, generates delinquent acts.

Miller has identified six focal concerns, or areas, to which lower-class males give persistent attention: trouble, toughness, smartness, excitement,

Cohen vs. Miller

Both Albert Cohen and Walter Miller argue that deviant subcultures develop among disadvantaged segments of society. Their theories diverge, however, when it comes to the association of these subcultures with the values of mainstream society. According to Cohen, delinquent subcultures are formed when disadvantaged youths cannot adhere to the same middle-class standards as their more-advantaged peers. In other words, deviant subculture develops in response to mainstream culture. Miller, on the other hand, hypothesizes that the subculture of violence develops in isolation from mainstream society. It is part of a more general culture that exists among the lower class, but it is not formed as a symbolic rejection of middle-class values and goals.

Overall, a comparison of Cohen and Miller's theories raises the question of whether it is disadvantage itself that leads to the formation of deviant subcultures or disadvantage *relative* to other segments of society.

In general, U.S. census data on poverty favors Cohen's theory. The United States has one of the highest violent-crime rates in the world, and it is also characterized by a mix of wealthy and impoverished segments of society. In 2006, 9.8 percent of families and 13.3 percent of individuals were living below the poverty line. At the same time, 19.1 percent of households were earning an annual income of $100,000 or more. The United States scored a 45 on the Gini index of income inequality.[1] When we consider concentrated poverty, however, the implications are less clear. Concentrated poverty, or the proportion of individuals living in high-poverty areas, declined between 1990 and 2000, but in 2000 it was still substantial at 10 percent and varied considerably depending on the region (see figure).[2] This can be interpreted as support for Miller or Cohen, depending on your perspective. On one hand, it indicates that a significant proportion of the United States is covered by clusters of impoverished communities where lower-class culture is likely to flourish in isolation from mainstream culture. On the other hand, the clustering of these communities together in space may make inhabitants more aware of the gap between themselves and the middle class.

International data are equally contradictory. Some international data support Cohen's theory. Between 1998 and 2001, South Africa had an average yearly homicide rate of 55.86 per 100,000 individuals, which is more than 10 times higher than that of the United States during roughly the same time period.[3] South Africa also has one of the largest wealth gaps in the world as measured by the Gini index of income inequality.[4] Other countries, such as China, have high income inequality but low crime rates.[5, 6] It appears that the direction of the relationship between inequality and crime varies by nation.

Aside from the international evidence, which provides no clear conclusions, one may ask which theory makes more intuitive sense. Does it seem possible for disadvantaged segments of society not only to be indifferent to mainstream culture, but also to be completely unaware of it? On the other hand, doesn't rejection of middle-class values suggest that disadvantaged youths have internalized them to some degree? In other words, if they do not care about mainstream values at all, wouldn't they retreat from them without hostility?

One may also point out that Cohen and Miller focus on the development of different types of subcultures—Cohen's theory explains delinquent subcultures, while Miller's explains violent subcultures. However, neither scholar offers any insight into why the two types of subcultures may develop differently from each other. Is this difference enough to reconcile the disparities between the two lines of thinking? Why might violent subcultures develop solely from lower-class culture and delinquent subcultures develop in response to middle-class standards?

If, according to Cohen, it is the inadequacy felt by disadvantaged youths when they are measured against the middle class that leads to delinquency, then why is this mentality limited to those individuals? Why does it not extend to middle-class youths when they compare themselves to upper-class peers, for example, or to upper-class youths when they compare themselves to celebrity children? Cohen would argue that the expectations of society are grounded in middle-class rather than upper-class standards and that it is the expectations of society rather than those of the individual that influence

luck, and autonomy. Concern over trouble is a major feature of lower-class life. Staying out of trouble and getting into trouble are daily preoccupations. Trouble can get a person into the hands of the authorities, or it can result in prestige among peers. Lower-class individuals are often evaluated by the extent of their involvement in activities such as fighting, drinking, and sexual misbehaving. In this case, the greater the involvement or the more extreme the performance, the greater the prestige or "respect" the person commands.

These young men are almost obsessively concerned with "toughness"; the code requires a show of masculinity, a denial of sentimentality, and a display of physical strength. Miller argues that this concern with toughness is related to the fact that a large proportion of lower-class males grow up in female-dominated households and have no male figure from whom to learn the male role. They join street gangs in order to find males with whom they can identify.

Claude Brown's classic 1965 autobiography, *Manchild in the Promised Land*, illustrates the

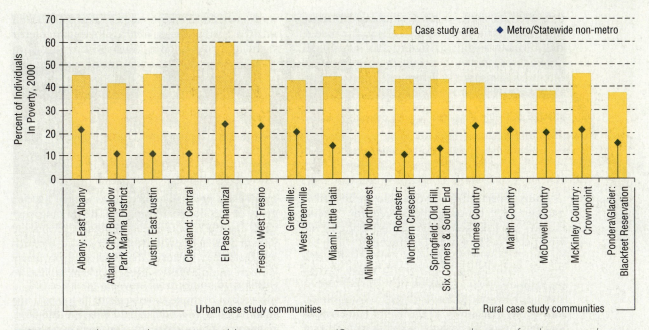

Poverty rates in the case study communities and their comparison areas. (Comparison areas are metropolitan areas for urban case study communities, and statewide nonmetropolitan areas for rural case study communities).

Sources: U.S. Census Bureau, Census 2000; Berube, A., Concentrated Poverty in America: An Overview. In D. Erickson et al., eds. *The Enduring Challenge of Concentrated Poverty in America: Case Studies from Communities across the U.S.*, p. 6, Figure 1A. © 2008 The Federal Reserve System and The Brookings Institution. Reprinted with permission. www.brookings.edu/metro.

subculture formation. Does this mean that awareness of an even higher standard has no influence? In other words, is it only expectations that matter, or do individual desires play a role as well? According to Miller, the question is irrelevant because deviant subculture is a product of membership in the lower class and thus does not apply to other individuals, regardless of their aspirations.

Sources

1. U.S. Census, 2008.
2. Paul Jargowsky, "Stunning Progress, Hidden Problems: The Dramatic Decline of Concentrated Poverty in the 1990s," *Living Cities Census Series,* Center on Urban and Metropolitan Studies (Washington, D.C.: Brookings Institute, 2003).
3. Gordon Barclay and Cynthia Tavares, "International Comparisons of Criminal Justice Statistics 2001," Home Office and Council of Europe, October 24, 2003.
4. Jens Martins, "A Compendium of Inequality: The Human Development Report 2005," FES briefing paper, October 2005.
5. Michael Yates, "Poverty and Inequality in the Global Economy," *Monthly Review* **55**(9), February, 2004, www.monthlyreview.org/0204yates.htm.
6. Yuri Andrienko, "Crime, Wealth, and Inequality: Evidence from International Crime Victim Surveys," Economics Education and Research Consortium, Moscow, November 2002.

Questions for Discussion

1. What is your position on the Cohen versus Miller debate? Explain.
2. What are the possible effects of attributing a "subculture of violence" to the lower class?

concerns about trouble and toughness among adolescents growing up in an urban slum:

> My friends were all daring like me, tough like me, dirty like me, ragged like me, cursed like me, and had a great love for trouble like me. We took pride in being able to hitch rides on trolleys, buses, taxicabs and in knowing how to steal and fight. We knew that we were the only kids in the neighborhood who usually had more than ten dollars in their pockets. . . . Somebody was always trying to shake us down or rob us. This was usually done by the older hustlers in the neighborhood or by storekeepers or cops. . . . We accepted this as a way of life.[41]

Another focal concern is "smartness"—the ability to gain something by outsmarting, outwitting, or conning another person. In lower-class neighborhoods, youngsters practice outsmarting each other in card games, exchanges of insults, and other trials. Prestige is awarded to those who demonstrate smartness.

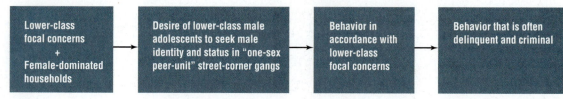

FIGURE 6.3 The relationship between delinquency and lower-class focal concerns.

Source: Donald J. Shoemaker, *Theories of Delinquency: An Examination of Explanations of Delinquent Behavior,* 4th ed. (2000), Figure 9 (p. 125). By permission of Oxford University Press, Inc. www.oup.com.

Many aspects of lower-class life are related to another focal concern, the search for "excitement." Youngsters alternate between hanging out with peers and looking for excitement, which can be found in fighting, getting drunk, and using drugs. Risks, danger, and thrills break up the monotony of their existence.

Fate, particularly "luck," plays an important role in lower-class life. Many individuals believe that their lives are subject to forces over which they have little control. If they get lucky, a rather drab life could change quickly. Common discussions center on whether lucky numbers come up, cards are right, or dice are good. Brown recalls:

> After a while [Mama] settled down, and we stopped talking about her feelings, then somebody came upstairs and told her she had hit the numbers. We just forgot all about her feelings. I forgot about her feelings. Mama forgot about her feelings. Everybody did. She started concentrating on the number. This was the first time she'd had a hit in a long time. They bought some liquor. Mama and Dad started drinking: everyone started making a lot of noise and playing records.[42]

Miller's final focal concern, "autonomy," stems from the lower-class person's resentment of external controls, whether parents, teachers, or police. This desire for personal freedom is expressed often in terms such as "No one can push me around" and "I don't need nobody."[43]

According to Miller, status in every class is associated with the possession of qualities that are valued. In the lower class, the six focal concerns define status. It is apparent that by engaging in behavior that affords status by these criteria, many people will be breaking the laws of the dominant society (Figure 6.3).

Tests of Miller's Theory

An obvious question is whether in our urban, heterogeneous, secular, technologically based society any isolated pockets of culture are still to be found. The pervasiveness of mass advertising, mass transit, and mass communication makes it seem unlikely that an entire class of people could be unaware of the dominant value system. Empirical research on opportunity theory has found that lower-class boys share the conventional success goals of the dominant culture. This finding suggests that the idea of isolation from the dominant system does not fit with reality. Empirical research has also found, however, that while gang boys may support middle-class values, they are willing to deviate from them. If an opportunity arises to gain prestige in a fight, gang boys are willing to take the chance that their act will not result in punishment.

Most empirical tests of values question young people on their attachment to middle-class values. Stephen Cernovich expanded this type of research by investigating attachment to lower-class focal concerns.[44] He found that toughness, excitement, trouble, and pleasure-seeking were related to self-reported delinquency in all classes. His findings also showed that boys of all classes were committed to delayed gratification, hard work, and education. Cernovich concluded that it is values, rather than class, that are associated with delinquency.

Evaluation: Miller's Theory

Criminologists have been disturbed by Miller's assumption that the lower-class lifestyle is generally focused on illegal activity. In making such an assumption, they say, Miller disregards the fact that most people in the lower class do conform to conventional norms. Moreover, some criminologists ask, if lower-class boys are conforming to their own value system, why would they suffer guilt or shame when they commit delinquent acts?[45]

Perhaps the best support for Miller's ideas is found in qualitative, rather than quantitative, accounts of life in a lower-class slum. In our discussion of cultural deviance and subcultural theories, we noted that the values and norms that define behavior in these areas do not change much over time or from place to place. Successive generations have to deal with the same problems. They typically demonstrate similar responses. Angela D'Arpa-Calandra, a former probation officer who now directs a Juvenile Intensive Supervision program, says she walked into a New York courtroom and "saw a mother and grandmother sitting with the 14-year-old offender. 'I had the grandmother in criminal court in 1963,' D'Arpa-Calandra says. 'We didn't stop it there. The grandmother was 14 when she was arrested. The mother had this child when she was 14. It's like a cycle we must relive.'"[46]

■ "Migrant Mother and Children," 1936. Dorothea Lange's photographic portrayal of the plight of a poor Southern family.

By and large, descriptions of life in poverty-stricken areas, whether written by people who have lived in them or by people who have studied them, reveal dreary routine, boredom, constant trouble, and incessant problems with drugs, alcohol, and crime. As the father tells his son in Eugene O'Neill's autobiographical play *Long Day's Journey into Night*, "There was no damned romance in our poverty."[47] O'Neill's words were captured by photographer Dorothea Lange, who startled and moved the world with images of the poor, destitute, and displaced during the Great Depression (1930–1939). The photograph above, in particular, inspired Steinbeck in *The Grapes of Wrath*—and millions of others—to consider the plight shown of the so very disadvantaged.[48]

GANGS AT THE TURN OF THE TWENTY-FIRST CENTURY

In Los Angeles:
A 7-year-old boy was slain and his 10-month-old brother seriously injured by stray bullets as members of the Crips gang opened fire in a parking lot to avenge shootings that had occurred two hours earlier.[49]

In New York:
An 11-year-old boy was killed as two gang members bicycled up to a crowded playground and opened fire. The goal was to kill a member of a rival gang.[50]

In Washington, D.C.:
An 18-year-old pleaded guilty to first-degree murder of a 12-year-old boy. He beat and shot the victim whom he had warned to stay out of the gang war. When the warning was not heeded, he concluded that the victim "wanted to be dead."[51]

In Santa Monica, California:
Within a 2-week period, gang wars left five people dead and three seriously injured. In the previous year Santa Monica had one homicide.[52]

In Houston, Texas:
A 16-year-old girl and member of the Hispanic gang Crazy Crew plunged a double-bladed knife with serrated edges into the heart of a 15-year-old boy and member of the rival gang MS-13, killing him.[53]

The new subculture that emerged in the 1980s and continues into the new century combines violence, which has become more vicious than in earlier years, with big business in drug trafficking. Many gangs have transitioned from turf-oriented to profit-driven organizations. Highly sophisticated gangs, such as the Latin Kings, Gangster Disciples, and Vice Lords, have forged relationships with Colombian and Dominican drug-trafficking organizations (DTOs) and are heavily involved in nearly every aspect of the retail drug trade, including smuggling, transportation, and the wholesale distribution of drugs nationwide.[54] The Latin Kings and Mara Salvatrucha (MS-13), for example, smuggle multikilogram-quantities of methamphetamine into the Southwest and transport the drug to previously untapped methamphetamine markets throughout the United States.[55] Meanwhile, it is estimated that one gang alone, the Eight Trey Gangster Crips, has distributed hundreds of kilos of crack and powdered cocaine worth over $10 million on the streets of Los Angeles and five other cities, as far east as Atlanta. The FBI reports that there are hundreds of similar drug networks operating across the country.

Gangs continue to control a significant portion of the illicit drug market in urban areas, as well as in rural and suburban areas. In fact, gangs are the principal distributors of illicit drugs in the United States, and drug trafficking is their primary source of financial equity. Research continues to demonstrate that as gangs become more entrenched in the drug market, the likelihood of criminal offending increases.[56] Movies like *Colors, American Me, Belly,* and *Baby Boy* capture the realities of life in a gang and, in some cases, provide models for gang activities.

Street Gangs

18th Street (National)

Formed in Los Angeles, 18th Street is a group of loosely associated sets or cliques, each led by an influential member. Membership is estimated at

Crime Surfing www

www.ncjrs.gov/
spotlight/gangs/
summary.html

Would you like to find out more about the prevalence of gangs in various areas?

30,000 to 50,000. In California approximately 80 percent of the gang's members are illegal aliens from Mexico and Central America. The gang is active in 44 cities in 20 states. Its main source of income is street-level distribution of cocaine and marijuana and, to a lesser extent, heroin and methamphetamine. Gang members also commit assault, auto theft, carjacking, drive-by shootings, extortion, homicide, identification fraud, and robbery.

Almighty Latin King and Queen Nation (National)

The Latin Kings street gang was formed in Chicago in the 1960s and consisted predominantly of Mexican and Puerto Rican males. Originally created with the philosophy of overcoming racial prejudice and creating an organization of "Kings," the Latin Kings evolved into a criminal enterprise operating throughout the United States under two umbrella factions—Motherland, also known as KMC (King Motherland Chicago), and Bloodline (New York). All members of the gang refer to themselves as Latin Kings and, currently, individuals of any nationality are allowed to become members. Latin Kings associating with the Motherland faction also identify themselves as "Almighty Latin King Nation (ALKN)," and make up more than 160 structured chapters operating in 158 cities in 31 states. The membership of Latin Kings following KMC is estimated to be 20,000 to 35,000. The Bloodline was founded by Luis Felipe in the New York State correctional system in 1986. Latin Kings associating with Bloodline also identify themselves as the "Almighty Latin King and Queen Nation (ALKQN)." Membership is estimated to be 2,200 to 7,500, divided among several dozen chapters operating in 15 cities in 5 states. Bloodline Latin Kings share a common culture and structure with KMC and respect them as the Motherland, but all chapters do not report to the Chicago leadership hierarchy. The gang's primary source of income is the street-level distribution of powder cocaine, crack cocaine, heroin, and marijuana. Latin Kings continue to portray themselves as a community organization while engaging in a wide variety of criminal activities, including assault, burglary, homicide, identity theft, and money laundering.

Asian Boyz (National)

Asian Boyz is one of the largest Asian street gangs operating in the United States. Formed in southern California in the early 1970s, the gang is estimated to have 1,300 to 2,000 members operating in at least 28 cities in 14 states. Members primarily are Vietnamese or Cambodian males. Members of Asian Boyz are involved in producing, transporting, and distributing methamphetamine as well as distributing MDMA and marijuana. In addition, gang members are involved in other criminal activities, including assault, burglary, drive-by shootings, and homicide.

Black P. Stone Nation (National)

Black P. Stone Nation, one of the largest and most violent associations of street gangs in the United States, consists of seven highly structured street gangs with a single leader and a common culture. It has an estimated 6,000 to 8,000 members, most of whom are African American males from the Chicago metropolitan area. The gang's main source of income is the street-level distribution of cocaine, heroin, marijuana and, to a lesser extent, methamphetamine. Members also are involved in many other types of criminal activity, including assault, auto theft, burglary, carjacking, drive-by shootings, extortion, homicide, and robbery.

Bloods (National)

Bloods is an association of structured and unstructured gangs that have adopted a single-gang culture. The original Bloods were formed in the early 1970s to provide protection from the Crips street gang in Los Angeles, California. Large, national-level Bloods gangs include Bounty Hunter Bloods and Crenshaw Mafia Gangsters. Bloods membership is estimated to be 7,000 to 30,000 nationwide; most members are African American males. Bloods gangs are active in 123 cities in 33 states. The main source of income for Bloods gangs is street-level distribution of cocaine and marijuana. Bloods members also are involved in transporting and distributing methamphetamine, heroin, and PCP (phencyclidine), but to a much lesser extent. The gangs also are involved in other criminal activity including assault, auto theft, burglary, carjacking, drive-by shootings, extortion, homicide, identity fraud, and robbery.

Crips (National)

Crips is a collection of structured and unstructured gangs that have adopted a common gang culture. Crips membership is estimated at 30,000 to 35,000; most members are African American males from the Los Angeles metropolitan area. Large, national-level Crips gangs include 107 Hoover Crips, Insane Gangster Crips, and Rolling 60s Crips. Crips gangs operate in 221 cities in 41 states. The main source of income for Crips gangs is the street-level distribution of powder cocaine, crack cocaine, marijuana, and PCP. The gangs also are involved in other criminal activity such as assault, auto theft, burglary, and homicide.

Florencia 13 (Regional)

Florencia 13 (F 13 or FX 13) originated in Los Angeles in the early 1960s; gang membership is estimated at more than 3,000 members. The gang operates primarily in California and increasingly in Arkansas, Missouri, New Mexico, and Utah. Florencia 13 is subordinate to the Mexican Mafia (La Eme) prison gang and claims Sureños (Sur 13) affiliation. A primary source of income for gang members is the trafficking of cocaine and methamphetamine. Gang members smuggle multikilogram quantities of powder cocaine and methamphetamine obtained from supply sources in Mexico into the United States for distribution. Also, gang members produce large quantities of methamphetamine in southern California for local distribution. Florencia members are involved in other criminal activities, including assault, drive-by shootings, and homicide.

Fresno Bulldogs (Regional)

Fresno Bulldogs is a street gang that originated in Fresno, California, in the late 1960s. Bulldogs is the largest Hispanic gang operating in central California, with membership estimated at 5,000 to 6,000. Bulldogs is one of the few Hispanic gangs in California that claim neither Sureños (Southern) nor Norteños (Northern) affiliation. However, gang members associate with Nuestra Familia (NF) members, particularly when trafficking drugs. The street-level distribution of methamphetamine, marijuana, and heroin is a primary source of income for gang members. In addition, members are involved in other criminal activity, including assault, burglary, homicide, and robbery.

Gangster Disciples (National)

The Gangster Disciples street gang was formed in Chicago, Illinois, in the mid-1960s. It is structured like a corporation and is led by a chairman of the board. Gang membership is estimated at 25,000 to 50,000; most members are African American males from the Chicago metropolitan area. The gang is active in 110 cities in 31 states. Its main source of income is the street-level distribution of cocaine, crack cocaine, marijuana, and heroin. The gang also is involved in other criminal activity, including assault, auto theft, firearms violations, fraud, homicide, the operation of prostitution rings, and money laundering.

Latin Disciples (Regional)

Latin Disciples, also known as Maniac Latin Disciples and Young Latino Organization, originated in Chicago in the late 1960s. The gang is composed of at least 10 structured and unstructured factions with an estimated 1,500 to 2,000 members and associate members. Most members are Puerto Rican males. Maniac Latin Disciples is the largest Hispanic gang in the Folk Nation Alliance. The gang is most active in the Great Lakes and southwestern regions of the United States. The street-level distribution of powder cocaine, heroin, marijuana, and PCP is a primary source of income for the gang. Members also are involved in other criminal activity, including assault, auto theft, carjacking, drive-by shootings, home invasion, homicide, money laundering, and weapons trafficking.

Mara Salvatrucha (National)

Mara Salvatrucha, also known as MS 13, is one of the largest Hispanic street gangs in the United States. Traditionally, the gang consisted of loosely affiliated groups known as cliques; however, law enforcement officials have reported increased coordination of criminal activity among Mara Salvatrucha cliques in the Atlanta, Dallas, Los Angeles, Washington, D.C., and New York metropolitan areas. The gang is estimated to have 30,000 to 50,000 members and associate members worldwide, 8,000 to 10,000 of whom reside in the United States. Members smuggle illicit drugs, primarily powder cocaine and marijuana, into the United States and transport and distribute the drugs throughout the country. Some members also are involved in alien smuggling, assault, drive-by shootings, homicide, identity theft, prostitution operations, robbery, and weapons trafficking.

Sureños and Norteños (National)

As individual Hispanic street gang members enter prison systems, they put aside former rivalries with other Hispanic street gangs and unite under the name Sureños or Norteños. The original Mexican Mafia members, most of whom were from southern California, considered Mexicans from the rural, agricultural areas of northern California weak and viewed them with contempt. To distinguish themselves from the agricultural workers or farmers from northern California, members of Mexican Mafia began to refer to the Hispanic gang members who worked for them as Sureños (Southerners). Inmates from northern California became known as Norteños (Northerners) and are affiliated with Nuestra Familia. Because of its size and strength, Fresno Bulldogs is the only Hispanic gang in the California Department of Corrections (CDC) that does not fall under Sureños or Norteños but remains independent. Sureños gang members' main sources of income are retail-level distribution of cocaine, heroin, marijuana, and methamphetamine within prison systems and in the community as well as extortion of drug distributors on the streets. Some members have direct links to Mexican DTOs and broker deals for Mexican Mafia as well as their own gang. Sureños gangs also are involved in other criminal activities such as assault, carjacking, home invasion, homicide, and robbery. Norteños gang members' main sources of income are the retail-level distribution of cocaine, heroin, marijuana, methamphetamine, and PCP within

The Girls in the Gang

Psychologist Anne Campbell studied female gangs in New York City and published her findings in her 1984 book, *The Girls in the Gang*. She summarizes some of her observations here:

All the girls in the gang come from families that are poor. Many have never known their fathers. Most are immigrants from Puerto Rico. As children the girls moved from apartment to apartment as they were evicted or burned out by arsonists. Unable to keep any friends they managed to make and alienated from their mothers, whose lack of English restricted their ability to control or understand their daughters' lives, the girls dropped out of school early and grew up on the streets. In the company of older kids and street-corner men, they graduated early into the adult world. They began to use drugs and by puberty had been initiated into sexual activity. By fifteen many were pregnant. Shocked, their mothers tried to pull them off the streets. Some sent their daughters back to relatives

in Puerto Rico while they had their babies. Abortion was out of the question in this Catholic world.

Those who stayed had "spoiled their identity" as good girls. Their reputations were marred before they ever reached adulthood. On the streets, among the gang members,

the girls found a convenient identity in the female gang. Often they had friends or distant relatives who introduced them as "prospects." After a trial period, they could undertake the initiation rite: they had to fight an established member nominated by the godmother.

■ *A portrait of Hispanic teen female members of the Pico Rivera gang, with one member holding her child.*

harmless as adherence to a particular dress code or as violent as a drive-by shooting. Experts have identified several types of suburban gangs.[71]

Delinquent Gangs

Delinquent gangs are similar to most inner-city gangs. Criminal activities include physical assaults, theft, burglary, and distribution of illegal drugs. The members seek money, peer recognition, the thrill of high-risk behavior, or even protection: "If you want to be able to walk the mall, you have to know you've got your boys behind you."[72] They typically adopt hand signals used by inner-city gangs.

Hate Gangs

These gangs, such as skinheads, attach themselves to an ideology that targets racial and ethnic groups. Vandalism, destruction of property, terrorist threats, physical assaults, and even murder are justified by their belief system. In 2003, three

men and a pregnant woman, all members of the Tacoma Skinhead Movement, beat and kicked a homeless man to death to achieve status and earn the right to wear red bootlaces—signifying that they have attacked an enemy of the white race. The number of racist skinheads is growing at an alarming rate. In 1988, 1,000 to 1,500 skinheads were operating in 12 states. By June 1993, the number was close to 3,500 spread across 40 states.[73] In 2006, the Anti-Defamation League identified 110 racist skinhead groups operating in every state, with as many as 10,000 members.[74] According to the FBI, there were 7,722 hate-crime incidents and 9,652 victims of hate crimes in 2006. Racial bias motivated 51.8 percent of the incidents, 18.9 percent were motivated by religious bias, crimes perpetrated based on sexual orientation accounted for 15.5 percent, and 12.7 percent were based on the ethnicity of the victim. Sixty percent of the hate crimes reported in 2006 were classified as person offenses.[75] Because of the difficulties

What was at issue was not winning or losing but demonstrating "heart," or courage. Gangs do not welcome members who join only to gain protection. The loyalty of other gang members has to be won by a clear demonstration of willingness to "get down," or fight.

Paradoxically, the female gang goes to considerable lengths to control the sexual behavior of its members. Although the neighborhood may believe they are fast women, the girls themselves do not tolerate members who sleep around. A promiscuous girl is a threat to the other members' relationships with their boyfriends. Members can take a boyfriend from among the male gang members (indeed, they are forbidden to take one from any other gang) but they are required to be monogamous. A shout of "Whore!" is the most frequent cause of fistfights among the female members.

On the positive side, the gang provides a strong sense of belonging and sisterhood. After the terrible isolation of their lives, the girls acquire a ready-made circle of friends who have shared many of their experiences and who are always willing to support them against hostile words or deeds by outsiders. Fighting together generates a strong sense of camaraderie and as a bonus earns them the reputation of being "crazy." This reputation is extremely useful in the tough neighborhoods where they live. Their reputation for carrying knives and for solidarity effectively deters outsiders from challenging them. They work hard at fostering their tough "rep" not only in their deeds but in their social talk. They spend hours recounting and embroidering stories of fights they have been in. Behind all this bravado it is easy to sense the fear they work so hard to deny. Terrified of being victims (as many of them have already been in their families and as newcomers in their schools), they make much of their own "craziness"—the violent unpredictability that frightens away anyone who might try to harm them.(1)

Campbell demonstrates the commonality of violence in the lives of female gang members in the early 1980s. Today there is growing concern over the increasing prevalence and severity of violence in some areas of the country.(2) The number of female gang members and the extent of changes in the use of violence are, however, still debated among researchers.(3)

Sources

1. Written by Anne Campbell. Adapted from Anne Campbell, *The Girls in the Gang* (New York: Basil Blackwell, 1984).
2. John M. Hagedorn, "Gang Violence in the Postindustrial Era," in *Youth Violence, Crime and Justice: A Review of Research*, vol. 24, eds. Michael Tonry and Mark H. Moore (Chicago: University of Chicago Press, 1998), pp. 365–419.
3. Margaret O'Brien, "At Least 16,000 Girls in Chicago's Gangs More Violent than Some Believe, Report Says," *Chicago Tribune*, September. 17, 1999, p. 5.

Questions for Discussion

1. How similar are Campbell's female gangs to the male gangs described in this chapter? Are there any significant differences?
2. Would you expect female gangs to become as involved in criminal activity as male gangs? Why or why not?

■ *Hate is shown by the demeanor and facial expressions of Denver skinheads at a demonstration against Martin Luther King Day.*

when neighborhood participants became involved in rent strikes, lawsuits charging discrimination, and public demonstrations. News of the conflict between supporters and opponents, and between the staff and the neighborhood it served, reached Congress, which made it clear that the point of the project was to reduce delinquency, not to reform society.

Little was done to evaluate the program's success. The project was eventually abandoned, and the commission that had established it ceased to exist. The political climate had changed, and federal money was no longer available for sweeping social programs. However, MOBY's failure does not disprove the opportunity theory on which it was based. In 1995, the Office of Juvenile Justice and Delinquency Prevention (OJJDP) launched the Comprehensive Gang Model, a pilot project based on the same principles as MOBY. Evaluations of the Comprehensive Gang Model reveal mixed results. The program has been shown to reduce arrests for serious violence and drugs in some sites. In others, however, it has had no significant effect on gang involvement or serious delinquency among participants compared to nonparticipants.[80]

Other Programs

Many other programs based on subcultural theory have attempted to change the attitudes and behavior of ghetto youngsters who have spent most of their lives learning unconventional street norms. Change is accomplished by setting up an extended-family environment for high-risk youths, one that provides positive role models, academic and vocational training, strict rules for behavior, drug treatment, health care, and other services. For many youths, these programs provide the first warm, caring living arrangement they have ever had.

One such program is the House of Umoja (a Swahili word for "unity") in Philadelphia. At any given time, about 25 black male teenage offenders live together as "sons" of the founder, Sister Fattah. Each resident signs a contract with Umoja obligating himself to help in the household, become an active part of the family group, study, and work in one of the program's businesses (a restaurant, a moving company, a painting shop) or elsewhere. By many measures this program is successful.

Programs similar to Umoja have spread throughout the country; they include Argus in New York's South Bronx; Violent Juvenile Offender Research and Development programs in Chicago, Dallas, New Orleans, Los Angeles, and San Diego; and Neighborhood Anticrime Self-Help programs in Baltimore, Newark, Cleveland, Boston, Miami, and Washington, D.C. All have the same mission: to provide a bridge

from a delinquent subcultural value system to a conventional one.[81]

Other means have been used to break up delinquent subcultures. Street workers, many of them former gang members (called "OGs," for "original gangsters"), serve as a "street-smart diplomatic corps" in many of the poorest ghettos in the country.[82] In Los Angeles, where gang members control many streets, the OGs work for the Community Youth Gang Service (a government-funded agency). Five nights a week, more than 50 of these street workers cover the city, trying to settle disputes between rival gangs and to discourage nonmembers from joining them. They look for alternatives to violence, in baseball games, fairs, and written peace treaties. During a typical evening, the street workers may try to head off a gang fight:

> *Parton [street worker]:* Hey, you guys, Lennox is going to be rollin' by here. . . .
>
> *Ms. Diaz [street worker]:* You with your back to the street, homeboy. They goin' to be lookin' for this car, some burgundy car.
>
> *Boy:* If they want to find me, they know where I'm at.
>
> *Ms. Diaz:* I'm tellin' you to be afraid of them. There are some girls here. You better tell them to move down the street. . . . We are goin' back over there to try to keep them there. Don't get lazy or drunk and not know what you're doin'. I know you don't think it's serious, but if one of your friends gets killed tonight, you will.
>
> *Boy:* It's serious, I know.
>
> *Ms. Diaz:* We're goin' to keep them in their 'hood, you just stay in yours for a while.
>
> *Boy:* All right.[83]

After 2 hours of negotiation, the fight was called off. There was plenty of work left for the team. They would continue the next day to help the gang members find jobs.

Getting Out: Gang Banging or the Morgue

The most difficult problem that counselors and street workers face is the power gangs have over their members. Gangs, through loyalty and terror, make it almost impossible for members to quit. Many gang members would gladly get out, but any move to leave leads to gang banging or the morgue. Second Chance Grace, a nonprofit organization in Meridian, Idaho, works with at-risk youth and young adults immersed in drugs, gangs, and other criminal activities. The organization has developed a program that offers laser tattoo removal free or at reduced cost to ex-gang members and former drug addicts.[84] A Wichita, Kansas, group, the church-sponsored Project Freedom, has created an "underground railroad," a network of local contacts that leads families with gang members to anonymity and freedom out of state.[85]

Gangs, once a local problem, have become a national concern. The federal antigang budget goes primarily to police and prosecution. In 1992, the Department of Justice spent $500 million on law enforcement. Crime has decreased overall in the last several years, yet gang-related crime continues to rise.[86] In 2007, Deputy U.S. Marshals and their task-force partners apprehended nearly 2,500 fugitives who were affiliated with gangs.[87] Despite this upward trend in gang activity, the Department of Justice was allocated $418,376 in antigang funds in 2008, and $386,713 for 2009.[88] Experts agree that unless we put more money into educational and socioeconomic programs, there is little likelihood that America's gang problems will lessen in the near future.

In the decade between the mid-1950s and mid-1960s, criminologists began to theorize about the development and content of youth subcultures and the gangs that flourish within them. Some suggested that lower-class males, frustrated by their inability to meet middle-class standards, set up their own norms by which they could gain status. Often these norms clashed with those of the dominant culture. Other investigators have refuted the idea that delinquent behavior stems from a rejection of middle-class values. They claim that lower-class values are separate and distinct from middle-class values and that it is the lower-class value system that generates delinquent behavior.

Gangs in the twenty-first century show increasing violence and reliance on guns, as is the case with MS-13. They are involved in large profit-making activities such as drug distribution. The number of homicides is rising.

Explanations of female delinquent subcultures and middle-class delinquency are an extension of subcultural explanations of lower-class delinquency. While the theories of reaction formation, the subculture of violence, and differential opportunity differ in some respects, they all share one basic assumption—that delinquent and criminal behaviors are linked to the values and norms of the areas where youngsters grow up.

"Many aspects of female gang functioning and the lives of female gang members remain a mystery because relatively few researchers have considered female gangs worthy of study. In addition, researchers face serious obstacles to the study of female gangs and, because of these obstacles, they often settle for unrepresentative samples. Gangs are highly suspicious of researchers and cooperate with them only under unusual circumstances. Female gang members, in particular, have been averse to talking about sexual abuse, whether it occurred at home or within the gang.... Unfortunately, female gang members have received little programmatic attention." (SOURCE: Joan Moore and John Hagedorn, *Female Gangs: A Focus on Research* [Washington, D.C.: OJJDP, 2001].)

Questions for Discussion Can you conceive of other reasons why female gangs have been overlooked? After reviewing the work of Professor Anne Campbell (See the box "Criminological Concerns: The Girls in the Gang"), what kinds of programs do you suppose would help female gang members make a transition to prosocial activities and lifestyles? In what ways must these programs differ from those proposed for male gang members?

You are a consultant called in to address the rise in female gang activity and violence. On what theory or theories would you base your intervention? Are the theories based on male delinquency sufficient? Are gender-based theories necessary?

The numbers next to the terms refer to the pages on which the terms are defined.

differential opportunity theory (142)

reaction formation (140)

subculture (139)

subcultures of violence (146)

the child participate and succeed in a social unit such as the school (by demonstrating good study habits, for example) and to reinforce conformity or punish violations of the group's norms. Results suggest that these initiatives decrease children's aggressiveness and increase parenting skills.[62]

School

A program called PATHE (Positive Action Through Holistic Education) operates in middle schools and high schools around the United States. Its objective is to reduce delinquency by strengthening students' commitment to school and attachment to conforming members—in other words, by bonding young people to the conventional system.[63]

Neighborhood

Historically, church and family have helped protect and maintain the social order in neighborhoods and instill a sense of pride and comfort in residents. This is no longer the case in many areas. The neighborhood as an institution of informal social control has been very much weakened. Various agencies have tried to reverse this trend with programs to prevent juvenile crime that are implemented through neighborhood-based organizations, for example, in Chicago, Dallas, Los Angeles, New Orleans, New York, and San Diego. Federally funded programs seek to reduce crime by strengthening neighborhood cohesion. Programs assess the needs of residents and then set up crisis-intervention centers, mediation (between youngsters and school, family, or police and between warring gangs), youth training, supervision programs, and family support systems.

Program evaluations reveal that serious juvenile crime decreases.[64] Hundreds of such community crime-prevention projects around the country have been organized by government agencies, private persons, and religious groups.[65] They have made a local impact, but they have not been able to change the national crime rate. The most successful models, however, may offer a plan for crime prevention on a broader, perhaps even a national, scale.

As our understanding of control theory evolves, so will our appreciation of the effects of control interventions. If nothing else, it is fair to say that social control programs and interventions are proliferating and may be found in every state. Here are just a few examples:

Homebuilders (Tacoma, Washington). A family preservation program that seeks to keep at-risk children at home.[66]

Families First (Michigan). A program that strengthens vulnerable families[67]

S.W.E.A.T. Team (Bridgeport, Connecticut). A project that employs teenagers to create new activities for children who may be tempted to join gangs or sell drugs[68]

Learnfare (Ohio, Virginia, Florida, Maryland, and Oklahoma). Programs that provide financial and social support for teenage welfare mothers who attend school[69]

Crime-prevention programs over the past decade have met with significant success. Most of these efforts are grounded in principles of social control.

CHAPTER 7

REVIEW The term "social control" has taken on a wide variety of meanings. In general, it describes any mechanism that leads to conformity to social norms. Mainstream studies of social control take one of two approaches. Macrosociological studies focus on formal systems of social control. Most contemporary criminological research takes the microsociological approach, which focuses on informal systems. Travis Hirschi's social control theory has had a long-lasting impact on the scholarly community. Hirschi identified four social bonds that promote adherence to society's values: attachment, commitment, involvement, and belief. The stronger these bonds, Hirschi claimed, the less the likelihood of delinquency.

According to the containment theory of Walter Reckless, every person has a containing external structure (a role in a social group with reasonable limits and responsibilities and alternative means of attaining satisfaction). In addition, each individual has a protective internal structure that depends on a good self-concept, self-control, a well-developed conscience, a tolerance for frustration, and a strong sense of responsibility.

Most investigators today believe that personal (inner) controls are as important as social (external) controls in keeping people from committing crimes. Albert Reiss found that personal controls reinforce social controls. Jackson Toby stressed the importance of a stake in conformity in keeping a person from responding to social disorganization with delinquent behavior. Recent efforts to integrate social control theories with other theories have resulted in developmental, integrated, and general theories of crime. All share one common variable—the social bonds that constitute social control theory. These efforts are notable, however, for their explanations of criminal behavior over the life course. More so than ever before, criminologists are examining the onset, continuance, desistance, and stability of criminal offending over the life course.

As part of an effort to reduce delinquency, a variety of programs at the local and regional levels help parents, schools, and neighborhood groups develop social controls.

CRIMINOLOGY & PUBLIC POLICY

In recent years, lawmakers at both the state and federal levels have passed legislation increasing penalties for criminal offenses, particularly violent crimes. These actions came in response to public concerns about crime and the belief that many serious offenders are released from prison too soon. Many such laws have come under the general label of "three strikes and you're out." The purpose of these laws is simple: Offenders convicted repeatedly of serious offenses should be removed from society for long periods of time, in many cases for life. For many years, most states have had provisions in their laws that included enhanced sentencing for repeat offenders. Yet between 1993 and 1995, 24 states and the federal government enacted new laws using the "three strikes" moniker, with similarly labeled bills introduced in a number of other states.

The rapid expansion of three-strikes laws, regardless of how they are defined, reflects the perception that existing laws did not adequately protect public safety in their application and/or outcome, that exceptional incidents had occurred that the new laws would address, or that the

intent of current laws was being frustrated by other factors such as prison crowding. Whether the perception was accurate and what the impact of the new laws will be are questions that cannot yet be answered. (SOURCE: John Clark, James Austin, and D. Alan Henry, *Three Strikes and You're Out: A Review of State Legislation* [Washington, D.C.: NIJ, 1997].)

Questions for Discussion Three-strikes laws can be harsh. Offenders committing petty thefts as their third strike may in some jurisdictions, for example, receive 25 or more years in prison as courts and prosecutors take their prior record into consideration. Such sentences were upheld by the U.S. Supreme Court in 2003. What concerns with three-strikes laws are raised by recent extensions to Hirschi's notion of social control—life course theories of offending? If the fundamental rationale of three-strikes laws is to protect the community from habitual offenders, are life course theories supportive? If we know what best predicts future offending and if programs can be created to address these causal factors, why rely on long prison sentences?

YOU BE THE CRIMINOLOGIST

The desire for stability, involvement, belief, and conformity can have a dark side. Consider how mechanisms of social control, narrowly conceived, can support new religious, political, and

psychosocial cults or sects. How does social control theory help explain the attraction to Heaven's Gate, the Aum Shinrikyo, the Order of the Solar Temple, or the Branch Davidians?

KEY TERMS

The numbers next to the terms refer to the pages on which the terms are defined.

attachment (167)
belief (168)
commitment (168)
conformity (173)
containment theory (173)
direct control (176)

drift (170)
indirect control (176)
internalized control (176)
involvement (168)
macrosociological studies (166)
microsociological studies (166)
social control theory (165)
synnomie (181)

8

Labeling, Conflict, and Radical Theories

■ Occupy Wall Street protest in New York City on February 29, 2012 (called "Shut Down the Corporations" by protesters).

Each era of social and political turmoil has produced profound changes in people's lives. Perhaps no such era was as significant for criminology as the 1960s. A society with conservative values was shaken out of its complacency when young people, blacks, women, and other disadvantaged groups demanded a part in the shaping of national policy. They saw the gaps between philosophical political demands and reality: Blacks had little opportunity to advance; women were kept in an inferior status; old politicians made wars in which the young had to die.

Rebellion broke out, and some criminologists joined the revolution.

These criminologists turned away from theories that explained crime by characteristics of the offender or of the social structure. They set out to demonstrate that individuals become criminals because of what people with power, especially those in the criminal justice system, do. Their explanations largely reject the consensus model of crime, on which all earlier theories rested. Their theories not only question the traditional explanations of the creation and enforcement of criminal law but also blame that law for the making of criminals (Table 8.1).

It may not sound so radical to assert that unless an act is made criminal by law, no person who performs that act can be adjudicated a criminal. The exponents of contemporary alternative explanations of crime grant that much. But—justifiably—they also ask, Who makes these laws in the first place? And why? Is breaking such laws the most important criterion for being a criminal? Are all people who break these laws criminals? Do all members of society agree that those singled out by the criminal law to be called "criminals" are criminals and that others are not?

LABELING THEORY

The 1950s were a period of general prosperity and pride for Americans. Yet some social scientists, uneasy about the complacency they saw, turned their attention to the social order. They noted that some of the ideals the United States had fought for in World War II had not been achieved at home. Human rights existed on paper but were often lacking in practice. It was clear that blacks continued to live as second-class citizens. Even though the Fourteenth Amendment to the Constitution guaranteed blacks equal rights, neither the law of the country nor the socioeconomic system provided them with equal opportunities.

Nowhere was this fact more apparent than in the criminal justice system. Social scientists and liberal lawyers pressed for change, and the Supreme Court, under Chief Justice Earl Warren, responded. In case after case, the Court found a pervasive influence of rules and customs that violated the concepts of **due process,** under which a person cannot be deprived of life, liberty, or property without lawful procedures; and **equal protection,** under which no one can be denied the safeguards of the law. The result of hundreds of Supreme Court decisions was that both black and white citizens now were guaranteed the right to counsel in all criminal cases, freedom from self-incrimination, and other rights enumerated in the first 10 amendments to the Constitution. Nevertheless, a great deal of social injustice remained.

In this social climate, a small group of social scientists, known as "labeling theorists," began to explore how and why certain acts were defined as criminal or, more broadly, as deviant behavior and others were not, and how and why certain people were defined as criminal or deviant. These theorists viewed criminals not as inherently evil

TABLE 8.1 Comparison of Four Criminological Perspectives

Perspective	Origin of Criminal Law	Causes of Criminal Behavior	Focus of Study
Traditional/consensus	Laws reflect shared values.	Psychological, biological, or sociological factors.	Biological and psychological factors (Chap. 4); unequal opportunity (Chap. 5); learning criminal behavior in disorganized neighborhoods (Chap. 5); subculture values (Chap. 6); social control (Chap. 7).
Labeling	Those in power create the laws, decide who will be the rule breakers.	The process that defines (or labels) certain persons as criminals.	Effects of stigmatizing by the label "criminal"; sociopolitical factors behind reform legislation; origin of laws; deviant behavior (Chap. 8).
Conflict	Powerful groups use laws to support their interests.	Interests of one group do not coincide with needs of another.	Bias and discrimination in criminal justice system; differential crime rates of powerful and powerless; development of criminal laws by those in power; relationship between rulers and ruled (Chap. 8).
Radical (Marxist)	Laws serve interests of the ruling class.	Class struggle over distribution of resources in a capitalist system.	Relationship between crime and economics; ways in which state serves capitalist interests; solution to crime problem based on collapse of capitalism (Chap. 8).

persons engaged in inherently wrong acts but rather as individuals who had had criminal status conferred upon them by both the criminal justice system and the community at large.

Viewed from this perspective, criminal acts themselves are not particularly significant; the social reaction to them, however, is. Deviance and its control involve a process of social definition in which the response of others to an individual's behavior is the key influence on subsequent behavior and on individuals' views of themselves. Sociologist Howard S. Becker has written:

> Deviance is not a quality of the act the person commits, but rather a consequence of the application by others of rules and sanctions to an "offender." The deviant is one to whom that label has successfully been applied; deviant behavior is behavior that people so label.[1]

In focusing on the ways in which social interactions create deviance, **labeling theory** declares that the reactions of other people and the subsequent effects of those reactions create deviance. Once it becomes known that a person has engaged in deviant acts, he or she is segregated from conventional society, and a label ("thief," "whore," "junkie") is attached to the transgressor. This process of segregation creates "outsiders" (as Becker called them), or outcasts from society, who begin to associate with others like themselves.[2]

As more people begin to think of these people as deviants and to respond to them accordingly, the deviants react to the response by continuing to engage in the behavior society now expects of them. Through this process, their self-images gradually change as well. So the key factor is the label that is attached to an individual: "If men define situations as real, they are real in their consequences."[3]

The Origins of Labeling Theory

The intellectual roots of labeling theory can be traced to the post–World War I work of Charles Horton Cooley, William I. Thomas, and George Herbert Mead. These scholars, who viewed the human self as formed through a process of social interaction, were called **social interactionists.** In 1918, Mead compared the impact of social labeling to "the angel with the fiery sword at the gate who can cut one off from the world to which he belongs."[4]

Labeling separates the good from the bad, the conventional from the deviant. Mead's interest in deviance focused on the social interactions by which an individual becomes a deviant. The person is not just a fixed structure whose action is the result of certain factors acting upon it. Rather, social behavior develops in a continuous process of action and reaction.[5] The way we perceive ourselves, our self-concept, is built not only on what we think of ourselves but also on what others think of us.

Somewhat later, historian Frank Tannenbaum (1893–1969) used the same argument in his study of the causes of criminal behavior. He described the creation of a criminal as a process: Breaking windows, climbing onto roofs, and playing truant are all normal parts of the adolescent search for excitement and adventure. Local merchants and others who experience these activities may consider them a nuisance or perhaps even evil. This conflict is the beginning of the process by which the evil act transforms the transgressor into an evil individual. From that point on, the evil individuals are separated from those in conventional society. Given a criminal label, they gradually begin to think of themselves as they have been officially defined.

Tannenbaum maintained that it is the process of labeling, or the "dramatization of evil," that locks a mischievous boy into a delinquent role ("the person becomes the thing he is described as being"). Accordingly, "the entire process of dealing with young delinquents is mischievous insofar as it identifies him to himself and to the environment as a delinquent person."[6] The system starts out with a child in trouble and ends up with a juvenile delinquent.

Basic Assumptions of Labeling Theory

In the 1940s, sociologist Edwin Lemert elaborated on Tannenbaum's discussion by formulating the basic assumptions of labeling theory.[7] He reminded us that people are constantly involved in behavior that runs the risk of being labeled delinquent or criminal. But although many run that risk, only a few are so labeled. The reason, Lemert contended, is that there are two kinds of deviant acts: primary and secondary.[8]

"Primary deviations" are the initial deviant acts that bring on the first social response. These acts do not affect the individual's self-concept. It is the "secondary deviations," the acts that follow the societal response to the primary deviation, that are of major concern. These are the acts that result from the change in self-concept brought about by the labeling process.[9] The scenario goes somewhat like this:

1. An individual commits a simple deviant act (primary deviation)—throwing a stone at a neighbor's car, for instance.

2. There is an informal social reaction: The neighbor gets angry.

3. The individual continues to break rules (primary deviations)—he lets the neighbor's dog out of the yard.

4. There is increased, but still primary, social reaction: The neighbor tells the youth's parents.

5. The individual commits a more serious deviant act—he is caught shoplifting (still primary deviation).

6. There is a formal reaction: The youth is adjudicated a "juvenile delinquent" in juvenile court.

7. The youth is now labeled "delinquent" by the court and "bad" by the neighborhood, by his conventional peers, and by others.

8. The youth begins to think of himself as "delinquent"; he joins other unconventional youths.

9. The individual commits another, yet more serious, deviant act (secondary deviation)—he robs a local grocery store with members of a gang.

10. The individual is returned to juvenile court, has more offenses added to his record, is cast out further from conventional society, and takes on a completely deviant lifestyle.

According to Lemert, secondary deviance sets in after the community has become aware of a primary deviance. Individuals experience "a continuing sense of injustice, which [is] reinforced by job rejections, police cognizance, and strained interaction with normals."[10] In short, deviant individuals have to bear the stigma of the "delinquent" label, just as English and American convicts, as late as the eighteenth century, bore stigmas, in the form of an "M" for murderer or a "T" for thief, burned or cut into their bodies to designate them as persons to be shunned.[11] Once such a label is attached to a person, a deviant or criminal career has been set in motion. The full significance of labeling theory was not recognized, either in Europe or in the United States, until political events provided the opportunity.[12]

Labeling in the 1960s

The 1960s witnessed a movement among students and professors to join advocacy groups and become activists in the social causes that were rapidly gaining popularity on college campuses across the nation, such as equal rights for minorities, liberation for women, and peace for humankind. The protests took many forms—demonstrations and rallies, sit-ins and teach-ins, beards and long hair, rock music and marijuana, dropping out of school, burning draft cards.

Arrests of middle-class youths increased rapidly; crime was no longer confined to the ghettos. People asked whether arrests were being made for behavior that was not really criminal. Were the real criminals the legislators and policy makers who pursued a criminal war in Vietnam while creating the artificial crime of draft card burning at home? Were the real criminals the National Guardsmen who shot and killed campus demonstrators at Kent State University? Labeling theorists made

■ *A Kent State University protestor grieving over the body of a fellow student shot and killed by National Guardsmen, Ohio, 1970.*

Crime Surfing

http://critcrim.org/
perspectives

Do critical
criminologists support
the death penalty, or
are they opposed?

surplus, high unemployment, and a burgeoning class of young urban migrants forced into the streets by poverty. London is said to have had at least 20,000 individuals who "rose every morning without knowing how they were to be supported through the day or where they were to lodge on the succeeding night, and cases of death from starvation appeared in the coroner's lists daily."[50] In other cities, conditions were even worse.

Engels and Marx

It was against this background that Friedrich Engels (1820–1895) addressed the effects of the Industrial Revolution. A partner in his father's industrial empire, Engels was himself a member of the class he attacked as "brutally selfish." After a 2-year stay in England, he documented the awful social conditions, the suffering, and the great increase in crime and arrests. All these problems he blamed on one factor—competition. In *The Condition of the Working Class in England,* published in 1845, he spelled out the association between crime and poverty as a political problem:

> The earliest, crudest, and least fruitful form of this rebellion was that of crime. The working man lived in poverty and want, and saw that others were better off than he. . . . Want conquered his inherited respect for the sacredness of property, and he stole.[51]

Though Karl Marx (1818–1883) paid little attention to crime specifically, he argued that all aspects of social life, including laws, are determined by economic organization. His philosophy reflects the economic despair that followed the Industrial Revolution. In his *Communist Manifesto* (1848), Marx viewed the history of all societies as a documentation of class struggles: "Freeman and slave, patrician and plebeian, lord and serf, guildmaster and journeyman, in a word, oppressor and oppressed, stood in constant opposition to one another."[52]

Marx went on to describe the most important relationship in industrial society as that between the capitalist bourgeoisie, who own the means of production, and the proletariat, or workers, who labor for them. Society, according to Marx, has always been organized in such a hierarchical fashion, with the state representing not the common interest but the interests of those who own the means of production. Capitalism breeds egocentricity, greed, and predatory behavior; but the worst crime of all is the exploitation of workers. Revolution, Marx concluded, is the only means to bring about change, and for that reason it is morally justifiable.

Many philosophers before Marx had noted the link between economic conditions and social problems, including crime. Among them were Plato, Aristotle, Virgil, Horace, Sir Thomas More, Cesare Beccaria, Jeremy Bentham, André Guerry, Adolphe Quételet, and Gabriel Tarde (several of whom we discussed in Chapter 3). But none of them had advocated revolutionary change. And none had constructed a coherent criminological theory that conformed with economic determinism. The cornerstone of the Marxist explanation is that people who are kept in a state of poverty will rebel by committing crimes. Not until 1905 can we speak of Marxist criminology.

Willem Adriaan Bonger

As a student at the University of Amsterdam, Willem Adriaan Bonger (1876–1940) entered a paper in a competition on the influence of economic factors on crime. His entry did not win, but its expanded version, *Criminality and Economic Conditions*, which appeared in French in 1905, was selected for translation by the American Institute of Criminal Law and Criminology. Bonger wrote in his preface, "[I am] convinced that my ideas about the etiology of crime will not be shared by a great many readers of the American edition."[53] He was right. Nevertheless, the book is considered a classic and is invaluable to students doing research on crime and economics.

Bonger explained that the social environment of primitive people was interwoven with the means of production. People helped each other. They used what they produced. When food was plentiful, everyone ate. When food was scarce, everyone was hungry. Whatever people had, they shared. People were subordinate to nature. In a modern capitalist society, people are much less altruistic. They concentrate on production for profit rather than for the needs of the community. Capitalism encourages criminal behavior by creating a climate that is less conducive to social responsibility. "We have a right," argued Bonger, "to say that the part played by economic conditions in criminality is predominant, even decisive."[54]

Willem Bonger died as he had lived, a fervent antagonist of the evils of the social order. An archenemy of Nazism and a prominent name on Hitler's list of people to be eliminated, he refused to emigrate even when the German army was at the border. On May 10, 1940, as the German invasion of Holland began, he wrote to his son: "I don't see any future for myself and I cannot bow to this scum which will now overmaster us."[55] He then took his own life. He left a powerful political and criminological legacy. Foremost among his followers were German socialist philosophers of the progressive school of Frankfurt.

Georg Rusche and Otto Kirchheimer

Georg Rusche and Otto Kirchheimer began to write their classic work at the University of Frankfurt. Driven out of Germany by Nazi persecution, they continued their research in exile in

Paris and completed it at Columbia University in New York in 1939. In *Punishment and the Social Structure,* they wrote that punishments had always been related to the modes of production and the availability of labor, rather than to the nature of the crimes themselves.

Consider galley slavery. Before the development of modern sailing techniques, oarsmen were needed to power merchant ships; as a result, galley slavery was a punishment in antiquity and in the Middle Ages. As sailing techniques were perfected, galley slavery was no longer necessary, and it lost favor as a sanction. By documenting the real purposes of punishments through the ages, Rusche and Kirchheimer made **penologists,** those who study the penal system, aware that severe and cruel treatment of offenders had more to do with the value of human life and the needs of the economy than with preventing crime.

The names Marx, Engels, Bonger, and Rusche and Kirchheimer were all but forgotten by mainstream criminologists of the 1940s and 1950s, perhaps because of America's relative prosperity and conservatism during those years. But when tranquillity turned to turmoil in the mid-1960s, the forgotten names provided the intellectual basis for American and European radical criminologists, who explicitly stated their commitment to Marxism.

Radical Criminology since the 1970s

Radical criminology (also called "critical," "new," and "Marxist criminology") made its first public appearance in 1968, when a group of British sociologists organized the National Deviancy Conference (NDC), a group of more than 300 intellectuals, social critics, deviants, and activists of various persuasions. What the group members had in common was a basic disillusionment with the criminological studies being done by the British Home Office, which they believed was system-serving and "practical." They were concerned with the way the system controlled people rather than with traditional sociological and psychological explanations of crime. They shared a respect for the interactionist and labeling theorists but believed that these theorists had become too traditional. Their answer was to form a new criminology based on Marxist principles.

The conference was followed by the publication in 1973 of *The New Criminology,* the first textual formulation of the new radical criminology. According to its authors, Ian Taylor, Paul Walton, and Jock Young, it is the underclass, the "labor forces of the industrial society," that is controlled through the criminal law and its enforcement, while "the owners of labor will be bound only by a civil law which regulates their competition between each other." The economic institution,

then, is the source of all conflicts. Struggles between classes always relate to the distribution of resources and power, and only when capitalism is abolished will crime disappear.[56]

About the time that Marxist criminology was being formulated in England, it was also developing in the United States, particularly at the School of Criminology of the University of California at Berkeley, where Richard Quinney, Anthony Platt, Herman and Julia Schwendinger, William Chambliss, and Paul Takagi were at the forefront of the movement. These researchers were also influenced by interactionist and labeling theorists, as well as by the conflict theories of Vold, Dahrendorf, and Turk.

Though the radical criminologists share the central tenet of conflict theory—that laws are created by the powerful to protect their own interests—they disagree on the number of forces competing in the power struggle. For Marxist criminologists, there is only one dominating segment, the capitalist ruling class, which uses the criminal law to impose its will on the rest of the people in order to protect its property and to define as criminal any behavior that threatens the status quo.[57] The leading American spokesperson for radical criminology is Richard Quinney. His earliest Marxist publications appeared in 1973: "Crime Control in Capitalist Society" and "There's a Lot of Us Folks Grateful to the Lone Ranger."[58] The second of these essays describes how Quinney drifted away from capitalism, with its folklore myths embodied in individual heroes like the Lone Ranger.[59]

In *Class, State, and Crime,* Quinney proclaims that "the criminal justice movement is . . . a state-initiated and state-supported effort to rationalize mechanisms of social control. The larger purpose is to secure a capitalist order that is in grave crisis, likely in its final stage of development."[60] Quinney challenges criminologists to abandon traditional ways of thinking about causation, to study what could be rather than what is, to question the assumptions of the social order, and to "ultimately develop a Marxist perspective."[61]

Marxist theory also can be found in the writings of other scholars who have adopted the radical approach to criminology. William Chambliss and Robert Seidman present their version in *Law, Order, and Power:*

> Society is composed of groups that are in conflict with one another and . . . the law represents an institutionalized tool of those in power (ruling class) which functions to provide them with superior moral as well as coercive power in conflict.[62]

They comment that if, in the operation of the criminal justice system by the powerful, "justice or fairness happen to be served, it is sheer coincidence."[63]

A male thief shoplifts from a store by slipping merchandise into his jacket.

criminals to use in committing their crimes. As people's daily work and leisure activities change with time, the location of property and personal targets also changes.

The logic of the routine-activity argument is straightforward: Routine patterns of work, play, and leisure time affect the convergence in time and place of motivated offenders who are not "handled," suitable targets, and the absence of guardians. If one component is missing, crime is not likely to be committed. And if all components are in place and one of them is strengthened, crime is likely to increase. Even if the proportions of motivated offenders and targets stay the same, changes in routine activities alone—for example, changes of the sort we have experienced since World War II—will raise the crime rate by multiplying the opportunities for crime. This approach has helped explain, among other things, rates of victimization for specific crimes, rates of urban homicide, and "hot spots"—areas that produce a disproportionate number of calls to police.[15]

Practical Applications of Situational Theories of Crime

The trio of approaches discussed here—environmental criminology, rational choice, and routine activities—often work together to explain why a person may commit a crime in a particular situation. We look now at how these theories of crime

are used to explain specific varieties of crime, and how the ideas that arise from these theories have practical applications.

Burglars and Burglary

Criminologists are increasingly interested in the factors that go into a decision to burglarize: the location or setting of the building, the presence of guards or dogs, the type of burglar alarms and external lighting, and so forth. Does a car in the driveway or a radio playing music in the house have a significant impact on the choice of home to burglarize? George Rengert and John Wasilchick conducted extensive interviews with suburban burglars in an effort to understand their techniques. They found significant differences with respect to several factors:[16]

- *The amount of planning* that precedes a burglary. Professional burglars plan more than do amateurs.

- The extent to which a burglar engages in *systematic selection of a home*. Some burglars examine the obvious clues, such as presence of a burglar alarm, a watchdog, mail piled up in the mailbox, newspapers on a doorstep. More experienced burglars look for subtle clues—for example, closed windows coupled with air conditioners that are turned off.

- The extent to which a burglar pays *attention to situational cues*. Some burglars routinely choose a corner property because it offers more avenues of escape, has fewer adjoining properties, and offers visibility.

Rengert and Wasilchick have also examined the use of time and place in burglary (Figure 9.3). Time is a critical factor to burglars, for three reasons:

- They must minimize the time spent in targeted places so as not to reveal their intention to burglarize.

- Opportunities for burglary occur only when a dwelling is unguarded or unoccupied, that is, during daytime. (Many burglars would call in sick so often that they would be fired from their legitimate jobs; others simply quit their jobs because the jobs interfered with their burglaries.)

- Burglars have "working hours"; that is, they have time available only during a limited number of hours (if they have a legitimate job).

Before committing their offenses, burglars take into account familiarity with the area, fear of recognition, concern over standing out as somebody who does not belong, and the possibility (following some successful burglaries) that a particular area is

■ *Thomas Crown (portrayed by Pierce Brosnan) crafted an extremely clever and well-planned theft of a painting from a well-guarded museum. Of course, not all burglars are so affluent and calculative.*

no longer cost-beneficial. Season, too, plays an important role. One experienced burglar stated that because neighborhoods are populated with children in the summer, he opted for winter months: "The best time to do crime out here is between 8:00 and 9:00 [A.M.]. All the mothers are taking the kids to school. I wait until I see the car leave. By the time she gets back, I've come and gone."[17]

Recent research demonstrates how important it is for burglars to have prior knowledge of their targets. They obtain such knowledge by knowing the occupants, by being tipped off about the occupants, or by observing the potential target. Some burglars even acquire jobs that afford them the opportunity to observe their potential victims' daily activities; others gain access to the interior of a house, search for valuable goods, and steal them at a later date. There are others, however, who come across burglary opportunities during the course of their daily routine instead of planning them. For these offenders, rational-choice decisions are made right before the criminal event.[18]

Robbers and Robberies

Richard Wright and Scott Decker conducted in-depth interviews with street robbers and found that they frequently victimize other street-involved individuals—drug dealers, drug users, and gang members—who, because they are criminals themselves, are unlikely to go to the police. These people are also targeted because they are believed to have a lot of money, jewelry, and other desirable items. Street robbers report that they sometimes specifically target people whom they do not like or people who have hurt or offended them in the past. When women are targeted, it is because robbers believe they will not resist and are not armed. On the other hand, women are not the desirable targets that men are because robbers think women do not carry as much money.[19]

Criminologists also study whether commercial robbers operate the same way as street robbers in their selection of targets. Robbers who target business establishments are interested in some of the same factors that concern burglars. Perpetrators carefully examine the location of the potential robbery, the potential gain, the capability of security personnel, the possibility of intervention by bystanders, and the presence of guards, cameras, and alarms.[20]

Criminologists have found that potential victims and establishments can do quite a bit to decrease the likelihood of being robbed. Following a series of convenience-store robberies in Gainesville, Florida, in 1985, a city ordinance required store owners to clear their windows of signs that obstructed the view of the interior, to position cash registers where they would be visible from the street, and to install approved electronic cameras.

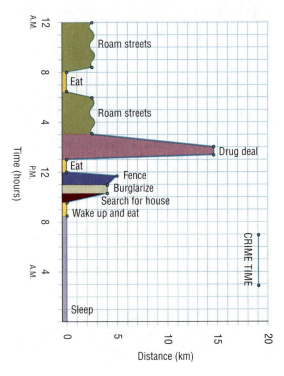

FIGURE 9.3 Crime day of burglar #26.

Source: From George Rengert and John Wasilchick, *Suburban Burglary: A Time and a Place for Everything*, 1985, p. 35. Courtesy of Charles C Thomas Publisher, Ltd., Springfield, Illinois.

TABLE 9.3   Sixteen Techniques of Situational Crime Prevention

Increasing Perceived Effort	Increasing Perceived Risks	Reducing Anticipated Rewards	Inducing Guilt or Shame
1. *Target hardening:* Slug-rejector device Steering locks Bandit screens	5. *Entry/exit screening:* Automatic ticket gates Baggage screening Merchandise tags	9. *Target removal:* Removable car radio Women's refuges Phone card	13. *Rule setting:* Harassment codes Customs declaration Hotel registrations
2. *Access control:* Parking lot barriers Fenced yards Entry phones	6. *Formal surveillance:* Burglar alarms Speed cameras Security guards	10. *Identifying property:* Property marking Vehicle licensing Cattle branding	14. *Strengthening moral condemnation:* "Shoplifting is stealing" Roadside speedometers "Bloody idiots drink and drive"
3. *Deflecting offenders:* Bus stop placement Tavern location Street closures	7. *Surveillance by employees:* Pay phone location Park attendants CCTV systems	11. *Reducing temptation:* Gender-neutral phone lists Off-street parking	15. *Controlling disinhibitors:* Drinking-age laws Ignition interlock Server intervention
4. *Controlling facilitators:* Credit card photo Caller ID Gun controls	8. *Natural surveillance:* Defensible space Street lighting Cab driver ID	12. *Denying benefits:* Ink merchandise tags PIN for car radios Graffiti cleaning	16. *Facilitating compliance:* Improved library checkout Public lavatories Trash bins

Crime Surfing WWW

http://www.ncjrs.gov/works/wholedoc.htm

John Eck, contributing to *Crime Prevention: What Works, What Doesn't, What's Promising*, compiled an extremely comprehensive literature review of research into the effectiveness of situational-crime-prevention strategies.

Situational Crime Prevention

Rational-choice theory provides the foundation for designing situational-crime-prevention techniques and their classification (Table 9.3). Situational crime prevention consists of the knowledge of how, where, and when to implement a specific measure that will alter a particular situation in order to prevent a crime from occurring. The routine-activity approach also aims at situational crime prevention by reducing the opportunities for likely offenders to commit crimes. Techniques include protecting suitable targets (making them less suitable) and increasing the presence of capable guardians. Measures such as steering-column locks, vandal-resistant construction, enhanced street lighting, and improved library checkout systems demonstrably decrease opportunities for crime. These are **target-hardening** techniques.

Rational-choice theorists have reviewed their situational-crime-prevention techniques and have added aspects of the offender's *perception* of a crime opportunity (Table 9.4) to the catalog of relevant factors, along with the element of guilt or shame.[62] The addition of the category of "perception" of opportunity was self-evident. After all, offenders act only in accordance with what they perceive. The addition of a category called "inducing guilt or shame," on the other hand, is a significant expansion of rational choice.[63] Techniques that induce guilt or shame include the installation of signs saying "shoplifting is stealing" or other measures calculated to prevent common crimes by increasing the personal and social cost in terms of shaming—especially after being caught in the act. For instance, if a high school student is leaving the school library with friends and the library checkout system detects a copy of *Rolling Stone* in his book bag (a magazine that is not allowed to leave the library), two things are expected to happen. First, the librarian will make the student surrender the magazine. Second, the student may be so embarrassed by having the librarian search his book bag while his friends stand by that he will not try to steal anything from the library again.

There are a number of successful examples of situational crime prevention. For example, situational-crime-prevention techniques have been successfully implemented to prevent crime at Disney World, to stop auto theft, to deter robberies at convenience stores, and to lessen crime in parking facilities.

The Phantom Crime Prevention at Disney World

Disney World, home of Donald Duck, Mickey and Minnie Mouse, Goofy, and their friends, provides us with an example of environmental/situational crime prevention. Illegal behavior is successfully controlled, yet in an environment that does not have the sterile, fortresslike appearance so often associated with security. How has this been accomplished?[64]

TABLE 9.4 Ten Factors Considered by Commercial Burglars in Suburban Philadelphia

1. *Revenues generated by burglary:*
   Is there a high "payoff"?

2. *Chances of being caught:*
   Can I get away with it?

3. *Location of target:*
   Is the target near a major road or thoroughfare?
   Commercial burglars like remote targets.

4. *Corner lot:*
   Is the target at the corner?
   Corner properties are easier to get into and out of.

5. *Shopping mall:*
   Is the target in a mall?
   Malls and large retail stores are ideal targets.

6. *Concentration of businesses:*
   Are there other businesses around?
   The more commercial establishments around, the greater the likelihood of burglary.

7. *Burglar alarm:*
   Is there a visible alarm or alarm sign?

8. *Exterior lighting:*
   How dark is the area around the target?

9. *Length of time the establishment has been in business:*
   Is this a new store?
   New commercial establishments are prime targets.

10. *Retail store:*
    Is the target retail?
    Retail is preferred over wholesale.

SOURCE: Simon Hakim and Yochanan Shachmurove, "Spatial and Temporal Patterns of Commercial Burglaries: The Evidence Examined," *American Journal of Economics and Sociology,* **55** (1996): 443–456.

■ *Even Goofy is part of the Disney crime prevention and control strategy, making Disneyland and Disney World two of the safest locations in the United States.*

Pakistan is World Leader in Stolen Cars

Islamabad: On an average, cars worth Rs 1 billion are stolen every month in Pakistan, said a report of the country's Interior Ministry, adding that cars worth Rs 18 billion were stolen in the past 18 months.

According to the report, 14,037 vehicles worth Rs 7 billion were stolen or snatched across the country during the first half of 2008, compared to 23,144 during 2007.

Thefts of vehicles are on the rise in the neigbouring country with clear indications that police and the vehicle registration offices are part of the mafia, reported The News.

A professional car lifter on condition of anonymity said that bigwigs in the police and the bureaucracy, besides top politicians, are directly involved in the lucrative business.

"I enjoy my job. I earn hundreds of thousands for a 3- to 4-minute effort. I can lift at least three vehicles in a day," the daring car lifter said.

He further said, "Toyota Corolla, Honda, Suzuki Mehran, Alto are the favourite vehicles to steal but we follow the demand of the receivers. Motorway is the safest way to take the stolen vehicles to Peshawar and Mardan."

According to him, Peshawar, Hazara and Mardan Divisions are havens for carjackers.

The mafia chiefs involved in this particular crime are known to the police, and so are their dens, mostly in the NWFP [North-West Frontier Province], but no one dares to take them to justice, added the paper.

According to the report, Punjab had the highest number of vehicle lifting incidents, as 7,432 vehicles were taken away in the first half of 2008.

A 49.07 percent increase of the crime was seen in Islamabad Capital Territory (ICT) as 401 vehicles were lifted during first two quarters of 2008 as compared to 269 during the same period in 2007.

Questions for Discussion

1. What, if anything, can Pakistan do to slow the rate of auto thefts?
2. How do the environmental conditions in Pakistan contribute to the auto theft problem in that country? How do these conditions differ from those in the United States?

SOURCE: ANI, "Pakistan is World Leader in Stolen Cars," *Mumbai Mirror,* August 19, 2008. Retrieved from http://www.mumbaimirror.com/index.aspx?Page=article&sectname=News%20-%20World&sectid=4&contentid=20080819200808190208054153512d75c7, Dec. 28, 2008.

DID YOU KNOW?

... that sometimes stealing might result from oversocialization and embarrassment rather than from undersocialization? Research into shoplifting from drugstores shows that the items most commonly stolen include condoms and other birth-control products, as well as medications, such as Preparation H, for "intimate conditions." Similarly, librarians surveyed said that books about sex are among the most stolen items from libraries, apparently because "readers were too embarrassed to borrow such stock legitimately."

The intricate web of security and crowd control (not visible to the untrained eye) starts at the parking lot with advice to lock your car and remember that you have parked at a particular lot, for example, "Donald Duck 1." With friendly greetings of "have a good time," watchful eyes surround visitors on the rubber-wheeled train into never-never land. Crowd control is omnipresent yet unobtrusive. Signs guide you through the maze of monorails, rides, and attractions. Physical barriers prevent injury and regulate the movement of adults and children alike. Mickey Mouse and Goofy monitor movements. Flower gardens, pools, and fountains are pretty to look at; they also direct people toward particular locations. Yet with all these built-in control strategies, few visitors realize the extent to which their choices of movement and action are limited.

Situational Prevention: Auto Theft

Information provided by the National Insurance Crime Bureau indicates the most-targeted vehicles for theft throughout the nation (Tables 9.5 and 9.6). Situational-crime-prevention practitioners are trained to analyze the vehicles and the specific situational factors that lead to their being targeted for theft. They then devise measures to block the opportunities that give rise to the theft of these particular vehicles—for example, side window panels that are particularly vulnerable, or key codes in the gas tank compartment (the thief simply writes down the key code and gets a replacement of the "lost" car key).[65]

Devising situational prevention measures, however, is usually not as easy as suggesting to a car manufacturer that the key code be placed in a more secure place. It is important that a researcher also analyze the type of offenders who steal cars (Table 9.7).

Convenience Stores

One of the most successful crime-prevention studies was the Tallahassee Convenience Store Study. In fact, it launched the concept of crime prevention through environmental design. It had long been known that convenience stores, like the 7-Eleven shops, were prime robbery targets. Researchers studied the vulnerability of these stores in great detail, assessing risks as well as losses, in terms of lives and property. The researchers recommended

TABLE 9.5 NICB's Top 10 Most Stolen Autos in 2010

1. 1994 Honda Accord
2. 1995 Honda Civic
3. 1991 Toyota Camry
4. 1997 Ford F-150 Pickup
5. 2004 Dodge Ram Pickup
6. 2000 Dodge Caravan
7. 1994 Chevrolet Pickup (Full Size)
8. 1994 Acura Integra
9. 2002 Ford Explorer
10. 2009 Toyota Corolla

SOURCE: National Insurance Crime Bureau, available at www. nicb.org.

TABLE 9.6 Top 10 Auto-Theft Cities in 2010

2010 Ranking	2009 Ranking
1. Fresno, California	5
2. Modesto, California	2
3. Bakersfield-Delano, California	3
4. Spokane, Washington	18
5. Vallejo-Fairfield, California	16
6. Sacramento/Arden-Arcade/ Roseville, California	11
7. Stockton, California	4
8. Visalia-Porterville, California	8
9. San Francisco/Oakland/ Fremont, California	7
10. Yakima, Washington	6

SOURCE: National Insurance Crime Bureau, available at www. nicb.org.

that stores have two or more clerks on duty, post "limited cash" signs, increase exterior lighting, and restrict escape routes and potential hiding places for robbers. The study led to the passage of the Florida Convenience Store Security Act (1990), which made certain security measures mandatory.[66] Convenience-store robberies in Florida have since dropped by two-thirds.

Parking Facilities[67]

Parking garages are said to be dangerous places: Individuals are alone in a large space, there are many hiding places, the amount of valuable property (cars and their contents) is high, they are open to the public, an offender's car can go unnoticed, and lighting is usually poor. Yet statistics indicate that because of the small amount of time and the relatively limited number of trips that each person takes to and from parking facilities, an individual's chances of being raped, robbed, or assaulted in a parking facility are very low. Nevertheless, the fear of victimization in these facilities is high. Efforts to improve conditions include better lighting, stairways and elevators that are open to the air or glass-enclosed, ticket-booth personnel monitoring drivers exiting and entering, color-coded signs designating parking areas, elimination or redesign of public restrooms, panic buttons and emergency phones, closed-circuit television, and uniformed security personnel.

Situational Crime Prevention— Pros and Cons

Despite the increasing popularity of situational crime prevention (SCP), the perspective has been the target of criticism by more traditional-minded criminologists. The debate on the merits of SCP techniques centers on a number of issues, including the following:

1. *SCP excludes "undesirables" from public places:*[68] For example, excluding would-be offenders from a mall by limiting shopping hours makes it more difficult for them to buy needed material goods.[69]

Response: The exclusion of "troublemakers" from public and semipublic places falls under order-maintenance duties of police officers, so it is not considered SCP.[70] "Deflecting offenders," which is one SCP technique identified by theorists, does have some exclusionary potential, but it is not meant to exclude undesirables; rather, the aim is to keep likely offenders away from suitable targets.

2. *SCP will only displace crime to new locations and times:* It may also lead to the escalation of crime to a more serious level, and the benefits of SCP are skewed toward more-advantaged classes who can afford security measures.[71]

Response: Behavior is influenced by situational factors, so there is no reason to assume that blocked crime at one location will lead to the commission of crime in a different situation. There will be different factors at play. Evidence also suggests that displacement is not as prevalent as critics claim, and the idea of escalation is inconsistent with many types of crime. For example, it is unlikely that reduced opportunities for shoplifting would lead offenders to start stealing shopping baskets from other customers.[72]

TABLE 9.7 Typologies of Frequent Auto Theft Offenders

ACTING-OUT JOYRIDER

- Most emotionally disturbed of the offenders—derives status from having his peers think he is crazy and unpredictable.

- Engages in outrageous driving stunts—dangerous to pursue—possesses a kamikaze attitude.

- Vents anger via car—responsible for large proportion of the totaled and burned cars.

- Least likely to be deterred—doesn't care what happens.

THRILL-SEEKER

- Heavily into drugs—doing crime is a way to finance the habit—entices others to feel the "rush" of doing crime.

- Engages in car stunts and willful damage to cars, but also steals them for transportation and to use in other crimes.

- Steals parts for sale in a loosely structured friendship network.

- Thrill-seeking behavior likely to be transferred to other activities and might be directed to legitimate outlets.

INSTRUMENTAL OFFENDER

- Doing auto theft for the money—most active of the offenders (five or more cars a week) but the smallest proportion of the sample—connected to organized theft operations.

- Rational, intelligent—does crimes with least risk—may get into auto theft from burglary—thinks about outcomes.

- Doing crime while young offender status affords them lenient treatment—indicate that they will quit crime at age 18.

SOURCE: Zachary Fleming, Patricia Brantingham, and Paul Brantingham, "Exploring Auto Theft in British Columbia," in *Crime Prevention Studies*, vol. 3, ed. Ronald V. Clarke (Monsey, N.Y.: Criminal Justice Press, 1994), p. 62. Reprinted by permission of the publisher.

3. *SCP inconveniences law-abiding citizens and infringes on their freedom:*[73] Crime-prevention efforts should focus on offenders—the burden should not be placed on law-abiding citizens.[74]

Response: Many SCP measures are unobtrusive, and human beings generally accept the need for implementing security measures in their own lives.[75]

4. *SCP treats the symptoms of the crime problem rather than the causes:*[76] Crime prevention should focus on the root causes of crime—unemployment, racial discrimination, and inadequate schooling, among others. Along the same lines, it is questionable whether the end (lower crime) justifies the means.[77] SCP is not necessarily the most appropriate way to deal with crime just because it is more efficient than other methods; it may not be if it prevents crime for the wrong reasons. For example, one way to reduce crime is by excluding everyone under the age of 21 from shopping malls because they are at highest risk for shoplifting. This measure reduces crime, but the means are questionable because they exclude these individuals from being able to shop freely.

Response: SCP avoids stigmatizing certain groups of individuals as likely criminals because it acknowledges that everyone is vulnerable to temptation.[78] Also, people change in response to

their experiences, so SCP has the potential to minimize or promote particular social practices.[79]

Despite the criticism, Felson and Clarke argue that situational crime prevention meets the three goals of crime control required by democratic standards—to provide crime prevention equally to all social groups, to respect individual rights, and to share responsibility for crime prevention with all parts of society—better than other crime policies.[80]

Displacement

One important question concerning crime-prevention measures remains. What will happen, for example, if these measures do prevent a particular crime from being committed? Will the would-be offender simply look for another target? Crime-prevention strategists have demonstrated that **displacement**—the commission of a quantitatively similar crime at a different time or place—does not always follow. German motorcycle helmet legislation demonstrates the point. As a result of a large number of accidents, legislation that required motorcyclists to wear helmets was passed and strictly enforced. It worked: Head injuries decreased. But there were additional, unforeseen consequences. Motorcycle theft rates decreased dramatically. The risks of stealing a motorcycle became too high because a would-be offender could not drive it away without wearing a helmet. At this point, researchers expected to see a rise in the number of cars or bikes stolen. They did not. In other words, there was very little displacement. Studies of hot-spots policing provide mixed evidence of displacement.[81] The research reveals a wide variety of types. Marcus Felson and Ronald Clarke propose five different forms:

1. Crime can be moved from one location to another (geographical displacement).

2. Crime can be moved from one time to another (temporal displacement).

3. Crime can be directed away from one target to another (target displacement).

4. One method of committing crime can be substituted for another (tactical displacement).

5. One kind of crime can be substituted for another (crime type displacement).[82]

Rarely noted but worthy of consideration is the fact that displacement can have positive as well as negative effects. These effects can take several forms:

- *Positive.* A crime is displaced to a less serious type of crime or a crime with greater risk, with lower rewards or less serious damage. It represents a success because it produces a net gain.

- *Neutral.* A crime is displaced to one of the same seriousness, the same risk, and the same rewards and damage.

- *Even-handed.* Prevention is concentrated on those who are repeatedly victimized in order to achieve a more equitable distribution of crime.

- *Negative.* A crime is displaced to a more serious crime, a crime with greater reward, or a crime with greater social cost.

- *Attractive.* Activities and/or places attract crime from other areas or activities (e.g., "red light" districts attract customers, as well as other criminal activities, from other areas).[83]

THEORY INFORMS POLICY

The study of targets and victims is crucial to preventing crime. Understanding how offenders make decisions helps policy makers allocate resources efficiently. For example, if it is possible to significantly reduce convenience-store robbery by relatively simple measures, isn't it better to spend time and money doing those things rather than trying to prevent crime by focusing exclusively on troubled people (who may or may not rob convenience stores anyway)? If we know that repeat victimization can be prevented by intervening with high-risk people and properties, isn't that the most cost-beneficial way to proceed?

We usually think of crime policy as being made by governments, for only they can control the police, courts, and corrections. Decisions about crime prevention, on the other hand, can be made by small communities, neighborhoods, schools, businesses, and individuals. We discussed how simple precautions lower the risk of convenience-store robbery. This knowledge not only encouraged governments to pass certain laws mandating that stores take those precautions, but led many in private industry to adopt the measures as well. Knowledge about crime prevention is especially valuable to all people because everyone can use these tools to reduce the chances of being a victim. Having discussed the application of theories of crime to conventional crime, we are left with the question of whether these theories are also applicable to unconventional crimes, such as terrorism.

This chapter focuses on situational theories of crime. These theories, which assume that there are always people motivated to commit crime, try to explain why crimes are being committed by a particular offender against a particular target. They analyze opportunities and environmental factors that prompt a potential perpetrator to act.

We discussed the three most prominent situational approaches to crime: environmental criminology, the rational-choice perspective, and the routine-activity approach. We noted that they have merged somewhat, particularly insofar as all these approaches aim at preventing victimization by altering external conditions that are conducive to crime.

Theories of victimization view crime as the dynamic interaction of perpetrators and victims (at a given time and place). Here, too, the aim is to find ways for potential victims to protect themselves. Research into lifestyles, victim-offender interaction, repeat victimization, hot spots, and geography of crime has vast implications for crime control in entire cities or regions. Situational theories of crime and theories of victimization are interrelated. Most of the theories and perspectives in this chapter can be used to explain and possibly predict the decision making of criminal organizations, including terrorist organizations.

REVIEW

Violent Crimes

■ Mark of violence: one of the first shots in a sniper spree that numbed the Washington, D.C., area in October 2002.

To millions of Americans, few things are more pervasive, more frightening, more real today than violent crime and the fear of being assaulted, mugged, robbed, or raped. The fear of being victimized by criminal attack has touched us all in some way. People are fleeing their residences in cities to the expected safety of suburban living. Residents of many areas will not go out on the street at night. Others have added bars and extra locks to windows and doors in their homes. Bus drivers in major cities do not carry cash because incidents of robbery have been so frequent. In some areas, local citizens patrol the streets at night to attain the safety they feel has not been provided. . . .

Manslaughter

Manslaughter is the unlawful killing of another person without malice. Manslaughter may be either voluntary or involuntary.

Voluntary Manslaughter

Voluntary manslaughter is a killing committed intentionally but without malice—for example, in the heat of passion or in response to strong provocation. Persons who kill under extreme provocation cannot make rational decisions about whether they have a right to kill. They therefore act without the necessary malice.[3]

Just as passion, fright, fear, or consternation may affect a person's capacity to act rationally, so may drugs or alcohol. In some states, a charge of murder may be reduced to voluntary manslaughter when the defendant was so grossly intoxicated as not to be fully aware of the implications of his or her actions. All voluntary-manslaughter cases have one thing in common: The defendant's awareness of the unlawfulness of the act was dulled or grossly reduced by shock, fright, consternation, or intoxication.

Involuntary Manslaughter

A crime is designated as **involuntary manslaughter** when a person has caused the death of another unintentionally but recklessly by consciously disregarding a substantial and unjustifiable risk that endangered another person's life. Many states have created an additional category, **negligent homicide,** to establish criminal liability for grossly negligent killing in situations where the offender assumed a lesser risk.

Manslaughter plays an increasingly prominent role in our society, with its high concentrations of population, high-tech risks, and chemical and even nuclear dangers. The reach of the crime of involuntary manslaughter was clearly demonstrated in the 1942 Coconut Grove disaster in Boston, in which 491 people perished because of a nightclub owner's negligence in creating fire hazards. The nightclub was overcrowded, it was furnished and decorated with highly flammable materials, and exits were blocked. The court ruled that a reasonable person would have recognized the risk. If the defendant is so "stupid" as not to have recognized the risk, he is nevertheless guilty of manslaughter.[4]

The Extent of Homicide

Social scientists who look at homicide have a different perspective from that of the legislators who define such crimes. Social scientists are concerned with rates and patterns of criminal activities. (For a rank ordering of violent crime rates, see Table 10.1.)

TABLE 10.1 Violent Crimes[1] Per 100,000 Population—2007

Rank[3]	State	Rate[2]
(X)	District of Columbia	1,414
1	South Carolina	788
2	Tennessee	753
3	Nevada	751
4	Louisiana	730
5	Florida	723
6	Delaware	689
7	New Mexico	664
8	Alaska	661
9	Maryland	642
10	Michigan	536
11	Illinois	533
12	Arkansas	529
13	California	523
14	Texas	511
15	Missouri	505
16	Oklahoma	500
17	Georgia	493
18	Arizona	483
19	North Carolina	466
20	Kansas	453
21	Alabama	448
22	Massachusetts	432
23	Pennsylvania	417
24	New York	414
25	Colorado	348
26	Ohio	343
27	Indiana	334
28	Washington	333
29	New Jersey	329
30	Nebraska	302
31	Kentucky	295
32	Iowa	295
33	Mississippi	291
34	Wisconsin	291
35	Minnesota	289
36	Oregon	288
37	Montana	288
38	West Virginia	275
39	Hawaii	273
40	Virginia	270
41	Connecticut	256
42	Idaho	239
43	Wyoming	239
44	Utah	235
45	Rhode Island	227
46	South Dakota	169
47	North Dakota	142
48	New Hampshire	137
49	Vermont	124
50	Maine	118

Symbol X Not applicable.
Notes: [1]Estimated number of violent crimes, which includes murder, forcible rape, robbery, and aggravated assault.
[2]Based on Census Bureau estimates as of July 1.
[3]For quality of ranking data see *Crime in the United States, 2007,* "Caution against Ranking."
SOURCE: U.S. Federal Bureau of Investigation, *Crime in the United States,* annual.

Homicide Rates in the Unite States Today

The murder rate in the United States is high, but steadily declining.

- An estimated 14,748 persons were murdered nationwide in 2010. This was a 4.2 percent decrease from the 2009 estimate, a 14.8 percent decrease from the 2006 figure, and an 8.0 percent decrease from the 2001 estimate.

- In 2010, there were 4.8 murders per 100,000 inhabitants, a 4.8 percent decrease from the 2009 rate. Compared with the 2006 rate, the murder rate decreased 17.4 percent, and compared with the 2001 rate, the murder rate decreased 15.0 percent.

- Nearly 44 percent (43.8) of murders were reported in the South, the most populous region, with 20.6 percent reported in the West, 19.9 percent reported in the Midwest, and 15.6 percent reported in the Northeast.

Homicide Rates over Time

Researchers have asked what happens to homicide rates over time when the composition of the population changes. Some scholars have found that changes in age and race structure play a modest role in explaining crime trends during the last several decades. According to James Fox, the age-race-sex structure accounted for about 10 percent of the 1990s decline in homicide rates, and Steven Levitt found that changes in the age distribution explain between 15 and 20 percent of variance in crime rates between 1960 and 1980 and between 1980 and 1995. Roland Chilton, using data on offenses committed in Chicago between 1960 and 1980 and census data for those years, found that about 20 percent of the total increase in homicide rates could be explained by increases in the nonwhite male population. The same correlation is found in most major cities in the United States. Chilton argues that the problem will remain because of the poverty and demoralization of the groups involved.[6]

In a 1996 article, "Work," sociologist William Julius Wilson explains why America's ghettos have descended into "ever-deeper poverty and misery." According to him,

> for the first time in the 20th century, a significant majority of adults in many inner-city neighborhoods are not working in a typical week. Inner cities have always featured high levels of poverty, but the current levels of joblessness in some neighborhoods are unprecedented. For example, in the famous black-belt neighborhood of Washington Park on Chicago's South Side, a majority of adults had jobs in 1950; by 1990, only 1 in 3 worked in a typical week. High neighborhood joblessness has a far more devastating effect than high neighborhood poverty. A neighborhood in which people are poor but employed is different from a neighborhood in which people are poor and jobless. Many of today's problems in the inner-city neighborhoods—crime, family dissolution, welfare—are fundamentally a consequence of the disappearance of work.[7]

Until conditions change, what has been poignantly referred to as "the subculture of exasperation" will continue to produce a high homicide rate among nonwhite inner-city males.[8] Coramae Mann has found that although black women make up about 11 percent of the female population in the United States, they are arrested for three-fourths of all homicides committed by females. She argues that given such a disproportionate involvement in violent crime, one has to question whether the subculture of exasperation alone is entirely responsible.[9] But so few studies have been done on the subject that we cannot reach any definitive conclusion. Other investigators agree that homicide rates cannot be explained solely by factors such as poverty; the rates are also significantly associated with cultural approval of a resort to violence.

The Nature of Homicide

Let us take a closer look at killers and their victims and see how they are related to each other. In the 1950s, Marvin Wolfgang studied homicide situations, perpetrators, and victims in the Philadelphia area. Victims and offenders were predominantly young black adults of low socioeconomic status. The offenses were committed in the inner city; they occurred primarily in the home of the victim or offender, on weekends, in the evening hours, and among friends or acquaintances.

Building on the pioneering work of Hans von Hentig,[10] Wolfgang found that many of the victims had actually initiated the social interaction that led to the homicidal response, in either a direct or subliminal way. He coined the term **victim precipitation** for such instances, which may account for as many as a quarter to a half of all intentional homicides. In such cases, it is the victim who, by insinuation, bodily movement, verbal incitement, or the actual use of physical force, initiates a series of events that results in his or her own death. For example:

> During an argument in which a male called a female many vile names, she tried to telephone the police. He grabbed the phone from her hands, knocked her down, kicked her, and hit her with a tire gauge. She ran to the kitchen, grabbed a butcher knife, and stabbed him in the stomach.[11]

A study by Richard Felson and Steven Messner found that victim precipitation is more often seen in cases where women kill their husbands as opposed to incidents in which men kill their

x-ray photographs of patients in the emergency rooms of 71 hospitals across the country over the course of a year, they found 300 cases of child abuse, of which 11 percent resulted in death and over 28 percent in permanent brain damage. Shortly thereafter, the women's movement rallied to the plight of the battered wife and, somewhat later, to the personal and legal problems of wives who were raped by their husbands.[61]

In the 1960s and 1970s, various organizations, fighting for the rights of women and children, exposed the harm that results from physical and psychological abuse in the home. They demanded public action and created public awareness of the extent of the problem. Psychologists, physicians, anthropologists, and social scientists, among others, increasingly focused attention on the various factors that enter into episodes of domestic violence. Such factors include the sources of conflict, arguments, physical attacks, injuries, and temporal and spatial elements.

Within three decades, family violence, the "well-kept secret," has come to be recognized as a major social problem.[62] Family violence shares some of the characteristics of other forms of violence, yet the intimacy of marital, cohabitational, or parent-child relationships sets family violence apart. The physical and emotional harm inflicted in violent episodes tends to be spread over longer periods of time and to have a more lasting impact on all members of the living unit. Moreover, such events tend to be self-perpetuating.

Spouse Abuse

In May 1998, Motley Crüe drummer Tommy Lee was sentenced to 6 months in jail and 3 years probation for battering his wife, former *Baywatch* beauty Pamela Anderson. Lee was also ordered to perform 200 hours of community service and donate $5,000 to a battered women's shelter. He had been arrested in February 1998 after Anderson called 911 to report a domestic dispute in which Lee had kicked her in the back while she was holding 7-week-old Dylan Jagger. Lee was charged with spousal abuse, child abuse, and unlawful possession of a firearm. As the result of a plea agreement, all charges except the spousal abuse charge were dropped.

Media celebrity and former star athlete O. J. Simpson was convicted in 1989 of assaulting his wife, Nicole Brown Simpson. For this offense, he served no time in prison, nor was he required to undergo counseling. On June 13, 1994, Nicole Brown Simpson and her friend Ronald Goldman were found lying dead in pools of their own blood, victims of a vicious knife attack. O. J. Simpson was accused of their murder. Following a lengthy, highly publicized, and much-discussed trial, Simpson was found not guilty by a jury of his peers. The verdict had a wide-reaching impact on various aspects of the criminal justice system. It also made

abused women fear for their lives. Concerned that a man who was a convicted batterer could be found not guilty of killing his ex-wife, despite what was perceived by many as convincing evidence, they wondered if they could eventually share the same fate as Nicole Brown Simpson.[63] O. J. Simpson was convicted of robbing two sports memorabilia dealers in 2008 and was sentenced to a minimum of 9 years in prison.

The Extent of Spouse Abuse

In a national sample of 6,002 households, Murray A. Straus and Richard J. Gelles found that about one of every six couples experiences at least one physical assault during the year.[64] While both husbands and wives perpetrate acts of violence, the consequences of their acts differ.[65] Men, who more often use guns, knives, or fists, inflict more pain and injury. About 60 percent of spousal assaults consist of minor shoving, slapping, and pushing; the other 40 percent are considered severe: punching, kicking, stabbing, choking.[66] According to the National Institute of Justice, partner violence is strongly linked to a variety of mental illnesses, a background of family adversity, dropping out of school, juvenile aggression, drug abuse, long-term unemployment, and cohabitation and/or parenthood at a young age. Research also suggests that women who have children by the age of 21 are two times more likely to be victims of domestic violence than are women who are not mothers, and that men who father children by age 21 are three times more likely to be perpetrators of abuse than are men who are not fathers.[67]

Researchers agree that assaultive behavior within the family is a highly underreported crime. Data from the National Crime Victimization Survey indicate:

- One-half of the incidents of domestic assault are not reported.

- The most common reason given for failure to report a domestic assault to the police was that the victim considered the incident a private matter.

- Victims who reported such incidents to the police did so to prevent future assaults.

- Although the police classified two-thirds of the reported incidents of domestic violence as simple assaults, half of them inflicted bodily injury as serious as, or more serious than, the injuries inflicted during rapes, robberies, and aggravated assaults.[68]

The Nature of Spouse Abuse

Before we can understand spouse abuse, we need information about abusers. Some experts have found that interpersonal violence is learned and transmitted from one generation to the next.[69]

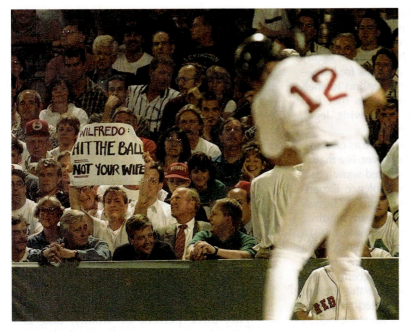

■ A spectator holds up a sign offering advice to Boston Red Sox batter Wilfredo Cordero as he pinch-hits for Reggie Jefferson in a game with the Toronto Blue Jays. The fans at Fenway Park, Boston, greeted him with boos as he stepped up to the plate.

Studies demonstrate that children who are raised by aggressive parents tend to grow up to be aggressive adults.[70] Other researchers have demonstrated how stress, frustration, and severe psychopathology take their toll on family relationships.[71] A few researchers have also explored the role of body chemistry; one investigation ties abuse to the tendency of males to secrete adrenaline when they feel sexually threatened.[72]

The relationship between domestic violence and the use of alcohol and drugs has also been explored. Abusive men with severe drug and alcohol problems are more likely to abuse their wives or girlfriends when they are drunk or high and to inflict more injury.[73]

Several studies of other societies demonstrate cultural support for the abuse of women. Moroccan researcher Mohammed Ayat reported that of 160 battered women, about 25 percent believed that a man who does *not* beat his wife must be under some magic spell; 8 percent believed that such a man has a weak personality and is afraid of his wife; 2 percent believed that he must be abnormal; and another 2 percent believed that he doesn't love her or has little interest in her.[74] Wife beating, then, appears to be accepted as a norm by over one-third of the women studied—women who are themselves beaten. It even appears to be an expected behavior. In fact, in a study of 90 cultures, spouse beating was rare or nonexistent in only 15.[75]

Spouse abuse has often been attributed to the imbalance of power between male and female partners. According to some researchers, the historical view of wives as possessions of their husbands persists even today.[76] Until recently, spousal abuse was perceived as a problem more of social service than of criminal justice.[77] Police responding to domestic disturbance calls typically do not make an arrest unless the assailant is drunk, has caused serious injury, or has assaulted the officers. Take, for example, the case of *Thurman v. Torrington*. Tracey Thurman had repeatedly requested police assistance because she feared her estranged husband. Even after he threatened to shoot her and her son, the police merely told her to get a restraining order. Eventually, the husband attacked Thurman, inflicting multiple stab wounds that caused paralysis from the neck down and permanent disfigurement. The police had delayed in responding to her call on that occasion, and the city of Torrington, Connecticut, was held liable for having failed to provide her with equal protection of the law. In the suit that followed, Ms. Thurman was awarded $2.3 million in damages.[78]

According to the U.S. Department of Justice, between 1998 and 2002:

- Of the almost 3.5 million violent crimes committed against family members, 49 percent were crimes against spouses.

- 84 percent of spouse abuse victims were female, and 86 percent of victims of dating partner abuse were female.

- Males made up 83 percent of spouse murderers and 75 percent of dating partner murderers.

- 50 percent of offenders in state prison for spousal abuse had killed their victims. Wives were more likely than husbands to be killed by their spouses: Wives comprised about half of all spouses in the population in 2002 but 81 percent of all persons killed by their spouse.[79]

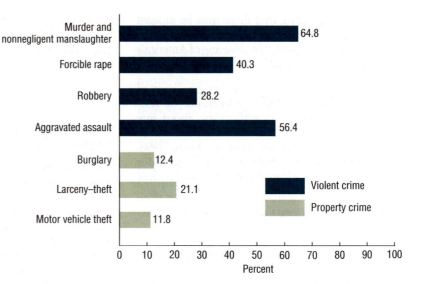

There is an arrest made for all types of forcible rape in about 40 percent of the cases (Figure 10.3).[105] Many stranger rapists remain at large because they commit their acts in ways that produce little tangible evidence as to their identities. They maintain a distance from the victim by not interacting with her before the attack. The serial rapist also attacks strangers, but because he finds his victims repeatedly in the same places, his behavior is more predictable and so leads to a better arrest rate.[106]

Who Are the Rapists?

Explanations of rape fall into two categories, psychological and sociocultural. While research in these areas has expanded over the last three decades, the causes of rape remain speculative.

Psychological Factors

Several experts view rapists as suffering from mental illness or personality disorders. They argue that some rapists are psychotic, sociopathic, or sadistic or feel deficient in masculinity. Most rapists show hostile feelings toward women, have histories of violence, and tend to attack strangers. They commit the offense because of anger, a drive for power (expressed as sexual conquest), or the enjoyment of maltreating a victim (sadism). Some rapists view women as sex objects whose role is to satisfy them.

Sociocultural Factors

Psychological explanations assume that men who rape are maladjusted in some way. But several studies done in the 1980s demonstrate that rapists are indistinguishable from other groups of offenders.[107] These studies generally conclude that rape is culturally related to societal norms that approve of aggression as a demonstration of masculinity (as we saw in Chapter 6) or that rape is the mechanism by which men maintain their power over women.

The social significance of rape has long been a part of anthropological literature. A cross-cultural study of 95 tribal societies found that 47 percent were rape-free, 35 percent intermediate, and 18 percent rape-prone. In the rape-prone societies, women had low status and little decision-making power, and they lived apart from men. The author of this study concluded: "Violence is socially, not biologically, programmed."[108]

Despite anthropologists' traditional interest in gender relationships, it was not until the feminist movement and radical criminology focused on the subject that the relationship of rape, gender inequality, and socioeconomic status was fully articulated. Writing from the Marxist perspective, which we explore in Chapter 8, Julia and Herman Schwendinger posited that "the impoverishment of the working class and the widening gap between rich and poor" create conditions for the prevalence of sexual violence.[109] A test of this hypothesis showed that while the incidence of sexual violence was not related to ethnic inequality, it was significantly related to general income inequality.[110]

A more recent study analyzed these findings and concluded that economic inequality was not the sole determinant of violent crime in our society. Forcible rape was found to be an added "cost" of many factors, including social disorganization.[111] In sum, many factors have been associated with the crime of rape: psychological problems, social factors, and even sociopolitical factors. Some experts suggest that boys are socialized to be aggressive and dominating, that the innate male sex drive leads to rape, and that pornography encourages men to rape by making sex objects of women, degrading women, and glamorizing violence against them. Rape has been explained in such a wide variety of ways that it is extremely difficult to plan preventive strategies and to formulate crime-control policy. Moreover, it has created major difficulties in the criminal justice system.

Rape and the Legal System

The difficulties of rape prosecutions have their roots in English common law. Sir Matthew Hale, a seventeenth-century jurist, explained in *Pleas of the Crown* (1685, 1736) how a jury was to be cautious in viewing evidence of rape: "[It] must be remembered . . . that it is an accusation easily to be made and hard to be proved, and harder to be defended, by the party accused, tho never so innocent."[112] This instruction, which so definitively protects the defendant, has until recently been a mandatory instruction to juries in the United States. Along with many other legal and policy changes, many jurisdictions have now cast it aside. The requirement of particularly stringent proof in rape cases had always been justified by the seriousness of the offense and the heavy penalties associated with it, plus the stigma attached to such a conviction.

Difficulties of Prosecution

Victims of rape have often been regarded with suspicion by the criminal justice system. The victim's testimony has not sufficed to convict the defendant, no matter how unimpeachable that testimony may have been. There had to be "corroborating evidence," such as semen, torn clothes, bruises, or eyewitness testimony.

Another major issue has been that of consent. Did the victim encourage, entice, or maybe even agree to the act? Was the attack forced? Did the victim resist? Martin Schwartz and Todd Clear sum up the reasons for such questions: "There is a widespread belief in our culture that women 'ask for it,' either individually or as a group." They compare rape victims to victims of other offenses: "Curiously, society does not censure the robbery victim for walking around with $10, or the burglary victim for keeping all of those nice things in his house, or the car theft victim for showing off his flashy new machine, just asking for someone to covet it."[113]

Because defendants in rape cases so often claim that the victim was in some way responsible for the attack, rape victims in the courtroom tend to become the "accused," required to defend their good reputations, their propriety, and their mental soundness. The severity of the assault, the injuries the victim sustains, whether or not the assailant was a stranger, and the victim's social support network all play a role in terms of the rape-reporting process.[114] Experts claim that as many as 60 percent of rapes are not reported.[115] In sum, so many burdens are placed on the victim that no one seriously wonders why so few rapes are reported and why so few men accused of rape are convicted.

Legislative Changes

The feminist movement has had a considerable impact on laws and attitudes concerning rape in our country. The state of Michigan was a leader in the movement to reform such laws by creating, in 1975, the new crime of "criminal sexual conduct" to replace the traditional rape laws. It distinguishes four degrees of assaultive sexual acts, differentiated by the amount of force used, the infliction of injury, and the age and mental condition of the victim.

The law is gender-neutral, in that it makes illegal any type of forcible sex, including homosexual rape. Other states have followed Michigan's lead. Schwartz and Clear have suggested that reform should go one step further. They argue that if rape were covered by the general assault laws rather than by a separate statute on sex crimes, the emphasis would be on the assault (the action of the offender) and not on the resistance (the action of the victim).

Some states have also removed many of the barriers women previously encountered as witnesses in the courtroom. Thus, in states with rape shield laws, women are no longer required to disclose their prior sexual activity, and corroboration requirements have been reduced or eliminated; as noted earlier, some states have reversed two centuries of legal tradition by striking down the "marital rape exemption" so that a wife may now charge her husband with rape.[116] But law reform has limits. Unfortunately, prejudices die hard.

Community Response

Women's advocates have taken an interest not only in legislative reform but also in the community's response to the victims of rape. In 1970, the first rape-specific support project, Bay Area Women Against Rape—a volunteer-staffed emergency phone information service—was established in Berkeley, California.[117] By 1973, similar projects had spread throughout the country. Run by small, unaffiliated groups, they handled crises, monitored agencies (hospitals, police, courts) that came in contact with victims, educated the public about the problems of victims, and even provided lessons in self-defense.

By the late 1970s, the number of these centers and their activities had increased dramatically. The mass media reported on their successes. Federal and, later, state and local support for such services rose. As the centers became more professional, they formed boards of directors, prepared detailed budgets to comply with the requirements of funding agencies, hired social workers and mental health personnel, and developed their political action component. But even with increased support, the demand for the services of rape crisis centers far outweighs the available resources.

KIDNAPPING

Kidnapping, as such, was not recognized as a felony under English common law; it was a misdemeanor. Some forms of kidnapping were later criminalized by statute. In the eighteenth century, the most frequent form of kidnapping, according to the great legal scholar Sir William Blackstone, was stealing children and sending them to servitude in the American colonies. Other forms of kidnapping were the "crimping," or shanghaiing, of persons for involuntary service aboard ships and the abduction of women for purposes of prostitution abroad.

All these offenses have elements in common, and together they define the crime of **kidnapping:** abduction and detention by force or fraud and transport beyond the authority of the place where the crime was committed. It was not until the kidnapping of Charles Lindbergh's infant son in 1932 that comprehensive kidnapping legislation was enacted in the United States. In passing the federal kidnapping statute—the so-called Lindbergh Act (now 18 U.S. Code Sec. 1201)—Congress made it a felony to kidnap and transport a victim across a state or national border. The crime was subject to the death penalty, unless the victim was released unharmed.

In the United States, kidnapping often involves the abduction of a child from one parent by the other. One interesting case recently appeared in the news. In October 1979, Stephen Fagan kidnapped his two daughters, Lisa (age 2) and Rachael (age 5), from Massachusetts and then moved to Florida. He told his daughters that their mother had died. It was not until 1998 that an anonymous tip led to his arrest in Florida, where he was living the high life as a socialite under the name Dr. William Martin. Fagan claimed that he took his daughters away from his ex-wife, Barbara Kurth, who he believed was an unfit and alcoholic mother. Kurth vehemently denied the allegation. Fagan was charged with kidnapping his daughters even though the crime had occurred 20 years earlier. In a plea agreement, Fagan was spared jail time; instead, he was fined $100,000 and received a suspended 3- to 5-year prison sentence. He was also required to serve probation for 5 years. The two daughters stood by their father and decided not to reunite with their mother.[118]

ROBBERY

Robbery is the taking of property from a victim by force and violence or by the threat of violence. The Model Penal Code (Section 222.1) grades robbery as a felony of the second degree, commanding a prison term of up to 10 years. If the robber has intentionally inflicted serious physical injury or attempted to kill, the sentence may be as long as life. In reality, however, the average sentence upon conviction for one charge of robbery is 6 years.[119] In 2007, the number of robbery offenses was 445,125, or 147.6 robberies per 100,000 population.[120]

There were an estimated 367,832 robberies in 2010. This is a 10 percent from the 2009 estimate and 18.1 percent from the 2006 estimate. The robbery rate of 119.1 percent 100,000 inhabitants reflected is a 10.5 percent decrease in one year. An estimated $456 million in losses were attributed to robberies in 2010. The average dollar value of property stolen per reported robbery was $1,239. The highest average dollar loss was for banks, which lost $4,410 per offense. Firearms were used in 41.4 percent of the robberies.[121]

Characteristics of Robbers

Criminologists have classified the characteristics of robbers as well as the characteristics of robberies. John Conklin detected four types of robbers:

- The *professional robber* carefully plans and executes a robbery, often with many accomplices; steals large sums of money; and has a long-term, deep commitment to robbery as a means of supporting a hedonistic lifestyle.

- The *opportunistic robber* (the most common) has no long-term commitment to robbery; targets victims for small amounts of money ($20 or less); victimizes elderly women, drunks, cab drivers, and other people who seem to be in no position to resist; and is young and generally inexperienced.

- The *addict robber* is addicted to drugs, has a low level of commitment to robbery but a high level of commitment to theft, plans less than professional robbers but more than opportunistic robbers, wants just enough money for a fix, and may or may not carry a weapon.

- The *alcoholic robber* has no commitment to robbery as a way of life, has no commitment to theft, does not plan his or her robberies, usually robs people after first assaulting them, takes few precautions, and is apprehended more often than other robbers.[122]

According to the Uniform Crime Reports, nearly 90 percent of those arrested for robbery in

2010 were males. Approximately 60 percent of the arrestees were under 25 years of age. In terms of race, blacks accounted for more than 50 percent of all robbery arrests, whites accounted for 45 percent, and all other races constituted the remaining 1 percent of all robbery arrests.[123]

The Consequences of Robbery

Robbery is a property crime as well as a violent crime. It is the combination of the motive for economic gain and the violent nature of robbery that makes it so serious.[124] An estimated $588 million was lost as a result of robbery in 2007 alone. The value of stolen property per incident averaged $1,321.[125] Loss of money, however, is certainly not the only consequence of robbery. The million-odd robberies that take place each year leave psychological and physical trauma in their wake, not to mention the pervasive fear and anxiety that have contributed to the decay of inner cities.

Not all criminologists agree, however, that the high level of fear is warranted. After examining trends in robbery-homicide data from 52 of the largest cities in the United States, one researcher found "little support for the fears that there is a new breed of street criminals who cause more serious injuries and deaths in robberies. Very recent trends point in the other direction. Killing a robbery victim appears to be going out of fashion."[126]

ORGANIZED CRIME

It's enough to make John Gotti turn in his grave—the feds are administering the last rites to his once-powerful Gambino crime family.

Only five days after the godfather's funeral, FBI agents yesterday pounced on 14 alleged family members and associates wanted for murder and racketeering crimes stretching back to the late '80s—a time when the Gambinos ruled New York's gangland with iron fists.

"It's a whole different world than it was," U.S. Attorney Jim Comey said, pointing proudly to a pyramid chart of rubbed-out Gambino mobsters with black crosses stamped on their faces.

"'This thing of ours'—La Cosa Nostra—is very, very different today."

The freshest black cross was on the head of one of the late Dapper Don's longest serving capos, Louis "Big Louie" Vallario, who was one of four men indicted for the 1989 execution of Staten Island businessman Fred Weiss.

One of the Gambinos' rising stars, Michael "Mikey Scars" DiLeonardo, was also arrested for the execution-style slaying. It was allegedly carried out as a favor to Gotti, who feared Weiss was cooperating with the feds.

Comey said the three indictments unsealed yesterday represented a "further dismantling of the Gambino family's leadership" and sent a signal that the feds will prevent the family from re-establishing its "violent, extortionate grip" over New York.

New York FBI assistant director Kevin Donovan described the busts as the "latest chapter in the decade-long saga of the decline of the Gambinos."

"Making money the mob way has always meant instilling fear through intimidation and violence, and it is not true that the victims of mob violence are just other mobsters," Donovan said.

Since Gotti was put away for the last time in June 1992, the Gambinos' grip over legitimate industries, such as garbage carting and the waterfront, has been pried loose.

And the family's ability to rebuild was dealt a further blow this month, when Peter Gotti, who took over from his ailing brother this year, was arrested along with 16 other soldiers and associates.

As part of the indictments unsealed yesterday, the feds claim to have busted a large-scale theft racket centered on a vegetable store in the Bronx, called Top Tomato. It was owned by Salvatore Sciandra, brother of Gambino member Carmine Sciandra, the indictment says.

Sciandra's wife, Margaret, and her mother, Mildred Scarpati, are also facing up to five years in prison after being charged with conspiracy to defraud Allstate Insurance by filing a bogus car-loss claim.

Three Gambino associates were also charged with extorting two Manhattan garment businesses.[127]

Earlier we noted that all forms of organizational criminality have in common the use of business enterprises for illegal profit. We have recognized some significant problems not only with existing definitions and conceptualizations of white-collar and corporate crime but also with the criminal justice response to such offenses. Similar problems arise in efforts to deal with organized crime. It, too, depends on business enterprises. And, like corporate crime, organized crime comes in so many varieties that attempts to define it precisely lead to frustration.

The difficulty of gaining access to information on organized crime has also hindered attempts to conceptualize the problems posed by this kind of law violation. Finally, law enforcement efforts have been inadequate to control the influence of organized crime. As will be evident, a greater effort must be made to uncover the nature, pattern, and extent of organized crime.

The History of Organized Crime

Organized crime had its origin in the great wave of immigrants from southern Italy (especially from Sicily) to the United States between 1875 and 1920. These immigrants came from an environment that historically had been hostile to them. Suppressed by successive bands of invaders and alien rulers dating back some 800 years before Christ, Sicily was first coveted by the Greeks and Phoenicians as a strategic location between major Mediterranean trade routes. In later centuries, Roman, Byzantine, Arab, Norman, German, Spanish, Austrian, and French soldiers all laid siege and claim to Sicily. Exploited by mostly absentee landlords with their armies, Sicilians had learned to survive by relying on the strength of their own families. Indeed, these families had undergone little change since Greco-Roman times, two millennia earlier.

A traditional Sicilian family has been described as an extended family, or clan; it includes lineal relations (grandparents, parents, children, grandchildren) and lateral relations through the paternal line—uncles, aunts, and cousins as far as the bloodline can be traced. This *famiglia* is hierarchically organized and administered by the head of the family, the *capo di famiglia* (the Romans called him *pater familias*), to whom all members owe obedience and loyalty. Strangers, especially those in positions of power in state or church, are not to be trusted. The importance of the family is evident in the famous Sicilian proverb *"La legge é per l ricchi, La forca é per l poveri, E la giustizie é per l buffoni."* (The law is for the rich, the gallows are for the poor, and justice is for the fools.) For Sicilians, all problems are resolved within the family, which must be kept strong. Its prestige, honor, wealth, and power have to be defended and strengthened, sometimes through alliances with more distant kin.[128]

Throughout history, these strong families have served each other and Sicily. Upon migration to the United States, members of Sicilian families soon found that the social environment in their new country was as hostile as that of the old. Aspirations were encouraged, yet legitimate means to realize them were often not available. And the new country seemed already to have an established pattern for achieving wealth and power by unethical means. Many of America's great fortunes—those of the Astors, the Vanderbilts, the Goulds, the Sages, the Stanfords, the Rockefellers, the Carnegies, the Lords, the Harrimans—had been made by cunning, greed, and exploitation.

As time passed, new laws were enacted to address conspiracies in restraint of trade and other economic offenses. Yet by the time the last wave of Sicilian immigrants reached the United States, the names of the great robber barons were connected with major universities, foundations, and charitable institutions.[129] At the local level, the Sicilian immigrants found themselves involved in a system of politics in which patronage and protection were dispensed by corrupt politicians and petty hoodlums from earlier immigrant groups—German, Irish, and Jewish. The Sicilian family structure helped its members survive in this hostile environment. It also created the organizational basis that permitted them to respond to the opportunity created when, on January 16, 1920, the Eighteenth Amendment to the Constitution outlawed the manufacture, sale, and transportation of alcoholic beverages.

Howard Abadinsky explains what happened:

> Prohibition acted as a catalyst for the mobilization of criminal elements in an unprecedented manner. Pre-prohibition crime, insofar as it was organized, centered around corrupt political machines, vice entrepreneurs, and, at the bottom, gangs. Prohibition unleashed an unparalleled level of competitive criminal violence and changed the order—the gang leaders emerged on top.[130]

During the early years of Prohibition, the names of the most notorious bootleggers, mobsters, and gangsters sounded German, Irish, and Jewish: Arthur Flegenheimer (better known as "Dutch Schultz"), Otto Gass, Bo and George Weinberg, Arnold Rothstein, John T. Nolen (better known as "Legs Diamond"), Vincent "Mad Dog" Coll, Waxey Gordon, Owney Madden, and Joe Rock. By the time Prohibition was repealed, Al Capone, Salvatore Luciana (better known as "Lucky Luciano"), Frank Costello, Johnny Torrio, Vito Genovese, Guiseppe Doto (better known as "Joe Adonis"), and many other Sicilians were preeminent in the underworld. They had become folk heroes and role models for young boys in the Italian ghettos, many of whom were to seek their own places in this new society.

Sicilian families were every bit as ruthless in establishing their crime empires as the earlier immigrant groups had been. They were so successful in their domination of organized crime that, especially after World War II, organized crime became virtually synonymous with the Sicilian Mafia.

The term "Mafia" appears to derive from an Arabic word denoting "place of refuge." The concept, which was adopted in Sicily during the era of Arab rule, gradually came to describe a mode of life and survival. Sicilians trace the word to a tale of revenge that took place on Easter Monday, 1282. On this day, a French soldier who was part of a band of marauding foreigners raped a Sicilian woman on her wedding day. Following the assault, bands of Sicilians went to the streets of Palermo to slaughter hundreds of Frenchmen, spurred on by the screams of the young girl's mother: *"Ma fia, ma fia"* ("My daughter, my daughter").[131]

■ On St. Valentine's Day, 1929, while Al Capone vacationed in Florida, his mobsters machine-gunned their rivals in Chicago. The victims were lured to this garage (to buy prohibited liquor) where the hit men, dressed in stolen police uniforms and driving a stolen police car, "raided" the place, told the victims to line up against the wall, and then opened fire.

Ultimately, the **Mafia** became the entirety of those Sicilian families that were loosely associated with one another in operating organized crime, both in America and in Sicily.[132] The first realistic depiction of the organization of the Mafia came with the testimony of Joseph Valachi before the Senate's McClellan Committee in 1963. Valachi, a disenchanted soldier in New York's Genovese crime family, was the first member of Italian organized crime to describe a quasi-military secret criminal syndicate. From that point on, the Mafia has also been referred to as *La Cosa Nostra*, literally translated as "this thing of ours."[133]

Despite Valachi's testimony and later revelations, some scholars still doubt the existence of a Sicilian-based American crime syndicate. To criminologist Jay Albanese, for instance,

> it is clear . . . that despite popular opinion which has for many years insisted on the existence of a secret criminal society called "the Mafia," which somehow evolved from Italy, many separate historical investigations have found no evidence to support such a belief.[134]

The Structure and Impact of Organized Crime

Americans have felt the impact of organized crime, and they have followed the media coverage of the mob wars and their victims with fascination. But little was known about the Mafia's actual structure in the United States until a succession of government investigations began to unravel its mysteries. The major investigations were conducted by the Committee on Mercenary Crimes, in 1932; the Special Senate Committee to Investigate Organized Crime in Interstate Commerce (the Kefauver crime committee), from 1950 to 1951; the Senate Permanent Subcommittee on Investigations (the McClellan committee), from 1956 to 1963; President Lyndon Johnson's Commission on Law Enforcement and Administration of Justice (the Task Force on Organized Crime), from 1964 to 1967; and the President's Commission on Organized Crime, which reported to President Reagan in 1986 and 1987.[135]

The findings of these investigations established the magnitude of organized crime in the United States. It had become an empire almost beyond the reach of government, with vast resources derived from a virtual monopoly on gambling and loan-sharking; drug trafficking; pornography and prostitution; labor racketeering; murder for hire; the control of local crime activities; and the theft and fencing of securities, cars, jewels, and consumer goods of all sorts.[136] Above all, it was found that organized crime had infiltrated a vast variety of legitimate businesses, such as stevedoring (the loading and unloading of ships), the fish and meat industries, the wholesale and retail liquor industry (including bars and taverns), the vending machine business, the securities and investment business, the waste disposal business, and the construction industry.[137]

Specific legislation and law enforcement programs have allowed governmental agencies to assert some measure of control over organized crime. Cases have been successfully prosecuted under the **Racketeer Influenced and Corrupt Organizations (RICO) Act** of 1970.[138] This statute attacks racketeering activities by prohibiting the investment of any funds derived from racketeering in any enterprise that is engaged in interstate commerce. In addition, the **Federal Witness Protection Program**, established under the Organized Crime Control Act of 1970 (also known as the Witness Security Program, or "Wit Sec"), has made it easier for witnesses to testify in court by

Nicholas Corozzo (right), head of the Gambino crime family, surrendered to federal agents in New York on May 29, 2008. He was charged with extorting construction companies, running an illegal gambling ring, and ordering a hit that also killed a bystander in 1996.

guaranteeing them a new identity, thus protecting them against revenge.[139] More than 7,500 witnesses and close to 10,000 family members have sought the services of this flagship program within the United States Marshals Service.

The information provided by the governmental commissions, in combination with scholarly research, has established that the structure of an organized crime group is similar to that of a Sicilian family. Family members are joined by "adopted" members; the family is then aided at the functional level by nonmember auxiliaries.[140] The use of military designations such as *caporegima* ("lieutenant") and "soldier" does not alter the fact that a criminal organization is rather more like a closely knit family business enterprise than like

"I TAKE IT YOU'RE ALSO IN THE FEDERAL WITNESS-PROTECTION PROGRAM."

Sidney Harris. ScienceCartoonsPlus.com.

an army.[141] On the basis of testimony presented by Joseph Valachi in 1963, the commission's Task Force on Organized Crime was able to construct an organization chart of the typical Mafia, or Cosa Nostra, family (Figure 10.4).

Relations among the various families, which formerly were determined in ruthlessly fought gang wars, have more recently been facilitated by a loosely formed coordinating body called "the Commission." By agreement, the country has been divided into territorial areas of jurisdiction, influence, and operation. These arrangements are subject to revision from time to time, by mutual agreement. Likewise, rules of conduct have become subject to control or regulation by the heads of the various crime families. They consider, for example, to what extent each family should enter the hard-drug market, how much violence should be used, and how each will deal with public officials and the police.[142]

Informants at the "convention" of the so-called Apalachin conspirators provided a rare opportunity to learn about the way crime families reach agreement on their operations. On November 14, 1957, 63 of the country's most notorious underworld figures were arrested in Apalachin, New York, at or near the home of Joseph M. Barbara, a well-known organized-crime figure. Participants included New York's Vito Genovese, Carlo Gambino, Paul Castellano, and Joe Bonanno. Also arrested were Florida's don, Santo Trafficante Jr.; Sam ("Momo") Giancana of Chicago; Detroit boss Joe Zerilli; and the boss of the Buffalo rackets, Stefano Magaddino. Apparently, they had congregated at Barbara's home to settle a dispute among the families, which 3 weeks earlier had resulted in the assassination of Mangano family boss Albert Anastasia (the Mangano family was predecessor to the largest contemporary crime family in the United States, the Gambino crime family)

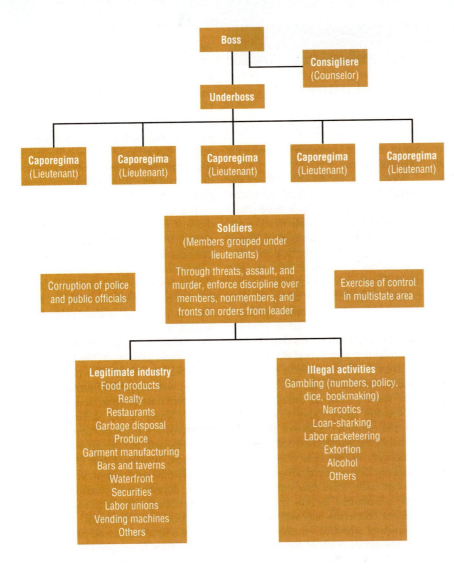

FIGURE 10.4 Organization chart of the typical Mafia family.

Source: President's Commission on Law Enforcement and Administration of Justice, *Task Force Report: Organized Crime* (Washington, D.C.: U.S. Government Printing Office, 1967), p. 9.

Boss

Consigliere (Counselor)

Underboss

Caporegima (Lieutenant)

Caporegima (Lieutenant)

Caporegima (Lieutenant)

Caporegima (Lieutenant)

Caporegima (Lieutenant)

Soldiers (Members grouped under lieutenants)

Through threats, assault, and murder, enforce discipline over members, nonmembers, and fronts on orders from leader

Corruption of police and public officials

Exercise of control in multistate area

Legitimate industry
Food products
Realty
Restaurants
Garbage disposal
Produce
Garment manufacturing
Bars and taverns
Waterfront
Securities
Labor unions
Vending machines
Others

Illegal activities
Gambling (numbers, policy, dice, bookmaking)
Narcotics
Loan-sharking
Labor racketeering
Extortion
Alcohol
Others

and the attempted murder in May 1957 of Francesco Castiglia, better known as Frank Costello, by the current godfather of the Genovese crime family, Vincent "The Chin" Gigante.

The presence of so many out-of-state license plates on brand-new Cadillacs and Lincolns in this small upstate New York town caught the attention of New York State police sergeant Edgar Croswell, an amateur organized-crime buff. Croswell, already somewhat suspicious of the true nature of Barbara's business dealings, put in a call to federal authorities and arranged to have a roadblock set up to guard against any of the participants leaving without being questioned. The police presence didn't go unnoticed by the gangsters, who rushed to make a quick escape back to their fiefdoms.

The comical scene of men in silk suits and fedora hats running through the forest was enough for Croswell. He caught as many as he could and placed them under arrest. None of the conspirators, however, publicly revealed the true nature of their meeting. Some suggested that, quite by coincidence, all had simply come to visit their sick friend Joe Barbara, who would die of a heart attack 2 years later. All were indicted and convicted for refusing to answer the grand jury's questions about the true purpose of the meeting. The convictions were subsequently reversed.[143]

Certain core business matters were decided at that meeting:

- Carlo Gambino was given the leadership of the New York crime family that still bears his name, a family made famous by the subsequent exploits of the late John Gotti.

- As a vote of confidence for Vito Genovese, Frank Costello was asked to go into semiretirement to pave the way for Genovese to take over the family that Lucky Luciano had started.

- A ban was placed on any "made man" trafficking in drugs. "If you deal, you die" was the slogan that resonated throughout organized crime as of the late 1950s. Although widely ignored, the ban still exists today.

The activities of the Mafia appear to have shifted from the once extremely violent bootlegging and street-crime operations to a far more sophisticated level of criminal activity.[144] Modern organized crime has assumed international dimensions.[145] It extends not only to international drug traffic, but also to legitimate enterprises such as real estate and trade in securities, as well as to many other lucrative business enterprises. This transition has been accomplished both by extortion and by entry with laundered money derived from illegitimate activity. It is tempting to wonder whether we may be witnessing the same kind of metamorphosis that occurred a century ago, when the robber barons became legitimate business tycoons and, ultimately, philanthropists.

The New Ethnic Diversity in Organized Crime

Organized crime is not necessarily synonymous with the Mafia. Other groups also operate in the United States. Foremost among them are the Colombian crime families, whose brutality is unrivaled by any other organized-crime group; and Bolivian, Peruvian, and Jamaican crime families, which since the 1970s have organized the production, transportation, and distribution within the United States of cocaine and marijuana.

Another form of organized crime, initiated by disillusioned veterans of the Korean War and reinforced by veterans of Vietnam, appears in the outlaw motorcycle gangs. Among them are the Hell's Angels, the Pagans, the Outlaws, the Sons of Silence, and the Bandidos. All are organized along military lines; all are devoted to violence; all are involved in the production and distribution of narcotics and other drugs. Many members

are also involved in other criminal activities, including extortion and prostitution, trafficking in stolen motorcycles and parts, and dealing in automatic weapons and explosives.

Among other organized groups engaged in various criminal activities are Chinese gangs (Figure 10.5), the so-called Israeli Mafia, the recently emerging Russian-Jewish Mafia, Jamaican posses, and the "Tattooed Men" of Japan's Yakuza, whose Yamaguchi-Gumi family alone has over 56,000 members, or nearly 20 times the number of fully initiated Italian organized-crime members in all the crews of all the families in the United States. All these groups have demonstrated potential for great social disruption.[146]

EMERGING PROBLEMS

Some of the more pressing issues we face today include global terrorism, an increase in hate crimes nationwide, the spread of racist and antigovernment militias, and deadly shootings in American schools. In recent years, largely as a result of media attention, these crimes have had a dramatic impact on the public's perception that violence has reached epidemic proportions. In reality, these crimes account for an extremely low proportion of all violent crimes, and rates for two of them (terrorism and violence in schools) have even gone down.

Terrorism

Many of those who worked in the South and North Towers of the World Trade Center arrived like clockwork—6:30 A.M., 7:00 A.M., 7:30 A.M., 8:00 A.M., and 8:30 A.M. They poured in from all

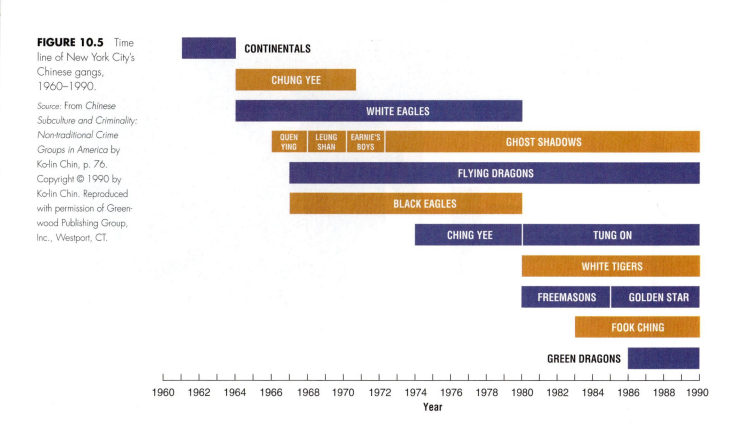

FIGURE 10.5 Time line of New York City's Chinese gangs, 1960–1990.

Source: From *Chinese Subculture and Criminality: Non-traditional Crime Groups in America* by Ko-lin Chin, p. 76. Copyright © 1990 by Ko-lin Chin. Reproduced with permission of Greenwood Publishing Group, Inc., Westport, CT.

over the tristate area (New York, New Jersey, and Connecticut) by car, rail, bus, ferry, and foot to ascend the two most visible symbols of New York.

Every day the mall on the ground floor was a teaming mass of blue- and white-collar workers—all marching toward one of two towers. It was no different on the morning of September 11, 2001. Secretaries were already checking e-mail at Nishi-Nippon Bank, Ltd., on the 102nd floor. Bond traders from Cantor Fitzgerald Securities were grabbing their morning coffee on the 105th floor. And waiters were setting the tables for a private function at the restaurant Windows on the World on the 107th floor.

Life was its usual fast pace for over 30,000 people working or visiting the World Trade Center—that is, until hijacked American Airlines Flight 11 crashed into the central core of the North Tower, raining a hail of debris over much of lower Manhattan. Witnesses said that the tall, sleek building literally swallowed the Boeing 767. Twenty-one minutes later, United Airlines Flight 175 collided with the South Tower, igniting a second fire that trapped helpless workers high above the New York City skyline. Desperate and with no means of escape, several hundred jumped to their tragic deaths.

At 10:00 A.M., the South Tower collapsed, the building imploding from the burning jet fuel and instantly killing thousands of workers, police, and firefighters. A thick and dark cloud enveloped Tribeca (the neighborhood in Manhattan represented by the *Triangle Below Canal Street*) like a fast-moving volcano. Thousands ran from lower Manhattan with an understandable mix of panic, fear, anger, confusion, and hysteria.

In a matter of seconds, everything and everybody left behind were covered in ash. It was, as some described it, like hell breaking loose or hell on Earth. After the thunderous crash of metal and concrete, the air had a strong and pungent smell of a chemical burn. The scene had all trappings of a movie set—a high-budget pyrotechnic war movie. Huge chunks of metal, tons of paper, and thick ash covered the deserted streets of a fallen city. Anyone approaching Liberty Street or West Street would see the unimaginable. Familiar landmarks were gone—buildings were no longer where they once were. Cars close to "Ground Zero" had literally melted to the ground from the heat of the fire and implosions.

People who had escaped from the North and South Towers, and those who emerged from adjoining buildings, were dazed. Some were in shock. Many were crying and consoling each other. Others were in desperate need of medical attention, with first- and second-degree burns. People who were bleeding from falling debris and choking from fumes rushed from lower Manhattan toward the Brooklyn Bridge, up Church Street and West Broadway. Many were crowded onto ferries to New Jersey. Everything that was typical, normal, and usual no longer was.

Emergency personnel from all five boroughs of New York City raced toward Tribeca and Ground Zero in a frenzied effort to put out the fire, to save and comfort the injured, to rescue the

6. Convention on the Physical Protection of Nuclear Material, signed in Vienna on October 26, 1979.
   Convention entered into force on February 8, 1987.
   Status: 130 parties.

7. Protocol for the Suppression of Unlawful Acts of Violence at Airports Serving International Civil Aviation, Supplementary to the Convention for the Suppression of Unlawful Acts against the Safety of Civil Aviation, signed in Montreal on February 24, 1988.
   Protocol entered into force on August 6, 1989.
   Status: 161 parties.

8. Convention for the Suppression of Unlawful Acts against the Safety of Maritime Navigation, done in Rome on March 10, 1988.
   Convention entered into force on March 1, 1992.
   Status: 147 parties.

9. Protocol for the Suppression of Unlawful Acts against the Safety of Fixed Platforms Located on the Continental Shelf, done in Rome on March 10, 1988.
   Protocol entered into force on March 1, 1992.
   Status: 136 parties.

10. Convention on the Marking of Plastic Explosives for the Purpose of Detection, done in Montreal on March 1, 1991.
    Convention entered into force on June 21, 1998.
    Status: 137 parties.

11. International Convention for the Suppression of Terrorist Bombings, adopted in New York on December 15, 1997.
    Convention entered into force on May 23, 2001.
    Status: 153 parties.

12. International Convention for the Suppression of the Financing of Terrorism, adopted in New York on December 9, 1999.
    Convention entered into force on April 10, 2002.
    Status: 160 parties.

13. International Convention for the Suppression of Acts of Nuclear Terrorism, adopted in New York on April 13, 2005.
    Convention entered into force on July 7, 2007.
    Status: 115 parties.[153]

These conventions, which provide for widespread international cooperation, cover a wide range of terrorist acts across a host of jurisdictions.

It appears that by 1989 several governments that had been supporting "freedom fighters" (elsewhere called "terrorist groups") had grown disenchanted with the groups' exercise of arbitrary violence against uninvolved civilian targets, such as airplane passengers, and had ceased to support such groups. In addition, the end of the cold war and the breakup of the Soviet bloc have deprived many of these groups of funding; consequently, they are on the decline. Rising in their stead is a new type of terrorist group, more difficult to monitor and perhaps even more dangerous. The old-style politically motivated mayhem has been replaced with ethnically and religiously inspired violence.

More recently, cults have sprung up whose members believe that a catastrophic war or natural disaster will land the "chosen few" in paradise. These doomsday cults can turn inward, leading to mass suicide or the murder of the membership. Eighty-six of David Koresh's followers at the Branch Davidian compound in Waco, Texas, died a fiery death after a lengthy siege by the FBI. It is still unclear whether the Branch Davidians set fire to the compound themselves or if the FBI was responsible. Other groups direct their actions at outsiders. In Japan, the Aum Shinrikyo ("Supreme Truth") sect was implicated in the deadly sarin nerve gas attack on the Tokyo subway, which killed 10 and injured over 5,000. The leader of the sect, Shoko Asahara, preached about the end of the world and claimed that sarin would be a primary weapon in the "final world war."[154]

Hate Crimes

In June 1998, James Byrd Jr., an African American, was dragged to his death in Jasper, Texas. Byrd was hitchhiking on a Saturday night when John William King and two friends chained him to their truck and pulled him, alive, for over 2 miles. His head was finally severed from his body. King, who was sentenced to death in March 1999, and his two friends were Ku Klux Klan (KKK) members.

An equally barbaric hate crime occurred in October 1998. Russell Henderson and Aaron McKinney posed as homosexuals and lured gay college student Matthew Shepard out of a bar in Wyoming. They robbed, pistol-whipped, and burned him with cigarettes before leaving him tied to a fence in near-freezing temperatures. Shepard died 5 days later in a hospital. The murder trial of Henderson and McKinney incited further displays of hate, with antigay demonstrators shouting and waving signs that read "God Hates Fags."[155] Only a few months later, in Alabama, Steven Mullins and Charles Butler lured Billy Jack Gaither, another gay male, out of a bar into a secluded area where they beat him and then dumped him into the trunk of their car. They

■ *Mary Nell Verrett remembers her brother, James Byrd Jr., who was brutally murdered in a hate crime in Jasper, Texas.*

18.5 percent targeted victims because of their sexual preferences, 982 were ethnically motivated, and 79 were disability motivated.[158] According to the Southern Poverty Law Center, the number of hate groups increased from 474 in 1997 to 1002 in 2010 (Figure 10.6).[159] It also appears that groups are recruiting more violent members to carry out their messages of hate nationwide. One of the most recent tools used to attract these members is the Internet. Since 1995, over 160 online hate sites have been identified.[160]

Although hate crimes make up only a small percentage of overall criminality, the viciousness of the acts and their impact on broad population groups give them prominence in the media and pose extraordinary challenges to the criminal justice system. Presently, some police departments are forming bias-crime units to further the investigation of these crimes.

Militias

Militias have come to the attention of the American public only within the last decade. Most of them are groups whose memberships consist of white, Christian, working- and middle-class Americans whose fundamental belief is that their constitutional right to bear arms (protected under the Second Amendment) is threatened. Members tend to have apocalyptic, paranoid views of U.S. politics and the federal government. Their antigovernment beliefs are intertwined with some forms of white supremacy. They believe leading Democratic politicians are "liberal elitists who betray traditional American values."[161] Members of these groups believe that the federal government is preparing for a war against its own citizens.[162] The movement is a collection of grassroots groups who call themselves Patriots, Militiamen, Freemen, Common-Law Advocates, and Strict Constitutionalists. Although they are often labeled "right-wing," members' backgrounds touch all points on the political spectrum. The movement is so fragmented that membership estimates are unreliable. The Southern Poverty Law Center says that members can be found in all 50 states.[163] Some estimates are that as many as 100,000 Americans are involved.[164]

Most militia groups are nonviolent. Members have a fondness for wearing battle fatigues, participating in paramilitary maneuvers, and stockpiling firearms. Yet there are growing indications of involvement in illegal activities. The Michigan Militia Corps, for example, one of the nation's largest, with an estimated membership of 10,000 to 12,000, has alleged ties to Timothy McVeigh and Terry Nichols, both charged in the Oklahoma City bombing.[165]

Long before this bombing focused attention on the radical right, the FBI had insiders and

drove about 15 miles, took him out of the trunk, and killed him with an ax handle. Mullins and Butler then placed Gaither's body on top of two old tires that they had set on fire.[156]

In August 1999, Buford O. Furrow, a former member of the Aryan Nation, walked into the lobby of the North Valley Jewish Community Center in the Granada Hills area of Los Angeles, shooting and wounding a receptionist, a camp counselor, and three children. After leaving the scene, Furrow carjacked a person's vehicle, drove to the residential area of Chatsworth, and shot Joseph Ileto, a Filipino-American postman who was in the middle of making his rounds. Furrow later turned himself in.[157]

During 2006, the United States experienced some of the most gruesome displays of hate-crime violence. According to the Uniform Crime Reports, there were 6,598 incidents of hate crimes, which involved 7,775 separate offenses reported from over 12,000 law enforcement agencies to the FBI. Of the incidents, 48.5 percent were racially motivated, 19.7 percent were religiously motivated,

The Extent of Firearm-Related Offenses

It is difficult to be certain how many guns there are in the United States. Before 1850, less than 10 percent of U.S. citizens were believed to own guns, and between 1800 and 1845, only about 15 percent of all violent deaths were caused by guns.[180] It is also unknown how many of the guns available in this country have been seized, destroyed, or lost, or do not work properly.[181] Law enforcement estimates that there are over 200 million firearms in circulation in the United States, including about 70 million handguns.[182] The rate of firearms crimes has dropped significantly over the past 30 years. In 1973, the rate was 172.1 per 100,000 population. Thirty-three years later, the rate was 129.9.[183]

In any case, firearm-related crime is still more prevalent in the United States than in other developed Western nations. According to the Task Force on Firearms of the National Commission on the Causes and Prevention of Violence, the rate of homicide by gun is 40 times higher in the United States than in England and Wales, and our rate of robbery by gun is 60 times higher.

The financial cost of gunshot injury and death, in terms of medical costs, lost productivity, and pain, suffering, and reduced quality of life, has been estimated at over $60 billion each year. The Centers for Disease Control and Prevention estimated that approximately 96,000 persons in the United States sustained gunshot wounds in 1997.[184]

Youths and Guns

Three young thugs boarded a city bus in Queens yesterday, brandished guns like Wild West bandits and staged a frontier-style holdup. They strode up and down the aisle, fired shots into the roof, terrorized and robbed 22 passengers, struck a girl in the face with a gun butt and escaped with $300 in cash and fistfulls of jewelry.

The outlaws—one armed with a silver revolver and another with a pair of guns, while a third carried a book bag—made no effort to conceal their faces as they boarded the Q-85 bus at 8:30 A.M. at 140th Avenue and Edgewood Avenue in Springfield Gardens, a residential neighborhood just northeast of Kennedy International Airport.[185]

The "bandits" were three youths ages 15 to 19. In a growing number of incidents across the United States, young people are using guns for robberies, gang warfare, initiation rites (drive-by shootings by wanna-be gang members), random shootings (in fact, James Jordan, father of former basketball star Michael Jordan, fell victim), and protection from their peers.[186]

Concern is mounting over adolescent illegal gun ownership and use. In 1995, the National Institute of Justice interviewed a sample of arrested individuals in Denver, the District of Columbia, Indianapolis, Los Angeles, Phoenix, St. Louis, and San Diego. The study found that juveniles are more likely than arrestees overall to commit crime with a gun. Of the juveniles interviewed, 20 percent said they carried a gun most or all of the time, 25 percent had stolen a gun, and 33 percent who owned a gun had used one in a crime (the percentages were considerably higher for gang members). Eighteen percent of the juveniles agreed that it was appropriate to use a gun "to shoot someone who disrespected you."[187]

Another study, of inner-city high schools in California, Illinois, Louisiana, and New Jersey, found a connection between involvement in drugs and gun carrying.[188] The same study sampled female students as well; 1 in 10 female students owned a gun at some time, and roughly the same percentage carried a gun.[189]

Why have youths turned to guns? When asked, many of them respond the way three teenagers did: "You fire a gun and you can just *hear* the power. It's like *yeah!*" or "It became cool to say you could get a gun," or "Nobody messes with you if they think you may have a gun."[190] While there are many studies on adolescent violent behavior, there are few on adolescent illegal gun use. One of the few, a study of ninth- and tenth-grade boys, 14- and 15-year-olds, in Rochester, New York, found that most boys who owned illegal guns had friends who owned guns, over half of the illegal gun owners were gang members, and selling drugs was a prime motivation for carrying a gun. Moreover, illegal gun ownership, friends' gun ownership, gang membership, and drug use were closely related to gun crime, street crime, and minor delinquency.[191] Illegal firearms have traditionally been used by youths in low-income urban neighborhoods. The problem, like that of school shootings, has now spread to the suburbs.

Controlling Handgun Use

While most people agree that gun-related crime is a particularly serious part of our crime problem, there is little agreement on what to do about it. Some want prohibition. Others want comprehensive licensing and registrations.[192] Civic organizations and police associations call for more laws prescribing mandatory sentences for the illegal purchase, possession, or use of firearms. Close to 20,000 laws that regulate firearms already exist in the United States.

A powerful protest plea outside the Denver NRA convention in 1999.

A variety of methods of controlling handgun use have been tried:

• In 1996 the Bureau of Alcohol, Tobacco and Firearms established the Youth Crime Gun Interdiction Initiative *to trace crime guns* (those illegally possessed or used in a crime) recovered by law enforcement. In its first year, 76,000 crime guns were traced. Almost half were recovered from persons under the age of 25.[193]

• A *prohibition against carrying guns* in public seemed to be related to a drop in gun crimes in Boston[194] and a leveling off of handgun violence in Detroit.[195]

• In Kansas City, Missouri, a *police gun-confiscation program* was implemented in gun-crime hot spots in the target area, which had a murder rate 20 times the national average. Gun seizures in the target area increased by over 65 percent, while gun crimes decreased by 49 percent. Homicides were also significantly reduced in the target area.[196]

• Some states have passed what are referred to as *sentence-enhancement statutes:* The punishment for an offense is more severe if a person commits it under certain conditions, such as by using a gun. The Massachusetts law (1975) mandates a minimum sentence of 1 year's incarceration upon conviction for the illegal carrying of a firearm.[197] Michigan created a new offense—commission of a felony while possessing a firearm—and added a mandatory 2-year prison sentence to the sentence received for the commission of the felony itself. The state mounted a widespread publicity campaign: "One with a gun gets you two," read the billboards and bumper stickers.[198]

• Sentence enhancement has been studied in six U.S. cities. Homicides committed with firearms decreased in all six after sentence-enhancement laws took effect, although the decline in homicides was large in some cities and small in others. Researchers studying sentence enhancement point out that its effectiveness is related to how closely judges follow the law. An additional 3 years in prison may deter criminals from using guns, while an additional month may not.

• Project Exile began in Richmond, Virginia, in 1997. This program specifies that any time a gun is found on a person, whether a drug dealer, drug user, convicted felon, or suspect in a crime, the case will be tried under federal statutes in federal court. By moving gun offenses into the federal system, offenders face mandatory sentences of 5 years without parole. Prison time is increased for repeat or aggravated offenses. This project is advertised all over the city on billboards that in bold letters say, "An Illegal Gun Gets You Five Years in Federal Prison." After implementation of this program, murders in Richmond dropped significantly, from 140 in 1997 to 94 in 1998 and 32 in the first 6 months of 1999. Project Exile also led to the recovery of almost 500 illegal handguns, indictments against about 400 people on gun charges, and a conviction rate of 86 percent through trials and plea bargains.[199] This Virginia program is being mirrored in other cities as well, with anticipation of a similar effect.[200] The National Rifle Association supports this program, claiming that it is the best alternative to restrictive gun laws.[201]

• A *total ban on handguns* was tried in Washington, D.C., beginning in 1976. Both gun homicides and gun suicides dropped visibly after the ban took effect, while no change occurred in homicides and suicides not committed with guns.[202]

• Some communities have tried *buy-back programs.* St. Louis, San Francisco, Philadelphia, New York, and several other cities have embarked on such programs to reduce the number of handguns in circulation in the community. Police departments buy guns, no questions

THEORY CONNECTS

Youths and Guns

How do subculture theories of delinquency (Chapter 6) help explain gun ownership among the young? In particular, does the notion of reaction formation reveal why so many adolescents are drawn to the violence of gang life?

Crime Surfing

www.atf.gov

The Bureau of Alcohol, Tobacco and Firearms provides information on firearms use, guns in circulation, and programs aimed at reducing the possession of illegal firearms.

rights and interests (crimes against property), as described in this chapter.

We have just explored some of the patterns of social interaction and the routine activities of daily life that set the stage for offenders to commit violent crimes and for other people—family members, acquaintances, strangers, airplane passengers—to become victims. We know that if we are to develop effective policies to prevent and control violent crime, we must have a thorough understanding of the characteristics of specific offenses; we need to know where, when, and how they are committed, and which individuals are most likely to commit them. The same is true for property offenses. To develop crime-prevention strategies, we need to study the characteristics that differentiate the various types of offenses that deprive people of their property.

Do offenses such as pocket-picking (pickpocketing), shoplifting, check forgery, theft by use of stolen credit cards, car theft, computer crimes, and burglary have different payoffs and risks? What kinds of resources are needed (weapons, places to sell stolen property)? Are any specific skills needed to carry out these offenses? The opportunities to commit property crime are all but unlimited. Studies demonstrate that if these opportunities are reduced, the incidence of crime is reduced as well.

The traditional property crimes are larceny (theft, or stealing); obtaining property by fraud of various sorts, including false pretenses, confidence games, forgery, and unauthorized use of credit cards; burglary, which does not necessarily involve theft; and arson, which not only deprives the owner of property but also endangers lives. New crime types, such as software piracy, online frauds, and computer viruses, are associated with high-technology equipment. We defer until Chapter 12 discussion of the crimes by which criminals deprive people of their property through organizational manipulations—individual white-collar crimes and corporate crimes.

LARCENY

Larceny (theft, stealing) is the prototype of all property offenses. It is also the most prevalent crime in our society; it includes contemporary forms such as purse-snatching, pickpocketing, shoplifting, art theft, and vehicle theft. In the thirteenth century, when Henry de Bracton set out to collect from all parts of England what was common in law—and thus, common law—he learned to his surprise that there was no agreement on a concept of larceny. He found a confusing variety of ancient Germanic laws. So he did what he always did in such circumstances: He remembered what he had learned about Roman law from Professor Azo in Bologna and simply inserted it into his new text of English law. Thus, our common law definition of larceny is virtually identical with the concept in Roman law.[1]

The Elements of Larceny

Here are the elements of **larceny** (or theft, or stealing):

A trespassory
Taking and
Carrying away of
Personal property
Belonging to another
With the intent to deprive the owner of the property permanently

Each of these elements has a long history that gives it its meaning. The first element is perhaps the easiest. There must be a trespass. "Trespass," a Norman-French term, has a variety of meanings. In the law of larceny, however, it simply means any absence of authority or permission for the taking. Second, the property must be taken: The perpetrator must exert authority over the property, as by putting a hand on a piece of merchandise or getting into the driver's seat of the targeted car.

Third, the property must be carried away. The slightest removal suffices to fulfill this element: moving merchandise from a counter, however slightly; loosening the brakes of a car so that it starts rolling, even an inch. Fourth, the property in question, at common law, has to be personal property. (Real estate is not subject to larceny.) Fifth, the property has to belong to another, in the sense that the person has the right to possess that property. Sixth, the taker must intend to deprive the rightful owner permanently of the property. This element is present when the taker (thief) intends to deprive the rightful owner of the property forever. In many states, however, the law no longer requires proof that the thief intended to deprive the owner "permanently" of the property.

The Extent of Larceny

Larceny, except for the most petty varieties, was a capital offense in medieval England.[2] Courts interpreted all its elements quite strictly—that is, in favor of defendants—so as to limit the use of

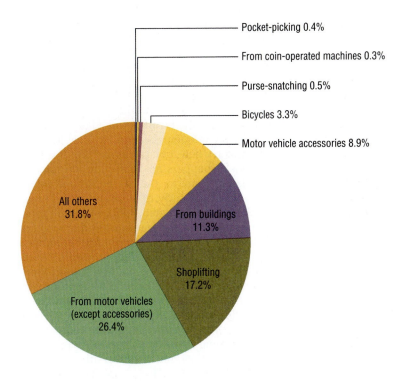

Pocket-picking 0.4%

From coin-operated machines 0.3%

Purse-snatching 0.5%

Bicycles 3.3%

Motor vehicle accessories 8.9%

All others 31.8%

From buildings 11.3%

Shoplifting 17.2%

From motor vehicles (except accessories) 26.4%

FIGURE 11.1 Distribution of larcenies known to police, 2010.

*Due to rounding the percentages may not add to 100

Source: United Crime Reports, 2010.

capital punishment. Only once did the courts expand the reach of larceny, when they ruled that a transporter who opens a box entrusted to him and takes out some items has committed larceny by "breaking bulk." For the other forms of deceptive acquisition of property, such as embezzling funds and obtaining property by false pretenses, Parliament had to enact separate legislation.

In the United States, the rate of larceny is extraordinarily high. The UCR reported 6.2 million thefts in 2010, or a rate of 2,003.8 for each 100,000 population.[3] The NCVS figure, 11.2 million, is nearly two times the UCR number, and neither figure includes automobile thefts.[4] The vast majority of thefts are, and always have been, committed furtively and without personal contact with the victims. Thefts involving personal contact—pickpocketing, purse-snatching, and other varieties of larceny—lag behind. Figure 11.1 shows the distribution of all larcenies known to the police in 2007. The estimated dollar value of stolen goods to victims nationally was over $5.1 billion.[5]

Who Are the Thieves?

Nobody knows exactly how many of the total number of thefts are committed by amateurs who lead rather conventional lives and how many are the work of professionals. According to some criminologists, the two types differ considerably.[6]

The Amateur Thief

Amateur thieves are occasional offenders who tend to be opportunists. They take advantage of a chance to steal when little risk is involved.

Typically, their acts are carried out with little skill, are unplanned, and result from some pressing situation, such as the need to pay the rent or a gambling debt.[7] In other words, amateurs resolve some immediate crisis by stealing. Most occasional offenders commit few crimes; some commit only one crime. Many are juveniles who do not go on to commit crimes in adulthood.

Amateur thieves do not think of themselves as professional criminals, nor are they recognized as such by those who do think of themselves as professionals. The lives of amateur thieves are quite conventional: Amateurs work, go to school, have conventional friends, and find little support or approval for their criminal behavior.

The Professional Thief

Professional thieves make a career of stealing. They take pride in their profession. They are imaginative and creative in their work and accept its risks. The most common crimes committed by professional thieves are pickpocketing, shoplifting, forgery, confidence swindling, and burglary. Professional thieves also are involved in art theft, motor vehicle theft, and fraud or theft by use of stolen or forged credit cards, among other crimes.

Thomas Bartholomew Moran, a professional thief who died in a Miami rescue mission in 1971, has been considered the best of American pickpockets. His career began in 1906, when, as a teenager, he started to pick women's purses. Under the careful guidance of Mary Kelly, a well-known pickpocket, he soon sharpened his skills until he could take wallets from pants, jeweled pins from clothing, and watches from vests

THEORY CONNECTS

Who Are the Thieves?

Situational theories of crime, such as rational choice and routine-activities theories, suggest that offenders calculate the costs and benefits of committing crimes. In what ways do these theories explain the behavior of professional thieves?

without alerting the victims. He devoted his life to shoplifting, forgery, and other forms of theft. In 1912, he boarded the *Titanic*, with the intention of profiting handsomely from proximity to

> the more than 300 first-class passengers whose collective wealth exceeded $250 million. His immediate ambitions were dimmed, however, when the Titanic brushed an iceberg in the North Atlantic [and sank] only two hours and forty minutes later. But Moran was among the 705 passengers who managed to find space in one of the ship's twenty lifeboats, and his career in crime continued to flourish for the better part of the 59 remaining years of his life.[8]

The most influential study of professional thieves was conducted by Edwin Sutherland in 1937. Sutherland found that professional thieves share five characteristics:

1. They have well-developed technical skills for their particular mode of operation.

2. They enjoy status, accorded to them by their own subculture and by law enforcement.

3. They are bound by consensus, a sharing of values with their own peers.

4. Not only do they learn from each other, but they also protect each other.

5. They are organized, however loosely.[9]

Subsequent studies have tended to confirm Sutherland's findings.

Shoplifting

Shoplifting, the stealing of goods from retail merchants, is a very common crime; it constitutes about 15 percent of all larcenies. A survey in Spokane, Washington, revealed that every twelfth shopper is a shoplifter and that men and women are equally likely to be offenders.[10] Perhaps shoplifting is so frequent because it is a low-risk offense, with a detection rate of perhaps less than 1 percent.[11] Shoppers are extremely reluctant to report shoplifters to the store management.[12] According to one study, of those apprehended for shoplifting, approximately 45.5 percent are actually prosecuted. It is also estimated that men are slightly more likely than women to be shoplifters, and that 41 percent of offenders are white, 29 percent are black, and 16 percent are Hispanic. More than half of shoplifting events occur between the hours of 12:00 P.M. and 6:00 P.M.[13] Interviews with 740 shoplifters in 50 Minneapolis stores revealed that almost half of those who expressed motivation for stealing said that they stole the merchandise because they liked it and did not have enough money to pay for it.[14] A Hayes International Retail Theft Survey revealed significant increases in apprehensions and recoveries over the past years of reporting[15] (Table 11.1).

Mary Owen Cameron found that professional shoplifters largely conform to Sutherland's five characteristics but that amateurs do not. She estimates that of all shoplifters, only 10 percent are professionals—people who derive most of their income from the sale of stolen goods.[16] A broad range of motivations may lead to shoplifting. Among amateurs, need and greed as well as

---

TABLE 11.1 Shoplifting Apprehensions Survey

Hayes International's 20th Annual Retail Theft Survey reports on over 620,000 shoplifting apprehensions taking place in just 24 large retail companies representing 19,151 stores with combined 2007 annual sales in excess of $689 billion.

| | Shoplifting | | Difference | |
	2006	**2007**	**Number/$**	**Percent**
Apprehensions	573,769	626,314	52,545	9.16%
Recoveries*	$77,299,608	$83,245,923	$5,946,315	7.69%
Average case value	$134.72	$132.91	($1.81)	(1.34%)
Hours per apprehension†	70.84	70.75	(0.09)	(0.13%)
Recoveries (no apprehensions made)‡	$26,528,990	$30,531,116	$4,002,126	15.09%

*For the 7th straight year, dollars recovered from shoplifting apprehensions increased.

†Eleven companies reporting.

‡For the 11th consecutive year, dollars recovered from shoplifters where no apprehension was made increased.

SOURCE: From "Theft Surveys." http://www.hayesinternational.com/thft_srvys.html.

you by
commo
in any
Chea
history
attitude
own in
pretens
have in

Confi

In an a
greed, a
tory off
cover th
legislat
somew
that the
induces
gain, a
makes
sense,
obtaini
To i
lying o
a man
should
son (C
pens t
loupe
ring, a
B gene

At the upscale Beverly Hills Saks Fifth Avenue on December 12, 2001, actress Winona Ryder is seen on a security surveillance tape released by the Los Angeles County Courts. On November 6, 2002, a jury found the two-time Oscar nominee guilty of grand theft and felony vandalism for stealing designer clothes worth about $5,000.

opportunity may precipitate the event.[17] Some researchers point to depression and other emotional disturbances and to the use of various prescription drugs.[18]

To most people, shoplifting is a rather insignificant offense. After all, how much can be stolen? On an individual basis, usually not very much: The average theft amount for each incident is roughly $133.[19] Taken together, however, all shoplifting incidents cost U.S. retail businesses over $37 billion every year.[20] Only a small percentage of stolen merchandise is recovered.

As shoplifters decrease store profits, the price of goods goes up; stepped-up security adds even more to costs. Stores typically hire more and more security personnel, although it has been demonstrated that physical or electronic methods of securing merchandise are more cost effective than the deployment of guards.[21] It is only the amateur shoplifter who is deterred by the presence of guards or store personnel, not the professional.[22]

Given the significantly high costs of shoplifting to retailers, what can be done to reclaim what has been stolen? One option, practiced quite often in the United Kingdom, is the use of civil recovery. Civil recovery is an administrative process that enables store owners to utilize the civil law in an attempt to collect restitution from shoplifters directly, whether the shoplifters are customers or store employees. This civil action operates parallel to the criminal process, meaning that stores can both report instances of shoplifting to the police and file separate civil complaints against the shoplifters to obtain restitution. Those apprehended for shoplifting can then either pay the civil penalty imposed upon them or appear before a civil court. Research has shown that for amateur shoplifters (as opposed to professionals), the use of civil recovery does not have a significant impact on their initial offense but does have an impact on preventing them from reoffending.[23]

Art Theft

At the high end of the larceny scale we find art theft. The public knows and seems to care little about art theft, yet it is as old as art itself. Looters have stolen priceless treasures from Egyptian tombs ever since they were built. As prices for antiques and modern art soar, the demand for stolen art soars. Mexico and other countries with a precious cultural heritage are in danger of losing their treasures to gangs of thieves who take what they can from archaeological sites and leave the rest in ruins.

One of the most grandiose art thefts occurred on May 21, 1986, when a gang of Irish thieves invaded an estate in Ireland with commando precision and made off with 11 paintings, among them a Goya, two Rubenses, a Gainsborough, and a Vermeer.

Art theft, particularly the illicit trade in objects of cultural heritage, has increased significantly worldwide in recent years. Art thieves use a variety of means, including forms of shoplifting, burglary, and robbery, to either steal individual works of art, illegally export pieces of art, or pillage archaeological sites.[24] Despite the widespread incidence of art theft, nobody knows the overall cost. Some paintings are worth $50, others $5,000, and others $50 million. Tens of thousands of paintings and other art objects are missing.[25]

In response to the increasing problem of art theft, the Federal Bureau of Investigation (FBI) has created the National Stolen Art File, which consists of a computerized index of stolen art and

Dar
fraud i

pleas, and two of the defendants were convicted on August 31, 2006, and January 28, 2008, respectively.

CHRISTOPHER CRAIG (SACRAMENTO): In May 2007, Christopher Craig of Auburn, California, pled guilty to bank fraud charges related to a foreclosure scheme. Craig approached home-owners who were on the verge of foreclosure and promised to loan them money. Instead, he created documents deeding away their properties to straw buyers, then applied for home equity loans from

Washington Mutual Bank. Washington Mutual disbursed $1.2 million in loan proceeds to Craig based on the false loan applications. Craig was sentenced in the Eastern District of California to five years in federal prison and ordered to pay $974,452 in restitution. Property and cash were also seized for asset forfeiture from Craig, including a 2007 GMC Hummer SUV.

Source

Federal Bureau of Investigation, Financial Crimes Report to the

Public, Fiscal Year 2007 (October 1, 2006—September 30, 2007). Available at http://www.fbi.gov/publications/financial/fcs_report2007/financial_crime_2007.htm.

Questions for Discussion

1. What role should the criminal law play in policing the subprime crisis?
2. How much blame should consumers assume for their failure to live up to their financial responsibilities?

■ U.S. Secret Service Director Mark Sullivan (left) and U.S. Attorney General Michael Mukasey (right) at a news conference on August 5, 2008, where charges were announced in a major credit card theft. The Department of Justice charged 11 people in connection with the hacking of nine major retailers, including Office Max and Boston Market, and the theft and sale of more than 40 million credit and debit card numbers.

Credit card fraud during the 1980s was associated primarily with counterfeiting and lost or stolen cards. Now many cards are stolen while in transit from the issuer to the cardholder or during cell phone transmissions of wireless refunds, or in large-scale thefts of retail store databases.[47] Other offenses are extremely elaborate (Figure 11.3).

The economic rewards of credit card fraud are quick and relatively easy. The risks are low. However, the banking industry has studied credit card schemes and has improved the electronic system with target-hardening responses. In 1971, Congress enacted legislation that limited the financial liability of owners of stolen credit cards to $50. Many states have enacted legislation making it a distinct offense to obtain property or services by means of a stolen or forged credit card, while others include this type of fraud under their larceny statutes.

Several fraud-prevention initiatives have been developed in response to the prevalence of credit card fraud. The use of laser-engraved photography

and signatures on credit cards makes impersonation more difficult. Other initiatives are the use of increased authorization levels on credit card transactions, as well as reduced floor limits above which transactions must be authorized to be guaranteed. Better technology has been developed to quickly transmit data on cards that have been reported lost and stolen to retailers worldwide. Further, with the ever-increasing "card not present" situations, such as when a person is purchasing items over the Internet, additional methods are being developed to verify the identity of the cardholder.[48]

Insurance Fraud

Insurance fraud is a major problem in the United States. Auto insurance, in particular, has been the target of many dishonest schemes. About $60 billion is paid in auto insurance claims annually. It is estimated that 10 percent of those claims are fraudulent.[49] The National Automobile Theft Bureau holds

United States Attorney's Office
Eastern District of Virginia

Alexandria   Newport News   Norfolk   Richmond

United States Attorney Chuck Rosenberg

FOR IMMEDIATE RELEASE
July 25, 2008

Jim Rybicki   Further Information Contact:
Public Information Officer   Kim Williams
Phone: (703) 842-4050 Fax: (703) 549-5202   Phone: (703) 299-3700
Email: usavae.press@usdoj.gov

Web Address: www.usdoj.gov/usao/vae

Ringleader of Credit Card and Mortgage Scam Sentenced to 212 Months in Prison, $5 Million in Forfeiture, and More Than $3 Million in Restitution

(Alexandria, Virginia)—Abdul Hameed, age 46, of Houston, Texas, was sentenced today to 212 months in prison following his conviction on May 5, 2008, on a 21-count superseding indictment charging him with conspiracy, engaging in a continuing financial crimes enterprise, mail fraud, aggravated identity theft, and credit card fraud. Chuck Rosenberg, United States Attorney for the Eastern District of Virginia, made the announcement following Hameed's sentencing before United States District Judge Leonie M. Brinkema.

The indictment alleged that Hameed and others conspired to devise a scheme to defraud in which the defendants used various fraudulent identities that they controlled to obtain numerous credit card accounts, personal and business bank accounts, and mortgage loan accounts. According to the indictment, the defendants also established multiple false businesses that were used to give the appearance that the false identities were employed by fabricating employment and salary documents for the false identities. The phony documents were then provided to credit card companies, leasing offices, mortgage companies, and financial institutions to obtain credit in the names of the false identities. Hameed and his co-conspirators also rented apartments and purchased properties using false identities. These locations were then used to receive mail from the lenders that was addressed to the false identities and false businesses. They also used these locations to receive shipments of goods purchased using credit cards in the names of the false identities. According to the indictment, Hameed organized, managed, and supervised a continuing financial crimes enterprise—that is, a series of violations of the mail fraud statute that affected a financial institution and was committed by at least four persons acting in concert—and received $5,000,000 or more in gross receipts from the criminal enterprise during a 24-month period from in or about May 2005 to May 2007. According to the indictment, hundreds of thousands of dollars obtained from the scheme were transferred by the defendants to accounts in Pakistan.

Hameed was also ordered to pay forfeiture of $5 million and more than $3 million in restitution to the victims.

The case was prosecuted by Assistant United States Attorneys James P. Gillis, Gordon D. Kromberg, and Karen L. Taylor, and was investigated by a team of law enforcement agents from the Federal Bureau of Investigation, the Fairfax County Police Department, and the U.S. Postal Inspection Service.

FIGURE 11.3   Press Release about a Credit Card and Mortgage Scam.

Source: The United States Attorney's Office for the Eastern District of Virginia; available at http://www.usdoj.gov/usao/vae.

manufacturers' records on 188 million vehicles (about 95 percent of U.S. cars); its theft and loss data indicate that 15 percent of all reported thefts are fraudulent.[50] Auto insurance schemes include:

- *Staged claims.* Parts of a car are removed, reported stolen, and later replaced by the owner.

- *Owner dumping.* The car is reported stolen; it is stripped by the owner, and the parts are sold.

- *Abandoned vehicles.* The car is left in a vulnerable spot for theft; then it is reported stolen.[51]

- *Staged accidents.* No collision occurs, but an "accident scene" is prepared with glass, blood, and so forth.

- *Intended accidents.* All parties to the "accident" are part of the scheme.

- *Caused accidents.* The perpetrator deliberately causes an innocent victim in a targeted car to crash into his or her car (often in the presence of "friendly" witnesses).[52]

There are many types of insurance fraud besides that involving automobiles. One rapidly

Insurance Fraud

The battle against insurance fraud is fought at the local, state, and federal levels. Increasingly, the Financial Crimes Section of the Federal Bureau of Investigation plays a central role. Its most recent fiscal year report (2010) appears here.

Insurance fraud continues to be an investigative priority for the FBI, due in large part to the insurance industry's significant role in the U.S. economy. The U.S. insurance industry consists of thousands of companies and collects nearly $1 trillion in premiums each year. The size of the industry, unfortunately, makes it a prime target for criminal activity; the Coalition Against Insurance Fraud (CAIF) estimates that the cost of fraud in the industry is as high as $80 billion each year. This cost is passed on to consumers in the form of higher premiums.

The downturn in the U.S. economy due to the financial crisis has led to an increase in insurance fraud. The FBI continues to identify the most prevalent schemes and the top echelon criminals defrauding the insurance industry in an effort to reduce insurance fraud. The FBI works closely with the National Association of Insurance Commissioners, NICB, CAIF, as well as state fraud bureaus, state insurance regulators, and other federal agencies to combat Insurance Fraud. In addition, the FBI is a member of the International Association of insurance fraud Agencies, an international nonprofit organization whose mission is to maintain an international presence to address insurance and insurance-related financial crimes on a global basis. Currently, the FBI is focusing a majority of its resources relating to insurance fraud on the following schemes:

Insurance-Related Corporate Fraud—Although corporate fraud is not unique to any particular industry, there have been instances involving insurance companies caught in the web of these schemes. The temptations for fraud within the corporate industry can be greater during periods of financial downturns. Insurance companies hold customer premiums which are forbidden from operational use by the company. However, when funding is needed, unscrupulous executives invade the premium accounts in order to pay corporate expenses. This leads to financial statement fraud because the company is required to "cover its tracks" to conceal the improper utilization of customer premium funds.

Premium Diversion/Unauthorized Entities—The most common type of fraud involves insurance agents and brokers diverting policyholder premiums for their own benefit. Additionally, there are a growing number of unauthorized and unregistered entities engaged in the sale of insurance-related products. As the insurance industry becomes open to foreign players, regulation becomes more difficult. Additionally, exponentially rising insurance costs in certain areas (i.e., terrorism insurance, directors'/officers' insurance, and corporations), increase the possibility for this type of fraud.

Viatical Settlement Fraud—A viatical settlement is a discounted, pre-death sale of an existing life insurance policy on the life of a person known to have a terminal condition. The parties to a viatical settlement include the insured party, insurance agent/broker, insurance company, viatical company/broker, and the investor. Viatical settlement fraud occurs when misrepresentations are made on the insurance policy applications, in effect, hiding the fact that the party applying for a policy has already been diagnosed with a terminal condition. On the investor end, the fraud occurs when misrepresentations are made to the investors by the viatical companies about life expectancies of insured parties and guaranteed high rates of return.

Workers' Compensation Fraud—The Professional Employer Organization (PEO) industry operates chiefly to provide workers' compensation insurance coverage to small businesses by pooling businesses together to obtain reasonable rates. Workers' compensation insurance accounts for as much as 46 percent of small business owners' general operating expenses. Due to this, small business owners have an incentive to shop workers' compensation insurance on a regular basis. This has made it ripe for entities that purport to provide workers' compensation insurance to enter the marketplace, offer reduced premium rates, and misappropriate funds without providing insurance. The focus of these investigations is on allegations that numerous entities within the PEO industry are selling unauthorized and nonadmitted workers' compensation coverage to businesses across the United States. This insurance fraud scheme has left injured and deceased

growing type involves filing fraudulent health insurance claims. Various terms have been created to describe the schemes that are used in medical fraud. "Overutilization" involves billing for superfluous and unnecessary tests and other services.[53] "Ping-Ponging" occurs when physicians refer patients to several practitioners when symptoms do not warrant such referrals. "Family ganging" takes place when a doctor extends several unnecessary services to all members of a patient's family. "Steering" is a practice in which doctors direct patients to the clinic's pharmacy to fill unneeded prescriptions.

Finally, "upgrading" occurs when a patient is billed for services more extensive than those that were actually performed.[54]

Credit card crimes and insurance schemes are comparatively recent types of fraud, but they are not the last opportunities for swindlers to deprive others of their property. Computer crime, for example, is a growing concern, and technological advances continue to offer new possibilities for theft. Opportunities will always challenge the imagination of entrepreneurs—illegitimate as well as legitimate.

victims without workers' compensation coverage to pay their medical bills.

With the cooperation of the insurance industry, through referrals from industry liaison and other law enforcement agencies, the FBI continues to target the individuals and organizations committing insurance fraud. The FBI continues to initiate and conduct traditional investigations as well as utilize sophisticated techniques, to include undercover investigations, to apprehend the fraudsters.

Disaster Fraud—When a disaster occurs, there are many organizations and individuals soliciting contributions for the victims of this disaster. Most of the organizations and individuals involved are legitimate; however, there are some who are not. Victims may be approached by unsolicited e-mails asking for donations to a legitimate-sounding organization. The schemer will instruct the victim to send a donation via a money transfer. Other types of disaster fraud include false or exaggerated claims by policyholders; misclassification of flood damage as wind, fire, or theft; claims filed by individuals residing hundreds of miles outside the disaster zone; bid-rigging by contractors; falsely inflating the cost of repairs; and contractors requiring up-front payment for services, then failing to perform the agreed upon repairs.

Staged Auto Accidents—Perpetrators of staged auto accidents will either stage an accident with co-conspirators, or maneuver innocent motorists into accidents. Although the resulting property damage may be small, the perpetrators make large—and illegal—claims for fake injuries

and property damage. This type of fraud results in higher insurance premiums for all drivers.

Property Insurance Fraud—Perpetrators of property insurance fraud seek to obtain payment that is higher than the value of the property damaged or destroyed, or intentionally destroy property that could not be sold. Common examples include arson, scuttling of boats, and the ditching of vehicles in lakes or canals.

III. SIGNIFICANT CASES

Israeli-Based Telemarketing Fraud (New York): This investigation centered on the activities of an Israeli-based boiler room. The perpetrators, all residents of Israel, contacted hundreds of elderly victims in the United States to inform them they had won substantial cash prizes in an international sweepstakes lottery, but in order to claim these prizes, they first needed to pay several thousand dollars in fees. Victims who had already sent money were often contacted again by the managers to send additional money in order to claim their prizes. The total fraud proceeds are estimated to be in excess of $2 million. During 2009, a total of eight subjects were arrested as a result of this investigation. This investigation was worked by FBI New York, in cooperation with the Tel Aviv Fraud Division of the Israel National Police. This case involves the largest number of Israeli citizens ever to be provisionally arrested by Israel in anticipation of extradition.

Vancouver-Based Telemarketing Fraud (Los Angeles): This investigation centered on the activities of a Vancouver-based fraudulent

telemarketing and money transfer operation. The perpetrators, residents of Vancouver, British Columbia, mailed letters to thousands of elderly U.S. victims that falsely represented they were winners of a monetary prize, such as a lottery or sweepstakes. Included with the letters was a fraudulent check, which the perpetrators claimed was sent to help them pay some required fees. The victims were instructed to utilize a money transfer service, such as MoneyGram, to pay these fees. Many victims wired these fees before realizing that the checks they received were fraudulent. As a result of this scheme, victims lost in excess of $10 million in money transfer payments. During 2009, two subjects were arrested as a result of this investigation.

This investigation was worked by FBI Los Angeles, in cooperation with the Royal Canadian Mounted Police Project Emptor Task Force, the USPIS, and FTC.

Source

Federal Bureau of Investigation, Financial Crimes Report to the Public, Fiscal Year 2007 (October 1, 2006—September 30, 2007). Available at http://www.fbi.gov/publications/financial/fcs_report2007/financial_crime_2007.htm.

Questions for Discussion

1. What type of punishment is appropriate for an insurance fraud offender?
2. What other types of laws and policies could be created in an attempt to prevent insurance fraud?

HIGH-TECH CRIMES: CONCERNS FOR TODAY AND TOMORROW

Orange County, California (September 15, 1999). Six Southern California telemarketers have been charged in connection with an Internet gaming scam. Federal prosecutors say the scam took in almost $5 million from more than 500 investors. The six worked for Gecko Holdings. They offered investors stock in Gecko, telling them it was an on-line gambling business about to go

public. Investors were promised that their shares, priced at two dollars, would double or triple the value in a few months. But the stock never went public. Instead, prosecutors say, the owners took off with the money. The six are charged with 26 counts each of mail and wire fraud.[55]

Crimes evolve with the environments we live in. The rise of computers and other high-technology equipment has paved the way for the genesis of new crime types. These present yet another set of

Crime Surfing WWW
www.cybercrime.gov

The Computer Crime & Intellectual Property Section of the U.S. Department of Justice prevents, investigates, and prosecutes computer crimes.

challenges for potential victims, law enforcement personnel, criminologists, and other criminal justice professionals.

What exactly is high-technology crime? While there may be debates over its definition, it is generally agreed that **high-tech crime** involves an attempt to pursue illegal activities through the use of advanced electronic media. We define "high technology" as "a form of sophisticated electronic device—computer, cell phone, or other digital communication—that is in common use today."[56] The new waves of computer crime are perhaps the most illustrative examples of high-technology crime, although sophisticated credit card fraud schemes and cell phone scams are also modern problems. In this section, we will refer to crimes relying on modern electronic technology as "high-tech crimes."

Characteristics of High-Tech Crimes

High-tech crimes have affected the nature of property crimes by taking on a few distinct characteristics.

Role of Victims, Type of Property

Criminals engaging in high-tech crimes no longer need actual direct contact with their victims; computers equipped with modems have unlimited range, enabling offenders to victimize people thousands of miles away. The reach of motivated offenders has been considerably extended. Physical movement has been replaced by virtual travel, especially with the recognition that computers are global networks.

The type of property that is stolen or affected is also very different in nature. While other property crimes (arson, vandalism, theft, larceny, burglary) victimize concrete targets, high-tech crimes involve less-visible and less-tangible kinds of property, such as information, data, and computer networks. In addition, many victims of high-tech crime realize they have been victimized only long after the crime has taken place. In most other property crimes, there is often little time between the actual crime and the realization that a crime has taken place (as in cases of burglary or arson, for example).

Profits of Crime

The profits from high-tech crimes are vast. The rise in the incidence of computer crime, for example, is a testament to its efficacy and the profit to be made. The British Banking Association in London estimates the cost of computer fraud worldwide to be about $8 billion a year.[57] With the increasing sophistication of equipment, computer hackers are able to steal greater amounts with greater ease, and sometimes a single act can victimize multiple people or places at once.

Detection

High-tech crime is also attractive to some individuals because they find evading detection and prosecution relatively easy. Few law enforcement agencies are equipped to detect the high-tech crimes occurring within their jurisdictions. Furthermore, because the nature of high-tech crime allows perpetrators to carry out their illegal activities without any geographic limitations, tracing high-tech criminal activity to the responsible individual is very difficult. Identifying the crime location becomes harder as street corners and physical space are replaced by airwaves, cyberspace, and other electronic media. Often, by the time illegal activity has been detected, the criminals have already moved on to a new target.

Degree of Criminal Complexity

Another important aspect of high-technology crimes involves the complicated nature of the crimes being committed. Every day, new crimes are being developed and refined by highly skilled computer users. Traditional law enforcement techniques are not designed to deal with such novel and complex crimes. High-tech criminals are, in a sense, sophisticated criminals. Stealing credit card numbers from the Internet for illicit purposes requires a certain degree of proficiency in Internet navigation, knowledge of how to break into the system to commit the thefts, and, finally, experience in using the stolen credit card numbers for criminal gain—all the while avoiding detection.

International Component

Phone companies and computer network systems often advertise that using their services will allow individuals to communicate with people located at the other side of the globe. Such ease of electronic travel is appealing to high-tech criminals, who now participate in a modern phenomenon: global criminality. High-tech crimes can easily go beyond national boundaries, making them transnational crimes—a criminal activity of serious concern for targeted countries. Using a computer, a high-tech criminal can make illegal international money transfers, steal information from a computer located in another country, or diffuse illicit information (such as child pornography or terrorist propaganda) worldwide. The ability to detect and successfully deal with such criminal activities is a major challenge for law enforcement agencies around the world.

Computers and the Internet: Types of Crimes

High-tech criminals have also created their own crime types. While some seek the same ends as more traditional property offenders (financial gain), modern technology allows for novel and totally new crimes.[58]

There are three main categories of computer crimes. First, the computer can be used as a storage or communication device whereby information can be created, stored, manipulated, and communicated electronically. In this instance, the computer is incidental, since it is not required for the crime itself but is used in some way that is connected to the criminal activity. An example is financial records kept on a drug dealer's computer.

Second, the computer can be used as an instrument or a tool of crime. In this case, the computer is used to commit traditional offenses, such as the creation of counterfeit money or official documents, or newer computer crime offenses, such as the distribution of child pornography, confidence schemes, and illegal gambling networks on the Internet.

Finally, a computer can be used as a weapon to commit attacks on the confidentiality, integrity, and availability of information, including theft of information, theft of services, and damage to computer systems.[59] This type of computer crime involves the widespread problem of viruses and other forms of siege attacks, such as those referred to as "denial of service" attacks. The purpose of a denial-of-service attack is to prevent the normal operation of a digital system. It is often committed by "cyber vandals." An increasing number of electronic siege attacks employing some form of denial of service have been initiated against organizations worldwide.[60]

The Internet Crime Complaint Center (IC3) received nearly 303,809 fraud complaints in 2010.[61] A wide range of frauds is reported regularly (Figure 11.4).

Computer Network Break-Ins

There are two types of computer network break-ins. The first is commonly known as "hacking." It is not practiced for criminal gain and therefore can be considered more mischievous than malicious. Nevertheless, network intrusions have been made illegal by the U.S. federal government. A hacker's reward is being able to tell peers that he or she has managed to break into a network, demonstrating superior computing ability, especially the ability to bypass security measures.

Hackers, for the most part, seek entry into a computer system and "snoop around," often leaving no sign of entry. It can be likened to an individual's stealthily gaining entry into another person's house, going through a few personal belongings, and carefully leaving without taking anything.

The second type of break-in is that done for illegal purposes. A criminal might break into a large credit card company's database to steal card numbers or into a network to steal data or sensitive information. Other criminal acts include computer vandalism, whereby individuals break into a system, alter its operating structure, delete important files, change passwords, or plant viruses that can destroy operating systems, software programs, and data.

Industrial Espionage

In an age where information can create power, it should not be surprising that competing industries are very curious to know what the others are doing. "Cyber spies" can be hired to break into a competitor's computer system and gather secret information, often leaving no trace of the intrusion. Once again, these spies have such powerful technology at their disposal that they are able to target computers and information that may be thousands of miles away, making detection even more difficult.

In response to the growing problem of industrial and economic espionage, Congress passed the Industrial Espionage Act of 1996. This law makes the theft, unauthorized appropriation, or other misuse of **proprietary economic information** a federal crime.

Proprietary economic information means all forms and types of financial, business, scientific, technical, economic, or engineering information, including data, plans, tools, mechanisms, compounds, formulas, designs, prototypes, processes, procedures, programs, codes, or commercial strategies, whether tangible or intangible, and whether stored, compiled, or memorialized physically, electronically, graphically, photographically, or in writing, that—

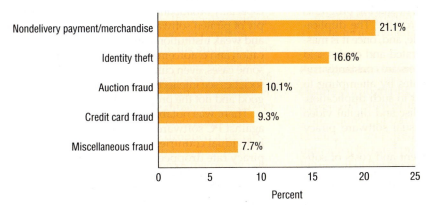

FIGURE 11.4 The top five referred to fraud complaints in 2010. Of the 303,809 complaints IC3 received in 2010, 121,710 were referred to law enforcement for further investigation.

Source: http://ic3report.nw3c.org/national_report.cfm.

Burglary

Rational-choice theories, when first imported to criminology, were used to explain residential burglary. What insights can you bring from rational-choice theory to the practical effort of crime prevention?

Today burglary is no longer limited to night attacks, although by statute the crime may be considered more serious if it is committed at night. Statutes have also added buildings other than dwellings to the definition. The United Crime Report (UCR) defines burglary simply as the unlawful entry into a structure (criminal trespass) to commit a felony or theft. The use of force to gain entry is not a required element of burglary under the UCR.

Burglary rates have consistently declined over the past decade. Even so, in 2010, almost 2.2 million burglaries were reported to the police, with an average loss of $2,119 per burglary. These crimes account for nearly a fifth of all Index offenses. Most burglaries are not cleared by arrests.[70]

Criminologists ask questions about the characteristics of offenders who commit burglaries and of the places that are burglarized. Neal Shover described the "good burglar" as one having competence, personal integrity, a specialty in burglary, financial success, and an ability to avoid prison.[71] Another study demonstrated that burglars are versatile, committing a wide range of offenses, but that they do specialize in burglary for short periods of time. Compared with male burglars, female burglars begin offending at a later age, more often commit burglaries with others, and have fewer contacts with the criminal justice system.[72]

Recent research on burglary asks questions not only about who is likely to commit a burglary or what distinguishes one burglar from another. In addition, as we note in Chapter 9, criminologists are looking, for instance, at the process that leads to the burglary of a particular house in a specific neighborhood—that is, how a burglar discriminates between individual areas and targets when there are so many alternatives—and at ways to make the process of burglary more difficult for any burglar.

FENCING: RECEIVING STOLEN PROPERTY

We are treating burglary as a property crime. An occasional burglar enters with the intention of committing rape, arson, or some other felony inside the building. But most burglars are thieves; they are looking for cash and for other property that can be turned into cash. Burglars and thieves depend on a network of fences to turn stolen property into cash.

Jonathan Wild controlled the London underworld from about 1714 until his hanging in 1725. For over 2½ centuries, he has captured the imagination of historians, social scientists, and writers. Henry Fielding wrote *The Life of Mr. Jonathan Wild, the Great*, and Mack the Knife in John Gay's *Beggar's Opera* was modeled on Wild. Wild was known as a "thief-taker." Thief-takers made an occupation of capturing thieves and claiming the rewards offered for their arrest. By law, thief-takers were allowed to keep the possessions of the thieves they caught, except objects that had been stolen, which were returned to their owners.

Wild added a devious twist to his trade: He bought stolen goods from thieves and sold them back to their rightful owners. The owners paid much more than the thief could get from the usual fences, so both Wild and the thief made a considerable profit. To thieves, he was a fellow thief; to honest people, he was a legitimate citizen helping them get back their property. Playing both roles well, he ran competing fencing operations out of business, employed about 7,000 thieves, and became the most famous fence of all time.[73]

A **fence** is a person who buys stolen property, on a regular basis, for resale. Fences, or dealers in stolen property, operate much like legitimate businesses: They buy and sell for profit. Their activity thrives on an understanding of the law governing the receiving of stolen property, on cooperation with the law when necessary, and on networking. The difference between a legitimate business and a fencing operation is that the channeling of stolen goods takes place in a clandestine environment (created by law enforcement and deviant associates) with high risks and with a need to justify one's activities in the eyes of conventional society.

Carl Klockars's *Professional Fence* and Darrell Steffensmeier's *Fence*, each focusing on the life of a particular fence, present us with fascinating accounts of this criminal business. The proprietors of such businesses deal in almost any commodity. "Oh, I done lots of business with him," said Klockars's fence, Vincent Swazzi. "One time I got teeth, maybe five thousand teeth in one action. You know, the kind they use for making false teeth—you see, you never know what a thief's gonna come up with." And many fences are quite proud of their positions in the community. Said Swazzi, "The way I look at it, this is actually my street. I mean I am the mayor. I walk down the street an' people come out the doors to say hello."[74]

Until recently, it was believed that professional thieves and fences were totally interdependent and that their respective illegal activities were mutually reinforcing. Recent research, however, demonstrates a change in the market for stolen goods. D'Aunn Webster Avery, Paul F. Cromwell, and James N. Olson conducted extensive interviews with 38 active burglars, shoplifters, and their fences and concluded that it is no longer the professional fence who takes care of stolen goods but, rather, occasional receivers—otherwise honest citizens—who buy from thieves directly or at flea markets.[75] This willingness to buy merchandise that the buyers must at least suspect has been stolen may indicate that the general public is more tolerant of stealing than previous generations were.

ARSON

The crimes against property that we have discussed so far involve the illegitimate transfer of possession. The property in question is "personal property" rather than real property, or real estate. Only two types of property crime are concerned with real property. Burglary is one; the other is arson.

The common law defined **arson** as the malicious burning of or setting fire to the dwelling of another person. Modern statutes have distinguished degrees of severity of the offense and have increased its scope to include other structures and even personal property, such as automobiles. The most severe punishments are reserved for arson of dwellings, because of the likelihood that persons in the building may be injured or die.

Arson has always been viewed as a more violent crime than burglary. In comparison with burglary, however, arson is a fairly infrequent offense. A total of 64,332 arson offenses were reported in 2007.[76] A national survey of fire departments, however, indicates that the actual number of arson incidents is likely to be far higher than the reported figure.[77]

Buildings were the most frequent targets (42.9 percent); 27.9 percent of the targets were mobile property (motor vehicles, trailers, and the like); and crops and timber constituted 29.2 percent.[78] The annual estimated property loss is well over $2 billion.[79]

The seriousness of this crime is demonstrated by a series of spectacular fires set in resort hotels in such cities as San Juan, Puerto Rico (in conjunction with a labor dispute), and Las Vegas, Nevada. Although these fires were not set with the intent to kill any of the people in the buildings, many lives were lost. The inferno created by arsonists in the Du Pont Plaza Hotel in San Juan in 1987 killed 97 people. The arson at the Las Vegas Hilton caused no deaths but did result in $14 million in damages, not including the loss of business.

While insurance fraudsters and organized-crime figures may be responsible for some of the more spectacular arsons, it is juveniles who account for the single most significant share. Why do children set fires?[80] Some research suggests that the motive may be psychological pain, anger, revenge, need for attention, malicious mischief, or excitement.[81] Juvenile fire setters have been classified in three groups: the playing-with-matches fire setter, the crying-for-help fire setter, and the severely disturbed fire setter.[82] Many juvenile fire setters are in urgent need of help. In

response to their needs, juvenile arson intervention programs have been established.[83]

An interesting English study found that while arsonists were in many respects comparable to offenders classified as violent, they had a lower incidence of interpersonal aggression and rated themselves as less assertive than did violent offenders—perhaps because, as the study showed, arsonists were taken into care at an earlier age.[84] The motives of adult arsonists are somewhat different from those of juveniles, though here, too, we find disturbed offenders (pyromaniacs) and people who set fires out of spite. We are also much more likely to encounter insurance fraudsters, as well as organized-crime figures who force compliance or impose revenge by burning establishments (the "torches").[85] One classification of fire setters by motive includes:

- Revenge, jealousy, and hatred

- Financial gain (mostly insurance fraud)

- Intimidation and/or extortion (often involving organized crime)

- Need for attention

- Social protest

- Arson to conceal other crimes

- Arson to facilitate other crimes

- Vandalism and accidental fire setting[86]

As arson continues to be a serious national problem, policy makers have been developing two distinct approaches for dealing with it. The offender-specific approach focuses on educational outreach in schools and the early identification of troubled children, for purposes of counseling and other assistance.[87] The offense-specific (geographic) approach focuses on places. It seeks to identify areas with a high potential for arson. The aim is to deploy arson specialists to correct problems and to stabilize endangered buildings and neighborhoods.[88]

COMPARATIVE CRIME RATES

The rates of property crime are much higher than those of the violent crime discussed in Chapter 10. It is interesting to compare these rates for various regions of the world. If we compare the property-owning, consumer-oriented countries of the industrialized Western world with the still largely agricultural but rapidly urbanizing countries of the Third World, we note a significant discrepancy: In 1990, the rate of thefts per 100,000 population in the developed countries was 4,200, while the rate in developing countries was 600.[89]

PFIZER INC. (Boston): Investigation was predicated in August 2004 upon the receipt of information from the FDA that Pfizer employees may have destroyed records sought in a federal civil investigation and that company employees had been engaged in a series of transactions involving off-label promotions and kickbacks. Between 2001 and 2005, Pfizer northeast regional manager Mary Holloway directed approximately 100 sales employees to market the painkiller Valdecoxib (Bextra) for uses specifically prohibited by the FDA. On March 30, 2009, Holloway pled by criminal information to one count of distribution of a misbranded drug. Holloway was sentenced to 24 months' probation and fined $75,000 on June 18, 2009. Holloway is the second subject convicted in this case. Thomas Farina, a New York-area sales manager for Pfizer, was indicted in March 2008, and pled guilty to obstruction later that month. In January 2009, Pfizer agreed to pay the U.S. government $2.3 billion to settle claims involving the drugs Bextra, Zyvox, Goedon, and Lyrica. Valdecoxib (Bextra) was a nonsteroidal anti-inflammatory prescription drug, administered in tablet form, used in the treatment of arthritis inflammation and pain, and menstrual discomfort. Bextra was approved by the FDA for distribution in the United States in 2001. Pfizer withdrew Bextra from the U.S. market in 2005, after the FDA cited increased incidence of heart attacks, strokes, and serious skin reactions to the drug.

PETTERS COMPANY, INC. (Minneapolis): Thomas J. Petters through his company Petters Group Worldwide LLC (PGW), obtained loans from hedge funds and investment groups for the stated purpose of financing sales to well-known big box retailers such as Costco and Sam's Club. The investigation revealed that the purchase and subsequent sale of merchandise to the retailers were actually fabricated transactions supported by fictional documentation. Thomas J. Petters was indicted for mail and wire fraud, conspiracy, and money laundering in December 2008 for his role in a $3.4 billion corporate fraud scheme. Six individuals have been indicted during the course of the investigation for various roles in the scheme, including the production of false banking transaction documentation. Petters' trial began on October 28, 2009, and Petters was convicted on December 2, 2009, following an 18-day trial, on all counts of the indictment. Petters was sentenced to 50 years in federal prison in April of 2010.

CREDIT SUISSE (New York): Credit Suisse, a global financial services company, advises clients across the globe in all aspects of finance. ST Microelectronics (STM) is a Switzerland-based semiconductor company with annual net revenue of US $9.85 billion in 2006. In 2006, STM invested $400 million with Credit Suisse in what were purportedly securities backed by student loans (to include investment statements); however, the funds were backed with subprime loans. Credit Suisse tried unsuccessfully to settle the matter for $280 million. The two managers, Eric Butler and Julian Tzolov, were indicted on securities fraud charges and arrested in June 2008. Tzolov pled guilty and testified as a key witness for the government in the trial against Butler. After several weeks of trial, Butler was convicted in August 2009 by the jury and later sentenced to five years in prison. Tzolov was sentenced to four years in prison.

WAYNE PUFF, AFFORDABLE HOMES CORP. (Newark): From 1998 to 2005, Puff and his co-conspirators recruited 1,200 investors from across the country, who poured $123.3 million into New Jersey Affordable Homes Corp. (NJAH). Mr. Puff drew investors by advertising guaranteed annual returns of 15 to 20 percent from his business of buying, renovating, and reselling real estate. The scheme relied on false claims of the company's profits and phony mortgage documents. Puff's co-conspirators included John Kurzel, an NJAH mortgage loan processor who was sentenced to 20 months in prison; Michael Meehan, a former licensed real estate appraiser, and

Anthony Natale, a closing attorney, who were both sentenced to 30 months in prison; Mitchell Fishman, an attorney, and Lucesita Santiago, an NJAH account manager, who were both sentenced to 18 months in prison; and Sydney Raposo, a paralegal for Natale, who was sentenced to six months' home detention. Two defendants are awaiting sentencing. On January 15, 2010, Wayne Puff, the founder of NJAH, a purported real estate investment business, was sentenced to 18 years in prison for defrauding mortgage lenders and investors.

ROBERT A. PENN, STEPHEN S. BROWN, TAMARA E. SCOTT (Indianapolis): Between November 2003 and August 2005, Penn, with the aid of Stephen Brown and Tamara Scott, solicited and obtained at least 136 loans from various lenders including Argent Mortgage Company, The MoneyStation, and People's Choice Mortgage/Countrywide Home Loans. Brown was responsible for submitting approximately 43 fraudulent loan applications supported by false documents and inflated appraisals, for which he received between $1,500 and $2,000 per application. Tamara Scott was responsible for attending the mortgage closings, signing fraudulent documents, and receiving checks for loan proceeds. Scott participated in approximately 130 of the fraudulent loans. Brown was sentenced to 37 months in prison and Scott was sentenced to 24 months. In addition, restitution was ordered to be paid by Penn in the amount of $11,411,722; Scott in the amount of $2,793,412; and Brown in the amount of $11,122,891. On January 7, 2010, Robert Penn was sentenced to seven years in prison for his role in brokering approximately $16 million on at least 136 fraudulent mortgages through his various business entities.[1]

What do these crimes have in common? All involve business enterprises.[2] It is the use of a legitimate or an illegitimate business enterprise for illegal profit that distinguishes organizational crimes from other types of offenses. Organizational offenses are also different in another important respect. Unlike violent crimes and property offenses, which the Model Penal Code classifies quite neatly, organizational offenses are a heterogeneous mix of crimes, ranging from homicide, fraud, and conspiracy to racketeering and the violation of a host of federal environmental statutes.

DEFINING WHITE-COLLAR CRIME

With a daily barrage of media reports on the latest corporate scandal—from allegations of fraud for selling subprime mortgages to evidence of widespread corruption in some of the most respected and admired multinational corporations—it is only natural to think that we are in the midst of an unprecedented wave of white-collar and corporate crime. Anecdotal evidence aside, there is no empirical evidence that much, if anything, has changed.

Not surprisingly, politicians seized the opportunity to call for corporate reforms in light of almost daily accusations of illegalities. With little reflection, President Bush signed the Sarbanes-Oxley Act of 2002 to quell public concerns over the legitimacy and integrity of the markets. This act adopts tough provisions to deter and punish corporate and accounting fraud and corruption.

According to a press release from the White House, the act "ensures justice for wrongdoers, and protects the interests of workers and shareholders. This bill improves the quality and transparency of financial reporting, independent audits, and accounting services for public companies."

■ Martha Stewart, an icon of good homemaking, was accused of selling thousands of shares of ImClone Systems, Inc., stock just prior to the company's announcement that it failed to receive Food and Drug Administration approval for an anticancer drug. Was this insider trading? Did she trade on material, nonpublic information?

TABLE 12.2 Victims of White-Collar Crime (NIBRS)

	Total	Property	Fraud	Bribery	Counterfeiting	Embezzlement
Total victims	5,886,566	4,069,324	103,993	198	110,545	21,356
Individual	3,998,310	2,621,843	47,826	143	45,270	3,006
Business	934,469	934,469	47,907	16	55,676	17,627
Financial institution	11,378	11,378	2,989	0	5,310	182
Government	73,623	73,623	3,844	36	2,949	260
Religious organization	10,794	10,794	70	0	104	35
Society or other	857,992	417,217	1,357	3	1,236	246

SOURCE: Cynthia Barnett, *The Measurement of White-Collar Crime Using Uniform Crime Reporting (UCR) Data* (Washington, D.C.: Department of Justice, 2000).

employee of an insurance company, for example, may write a favorable claim assessment in exchange for half of the insurance payment.

• Taking advantage of the complexity and anonymity of a large organization, such as a corporation, employees may abuse the systems available to them or the power they hold within the structure for purposes of unlawful gain, as by embezzlement.

• Members of the public who have to deal with a large organization do not have the faith and trust they had when they dealt with individual merchants. If they see an opportunity to defraud a large organization, they may seize it in the belief that the organization can easily absorb the loss and nobody will be hurt.

• Because the relation of buyer to seller (or of service provider to client) has become increasingly less personal in an age of medical group practice, HMOs, large law firms, and drugstore chains, opportunities for **occupational crimes**—crimes committed by individuals for themselves in the course of rendering a service—have correspondingly increased. Medicare fraud, misuse of clients' funds by lawyers and brokers, substitution of inferior goods—all such offenses are occupational crimes.[11]

Types of White-Collar Crimes

White-collar crimes are as difficult to detect as they are easy to commit.[12] The detection mechanisms on which police and government traditionally rely seem singularly inadequate for this vast new body of crimes. Moreover, though people have learned through the ages to be wary of strangers on the street, they have not yet learned to protect themselves against vast enterprises. Much more scientific study has to be undertaken on the causes, extent, and characteristics of white-collar crimes before we can develop workable prevention strategies (Figure 12.1).[13]

Eight categories of white-collar offenses committed by individuals can be identified:

• Securities-related crimes

• Bankruptcy fraud

• Fraud against the government

• Consumer fraud

Ricky Churchwell, a former chancery clerk from Lucedale, Mississippi, was indicted on 15 counts of embezzlement in July 2002. Churchwell is the fourth clerk in 4 years to be indicted in Mississippi.

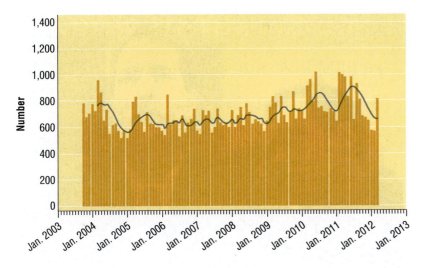

FIGURE 12.1 Criminal white-collar crime prosecutions over the past decade.

Source: White Collar Crime Prosecutions. Transactional Records Access Clearinghouse (TRAC) at Syracuse University. (http://trac.syr.edu). © 2012, TRAC Reports, Inc. Reprinted with permission.

- Insurance fraud

- Tax fraud

- Bribery, corruption, and political fraud

- Insider-related fraud[14]

Let us briefly examine each type of crime.

Securities-Related Crimes

State and federal securities laws seek to regulate both the registration and issuance of a security and the employment practices of personnel in the securities industries. After the stock market crash on October 26, 1929, the federal government enacted a series of regulatory laws, including the Securities Act of 1933 and the Securities Exchange Act of 1934, aimed at prohibiting manipulation and deceptive practices. The 1934 act provided for the establishment of the Securities and Exchange Commission (SEC), an organization with broad regulatory and enforcement powers. The SEC is empowered to initiate civil suits and administrative actions and to refer criminal cases to the U.S. Department of Justice.

Crime in the securities field remains common. The problem of securities fraud was made more apparent in recent years with some notable cases. The significance of the problem, however, is highlighted by the sheer size of the equities market.

Four kinds of offenses are prevalent: churning, trading on insider information, stock manipulation, and boiler-room operations.

Churning is the practice of trading a client's shares of stock frequently in order to generate large commissions. A broker earns a commission on every trade, so whether the stock traded increases or decreases in value, the broker makes money. Churning is difficult to prove, because brokers typically are allowed some discretion. Therefore, unless the client has given the broker specific instructions in writing, a claim of churning often amounts to no more than the client's word against the broker's.

Insider trading is the use of material, nonpublic financial information to obtain an unfair advantage in trading securities.[15] A person who has access to confidential corporate information may make significant profits by buying or selling stock on the strength of that information. The prototype case of insider trading was that against Dennis Levine. Levine, a 34-year-old managing director of the securities firm formerly known as Drexel Burnham Lambert, used insider information to purchase stock for himself and others in corporations such as International Telephone and Telegraph, Sperry Corporation, Coastal Corporation, American National Resources, and McGraw Edison. After the SEC found out, Levine implicated other Wall Street executives—including Ivan Boesky, who had made millions of dollars in illegal profits.

◼ *Dr. Samuel Waksal, former chief executive officer, ImClone Systems, Inc., testifies before the U.S. House Energy and Commerce Subcommittee on Oversight and Investigations hearing on "An Inquiry into the ImClone Cancer-Drug Story" in Washington on June 13, 2002. On June 10, 2003, he was sentenced to over 7 years in jail and ordered to pay $4 million in back taxes and fines.*

with god's glory prevented America from controlling a large segment of the Iraqi oil which they hoped would compensate for their economic losses in September 11th. While currently they control the oil in Saudi Arabia which amounts to two thirds of the pie, they hoped to control the whole pie after they controlled Iraq.

Any operation targeting a field of infrastructure in a new country that does not have a history of countering these operations is considered as bleeding to the greater enemy America and the targeted nation itself. It is so because these nations will be required to protect all similar potential targets which results in economic exhaustion. More so, the effect will be on America when the target nation is incapable of doing so, they will turn over the mission to the Americans who will need to personally defend their interests. This is what is occurring in a number of countries like some of the African nations. For example if a hotel that caters to western

tourists in Indonesia is targeted, the enemy will be required to protect all hotels that cater to western tourists in all countries which may become a target of similar attacks. You can say the same thing about residential buildings, economic establishments, embassies and others.

I conclude by taking a look at future operations of al-Qaeda which I can predict based on their communiqués and past operations. I predict they will concentrate on the oil infrastructure in one of the following three nations (Kuwait—Venezuela—Saudi Arabia). In addition, there is a possibility that al-Qaeda will, one way or another, target the Wall Street stock exchange which signifies the nerve of domestic American economy. Finally, continuing to prevent the American thieves from benefiting from Iraqi oil by concentrating a large effort on the following, with the possibility of partial American withdrawal from Iraq.

Warning:

When I indicated that the battle with the U.S. and others is economic I do not mean that it is for the sake of the economy itself; rather, because they use the economy to control the Muslims and destroy them. This is first and foremost a religious war in all its forms.

Source

Abu Mus'ab al-Najadi, "Al-Qaeda's Battle Is Economic not Military," Oct. 3, 2005.

Questions for Discussion

1. To what extent can the United States harden economic targets so that they are protected from terrorist attack?
2. What kinds of crimes can we expect from terrorist groups seeking to further compromise our economic strength?

Operation Total Disclosure alone resulted in the arrest of 110 bankruptcy fraud subjects.

Fraud against the Government

Governments at all levels are victims of a vast amount of fraud, which includes collusion in bidding, payoffs and kickbacks to government officials, expenditures by a government official that exceed the budget, the filing of false claims, the hiring of friends or associates formerly employed by the government, and offers of inducements to government officials.

Consider, for example, the fall of Wedtech—a military contractor with annual sales in excess of $100 million. At one time the Wedtech Corporation was hailed as the first major employer of blacks and Hispanics in New York City's blighted South Bronx. Before its fall from grace, Wedtech was a highflier on the New York Stock Exchange. What fueled the company? As a minority-controlled business, it won defense contracts without the need to bid. But in early 1986, Wedtech lost its status as a minority business, and by the end of that year the company was in ruins.

Wedtech officials had used fraudulent accounting methods, issued false financial reports, and

counted profits before they were received. Caught in the cross fire of charges was Congressman Mario Biaggi, who was later convicted of soliciting bribes in order to obtain special government support for Wedtech. Other company and government officials either pled guilty or were convicted.[16]

Is the Wedtech scandal an isolated case? Clearly not. From 1986 through 1994, the Department of Defense reported that 138 defense contractors made 325 voluntary disclosures of potential procurement fraud. Recoveries from these disclosures amounted to $290 million.[17]

An important step to curb government contract fraud was taken with the passage of the Major Fraud Act (1988), creating a separate offense of government contract fraud in excess of $1 million. What kinds of activities does this act cover? Federal prosecutors seek indictments against contractors who engage in deceptive pricing or overcharging by submitting inaccurate cost and pricing data; mischarging by billing the government for improper or nonallowable charges; collusion in bidding (a conspiracy between presumed competitors to inflate bids); product substitution or the delivery of inferior, nonconforming, or untested goods; or the use of bribes, gratuities, conflicts of interest, and a whole range of other techniques designed to influence procurement officials.

Clearly there is more to government-related fraud than the manipulation of contractors and consultants.[18] The Inspector General's Office in the Department of Health and Human Services reported that an estimated $20 billion may be lost annually to fraud in the Medicare program alone.[19]

Consumer Fraud

Consumer fraud is the act of causing a consumer to surrender money through deceit or a misrepresentation of a material fact. These offenses range from health care fraud to Internet auction fraud (Table 12.3). Consumer frauds often appear as confidence games and may take some of the following forms:

- *Home-improvement fraud.* Consumers have been defrauded through the promise of low-cost home renovation. The home owners give sizable down payments to the contractors, who have no plans to complete the job. In fact, contractors often leave the jurisdiction or declare bankruptcy.

- *Deceptive advertising.* Consumers are often lured into a store by an announcement that a product is priced low for a limited period of time. Once in the store, the customer is told that the product is sold out, and he or she is offered a substitute, typically of inferior quality or at a much higher price. Such schemes are known as "bait-and-switch advertising."

- *Telemarketing fraud.* You are no doubt familiar with the old adage "If a deal sounds too good to be true, it probably is!" Each day, countless phone calls are made to homes around the United States with a very familiar opening script: "Congratulations! You are a grand prize winner." "Please donate money to _____ fund or _____ charity." Telemarketers lure consumers by making attractive offers (e.g., vacations, prizes, discounts on household items) that are nothing more than scams. Once you pay, your name is often added to a "sucker list" that may be sold to other scam telemarketers.

Of course, not all telemarketing is fraudulent. The New York State Attorney General, for example, estimates that approximately 10 percent of over 140,000 New York businesses using telemarketing to sell their products are frauds. (See Table 12.4.)

- *Land fraud.* Consumers are easy prey for land fraud swindlers. Here the pitch is that a certain piece of vacation or retirement property is a worthy investment, many improvements to the property will be made, and many facilities will

TABLE 12.3 The Top Categories of Consumer Fraud Complaints in 2005

- Internet auctions
- Foreign money offers
- Shop-at-home/catalog sales
- Prizes/sweepstakes and lotteries
- Internet services and computer complaints
- Business opportunities and work-at-home plans
- Advance fee loans and credit protection
- Telephone services
- Other

be made available in the area. Consumers often make purchases of worthless or overvalued land.

- *Business opportunity fraud.* The objective of business opportunity fraud is to persuade a consumer to invest money in a business concern through misrepresentation of its actual worth. Work-at-home frauds are common: Victims are told they can make big money by addressing envelopes at home or performing some other simple task. Consumers lose large sums of money investing in such ventures.

Insurance Fraud

There are many varieties of insurance fraud: Policyholders defraud insurers, insurers defraud the public, management defrauds the public, and third parties defraud insurers. Policyholder fraud is most often accomplished by the filing of false claims for life, fire, marine, or casualty insurance. Sometimes an employee of the insurance company is part of the fraud and assists in the preparation of the claim. The fraud may be simple—a false death claim—or it may become complex when multiple policies are involved.

A different type of insurance fraud is committed when a small group of people create a "shell" insurance firm without true assets. Policies are sold with no intent to pay legitimate claims. In fact, when large claims are presented to shell insurance companies, the firms disband, leaving a trail of policyholder victims. In yet another form of insurance fraud, middle- and upper-level managers of an insurance company loot the firm's assets by removing funds and debiting them as payments of claims to legitimate or bogus policyholders.[20]

TABLE 12.4 Common Telemarketing Scams

ADVANCE-FEE LOAN OR CREDIT SCHEMES

Telemarketers seek out people with bad credit and offer them loans or credit cards in exchange for fees. Victims offered loans never receive them. Victims offered credit cards usually only get a standard application form or generic information on how to apply.

FOREIGN LOTTERY SCHEMES

Telemarketers offer victims the opportunity to "invest" in tickets in well-known foreign lotteries (e.g., Canada or Australia), or give them a "one in six" chance of winning a substantial prize. This is a common cross-border offense since it plays upon the ignorance of victims of the rules (or even the existence) of foreign lotteries. If offenders purport to sell real lottery chances but deceive victims about their chances of winning, it may be both a gambling offense and fraud. If real chances are sold without deception, it may still be a gambling offense.

INVESTMENT SCHEMES

Victims are sold "investments" in a wide range of merchandise or securities that appear to offer high profit margins. The fraud lies in misrepresenting the true value (or actual existence) of what is being sold, and/or the true extent of the risk in buying it. Common "opportunities" have involved stocks or securities, investment-grade gemstones, precious or strategic metals or minerals, and business opportunities such as oil and gas ventures, pizza ovens, and ostrich farms. These schemes commonly defraud victims more than once (see "reloading" schemes). Once funds have been committed, the victim can be induced to make additional payments to increase the value of the "investment" or avoid its loss (e.g., "margin calls"). Since legitimate investments normally tie up assets for extended periods, victims often do not realize for some time that they have been defrauded.

PRIZE PROMOTION

Telemarketers "guarantee" that the victims have won valuable prizes or gifts, such as vacations or automobiles, but require victims to submit one or more payments for non-existent shipping, taxes, customs or bonding fees, or anything else the offender thinks plausible. Some schemes never provide their victims with any prize or gift, while others provide inexpensive items, often called "gimme gifts" by U.S. telemarketers and "cheap gifts" by Canadian telemarketers.

TELEFUNDING SCHEMES

These prey on the charity of victims by soliciting donations for worthy causes such as antidrug programs or victims of natural disasters. The pitch may simply ask for donations or it may include other inducements, such as donor eligibility for valuable prizes, which never materialize (see "prize promotion" schemes). Charitable donors do not usually expect something in return for their contribution and thus may never become aware that they have been defrauded.

TRAVEL-RELATED SCHEMES

Fraudulent telemarketers purporting to be travel agencies offer substantial travel packages at comparatively low cost. The use of travel as a commodity makes the long-distance nature of the transaction plausible. The fraud usually involves lies, misrepresentations, or non-disclosure of information about the true value of travel and accommodations, limitations or restrictions on when or where purchasers may go, or what awaits them at the destination. In some cases, the travel proves to be a complete fabrication or has so many terms and conditions as to be completely unusable.

RELOADING AND RECOVERY ROOM SCHEMES

These target the same victims again and again. Persons victimized once are most likely to be deceived repeatedly. Unfortunately, victims' understandable desires to recover their original losses make them more vulnerable to further schemes. This is known as "reloading" or "loading." Those who "invest" money are "reloaded" for more to protect or increase their investment, those asked for customs or shipping fees are "reloaded" for additional charges, and those who give to a spurious "worthy cause" are often "reloaded" for further donations.

Recovery room schemes exploit the victim's desire to recover losses from previous frauds. Offenders, often from the same organization which defrauded the victim in the first place, call with inside knowledge of the fraud and a promise to recover the losses if "taxes" or "fees" are paid. A common tactic of callers is to represent themselves as law enforcement or other government or professional employees (e.g., bank or stock-exchange officials), using inside knowledge of the victim and the fraud to establish credibility. Recovery room operations frequently deprive victims of their last remaining funds.

SOURCE: http://www.fbi.gov.

Criminologists Paul Tracy and James Fox conducted a field experiment to find out how many auto-body repair shops in Massachusetts inflate repair estimates to insurance companies, and by how much. These researchers rented two Buick Skylarks with moderate damage, a Volvo 740 GLE with superficial damage, and a Ford Tempo with substantial damage. They then obtained 191 repair estimates, some with a clear understanding that the car was insured, others with the understanding that there was no insurance coverage. The results were unequivocal: Repair estimates for insured vehicles were significantly higher than those for noncovered cars. This finding is highly suggestive of fraud.[21]

Tax Fraud

The Internal Revenue Code makes willful failure to file a tax return a misdemeanor. An attempt to evade or defeat a tax, nonpayment of a tax, or willful filing of a fraudulent tax return is a felony. What must the government prove? In order to sustain a conviction, the government must present evidence of income tax due and owing, willful avoidance of payment, and an affirmative act toward tax evasion.[22] How are tax frauds accomplished? Consider the following techniques:

- *Keeping two sets of books.* A person may keep one set of books reflecting actual profits and losses and another set for the purpose of misleading the Internal Revenue Service.

- *Shifting funds.* In order to avoid detection, tax evaders often shift funds continually from account to account, from bank to bank.

- *Faking forms.* Tax evaders often use faked invoices, create fictitious expenses, conceal assets, and destroy books and records.

The IRS lacks the resources to investigate all suspicious tax forms. When the difficulty of distinguishing between careless mistakes and willful evasion is taken into account, the taxes that go uncollected each year are estimated to exceed $100 billion.[23]

Bribery, Corruption, and Political Fraud

Judges who fix traffic tickets in exchange for political favors, municipal employees who speculate with city funds, businesspeople who bribe local politicians to obtain favorable treatment—all are part of the corruption in our municipal, state, and federal governments. The objectives of such offenses vary—favors, special privileges, services, business. The actors include officers of corporations as well as of government; they may even belong to the police or the courts.

Bribery and other forms of corruption are ingrained in the political machinery of local and state governments. Examples abound: Mayors of large cities attempt to obtain favors through bribes; manufacturers pay off political figures for favors; municipal officials demand kickbacks from contractors.[24] In response to the seriousness of political corruption and bribery, Congress established two crimes: It is now a felony to accept a bribe or to provide a bribe.[25] Of course, political bribery and other forms of corruption do not stop at the nation's borders. Kickbacks to foreign officials are common practice, and countries develop reputations for both facilitating and tolerating corruption.[26] Business sectors develop reputations for corruption as well.

Corruption can also be found in private industry. One firm pays another to induce it to use a product or service; a firm pays its own board of directors or officers to dispense special favors; two or more firms, presumably competitors, secretly agree to charge the same prices for their products or services.

Insider-Related Fraud

Insider-related fraud involves the use and misuse of one's position for pecuniary gain or privilege. This category of offenses includes embezzlement, employee-related theft, and sale of confidential information.

Embezzlement is the conversion (misappropriation) of property or money with which one is entrusted or for which one has a fiduciary responsibility. Yearly losses attributable to embezzlement are estimated at over $1 billion.[27]

Employee-related thefts of company property are responsible for a significant share of industry losses. Estimates place such losses between $4 billion and $13 billion each year. Criminologists John Clark and Richard Hollinger have estimated that the 35 percent rate of employee pilferage in some corporations results primarily from vocational dissatisfaction and a perception of exploitation.[28] And not only goods and services are taken; time and money are at risk as well. Phony payrolls, fictitious overtime charges, false claims for business-related travel, and the like are common.

Finally, in a free marketplace where a premium is placed on competition, corporations must guard against the *sale of confidential information* and trade secrets. The best insurance policy is employee loyalty. Where there is no loyalty, or where loyalty is compromised, abuse of confidential information is possible. The purchase of confidential information from employees willing to commit industrial espionage is estimated to be a multimillion-dollar business.[29]

CORPORATE CRIME

The idea of white-collar crime is straightforward. Employees in a business step over the line by pocketing corporate funds. Tax avoiders become tax evaders. Home owners file fraudulent insurance claims. The crimes of white-collar criminals make fascinating television and movie scripts, from complex insider trading scandals to smoke-filled, boiler-room stock frauds. There are, however, other kinds of crimes that take place in the course of a respected and legitimate business enterprise. For the balance of this chapter, we will consider crimes by one or more employees of a corporation that are attributed to the organization itself—corporate crimes. The concept of **corporate crime** may be familiar if you have heard or read about the fall of Arthur Andersen and other companies that have been convicted—as corporations—of a host of criminal law violations. In fact, the concept of a "corporate" crime is more than a century old.

Frequency and Problems of Definition

There is no central repository for data on the number of cases of corporate crime in either state or federal courts. The best source of data, the United States Sentencing Commission, is less than ideal. The commission compiles information on cases of corporations that have been convicted of a federal crime.

On average, between 200 and 350 corporations are convicted each year in federal courts for offenses ranging from tax law violations to environmental crimes. The vast majority of these companies are small- to medium-size privately held corporations. In fact, between November 1, 1996, and June 30, 2005, nearly 92 percent of all corporations convicted had fewer than 50 employees. Less than 5 percent of all convicted corporations had more than 500 employees.

One problem with corporate crime is defining it. In 1989, the supertanker *Exxon Valdez* ran aground in Prince William Sound, Alaska, spilling 250,000 barrels of oil. The spill became North America's largest ecological disaster. Prosecutors were interested in determining the liability of the captain, his officers, and his crew. But there were additional and far-reaching questions. Was the Exxon Corporation liable? If so, was this a corporate crime? The same problem presented itself with the filing of criminal charges against Arthur Andersen. Should the firm bear the brunt of the crimes of its employees?

During the Great Depression, thousands of unemployed people heard that there was work to be had in the little West Virginia town of Hawk's Nest, where a huge tunnel was to be dug. Thousands of people came to work for a pittance. The company set the men up in crude camps and put them to work drilling rock for the tunnel project—without masks or other safety equipment. The workers breathed in the silicon dust that filled the air. Many contracted silicosis, a chronic lung disease that leads to certain death. They died by the dozens. Security guards dragged the bodies away and buried them secretly. No one was to know. The work went on. The deaths multiplied. Who was to blame? The corporation?[30]

Phases of Corporate Criminal Law

Corporate criminal law has moved through five distinct phases over the past century (Figure 12.2). In the first phase, courts wrestled with the idea that a corporation may be a "person" who is criminally liable. But can a corporation have a soul? Judges concluded that the idea that a corporation, without a soul, intended harm was too much of a fiction. Between 1850 and 1910, however, rising concerns over the possibility of corporate abuses captured the public's attention. Corporate criminal liability, no matter how illusory or illogical, became increasingly appealing as a hedge against the abuses considered inevitable with the rise of corporate power.

In the second phase, initiated by the decision of *New York Central Railroad* (1909), courts reviewed a wide variety of criminal cases against corporations.[31] Corporate regulation in this new world of interstate commerce required a more powerful and formal social control. This was all the more true as the first wave of mergers ended and large corporations increasingly spun off divisions—decentralizing. Centralized functions were now specialized and complex. In the years leading up to *New York Central Railroad*, concerns emerged that as corporations grew large, managerial oversight and control of employees would diminish.[32] Holding management responsible, through vicarious corporate criminal liability, soon became the rule of law in all federal courts.

Perceptions that this rule was unduly harsh prompted pleas by firms that they should be given a break for attempting compliance with laws.[33] Within 4 years of *New York Central Railroad*, corporations were telling courts that they were doing everything possible to comply with the law—even if they sometimes failed.

The third phase of the corporate criminal law saw a significant rise in the power of government regulators and, not surprisingly, the reach of regulatory law. Getting companies to comply with laws replaced punishment as the preferred sanction. Literally hundreds of thousands of criminal provisions were found in a wide range of federal statutory laws.[34] Marshall Clinard and his colleagues captured a glimpse of the effects of this

FIGURE 12.2 The five phases of the corporate criminal law, 1850–present.

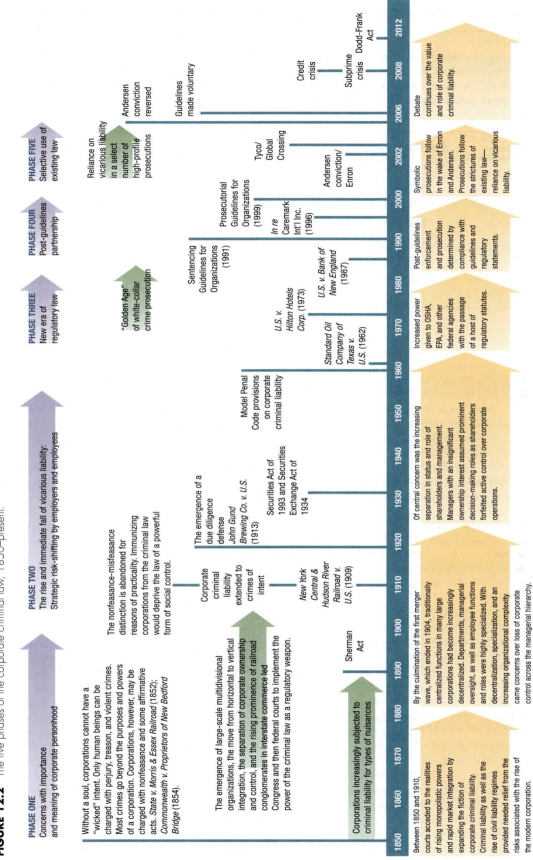

In Tyler, Texas, Jim and Kathy Taylor hold a photo of their daughter Jessica, a cheerleader who died in a tire blowout crash on her way to a game. In the background, their lawyer, Randell Roberts, holds a Firestone tire from the SUV. Subsequently, Firestone recalled 6.5 million of its most widely used product.

In February 2009, chief executives from major banks and other financial institutions that received federal money in the wake of the economic crisis that began in 2008 testified before the House Financial Services Committee in Washington. Companies represented at the hearing included, among others, Goldman Sachs, Bank of America, and Morgan Stanley.

new regulatory state on large corporations in their influential work *Illegal Corporate Behavior*.[35]

In the fourth phase, defined by the passage of the Sentencing Guidelines for Organizations, corporations joined with the government in routing out crime (Figure 12.3). Following significant lobbying from business associations, a congressionally appointed body—the United States Sentencing Commission—announced guidelines that govern the sentencing of corporations in federal courts. Drafters of the sentencing guidelines wanted corporations to face the threat of significant punishment and, at the same time, the possibility of mitigation, leniency, and amnesty (Table 12.5). This was the incentive for corporations to help ferret out crime.

The sentencing guidelines require judges to consider a fine multiplied by a score reflecting factors that make the corporation more or less blameworthy. A corporation's willingness to accept responsibility, cooperate with authorities, and implement a compliance reveals corporate due diligence and mitigates a sanction. To help companies understand how to best position themselves relative to prosecutors and regulators, consultants for a new and emerging industry—the corporate compliance industry—offered their skills.

The compliance industry markets the story that evidence of **organizational due diligence** (cooperating with authorities, creating an ethics code, hiring ethics officers, etc.) likely forestalls a criminal investigation, minimizes the likelihood

FIGURE 12.3 The development of the corporate criminal law, preguidelines–present.

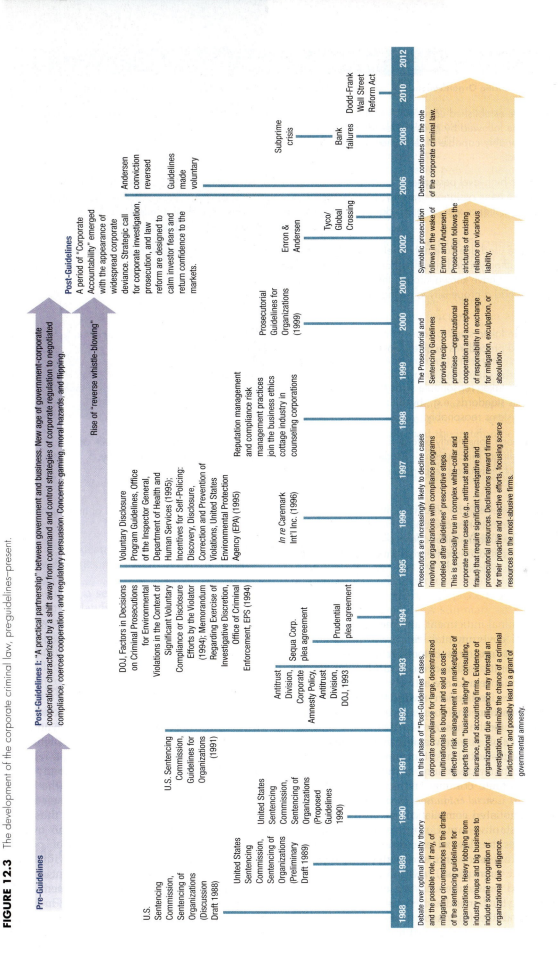

temptation too great for the governments of many developing countries to resist. They would rather have employment opportunities that pollute air and water than unemployment in a clean environment. Government officials in some Third World countries can be bribed to create or maintain a legal climate favorable to the business interests of the corporation, even though doing so may be detrimental to the people of the host country.

The work of Sutherland, Clinard, and Yeager and other traditional scholars, as well as that of a group of radical criminologists;[44] hearings on white-collar and corporate crime held by the Subcommittee on Crime of the House Judiciary Committee, under the leadership of Congressman John Conyers Jr. in 1978; the consumer protection movement, spearheaded by Ralph Nader; and investigative reporting by the press have all contributed to public awareness of large corporations' power to inflict harm on large population groups.

In 1975, James Q. Wilson still considered such crime to be insignificant,[45] but more recent studies show that the public considers corporate criminality at least as serious as, if not more serious than, street crime. Marvin Wolfgang and his associates found in a national survey that Americans regard illegal retail price-fixing (the artificial setting of prices at a high level, without regard for the demand for the product) as a more serious crime than robbery committed with a lead pipe.[46] Within the sphere of corporate criminality, perhaps no other group of offenses has had as great an impact on public consciousness as crimes against the environment. As we shall see, however, enforcement of major environmental statutes has been weak in the past. There is some evidence that this is changing.

Environmental Crimes

The world's legal systems include few effective laws and mechanisms to curb destruction of the environment. The emission of noxious fumes into the air and the discharge of pollutants into the water have until recently been regarded as common law nuisances at the level of misdemeanors, usually commanding no more than a small fine. Industrial polluters could easily absorb such a fine and tended to regard it as a kind of business tax. In 1969, Congress passed the National Environmental Policy Act (NEPA). Among other things, the act created the Environmental Protection Agency (EPA). It requires environmental impact studies so that any new development that would significantly affect the environment can be prevented or controlled.

The EPA is charged with enforcing federal statutes and assisting in the enforcement of state laws enacted to protect the environment. The agency monitors plant discharges all over the country and may take action against private industry or municipal governments. Yet during the first 5 years of its existence, the EPA referred only 130 cases to the U.S. Department of Justice for criminal prosecution, and only 6 of those involved major corporate offenders.[47] The government actually charged only one of the corporations, Allied Chemical, which admitted responsibility for 940 misdemeanor counts of discharging toxic chemicals into the Charles River in Virginia, thereby causing 80 people to become ill.[48]

A 1979 report of the General Accounting Office stated that the EPA inadequately monitored, inaccurately reported, and ineffectively enforced the nation's basic law on air pollution, although the agency's chief at that time contended that corrective action had been taken during the previous year.[49] The situation improved during the 1990s, but the environment is far from safe. Catastrophic releases of toxic and even nuclear substances, usually attributable to inadequate safeguards and human negligence, pose a particularly grave hazard, as the disasters at Bhopal in India and at Chernobyl in the former Soviet Union have demonstrated.

The effects of environmental crimes touch more than the environment. Employees in "culpable" companies may be victims as well. Consider, for example, the criminal investigation and prosecution of Darling International, Inc., a meat and meat-processing company located in Minnesota, for violations of the Clean Water Act.[50] The case of *United States v. Darling* is often thought of as representing a trend of management to exchange or trade culpable employees for corporate leniency.[51]

In 1989, Darling International bought a rendering plant in Blue Earth, Minnesota. Under significant pressure to increase production to meet sales objectives, its wastewater system soon became overloaded. Beginning in 1991, employees sought to remedy this situation by illegally dumping millions of gallons of ammonia and blood-contaminated water into the Blue Earth River, causing significant environmental damage. Soon thereafter, on orders of the plant manager and with the knowledge of the vice president of environmental affairs, employees attempted to hide the illegal dumping by diluting and tampering with at least nine wastewater samples sent to state pollution control authorities. The government had evidence that employees also fabricated and submitted discharge-monitoring reports and related documents that were later sent to state regulators.

The federal government's investigation into these environmental crimes stalled until Darling's board required retained counsel to cooperate with authorities and provide evidence of any criminal acts by its employees. With newly offered evidence, prosecutors obtained criminal convictions of four employees, all of whom had been fired by Darling after fully cooperating with counsel retained by the company and federal prosecutors. Darling entered into a plea agreement, and prosecutors recognized the company's cooperation by recommending a significantly mitigated fine— one quarter of the originally recommended fine.

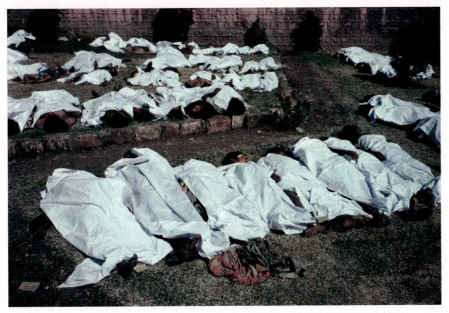

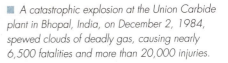

A catastrophic explosion at the Union Carbide plant in Bhopal, India, on December 2, 1984, spewed clouds of deadly gas, causing nearly 6,500 fatalities and more than 20,000 injuries.

The company promptly implemented an environmental compliance program, adopted a code of business conduct, and created a corporate ombudsman's position to "encourage employees to report suspected problems even when they are reluctant to go directly to their supervisors, legal counsel, or someone else in management."[52]

Darling is notable for many reasons: the complicity and knowledge of management, the distance between the employees held responsible and those cooperating with authorities, the absence of compliance initiatives or programs, and a culture that permitted scapegoating and the deception that can and often does accompany it. Simply put, existing principles and practices of corporate criminal law offer a less-than-optimal solution and remedy.

Enforcing Legislation

The difficulties of enforcing legislation designed to protect the environment are enormous. Consider the 250,000 barrels of oil spilled by the *Exxon Valdez* in 1989. What legislation could have prevented the disaster? Developing effective laws to protect the environment is a complex problem. It is far easier to define the crimes of murder and theft than to define acts of pollution, which are infinitely varied. A particular challenge is the separation of harmful activities from socially useful ones. Moreover, pollution is hard to quantify. How much of a chemical must be discharged into water before the discharge is considered noxious and subjects the polluter to punishment? Discharge of a gallon by one polluter may not warrant punishment, and a small quantity may not even be detectable. But what do we do with a hundred polluters, each of whom discharges a gallon?

Many other issues must be addressed as well. For instance, should accidental pollution warrant the same punishment as intentional or negligent pollution? Since many polluters are corporations, what are the implications of penalties that force a company to install costly antipollution devices? To cover the costs, the corporation may have to increase the price of its product, so the consumer pays. Should the company be allowed to lower plant workers' wages instead? Should the plant be forced or permitted to shut down, thereby increasing unemployment in the community? The company may choose to move its plant to another state or country that is more hospitable.

Addressing Sensitive Issues

Fines imposed on intentional polluters have been increased so that they can no longer be shrugged off as an ordinary cost of doing business. General Electric Company was fined $7 million and Allied Chemical Corporation $13.2 million for pollution offenses. Fines of such magnitude are powerful incentives to corporations to limit pollution. But because many of the enterprises that are likely to pollute are in the public sector, or produce for the public sector, the public ultimately will have to pay the fine in the form of increased gas or electricity bills.[53]

In the Third World, the problems of punishing and preventing pollution are enormous. Industries preparing to locate there have the power to influence governments and officials, surreptitiously and officially, into passing legislation favorable to the industry. The desire to industrialize outweighs the desire to preserve the environment. Some countries find ways to address the problem, only to relinquish controls when they prove irksome. While Japan was trying to establish its industrial dominance, for example, it observed a constitutional provision stating, "The conservation of life environment shall be balanced against the needs of economic development."[54]

Curbing Corporate Crime

Laws and regulations prescribing criminal sanctions have been passed and continue to be passed to guard the public against the dangers rooted in the power of corporate enterprise. As we noted, Congress passed sentencing guidelines that significantly increased corporate sanctions but at the same time allowed for reductions in fines where there was evidence of organizational due diligence—that is, implementation of effective ethics **corporate compliance programs.**[56] While such laws, regulations, and guidelines may provide some disincentives for illegal acts, many governments recognize that criminal justice systems are not well prepared to deal with economic crimes, in terms of either strategy or resources.[57] They also recognize the importance of attacking this problem at the international level, perhaps by designing strategies, standards, and guidelines that may be helpful to all governments.[58]

A disturbing thought remains: Is imposing criminal liability on the corporations themselves for their conduct really the best way to curb corporate misconduct? If corporations act on the decisions of their principal officers or agents, might it not be appropriate to restrict the reach of the law to these corporate actors rather than to subject the innocent and uninformed shareholders to financial loss? Why not rely more on administrative and civil proceedings? Both can and often do contain penalties that exceed those of the criminal law.

The recent spate of corporate scandals has brought about new legislation to combat corporate crime. Of particular note is the Sarbanes-Oxley Act of 2002. At the center of this act are provisions that mandate auditor independence and increased penalties for securities fraud.

Curbing corporate crime is as much a matter of politics as of careful law reform. As the effects of new legislation take place, we will see whether critics are right that these first few steps are not enough.

The Future of White-Collar and Corporate Crime

Some of the most respected names on Wall Street are under investigation or indictment or lie in ruins, bankrupt. Others have been criminally convicted and are desperately reinventing themselves. From WorldCom to Lehman Brothers, the very companies that made billions for investors in the 1990s are both perpetrators and victims of fraud, mismanagement, and conflicts of interest. And repercussions from the scandals continue in an economy that brings back memories of the Great Depression.

The icon of this wave of corporate scandals is a company that now lies in ruin. Its property was put up for auction. Its employees desperately searched for jobs. If you go on eBay, you can buy a copy of the company's ethics code put up for

■ Mary Shapiro, appointed by President Barack Obama, was sworn in on January 27, 2009 as the 29th chairman of the Securities and Exchange Commission.

sale by former employees looking to make a couple of dollars and prove the point that what companies say they are doing and what they actually do are often two very different things. In 2000, this company had worldwide assets of more than $65 billion and revenue of $101 billion. As of 2000, *Fortune* magazine called it "the Most Innovative Company in America." That year, the same magazine ranked it 22nd of the "100 Best Companies to Work for in America."

One cannot imagine working for a more ethical and socially minded company. In its 2000 Corporate Responsibility Annual Report, the chairman and CEO of this company, Kenneth Lay, articulated four of its guiding principles:

Respect: We will work to foster mutual respect with communities and stakeholders who are affected by our operations; we will treat others as we would like to be treated ourselves.

Integrity: We will examine the impacts, positive and negative, of our business on the environment and on society, and will integrate human health, social, and environmental considerations into our internal management and value system.

Communication: We will strive to foster understanding and support with our stakeholders and communities, as well as measure and communicate our performance.

Excellence: We will continue to improve our performance and will encourage our business partners and suppliers to adhere to the same standards.

The name of this company, in case you have not yet guessed it, is Enron Corporation. Enron was created in 1985 following a merger of Houston Natural Gas and InterNorth, a natural gas company with headquarters in Omaha, Nebraska.

Both companies were in the business of transporting and selling natural gas, and their merger created a network of more than 37,000 miles of gas pipeline. Soon after the merger, however, deregulation of the nation's energy markets, including the natural gas market, posed a significant challenge for Enron's business model. With the help of the large and prestigious consulting firm of McKinsey & Co., Enron diversified, going into the business of creating its own natural gas market, that is, buying and selling gas through contracts while controlling costs and prices.

Jeff Skilling, the young McKinsey consultant who brought the idea of Enron's creating its own energy market, was hired as chairman and CEO of Enron Finance Corporation, later becoming president and chief operating officer of Enron. The rest is history—a very sad page of business history. The history of Enron is marked by a single employee corporate **whistle-blower,** Sherron Watkins, who sent a one-page anonymous letter to Ken Lay (then chief executive officer) immediately after Jeff Skilling unexpectedly resigned. Portions of it read:

Has Enron become a risky place to work? For those of us who didn't get rich over the last few years, can we afford to stay? . . . The spotlight will be on us, the market just can't accept that Skilling is leaving his dream job. I think that the valuation issues can be fixed and reported with other good will write-downs to occur in 2002. How do we fix the Raptor and Condor deals? They unwind in 2002 and 2003, we will have to pony up Enron stock and that won't go unnoticed.

To the layman on the street, it will look like we recognized funds flow of $800 million from merchant asset sales in 1999 by selling to a vehicle (Condor) that we capitalized with a promise of Enron stock in later years. Is that really funds flow or is it cash from equity issuance?

We have recognized over $550 million of fair value gains on stocks via our swaps with Raptor. Much of that stock has declined significantly—Avici by 98 percent from $178 million, to $5 million; the New Power Company by 80 percent from $40 a share, to $6 a share. The value in the swaps won't be there for Raptor, so once again Enron will issue stock to offset these losses. Raptor is an LJM entity. It sure looks to the layman on the street that we are hiding losses in a related company and will compensate that company with Enron stock in the future.

I am incredibly nervous that we will implode in a wave of accounting scandals. My eight years of Enron work history will be worth nothing on my résumé, the business world will consider the past successes as nothing but an elaborate accounting hoax. Skilling is resigning now for "personal reasons" but I would think he wasn't having fun, looked down the road and knew this stuff was unfixable and would rather abandon ship now than resign in shame in two years.

You need not understand the accounting alchemy that Enron used to defraud investors—for example, special-purpose entities like Raptor or Condor and "related party transactions and disclosures." Many accountants still find these technicalities difficult to explain. Suffice it to say, Enron was built on an accounting house of cards. When that house tumbled down, a host of victims emerged, from the thousands of loyal and hardworking Enron employees to countless investors whose pensions and retirement plans dramatically lost value. Once nearly a $90-per-share stock, Enron stock certificates trade on eBay as collectors' items. The accounting firm that offered advice and counsel to Enron, Arthur Andersen, LLP, was indicted and convicted of obstruction of justice for shredding thousands of documents related to Enron audits. They, too, suffered corporate death. Tens of thousands of Andersen employees sought employment elsewhere as the accounting world watched in horror. It was common to refer to Andersen as one of the top five accounting firms. Now there are four.

Most important, Enron and the fall of Arthur Andersen sent a strong signal that Wall Street had a problem with corporate governance, that is, the way in which a corporation is managed and overseen. Principles of corporate governance require that both senior management and the board of directors participate in the affairs of the company. But they do so differently. Senior managers run the day-to-day operations of the company. The board of directors has the special function of providing an independent oversight of senior management—an independent check on managers. This is accomplished through governance and nominating committees, audit committees, finance committees, and compensation committees that tirelessly review the health of the company. In recent years, boards have been called upon to see that systems of internal controls are implemented and monitored.

What happened to the systems of control and governance structures of Enron? Why and how did all of the gatekeepers (accountants, lawyers, credit-rating agencies) fail? Answers are difficult to find, particularly because Enron followed many of the "best practices" of corporate governance, including an independent board of directors of competent outsiders. Enron had all the trappings of an ethical, Fortune 500 company with a bright future. Enron hired the best accountants and lawyers. Until answers to the many questions about Enron emerge, it is only fair to ask, How significant is the problem of corporate misgovernance in the United States? To this question the only answer is that the future of Wall Street and its perceived legitimacy hang in the balance.

Myers-Powell, 53, hasn't just spent the last decade finding her footing, which would be laudable alone. Having found her voice, she has become a tireless advocate in preventing young girls from entering the sex trade and helping those who are entrenched burrow their way out.

One day last week exemplified her mission. She spent the early morning in Cook County Jail with the Prostitutes Anonymous group she runs as part of her job as a member of the Cook County Sheriff's Department's prostitution intervention team.

She spent the late afternoon at an Englewood library with girls involved in the Dreamcatcher Foundation, the nonprofit she co-founded in 2008 that currently needs a home.

In addition, she has co-written research projects for DePaul University. She conducted the most recent study, "From Victims to Victimizers: Interviews with 25 Ex-Pimps in Chicago," with law professor and senior research fellow Jody Raphael.

Like most girls (and boys) who enter prostitution, Myers-Powell said, she grew up in a house in which she was sexually abused. She said her earliest memory of being raped goes back to when she was 4.

"As I grew up, I remember identifying with the women on the street corner because they wore shiny clothes and I wanted to be and feel shiny," she said. "I asked what they were doing, and my grandmother told me they were taking their panties off and men were giving them money."

"I could identify with that scenario, too, because men had been taking my panties off. And I thought, 'Wow I'll probably do that one day.' It seemed inevitable."

She said people are reluctant to help those caught up in the sex trade because they don't see prostitutes as being salvageable. Also, most people think of prostitution as something that doesn't happen in their neighborhood.

"But if you have the Internet, your child probably has been approached by someone in prostitution or exposed to it in some way," she said. "And because of the way sex is viewed in popular culture, some young girls don't call having sex for money prostitution. They call it 'just getting paid.'"

She said pimps have employed the Internet to lure girls into prostitution in increasingly creative ways. They often pose as rap video producers who offer young women an opportunity to be in a video with a famous rapper.

"They say, 'Send me some pictures to see if you qualify,'" she said. "It looks professional and then he will send her plane fare to go to Miami, Atlanta or Las Vegas and the next thing you know you don't see your child for a while—if you see her again."

Myers-Powell said she decided to leave prostitution after a client dragged her for six blocks in his car when he decided he didn't want to pay. She was in the hospital for a week with injuries to her left side and most of her face. She almost lost her left eye.

She tells young women she counsels that she understands how difficult it is to change their lives.

"She feels like she's damaged goods. But I tell them, 'Yes, you are still great and beautiful and yes, you can go back home and recover from this.'"

And more than counseling, she provides necessities such as bus passes and critical telephone numbers to help women transition off the streets.

"These traffickers and pimps, they know what they're doing, such as the manipulation, the brainwashing," she said. "They make the girls believe that the only way the girl can be successful is through (the pimp's) direction. Otherwise, the girls are worthless and they have no value."

Without changing the thinking, she said the women—even those counseled during jail stays—find their way back to the streets.

Myers-Powell has been married for six years and lives with her husband and 4-year-old foster son outside the city.

"A woman like myself who started as a youth in prostitution and didn't get out until I was 39 years, proves that if it can happen to me, it can happen to anybody," she said. "You're never too young or too old to start a new life."[1]

In cities across the country and around the world, people buying and selling illicit goods and services congregate in certain areas easily identifiable by storefronts that boldly advertise live sex shows. Shops feature everything from the latest DVD pornography to sex toys of every sort. Prostitutes openly solicit; drunks propped up in doorways clutch brown bags; drug addicts deal small amounts of whatever they can sell to support their habit. The friendly locals will deliver virtually any service to visitors at any price.

Cities across the country and around the world also are home to an underground market—on the Internet, in informal "shadow" markets in developing nations, and in the living rooms and bedrooms of suburban America—where people buying and selling illicit goods and services seek to avoid the scrutiny of law enforcement, exploit lax enforcement of laws, and avoid detection or apprehension because of the sheer number of law violators. From prostitution to the purchase of child pornography, from "recreational" drug use to the transport of cocaine or heroin across international borders, the crimes are varied. They are generally increasing in rate, entail vastly different degrees of harm and extent of victimization, and are as global as any form of commerce. As we shall see, to call these offenses "public order crimes" does not capture their breadth, scale, or complexity.

DRUG ABUSE AND CRIME

Crime Surfing www

www.whitehousedrug policy.gov

Find out more about the national drug control policy.

An 82-year-old woman from Bogota who struggled economically to care for her mentally retarded son was convinced by narco-traffickers that one trip to New York as a "drug mule" would supply her with enough money for her son's future. But her dream ended when a pellet full of narcotics ruptured in her stomach as she got into a cab at John F. Kennedy Airport in New York. She died before the cab could reach a hospital.[2] In New York City, a heroin addict admits that "the only livin' thing that counts is the fix . . . : Like I would steal off anybody—anybody, at all, my own mother gladly included."[3] In Chicago, crack cocaine has transformed some of the country's toughest gangs into ghetto-based drug-trafficking organizations that guard their turf with automatic weapons and assault rifles.[4]

On a college campus in the northeast, a crowd sits in the basement of a fraternity house drinking beer and smoking pot through the night. At a beachfront house in Miami, three young professional couples gather for a barbecue. After dinner they sit down at a card table in the playroom. On a mirror, someone lines up a white powdery substance into rows about ⅛ inch wide and 1 inch long. Through rolled-up paper they breathe the powder into their nostrils and await the "rush" of the coke. In a quiet suburban home, two middle-school students inhale paint thinner after school.

These incidents demonstrate that when we speak of the "drug problem," we are talking about a wide variety of conditions that stretch beyond our borders, that involve all social classes, that in one way or another touch most people's lives, and that cost society significant sums of money (Figure 13.1). The drug scene includes manufacturers, importers, primary distributors (for large geographical areas), smugglers (who transport large quantities of drugs from their place of origin), dealers (who sell drugs on the street and in crack houses), corrupt criminal justice officials, and users who endanger other

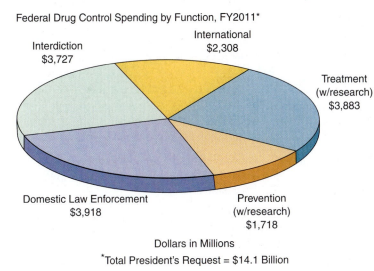

Federal Drug Control Spending by Function, FY2011*

Interdiction $3,727
International $2,308
Treatment (w/research) $3,883
Domestic Law Enforcement $3,918
Prevention (w/research) $1,718
Dollars in Millions
*Total President's Request = $14.1 Billion

FIGURE 13.1 National spending for drug control.

Source: National Drug Control Strategy, 2011 Annual Report (Washington, D.C.: The White House, 2011).

people's lives through negligence (train engineers, pilots, physicians) (Table 13.1).

The drug problem is further complicated by the wide diversity of substances abused, their varying effects on the mind and body, and the kinds of dependencies users develop. There is also the much-debated issue of the connection between drug use and crime—an issue infinitely more complex than the stereotype of maddened addicts committing heinous acts because they either are under the influence of drugs or need to get the money to support a habit. Many of the crimes we have discussed in earlier chapters are part of what has been called the nation's (or the world's) drug problem. Let us examine this problem in detail.

The History of Drug Abuse

The use of chemical substances that alter physiological and psychological functioning dates back to the Old Stone Age.[5] Egyptian relics from 3500 B.C. depict the use of opium in religious rituals. By 1600 B.C., an Egyptian reference work listed

TABLE 13.1 Roles and Functions in the Drug Distribution Business Compared with Those in Legitimate Industry

Approximate Role Equivalents in Legal Markets	Roles by Common Names at Various Stages of the Drug Distribution Business	Major Functions Accomplished at This Level
PROVIDERS		
Grower producer	Coca farmer, opium farmer, marijuana grower	Grow coca, opium, marijuana—the raw materials
Manufacturer	Collector, transporter, elaborator, chemist, drug lord	All stages for preparation of heroin, cocaine, marijuana as commonly sold
TRAFFICKERS		
Importer	Multikilo importer, mule, airplane pilot, smuggler, trafficker, money launderer	Smuggling of large quantities of substances into the United States
Wholesale distributor	Major distributor, investor, "kilo connection"	Transportation and redistribution of multi-kilograms and single kilograms
DEALERS		
Regional distributor	Pound and ounce men, weight dealers	Adulteration and sale of moderately expensive products
Retail store owner	House connections, suppliers, crack house supplier	Adulteration and production of retail-level dosage units (bags, vials, grams) in very large numbers
Assistant manager, security chief, or accountant	"Lieutenant," "muscle man," transporter, crew boss, crack-house manager/proprietor	Supervises three or more sellers, enforces informal contracts, collects money, distributes multiple dosage units to actual sellers
SELLERS		
Store clerk, salesmen (door-to-door and phone)	Street drug seller, runner, juggler	Makes actual direct sales to consumer; private seller responsible for both money and drugs
LOW-LEVEL DISTRIBUTORS		
Advertiser, security guard, leaflet distributor	Steerer, tout, cop man, lookout, holder runner, help friend, guard, go-between	Assists in making sales, advertises, protects seller from police and criminals, solicits customers; handles drugs or money but not both
Servant, temporary employee	Run shooting gallery, injector (of drugs), free-baser, taster, apartment cleaner, drug bagger, fence, money launderer	Provides short-term services to drug users or sellers for money or drugs; not responsible for money or drugs

SOURCE: From Bruce D. Johnson, Terry Williams, Kojo A. Dir, and Harry Sanabria, "Drug Abuse in the Inner City: Impact on Hard-Drug Users and the Community," in *Drugs and Crime*, vol. 13: *Crime and Justice*, eds. Michael Tonry and James Q. Wilson (Chicago: University of Chicago Press, 1990), p. 19. Copyright © 1990 by the University of Chicago. All rights reserved. Reprinted by permission of the University of Chicago Press.

opium as an analgesic, or painkiller. The Incas of South America are known to have used cocaine at least 5,000 years ago. Cannabis, the hemp plant from which marijuana and hashish are derived, also has a 5,000-year history.[6]

Since antiquity, people have cultivated a variety of drugs for religious, medicinal, and social purposes. The modern era of drug abuse in the United States began with the use of drugs for medicinal purposes. By the nineteenth century, the two components of opium, which is derived from the sap of the opium poppy, were identified and given the names "morphine" and "codeine." Ignorant of the addictive properties of these drugs, physicians used them to treat a wide variety of human illnesses. So great was their popularity that they found their way into almost all patent medicines used for pain relief and were even incorporated into soothing syrups for babies (Mother Barley's Quieting Syrup and Mumm's Elixir were very popular).

During the Civil War, the use of injectable morphine to ease the pain of battle casualties was so extensive that morphine addiction among veterans came to be known as the "soldier's disease."[7] By the time the medical profession and the public recognized just how addictive morphine was, its use had reached epidemic proportions. Then, in 1898, the Bayer Company in Germany introduced a new opiate, supposedly a nonaddictive substitute for morphine and codeine. It came out under the trade name Heroin; it proved to be even more addictive than morphine.[8]

When cocaine, which was isolated from the coca leaf in 1860, appeared on the national drug scene, it, too, was used for medicinal purposes. (Its use to unblock the sinuses initiated the "snorting" of cocaine into the nostrils.) Its popularity spread, and soon it was used in other products: Peruvian Wine of Coca ($1 a bottle in the Sears, Roebuck catalog); a variety of tonics; and, the most famous of all, Coca-Cola, which was made with coca until 1903.[9]

As the consumption of opium products (narcotics) and cocaine spread, states passed a variety of laws to restrict the sale of these substances. Federal authorities estimated that there were 200,000 addicts in the early 1900s. Growing concern over the increase in addiction led in 1914 to the passage of the Harrison Act, designed to regulate the domestic use, sale, and transfer of opium and coca products. Though this legislation decreased the number of addicts, it was a double-edged sword: By restricting the importation and distribution of drugs, it paved the way for the drug smuggling and black-market operations that are so deeply entrenched today.

It was not until the 1930s that the abuse of marijuana began to arouse public concern. Because marijuana use was associated with groups outside the social mainstream—petty criminals, jazz musicians, bohemians, and, in the Southwest, Mexicans—a public outcry for its regulation arose.[10] Congress responded with the Marijuana Tax Act of 1937, which placed a prohibitive tax of $100 an ounce on the drug. With the passage of the Boggs Act in 1951, penalties for possession of and trafficking in marijuana (and other controlled substances) increased. Despite all the legislation, the popularity of marijuana continued.

As the drugs being used proliferated to include glue, tranquilizers (such as Valium and Librium), LSD, and many other substances, the public became increasingly aware of the dangers of drug abuse. In 1970, another major drug law, the Comprehensive Drug Abuse Prevention and Control Act (the Controlled Substances Act), updated all federal drug laws since the Harrison Act.[11] This act placed marijuana in the category of the most serious substances. The 1970 federal legislation made it necessary to bring state legislation into conformity with federal law. The Uniform Controlled Substances Act was drafted and now is the law in 48 states, the District of Columbia, Puerto Rico, the Virgin Islands, and Guam.

Most of the basic federal antidrug legislation has been drawn together in Title 21 of the United States Code, the collection of all federal laws. It includes many amendments passed since 1970, especially the Anti-Drug Abuse Act of 1988, which states, "It is the declared policy of the United States Government to create a drug-free America by 1995."[12]

Title 21, as amended, has elaborate provisions for the funding of national and international drug programs; establishes the Office of National Drug Control Policy, headed by a so-called drug czar; and provides stiff penalties for drug offenses. The manufacture, distribution, and dispensing of listed substances in stated (large) quantities are each subject to a prison sentence of 10 years to life and a fine (for individuals) of $4 million to $10 million. Even simple possession now carries a punishment of up to 1 year in prison and a $100,000 fine. Title 21, along with other recent crime-control legislation, defines many other drug crimes as well and provides for the forfeiture of any property constituting or derived from the proceeds of drug trading.

The Extent of Drug Abuse

The National Survey on Drug Use and Health (NSDUH) provides some of the best estimates of drug use and drug use trends for the United States.[13] According to the 2010 NSDUH survey, an estimated 22.6 million Americans (8.9 percent) age 12 and older are current users. The 2010 NSDUH survey revealed a near across-the-board leveling off in drug use. Estimates of marijuana use or dependence among youths 12 to 17 remained stable from 6.7 percent in 2007 to 6.9 percent in 2010. (See Table 13.2 for more survey findings.)

The therapeutic community is a 24-hour, total-care facility where former addicts and professionals work together to help addicts become drug-free. In methadone maintenance programs, addicts are given a synthetic narcotic, methadone, that prevents withdrawal symptoms (physical and psychological pain associated with giving up drugs) while addicts reduce their drug intake slowly over a period of time. Throughout the program, addicts receive counseling designed to help them return to a normal life.

It is difficult to assess the success of most treatment programs. Even if individuals appear to be drug-free within a program, it is hard to find out what happens to them once they leave it (or even during a week when they do not show up). In addition, it may well be that the addicts who succeed in drug treatment programs are those who have already resolved to stop abusing drugs before they voluntarily come in for treatment; the real hard-core users may not even make an effort to become drug-free.

A program to divert drug offenders (users and purchasers) from criminal careers is the drug court, in which the judge has the option to divert nonviolent drug offenders to a counseling program in lieu of incarceration. Since the first drug court was established in Dade County, Florida, in 1989, more than 2,100 similar courts have been established in counties throughout the country (see Figure 13.3). The S.T.O.P. program in Portland, Oregon, diverted 944 cases within an 18-month period and has a rearrest rate of 6 percent for the first year following completion of the program. Other drug courts enjoy similar success rates.[37]

Education

While drug treatment deals with the problem of addiction after the fact, education tries to prevent people from taking illegal drugs in the first place. The idea behind educational programs is straightforward: People who have information about the harmful effects of illegal drugs are likely to stay away from them. Sometimes the presentation of the facts has been coupled with scare tactics. Some well-known athletes and entertainers have joined the crusade with public-service messages ("a questionable approach," says Howard Abadinsky, "given the level of substance abuse reported in these groups").[38]

The educational approach has several drawbacks. Critics maintain that most addicts are quite knowledgeable about the potential consequences of taking drugs but think of them as just a part of the "game."[39] Most people who begin to use drugs believe they will never become addicted, even when they have information about addiction.[40] Inner-city youngsters do not lack information about the harmful effects of drugs. They learn about the dangers from daily exposure to addicts desperately searching for drugs, sleeping on the streets, going through withdrawal, and stealing family belongings to get money.[41]

Legalization

Despite increases in government funding for an expanded war on drugs, the goal of a drug-free society in the 1990s was not achieved and is hardly likely to be achieved within the next decade. There is much evidence that all the approaches, even the "new" ones, have been tried before with little or no effect. Some experts are beginning to advocate a very different approach—legalization. Their reasoning is that because the drug problem seems to elude all control efforts, why not deal with heroin and cocaine the same way we deal with alcohol and tobacco? In other words, why not subject these drugs to some government control and restrictions but make them freely available to all adults?[42]

They argue that current drug-control policies impose tremendous costs on taxpayers without demonstrating effective results. In addition to spending less money on crime control, the government would make money on tax revenue from the sale of legalized drugs. This is, of course, a hotly debated issue. Given the dangers of drug abuse and the moral issues at stake, legalization surely offers no easy solution and has had little public support. However, the surgeon general of the United States, in 1994, mentioned the option of legalization—only to be rebuffed by the president.

ALCOHOL AND CRIME

Alcohol is another substance that contributes to social problems. One of the major differences between alcohol and the other drugs we have been discussing is that the sale and purchase of alcohol are legal in most jurisdictions of the United States. The average annual consumption of alcoholic beverages by each individual 14 years of age and over is equivalent to 591 cans of beer, or 115 bottles of wine, or 35 fifths of liquor; this is more than the average individual consumption of coffee and milk.[43] Alcohol is consumed at recreational events, business meetings, lunches and dinners at home, and celebrations; in short, drinking alcohol has become the expected behavior in many social situations.

Drinking is widespread among young people. While the rate of use has been fairly steady since 1994, the percentage of drinkers in 2010 was 51.8 percent of the population above 12 years old. Recent research demonstrates that 13.6 percent of current drinkers were 12 to 17 years old. Of this group, 7.8 percent were binge drinkers, and 1.7 percent were classified as heavy drinkers.[44] (See Table 13.2.)

FIGURE 13.3 Timeline of drug courts and other problem-solving courts in the United States, 1989–2007.

Source: Figure 1 from C. West Huddleston III, Douglas B. Marlowe, J.D., Ph.D., and Rachel Casebolt, *Painting the Current Picture: A National Report Card on Drug Courts and Other Problem-Solving Court Programs in the United States*, Volume II, Number 1, May 2008. Washington, D.C.: National Drug Court Institute, p. 1. Copyright © 2008 National Drug Court Institute. Reprinted with permission.

The History of Legalization

Alcohol consumption is not new to our culture; in colonial days alcohol was considered safer and healthier than water. Still, the history of alcohol consumption is filled with controversy. Many people through the centuries have viewed it as wicked and degenerate. By the turn of the twentieth century, social reformers linked liquor to prostitution, poverty, the immigrant culture, and corrupt politics.

Various lobbying groups, such as the Women's Christian Temperance Union and the American Anti-Saloon League, bombarded politicians with demands for the prohibition of alcohol.[45] On January 16, 1920, the Eighteenth Amendment to the Constitution went into force, prohibiting the

conduct in Anglo-American law has been greatly influenced by both the Old and the New Testaments. In the Middle Ages, the enforcement of laws pertaining to sexual morality was the province of church courts. Today, to the extent that immorality is still illegal, it is the regular criminal courts that enforce such laws.

Morality laws have always been controversial, whether they seek to prevent alcohol abuse or to prohibit certain forms of sexual behavior or its public display or depiction. Sexual activity other than intercourse between spouses for the purpose of procreation has been severely penalized in many societies and until only recently in the United States. Sexual intercourse between unmarried persons ("lewd cohabitation"), seduction of a female by promise of marriage, and all forms of "unnatural" sexual relations were serious crimes—some carrying capital sentences—as late as the nineteenth century. In 1962, the Model Penal Code proposed some important changes. Fornication and lewd cohabitation were dropped from the list of offenses, as was homosexual intercourse between consenting adults.

The idea behind these changes is that the sexual relations of consenting adults should be beyond the control of the law, not only because throughout history such legal efforts have proved ineffective but also because the harm to society, if any, is too slight to warrant the condemnation of law. "The state's power to regulate sexual conduct ought to stop at the bedroom door or at the barn door," said sex researcher Alfred Kinsey four decades ago.[63]

Although the Model Penal Code (MPC) has removed or limited sanctions for conduct among consenting adults, the code retains strong prohibitions against sexual activities involving children. Penalties are severe for **statutory rape** (illegal sexual activity between two people when it would otherwise be legal if not for their age), deviate sexual intercourse with a child, corruption of a minor, sexual assault, and endangering the welfare of a child. Of course, the recommendations of the American Law Institute are not always accepted by state legislatures.

Let us take a close look at three existing offenses involving sexual morality: deviate sexual intercourse by force or imposition, prostitution, and pornography.

Deviate Sexual Intercourse by Force or Imposition

The Model Penal Code defines "deviate sexual intercourse" as "sexual intercourse per os or per anum [by mouth or by anus] between human beings who are not husband and wife, and any form of sexual intercourse with an animal" [sec. 213.2(1)]. The common law called such sexual acts **sodomy,** after the biblical city of Sodom, which the Lord destroyed for its wickedness, presumably because its citizens had engaged in such acts. The common law dealt harshly with sodomy, making it a capital offense and referring to it as *crimen innominatum*—a crime not to be mentioned by name.

Yet other cultures, including ancient Greece, did not frown on homosexual activities. And Alfred Kinsey reminded us that homosexual (from the Greek word *homos*, meaning "same") relations are common among all mammals, of which humans are but one species.[64] The MPC subjects "deviate sexual intercourse" between two human beings to punishment only if it is accomplished by severe compulsion or if the other person is incapable of granting consent or is a child less than 10 years old. To conservative lawmakers, this model legislation is far too liberal; to liberals, it does not go far enough. Generally, liberal thinkers prefer the law not to interfere with the sexual practices of consenting adults at all.

The gay and lesbian rights movement has done much to destigmatize consensual, private adult sexual relationships for the lesbian, gay, bisexual, and transgender (LGBT) community. Legislatures have been slow to respond, and the U.S. Supreme Court has taken a conservative stance as well. Laws on same-sex relationships and marriage are being debated in state legislatures, however, and are changing. New laws with respect to "marriage equality" and "civil unions" have been passed in several states, including Massachusetts, Connecticut, Maine, Iowa, and Vermont. Many other states, such as California, are in the midst of a long and protracted debate over the constitutionality of same-sex marriage.

Prostitution

Not so long ago it was a crime to be a prostitute.[65] The law punished women for a status acquired on the basis of sexual intercourse with more than one man. Under some statutes it was not even necessary to prove that money was paid for the sexual act. The Supreme Court ruled in 1962—in a case involving the status of being a drug addict—that criminal liability can be based only on conduct, that is, on doing something in violation of law.[66] This decision would seem to apply to prostitution as well. Therefore, one can no longer be penalized for being a prostitute. But soliciting for sex is an act, not a status, and nearly all states make solicitation of sex for money the misdemeanor of **prostitution.**

The Uniform Crime Reports recorded 62,668 arrests for prostitution and commercialized vice during 2010.[67] The number would be extremely high if we were to include all acts of sexual favor granted in return for some gratuity. Even if the number were limited to straightforward cash transactions (including, nowadays, credit card transactions), there is no way of arriving at a figure. Many persons may act as prostitutes for a while and then return to legitimate lifestyles. There are part-time

and full-time prostitutes, male and female prostitutes, itinerant and resident prostitutes, street hookers and high-priced escorts who do not consider themselves prostitutes.[68]

Many law enforcement agencies do not relish the task of suppressing prostitution. In some jurisdictions, the police have little time to spend on vice control, given the extent of violent and property crimes. Thus, when prostitutes are arrested, it is likely to be in response to demands by community groups, business establishments, or church leaders to "clean up the neighborhood." Occasionally, the police find it expedient to arrest prostitutes because they may divulge information about unsolved crimes, such as narcotics distribution, theft, receiving stolen property, or organized crime.

Prostitution encompasses a variety of both acts and actors. The prostitute, female or male, is not alone in the business of prostitution. A **pimp** provides access to prostitutes and protects and exploits them, living off their proceeds. There are still madams who maintain houses of prostitution. And, finally, there are the patrons of prostitutes, popularly called "johns." Ordinarily, it is not a criminal offense to patronize a prostitute, yet the framers of the MPC proposed to criminalize this act. The section was hotly debated before the American Law Institute. A final vote of the members rejected criminalization.

Researchers have found that many prostitutes come from broken homes and poor neighborhoods and are school dropouts. Yet all social classes contribute to the prostitution hierarchy. High-priced call girls, many of them well-educated women, may operate singly or out of agencies. The television "blue channels" that broadcast after midnight in most metropolitan areas carry commercials

advertising the availability of call girls, their phone numbers, and sometimes their specialties. At the next lower level of the prostitution hierarchy are the massage-parlor prostitutes. When Shirley, a masseuse, was asked, "Do you consider yourself a prostitute?" she answered: "Yes, as well as a masseuse,

Cyberporn: Where Do We (Should We) Draw the Line?

- The dean of the Harvard Divinity School resigned his post after a computer tech discovered an extensive collection of hard-core pornography on his Harvard-owned computer. This Lutheran minister, divinity school dean, scholar, and father of two committed no crime, but his actions violated the school's ban on having materials that are "inappropriate, obscene, bigoted or abusive" on school computers.(1) The case received widespread media coverage.

- A deputy sheriff from Palmdale, California, was indicted on federal charges for child pornography. The evidence was found on his hard drive. Also, he allegedly tried to solicit sex via the Internet from a person he thought was a 13-year-old girl. The deputy sheriff faced up to 15 years in prison if convicted.(2)

- A Cub Scout leader from Long Island was arrested for having child pornography on his computer, which he downloaded from the Internet and reportedly swapped with other porn peddlers.(3)

- A 23-year-old woman started her own porn website as a hobby. She expected to make about $50,000 a week on the site in the first year. This money would allow her to cut back on making movies and dancing at clubs. She is one of many women in the porn industry who have set up their own websites as alternative businesses.(4)

- Some men find themselves "addicted" to cyberporn, spending as much as 80 hours per week online. Their real sex lives and relationships are damaged as online sex becomes more important and fulfilling than the real thing, leading some marriages to end in divorce.(5)

The Internet provides an ever-increasing number of avenues for the distribution of pornography. For entrepreneurs setting up porn sites, the Internet is proving quite lucrative. However, some of those who use it find themselves in legal trouble when they go beyond legal pornography to child pornography or use sex chat rooms to solicit sex with children. Even those who stick to legal porn may face problems related to their jobs or their personal relationships. It is unlikely that pornography—both legal and illegal—on the Internet will decrease in the years to come.

Of all the issues regarding pornography on the Internet, one of the most hotly debated is censorship. While some programs exist that limit access to porn sites, they do not prevent the exploitation of children or keep those who wish to access the sites from doing so. Child pornographers are creative and adaptable, shying away from explicit child pornography. Many frequent preteen and teen nudism news groups and sites, where thousands of photographs of nude children await them in an apparently "constitutionally protected" cyberspace. The question remains as to what can be done to limit children's access to pornographic sites as well as to prevent their exploitation on the Internet while still protecting freedom of speech. Where should courts draw the line?

Few criminologists have attempted to answer this question or to delve into the world of pornography—including child pornography—in spite of the complex and important issues associated with it. Perhaps the best-known and most competent work in this area has been done by Philip Jenkins. In his work *Beyond Tolerance: Child Pornography on the Internet*, Jenkins raises and wrestles with the more significant issues facing the regulation of this phenomenon. In his own words:

Child pornography is a substantial presence on the Internet, and its potential audience is likely to grow rapidly as Internet usage expands. Given this fact, what, if anything, can be done? Is it possible to suggest solutions or responses that would not sabotage many of the positive aspects of the Internet? In other words, is there a cure that is not worse than the disease? Trafficking in Internet child porn may be so securely protected that total eradication could be achieved only by means that could not fail to damage many innocent users. Deciding which means are too severe or intrusive to combat this problem produces some troubling ethical debates. Briefly, do civil liberties and privacy rights end when one accesses the Internet? Some citizens may well place such a high value on child protection that they would accede to granting police or government the right to observe all Web traffic, to read all mail at random. Most of us, however, would be appalled by such an idea. So what is the proper balance between given technologies being both effective and tolerable?

This is not a simple transaction, a straightforward equation of "how many rights are you prepared to give up to safeguard children?" Repressive new laws theoretically directed against

and a healer, and a couple of other things."[69] One rung lower on the prostitution ladder are the "inmates" (a term used by the MPC) of the houses of prostitution, locally called "bordellos," "whorehouses," "cathouses," or "red-light houses."

According to people "in the life" (prostitution), the streetwalkers are the least-respected class in the hierarchy. They are the "working girls" or "hookers." They are found clustered on their accustomed street corners, on thoroughfares, or in truck and bus depots, dressed in bright attire, ready to negotiate a price with any passerby. Sexual services are performed in vehicles or in nearby "hot-sheet" hotel rooms. Life for these prostitutes—some of whom are transvestite males—is dangerous and grim. Self-reports suggest that many are drug addicts and have been exposed to HIV.[70] Other varieties of prostitution range from the legal houses that a few counties permit to operate in Nevada to troupes of prostitutes who travel from one place of

child porn might well cause injustice and inconvenience without having the slightest impact on that traffic. Recognizing a serious problem is one thing: using it as an excuse to implement dangerously bad laws is quite another. The answer to child porn is not to be found by adding ever more legal weapons to an already bulging police arsenal but rather in the proper deployment of existing powers and technologies.

From the outset, we have to realize what goals are achievable, and the total elimination of electronic child porn simply may not be within the bounds of possibility. That does not mean that we have to learn to accept or live with the problem, and we might well achieve a massive reduction of production and availability, on the lines of what was accomplished in the 1980s. The great majority of child porn users are rational enough to be deterred, if the proper methods are applied. If we could achieve, say, a 90 or 95 percent reduction of availability, that would be a massive victory in its own right. The fact that some residual trade will continue indefinitely should not provide grounds for ever-increasing encroachments on the liberties of law-abiding Netizens.

To illustrate just how intractable the child porn problem is, let us imagine a means by which this material could be removed or destroyed entirely. Purely as a fantasy, let us suggest that the Internet should simply be prohibited, along with private communication over computer networks. Such a desperate solution was briefly discussed in Mike Cane's Computer Phone Book in the mid-1980s, when he reacted angrily to sysops who "resent having the government come into their domain because of systems for child molesters." Cane argued simply, "If there's a

choice between most BBS's existing or protecting innocent children, I'll be the first to throw away my modem. How about you?" Nobody was suggesting such a scheme seriously, and that was long before the Internet came to occupy its present hegemonic position in the U.S. economy. Put bluntly, the vast majority of citizens would not be prepared to throw away their modems in the quest for child protection, even if such a scheme were vaguely conceivable. And if a hypothetical government did prohibit computer networks, it still would not eliminate child porn. Such a ban could be enforced only by computers in the hands of police or security forces, and many precedents indicate that these government employees would surreptitiously be sharing pornographic images. If there are computers, there will be computerized child pornography.

To take a marginally less outrageous solution, consider the experience of China, which, like many authoritarian nations, faces a fundamental paradox in its attitudes toward Internet technology. The Chinese want the massive economic benefits of the Net and also realize the military implications of having a computer-literate populace. The ongoing cold war between the People's Republic of China (PRC) and Taiwan is increasingly fought in the form of hacker attacks on each other's electronic installations. At the same time, the PRC's rulers are nervous about the democratic implications of the Internet, the ability of ordinary citizens to form political or cultural groupings online and to circulate information critical of the state. In response to this dilemma, the Chinese government has ordained that all Internet traffic must pass through two portals, both run by the state. The authorities strictly limit what sites can be accessed and keep detailed records of who is

visiting what site. All ISPs and Internet users have to register with authorities. Under present arrangements, "Chinese in the People's Republic can now log onto the China Wide Web and find links with the Chinese version of Yahoo, but without the freedom to connect with sites the government does not wish them to see." Even stricter laws have been proposed: under a recent measure, "the use of e-mail to transmit what might be regarded as secret information is expressly forbidden. The regulations also put operators of chat rooms on notice that they will be held liable for their content. And Internet sites are required to submit to 'examination and approval by the appropriate secrecy work offices,' although the rules do not specify what that process involves. . . . A basic principle of the new regulations is that 'whoever puts it on the Internet assumes responsibility.'"

Anyone using encryption technology is required to notify a government agency of that fact. Other countries with comparably strict laws are Singapore, Saudi Arabia, and Vietnam, and one state has taken the principle of control to its logical extent: "Burma [Myanmar] has taken the strongest measures by outlawing the use of the Internet and making ownership of an unregistered computer with networking capabilities illegal."

With such a model, much child pornography could indeed be kept off the Internet and its aficionados rounded up or terrorized into inactivity. The difficulty is that a Western nation would find such a solution unacceptable from a myriad [of] different perspectives, not least because it would hamstring the whole Internet and introduce controls that most members of a democratic society would regard as utterly

(continued)

opportunity to another (work projects, farm labor camps, construction sites) and bar ("B") girls who entertain customers in cocktail lounges and make themselves available for sexual activities for a price.

Popular, political, and scientific opinions on prostitution have changed, no doubt largely because prostitution has changed. Around the turn of the century, it probably was true that a large number of prostitutes had been forced into

the occupation by unscrupulous men. Indeed, it was this pattern that led to the enactment of the White Slave Traffic Act (called the Mann Act, after the senator who proposed the bill), prohibiting the interstate transportation of females for purposes of prostitution. There is some evidence that today the need for money, together with limited legitimate opportunities to obtain it, prompts many young women and men to become prostitutes.

intolerable. But would it even work? China has an age-old tradition of technological innovation, while successive generations of Chinese dissidents over long centuries have devised ever more imaginative means of outwitting repressive governments and distributing their own propaganda. Not surprisingly, the latest restrictions do not appear too burdensome in practice. Chinese computer users access forbidden sites by means of proxy servers, of which there are far too many to permit concerted government action against them. Users also make extensive use of Internet cafés rather than private machines, so even if authorities note that an unregulated site has been accessed, the odds of detecting a specific individual are slight. The Chinese experience neatly illustrates the remark of Internet pioneer John Gilmore that "the Internet interprets censorship as damage and routes around it." As Ian Buruma notes after describing a recent harsh crackdown on Internet dissidents, "these are desperate measures which cannot stop thousands of others from surfing in forbidden areas." Once again, too, we face the issue of "who guards the guards?" We may wonder what frivolous, decadent, and obscene websites are regularly frequented by the guardians of electronic morality in socialist China.

While a Chinese (or Burmese) solution is inconceivable in the West, it is scarcely less Orwellian than some of the ideas that have been floated, however speculatively. Given the nature of the child porn trade, the only policies that might conceivably attempt eradication would involve wide-ranging surveillance of Web traffic by official agencies. This effort might be carried out in a directed way under the approval of court warrants or randomly through general fishing expeditions undertaken against the sort of people thought likely to offend in this particular way. The British example of GTAC and the extravagant powers granted to MI5 indicate that something like this may not be too far away. Yet, as the Chinese example indicates, even such an intolerable set of burdens probably would not eliminate the underlying problem.(6)

Sources

1. Trent Gegax, "An Odd Fall from Grace: Computer Porn Undoes a Divinity-School Dean," *Newsweek*, May 31, 1999, p. 70.
2. "Deputy in Custody Allegedly Tried to Solicit Sex in Internet Chat Room," *City News Service*, Oct. 22, 1999.
3. "Scout Leader Accused of Child Pornography," *New York Times*, Oct. 22, 1999, p. B14.
4. John Leland, "More Bang for the Buck: How Sex on the Internet Has Transformed the Business of Pornography," *Newsweek*, Oct. 11, 1999, p. 73.
5. Greg Gutfield, "The Sex Drive: Web Pornography Has Turned Computers into Sex Objects, and Men, by the Millions, Are Hooking Up, Should You?" *Men's Health*, Oct. 1, 1999, p. 116.
6. From Philip Jenkins, *Beyond Tolerance: Child Pornography on the Internet*, pp. 204–208. Copyright © 2001 by New York University. Reprinted by permission of New York University Press.

Questions for Discussion

1. Why do you think seemingly normal individuals procure child pornography on the Internet or become "addicted" to cyberporn?
2. What can society do to limit the damage done to children by child pornographers who use the Internet as a means of distribution? What should be done with those who are caught?

Sex researcher Paul Gebhard found in 1969 that only 4 percent of U.S. prostitutes were forced into prostitution. More recently, Jennifer James found that the majority entered the life because of its financial rewards.[71] Whatever view we take of adult prostitutes as victims of a supposedly victimless criminal activity, one subgroup clearly is a victimized class: children, female and male, who are enticed and sometimes forced into prostitution, especially in large cities. Some are runaways, picked up by procurers at bus depots; some are simply "street children"; and others have been abused and molested by the adults in their lives.[72]

Pornography

Physical sexual contact is a basic component of both sodomy and prostitution. **Pornography** requires no contact at all; it simply portrays sexually explicit material. Statutes in all states make it a criminal offense to produce, offer for sale, sell, distribute, or exhibit certain kinds of pornographic (sometimes called "obscene," "lewd," or "lascivious") material. Federal law prohibits the transportation of illegal material in interstate commerce and outlaws the use of the mails, the Internet, the telephone, radio, and television for the dissemination of pornographic material.[73]

The Problem of Definition

The term "pornographic" is derived from the Greek *pornographos* ("writing of harlots," or descriptions of the acts of harlots). The term "obscene" comes from the Latin *ob* ("against," "before") plus *caenum* ("filth"), or possibly from *obscena* ("offstage"). In Roman theatrical performances, disgusting and offensive parts of plays took place offstage, out of sight but not out of hearing of the audience.[74] Courts and legislators have used the two terms interchangeably, but nearly all statutes and decisions deal with pornography (with the implication of sexual arousal) rather than with obscenity (with its implication of filth).[75]

Scholars generally agree that the statutes in existence appear to be addressed primarily to

Preventing Child Pornography

In late November about 3,500 people from some 170 governments and from international and nongovernmental organizations attended the third World Congress Against Sexual Exploitation of Children and Adolescents in Rio de Janeiro. The conference declared that accessing, downloading, storing or viewing child pornography on the Internet is a crime. It urged governments to legally prohibit such acts.

Justice and home affairs ministers of the Group of Eight nations declared in June: "We strongly condemn and denounce all forms of sexual exploitation of children, including the practice of persons travelling abroad and engaging in sexual conduct with children, as well as the alarming flood of images of sexual abuse of children—so-called child pornography—on the Internet."

In Japan and Russia, the possession of child porn is not punishable if it is not for sale or offering. The international community accuses Japan of being a major child porn exporter. Around the time of the Rio de Janeiro conference, there was reportedly heavy access from abroad and home after file-swapping software used in Japan allowed child porn to be placed on the Net.

In June the ruling bloc submitted a bill to the Diet that would call for the imprisonment of up to one year or a fine of up to ¥1 million [1 million yen] if a person possesses child pornography to satisfy his or her sexual curiosity. It also calls on Internet providers to cooperate with the police and take steps to prevent the spread of child porn.

The Democratic Party of Japan submitted its own bill, thinking that the ruling bloc's bill could lead to arbitrary investigations. Under the DPJ bill, a person could be imprisoned for up to three years or fined up to ¥3 million [3 million yen] if he or she buys child porn or obtains it repeatedly. Both bills are to revise a 1999 law that protects children under 18 against sexual exploitation.

Although the Rio de Janeiro declaration is not legally binding, it is an international call for Japan to strengthen regulations against child pornography. The ruling bloc and the DPJ should act quickly to find a common ground for effective regulation.

Questions for Discussion

1. How did the Rio de Janeiro conference affect the laws about child pornography in Japan?
2. What role should the global community take in policing child pornography?

SOURCE: Editorial, "Preventing Child Pornography," *The Japan Times*, December 25, 2008. Reprinted by permission of The Japan Times.

---

pornographic materials.[76] What, then, is the contemporary meaning of "pornography"? The Model Penal Code (1962) says that a publication is pornographic (obscene or indecent) "if, considered as a whole, its predominant appeal is to prurient interests" and if, "in addition, it goes substantially beyond customary limits in describing or representing such matters" (sec. 251.4). This definition, which is full of ambiguities, was to play a major role in several Supreme Court decisions.

Two presidential commissions were no more successful in defining the term. The Commission on Obscenity and Pornography (1970) avoided a definition and used instead the term "explicit sexual material."[77] The Attorney General's Commission on Pornography (1986) gave no definition.[78] The definition created by a British parliamentary committee in 1979 seems to describe pornography best:

A pornographic representation combines two features: It has a certain function or intention, to arouse its audience sexually, and also a certain content, explicit representation of sexual materials (organs, postures, activity, etc.).[79]

This definition indicates nothing about any danger inherent in pornography. The law will step in only when pornography is exhibited or distributed in a manner calculated to produce harm.

Historically, that harm has been seen as a negative effect on public morals, especially those of children. That was the stance taken by many national and local societies devoted to the preservation of public morality in the nineteenth century. More recently, the emphasis has shifted to the question of whether the availability and use of pornography produce actual, especially violent, victimization of women, children, or, for that matter, men.

Pornography and Violence

The National Commission on Obscenity and Pornography in 1970 and the Attorney General's Commission on Pornography in 1986 reviewed the evidence of an association between pornography, on one hand, and violence and crime, on the other. The National Commission provided funding for more than 80 studies to examine public attitudes toward pornography, experiences with pornography, the association between the availability of pornography and crime rates, the experience of sex offenders with pornography, and the relation between pornography and behavior. The commission concluded:

> [E]mpirical research designed to clarify the question has found no evidence to date that exposure to explicit sexual materials plays a significant role in the causations of delinquent or criminal behavior among youth or adults. The Commission cannot conclude that exposure to erotic materials is a factor in the causation of sex crimes or sex delinquency.[80]

Between 1970 (when the National Commission reported its findings) and 1986 (when the Attorney General's Commission issued its report), hundreds of studies had been conducted on this question. For example:

- Researchers reported in 1977 that when male students were exposed to erotic stimuli, those stimuli neither inhibited nor had any effect on levels of aggression. When the same research team worked with female students, they found that mild erotic stimuli inhibited aggression and that stronger erotic stimuli increased it.[81]

- Researchers who exposed students to sexually explicit films during six consecutive weekly sessions in 1984 concluded that exposure to increasingly explicit erotic stimuli led to a decrease in both arousal responses and aggressive behavior. In short, these subjects became habituated to the pornography.[82]

After analyzing such studies, the Attorney General's Commission concluded that nonviolent and nondegrading pornography is not significantly associated with crime and aggression. It did conclude, however, that exposure to pornographic materials

> (1) leads to a greater acceptance of rape myths and violence against women; (2) results in pronounced effects when the victim is shown enjoying the use of force or violence; (3) is arousing for rapists and for some males in the general population; and (4) has resulted in sexual aggression against women in the laboratory.[83]

The Feminist View: Victimization

To feminists, these conclusions supported the call for greater restrictions on the manufacture and dissemination of pornographic material. Historian Joan Hoff has coined the term "pornerotic," meaning

> any representation of persons that sexually objectifies them and is accompanied by actual or implied violence in ways designed to encourage readers or viewers that such sexual

subordination of women (or children or men) is acceptable behavior or an innocuous form of sex education.[84]

Hoff's definition also suggests that pornography, obscenity, and erotica may do far more than offend sensitivities. Such material may victimize not only the people who are depicted but all women (or men or children, if they are the people shown). Pornographers have been accused of promoting the exploitation, objectification, and degradation of women. Many people who call for the abolition of violent pornography argue that it also promotes violence toward women. Future state and federal legislation is likely to focus on violent and violence-producing pornography, not on pornography in general.

The Legal View: Supreme Court Rulings

Ultimately, defining pornographic acts subject to legal prohibition is a task for the U.S. Supreme Court. The First Amendment to the Constitution guarantees freedom of the press. In a series of decisions culminating in *Miller v. California* (1973), however, the Supreme Court articulated the view that obscenity, really meaning pornography, is outside the protection of the Constitution. Following the lead of the Model Penal Code and reinterpreting its own earlier decisions, the Court announced the following standard for judging a representation as obscene or pornographic:

- The average person, applying contemporary community standards, would find that the work, taken as a whole, appeals to prurient interests.

- The work depicts or describes, in a patently offensive way, sexual conduct specifically defined by the applicable state law.

- The work, taken as a whole, lacks serious literary, artistic, political, or scientific value.[85]

While this proposed standard is flexible enough to be expanded or contracted as standards change over time and from place to place, its terms are so vague that they give little guidance to local law enforcement officers or to federal and state courts. In 1987, the Supreme Court addressed this problem and modified the Miller decision. In *Pope v. Illinois*, the Court ruled that the third aspect of Miller (that the work has "no value") may be judged by an objective test rather than by local community standards. Justice Byron White wrote for the majority:

> The proper inquiry is not whether an ordinary person of any given community will find serious literary, artistic, political, or scientific value in the allegedly obscene material, but whether a reasonable person would find such value in the material, taken as a whole.[86]

Whether this test makes juries' tasks easier when they must decide whether a film or magazine is pornographic or obscene is still not clear.

Pornography and the Internet

Any child with basic knowledge of a computer and a minimal amount of curiosity can, with a few clicks of a mouse, open a doorway to the world of cyberporn: pictures of adults having sexual intercourse, adults having intercourse with animals, video clips of adults having sex with children, and guides to bordellos, massage parlors, and various pleasure districts—both local and international.[87]

Censorship of the Internet has been a heavily debated issue in recent times. Almost everyone agrees that access of minors to pornographic material over the Internet should be restricted, but the primary point of contention remains: Who should be responsible for policing access to such material? Parents? Educators? The government? Responding to a nationwide outcry, Congress passed the Communications Decency Act (CDA) on February 8, 1996. This portion of the Telecommunications Decency Act of 1996 made it a felony to "knowingly use a telecommunications device or interactive computer to send an indecent communication to a child or to use a computer to display indecent material in a manner accessible to a child." Violations of this act are punishable by up to 2 years' imprisonment and a fine of $250,000.

Four months after the passage of this law, however, a federal court in Philadelphia ruled that it is in conflict with the constitutional right to free speech. According to the court, blocking enforcement of the CDA was justified because (1) the term "indecent" was found to be impermissibly vague and (2) while the CDA could restrict Americans from disseminating "indecent" material, it had no jurisdiction over communications originating outside the United States and would thus be ineffective. Existing federal and state laws, however, still ban the sale and possession of child pornography.

One of the biggest issues surrounding government regulation of pornography on the Internet is the lack of global cooperation. The 1998 conviction of the head of the German division of the American online service CompuServe for the spread of child pornography on the Internet highlights this fact. Legislation on pornography varies around the world, and this means that pornography can be easily sent across borders. Strategies are currently being developed by several international agencies to increase communication, provide hotlines for users to report illegal material, make laws more unified, and prevent the exploitation of children on a global scale.

Another significant issue is the fine line between what some call eroticism and others call child pornography. Perhaps the most famous photographer of young girls—David Hamilton—prides himself on belonging to an elite group of art photographers. His books—which no doubt appeal to child pornographers—are carried by most large chain bookstores and are on the Internet. But is this art or child pornography? Is it constitutionally protected, or should it be criminally prosecuted? These two questions will be at the forefront of a debate about pornography on and off the Web.

In the wake of the continued controversy over "cybersmut," several computer programs have been developed to assist parents and educators in regulating children's access to the Internet.

Crime Surfing

http://internet-filter-review.toptenreviews.com/internet-pornography-statistics.html

Check out these statistics on Internet pornography.

■ Anyone with a computer and a modem can access cyber pornography, even children. The FBI, U.S. Customs Service, Department of Justice, and U.S. Postal Service have committed significant resources to investigate and prosecute distributors and consumers of child pornography.

■ *Pandemonium at a Moscow theater where 41 Chechen terrorists held 800 people hostage for 57 hours.*

towers and damage the Pentagon on September 11, 2001, with a loss of thousands of lives (see Chapter 10).[72]

Much scholarly inquiry has been directed at understanding and explaining international terrorism.[73] And there have been legislative responses. As a matter of fact, a network of international conventions is in place to deal with international terrorism. International judicial collaboration and police cooperation have been vastly improved. Yet there is no international machinery in operation to ensure the arrest or adjudication of international terrorists, and criminologists have yet to arrive at theoretically sound explanations that would help nations deal with a problem that knows no boundaries.

3. *Theft of art and cultural objects.* This category ranked third because of its potential for robbing entire cultures and nations of their cultural heritage. Tombs and monuments have been plundered since the time of the pharaohs. But with the development of modern tools and the high demand for cultural objects, as well as the ease of transport, international thieves have developed systems that can strip an entire region or country of its heritage—as well as the work of contemporary artists. Every country has been victimized. An estimated $4.5 billion worth of fine art is stolen every year for sale on the international market. A database lists 45,000 stolen art objects, with 2,000 items added each month.[74] With few exceptions,[75] criminologists have paid scant attention to this phenomenon, though the art industry has endeavored to come up with some practical solutions.[76]

4. *Theft of intellectual property.* Theft of intellectual property includes the unauthorized use of the rights of authors and performers and of copyrights and trademarks. There is obviously a great temptation to reproduce works of protected originators at a fraction of franchise (or similar) costs, especially in countries with relatively unregulated economies. Yet the destructive impact on the economies of producing or originating countries is immediately apparent. Intellectual property theft costs

American corporations billions every year. How many billions is not clear. The Motion Picture Association of America (MPAA) estimated that the movie industry lost $58 billion in 2000, the Recording Industry Association of America (RIAA) estimated losses in the music industry of roughly $12.5 billion; and the U.S. Software Publishers Association estimated losses of $7.5 billion. Intellectual theft also includes counterfeit versions of pharmaceuticals, automotive parts, and electrical equipment, which pose significant health and safety issues in addition to economic losses.[77] Despite international agreements, this transnational crime category remains a problem without a solution.

5. *Illicit traffic in arms.* Local, regional, or national armed conflicts, which today plague every part of the globe, would be unimaginable without an international network of weapons producers and suppliers. This is a shadowy world beyond the reach of statistical assessment. Criminological information on the illegal arms trade is also lacking. Yet the largest portion of the world's homicides potentially is traceable to the illegal traffic in arms.

The most lethal part of the world's illegal arms trade involves the transfer of nuclear materials. It has become clear that several relatively small quantities of nuclear material, including pure plutonium, have been diverted from nuclear facilities in former Soviet republics and offered for sale in Germany and other countries west of Russia.

First indications are that the diversions of nuclear material that have occurred so far were carried out by small groups of individuals, rather than organized crime, for motives of individual gain (or possibly to assist in financing underfunded former Soviet laboratories and scientists). Most of the efforts were amateurish, and none of the material apparently reached a viable buyer. Indeed, most ended up in sting operations. However, the quantities of nuclear material seized by authorities are not insubstantial. In September 1999, Georgian authorities seized 2.2 pounds of uranium 235 at the Georgian-Turkish border.[78] In several cases, the thieves, transporters, and the public have been exposed to radiation hazards—in itself a substantial danger.[79] Criminologists have been caught by surprise. As yet, there have been few criminological responses.[80] At this point, governments have cooperated to control nuclear materials at the source.

6. *Aircraft hijacking.* The system for curbing and responding to the illegal interception of aircraft is in place and has proved somewhat effective. The number of hijackings has declined significantly, yet incidents still occur with regularity, as the events of September 11, 2001, have horribly demonstrated.

The airline industry had been plagued by aircraft hijackings in the 1970s and into the 1980s. While a few such incidents were attributable to individuals who demanded ransom, most were political statements with typical terrorist characteristics, aimed at demonstrating the ability of the terrorist organization to strike at vulnerable targets almost anywhere in the world.

Because the entire world community was affected—especially diplomats and politicians, whose mobility depends on air travel—the reaction to the flood of hijackings was swift. The industry itself reacted by increasing security measures.

The criminological literature on this phenomenon is considerable, centering on the profiles of hijackers, causes, regions, carriers involved, and the like, all of which has led to the improvement of controls.

7. *Sea piracy.* Virtually forgotten until the mid-1970s, sea piracy has resurfaced:

• Illegal narcotics drug smuggling from South and Central America into the United States initially relied heavily on yachts and fishing vessels captured at sea or in port, after owners and crews were killed. Several thousand vessels were victimized. As the drug trade became prosperous, smugglers began to rely on purchased or illegally chartered vessels.

• At the roadstead of Lagos, Nigeria, and the narrow shipping channel of the Malacca Straits—as well as in several comparable sea lanes—the opportunity of deriving some benefit by attacking commercial vessels at anchor or slow speed attracted thousands of marginalized young men in Africa, Southeast Asia, and Latin America. Such piracies (often not piracies in the international law sense, since they occurred in the territorial waters of states) reached a high level of frequency (one a day in the 1980s) but are now on the decline, thanks largely to the research and policy activities of the International Maritime Bureau (London) of the International Chamber of Commerce (Paris), the International Maritime Organization (UN), and a number

of criminologists.[81] (See "Debatable Issues," Chapter 11.)

• There has been a major increase in piracy off the Somali coast. An estimated 230 foreign sailors were being held hostage for ransom in ships off the coast of Somalia as of June 2009. More than a dozen warships from navies around the world have joined in the hunt. Prudent shipping lines order "piracy watches" on their vessels in affected waters. National and regional maritime law enforcement agencies maintain closer watch, and the International Maritime Bureau maintains a special branch office in Kuala Lumpur, Malaysia, to monitor developments. Worldwide attention to the problem of piracy was heightened in April 2009 with the daring high seas rescue of Captain Richard Phillips. Phillips was held hostage for four days after pirates boarded his container ship.

8. *Land hijacking.* The inclusion of land hijacking in the list of transnational crimes was a surprise. At the national level, hijacking of trucks had been well documented as a form of robbery or theft. But the world economy shifted. Long-distance trucking from eastern to western Europe or from the central Asian republics to the Baltic States now is a reality and involves a high percentage of goods transported transnationally. The opportunity to divert such cargos has increased proportionately.

It is telling that only four countries responded to this item on the UN questionnaire. At this point, the evidence is entirely episodic but seems to point to the involvement of organized groups. Predictably, the problem will increase as a result of the openness of borders, the growth of organized crime (especially in eastern Europe), and the lack of data and criminological analysis.

9. *Insurance fraud.* The insurance industry is internationally linked, especially through reinsurance and other methods of spreading risks and benefits. Thus, local insurance fraud ultimately affects all insurers, and all insured, worldwide. The global dimensions of the problem have not been calculated, but for the United States alone, the loss likely exceed $100 billion annually.[82]

10. *Computer crime.* The Internet serves legitimate commerce, governments, and researchers. But the global Internet also presents a host of opportunities for criminals, including exploitation, criminal schemes, and wide use by organized crime. Current estimates of losses through computer crime range up to $8 billion annually.[83] Unfortunately, we lack information on this issue, though criminologists are taking an increasing interest in the development of legal and other protections.

11. *Environmental crime.* Well into the middle of the twentieth century, harming the environment was regarded as a matter to be controlled by local authorities. It was not until the United Nations

38. Philippe Pinel, *A Treatise on Insanity* (1806; New York: Hafner, 1962).

39. Peter Scott, "Henry Maudsley," *Journal of Criminal Law, Criminology, and Police Science,* **46** (March–April 1956): 753–769.

40. Henry H. Goddard, *The Criminal Imbecile* (New York: Macmillan, 1915), pp. 106–107.

41. Adolphe Quételet, *A Treatise on Man,* facs. ed. of 1842 ed., trans. Salomon Diamond (1835; Gainesville, Fla.: Scholars Facsimiles and Reprints, 1969), p. 97.

42. Quételet, *A Treatise on Man,* p. 103. For Quételet's influence on modern scholars, see Derral Cheatwood, "Is There a Season for Homicide?" *Criminology,* **26** (1988): 287–306.

43. Gabriel Tarde, *Penal Philosophy,* trans. R. Howell (Boston: Little, Brown, 1912), p. 252.

44. Gabriel Tarde, *Social Laws: An Outline of Sociology* (New York: Macmillan, 1907).

45. Émile Durkheim, *The Rules of Sociological Method,* ed. George E. G. Catlin (Chicago: University of Chicago Press, 1938), p. 71.

46. T. S. Kuhn, *The Structure of Scientific Revolutions* (Chicago: Chicago University Press, 1962), p. 10

47. Gary LaFree, "Expanding Criminology's Domain: The American Society of Criminology 2006 Presidential Address," *Criminology,* **45** (2007): 1–31.

48. Richard Rosenfeld, "The Big Picture: 2010 Presidential Address to the American Society of Criminology," *49,* pp. 1–26.

CHAPTER 4

1. http://www.cnn.com/2005/LAW/06/27/btk/index.html.

2. http://www.cnn.com/2005/LAW/06/28/victims.son/index.html.

3. See Ronald Blackburn, *The Psychology of Criminal Conduct: Theory, Research, and Practice* (Chichester, England: Wiley, 1993); and Hans Toch, *Violent Men: An Inquiry into the Psychology of Violence,* rev. ed. (Washington, D.C.: American Psychological Association, 1992).

4. See, e.g., Cathy Spatz Widom, "Cycle of Violence," *Science,* **244** (1989): 160–165; and Nathaniel J. Pallone and J. J. Hennessy, *Criminal Behavior: A Process Psychology Analysis* (New Brunswick, N.J.: Transaction, 1992).

5. See, generally, A. J. Reiss Jr., K. A. Klaus, and J. A. Roth, eds., *Biobehavioral Influences:* vol. 2, *Understanding and Preventing Violence* (Washington, D.C.: National Academy Press, 1994); M. Hillbrand and N. J. Pallone, "The Psychobiology of Aggression: Engines, Measurement, Control," *Journal of Offender Rehabilitation,* **21** (1994): 1–243; and J. T. Tedeschi and R. B. Felson, *Violence, Aggression, and Coercive Actions* (Washington, D.C.: American Psychological Association, 1994).

6. J. Puig-Antich, "Biological Factors in Prepubertal Major Depression," *Pediatric Annals,* **12** (1986): 867–878.

7. See, e.g., Guenther Knoblich and Roy King, "Biological Correlates of Criminal Behavior," in *Facts, Frameworks, and Forecasts: Advances in Criminological Theory,* vol. 3, ed. J. McCord (New Brunswick, N.J.: Transaction, 1992); Diana H. Fishbein, "Biological Perspectives in Criminology," *Criminology,* **28** (1990): 17–40; David Magnusson, Britt af Klinteberg, and Hakan Stattin, "Autonomic Activity/Reactivity, Behavior, and Crime in a Longitudinal Perspective," in McCord, *Facts, Frameworks, and Forecasts;* Frank A. Elliott, "Violence: The Neurologic Contribution: An Overview," *Archives of Neurology,* **49** (1992): 595–603; L. French, "Neuropsychology of Violence," *Corrective and Social Psychiatry and Journal of Behavior Technology Methods and Therapy,* **37** (1991): 12–17; and Elizabeth Kandel and Sarnoff A. Mednick, "Perinatal Complications Predict Violent Offending," *Criminology,* **29** (1991): 519–530.

8. Edward O. Wilson, *Sociobiology: The New Synthesis* (Cambridge, Mass.: Harvard University Press, 1975).

9. C. Ray Jeffery, *Biology and Crime* (Beverly Hills, Calif.: Sage, 1979).

10. P. A. Brennan and S. A. Mednick, "Genetic Perspectives on Crime," *Acta Psychiatria Scandinavia,* **370** (1993): 19–26.

11. See Sarnoff A. Mednick, Terrie E. Moffitt, and Susan A. Stack, *The Causes of Crime: New Biological Approaches* (New York: Cambridge University Press, 1987).

12. A. A. Sandberg, G. F. Koepf, and T. Ishihara, "An XYY Human Male," *Lancet* (August 1961): 488–489.

13. Herman A. Witkin et al., "Criminality, Aggression, and Intelligence among XYY and XXY Men," in *Biosocial Bases of Criminal Behavior,* eds. Sarnoff A. Mednick and Karl O. Christiansen (New York: Wiley, 1977).

14. Johannes Lange, *Verbrechen als Schicksal* (Leipzig: Georg Thieme, 1929).

15. Cf. Gregory Carey, "Twin Imitation for Antisocial Behavior: Implications for Genetic Environment Research," *Journal of Abnormal Psychology,* **101** (1992): 18–25.

16. See Karl O. Christiansen, "A Preliminary Study of Criminality among Twins," in Mednick and Christiansen, *Biosocial Bases of Criminal Behavior.*

17. David C. Rowe and D. Wayne Osgood, "Heredity and Sociological Theories of Delinquency: A Reconsideration," *American Sociological Review,* **49** (1986): 526–540; David C. Rowe, "Genetic and Environmental Components of Antisocial Behavior: A Study of 256 Twin Pairs," *Criminology,* **24** (1986): 513–532.

18. Sarnoff A. Mednick, William Gabrielli, and Barry Hutchings, "Genetic Influences in Criminal Behavior: Evidence from an Adoption Court," in *Prospective Studies of Crime and Delinquency,* ed. K. Teilmann et al. (Boston: Kluwer-Nijhoff, 1983).

19. These and other studies are reviewed in Mednick et al., *The Causes of Crime.*

20. Hannah Bloch and Dick Thompson, "Seeking the Roots of Violence," *Time,* Apr. 19, 1993, pp. 52–53.

21. Daniel Goleman, "New Storm Brews on Whether Crime Has Roots in Genes," *New York Times,* Sept. 15, 1992, p. C1.

22. Bloch and Thompson, "Seeking the Roots of Violence."

23. Study Group on Serious and Violent Juvenile Offenders, Office of Juvenile Justice and Delinquency Prevention (Washington, D.C.: NIJ, 1998); Fox Butterfield, "Study Cites Biology's Role in Violent Behavior," *New York Times,* Nov. 13, 1992, p. A7.

24. Goleman, "New Storm Brews on Whether Crime Has Roots in Genes."

25. Ibid.

26. Hugo Munsterberg, *On the Witness Stand* (New York: Doubleday, 1908); Henry H. Goddard, *Feeble-Mindedness: Its Causes and Consequences* (New York: Macmillan, 1914).

27. Edwin H. Sutherland, "Mental Deficiency and Crime," in *Social Attitudes,* ed. K. Young (New York: Henry Holt, 1931).

28. Robert H. Gault, "Highlights of Forty Years in the Correctional Field—and Looking Ahead," *Federal Probation,* **17** (1953): 3–4.

29. Arthur Jensen, *Bias in Mental Testing* (New York: Free Press, 1979).

30. Ibid.; Richard J. Herrnstein, *IQ in the Meritocracy* (Boston: Atlantic–Little, Brown, 1973).

31. Travis Hirschi and Michael J. Hindelang, "Intelligence and Delinquency: A Revisionist Review," *American Sociological Review,* **42** (1977): 571–586.

32. Travis Hirschi, *Causes of Delinquency* (Berkeley: University of California Press, 1969).

33. Marvin E. Wolfgang, Robert F. Figlio, and Thorsten Sellin, *Delinquency in a Birth Cohort* (Chicago: University of Chicago Press, 1972).

34. Albert J. Reiss and Albert L. Rhodes, "The Distribution of Juvenile Delinquency in the Social Class Structure," *American Sociological Review,* **26** (1961): 720–732.

35. See M. Rutter, T. E. Moffitt, and A. Caspi, "Gene-Environment Interplay and Psychopathology: Multiple Varieties but Real Effects," *Journal of Child Psychology and Psychiatry,* **47** (2006): 226–261; T. E. Moffitt, A. Caspi, and M. Rutter, "Measured Gene-Environment Interactions in Psychopathology: Concepts, Research Strategies, and Implications for Research, Intervention, and Public Understanding of Genetics," *Perspectives on Psychological Science,* **1** (2006): 5–27. See also James Q. Wilson and Richard Herrnstein, *Crime and Human Nature* (New York: Simon & Schuster, 1985); Deborah W. Denno, "Sociological and Human Developmental Explanations of Crime: Conflict or Consensus?" *Criminology,* **23** (1985): 711–740; and Deborah W. Denno, "Victim, Offender, and Situational Characteristics of Violent Crime," *Journal of Criminal Law and Criminology,* **77** (1986): 1142–1158.

36. "Taking the Chitling Test," *Newsweek,* July 15, 1968.

37. Sandra Scarr and Richard Weinberg, "I.Q. Test Performance of Black Children Adopted by White Families," *American Psychologist,* **31** (1976): 726–739.

38. See Doris J. Rapp, *Allergies and the Hyperactive Child* (New York: Simon & Schuster, 1981).

39. Diana H. Fishbein and Susan Pease, "The Effects of Diet on Behavior: Implications for Criminology and Corrections," *Research on Corrections,* **1** (1988): 1–45.

40. Stephen Schoenthaler, "Diet and Crime: An Empirical Examination of the Value of Nutrition in the Control and Treatment of Incarcerated Juvenile Offenders," *International Journal of Biosocial Research,* **4** (1982): 25–39.

41. Heather M. Little, "Food May Be Causing Kids' Problems," *Chicago Tribune,* Oct. 29, 1995, p. 1; Abram Hoffer, "The Relation of Crime to Nutrition," *Humanist in Canada,* **8** (1975): 2–9.

42. Benjamin F. Feingold, *Why Is Your Child Hyperactive?* (New York: Random House, 1975).

43. James W. Swanson and Marcel Kinsbourne, "Food Dyes Impair Performance of Hyperactive Children on a Laboratory Test," *Science,* **207** (1980): 1485–1487.

44. Anthony R. Mawson and K. W. Jacobs, "Corn Consumption, Tryptophan, and Cross-National Homicide Rates," *Journal of Orthomolecular Psychiatry,* **7** (1978): 227–230.

45. "Toddler Dies after Being Thrown in Lake by Dad in Diabetic Seizure," *Chicago Tribune,* July 10, 1995, p. 9.

46. Matti Virkkunen, "Insulin Secretion during the Glucose Tolerance Test among Habitually Violent and Impulsive Offenders," *Aggressive Behavior,* **12** (1986): 303–310.

47. E. A. Beeman, "The Effect of Male Hormones on Aggressive Behavior in Mice," *Physiological Zoology,* **20** (1947): 373–405.

48. D. A. Hamburg and D. T. Lunde, "Sex Hormones in the Development of Sex Differences," in *The Development of Sex Differences,* ed. Eleanor E. Maccoby (Stanford, Calif.: Stanford University Press, 1966).

49. A. Booth and D. W. Osgood, "The Influence of Testosterone on Deviance in Adulthood: Assessing and Explaining the Relationship," *Criminology,* **31** (1993): 93–117; L. E. Kreuz and R. M. Rose, "Assessment of Aggressive Behavior and Plasma Testosterone of a Young Criminal Population," *Psychosomatic Medicine,* **34** (1972): 321–332; R. T. Rada, D. R. Laws, and R. Kellner, "Plasma Testosterone Levels in the Rapist," *Psychosomatic Medicine,* **38** (1976): 257–268.

50. Katharina Dalton, *The Premenstrual Syndrome* (Springfield, Ill.: Charles C Thomas, 1971).

51. Julie Horney, "Menstrual Cycles and Criminal Responsibility," *Law and Human Behavior,* **2** (1978): 25–36.

52. *Regina v. Charlson,* 1 A11. E.R. 859 (1955).

53. L. P. Chesterman et al., "Multiple Measures of Cerebral State in Dangerous Mentally Disordered Inpatients," *Criminal Behavior and Mental Health,* **4** (1994): 228–239; Lee Ellis, "Monoamine Oxidase and Criminality: Identifying an Apparent Biological Marker for Antisocial Behavior," *Journal of Research in Crime and Delinquency,* **28** (1991): 227–251.

54. A. Raine, M. S. Buchsbaum, and L. LaCasse, "Brain Abnormalities in Murderers Indicated by Positron Emission Tomography," *Biological Psychiatry,* **42** (1997): 496–508.

55. A. Raine, J. R. Meloy, S. Bihrle, J. Stoddard, L. LaCasse, and M. S. Buchsbaum, "Reduced Prefrontal and Increased Subcortical Brain Functioning Assessed Using Positron Emission Tomography in Predatory and Affective Murderers," *Behavioral Sciences and the Law,* **16** (1998): 319–332.

56. A. Raine, T. Lencz, S. Bihrle, L. LaCasse, and P. Colletti, "Reduced Prefrontal Gray Matter Volume and Reduced Autonomic Activity in Antisocial Personality Disorder," *Archives of General Psychiatry,* **57** (2000): 119–127.

57. Raine, Buchsbaum, and LaCasse, "Brain Abnormalities in Murderers."

58. A. Raine and Y. Yang, "The Neuroanatomical Bases of Psychopathy: A Review of Brain Imaging Findings," in *Handbook of Psychopathy,* ed. C. J. Patrick (New York: Guilford Press, 2006), pp. 278–295.

59. H. Forssman and T. S. Frey, "Electroencephalograms of Boys with Behavior Disorders," *Acta Psychologica et Neurologia Scandinavica,* **28** (1953): 61–73; H. de Baudouin et al., "Study of a Population of 97 Confined Murderers," *Annales Medico-Psychologique,* **119** (1961): 625–686.

60. Sarnoff A. Mednick, Jan Volavka, William F. Gabrielli, and Turan M. Itil, "EEG as a Predictor of Antisocial Behavior," *Criminology,* **19** (1981): 219–229.

61. Jan Volavka, "Electroencephalogram among Criminals," in Mednick et al., *The Causes of Crime.* See also J. Volavka, *Neurobiology of Violence* (Washington, D.C.: American Psychiatric Press, 1995); Adrian Raine, Monte Buchsbaum, and Lori LaCasse, "Brain Abnormalities in Murderers Indicated by Positron Emission Tomography," *Biological Psychiatry,* **42** (1997): 495–508; and Adrian Raine, J. Reid Meloy, Susan Bihrle, Jackie Stoddard, Lori LaCasse, and Monte S. Buchsbaum, "Reduced Prefrontal and Increased Subcortical Brain Functioning Assessed Using Positron Emission Tomography in Predatory and Affective

in *American Cities* (Chicago: University of Chicago Press, 1969). See also Frederick M. Thrasher, *The Gang* (Chicago: University of Chicago Press, 1927).

51. Ralph B. Taylor, "The Impact of Crime on Communities," *The Annals of the American Academy,* **539** (1995): 28–45.

52. Ralph B. Taylor, Steve D. Gottfredson, and Sidney Brower, "Attachments to Place: Discriminant Validity and Impacts of Disorder and Diversity," *American Journal of Community Psychology,* **13** (1985): 525–542.

53. Michael Marriott, "Living in 'Lockdown,'" *Newsweek,* Jan. 23, 1995, p. 57.

54. Lynn Newhart Smith and Gary D. Hill, "Victimization and Fear of Crime," *Criminal Justice and Behavior,* **18** (1991): 217–239. See also Fred E. Markowitz, Paul E. Bellair, Allen E. Liska, and Jianhong Liu, "Extending Social Disorganization Theory: Modeling the Relationships between Cohesion, Disorder, and Fear," *Criminology,* **39** (2001): 293–319; and Randy L. LaGrange, Kenneth F. Ferraro, and Michael Supancic, "Perceived Risk of Fear of Crime: Role of Social and Physical Incivilities," *Journal of Research in Crime and Delinquency,* **29** (1992): 311–334. For research that measures safety and perceived safety resources in the context of other environmental concerns (as an alternative to measuring fear of crime), see John J. Gibbs and Kathleen J. Hanrahan, "Safety Demand and Supply: An Alternative to Fear of Crime," *Justice Quarterly,* **10** (1993): 369–394.

55. Ralph Taylor and Jeanette Covington, "Community Structural Change and Fear of Crime," *Social Problems,* **40** (1993): 374–392.

56. Douglas A. Smith, "The Neighborhood Context of Police Behavior," in *Communities and Crime,* eds. Albert J. Reiss and Michael Tonry (Chicago: University of Chicago Press, 1986), pp. 313–341; Terance D. Miethe, Michael Hughes, and David McDowall, "Social Change in Crime Rates: An Evaluation of Alternative Theoretical Approaches," *Social Forces,* **70** (1991): 165–185; E. Britt Paterson, "Poverty, Income Inequality, and Community Crime Rates," *Criminology,* **29** (1991): 755–776; Josefina Figueira-McDonough, "Community Structure and Delinquency: A Typology," *Social Service Review,* **65** (1991): 65–91; Denise C. Gottfredson, Richard J. McNeil, and Gary D. Gottfredson, "Social Area Influence on Delinquency: A Multilevel Analysis," *Journal of Research in Crime and Delinquency,* **28** (1991): 197–226.

57. Dina R. Rose and Todd R. Clear, "Incarceration, Social Capital, and Crime: Implications for Social Disorganization Theory," *Criminology,* **36** (1998): 441–479.

58. Robert J. Sampson and Dawn Jeglum Bartusch, *Attitudes toward Crime, Police, and the Law: Individual and Neighborhood Differences,* National Institute of Justice Research Preview, June 1999.

59. Steve J. South and Gary D. Deane, "Race and Residential Mobility: Individual Determinants and Structural Constraints," *Social Forces,* **72** (1993): 147–167.

60. See Faith Peeples and Rolf Loeber, "Do Individual Factors and Neighborhood Context Explain Ethnic Differences in Juvenile Delinquency?" *Journal of Quantitative Criminology,* **10** (1994): 141–157; and Thomas A. Petee, Gregory S. Kowlaski, and Don W. Duffield, "Crime, Social Disorganization, and Social Structure: A Research Note on the Use of Interurban Ecological Models," *American Journal of Criminal Justice,* **19** (1994): 117–132. For generalizability of social

disorganization theory to nonurban areas, see D. Wayne Osgood and Jeff M. Chambers, "Social Disorganization Outside the Metropolis: An Analysis of Rural Youth Violence," *Criminology,* **38** (2000): 81–115.

61. Taylor, "The Impact of Crime on Communities," p. 36.

62. Andrew J. Buck, Simon Hakim, and Ulrich Spiegel, "Casinos, Crime, and Real Estate Values: Do They Relate?" *Journal of Research in Crime and Delinquency,* **28** (1991): 288–303.

63. Robert J. Bursik and Harold G. Grosmick, *Neighborhoods and Crime* (New York: Lexington Books, 1993).

64. Anthony Sorrentino and David Whittaker, "The Chicago Area Project—Addressing the Gang Problem," *FBI Law Enforcement Bulletin,* **63** (1994): 8–12; "Philadelphia Settles with Estates of MOVE Members," *Jet,* Feb. 17, 1997, p. 40; Steven Schlossman, Goul Zellman, and Richard Shavelson, "Delinquency Prevention in South Chicago: A Fifty-Year Assessment of the Chicago Area Project," report prepared for the National Institute of Education by the Rand Corporation, May 1984, p. 1; Solomon Kobrin, "The Chicago Area Project: 25 Years of Assessment," *Annals of the American Academy of Political and Social Science,* **332** (1959): 20–29.

65. Terence Dunworth and Gregory Mills, *National Evaluation of Weed and Seed,* NIJ Research in Brief, June 1999.

66. M. Isolina Ferre, "Prevention and Control of Violence through Community Revitalization, Individual Dignity, and Personal Self-Confidence," *Annals of the American Academy of Political and Social Science,* **494** (1987): 27–36.

67. Edwin H. Sutherland, *Principles of Criminology,* 3d ed. (Philadelphia: Lippincott, 1939).

68. William Chambliss, *Boxmen* (New York: Harper & Row, 1972).

69. James F. Short, "Differential Association as a Hypothesis: Problems of Empirical Testing," *Social Problems,* **8** (1960): 14–15.

70. Travis Hirschi, *Causes of Delinquency* (Berkeley: University of California Press, 1969), p. 95.

71. Beth Bjerregaard and Carolyn Smith, "Patterns of Male and Female Gang Membership," working paper no. 13, Rochester Youth Development Study (Albany, N.Y.: Hindelang Criminal Justice Research Center, 1992), p. 20. For contradictory findings, see Mark D. Reed and Pamela Wilcox Roundtree, "Peer Pressure and Adolescent Substance Abuse," *Journal of Quantitative Criminology,* **13** (1997), 143–180. For the relationship of delinquents to their delinquent siblings, see Janet L. Lauritsen, "Sibling Resemblance in Juvenile Delinquency: Findings from the National Youth Survey," *Criminology,* **31** (1993): 387–409.

72. Mark Warr, "Age, Peers, and Delinquency," *Criminology,* **31** (1993): 17–40.

73. Charles Tittle, *Sanctions and Social Deviance* (New York: Praeger, 1980).

74. Clayton A. Hartjen, *Crime and Criminalization* (New York: Praeger, 1974), p. 51.

75. Ross L. Matsueda, "The Current State of Differential Association," *Crime and Delinquency,* **34** (1988): 277–306; Craig Reinarman and Jeffrey Fagan, "Social Organization and Differential Association: A Research Note from a Longitudinal Study of Violent Juvenile Offenders," *Crime and Delinquency,* **34** (1988): 307–327.

76. Susan Chira, "A Program That Works for Teen-Age Mothers," *New York Times,* Apr. 28, 1993, p. A12.

77. Fox Butterfield, "Programs Seek to Stop Trouble before It Starts," *New York Times*, Dec. 30, 1994, p. A25.

78. Thorsten Sellin, *Culture, Conflict and Crime*, Bulletin 41 (New York: Social Science Research Council, 1938); Avison and Loring, "Population Diversity and Cross-National Homicide"; Mark R. Pogrebin and Eric D. Poole, "Culture Conflict and Crime in the Korean-American Community," *Criminal Justice Policy Review*, **4** (1990): 69–78; Ira Sommers, Jeffrey Fagan, and Deborah Baskin, "The Influences of Acculturation and Familism on Puerto Rican Delinquency," *Justice Quarterly*, **11** (1994): 207–228.

CHAPTER 6

1. Federal Bureau of Investigation, "The MS-13 Threat: A National Assessment" available at www.fbi.gov/page2/jan08/ms13_011408.html.

2. Excerpts from *2011 National Gang Threat Assessment* (Washington, D.C.: Bureau of Justice Assistance, 2012), available at: http://www.fbi.gov/stats-servicas/publications/2011_national_gang_threat_assessment.

3. Albert K. Cohen, *Delinquent Boys: The Culture of the Gang* (Glencoe, Ill.: Free Press, 1955).

4. For example, James F. Short Jr. and Fred L. Strodtbeck, *Group Process and Gang Delinquency* (Chicago: University of Chicago Press, 1965).

5. Kenneth Polk and Walter B. Schafer, eds., *School and Delinquency* (Englewood Cliffs, N.J.: Prentice-Hall, 1972); Alexander Liazos, "School, Alienation, and Delinquency," *Crime and Delinquency*, **24** (1978): 355–370.

6. Travis Hirschi, *Causes of Delinquency* (Berkeley: University of California Press, 1969).

7. Delbert S. Elliott and Harwin L. Voss, *Delinquency and Dropout* (Lexington, Mass.: Lexington Books, 1974).

8. G. Roger Jarjoura, "Dropping Out of School Enhances Delinquent Involvement? Results from a Large-Scale National Probability Sample," *Criminology*, **31** (1993): 149–172.

9. Albert J. Reiss and Albert L. Rhodes, "Deprivation and Delinquent Behavior," *Sociological Quarterly*, **4** (1963): 135–149.

10. Marvin Krohn, R. L. Akers, M. J. Radosevich, and L. Lanza-Kaduce, "Social Status and Deviance," *Criminology*, **18** (1980): 303–318.

11. Mark Warr, "Organization and Instigation in Delinquent Groups," *Criminology*, **34** (1996): 11–37.

12. David F. Greenberg, "Delinquency and the Age Structure of Society," *Contemporary Crisis*, **1** (1977): 189–223.

13. John I. Kitsuse and David C. Dietrick, "Delinquent Boys: A Critique," *American Sociological Review*, **24** (1959): 208–215.

14. David J. Bordua, "Delinquent Subcultures: Sociological Interpretations of Gang Delinquency," *Annals of the American Academy of Political and Social Science*, **338** (1961): 119–136.

15. Albert K. Cohen and James F. Short Jr., "Research in Delinquent Subcultures," *Journal of Social Issues*, **14** (1958): 20–37.

16. Richard A. Cloward and Lloyd E. Ohlin, *Delinquency and Opportunity* (Glencoe, Ill.: Free Press, 1960).

17. Clifford R. Shaw, *The Jack-Roller* (Chicago: University of Chicago Press, 1930), p. 54.

18. James R. David, *Street Gangs* (Dubuque, Iowa: Kendall/Hunt, 1982).

19. Hirschi, *Causes of Delinquency*, p. 227.

20. John M. Hagedorn, "Homeboys, Dope Fiends, Legits, and New Jacks," *Criminology*, **32** (1994): 197–219.

21. James Short, Ramon Rivera, and Ray Tennyson, "Perceived Opportunities, Gang Membership, and Delinquency," *American Sociological Review*, **30** (1965): 56–57.

22. Lecture by Ko-lin Chin, Rutgers University, Nov. 22, 1993. See also K. Chin, *Chinese Subculture and Criminality: Nontraditional Crime Groups in America*, Criminology and Penology Series, vol. 29 (Westport, Conn.: Greenwood, 1990); Mark Warr, "Organization and Instigation in Delinquent Groups," *Criminology*, **34** (1996): 11–37; and Kevin M. Thompson, David Brownfield, and Ann Marie Sorenson, "Specialization Patterns of Gang and Nongang Offending: A Latent Structure Analysis," *Journal of Gang Research*, **3** (1996): 25–35.

23. Finn-Aage Esbensen and David Huizinga, "Gangs, Drugs, and Delinquency in a Survey of Urban Youth," *Criminology*, **31** (1993): 565–587; Terence P. Thornberry, Marvin D. Krohn, Alan J. Lizotte, and Deborah Chard-Wierschem, "The Role of Juvenile Gangs in Facilitating Delinquent Behavior," *Journal of Research in Crime and Delinquency*, **30** (1993): 55–87; Malcolm Klein, Cheryl L. Maxson, and Lea C. Cunningham, "'Crack,' Street Gangs, and Violence," *Criminology*, **29** (1991): 623–650.

24. K. Chin and J. Fagan, "Social Order and Gang Formation in Chinatown," in *Advances in Criminological Theory*, vol. 6, eds. Freda Adler and William S. Laufer (New Brunswick, N.J.: Transaction, 1994).

25. George W. Knop, Edward D. Tromanhauser, James G. Houston, et al., *The Economics of Gang Life: A Task Force Report of the National Gang Crime Research Center* (Chicago: National Crime Research Center, 1995).

26. Ibid., p. ii.

27. John P. Hoffman and Timothy Ireland, "Cloward and Ohlin's Strain Theory Reexamined: An Elaborated Theoretical Model," in *Advances in Criminological Theory*, vol. 6.

28. Marvin E. Wolfgang and Franco Ferracuti, *The Subculture of Violence* (London: Tavistock, 1967).

29. Elijah Anderson, *Code of the Street* (New York: W. W. Norton & Company, 1999); T. Brezina, Robert Agnew, and F. T. Cullen, "The Code of the Street: A Quantitative Assessment of Elijah Anderson's Subculture of Violence Thesis and Its Contribution to Youth Violence Research," *Youth Violence and Juvenile Justice*, **2(4)** (2004): 303–328; Liqun Cao, Anthony Adams, and Vickie J. Jensen, "A Test of the Black Subculture of Violence Thesis: A Research Note," *Criminology*, **35(2)** (1997): 367–379; Lance Hannon, "Race, Victim-Precipitated Homicide, and the Subculture of Violence Thesis," *Social Science Journal*, **41** (2004): 115–121; Howard S. Erlanger, "The Empirical Status of the Subcultures of Violence Thesis," *Social Problems*, **22** (1974): 280–292. For the relationship of the thesis to routine activities, see Leslie W. Kennedy and Stephen W. Baron, "Routine Activities and a Subculture of Violence: A Study on the Street," *Journal of Research in Crime and Delinquency*, **30** (1993): 88–112. For a look at regional differences in punitiveness, see Marian J. Borg, "The Southern Subculture of Punitiveness? Regional Variation in Support for Capital Punishment," *Journal of Research in Crime and Delinquency*, **34** (1997): 25–45.

30. William G. Doerner, "A Regional Analysis of Homicide Rates in the United States," *Criminology*, **13** (1975): 90–101.

31. Jo Dixon and Alan J. Lizotte, "Gun Ownership and the Southern Subculture of Violence," *American Journal of Sociology*, **93** (1987): 383–405.

69. Jackson Toby, "The New Criminology Is the Old Sentimentality," *Criminology*, **16** (1979): 516–526; Jim Thomas and Aogan O'Maolchatha, "Reassessing the Critical Metaphor: An Optimistic Revisionist View," *Justice Quarterly*, **6** (1989): 143–171; David Brown and Russell Hogg, "Essentialism, Radical Criminology and Left Realism," *Australian and New Zealand Journal of Criminology*, **25** (1992): 195–230.

70. Carl B. Klockars, "The Contemporary Crises of Marxist Criminology," *Criminology*, **16** (1979): 477–515.

71. Ibid.

72. Richard F. Sparks, "A Critique of Marxist Criminology," in *Crime and Justice: An Annual Review of Research*, ed. Norval Morris and Michael Tonry (Chicago: University of Chicago Press, 1980), p. 159.

73. Milton Mankoff, "On the Responsibility of Marxist Criminology: A Reply to Quinney," *Contemporary Crisis*, **2** (1978): 293–301.

74. Austin T. Turk, "Analyzing Official Deviance: For Nonpartisan Conflict Analysis in Criminology," in *Radical Criminology: The Coming Crisis*, ed. James A. Inciardi (Beverly Hills, Calif.: Sage, 1980), pp. 78–91. See also Sykes, "The Rise of Critical Criminology," p. 212.

75. Philip L. Reichel and Andrzej Rzeplinski, "Student Views of Crime and Criminal Justice in Poland and the United States," *International Journal of Comparative and Applied Criminal Justice*, **13** (1989): 65–81.

76. Quinney, *Class, State, and Crime*, p. 40.

77. R. Weitzer, "Flawed Theory and Method in Studies of Prostitution," *Violence against Women*, **11(7)** (2005): 934–949.

78. J. Raphael and D. Shapiro, "Violence in Indoor Prostitution Venues," *Violence against Women*, **10** (2004): 126–139.

79. M. Farley, "Prostitution: Factsheet on Human Rights Violations," (San Francisco: Prostitution Research and Education, 2000).

80. M. Farley, "Bad for the Body, Bad for the Heart: Prostitution Harms Women Even if Legalized or Decriminalized," *Violence against Women*, **10** (2004): 1087–1125.

81. R. Weitzer, "Flawed Theory and Method in Studies of Prostitution," *Violence against Women*, **11(7)** (2005): 934–949.

82. K. Martin, L. M. Vieraitis and S. Britto, "Gender Equality and Women's Absolute Status: A Test of the Feminist Models of Rape," *Violence against Women*, **12(4)** (2006): 321–339.

83. Martin D. Schwartz and Walter S. DeKeseredy, "Left Realist Criminology: Strengths, Weaknesses and the Feminist Critique," *Crime, Law and Social Change*, **15** (1991): 51–72; John Lowman and Brian D. MacLean, eds., *Realist Criminology: Crime Control and Policing in the 1990s* (Ontario: University of Toronto Press, 1990); Walter S. DeKeseredy and Martin D. Schwartz, "British and U.S. Left Realism: A Critical Comparison," *International Journal of Offender Therapy and Comparative Criminology*, **35** (1991): 248–262.

84. Jock Young, "Ten Points of Realism," in *Rethinking Criminology: The Realist Debate*, ed. J. Young and R. Matthews (London: Sage, 1992), pp. 24–28.

85. Pepinsky and Quinney, eds., *Criminology as Peace-Making*; Richard Quinney, "Socialist Humanism and the Problem of Crime," *Crime, Law and Social Change*, **23** (1995): 147–156; Robert Elias et al., Special Issue, "Declaring Peace on Crime," *Peace Review: A Transnational Quarterly*, **6** (1994): 131–254.

86. B. A. Arrigo and Y. Takahashi, "Recommunalization of the Disenfranchised: A Theoretical and Critical Criminological Inquiry," *Theoretical Criminology*, **10(3)** (2006): 307–336.

CHAPTER 9

1. Bruce Golding, "Jeweler Held in Botched Heist," *New York Post*, December 9, 2008, p. 7.

2. Richard Winton, "Car-to-Car Shooting Leaves Woman Dead," *Los Angeles Times*, December 9, 2008, p. B2.

3. Theodore Decker, "Rapist Blamed for 7th Attack: Nov. 2 Crime Took Place Near Site of Oct. 5 Assault," *Columbus Dispatch*, November 12, 2008.

4. Paul J. Brantingham and Patricia L. Brantingham, "Introduction: The Dimensions of Crime," in *Environmental Criminology*, ed. Brantingham and Brantingham (Prospect Heights, Ill.: Waveland, 1991), p. 8. For a discussion on the application of environmental criminology to urban planning, see Paul J. Brantingham and Patricia L. Brantingham, "Environmental Criminology: From Theory to Urban Planning Practice," *Studies on Crime and Crime Prevention*, **7** (1998): 31–60.

5. André M. Guerry, *Essai sur la Statistique Morale de la France* (Paris: Crochard, 1833).

6. Adolphe Quételet, *A Treatise on Man* (Edinburgh: Chambers, 1842), reprinted excerpt Adolphe Quételet, "Of the Development of the Propensity to Crime," in *Criminological Perspectives: A Reader*, ed. John Muncie, Eugene McLaughlin, and Mary Langan (Thousand Oaks, Calif.: Sage, 1996), p. 19.

7. Ronald Clarke and Derek Cornish, "Modeling Offenders' Decisions: A Framework for Research and Policy," in *Crime and Justice*, vol. 6, ed. Michael Tonry and Norval Morris (Chicago: University of Chicago Press, 1985), pp. 147–185; Derek B. Cornish and Ronald V. Clarke, eds., *The Reasoning Criminal* (New York: Springer Verlag, 1986).

8. Jeremy Bentham, *On the Principles and Morals of Legislation* (New York: Kegan Paul, 1789) [reprinted 1948]; Gary S. Becker, "Crime and Punishment: An Economic Approach," *Journal of Political Economy*, **76** (1968): 169–217.

9. David Weisburd, Tomer Enat, and Matt Kowalski, "The Miracle of the Cells: An Experimental Study of Interventions to Increase Payment of Court-Ordered Financial Obligations," *Criminology & Public Policy*, **7(1)** (2008): 5–8.

10. Bradley R. E. Wright, Avshalom Caspi, Terrie E. Moffitt, and Raymond Paternoster, "Does the Perceived Risk of Punishment Deter Criminally-Prone Individuals? Rational Choice, Self-Control, and Crime," *Journal of Research in Crime and Delinquency*, **41** (2004): 180–213.

11. Daniel S. Nagin, "Thoughts on the Broader Implications of the Miracle of the Cells," *Criminology & Public Policy*, **7(1)** (2008): 37–42.

12. Lawrence E. Cohen and Marcus Felson, "Social Change and Crime Rate Trends: A Routine Activity Approach," *American Sociological Review*, **44** (1979): 588–608; Marcus Felson, "Linking Criminal Choices, Routine Activities, Informal Control, and Criminal Outcomes," in *The Reasoning Criminal: Rational Choice Perspectives on Offending*, ed. Derek B. Cornish and Ronald V. Clarke (New York: Springer-Verlag, 1986), pp. 119–128.

13. Marcus Felson, *Crime and Everyday Life: Insights and Implications for Society* (Thousand Oaks, Calif.: Pine Forge Press, 1994), pp. 20–21, 35.

14. Mangai Natarajan, "Telephones as Facilitators of Drug Dealing," paper presented at the Fourth International Seminar on Environmental Criminology and Crime Analysis, July 1995, Cambridge, England; Mangai Natarajan, Ronald V. Clarke and Mathieu Belanger, "Drug Dealing and Pay Phones: The Scope for Intervention," *Security Journal, 7* (1996): pp. 245–251.

15. Lawrence W. Sherman, Patrick R. Gartin, and Michael E. Buerger, "Hot Spots of Predatory Crime: Routine Activities and the Criminology of Place," *Criminology, 27* (1989): 27–55; Ronald V. Clarke and Patricia M. Harris, "A Rational Choice Perspective on the Targets of Automobile Theft," *Criminal Behaviour and Mental Health, 2* (1992): 25–42. See also the following articles in Ronald V. Clarke and Marcus Felson, eds., *Routine Activity and Rational Choice, Advances in Criminological Theory,* vol. 5 (New Brunswick, N.J.: Transaction, 1993): Raymond Paternoster and Sally Simpson, "A Rational Choice Theory of Corporate Crime," pp. 37–58; Richard W. Harding, "Gun Use in Crime, Rational Choice, and Social Learning Theory," pp. 85–102; Richard B. Felson, "Predatory and Dispute-Related Violence: A Social Interactionist Approach," pp. 103–125; Nathaniel J. Pallone and James J. Hennessy, "Tinderbox Criminal Violence: Neurogenic Impulsivity, Risk-Taking, and the Phenomenology of Rational Choice," pp. 127–157; Max Taylor, "Rational Choice, Behavior Analysis, and Political Violence," pp. 159–178; Pietro Marongiu and Ronald V. Clarke, "Ransom Kidnapping in Sardinia, Subcultural Theory and Rational Choice," pp. 179–199; Bruce D. Johnson, Mangai Natarajan, and Harry Sanabria, "'Successful' Criminal Careers: Toward an Ethnography within the Rational Choice Perspective," pp. 201–221.

16. George Rengert and John Wasilchick, *Suburban Burglary: A Time and a Place for Everything* (Springfield, Ill.: Charles C Thomas, 1985).

17. Paul F. Cromwell, James N. Olson, and D'Aunn Webster Avary, *Breaking and Entering: An Ethnographic Analysis of Burglary* (Newbury Park, Calif.: Sage, 1991), pp. 45–46.

18. Clarke and Felson, *Routine Activity and Rational Choice;* Richard T. Wright and Scott H. Decker, *Burglars on the Job: Streetlife and Residential Break-Ins* (Boston: Northeastern University Press, 1994), pp. 63–68; Alex Piquero and George F. Rengert, "Studying Deterrence with Active Residential Burglars: A Research Note," *Justice Quarterly, 16* (1999): 451–472.

19. Richard T. Wright and Scott Decker, *Armed Robbers in Action: Stickups and Street Culture* (Boston: Northeastern University Press, 1994). For a feminist analysis of Wright and Decker's ethnographic work on street robbers, see Jody Miller, "Up It Up: Gender and the Accomplishment of Street Robbery," *Criminology, 36* (1998): 37–66.

20. Philip J. Cook, *Robbery in the United States: An Analysis of Recent Trends and Patterns,* U.S. Department of Justice (Washington, D.C.: U.S. Government Printing Office, 1983).

21. Wayland Clifton Jr., *Convenience Store Robbery in Gainesville, Florida* (Gainesville, Fla.: Gainesville Police Department, 1987), p. 15.

22. Cohen and Felson, "Social Change and Crime Rate Trends."

23. Ronald V. Clarke, *Hot Products: Understanding, Anticipating and Reducing Demand for Stolen Goods,* Policing and Reducing Crime Unit, Police Research Series Paper 112 (London: Home Office, 1999). For discussions of what drives shoplifters, see Read Hayes, "Shop Theft: An Analysis of Shoplifter Perceptions and Situational Factors," *Security Journal, 12* (1999): 7–18; and David P. Farrington, "Measuring, Explaining, and Preventing Shoplifting: A Review of British Research," *Security Journal, 12* (1999): 9–28. For details on measuring and preventing crime against retail business, see a special issue of *Security Journal, 7* (1996): 1–75.

24. Bonnie S. Fisher, John J. Sloan, Francis T. Cullen, and Chunmeng Lu, "Crime in the Ivory Tower: The Level and Sources of Student Victimization," *Criminology, 36* (1998): 671–710. For additional research supporting the routine-activity approach, see also Verna A. Henson and William E. Stone, "Campus Crime: A Victimization Study," *Journal of Criminal Justice, 27* (1999): 295–308.

25. Hans von Hentig, "Remarks on the Interaction of Perpetrator and Victim," *Journal of Criminal Law and Criminology, 31* (1941): 303–309.

26. Hans von Hentig, *The Criminal and His Victim* (New Haven, Conn.: Yale University, 1948).

27. See Beniamin Mendelsohn, "The Origin of the Doctrine of Victimology," in *Victimology,* ed. Israel Drapkin and Emilio Viano (Lexington, Mass.: Lexington Books, 1974), pp. 3–4.

28. Frederic Wertham, *The Show of Violence* (Garden City, N.Y.: Country Life Press, 1948), p. 259.

29. Ezzat A. Fattah, "Victims and Victimology: The Facts and the Rhetoric," *International Review of Victimology, 1* (1989): 44–66, at p. 44.

30. Ezzat A. Fattah, "The Rational Choice/Opportunity Perspective as a Vehicle for Integrating Criminological and Victimological Theories," in Clarke and Felson, *Routine Activity and Rational Choice,* pp. 230–231. For an examination of the relationship between lifestyle factors and the victimization of prostitutes, see Charisse Coston and Lee Ross, "Criminal Victimization of Prostitutes: Empirical Support for the Lifestyle/Exposure Model," *Journal of Crime and Justice, 21* (1998): 53–70.

31. Fattah, "Victims and Victimology," p. 54.

32. Michael J. Hindelang, Michael R. Gottfredson, and James Garofalo, *Victims of Personal Crime: An Empirical Foundation for a Theory of Personal Victimization* (Cambridge, Mass.: Ballinger, 1978), p. 245.

33. Ibid., pp. 251–265.

34. Marvin E. Wolfgang, *Patterns in Criminal Homicide* (Philadelphia: University of Pennsylvania Press, 1958), p. 253.

35. James T. Tedeschi and Richard B. Felson, *Violence, Aggression, and Coercive Actions* (Washington, D.C.: American Psychological Association, 1994).

36. Richard B. Felson, "Big People Hit Little People: Sex Differences in Physical Power and Interpersonal Violence," *Criminology, 34* (1996): 433–452.

37. Dan Olweus, "Aggressors and Their Victims: Bullying at School," in *Disruptive Behaviors in Schools,* ed. N. Frude and H. Gault (New York: Wiley, 1984), pp. 57–76.

38. Alan Trickett, Dan Ellingworth, Tim Hope, and Ken Pease, "Crime Victimization in the Eighties: Changes in Area and Regional Inequality," *British Journal of Criminology, 35* (1995): 343–359; Graham Farrell, "Preventing Repeat Victimization," in *Building a Safer Society: Strategic Approaches to Crime Prevention, Crime and Justice,* vol. 19, ed. Michael Tonry and David P. Farrington (Chicago: University of Chicago Press, 1995), pp. 469–534.

39. Dan Ellingworth, Graham Farrell, and Ken Pease, "A Victim Is a Victim Is a Victim? Chronic Victimization in Four Sweeps of the British Crime Survey," *British Journal of Criminology,* **35** (1995): 360–365.

40. William Spelman, "Once Bitten, Then What? Cross-Sectional and Time-Course Explanations of Repeat Victimization," *British Journal of Criminology,* **35** (1995): 366–383.

41. Natalie Polvi, Terah Looman, Charlie Humphries, and Ken Pease, "The Time-Course of Repeat Burglary Victimization," *British Journal of Criminology,* **31** (1991): 411–414.

42. Graham Farrell, Coretta Phillips, and Ken Pease, "Like Taking Candy: Why Does Repeat Victimization Occur?" *British Journal of Criminology,* **35** (1995): 384–399.

43. James P. Lynch, Michael L. Berbaum, and Mike Planty, *Investigating Repeated Victimization with the NCVS* (Washington, D.C.: National Institute of Justice, 1998).

44. Lawrence W. Sherman, Patrick R. Gartin, and Michael E. Buerger, "Hot Spots of Predatory Crime: Routine Activities and the Criminology of Place," *Criminology,* **27** (1989): 27–55.

45. See, e.g., Kate J. Bowers, Shane D. Johnson, and Ken Pease, "Prospective Hot-Spotting: The Future of Crime Mapping?" *British Journal of Criminology,* **44** (2004): 641–658.

46. Dennis W. Roncek and Donald Faggiani, "High Schools and Crime: A Replication," *Sociological Quarterly,* **26** (1985): 491–505.

47. Dennis W. Roncek and Pamela A. Maier, "Bars, Blocks, and Crimes Revisited: Linking the Theory of Routine Activities to the Empiricism of 'Hot Spots,' " *Criminology,* **29** (1991): 725–753.

48. Richard L. Block and Carolyn R. Block, "Space, Place and Crime: Hot Spot Areas and Hot Places of Liquor-Related Crime," in *Crime and Place: Crime Prevention Studies,* vol. 4, ed. John E. Eck and David Weisburd (Monsey, N.Y.: Criminal Justice Press; Washington, D.C.: The Police Executive Research Forum, 1995), pp. 145–183.

49. Per-Olof Wikström, "Preventing City-Center Street Crimes," in Tonry and Farrington, *Building a Safer Society,* vol. 19, pp. 429–468.

50. William Spelman, "Abandoned Buildings: Magnets for Crime?" *Journal of Criminal Justice,* **21** (1993): 481–495.

51. Dennis W. Roncek and Ralph Bell, "Bars, Blocks, and Crimes," *Journal of Environmental Systems,* **11** (1981): 35–47; Roncek and Faggiani, "High Schools and Crime."

52. Jeffrey Peck, G. O. W. Mueller, and Freda Adler, "The Vulnerability of Ports and Marinas to Vessel and Equipment Theft," *Security Journal,* **5** (1994): 146–153.

53. David Weisburd and Lorraine Green with Frank Gajewski and Charles Bellucci, Jersey City Police Department, "Defining the Street Level Drug Market," in *Drugs and Crime: Evaluating Public Policy Initiatives,* ed. Doris Layton MacKenzie and Craig Uchida (Newbury Park, Calif.: Sage, 1994), pp. 61–76. For a discussion of the role of place managers in controlling drug and disorder problems, see Lorraine Green Mazerolle, Colleen Kadleck, and Jan Roehl, "Controlling Drug and Disorder Problems: The Role of Place Managers," *Criminology,* **36** (1998): 371–404. For an analysis of problem-oriented policing in troubled areas, see Anthony A. Braga, David L. Weisburd, Elin J. Waring, Lorraine Green Mazerolle, William Spelman, and Francis Gajewski, "Problem-Oriented Policing in Violent Crime Places: A Randomized Controlled Experiment," *Criminology,* **37** (1999): 541–580.

54. Lawrence W. Sherman, "Hot Spots of Crime and Criminal Careers of Places," in Eck and Weisburd, *Crime and Place,* vol. 4, pp. 35–52.

55. See Fattah, "The Rational Choice/Opportunity Perspective," in Clarke and Felson, *Routine Activity and Rational Choice,* pp. 225–258.

56. James R. Lasley, "Drinking Routines/Lifestyles and Predatory Victimization: A Causal Analysis," *Justice Quarterly,* **6** (1989): 529–542.

57. Martin D. Schwartz and Victoria L. Pitts, "Exploring a Feminist Routine Activities Approach to Explaining Sexual Assault," *Justice Quarterly,* **12** (1995): 9–31.

58. Robert F. Meier and Terance D. Miethe, "Understanding Theories of Criminal Victimization," in *Crime and Justice: A Review of Research,* vol. 17, ed. Michael Tonry (Chicago: University of Chicago Press, 1993), pp. 459–499; Richard Titus, "Bringing Crime Victims Back into Routine Activities Theory/Research," paper presented at Fourth International Seminar on Environmental Criminology and Crime Analysis, July 1995, Cambridge, England.

59. C. Ray Jeffery, *Crime Prevention through Environmental Design* (Beverly Hills, Calif.: Sage, 1971).

60. Oscar Newman, *Defensible Space: Crime Prevention through Urban Design* (New York: Macmillan, 1972).

61. Ronald V. Clarke, "Introduction," in *Situational Crime Prevention: Successful Case Studies,* ed. Ronald V. Clarke (New York: Harrow and Heston, 1992), pp. 3–36.

62. Ronald V. Clarke and Ross Homel, "A Revised Classification of Situational Crime Prevention Techniques," in *Crime Prevention at a Crossroads,* ed. Steven P. Lab (Cincinnati: Anderson, 1997). For a discussion of precipitating factors and opportunity, see Richard Wortley, "A Two-Stage Model of Situational Crime Prevention," *Studies on Crime and Crime Prevention,* **7** (1998): 173–188.

63. See Gresham M. Sykes and David Matza, "Techniques of Neutralization: A Theory of Delinquency," *American Sociological Review,* **22** (1957): 664–670; Harold G. Grasmick and Robert J. Bursik, "Conscience, Significant Others, and Rational Choice," *Law and Society Review,* **34** (1990): 837–861; and John Braithwaite, *Crime, Shame and Reintegration* (Cambridge: Cambridge University, 1989).

64. Clifford D. Shearing and Phillip C. Stenning, "From the Panopticon to Disney World: The Development of Discipline," in *Perspectives in Criminal Law: Essays in Honour of John L. J. Edwards,* ed. Anthony N. Doob and Edward L. Greenspan (Aurora: Canada Law Book, 1984), pp. 335–349.

65. Kim Hazelbaker, "Insurance Industry Analyses and the Prevention of Motor Vehicle Theft," paper presented at the Business and Crime Prevention Conference, an International Seminar Sponsored by the National Institute of Justice and Rutgers, State University of New Jersey, New Brunswick, N.J., 1996.

66. Ronald D. Hunter and C. Ray Jeffery, "Preventing Convenience Store Robbery through Environmental Design," in Clarke, *Situational Crime Prevention,* pp. 194–204. See also Lisa C. Bellamy, "Situational Crime Prevention and Convenience Store Robbery," *Security Journal,* **7** (1996): 41–52.

67. All information for this section abstracted from Mary S. Smith, *Crime Prevention through Environmental Design in Parking Facilities,* Research in Brief, for

National Institute of Justice (Washington, D.C.: U.S. Government Printing Office, 1996).

68. Ronald V. Clarke, "Situational Prevention, Criminology and Social Values," in *Ethical and Social Perspectives on Situational Crime Prevention*, eds. A. von Hirsch, D. Garland, and A. Wakefield (Portland, Ore.: Hart Publishing, 2000).

69. R. A. Duff and S. E. Marshall, "Benefits, Burdens and Responsibilities: Some Ethical Dimensions of Situational Crime Prevention," in von Hirsch et al., *Ethical and Social Perspectives*.

70. Clarke, "Situational Prevention, Criminology and Social Values."

71. Ibid.; Richard Wortley, "Reconsidering the Role of Opportunity in Situational Crime Prevention," in *Rational Choice and Situational Crime Prevention*, eds. G. Newman, R. V. Clarke, and S. G. Shoham (Aldershot, U.K.: Dartmouth, 1997).

72. Ibid.

73. Clarke, "Situational Prevention, Criminology and Social Values."

74. Marcus Felson and Ronald V. Clarke, "The Ethics of Situational Crime Prevention," in Newman et al., *Rational Choice and Situational Crime Prevention*.

75. Clarke, "Situational Prevention, Criminology and Social Values."

76. Felson and Clarke, "The Ethics of Situational Crime Prevention."

77. Duff and Marshall, "Benefits, Burdens and Responsibilities."

78. Felson and Clarke, "The Ethics of Situational Crime Prevention"; Graeme Newman, "Introduction: Towards a Theory of Situational Crime Prevention," in Newman et al., *Rational Choice and Situational Crime Prevention*.

79. David J. Smith, "Changing Situations and Changing People," in von Hirsch et al., *Ethical and Social Perspectives*.

80. Felson and Clarke, "The Ethics of Situational Crime Prevention."

81. David Weisburd et al., *Does Crime Just Move around the Corner? A Study of Displacement and Diffusion in Jersey City, NJ* (Washington, D.C.: National Institute of Justice, 2005).

82. M. Felson and R. V. Clarke, *Opportunity Makes the Thief: Practical Theory for Crime Prevention*. Police Research Series paper 98. (London: Home Office, 1998).

83. Home Office, *A Practical Guide to Crime Prevention for Local Partnerships*. (London: Home Office, 1993).

CHAPTER 10

1. *Crimes of Violence: A Staff Report Submitted to the National Commission on the Causes and Prevention of Violence* (Washington, D.C.: U.S. Government Printing Office, December 1969), vol. 12, p. xxvii; vol. 11, p. 4.

2. G. O. W. Mueller, "Where Murder Begins," *New Hampshire Bar Journal*, **2** (1960): 214–224; G. O. W. Mueller, "On Common Law Mens Rea," *Minnesota Law Review*, **42** (1958): 1043–1104.

3. Wayne R. LaFave and Austin W. Scott, *Handbook on Criminal Law* (St. Paul, Minn.: West, 1972), pp. 572–577.

4. *Commonwealth v. Welansky*, 316 Mass. 383, N.E. 2d 902 (1944), at pp. 906–907. See G. O. W. Mueller, "The Devil May Care—Or Should We? A Reexamination of Criminal Negligence," *Kentucky Law Journal*, **55** (1966–1967): 29–49.

5. See, Uniform Crime Reports, 2010, available at: www.fbi.gov/about-us/cjis/ucr/ucr.

6. James Alan Fox and Alex R. Piquero, "Deadly Demographics: Population Characteristics and Forecasting Homicide Trends," *Crime and Delinquency*, July 2003; Steven D. Levitt, "Understanding Why Crime Fell in the 1990s: Four Factors That Explain the Decline and Six That Do Not," *Journal of Economic Perspectives*, **18** (2004): 163–190. See also James Alan Fox, "Demographics and U.S. Homicide," in *The Crime Drop in America*, ed. A. Blumstein and J. Wallman (Cambridge: Cambridge University Press, 2000), pp. 288–317; Steven D. Levitt, "The Limited Role of Changing Age Structure in Explaining Aggregate Crime Rates," *Criminology*, **37(3)** (1999): 581–597; and Roland Chilton, "Twenty Years of Homicide and Robbery in Chicago: The Impact of the City's Changing Racial and Age Composition," *Journal of Quantitative Criminology*, **3(3)** (1987): 195–214.

7. William Julius Wilson, "Work," *New York Times Magazine*, Aug. 18, 1996, pp. 27, 28.

8. William B. Harvey, "Homicide among Young Black Adults: Life in the Subculture of Exasperation," in *Homicide among Black Americans*, ed. Darnell F. Hawkins (Lanham, Md.: University Press of America, 1986), pp. 153–171. See also Robert L. Hampton, "Family Violence and Homicide in the Black Community: Are They Linked?" in *Violence in the Black Family*, ed. Hampton (Lexington, Mass.: Lexington Books, 1987), pp. 135–156.

9. Coramae Richey Mann, "Black Women Who Kill," in *Homicide among Black Americans*, pp. 157–186.

10. Hans von Hentig, *The Criminal and His Victim* (New Haven, Conn.: Yale University Press, 1948).

11. Marvin E. Wolfgang, *Patterns in Criminal Homicide* (Philadelphia: University of Pennsylvania Press, 1958), p. 253. See also Marvin E. Wolfgang, "A Sociological Analysis of Criminal Homicide," in *Studies in Homicide*, ed. Wolfgang (New York: Harper & Row, 1967), pp. 15–28.

12. Richard B. Felson and Steven F. Messner, "Disentangling the Effects of Gender and Intimacy on Victim Precipitation in Homicide," *Criminology*, **36** (1998): 405–423.

13. Robert A. Silverman and Leslie W. Kennedy, "Relational Distance and Homicide: The Role of the Stranger," *Journal of Criminal Law and Criminology*, **78** (1987): 272–308. See also Nanci Koser Wilson, "Gendered Interaction in Criminal Homicide," in *Homicide: The Victim/Offender Connection*, ed. Anna Victoria Wilson (Cincinnati: Anderson, 1993), pp. 43–62.

14. Margaret A. Zahn and Philip C. Sagi, "Stranger Homicides in Nine American Cities," *Journal of Criminal Law and Criminology*, **78** (1987): 377–397.

15. Uniform Crime Reports, 2010, available at: www.fbi.gov/about/us/cjis/ucr/ucr.

16. Marc Riedel, "Stranger Violence: Perspectives, Issues, and Problems," *Journal of Criminal Law and Criminology*, **78** (1987): 223–258.

17. Kenneth Polk, "Observations on Stranger Homicide," *Journal of Criminal Justice*, **21** (1993): 573–582.

18. Coramae Richey Mann, *When Women Kill* (Albany: State University of New York Press, 1996).

19. See, e.g., Colin Loftin, Karen Kindley, Sandra L. Norris, and Brian Wiersema, "An Attribute Approach to Relationships between Offenders and Victims in Homicide," *Journal of Criminal Law and Criminology*, **78** (1987): 259–271.

Weisburd (Boston: Northeastern University Press, 1992), describe corporations as being given a life and a moral personhood that clouds the distinction between crimes attributable to individuals (hourly employees, line managers, corporate officers, etc.) and those attributable to the corporate entity. See also John Braithwaite and Brent Fisse, "On the Plausibility of Corporate Crime Theory," in *Advances in Criminological Theory,* vol. 2.

31. William S. Laufer, "Corporate Bodies and Guilty Minds," *Emory Law Journal,* **43** (1994): 647, 651–58 (discusses origins of corporate criminal liability).

32. See generally Richard S. Gruner, *Corporate Crime and Sentencing* (Charlottesville, Va.: Michie, 1994).

33. William S. Laufer, "Corporate Liability, Risk Shifting, and the Paradox of Compliance," *Vanderbilt Law Review,* **52** (1999): 1343.

34. William S. Laufer, "Culpability and the Sentencing of Corporations," *Nebraska Law Review,* **71** (1992): 1049.

35. Marshall Clinard, Peter C. Yeager, Jeanne Brissette, David Petrashek, and Elizabeth Harries, *Illegal Corporate Behavior* (Washington, D.C.: U.S. Government Printing Office, 1979).

36. Nearly a century ago, D. R. Richberg asked the question, "Should it not be the effort of all legislation dealing with corporations, to place them as nearly as possible on a plane of equal responsibility with individuals?" D. R. Richberg, "The Imprisonment of the Corporation," *Case and Comment,* **18** (1912): 512–529. Saul M. Pilchen discovered that although notions of corporate criminal culpability have been broadened over the years, initial prosecutions under the federal sentencing guidelines for organizations generally have been limited in scope. Saul M. Pilchen, "When Corporations Commit Crimes: Sentencing under the Federal Organizational Guidelines," *Judicature,* **78** (1995): 202–206. See Daniel R. Fischel and Alan O. Sykes, "Corporate Crime," *Journal of Legal Studies,* **xxv** (1996): 319–349. Ronald L. Dixon believes, "No corporation should be unaware of these statutes or of the theories upon which criminal liability can be established. Corporations must realize that no one is immune from criminal liability, and corporate practices must reflect this fact." Ronald L. Dixon, "Corporate Criminal Liability," in *Corporate Misconduct: The Legal, Societal, and Management Issues,* ed. Margaret P. Spencer and Ronald R. Sims (Westport, Conn.: Quorum Books, 1995). For a British perspective on corporate liability, see "Great Britain, The Law Commission," in *Criminal Law: Involuntary Manslaughter: A Consultation Paper,* no. 135 (London: Her Majesty's Stationery Office, 1994). For a general overview of the corporate crime problem, see Francis T. Cullen, William J. Maakestad, and Gray Cavender, *Corporate Crime under Attack: The Ford Pinto Case and Beyond* (Cincinnati: Anderson, 1987), pp. 37–99.

37. Sherman Antitrust Act, Act of July 2, 1890, c. 647, 26 Stat. 209, 15 U.S.C. §§ 1–7 (1976).

38. Clayton Antitrust Act, Act of Oct. 15, 1914, c. 322, 38 Stat. 730, 15 U.S.C. §§ 12–27 (1976); Robinson-Patman Act, Act of June 19, 1936, c. 592, § 1, 49 Stat. 1526, 15 U.S.C. § 13(a) (1973). See also Brickey, *Corporate Criminal Liability.*

39. Phillip Knightly, Harold Evans, Elaine Potter, and Marjorie Wallace, *Suffer the Children: The Story of Thalidomide* (New York: Viking, 1979).

40. The Ford Pinto case is fully described in Cullen et al., *Corporate Crime under Attack.* For more information on crimes against consumer safety, see Raymond J. Michalowski, *Order, Law, and Crime* (New York: Random House, 1985), pp. 334–340. For a description of corporate greed in its most vile form, see James S. Kunen, *Reckless Disregard: Corporate Greed, Government Indifference, and the Kentucky School Bus Crash* (New York: Simon & Schuster, 1994).

41. For an examination of corporate criminality in the United States and the response of the criminal justice system of America, see Spencer and Sims, *Corporate Misconduct.* See also Russell Mokhiber, *Corporate Crime and Violence: Big Business Power and the Abuse of the Public Trust* (San Francisco: Sierra Club, 1988); Susan P. Shapiro, *Wayward Capitalists: Target of the Securities and Exchange Commission* (New Haven, Conn.: Yale University Press, 1984); M. David Ermann and Richard J. Lundman, *Corporate and Governmental Deviance: Problems of Organizational Behavior in Contemporary Society,* 2d ed. (New York: Oxford University Press, 1982); Cullen et al., *Corporate Crime under Attack;* Knightly et al., *Suffer the Children;* and W. Byron Groves and Graeme Newman, *Punishment and Privilege* (New York: Harrow & Heston, 1986).

42. See Edwin Sutherland, *White Collar Crime* (New York: Dryden, 1949). Sutherland had earlier published articles on the topic, including "White Collar Criminality" and "Is White Collar Crime 'Crime'?" *American Sociological Review,* **10** (1945): 132–139.

43. See Gary E. Reed and Peter Cleary Yeager, "Organizational Offending and Neoclassical Criminology: Challenging the Reach of a General Theory of Crime," *Criminology,* **34** (1996): 357–382; and Clinard and Yeager, *Corporate Crime,* p. 116. See also Peter C. Yeager, "Analysing Corporate Offences: Progress and Prospects," *Research in Corporate Social Performance and Policy,* **8** (1986): 93–120. For similar findings in Canada, see Colin H. Goff and Charles E. Reasons, *Corporate Crime in Canada* (Scarborough, Ontario: Prentice-Hall, 1978).

44. Richard Quinney, *Critique of Legal Order: Crime Control in Capitalist Society* (Boston: Little, Brown, 1974); Richard Quinney, *Class, State, and Crime: On the Theory and Practice of Criminal Justice* (New York: David McKay, 1977); Ian Taylor, Paul Walton, and Jock Young, *The New Criminology: For a Social Theory of Deviance* (London: Routledge & Kegan Paul, 1973); William Chambliss and Robert Seidman, *Law, Order, and Power,* 2d ed. (Reading, Mass.: Addison-Wesley, 1982).

45. James Q. Wilson, *Thinking about Crime* (New York: Basic Books, 1975). For a competing school of thought, see Gilbert Geis, "Criminal Penalties for Corporate Criminals," *Criminal Law Bulletin,* **8** (1972): 377–392; Chamber of Commerce of the United States, *White Collar Crime* (Washington, D.C.: U.S. Government Printing Office, 1974); John Collins Coffee Jr., "Beyond the Shut-Eyed Sentry: Toward a Theoretical View of Corporate Misconduct and an Effective Legal Response," *Virginia Law Review,* **63** (1977): 1099–1278; Gilbert Geis and Robert F. Meier, *White-Collar Crime: Offenses in Business, Politics, and the Professions* (New York: Free Press, 1977); Marshall B. Clinard, *Illegal Corporate Behavior* (Washington, D.C.: U.S. Government Printing Office, 1979); Miriam S. Saxon, *White-Collar Crime: The Problem and the Federal Response* (Report no. 80-84 EPW, Library of Congress, Congressional Research Service, Washington, D.C., Apr. 14, 1980); and Laura S. Schrager and James F. Short Jr., "How Serious a Crime? Perceptions of Organizational and Common

Crimes," in *White-Collar Crime: Theory and Research,* ed. Gilbert Geis and Ezra Stotland (Beverly Hills, Calif.: Sage, 1980). More recent works include James W. Coleman, *The Criminal Elite: The Sociology of White-Collar Crime* (New York: St. Martin's Press, 1989); Laureen Snider, "The Regulatory Dance: Understanding Reform Processes in Corporate Crime," *International Journal of the Sociology of Law,* **19** (1991): 209–236; Kip Schlegel and David Weisburd, *White-Collar Crime: The Parallax View* (Boston: Northeastern University Press, 1993); Michael Tonry and Albert J. Reiss, *Beyond the Law: Crime in Complex Organizations* (Chicago: University of Chicago Press, 1993); and Robert Tillman and Henry Pontell, "Organizations and Fraud in the Savings and Loan Industry," *Social Forces,* **73** (1995): 1439–1463.

46. Patsy Klaus and Carol Kalish, *The Severity of Crime,* Bureau of Justice Statistics Bulletin NCJ-92326 (Washington, D.C.: U.S. Government Printing Office, 1984). See also Schrager and Short, "How Serious a Crime?"; Francis Cullen, B. Link, and C. Polanzi, "The Seriousness of Crime Revisited," *Criminology,* **20** (1982): 83–102; Francis Cullen, R. Mathers, G. Clark, and J. Cullen, "Public Support for Punishing White Collar Crime: Blaming the Victim Revisited," *Journal of Criminal Justice,* **11** (1983): 481–493; and Richard Sparks, Hazel G. Genn, and David Dodd, *Surveying Victims* (New York: Wiley, 1977).

47. Mark A. Cohen, "Environmental Crime and Punishment: Legal/Economic Theory and Empirical Evidence on Enforcement of Federal Environmental Statutes," *Journal of Criminal Law and Criminology,* **82** (1992): 1054–1108. See, for an early treatment, Timothy R. Young, "Criminal Liability under the Refuse Act of 1899 and the Refuse Act Permit Program," *Journal of Criminal Law, Criminology and Police Science,* **63** (1972): 366–376. For a global perspective on the prevention of environmental crimes, see Boon Khoo Hui, Prathan Watanavanich, Edgar Aglipay, et al., *Effective Countermeasures against Crimes Related to Urbanization and Industrialization: Urban Crime, Juvenile Delinquency and Environmental Crime* (Tokyo: Report for 1993 and Resource Material Series no. 45, UNAFEI, 1994).

48. Clinard and Yeager, *Corporate Crime,* p. 92, citing *New York Times* survey of July 15, 1979.

49. Gerhard O. W. Mueller, "Offenses against the Environment and Their Prevention: An International Appraisal," *Annals of the American Academy of Political and Social Science,* **444** (1979): 56–66.

50. 33 U.S.C. § 1251 (2001).

51. *United States v. Darling Int'l Inc.,* No. CR 4-96-162 (D. Minn. July 10, 1997) (factual basis statement, plea agreement, and sentencing stipulations on file with author); see also Barry Shanoff, "Company Incriminates Employees: Darling International." *World Wastes* **40** (1997): 64, 65 ("The Darling case is part of a pattern throughout the country. Companies under scrutiny are winning leniency for themselves by 'giving up' their employees."); Tom Meersman, "Company Fined $4 Million for Polluting," *Star Tribune,* Dec. 17, 1996, p. 1B ("[S]ome of the most serious charges resulted from the company 'blowing the whistle on itself.'"); and Dean Starkman, "Pollution Case Highlights Trend to Let Employees Take the Rap," *The Wall Street Journal,* Oct. 9, 1997, p. B10 ("What happened in the Darling case is being repeated across the country. Corporations under government investigation are increasingly turning on their employees to win leniency for themselves.")

52. Defendant's Sentencing Memorandum, at 8–9 (on file with author).

53. Mueller, "Offenses against the Environment," p. 60.

54. Ryuichi Hirano, "The Criminal Law Protection of Environment: General Report," Tenth International Congress of Comparative Law, Budapest, 1978. For a discussion of the problems of multinational corporations operating in developing countries, see Richard Schaffer, Beverly Earle, and Filiberto Agusti, *International Business Law and Its Environment,* 2d ed. (St. Paul, Minn.: West, 1993). For a discussion of corporate crime in Japan, see Harold R. Kerbo and Mariko Inoue, "Japanese Social Structure and White Collar Crime: Recruit Cosmos and Beyond," *Deviant Behavior,* **11** (1990): 139–154.

55. Kerbo and Inoue, "Japanese Social Structure and White Collar Crime."

56. John Braithwaite, "Challenging Just Deserts: Punishing White-Collar Criminals," *Journal of Criminal Law and Criminology,* **73** (1982): 723–763; Stanton Wheeler, David Weisburd, and Nancy Boden, "Sentencing the White-Collar Offender," *American Sociological Review,* **47** (1982): 641–659. For a thoughtful analysis of corporate illegality, see Nancy Frank and Michael Lombness, *Corporate Illegality and Regulatory Justice* (Cincinnati: Anderson, 1988); Kip Schlegel, *Just Deserts for Corporate Criminals* (Boston: Northeastern University Press, 1990); and John C. Coffee Jr., Mark A. Cohen, Jonathan R. Macey, et al., "A National Conference on Sentencing of the Corporation," *Boston University Law Review,* **71** (1991): 189–453.

57. Sally S. Simpson and Christopher S. Koper, "Deterring Corporate Crime," *Criminology,* **30** (1992): 347–375; Genevra Richardson, *Policing Pollution: A Study of Regulation and Enforcement* (Oxford: Clarendon, 1982); Albert J. Reiss and Albert D. Biderman, *Data Sources on White-Collar Law-Breaking* (Washington, D.C.: National Institute of Justice, 1980); Susan Shapiro, "Detecting Illegalities: A Perspective on the Control of Securities Violations," Ph.D. dissertation, Yale University (University Microfilms), 1980. See also Brian Widlake, *Serious Fraud Office* (London: Little, Brown, 1995).

58. Dan Magnuson, ed., *Economic Crime: Programs for Future Research* (Stockholm: National Council for Crime Prevention, 1985); Michael L. Benson, Francis T. Cullen, and William A. Maakestad, *Local Prosecutors and Corporate Crime: Final Report* (Washington, D.C.: National Institute of Justice, 1991); Michael L. Benson, Francis T. Cullen, and William J. Maakestad, "Local Prosecutors and Corporate Crime," *Crime and Delinquency,* **36** (1990): 356–372.

CHAPTER 13

1. Dawn Turner Trice, Life after 25 years of prostitution: After 25 years in prostitution, woman helps others escape sex trade, Chicago Tribune, March 14, 2011.

2. Carmen Sesin, "Caring for 'drug mules' who perish on the job," MSNBC, May 25, 2004; available at http://www.msnbc.msn.com/id/5050399/.

3. Arthur Santana, "For Liz, a Heroin User, Time Is Running Out—Health Officials Estimate 15,000 Addicts in King County," *Seattle Times,* July 12, 1999, p. B1.

4. David Heinzmann, "Violence No Stranger Where Boy Shot; 4-Year-Old Victim of Gun Battle in Good Condition," *Chicago Tribune,* Oct. 9, 1999, p. 5. See also Robert C. Davis and Arthur J. Lurigio, *Fighting Back: Neighborhood Antidrug Strategies* (Thousand Oaks, Calif.: Sage, 1996); Bureau of Justice Statistics, *Guns*

Used in Crime (Washington, D.C.: U.S. Department of Justice, 1995); and Susan J. Popkin, Lynn M. Olson, Arthur J. Lurigio, et al., "Sweeping Out Drugs and Crime: Residents' Views of the Chicago Housing Authority's Public Housing Drug Elimination Program," *Journal of Research in Crime and Delinquency,* **41** (1995): 73–99.

5. Mark D. Merlin, *On the Trail of the Ancient Opium Poppy* (Rutherford, N.J.: Fairleigh Dickinson University Press, 1984). For a historic account of alcohol consumption, see Harvey A. Siegal and James A. Inciardi, "A Brief History of Alcohol," in *The American Drug Scene: An Anthology,* ed. James A. Inciardi and Karen McElrath (Los Angeles: Roxbury, 1995).

6. Howard Abadinsky, *Drug Abuse: An Introduction* (Chicago: Nelson Hall, 1989), pp. 30–31, 54. For the medicinal benefits of marijuana, see Lester Grinspoon and James Bakalar, "Marijuana: The Forbidden Medicine," in Inciardi and McElrath, *The American Drug Scene.*

7. Michael D. Lyman, *Narcotics and Crime Control* (Springfield, Ill.: Charles C Thomas, 1987), p. 8. See also F. E. Oliver, "The Use and Abuse of Opium," in *Yesterday's Addicts: American Society and Drug Abuse, 1865–1920,* ed. H. Wayne Morgan (Norman: University of Oklahoma Press, 1974).

8. W. Z. Guggenheim, "Heroin: History and Pharmacology," *International Journal of the Addictions,* **2** (1967): 328. For a history of heroin use in New York City, from just after the turn of the twentieth century into the late 1960s, see Edward Preble and John J. Casey, "Taking Care of Business: The Heroin Addict's Life on the Street," *International Journal of the Addictions,* **4** (1969): 1–24.

9. Abadinsky, *Drug Abuse,* p. 52.

10. Ibid., p. 56.

11. Lyman, *Narcotics and Crime Control,* p. 10.

12. Public Law 100-690, of Nov. 18, 1988, 102 Stat. 4187.

13. *2010 National Survey on Drug Use and Health: National Findings* (Washington, D.C.: Department of Health and Human Services, 2011).

14. Lisa Maher, Eloise Dunlap, Bruce D. Johnson, and Ansley Hamid, "Gender, Power, and Alternative Living Arrangements in the Inner-City Crack Culture," *Journal of Research in Crime and Delinquency,* **33** (1996): 181–205; H. Virginia McCoy, Christine Miles, and James A. Inciardi, "Survival Sex: Inner-City Women and Crack-Cocaine," in Inciardi and McElrath, *The American Drug Scene;* Jody Miller, "Gender and Power on the Streets: Street Prostitution in the Era of Crack Cocaine," *Journal of Contemporary Ethnography,* **23** (1995): 427–452; Ann Sorenson and David Brownfield, "Adolescent Drug Use and a General Theory of Crime: An Analysis of a Theoretical Integration," *Canadian Journal of Criminology,* **37** (1995): 19–37. For a summary of psychiatric approaches, see Marie Nyswander, *The Drug Addict as a Patient* (New York: Grune & Stratton, 1956), chap. 4.

15. Richard Cloward and Lloyd Ohlin, *Delinquency and Opportunity* (New York: Free Press, 1960), pp. 178–186. See also Jeffrey A. Fagan, "The Social Organization of Drug Use and Drug Dealing among Urban Gangs," *Criminology,* **27** (1989): 633–669. See also Marcia R. Chaiken, *Identifying and Responding to New Forms of Drug Abuse: Lessons Learned from "Crack" and "Ice"* (Washington, D.C.: National Institute of Justice, 1993).

16. D. F. Musto, "The History of Legislative Control over Opium, Cocaine, and Their Derivatives," in *Dealing with Drugs,* ed. Ronald Hamowy (Lexington, Mass.: Lexington Books, 1987), pp. 37–73.

17. Marsha Rosenbaum, *Women on Heroin* (New Brunswick, N.J.: Rutgers University Press, 1981), pp. 14–15; Jeannette Covington, "Theoretical Explanations of Race Differences in Heroin Use," in *Advances in Criminological Theory,* vol. 2, ed. William S. Laufer and Freda Adler (New Brunswick, N.J.: Transaction). See also U.S. Senate Judiciary Committee, Subcommittee to Investigate Juvenile Delinquency, *The Global Connection: Heroin Entrepreneurs. Hearings, July 28 and August 5, 1976* (Washington, D.C.: U.S. Government Printing Office, 1976).

18. Freda Adler, Arthur D. Moffett, Frederick G. Glaser, John C. Ball, and Diana Horwitz, *A Systems Approach to Drug Treatment* (Philadelphia: Dorrance, 1974).

19. Erich Goode, *Drugs in American Society* (New York: Basic Books, 1972). See also Ned Polsky, *Hustlers, Beats, and Others* (Chicago: Aldine, 1967).

20. Norman E. Zinberg, "The Use and Misuse of Intoxicants: Factors in the Development of Controlled Abuse," in Hamowy, *Dealing with Drugs,* p. 262.

21. Abadinsky, *Drug Abuse,* p. 53. See also, as an early treatment, Hope R. Victor, Jan Carl Grossman, and Russell Eisenman, "Openness to Experience and Marijuana Use in High School Students," *Journal of Consulting and Clinical Psychology,* **41** (1973): 78–85; U.S. Narcotics and Dangerous Drugs Bureau, *Marijuana: An Analysis of Use, Distribution and Control* (Washington, D.C.: U.S. Government Printing Office, 1971); California Department of Public Health and Welfare, Research and Statistics Section, *Five Mind-Altering Drugs: The Use of Alcoholic Beverages, Amphetamines, LSD, Marijuana, and Tobacco, Reported by High School and Junior High School Students, San Mateo County, California, Two Comparable Surveys, 1968 and 1969* (San Mateo: California Department of Public Health, 1969); Erich Goode, "Multiple Drug Use among Marijuana Smokers," *Social Problems,* **17** (1969): 48–64.

22. Bruce A. Jacobs, "Crack Dealers' Apprehension Avoidance Techniques: A Case of Restrictive Deterrence," *Justice Quarterly,* **13** (1996): 359–381; Bruce A. Jacobs, "Crack Dealers and Restrictive Deterrences: Identifying Narcs," *Criminology,* **34** (1996): 409–431; Bruce D. Johnson, Andrew Golub, and Jeffrey Fagan, "Careers in Crack, Drug Use, Drug Distribution, and Nondrug Criminality," *Journal of Crime and Delinquency,* **41** (1995): 275–295; Abadinsky, *Drug Abuse,* p. 83. See also Jeffrey A. Fagan, "Initiation into Crack and Powdered Cocaine: A Tale of Two Epidemics," *Contemporary Drug Problems,* **16** (1989): 579–618; Jeffrey A. Fagan, Joseph G. Weis, and Y. T. Cheng, "Drug Use and Delinquency among Inner City Youth," *Journal of Drug Issues,* **20** (1990): 349–400; James A. Inciardi et al., "The Crack Epidemic Revisited," *Journal of Psychoactive Drugs,* **24** (1992): 305–416; and B. D. Johnson, M. Natarajan, E. Dunlap, and E. Elmoghazy, "Crack Abusers and Noncrack Abusers: A Comparison of Drug Use, Drug Sales, and Nondrug Criminality," *Journal of Drug Issues,* **24** (1994): 117–141. Smoking crack is certainly not limited to the inner cities of America. For a description of crack use in the tropical paradise of Hawaii, see Gordon James Knowles, "Dealing Crack Cocaine: A View from the Streets of Honolulu," *The FBI Law Enforcement Bulletin,* July 1996, pp. 1–7.

23. Michael Marriott, "Potent Crack Blend on the Streets Lures a New Generation to Heroin," *New York Times,* July 13, 1989, pp. A1, B3.

24. James Inciardi, "Heroin Use and Street Crime," *Crime and Delinquency,* **25** (1979): 335–346; Bruce D. Johnson, Paul J. Goldstein, Edward Preble, James Schmeidler, Douglas S. Lyston, Barry Spunt, and Thomas Miller, *Taking Care of Business: The Economics of Crime by Heroin Abusers* (Lexington, Mass.: Heath, 1985); James Inciardi, *The War on Drugs: Heroin, Cocaine, Crime, and Public Policy* (Palo Alto, Calif.: Mayfield, 1986); Eric Wish and Bruce Johnson, "The Impact of Substance Abuse on Criminal Careers," in *Criminal Careers and Career Criminals,* ed. Alfred Blumstein, Jacqueline Cohen, Jeffrey A. Roth, and Christy A. Visher (Washington, D.C.: National Academy Press, 1986), pp. 52–58.

25. Office of National Drug Control Policy, "Drug Facts. Marijuana, 2002" (www.whitehousedrugpolicy.gov/drugfact/marijuana/index.html).

26. For a determination of the causal link between drug use and crime, see Bruce L. Benson and David W. Rasmussen, *Illicit Drugs and Crimes* (Oakland, Calif.: The Independent Institute, 1996); James A. Inciardi, Duane C. McBride, and James E. Rivers, *Drug Control and the Courts* (Thousand Oaks, Calif.: Sage, 1996); Inciardi and McElrath, *The American Drug Scene;* and Sybille M. Guy, Gene M. Smith, and P. M. Bentler, "The Influence of Adolescent Substance Use and Socialization on Deviant Behavior in Young Adulthood," *Criminal Justice and Behavior,* **21** (1994): 236–255.

27. George Speckart and M. Douglas Anglin found that criminal records preceded drug use; see their "Narcotics Use and Crime: An Overview of Recent Research Advances," *Contemporary Drug Problems,* **13** (1986): 741–769, and "Narcotics and Crime: A Causal Modeling Approach," *Journal of Quantitative Criminology,* **2** (1986): 3–28. See also Cheryl Carpenter, Barry Glassner, Bruce D. Johnson, and Julia Loughlin, *Kids, Drugs, and Crime* (Lexington, Mass.: Heath, 1988); and Louise L. Biron, Serge Brochu, and Lyne Desjardins, "The Issue of Drugs and Crime among a Sample of Incarcerated Women," *Deviant Behavior,* **16** (1995): 25–43.

28. James A. Inciardi and Anne E. Pottieger, "Kids, Crack, and Crime," *Journal of Drug Issues,* **21** (1991): 257–270; David N. Nurco, Thomas E. Hanlon, Timothy W. Kinlock, and Karen R. Duszynski, "Differential Criminal Patterns of Narcotics Addicts over an Addiction Career," *Criminology,* **26** (1988): 407–423; M. Douglas Anglin and George Speckart, "Narcotics Use and Crime: A Multisample, Multimethod Analysis," *Criminology,* **26** (1988): 197–233; M. Douglas Anglin and Yining Hser, "Addicted Women and Crime," *Criminology,* **25** (1987): 359–397.

29. Paul Goldstein, "Drugs and Violent Crime," in *Pathways to Criminal Violence,* ed. Neil Alan Weiner and Marvin E. Wolfgang (Newbury Park, Calif.: Sage, 1989), pp. 16–48.

30. Colin McMahon, "Panama's Future Uncertain as Ever; Corruption Persists in Post-Noriega Era," *Chicago Tribune,* Aug. 25, 1996, p. 17.

31. United Nations, "Commission on Narcotic Drugs, Comprehensive Review of the Activities of the United Nations Fund for Drug Abuse Control in 1985," E/CN.7/1986/CRP.4, Feb. 4, 1986. See also Elaine Sciolino, "U.N. Report Links Drugs, Arms, and Terror," *New York Times,* Jan. 12, 1987.

32. John Warner, "Terrorism and Drug Trafficking: A Lethal Partnership," *Security Management,* **28** (1984): 44–46.

See, as an early treatment, U.S. Congress, House Public Health and Environment Subcommittee, *Production and Abuse of Opiates in the Far East* (Washington, D.C.: U.S. Government Printing Office, 1971).

33. For a review of drug enforcement policies aimed directly at the users of illicit narcotics, see Richard Lawrence Miller, *Drug Warriors and Their Prey: From Police Power to Police State* (Westport, Conn.: Praeger, 1996). For a comprehensive guide to state agencies that address drug abuse concerns, see Bureau of Justice Statistics, *State Drug Resources: 1994 National Directory* (Washington, D.C.: U.S. Department of Justice, 1994).

34. James A. Inciardi, *The War on Drugs II: The Continuing Epidemic of Heroin, Cocaine, Crack, Crime, AIDS, and Public Policy* (Mountain View, Calif.: Mayfield, 1992).

35. Even before President Bush's drug initiatives, government agencies recognized the ineffectiveness of narcotic countermeasures during the 1970s; see U.S. Comptroller General, *Gains Made in Controlling Illegal Drugs, Yet the Drug Trade Flourishes* (Washington, D.C.: U.S. Government Printing Office, 1979).

36. See Rae Sibbitt, *The Ilps Methadone Prescribing Project* (London: Home Office, 1996); Paul J. Turnbull, Russell Webster, and Gary Stillwell, *Get It While You Can: An Evaluation of an Early Intervention Project for Arrestees with Alcohol and Drug Problems* (London: Home Office, 1996); Ira Sommers, Deborah R. Baskin, and Jeffrey Fagan, "Getting out of the Life: Crime Desistance by Female Street Offenders," *Deviant Behavior,* **15** (1994): 125–149; and Sandra L. Tunis, *The State of the Art in Jail Drug Treatment Programs* (San Francisco: National Council on Crime and Delinquency, 1994).

37. See Peter Finn and Andrea K. Newlyn, *Miami's "Drug Court,"* National Institute of Justice (Washington, D.C.: U.S. Government Printing Office, 1993), for Dade County; see Christopher S. Wren, "Arizona Finds Cost Savings in Treating Drug Offenders," *New York Times,* Apr. 21, 1999, for Arizona; see also Bureau of Justice Assistance, *Two Special Drug Court Models: Dedicated Drug Treatment vs. Speedy Trial and Differentiated Case Management (DCM)—The Program Concept* (Washington, D.C.: U.S. Government Printing Office, 1998); and Jonathan Alter, "The Buzz on Drugs," *Newsweek,* September 6, 1999, pp. 25–28.

38. Abadinsky, *Drug Abuse,* p. 171.

39. David N. Nurco, Norma Wegner, Philip Stephenson, Abraham Makofsky, and John W. Shaffer, *Ex-Addicts' Self-Help Groups: Potentials and Pitfalls* (New York: Praeger, 1983); Harold I. Hendler and Richard C. Stephens, "The Addict Odyssey: From Experimentation to Addiction," *International Journal of the Addictions,* **12** (1977): pp. 25–42.

40. For a perspective on how corporate America educates employees on the risks of drug abuse, see Mark A. de Bernardo, *What Every Employee Should Know about Drug Abuse* (Washington, D.C.: Institute for a Drug-Free Workplace, 1993); see also Troy Duster, *The Legislation of Morality: Law, Drugs, and Moral Judgment* (New York: Free Press, 1970), p. 192.

41. Dan Waldorf, "Natural Recovery from Opiate Addiction," *Journal of Drug Issues,* **13** (1983): 237–280.

42. See James A. Inciardi, Duane C. McBride, Clyde B. McCoy, et al., "Violence, Street Crime and the Drug Legalization Debate: A Perspective and Commentary on the U.S. Experience," *Studies on Crime and Crime Prevention,* **4** (1995): 105–118; Steven Foy Luper, Curtis Brown, et al., *Drugs, Morality, and the Law* (New York: Garland, 1994); Robert J. MacCoun, James P. Kahan,

(Bloomington: Indiana University Press, 1989), p. 18. See also Franklin Mark Osanka and Sara Lee Johann, "Pornography Contributes to Violence against Women," in Swisher, Wekesser, and Barbour, *Violence against Women*.

85. *Miller v. California*, 413 U.S. 15 (1973). See also Laura Lederer, Richard Delgado, et al., *The Price We Pay: The Case against Racist Speech, Hate Propaganda, and Pornography* (New York: Hill and Wang, 1995).

86. *Pope v. Illinois*, 481 U.S. 497 (1987). See also Adele M. Stan et al., *Debating Sexual Correctness: Pornography, Sexual Harassment, Date Rape, and the Politics of Sexual Equality* (New York: Dell, 1995); Bill Thompson, *Soft Core: Moral Crusades against Pornography in Britain and America* (London: Cassell, 1994); and Catherine Itzen et al., *Pornography: Women, Violence and Civil Liberties* (Oxford: Oxford University Press, 1993).

87. Laura Davis, Marilyn D. McShane, and Frank P. Williams III, "Controlling Computer Access to Pornography: Special Conditions for Sex Offenders," *Federal Probation*, **59** (1995): 43–48; Marty Rimm, "Marketing Pornography on the Information Superhighway: A Survey of 917,410 Images, Descriptions, Short Stories and Animations Downloaded 8.5 Million Times by Consumers in Over 2,000 Cities in Forty Countries, Provinces, and Territories," *Georgetown Law Journal*, **83** (1995): 1849–2008; Great Britain House of Commons, *Computer Pornography* (London: Her Majesty's Stationery Office, 1994). For a perspective on the government's plan to police the Internet's superhighway, see James Aley, "How Not to Help High Tech," *Fortune Magazine*, May 16, 1994, p. 100.

88. Kinsey et al., *Sexual Behavior in the Human Male*.

89. Alfred C. Kinsey, Wardel B. Pomeroy, Clyde E. Martin, and Paul H. Gebhard, *Sexual Behavior in the Human Female* (Philadelphia: Saunders, 1953), p. 453.

90. Morton M. Hunt, *Profiles of Social Research: The Scientific Study of Human Interactions* (New York: Russell Sage Foundation, 1985).

CHAPTER 14

1. R. J. Estes and N. A. Weiner, *The Commercial Sexual Exploitation of Children in the U.S., Canada, and Mexico.* (Philadelphia: University of Pennsylvania, School of Social Work, Center for the Study of Youth Policy, 2002), available at http://www.sp2.upenn.edu/~restes/CSEC_Files/Complete_CSEC_020220.pdf (retrieved June 20, 2008).

2. UNICEF, *Combating Child Trafficking: Handbook for Parliamentarians* (Inter-Parliamentary Union & UNICEF, 2005).

3. Ibid.

4. U. S. Department of State, "The Facts about Child Sex Tourism" (2005), available at http://www.state.gov/documents/organization/51459.pdf (retrieved June 25, 2008).

5. UNICEF, *Combating Child Trafficking.*

6. Piers Beirne and David Nelken, eds., *Issues in Comparative Criminology* (Aldershot, U.K.: Dartmouth, 1997), is a useful anthology of scientific issues in comparative criminology.

7. The term "comparative criminology" appears to have been coined by Sheldon Glueck. See Sheldon Glueck, "Wanted: A Comparative Criminology," in *Ventures in Criminology*, ed. Sheldon Glueck and Eleanor Glueck (London: Tavistock, 1964), pp. 304–322.

8. James O. Finckenauer, *Russian Youth: Law, Deviance and the Pursuit of Freedom* (New Brunswick, N.J.: Transaction, 1995); Nanci Adler, "Planned Economy and Unplanned Criminality: The Soviet Experience," *International Journal of Comparative and Applied Criminal Justice*, **17** (1993): 189–201; Wojciech Cebulak, "White-Collar Crime in Socialism: Myth or Reality?" *International Journal of Comparative and Applied Criminal Justice*, **15** (1991): 109–120; Klaus Sessar, "Crime Rate Trends before and after the End of the German Democratic Republic—Impressions and First Analyses," in *Fear of Crime and Criminal Victimization*, ed. Wolfgang Bilsky, Christian Pfeiffer, and Peter Wetzels (Stuttgart, Germany: Ferdinand Enke Verlag, 1993), pp. 231–244; Louise I. Shelley et al., "East Meets West in Crime," *European Journal on Criminal Policy and Research*, **3** (1995): 7–107. As China is undergoing a transformation, mostly economic, changes in that country are noteworthy. See Yue Ma, "Crime in China: Characteristics, Causes and Control Strategies," *Journal of Comparative and Applied Criminal Justice*, **34** (1994): 54–68.

9. Martin Killias et al., "Cross-Border Crime," *European Journal on Criminal Policy and Research*, **1** (1993): 7–134.

10. William F. McDonald, "The Globalization of Criminology: The New Frontier Is the Frontier," *Transnational Organized Crime*, **1** (1995): 1–12.

11. Piers Beirne and Joan Hill, *Comparative Criminology—An Annotated Bibliography* (New York: Greenwood, 1991), pp. vii–viii.

12. Dae H. Chang, *Criminology: A Cross-Cultural Perspective*, 2 vols. (Durham, N.C.: Carolina Academic Press, 1976); George F. Cole, Stanislaw J. Frankowski, and Marc G. Gertz, *Major Criminal Justice Systems—A Comparative Survey*, 2d ed. (Newbury Park, Calif.: Sage, 1987); Richard J. Terrill, *World Criminal Justice Systems*, 2d ed. (Cincinnati: Anderson, 1985); Robert Heiner, ed., *Criminology—A Cross-Cultural Perspective* (Minneapolis/St. Paul: West, 1996); Obi N. I. Ebbe, ed., *Comparative and International Criminal Justice Systems* (Boston: Butterworth-Heinemann, 1996); Charles B. Fields and Richter H. Moore, eds., *Comparative Criminal Justice: Traditional and Non-traditional Systems of Law and Control* (Prospect Heights, Ill.: Waveland Press, 1996).

13. G. O. W. Mueller, *World Survey on the Availability of Criminal Justice Statistics*, Internet-UNCJIN-ftp238.33.18WSAYL. See also G. O. W. Mueller, "International Criminal Justice: Harnessing the Information Explosion—Coasting down the Electronic Superhighway," *Journal of Criminal Justice Education* 7(2) (Fall 1996): 253–261.

14. Interpol, located in Lyons, France, has published the crime statistics supplied to it by member states since 1951.

15. First survey: 1970–1975, A/32/199; second survey: 1975–1980, A/Conf. 121/18; third survey: 1980–1986, A/Conf. 144/6; fourth survey: 1986–1990, A/Conf. 169/15 and Add. 1; fifth survey (see United Nations, Office on Drugs and Crime, *Global Report on Crime and Justice*, ed. Graeme Newman (New York: Oxford University Press, 1999).

16. World Health Organization, "Homicide Statistics," in *World Health Statistics* (Geneva: World Health Organization, annually).

17. Dane Archer and Rosemary Gartner, *Violence and Crime in Cross-National Perspective* (New Haven, Conn.: Yale University Press, 1984).

18. Richard R. Bennett, *Correlates of Crime: A Study of Nations, 1960–1984* (Ann Arbor, Mich.: Inter-University Consortium for Political and Social Research, 1989).

19. Richard R. Bennett and James P. Lynch, "Does a Difference Make a Difference?" *Criminology*, **28** (1990): 155–182; Carol B. Kalish, *International Crime Rates* (Washington, D.C.: Bureau of Justice Statistics, 1988).

20. Jan J. M. Van Dijk, Pat Mayhew, and Martin Killias, *Experiences of Crime across the World: Key Findings from the 1989 International Crime Survey* (Deventer, Netherlands: Kluwer, 1990); Richard R. Bennett and R. Bruce Wiegand, "Observations on Crime Reporting in a Developing Nation," *Criminology, 32* (1994): 135–148; Ugljesa Zvekic and Anna Albazzi del Frate, eds., *Criminal Victimization in the Developing World* (Rome: United Nations Interregional Crime and Justice Research Institute, 1995); Gail Travis et al., "The International Crime Surveys: Some Methodological Concerns," *Current Issues in Criminal Justice, 6* (1995): 346–361; Van Dijk, Box 0.9 in United Nations, *Global Report on Crime and Justice*, p. 9.

21. Josine Junger-Tas, Gert-Jan Terlouw, and Malcolm W. Klein, *Delinquent Behavior among People in the Western World* (Amsterdam: RDC Ministry of Justice, Kugler Publ., 1994); Junger-Tas, Box 0.10 in United Nations, *Global Report on Crime and Justice*, p. 16.

22. Hermann Mannheim, *Comparative Criminology* (Boston: Houghton Mifflin, 1965).

23. See Jerome L. Neapolitan, *Cross-National Crime—A Research Review and Sourcebook* (Westport, Conn.: Greenwald Press, 1997); Dennis Benamati, Phyllis Schultze, Adam Bouloukos, and Graeme Newman, *Criminal Justice Information: How to Find It, How to Use It* (Phoenix, Ariz.: Onyx Press, 1997); Harry R. Dammer and Philip L. Reichel, eds., *Teaching about Comparative/International Criminal Justice—A Resource Manual* (Highland Heights, N.Y.: Academy of Criminal Justice Sciences, 1997).

24. Elmer H. Johnson, ed., *International Handbook of Contemporary Developments in Criminology*, 2 vols. (Westport, Conn.: Greenwood Press, 1983); George F. Cole, Stanislaw J. Frankowski, and Marc G. Gertz, *Major Criminal Justice Systems—A Comparative Survey*, 2d ed. (Newbury Park, Calif.: Sage, 1987); Richard J. Terrill, *World Criminal Justice Systems: A Survey* (Cincinnati: Anderson, 1984); Obi N. Ignatius Ebbe, *Comparative and International Criminal Justice Systems* (Boston: Butterworth, 1996); Philip L. Reichel, *Comparative Criminal Justice Systems: A Topical Approach* (Upper Saddle River, N.J.: Prentice Hall, 1994); Brunon Holyst, *Comparative Criminology* (Lexington, Mass.: Lexington Books, 1979); Louise I. Shelley, ed., *Readings in Comparative Criminology* (Carbondale: Southern Illinois University Press, 1981).

25. United Nations, *The United Nations Crime Prevention and Criminal Justice Program: Formulation of Standards and Efforts at Their Implementation* (Philadelphia: University of Pennsylvania, 1994); Benedict Alper and Jerry F. Boren, *Crime: International Agenda* (Lexington, Mass.: Lexington Books, 1972); Ethan N. Nadelman, *Cops across Borders* (University Park: Penn State Press, 1993); André Bossard, *Transnational Crime and Criminal Law* (Chicago: Office of International Criminal Justice, 1990).

26. United Nations, *Global Report on Crime and Justice*. See also *The United Nations and Crime Prevention: Seeking Security and Justice for All* (New York: UNDPI, 1996); and *The United Nations and Criminal Justice, 1946–1996: Resolutions, Reports, Documents and Publications*, *International Review of Criminal Policy*, Issue 47–48 (Vienna: United Nations, 1996/97).

27. G. O. W. Mueller, Michael Gage, and Lenore R. Kupperstein, *The Legal Norms of Delinquency: A Comparative Study*, Criminal Law Education and Research Center Monograph Series, vol. 1 (South Hackensack, N.J.: Fred B. Rothman, 1969).

28. Anastassios Mylonas, *Perception of Police Power: A Study in Four Cities*, Comparative Criminal Law Project Monograph Series, vol. 8 (South Hackensack, N.J.: Fred B. Rothman, 1973).

29. Setsuo Miyazawa, "The Enigma of Japan as a Testing Ground for Cross-Cultural Criminological Studies," *Annales Internationales de Criminologie, 32* (1994): 81–103; B. Hebenton and J. Spencer, "The Contribution and Limitations of Anglo-American Criminology to Understanding Crime in Central-Eastern Europe," *European Journal of Crime, Criminal Law and Criminal Justice, 2* (1994): 50–61.

30. Sheldon Glueck and Eleanor Glueck, *Unraveling Juvenile Delinquency* (New York: The Commonwealth Fund; Cambridge, Mass.: Harvard University Press, 1950).

31. Sheldon Glueck and Eleanor Glueck, *Of Delinquency and Crime—A Panorama of Years of Search and Research*, Publications of the Criminal Law Education and Research Center, vol. 8 (Springfield, Ill.: Charles C Thomas, 1974), p. 332.

32. Obi N. I. Ebbe, "Juvenile Delinquency in Nigeria: The Problem of Application of Western Theories," *International Journal of Comparative and Applied Criminal Justice, 16* (1992): 353–370.

33. Rosemary Gartner, "The Victims of Homicide: A Temporal and Cross-National Comparison," *American Sociological Review, 55* (1990): 92–106.

34. Gary LaFree and Christopher Birkbeck, "The Neglected Situation: A Cross-National Study of the Situational Characteristics of Crime," *Criminology, 29* (1991): 73–98.

35. Richard R. Bennett, "Routine Activities: A Cross-National Assessment of a Criminological Perspective," *Social Forces, 70* (1991): 147–163.

36. Richard R. Bennett and P. Peter Basiotis, "Structural Correlates of Juvenile Property Crime: A Cross-National, Time-Series Analysis," *Journal of Research in Crime and Delinquency, 28* (1991): 262–287.

37. Sam S. Souryal, "Juvenile Delinquency in the Cross-Cultural Context: The Egyptian Experience," *International Journal of Comparative and Applied Criminal Justice, 16* (1992): 329–352.

38. Adel Helal and Charisse T. M. Coston, "Low Crime Rates in Bahrain: Islamic Social Control—Testing the Theory of Synnomie," *International Journal of Comparative and Applied Criminal Justice, 15* (1991): 125–144.

39. Gregory C. Leavitt, "General Evaluation and Durkheim's Hypothesis of Crime Frequency: A Cross-Cultural Test," *Sociological Quarterly, 33* (1992): 241–263; Suzanne T. Ortega, Jay Corzine, and Cathleen Burnett, "Modernization, Age Structure, and Regional Context: A Cross-National Study of Crime," *Sociological Spectrum, 12* (1992): 257–277.

40. Christopher Birkbeck, "Against Ethnocentrism: A Cross-Cultural Perspective on Criminal Justice

Glossary

Accommodate In regard to achieving the American dream, to adjust noneconomic needs so that they are secondary to and supportive of economic ones.

Accomplice A person who helps another commit a crime.

Aggravated assault An attack on another person in which the perpetrator inflicts serious harm on the victim or uses a deadly weapon.

Aging-out phenomenon A concept that holds that offenders commit less crime as they get older because they have less strength, initiative, stamina, and mobility.

Anomie A societal state marked by normlessness, in which disintegration and chaos have replaced social cohesion.

Arraignment First stage of the trial process, at which the indictment or information is read in open court and the defendant is requested to respond.

Arson At common law, the malicious burning of the dwelling house of another. This definition has been broadened by state statutes and criminal codes to cover the burning of other structures or even personal property.

Assault At common law, an unlawful offer or attempt with force or violence to do a corporal hurt to another or to frighten another.

Atavistic stigmata Physical features of a human being at an earlier stage of development, which—according to Cesare Lombroso—distinguish a born criminal from the general population.

Attachment The bond between a parent and child or between individuals and their family, friends, and school.

Bankruptcy fraud A scam in which an individual falsely attempts to claim bankruptcy (and thereby erase financial debts) by taking advantage of existing laws.

Battery A common law crime consisting of the intentional touching of or inflicting of hurt on another.

Behavioral modeling Learning how to behave by fashioning one's behavior after that of others.

Belief The extent to which an individual subscribes to society's values.

Biocriminology The subdiscipline of criminology that investigates biological and genetic factors and their relation to criminal behavior.

Birth cohort A group consisting of all individuals born in the same year.

Boiler rooms Operations run by one or more stock manipulators who, through deception and misleading sales techniques, seduce the unsuspecting and uninformed public into buying stocks in obscure and often poorly financed corporations.

Born criminal According to Lombroso, a person born with features resembling an earlier, more primitive form of human life, destined to become a criminal.

Burglary A common law felony; the nighttime breaking and entering of the dwelling house of another, with the intention to commit a crime (felony or larceny) therein.

Case study An analysis of all pertinent aspects of one unit of study.

Certiorari, writ of A writ issued by a higher court directing a lower court to prepare the record of a case and send it to the higher court for review.

Challenges for cause Challenges to remove a potential juror because of his or her inability to render a fair and impartial decision in a case. *See also* Peremptory challenges; Voir dire.

Check forging The criminal offense of making or altering a check with intent to defraud.

Chromosomes Basic cellular structures containing genes, i.e., biological material that creates individuality.

Churning Frequent trading, by a broker, of a client's shares of stock for the sole purpose of generating large commissions.

Classical school A criminological perspective suggesting that (1) people have free will to choose criminal or conventional behavior, (2) people choose to commit crime for reasons of greed or personal need, and (3) crime can be controlled by criminal sanctions, which should be proportionate to the guilt of the perpetrator.

Commitment A person's support of and participation in a program, cause, or social activity, which ties the individual to the moral or ethical codes of society.

Community policing A strategy that relies on public confidence and citizen cooperation to help prevent crime and make the residents of a community feel more secure.

Comparative criminology The study of crime in two or more cultures in an effort to gain broader information for theory construction and crime-control modeling.

Conditioning The process of developing a behavior pattern through a series of repeated experiences.

Conduct norms Norms that regulate the daily lives of people and that reflect the attitudes of the groups to which they belong.

Confidence game A deceptive means of obtaining money or property from a victim who is led to trust the perpetrator.

Conflict model A model of crime in which the criminal justice system is seen as being used by the ruling class to control the lower class. Criminological investigation of the conflicts within society is emphasized.

Conflict theory A theory that holds that the people who possess the power work to keep the powerless at a disadvantage.

Conformity Correspondence of an individual's behavior to society's patterns, norms, or standards.

Conjugal visits A program that permits prisoners to have contact with their spouses or significant others in order to maintain positive relationships.

Consensus model A model of criminal lawmaking that assumes that members of society agree on what is right and wrong and that law is the codification of agreed-upon social values.

Constable An officer, established by the Statute of Winchester in 1285, who was responsible for suppressing

Involvement An individual's participation in conventional activities.

Just deserts A philosophy of justice which asserts that the punishment should fit the crime and culpability of the offender. *See also* Retribution.

Justices of the peace Originally (established in 1326), untrained men, usually of the lower nobility, who were assigned to investigate and try minor cases; presently, judges of a lower local or municipal court with limited jurisdiction.

Justifiable homicide A homicide, permitted by law, in defense of a legal right or mandate.

Kidnapping A felony consisting of the seizure and abduction of a person by force or threat of force and against the victim's will. Under federal law, the victim of a kidnapping is one who has been taken across state lines and held for ransom.

Labeling theory A theory that explains deviance in terms of the process by which a person acquires a negative identity, such as "addict" or "ex-con," and is forced to suffer the consequences of outcast status.

Larceny The trespassory (unconsented) taking and carrying away of personal property belonging to another with the intent to deprive the owner of the property permanently.

Laws of imitation An explanation of crime as learned behavior. Individuals are thought to emulate behavior patterns of others with whom they have contact.

Longitudinal studies Analyses that focus on studies of a particular group conducted repeatedly over a period of time.

Macrosociological studies The study of overall social arrangements, their structures, and their long-term effects.

Mafia The entirety of those Sicilian families which, in both the United States and Sicily, are loosely associated with one another in operating organized crime.

Malice aforethought The mens rea requirement for murder, consisting of the intention to kill with the awareness that there is no right to kill. *See also* Mens rea.

Mandatory sentence A sentence that is specified by law and that a judge has no power to alter.

Manslaughter Criminal homicide without malice, committed intentionally after provocation (voluntary manslaughter) or recklessly (involuntary manslaughter).

Mass murder The killing of several persons, in one act or transaction, by one perpetrator or a group of perpetrators.

Mens rea (Latin, "guilty mind") Awareness of wrongdoing; the intention to commit a criminal act or behave recklessly.

Microsociological studies The study of everyday patterns of behavior and personal interactions.

Minimal brain dysfunction (MBD) An attention-deficit disorder that may produce such asocial behavior as impulsivity, hyperactivity, and aggressiveness.

Miranda warning A warning that explains the rights of an arrestee. An arresting officer is required by law to recite the warning at the time of the arrest.

Misdemeanors Crimes less serious than a felony and subject to a maximum sentence of 1 year in jail or a fine.

Money laundering The process by which money derived from illegal activities (especially drug sales) is unlawfully taken out of the country, placed in a numbered account abroad, and then transferred as funds no longer "dirty."

Monozygotic (MZ) twins Identical twins, who develop from a single fertilized egg that divides into two embryos. *See also* Dizygotic twins.

Motions Oral or written requests to a judge that ask the court to make a specified ruling, finding, decision, or order. May be presented at any appropriate moment from arrest until the end of the trial.

Motion to dismiss A request by the defense that the trial proceedings be terminated.

Murder The unlawful (usually intentional) killing of a human being with malice aforethought.

Negligent homicide A homicide designation used by some states to differentiate between involuntary manslaughter and situations in which the offender assumed a lesser risk.

Neuroticism A personality condition marked by low self-esteem, excessive anxiety, and wide mood swings (Eysenck).

Night watchmen Originally, thirteenth-century untrained citizens who patrolled at night on the lookout for disturbances.

Nonparticipant observation A study in which investigators observe closely but do not become participants.

Occupational crimes Crimes committed by an individual for his or her own benefit, in the course of performing a profession.

Organizational due diligence Implementation of effective ethics corporate compliance programs, which may include cooperating with authorities, creating an ethics code, and hiring ethics officers.

Parens patriae (Latin, "father of the fatherland") Assumption by the state of the role of guardian over children whose parents are deemed incapable or unworthy.

Parole Supervised conditional release of a convicted prisoner before expiration of the sentence of imprisonment.

Participant observation Collection of information through involvement in the social life of the group a researcher is studying.

Penitentiary A prison or place of confinement and correction for persons convicted of felonies; originally, a place where convicts did penance.

Penologists Social scientists who study and apply the theory and methods of punishment for crime.

Peremptory challenges Challenges (limited in number) by which a potential juror may be dismissed by either the prosecution or the defense without assignment of reason. *See also* Challenges for cause; Voir dire.

Phrenology A nineteenth-century theory based on the hypothesis that human behavior is localized in certain specific brain and skull areas. According to this theory, criminal behavior can be determined by the bumps on the head.

Physiognomy The study of facial features and their relation to human behavior.

Pimp A procurer or manager of prostitutes who provides access to prostitutes and protects and exploits them, living off their proceeds.

Plea bargaining Making an agreement between defense and prosecution for certain leniencies in return for a guilty plea.

Plead To respond to a criminal charge. Forms of pleas are guilty, not guilty, and nolo contendere.

Police subculture The result of socialization and bonding among police officers due to the stress and anxiety produced on the job.

Population A large group of persons in a study.

Pornography The portrayal, by whatever means, of lewd or obscene (sexually explicit) material prohibited by law.

Positivist school A criminological perspective that uses the scientific methods of the natural sciences and suggests that human behavior is a product of social, biological, psychological, or economic forces.

Preliminary hearing A preview of a trial held in court before a judge, in which the prosecution must produce sufficient evidence of guilt for the case to be bound over for the grand jury or to proceed to trial.

Presumptive sentence A sentence whose length is specified by law but that may be modified by a judge under limited circumstances.

Prima facie case A case in which there is as much evidence as would warrant the conviction of the defendant if properly proved in court, unless contradicted; a case that meets evidentiary requirements for grand-jury indictment.

Primary data Facts and observations that researchers gather by conducting their own measurements for a study.

Prisonization A socialization process in which new prisoners learn the ways of prison society, including rules, hierarchy, customs, and culture.

Proactive corporate fault The failure of a corporation to prevent ethical or legal violations.

Probable cause A set of facts that would induce a reasonable person to believe that an accused person committed the offense in question; the minimum evidence requirement for an arrest, according to the Fourth Amendment to the U.S. Constitution.

Probation An alternative to imprisonment, allowing a person found guilty of an offense to stay in the community, under conditions and with supervision.

Problem-oriented policing A strategy to enhance community relations and to improve crime prevention whereby police work with citizens to identify and respond to problems in a given community.

Proprietary economic information Any information, whether tangible or intangible, that a corporation has made reasonable efforts to keep confidential.

Prosecutor An attorney and government official who represents the people in proceedings against persons accused of criminal acts.

Prostitution The practice of engaging in sexual activities for hire.

Psychoanalytic theory In criminology, a theory of criminality that attributes delinquent and criminal behavior to a conscience that is either so overbearing that it arouses excessive feelings of guilt or so weak that it cannot control the individual's impulses.

Psychopathy A condition in which a person appears to be psychologically normal but in reality has no sense of responsibility, shows disregard for truth, is insincere, and feels no sense of shame, guilt, or humiliation (also called "sociopathy").

Psychosis A mental illness characterized by a loss of contact with reality.

Psychoticism A dimension of the human personality describing individuals who are aggressive, egocentric, and impulsive (Eysenck).

Racketeer Influenced and Corrupt Organizations (RICO) Act A federal statute that provides for forfeiture of assets derived from a criminal enterprise.

Radical criminology A criminological perspective that studies the relationships between economic disparity and crime, avers that crime is the result of a struggle between owners of capital and workers for the distribution of power and resources, and posits that crime will disappear only when capitalism is abolished.

Random sample A sample chosen in such a way as to ensure that each person in the population to be studied has an equal chance of being selected. *See also* Sample.

Rape At common law, a felony consisting of the carnal knowledge (intercourse), by force and violence, by a man of a woman (not his wife) against her will. The stipulation that the woman not be the man's wife is omitted in modern statutes. Many states now call rape "sexual assault."

Rational choice A theory stating that crime is the result of a decision-making process in which the offender weighs the potential penalties and rewards of committing a crime.

Reaction formation An individual response to anxiety in which the person reacts to a stimulus with abnormal intensity or inappropriate conduct.

Reactive corporate fault The failure of a corporation to respond responsibly to the discovery of an ethical or legal violation.

Reasonable suspicion Warranted suspicion (short of probable cause) that a person may be engaged in the commission of a crime.

Rehabilitation A punishment philosophy that asserts that through proper correctional intervention, a criminal can be reformed into a law-abiding citizen.

Restorative justice An approach to sentencing that seeks both to restore those who have suffered from a crime to their original sense of well-being and to make it clear that justice itself is being restored.

Retribution An "eye for an eye" philosophy of justice. *See also* Just deserts.

Robbery The taking of the property of another, or out of his or her presence, by means of force and violence or the threat thereof.

Routine activity A theory stating that an increase or decrease in crime rates can be explained by changes in the daily habits of potential victims; based on the expectation that crimes will occur where there is a suitable target unprotected by guardians.

Sample A selected subset of a population to be studied. *See also* Random sample.

Secondary data Facts and observations that were previously collected for a different study.

Selective incapacitation The targeting of high-risk and recidivistic offenders for rigorous prosecution and incarceration.

Self-report surveys Surveys in which respondents answer in a confidential interview or, most often, by completing an anonymous questionnaire.

Sentencing commissions Independent agencies authorized by a legislature to create sentencing guidelines.

Serial murder The killing of several victims over a period of time by the same perpetrator(s).

Sheriff The principal law enforcement officer of a county.

Sherman Antitrust Act An act (1890) of Congress prohibiting any contract, conspiracy, or combination of business interests in restraint of foreign or interstate trade.

Shock incarceration (SI) Short-term, high-intensity confinement intended to shock convicts into disciplined lifestyles.

Shoplifting Stealing goods from stores or markets.

Simple assault An attack that inflicts little or no physical harm on the victim.

Social control theory An explanation of criminal behavior that focuses on control mechanisms, techniques, and strategies for regulating human behavior, leading to conformity or obedience to society's rules, and which posits that deviance results when social controls are weakened or break down, so that individuals are not motivated to conform to them.

Social disorganization theory A theory of criminality in which the breakdown of effective social bonds, primary-group associations, and social controls in neighborhoods and communities is held to result in development of high-crime areas.

Social interactionists Scholars who view the human self as formed through a process of social interaction.

Social learning theory A theory of criminality that maintains that delinquent behavior is learned through the same psychological processes as nondelinquent behavior, e.g., through reinforcement.

Social norms Perceived standards of acceptable behavior prevalent among members of a society.

Sociopaths Persons who have no sense of responsibility; show disregard for truth; are insincere; and feel no sense of shame, guilt, or humiliation.

Sodomy Sexual intercourse by mouth or anus; a felony at common law.

Somatotype school A criminological perspective that relates body build to behavioral tendencies, temperament, susceptibility to disease, and life expectancy.

Statutory rape Sexual intercourse with a person incapable of giving legally relevant consent, because of immaturity (below age) or mental or physical condition.

Sting operation An undercover operation in which police officers attract likely perpetrators by posing as criminals.

Stock manipulation An illegal practice of brokers in which clients are led to believe that the price of a particular stock will rise, thus creating an artificial demand for it.

Strain theory A criminological theory positing that a gap between culturally approved goals and legitimate means of achieving them causes frustration that leads to criminal behavior.

Stranger homicide Criminal homicide committed by a person unknown and unrelated to the victim.

Strict liability Liability for a crime or violation imposed without regard to the actor's guilt; criminal liability without mens rea. *See also* Mens rea.

Subculture A subdivision within the dominant culture that has its own norms, beliefs, and values.

Subcultures of violence Subcultures with values that demand the overt use of violence in certain social situations.

Superego In psychoanalytic theory, the conscience, or those aspects of the personality that threaten the person or impose a sense of guilt or psychic suffering and thus restrain the id.

Survey The systematic collection of information by asking questions in questionnaires or interviews.

Synnomie A societal state, the opposite of anomie, marked by social cohesion achieved through the sharing of values.

Target hardening A crime-prevention technique that seeks to make it more difficult to commit a given offense, by better protecting the threatened object or person.

Team policing A strategy for improving contacts between citizens and police, whereby a team of officers is responsible for a specific neighborhood on a 24-hour basis.

Terrorism The use of violence against a target to create fear, alarm, dread, or coercion for the purpose of obtaining concessions or rewards or commanding public attention for a political cause.

Theories of victimization Theories that explain the role that victims play in the crimes that happen to them.

Theory A coherent group of propositions used as principles in explaining or accounting for known facts or phenomena.

Tithing In Anglo-Saxon law, an association of 10 families bound together by a frankpledge, for purposes of crime control. *See also* Frankpledge.

Torts Injuries or wrongs committed against another, subject to compensation; infringements of the rights of an individual that are not founded on either contract or criminal law prohibition.

Transnational crime A criminal act or transaction violating the laws of more than one country or having an impact on a foreign country.

Utilitarianism A criminological perspective positing that crime prevention and criminal justice must serve the end of providing the greatest good for the greatest number;

specific brain and skull areas. According to this theory, criminal behavior can be determined by the bumps on the head.

Physiognomy The study of facial features and their relation to human behavior.

Pimp A procurer or manager of prostitutes who provides access to prostitutes and protects and exploits them, living off their proceeds.

Plea bargaining Making an agreement between defense and prosecution for certain leniencies in return for a guilty plea.

Plead To respond to a criminal charge. Forms of pleas are guilty, not guilty, and nolo contendere.

Police subculture The result of socialization and bonding among police officers due to the stress and anxiety produced on the job.

Population A large group of persons in a study.

Pornography The portrayal, by whatever means, of lewd or obscene (sexually explicit) material prohibited by law.

Positivist school A criminological perspective that uses the scientific methods of the natural sciences and suggests that human behavior is a product of social, biological, psychological, or economic forces.

Preliminary hearing A preview of a trial held in court before a judge, in which the prosecution must produce sufficient evidence of guilt for the case to be bound over for the grand jury or to proceed to trial.

Presumptive sentence A sentence whose length is specified by law but that may be modified by a judge under limited circumstances.

Prima facie case A case in which there is as much evidence as would warrant the conviction of the defendant if properly proved in court, unless contradicted; a case that meets evidentiary requirements for grand-jury indictment.

Primary data Facts and observations that researchers gather by conducting their own measurements for a study.

Prisonization A socialization process in which new prisoners learn the ways of prison society, including rules, hierarchy, customs, and culture.

Proactive corporate fault The failure of a corporation to prevent ethical or legal violations.

Probable cause A set of facts that would induce a reasonable person to believe that an accused person committed the offense in question; the minimum evidence requirement for an arrest, according to the Fourth Amendment to the U.S. Constitution.

Probation An alternative to imprisonment, allowing a person found guilty of an offense to stay in the community, under conditions and with supervision.

Problem-oriented policing A strategy to enhance community relations and to improve crime prevention whereby police work with citizens to identify and respond to problems in a given community.

Proprietary economic information Any information, whether tangible or intangible, that a corporation has made reasonable efforts to keep confidential.

Prosecutor An attorney and government official who represents the people in proceedings against persons accused of criminal acts.

Prostitution The practice of engaging in sexual activities for hire.

Psychoanalytic theory In criminology, a theory of criminality that attributes delinquent and criminal behavior to a conscience that is either so overbearing that it arouses excessive feelings of guilt or so weak that it cannot control the individual's impulses.

Psychopathy A condition in which a person appears to be psychologically normal but in reality has no sense of responsibility, shows disregard for truth, is insincere, and feels no sense of shame, guilt, or humiliation (also called "sociopathy").

Psychosis A mental illness characterized by a loss of contact with reality.

Psychoticism A dimension of the human personality describing individuals who are aggressive, egocentric, and impulsive (Eysenck).

Racketeer Influenced and Corrupt Organizations (RICO) Act A federal statute that provides for forfeiture of assets derived from a criminal enterprise.

Radical criminology A criminological perspective that studies the relationships between economic disparity and crime, avers that crime is the result of a struggle between owners of capital and workers for the distribution of power and resources, and posits that crime will disappear only when capitalism is abolished.

Random sample A sample chosen in such a way as to ensure that each person in the population to be studied has an equal chance of being selected. *See also* Sample.

Rape At common law, a felony consisting of the carnal knowledge (intercourse), by force and violence, by a man of a woman (not his wife) against her will. The stipulation that the woman not be the man's wife is omitted in modern statutes. Many states now call rape "sexual assault."

Rational choice A theory stating that crime is the result of a decision-making process in which the offender weighs the potential penalties and rewards of committing a crime.

Reaction formation An individual response to anxiety in which the person reacts to a stimulus with abnormal intensity or inappropriate conduct.

Reactive corporate fault The failure of a corporation to respond responsibly to the discovery of an ethical or legal violation.

Reasonable suspicion Warranted suspicion (short of probable cause) that a person may be engaged in the commission of a crime.

Rehabilitation A punishment philosophy that asserts that through proper correctional intervention, a criminal can be reformed into a law-abiding citizen.

Restorative justice An approach to sentencing that seeks both to restore those who have suffered from a crime to their original sense of well-being and to make it clear that justice itself is being restored.

Retribution An "eye for an eye" philosophy of justice. *See also* Just deserts.

Robbery The taking of the property of another, or out of his or her presence, by means of force and violence or the threat thereof.

Routine activity A theory stating that an increase or decrease in crime rates can be explained by changes in the daily habits of potential victims; based on the expectation that crimes will occur where there is a suitable target unprotected by guardians.

Sample A selected subset of a population to be studied. *See also* Random sample.

Secondary data Facts and observations that were previously collected for a different study.

Selective incapacitation The targeting of high-risk and recidivistic offenders for rigorous prosecution and incarceration.

Self-report surveys Surveys in which respondents answer in a confidential interview or, most often, by completing an anonymous questionnaire.

Sentencing commissions Independent agencies authorized by a legislature to create sentencing guidelines.

Serial murder The killing of several victims over a period of time by the same perpetrator(s).

Sheriff The principal law enforcement officer of a county.

Sherman Antitrust Act An act (1890) of Congress prohibiting any contract, conspiracy, or combination of business interests in restraint of foreign or interstate trade.

Shock incarceration (SI) Short-term, high-intensity confinement intended to shock convicts into disciplined lifestyles.

Shoplifting Stealing goods from stores or markets.

Simple assault An attack that inflicts little or no physical harm on the victim.

Social control theory An explanation of criminal behavior that focuses on control mechanisms, techniques, and strategies for regulating human behavior, leading to conformity or obedience to society's rules, and which posits that deviance results when social controls are weakened or break down, so that individuals are not motivated to conform to them.

Social disorganization theory A theory of criminality in which the breakdown of effective social bonds, primary-group associations, and social controls in neighborhoods and communities is held to result in development of high-crime areas.

Social interactionists Scholars who view the human self as formed through a process of social interaction.

Social learning theory A theory of criminality that maintains that delinquent behavior is learned through the same psychological processes as nondelinquent behavior, e.g., through reinforcement.

Social norms Perceived standards of acceptable behavior prevalent among members of a society.

Sociopaths Persons who have no sense of responsibility; show disregard for truth; are insincere; and feel no sense of shame, guilt, or humiliation.

Sodomy Sexual intercourse by mouth or anus; a felony at common law.

Somatotype school A criminological perspective that relates body build to behavioral tendencies, temperament, susceptibility to disease, and life expectancy.

Statutory rape Sexual intercourse with a person incapable of giving legally relevant consent, because of immaturity (below age) or mental or physical condition.

Sting operation An undercover operation in which police officers attract likely perpetrators by posing as criminals.

Stock manipulation An illegal practice of brokers in which clients are led to believe that the price of a particular stock will rise, thus creating an artificial demand for it.

Strain theory A criminological theory positing that a gap between culturally approved goals and legitimate means of achieving them causes frustration that leads to criminal behavior.

Stranger homicide Criminal homicide committed by a person unknown and unrelated to the victim.

Strict liability Liability for a crime or violation imposed without regard to the actor's guilt; criminal liability without mens rea. *See also* Mens rea.

Subculture A subdivision within the dominant culture that has its own norms, beliefs, and values.

Subcultures of violence Subcultures with values that demand the overt use of violence in certain social situations.

Superego In psychoanalytic theory, the conscience, or those aspects of the personality that threaten the person or impose a sense of guilt or psychic suffering and thus restrain the id.

Survey The systematic collection of information by asking questions in questionnaires or interviews.

Synnomie A societal state, the opposite of anomie, marked by social cohesion achieved through the sharing of values.

Target hardening A crime-prevention technique that seeks to make it more difficult to commit a given offense, by better protecting the threatened object or person.

Team policing A strategy for improving contacts between citizens and police, whereby a team of officers is responsible for a specific neighborhood on a 24-hour basis.

Terrorism The use of violence against a target to create fear, alarm, dread, or coercion for the purpose of obtaining concessions or rewards or commanding public attention for a political cause.

Theories of victimization Theories that explain the role that victims play in the crimes that happen to them.

Theory A coherent group of propositions used as principles in explaining or accounting for known facts or phenomena.

Tithing In Anglo-Saxon law, an association of 10 families bound together by a frankpledge, for purposes of crime control. *See also* Frankpledge.

Torts Injuries or wrongs committed against another, subject to compensation; infringements of the rights of an individual that are not founded on either contract or criminal law prohibition.

Transnational crime A criminal act or transaction violating the laws of more than one country or having an impact on a foreign country.

Utilitarianism A criminological perspective positing that crime prevention and criminal justice must serve the end of providing the greatest good for the greatest number;

based on the rationality of lawgivers, law enforcers, and the public at large.

Variables Changeable factors.

Vicarious liability The imputation of liability from an agent to a principal, e.g., from an employee to an employer.

Victim precipitation Opening oneself up, by either direct or subliminal means, to a criminal response.

Victimization surveys Surveys that measure the extent of crime by interviewing individuals about their experiences as victims.

Vindication Condemnation of the commission of offenses.

Violations Minor criminal offenses, usually under a city ordinance, commonly subject only to a fine.

Voir dire A process in which lawyers and a judge question potential jurors in order to select those who are acceptable, that is, those who are unbiased and objective in relation to the particular trial. *See also* Challenges for cause; Peremptory challenges.

Voluntary manslaughter Homicide in which the perpetrator intentionally, but without malice, causes the death of another person, as in the heat of passion, in response to strong provocation, or possibly under severe intoxication.

Whistle-blower An employee, or interested party, who reports corporate illegalities to authorities.

White-collar crime A sociological concept encompassing any violation of the law committed by a person or group of persons in the course of an otherwise respected and legitimate occupation or business enterprise.

Credits

PHOTO CREDITS

Name Index

Italicized page numbers indicate material in captions, tables, and figures. Page numbers followed by "n." indicate source notes in text; those preceded by "N" indicate material in "Notes" section.

A

Abadinsky, Howard, 256, 350, N–27, N–36
Abdel-aziz, Atiqui, N–25
Abraham, Nathaniel, *178*
Abrahamsen, David, N–24
Adams, Anthony, N–13
Adams, Reed, N–9
Adler, Amy, 365n.
Adler, Freda, 51, 61n., 121, 180–181, 181n., 195, 289n., N–1, N–4, N–11, N–15, N–17, N–19, N–22, N–31, N–36, N–42, N–43
Adler, Jeffrey S., N–19
Adler, Jerry, N–29
Adler, Nanci, N–1, N–40
Adrian, Raine, N–7
Africa, John, 135
Ageton, Suzanne S., 52, N–3, N–10, N–17
Aglipay, Edgar, N–35
Agnew, Robert, 121, 169, *177*, 180–181, N–4, N–10, N–11, N–13, N–16, N–17
Agusti, Filiberto, N–35
Ahlstrom-Laakso, S., N–38
Aichhorn, August, N–8
Aigner, Stephen M., N–4
Akers, Ronald L., 99, 169, 192, N–9, N–13, N–18
Alamo, Tony, *301*
Albanese, Jay S., 257, N–27, N–28
Albini, Joseph, N–27
Albonetti, Celesta A., N–19
Albrecht, Steve W., N–32
Alder, Christine, N–26
Alexander, Shana, N–27
Aley, James, N–40
Alper, Benedict, N–41
Alter, Jonathan, N–37
Amaechi, Rotimi, 161
Ames, M. Ashley, N–25
Amir, Menachem, 251, N–26, N–38
Anastasia, Albert, 258
Ancel, Marc, N–5
Anderson, Annelise Graebner, N–27
Anderson, Bo, N–15
Anderson, Elijah, 146, N–13
Anderson, Pamela, 246
Anderson, Terry M., *105n.*
Andrews, D. W., N–9
Andrienko, Yuri, 149n.

B

Baarda, B., N–9
Bacher, J.-L., 33, N–2
Bachman, Jerald, N–2
Bacich, Anthony R., N–25
Bai, Matt, N–29
Bailey, William C., N–26
Bakalar, James, N–36
Baker, Al, 189n.
Baker, Raymond, 6n.
Baker, Rodger, 261n.
Ball, John C., N–36
Ball, Richard A., N–16
Balladares, Ernesto Perez, 347
Balliofyne, Scott, N–42
Balsamo, William, N–27
Bamfield, Joshua, N–30
Bandura, Albert, 97, 99, N–8
Barbara, Joseph, 258–259
Barclay, Gordon, 149n.
Barnes, H. V., N–2, N–5
Barnes, Harry Elmer, 59
Barnett, Cynthia, *313n.*, *314n.*
Barnett, W. Steven, N–11
Baron, Stephen W., N–13
Barovick, Harriet, 174n.
Barron, R. A., N–39
Barton, Mark O., 239
Bartusch, Dawn R. Jeglum, N–3, N–12

Anglin, Deirdre, N–24
Anglin, M. Douglas, N–9, N–37
Applegate, Brandon K., N–38
Applewhite, Marshall, 132–133
Arbuthnot, Jack, N–8
Archer, Dane, N–24, N–40
Argomaniz, J., N–2
Aristotle, 196
Arlacchi, Pino, N–27
Arneklev, B. J., N–17
Arnold, Rolf, N–33
Arrigo, Bruce A., 203, N–20
Arthur, John A., N–30, N–42
Asahara, Shoko, *133*, 268
Aultman, Madeline G., N–17
Austin, James, 183n.
Austin, Roy L., N–3
Austin, W. Timothy, N–17
Avary, D'Aunn Webster, 306, N–21, N–31
Avison, William R., N–11
Awlaki, Anwar al-, 5
Ayat, Mohammed, 247, N–25

Barzini, Luigi, N–27
Bashir, Omar Hassan Ahmed, 198–199
Basiotis, P. Peter, N–41
Baskin, Deborah R., N–13, N–37
Bassiouni, M. Cherif, N–43
Baucus, Melissa, N–32
Baudouin, H. de, N–7
Baum, K., 219n.
Baumer, Eric P., *120n.*
Baumer, Terry L., N–26
Baus, Stephanie A., N–39
Beccaria, Cesare, 1, 57–63, *59*, *74*, 76, 196, N–5
Becker, Ed, N–27
Becker, Gary S., N–20
Becker, Howard S., 186, 188–189, 192, N–18
Beeman, E. A., N–7
Beha, James A., II, N–29
Beirne, Piers, N–5, N–40
Belanger, Mathieu, N–21
Bell, P. A., N–39
Bell, Ralph, N–22
Bellair, Paul E., N–12
Bellamy, Lisa C., N–22
Bellis, David J., N–39
Belliston, Lara M., N–17
Bellucci, Charles, N–22
Benamati, Dennis, N–41
Bennett, Nathan, N–26
Bennett, Wayne W., N–31
Bennett, William, 55
Benson, Bruce L., N–37
Benson, Michael L., N–32, N–35
Bentham, Jeremy, 58, 62–64, 63n., *74*, 196, N–5, N–20
Bentler, P. M., N–37
Bequai, August, N–32
Berbaum, Michael L., N–22
Berger, Dale E., N–42
Berger, Herbert, N–38
Berger, Phil, N–33
Berk, Richard A., 25, 357, 357n., N–25
Berkey, Martha Lou, N–31
Berkowitz, David "Son of Sam," 235
Bernard, Thomas J., N–10, N–11
Bernardo, Mark A. de, N–37
Berrueta-Clement, John R., N–11
Bersten, Michael, N–32
Berthelsen, Christian, N–26

Lemaitre, Andre, N–33
Lemaitre, Rolf, N–33
Lemert, Edwin M., 186–187, N–18
Lemert, Edwin W., 291, N–31
Lencz, T., N–7
Lenin, V. I., 9
Lensing, H., N–42
Leonard, Kenneth E., N–25, N–38
Leonard, Kimberly K., N–16
Leon Radzinowicz, N–5
Leung, Rebecca, N–28
Levi, Michael, N–31
Levin, Jack, 239, N–24, N–42
Levine, Betti Jane, N–16
Levine, Dennis, 315
Levine, James, N–2
Levinson, David, N–25
Levitt, Steven D., 233, N–23
Levung, Shirley, 133n.
Lewis, Matthew W., N–38
Lewis, Michael, N–8
Lewis, Norman, N–27
Lewis, Oscar, 113, N–10
Liazos, Alexander, N–13, N–18
Lieberman, Alicia F., N–8
Liebl, Karlhans, N–32
Lightner, Candy, 353
Lightner, Cari, 353
Lindbergh, Charles, 254
Linden, R., N–38
Link, Bruce G., N–18, N–35, N–38
Linquist, P., N–38
Lipstadt, Deborah, 198, 199n.
Liska, Allen E., N–12, N–16
Little, G. L., N–8
Little, Heather M., N–7
Littman, R. A., N–9
Litton, Roger, N–33
Liu, Jianhong, N–12
Lizotte, Alan J., 195, 277, N–13, N–14, N–17, N–19, N–29
Lobi, Nadya, N–29
Locke, John, 59
Loeber, Rolf, N–12
Loftin, Colin, 146, N–14, N–23, N–29
Lofvers, Jeff, 168, N–16
Logan, John, *288*
Lohan, Lindsay, 18–19
Lombness, Michael, N–35
Lombroso, Cesare, 1, 12, 50–51, 65–67, *67*, 71, *74*, 81, 82, N–4, N–5
Lombroso, Gina, 103
Looman, Terah, N–22
Lopez, Pedro Alonso "Monster of the Andes," 235

Loring, Pamela L., N–11
Loughlin, Julia, N–37
Louis XV, 59
Lovell, Constance, 102, N–9
Lowney, Jeremiah, N–39
Lu, Chunmeng, N–21
Lucania, Salvatore "Lucky Luciano," 256, 259
Luckenbill, David F., N–24, N–39
Lunde, D. T., N–7
Lundman, Richard J., N–33, N–34
Luper, Steven Foy, N–37
Lupsha, Peter A., N–27
Lurigio, Arthur J., N–35, N–36
Lyman, Michael D., N–36
Lynch, James P., N–22, N–41
Lynum, Donald R., N–3
Lyston, Douglas S., N–37

M

Ma, Yue, N–40
Maahs, Jeff, N–11
Maakestad, William J., N–34, N–35
Maas, Peter, N–27
MacCoun, Robert J., N–37
MacDonald, John M., N–17, N–31
Macey, Jonathan R., N–35
MacKenzie, D. L., 33, N–2
Macphail, Daniel D., N–8
Madden, Owney, 256
Madoff, Bernard L., 309, *309*, 377
Maestro, Marcello T., N–5
Magaddino, Stefano, 258
Magedanz, T., N–38
Magnuson, Dan, N–35
Magnusson, David, N–6
Mahar, Maggie, *347n.*
Maher, Lisa, N–32, N–36, N–39
Maier, Pamela A., N–22
Makofsky, Abraham, N–37
Malekian, Farhad, N–43
Malle, Louis, 109
Malvo, John Lee, 236
Manchin, R., 48n.
Mankoff, Milton, N–20
Mann, Coramae Richey, 233, N–4, N–23, N–24
Mannheim, Hermann, 371, N–5, N–41
Manning, Wendy D., 175n.
Manson, Charles, 132
Manuel, Yolanda, *230*
Marcial, Gene G., N–33
Margaryan, Satenik, N–17
Marie Antoinette, *58*

Markowitz, Fred E., N–12
Marlowe, Douglas B., *351n.*
Marolla, J., N–26
Marongiu, Pietro, N–5, N–21
Marriott, Michael, 119n., N–12, N–37
Marshall, Ineke Haen, N–3
Marshall, S. E., N–23
Martens, Frederick T., N–43
Martin, Clyde E., N–38, N–40
Martin, Kimberly, 201, N–20
Martin, R. D., N–9
Martin, William, 254
Martins, Jens, 149n.
Marx, Karl, 196, 197, 201, N–19
Massey, James L., N–16
Mastrofski, Stephen D., N–38
Mathers, R., N–35
Matsueda, Ross L., N–12, N–16, N–17, N–18
Matza, David, 117, 170, N–11, N–14, N–16, N–18, N–22
Maudsley, Henry, 71, *74*
Mawson, Anthony R., 87, N–7
Maxfield, Michael G., N–2
Maxson, Cheryl L., N–13, N–24
Mayer, Martin, N–33
Mayfield, D., N–38
Mayhew, Pat, N–41
Mazerolle, Charles W., 175n.
Mazerolle, Lorraine Green, N–2, N–22
Mazerolle, Paul, N–11
Mazumdar, Sundip, 111
McBarnet, Doreen, N–33
McBride, Duane C., N–37
McCaffrey, Barry, 348
McCaghy, Charles, N–30
McCall, Patricia L., N–11
McClintock, F. H., N–42
McCord, Joan, 97, N–8, N–10, N–16, N–25
McCord, William, N–10
McCoy, Clyde B., N–37
McCoy, H. Virginia, N–36
McDevitt, Jack, N–42
McDonald, Mark, 289n.
McDonald, William F., N–40
McDowall, David, 277, N–12, N–14, N–29
McFadden, Robert D., N–29
McFarland, Bentson, N–32
McGuffog, Carolyn, N–8
McGuire, J., 33, N–2
McKay, Henry D., 126–127, 129, 130, N–11
McKenzie, Doris, N–11
McKinley, James C., Jr., N–3
McKinney, Aaron, 268
McMahon, Colin, N–37

Rook, Karen S., N–16
Roosevelt, Theodore, 330
Rose, Dina R., 127, N–12
Rose, R. M., N–7
Rosen, Lawrence, N–16
Rosenbaum, Jill Leslie, N–14, N–16
Rosenbaum, Marsha, N–36
Rosenbaum, Ron, 71n.
Rosenblatt, Roger, N–29
Rosenfeld, Richard, 75, *120*, 120–121, 136n., N–2, N–6, N–11
Rosenhan, D. L., N–18
Ross, E. A., 165, 338
Ross, Lee, N–21
Roth, Jeffrey A., N–3, N–6, N–37
Rothstein, Arthur, 256
Roundtree, Pamela Wilcox, N–12
Roussean, Jean-Jacques, 59
Rowe, Daryl, N–26
Rowe, David C., 83, N–6
Ruback, Barry R., N–24
Rude, George, N–5
Rudovsky, David, 56n.
Rusche, Georg, 196–197, N–19
Ruth, David E., N–27
Rutter, Michael, N–7, N–8
Ryder, Winona, *285*
Rymond-Richmond, Wenona, 199n.
Rzeplinski, Andrzej, N–20

S
Sagarin, Edward, 90, N–8
Sagi, Philip C., 234, N–23
Salama, Sammy, 217n.
Salerno, Ralph, N–33
Samenow, Stanton, 102, N–9
Samper, Ernesto, 347
Sampson, Robert J., *177*, 177–179, 192, N–3, N–5, N–12, N–17, N–18
Sanabria, Harry, *342n.*, N–21
Sanchez, Rene, N–14
Sanday, P. R., N–26
Sandberg, A. A., N–6
Sanders, Joseph, N–42
Santana, Arthur, N–35
Santino, Umberto, N–28
Savona, Ernesto U., N–27
Saxon, Miriam S., N–34
Scarpati, Mildred, 255
Scarpitti, Frank R., N–16, N–27
Scarr, Sandra, 85–86, N–7
Scatchard, Dave, *103*
Schafer, Walter B., N–13
Schaffer, Richard, N–35
Schatzberg, Rufus, N–28

Scheffer, David, 198, 199n.
Schlegel, Kip, N–35
Schlossman, Steven, N–12
Schmeidler, James, N–37
Schmidt, Janell D., N–25
Schneider, Hans Joachim, N–42
Schneider, Paul Schäfer, 132
Schoenberg, Robert J., N–27
Schoenthaler, Stephen, 86, N–7
Scholar, Michael, 38–39
Schott, Ian, N–27
Schrag, Clarence, 176–177, N–16
Schrager, Laura S., N–34
Schuessler, Karl E., 102, N–9
Schulenburg, Caroline, N–9
Schultz, Dutch (Arthur Flegenheimer), 256, 352
Schultze, Phyllis, N–41
Schuman, Karl, N–42
Schur, Edwin M., 188, N–18
Schwartz, Martin D., 253, N–20, N–22, N–26
Schwartz, Richard D., 190, N–18
Schweinhart, Lawrence J., N–2, N–11
Schwendinger, Herman, 197, 200, 252, N–19, N–26
Schwendinger, Julia R., 197, 200, N–19, N–26
Schwind, Hans-Dieter, N–42
Sciandra, Carmine, 255
Sciandra, Margaret, 255
Sciandra, Salvatore, 255
Sciolino, Elaine, N–37
Scott, Austin W., N–23
Scott, Heather, N–39
Scott, Peter, N–6
Scott, Richard O., N–29
Scott, Tamara E., 311
Scronce, Christine A., N–38
Scully, D., N–26
Sears, Kenneth C., N–31
Seda, Heriberto "New York Zodiac Killer," *79*, 79–80, 235
Sees, Karen L., N–2
Seidman, Robert, 197, N–19, N–34
Sellin, Thorsten, 49, 67, 134–135, N–3, N–5, N–7, N–13, N–14
Selva, Lance H., N–19
Semler, P. K., N–1
Sennewald, Charles A., N–30
Seper, Jerry, N–1
Serrill, Michael S., 357n.
Sesin, Carmen, N–35
Sessar, Klaus, N–40
Seydlitz, Ruth, N–16
Shackmurove, Yochanan, *221n.*
Shaffer, John W., N–37
Shakespeare, William, 65

Shakur, Tupac Amaru, 118–119, *119*, 119n.
Shannon, Elaine, N–29
Shanoff, Barry, N–35
Shapiro, D., N–20
Shapiro, Mary, *336*
Shapiro, Susan P., N–32, N–34, N–35
Shavelson, Richard, N–12
Shaw, Bud, 174n.
Shaw, Clifford R., 126–127, 129, 130, N–11, N–13
Shaw, James W., N–29
Shearing, Clifford D., N–22
Shedd, Ed, N–27
Sheldon, William H., 68–70, 74, N–5
Sheley, Joseph F., N–29
Shelley, Louise I., N–27, N–40, N–42
Shelly, Peggy, N–30
Shelton, D., N–15
Shenou, Philip, N–1
Shepard, Matthew, 268
Sherman, Lawrence W., 25, 32, 36–37, 214, N–2, N–11, N–21, N–22, N–25, N–29
Shichor, David, N–42
Shipman, Colleen, *52*
Shoemaker, Donald J., *125n.*, *141n.*, *143n.*, *150n.*, N–14, N–16
Short, James F., Jr., 131, 142, 156, N–10, N–12, N–13, N–16, N–34
Shover, Neal, 306, N–3, N–31
Sibbitt, Rae, N–37
Sickmund, M., *43n.*, N–3
Siegal, Harvey A., N–36
Sigler, Robert, N–26
Silas, Faye, N–38
Silva, Phil A., N–3, N–4, N–10
Silver, H. K., N–24
Silverman, Eli, 45
Silverman, F. N., N–24
Silverman, Robert A., 234, N–23
Silverstein, Martin E., N–14
Simmons, Christopher, 92
Simon, Jeffrey D., N–28
Simon, Patricia M., N–39
Simon, Rita James, 51, N–4
Simons, Marlise, 357n.
Simons, Ronald L., N–4
Simpson, John, N–4, N–16
Simpson, Nicole Brown, 18, 246
Simpson, O. J., 18–19, 246
Simpson, Sally S., N–4, N–21, N–32, N–35
Sinclair, Upton, 338
Singer, Peter, 62–63, 63n.

Subject Index

Note: *Italicized* page numbers indicate material in captions, tables, and figures. Page numbers followed by "n." indicate source notes.

choice structuring properties, 208

chop shops, 287, *288*

chromosomes
  defined, 82
  XYY syndrome, 82–83, *105*

churning, 315

Cinderella fairy tale, 16

Citigroup, *324*, 334

Civil War, 343

Class, State, and Crime (Quinney), 197

classical school of criminology, 57–64, *74*

Clayton Antitrust Act of 1914, 330

Clean Water Act, 332–333

Coalition Against Insurance Fraud (CAIF), 296

Coalition for Evidence-Based Policy, 32

Coca-Cola, 343

cocaine, 5, *146*, 151–154, 341–343, 345–346, 347, 348, 350

Cocaine Anonymous, 348

Coconut Grove disaster (1942; Boston), 232

codeine, 343

Code of Hammurabi (Babylon), 14, *16*

college campus crime
  date rape, 251
  drug use and abuse, 341
  relationship violence, 248
  situational theories of crime, 212

Colombia
  coca trade, 5
  drug trafficking, 151, 347, 348
  mass murder, 235, *236*
  organized crime in, 260–261

Colorado
  Columbine High School shootings (1999; Colorado), 236, 271, 273
  Denver Youth Survey, 144

Columbine High School shootings (1999; Colorado), 236, 271, 273

commitment, as social bond, 168, 169

Communications Decency Act (CDA) of 1996, 363

Communist Manifesto (Marx), 196

community-based treatment programs
  drug control, 348–350
  evidence-based policy on, 33
  just-community intervention approach in schools, 96
  rape and, 253–254

Community Tolerance Study, 117

Comparative Crime Data File, 370

comparative criminology, 368–383. *See also* international criminology
  comparative research issues, 370–372
  defined, 368
  globalization versus ethnic fragmentation, 382, 383
  goals of comparative research, 370
  history of, 368–370
  international crime, 373–374, 381–382
  practical goals of, 373–382
  theory testing, 372–373
  transnational crime, 4–11, 20–21, 374–381

Comparative Criminology (Mannheim), 371

Comprehensive Drug Abuse Prevention and Control Act of 1970, 343

CompuServe, 363

computer crime. *See* high-tech crimes

concurrence requirement for crime, 28

condition, act versus, 26

conditioning theory, 102–103

Condition of the Working Class, The (Engels), 196

conduct norms, 134–135

confidence games, 291

confidential information, 299–300, 321

conflict model of law and crime, 14–16, 193–195

conflict theory, 193–195
  comparison with other criminological perspectives, *185*
  conflict model of, 14–16, 193–195
  consensus model of, 14–16, 193
  criminology and, 194–195
  empirical evidence for, 195

conformity
  defined, 173
  in gangs, 162–163
  as mode of adaptation, *114*, 114
  personal stake in, 172–173

ConocoPhillips, *324*

consensus model of law and crime, 14–16, 193

constructive corporate culpability (CCC), 329, *330*

consumer fraud, 319

containment theory, 173–177
  evaluation of, 176–177
  "in your face" attitudes in football, 174
  probability of deviance and, 173, *173*
  tests of, 176

control theories. *See* social control theory

convenience stores, situational crime prevention, 222–223, 225

conventional morality (Kohlberg), 94–96

corn-based diet, 87

corner boys, 140

corporate compliance programs, 336

corporate crime, 322–337
  corporate fraud, 296, 334–335, 336–337, 376–377
  corporate power and, *324–325*
  curbing, 336
  defining, 322
  environmental crimes, 322, 331, 332–335, 373, 379–380
  frequency of, 322
  future of, 336–337
  government control of corporations, 330–331
  investigating, 331–332
  models of corporate culpability, 329, *330*
  nature of corporation, 328–329
  phases of corporate criminal law, 322–328
  sentencing guidelines, 322, 326–328, *328*, 336
  theories of corporate liability, 328–329

corporate ethos (CE), 329, *330*

corporate fraud, 296, 334–335, 336–337, 376–377

corporate policy (CP), 329, *330*

Correlates of Crime, 370

corruption, 190–191, 321, 381

Corruption Perceptions Index (CPI), 190–191

cortical arousal, 103

Costa Rica, crime rates, 181

Costco Wholesale, 310, *325*

counteraggression, 99

Countrywide Home Loans, 293

Course in Positive Philosophy (Comte), 64

crack cocaine, *146*, 151, 152, 153, 157, 341, 346

deviance, 124–125
  crime versus, 13
  defined, 12
  labeling theory and, 186–187
  in making of laws, 12–13
  modes of deviant behavior, *116*
  probability of, in containment theory, 173, *173*
  tunnel of, *13*
diet, in biocriminology, 82, 86–87, *105*
differential association-reinforcement, 99–101
differential association theory, 124, 130–134, 139
  evaluation of, 131–134
  public policy and, 134
  of Sutherland, 130–131
  tests of, 131
differential opportunity theory, 142–145, 161–162
  evaluation of, 145
  tests of, 144–145
direct control, 176
direct experience, in social learning theory, 99
dirty money. *See* money laundering
disaster fraud, 297
disasters
  ecocide, 11, 332, *333*, 373
  natural, 3–4
Disney World, phantom crime prevention, 220–222
displacement
  in gun control, 278
  in situational crime prevention, 224–225
Division of Labor (Durkheim), 72–73
dizygotic (DZ) twins, 83
Doctors Without Borders, 161
Dodd-Frank Wall Street Reform and Consumer Protection Act, 312, 328
domestic violence, 246–248, 352
Dominican Republic, drug-trafficking organizations (DTOs), 151
dramatization of evil (Tannenbaum), 186
Dreamcatcher Foundation, 340
Drexel Burnham Lambert, 315
drift, 170
drive-by shootings, 154–155, 157, 205–206, *233*, 236, 239
driving under the influence (DUI), 18–19, 352–353, 373

dropout-delinquency relationship, 141
drug abuse and crime, 341–350
  age and, 53–54, 341
  date rape, 251
  domestic violence, 247
  drug control, 348–350
  drug trafficking, 5–7, *146*, 151–154, 157, 260–262, *342*, 346–348, 373–374, 380
  education, 350
  extent of drug abuse, 343, *344*
  fame and, 18–19
  history of drug abuse, 342–343
  international, 346–348
  legalization, 350
  medicinal use of drugs, 343
  money laundering, 346–347
  organized crime and, 260–262
  patterns of drug abuse, 345–346
  piracy and, 289
  political impact, 347–348, *349*
  treatment, 348–350
Drug Enforcement Agency (DEA), 34
Drug Use Forecasting, 346
due process, 185

E
early childhood development, 53, 54
East Jersey State Prison (New Jersey), Juvenile Awareness Program/Scared Straight, 24–25, *32*
ecocide, 11, 114, 332, *333*, 373
ecology, 125
economic issues. *See also* corporate crime; white-collar crime
  collapse of economic order under Marxist theory, 200–201
  comparative socioeconomic development in perspective, 372–373
  economic choice theory, 208–209
  economic terrorism, 317–318, 374–375
  social disorganization theory and, 127–128
ectomorphy, 68–69, 70–71
education
  and crime, 53, 54
  in drug control, 350
EEG (electroencephalogram) studies, 89–90

ego, 91–94
Egypt, ancient, 342–343
18th Street National, 151–152
Eighteenth Amendment, 256, 351–352
Eighth Amendment, 26, 92
Eight Trey Gangster Crips, 151
elder abuse, 250–251
embezzlement, 321
employee-related thefts, 321
endomorphy, 68–69, 70–71
English law, 29, 290, 291
Enron Corporation, *316*, 336–337
environmental crimes, 322, 331, 332–335, 373, 379–380
environmental criminology, 207, 218–219
environmental disasters, 3–4, 11, 322, 333, 373
Environmental Protection Agency (EPA), 332
equal protection, 185
espionage, industrial, 299–300, 321
ethical review boards (ERBs), 35
ethics
  genetic studies and, 84–85
  in research, 34–35
ethnic cleansing, 198–199
eugenics, 69
experiments, 30, 31–33, 35
extroversion, 102–103
Exxon Corporation, 322
Exxon Mobil, *324*
Exxon Valdez oil spill (1989), 11, 322, 333
Eysenck Personality Questionnaire (EPQ), 102–103

F
fairy tales, 16–17
false premises, obtaining property by, 290–291
Families First (Michigan), 182
family
  attachment theory, 96–97
  delinquency and family atmosphere, 97, *98*
  family-related crimes, 245–251
  homicide in, 234–235
  role in crime prevention, *98*, 181–182
  same-sex marriage and, 354, *355*
Fannie Mae, 10, *324*

Federal Bureau of Investigation
(FBI), 35, 44
bankruptcy fraud, 316–318
corporate fraud, 334–335
Financial Crimes Section, 296
National Crime Information
Center, 289–290
National Joint Task Force, 138
National Stolen Art File,
285–286
Stolen Boat File, 289
Suspicious Activity Reports
(SARs), 292–294
Federal Bureau of Prisons, 34
Federal Corrupt Practices Act,
330
Federal Election Campaign Act,
330
Federal Witness Protection
Program, 257–258
felonies, 28
felony murder, 231
female gangs, 156–157, 158–159,
163
Female Offender, The (Lombroso
and Ferrero), *50*
feminism
pornography and, 362
radical, 201
rape and legal system, 253
Fence (Steffensmeier), 306
fencing, 306–307
field experiments, 31–33
Fifth Amendment, 23
FinCEN (Financial Crimes
Enforcement Network), 293
Finland, hypoglycemia and
crime, 88
Firestone, *326*
First Amendment, 133, 362–363
first degree murder, 231
Florencia 13, 152–153
food additives and dyes, 87
food allergies, 86
football, "in your face" attitude,
174
Ford Motor, *324*
foreign lottery schemes, *320*
fornication, 354
Fourteenth Amendment, 92, 185
Fourth Amendment, 23
fraud, 290–297
bankruptcy, 316–318, 380
check forgery, 291
confidence games, 291
consumer, 319
corporate, 296, 334–335,
336–337, 376–377
credit card crimes, 291–294,
296

against the government,
318–319
insider-related, 321
insurance fraud, 33, 288,
294–297, 319–321, 379
land, 319
mortgage fraud, 292–294,
310–311
obtaining property by false
pretenses, 290–291
political, 321
tax, 321
telemarketing, 297, 319, *320*
Freedom Financial, 293–294
Freemen of Montana, 270–272
free will, 57–64, *74*
French law, 29, 58–59
French Revolution of 1789,
58–59
Fresno Bulldogs, 153
Fulcher v. State, 105
Fundamentalist Church of Jesus
Christ of Latter-Day Saints
(FLDS Church), 132
fundamental psychological
error, 104–105

G
gangs, 137–139. *See also names of
specific gangs*
Cohen's theory of, 140–142
current status of, 151–155
differential association theory,
131
differential opportunity
theory, 142–145, 161–162
drug trafficking, *146*, 151–154,
157, 341
female, 34, 156–157, 158–159,
163
focal concerns of members,
147–151
gang murder, 239
guns and, 146, 154–155
Miller's theory of, 148–151
motorcycle gangs, 124–125,
139, 262
new ethnic diversity in, 262
Nigerian, 160–161
power over members,
162–163
public policy on, 161–162
risk factors for membership
in, *171–172*
street gangs, 137–139, 151–154
subculture of violence,
145–147
types of, 143–144
gangsta rap, 118–119
Gangster Disciples, 153

Gecko Holdings, 297
gender and crime, 49–51
in biological determinism,
66–67
female burglars, 306
female gangs, 34, 156–157,
158–159, 163
homicide, 234
juvenile offenders, *50*
serial killers, 235
General Electric Company, *324*,
333
General Motors, *324*, 334
general strain theory, 121
general theory of crime, *177*,
179–181
General Theory of Crime, A (Hirschi
and Gottfredson), 179–180
genetics and criminality, 82–86
adoption studies, 83–84
controversy over violence
and genes, 84–85
environment versus, 85–86
IQ debate, 85–86
twin studies, 83
XYY syndrome, 82–83, *105*
genocide, 21, 198–199, 381, 382,
383
geography of crime, 214–216
Germany
crime rates, 180
fronts for terrorism, 7
genetic studies in, 83
Grimm brother fairy tales,
16–17
Nazi, 9, 67, 196–197, 198
Girls in the Gang, The
(Campbell), 156–157,
158–159
globalization, 382
global village, 20–21
glue, 343
Gods Must Be Crazy, The
(movie), 281, *281*, 308
Goldman Sachs, *326*
Good Samaritan, 26
government
control of corporations,
330–331
fraud against, 318–319
Great Britain. *See also* Ireland
arsonist characteristics, 307
British Crime Survey, 214
Cambridge Study in
Delinquent Development,
97, 178–179
Great Depression (1930 - 1939),
112, 151, 322, 336
Greece, ancient, 57, 64–65, 354,
360, 368

breaking of laws, 17–18, 20–21
concept of crime and, 13–14
consensus and conflict views
of, 14–16, 193–195
defenses, 29, 86–87, *88*, 92,
105, 105–107
ingredients of crime, 25,
26–28
legality requirement for
crime, 26–27, 29
making of laws, 12–17
organized crime and. *See*
organized crime
problems with high-tech
crimes, 305
rape and. *See* rape and sexual
assault
sentencing, 275, 322, 326–328,
328, 336
society's reaction to the
breaking of laws, 18–21
Law of the Twelve Tables
(Rome), 14
laws of imitation, 72
LEAP (for learning, earning,
and parenting), 134
Learnfare (Ohio, Virginia,
Florida, Maryland,
Oklahoma), 134, 182
learning theory, differential
association-reinforcement,
99–101
left realism, 201–202
legality requirement for crime,
26–27, 29
legalization
of alcohol, 351–352
of drugs, 350
Lehman Brothers, 10, 312, 336
lewd cohabitation, 354
life course/developmental
theory of crime, *177*,
177–179
life-course perspective, 47–49
*Life of Mr. Jonathan Wild the
Great, The* (Fielding), 306
lifestyle theories of
victimization, 213
Life You Can Save, The (Singer), 63
Lindbergh Act, 254
locations of criminal acts, 43
lockdown, 127
Lo-Jack, 288
longitudinal studies, 48
Lord of the Flies (Golding), 164
Los Angeles. *See also* California
gangs, 151–153
riots of 1992, 128
Vancouver-based
telemarketing fraud, 297
LSD, 345

M

macrosociological studies, 166
Mafia/La Cosa Nostra, 255–262
mail bombings, 303
mail-order brides, 367
Major Fraud Act (1988), 318–319
malice aforethought, 230–231
Manchild in the Promised Land
(Brown), 148–149
Maniac Latin Disciples, 153
Mann Act, 359
manslaughter
involuntary, 232
voluntary, 232
Manson Family, 132
mapping crimes, 207, 214
Mara Salvatrucha (MS-13),
137–139, 151, 153
Marathon Oil, *325*
marijuana, *146*, 152–154, 343,
344, 345
Marijuana Tax Act of 1937, 343
Martha Stewart Omnimedia, 52
Marxist theory. *See* radical
(Marxist) theory
mass murder, 235–237
Master-Thief fairy tale, 16
maternal deprivation, 96–97
McDonald's, 113–114, 235–236
McKesson, *324*
McKinsey & Co., 337
MDMA, *146*, 152, 154
measuring crime, 30–35
data collection methods,
30–34
ethics and researcher, 34–35
severity of crime, 43, *46*
Medco Health Solutions, *325*
*Medical Jurisprudence of Insanity,
The* (Ray), 71
mens rea, 27–28, 329
mental disorders, 103–107
civil commitment for sexual
predators, 107–108
insanity defense, 29, 86–87,
88, *105*, 105–107
mass murder and, 239
psychological causation,
104–105
psychopathy, 100–101,
103–104
psychosis, 102, 103
serial murder and, 239
mesomorphy, 68–69, 70–71
methamphetamine, *146*, 151–
154, *344*
MetLife, *325*
Mexico
gang members from, 151–152
gangs from, 153–154
organized crime in, 260–261

Michael Jordan Restaurants, 114
Michigan, Families First, 182
microsociological studies, 166–
170, 181–182
empirical tests of Hirschi's
theory, 168–170
evaluation of Hirschi's theory,
170
Middle Ages, 11, 16–17, 18–19,
59, 65, 197, 282, 354, 368
middle class
labeling theory and, 187–188
as measuring rod, 140
middle-class delinquency,
157–161
militias, 269–271
Milk (movie), 86–87
Miller v. California, 362
minimal brain dysfunction
(MBD), 90
Minneapolis
Minneapolis Domestic
Violence Experiment, 31,
248
Minneapolis Police
Department, 25
Minuteman Project, *270*
misdemeanors, 28, 29
mistake of fact defense, 29
Mobilization for Youth (MOBY),
161–162
modeling instigators, 99
Model Penal Code, 29, 100, 254,
354
money laundering, 5–7, *7*, 346–
347, 375–376, *377*
MoneyStation, The, 311
monopoly, 330
monozygotic (MZ) twins, 83
moral development, 94–96,
100–101
moral insanity (Pinel), 71
Morgan Stanley, *325*, *326*
morphine, 343
mortgage fraud, 292–294,
310–311
Motherland, 152
Mothers Against Drunk Driving
(MADD), 353
Motion Picture Association of
America (MPAA), 378
Motley Crüe, 246
motorcycle gangs, 124–125, 139,
262
motorcycle theft, 224–225
motor vehicle theft, 287–289
insurance fraud, 294–295, 297
most popular stolen autos,
223, 287–288
most popular U.S. cities, *223*,
287, 287–288

Panama, drug trafficking, 347
panel studies, 31
Parents Anonymous, 250
Parents Television Council, 98–99
parking facilities, situational crime prevention, 223
Parrot Middle School (Florida) after-school program, 168
participant observation, 30, 33–34
partner violence, 246
password sniffers, 304
PATHE (Positive Action Through Holistic Education), 182
PCP (phencyclidine), 152, 153–154
peacemaking criminology, *202*, 202–203
Penny Stock Reform Act of 1990, 316
Pentagon
Information Awareness Office (IAO), Total Information Awareness, 279
terrorist attack (2001), 5, 8–9, 22–23, 216–217, 262–264, 317, 376–378, 379
People's Choice Mortgage/ Countrywide Home Loans, 311
People's Temple, 133
Permanent International Criminal Court, 381
Perry Preschool Project, 122, *123*, 134
personal control theory, 170–173
failure of control mechanisms, 172
stake in conformity, 172–173
personality and criminology, 101–103
Eysenck's conditioning theory, 102–103
types of research studies on, 101–102
Peru
crime rates, 181
drug trafficking, 347, 348
mass murder, 235
Petters Company Inc., 310
Pfizer Inc., 310, *325*
phantom crime prevention, 220–222
phencyclidine (PCP), 152, 153–154
Philadelphia
After-School Activities Partnerships, 168

Communications Decency Act (CDA) of 1996 and, 363
homicide in, 233–234, 352
phrenology, 65, *66*
physiognomy, 65
pickpockets, 283–284
pimps, 355
piracy
movie/music, 378
sea, 289, 379
software, 300–301, 378
Pleas of the Crown (Hale), 253
police
Los Angeles riots of 1992, 128
police statistics, 35–37
racial profiling, 55–56, 188–189
social disorganization theory and, 127, 128
stop-and-frisk and labeling theory, 188–189
Police Foundation, 25
Polish Peasant in Europe and America, The (Thomas and Znaniecki), 125
political fraud, 321
polygamy, 132
Ponzi schemes, 309, 334, 377
Pope v. Illinois, 362
populations, 31
pornography, 360–364
child, *301, 304*, 358, 361, 363–365
definition problem, 360–361, 363–364
feminist view of, 362
online, 301–303, *304*, 358–360, 361, 363–364
Supreme Court rulings, 362–363
violence and, 361–362
positivist school, 58, 64, 69
positron emission tomography (PET) brain imaging, 90
postconventional morality (Kohlberg), 94–96
Potrero Hill Posse (PHP), 157
poverty and crime, 53, 54. *See also* social class and crime
strain theory and, 111, 112–123
subculture of exasperation, 233
subculture of violence theory, 147–151
power
conflict theory and, 194
corporate, *324–325*
of gangs over members, 162–163
spouse abuse and, 247

preconventional morality (Kohlberg), 94–96
predatory rape, 251
premeditation and deliberation, 230–231
premenstrual syndrome (PMS), 88, 105
premium diversion, 296
President's Commission on Law Enforcement and Administration of Justice, 20
President's Commission on the Causes and Prevention of Violence, 146
primary conflict (Sellin), 135
primary data, 30
primary deviations, 186–187
Principles of Criminology, The (Sutherland), 130
prison
Cradle to Prison Pipeline Campaign, 52–54
denying convicted felons voting rights, 203–204
just-community intervention approach, 96
Scared Straight program, 24–25, 31, *32*
smoke-free rules by state, 166
social class and, 52
social disorganization theory and, 127
privacy, background checks, 276–277, 279
prize promotion scams, *320*
proactive corporate fault (PCF), 329, *330*
Procter & Gamble, *325*
Professional Fence (Klockars), 306
Professional Thief, The (Sutherland), 34
professional thieves, 34, 283–285
profiling, 55–56, 188–189
prohibition, 351–352
Project Exile, 275
Project Freedom, 162–163
property crimes, 281–308
arson, 307
burglary, 210–211, 214, *221*, 305–306
comparative crime rates, 307–308
fencing, 306–307
fraud, 290–297
high-tech crimes, 297–305
larceny, 282–290
rape and sexual assault as, 251
robbery, 254–255
property insurance fraud, 297
proprietary economic information, 299–300, 321, 378

prostitution, 339–341, 354–360
  child, 356–357, 366–368
  gangs, 156
  kidnapping and, 254
protetariat, 196
psychoanalytic theory, 91–94
psychological determinism, 71,
    74
psychology and criminality, 81,
    91–107
  family-based crime
    prevention, *98*
  insanity defense, 29, 86–87,
    88, 105, 105–107
  integrated theory of, 107
  maternal deprivation and
    attachment theory, 96–97
  mental disorders, 100–101,
    103–107
  moral development, 94–96,
    100–101
  personality factors, 101–103
  psychological development,
    91–94
  rapist characteristics, 252
  social disorganization theory,
    127
  social learning theory, 97–101
psychopathy, 100–101, 103–104
psychosis, 102, 103
psychoticism, 102–103
public order crimes. *See* alcohol
    and crime; drug abuse
    and crime; sexual morality
    offenses
public punishment, *58, 59*
Puerto Rico
  arson in, 307
  gang members from, 151–152
*Punishment and the Social
    Structure* (Rusche and
    Kirchheimer), 196–197
punishment requirement for
    crime, 28

Q
Quantum 3D, 300

R
race and crime, 54–55. *See
    also* African Americans;
    Latinos/Latinas
  Cradle to Prison Pipeline
    Campaign, 52–54
  labeling theory and, 185–192
  racial profiling, 55–56, 188–189
  strain theory of, 117–118
Racketeer Influenced and
    Corrupt Organizations
    (RICO) Act of 1970, 257, 330

radical criminology, 197–200, 332
radical feminism, 201
radical (Marxist) theory,
    195–203
  abolitionist criminology, 202
  anarchist criminology, 202
  comparison with other
    criminological perspectives,
    185
  evaluation of, 200–201
  intellectual heritage of
    Marxist criminology,
    195–197
  labeling theory versus, 192
  left realism, 201–202
  peacemaking criminology,
    202, 202–203
  radical criminology and,
    197–200, 332
  radical feminist theory, 201
  since the 1970s, 197–200
  voting rights of convicted
    felons, 203–204
Raëlians, 132
Rahway State Prison (New
    Jersey), Scared Straight
    program, 24–25, *32*
rain forests, 115
Rand Corporation, 189
randomized controlled trials
    (RCT), 31–33
random samples, 31–33
rap, 118–119
rape and sexual assault, 250,
    251–254
  characteristics of rape event,
    251–252
  characteristics of rapist,
    252–253
  community response to,
    253–254
  as form of genocide, 198–199
  legal systems and, 253–254
  serial, 206
rational-choice perspective,
    208–209, 216–217
reaction formation, 140, *141n.*
reactive corporate fault (RCF),
    329, *330*
real estate
  arson, 307
  land fraud, 319
  mortgage fraud, 292–294,
    310–311
  subprime loan crisis, 9–10,
    310, 334–335
rebellion, as mode of
    adaptation, *114,* 116
Recording Industry Association
    of America (RIAA), 378

Red Riding Hood fairy tale, 16
relative and acquaintance
    violence, 234–235, 245–251
  child abuse and neglect,
    249–250
  date rape, 251
  elder abuse, 250–251
  relationship violence, 248
  spouse abuse, 246–248, 352
reloading and recovery room
    schemes, *320*
repeat victimization, 214
Republic of Ireland. *See* Ireland
retreatism, as mode of
    adaptation, *114,* 116
Revolutionary War, 69
Richmond Youth Study, 117
Rikers Island, 154
riots, 55, 128
ritualism, as mode of
    adaptation, *114,* 116
robbers and robbery, 254–255
  armed robbery, 205, 206
  carjacking as, 288
  characteristics of robbers,
    254–255
  consequences of, 255
  situational theories of crime,
    211–212
  types of robbers, 254
Robinson v. California, 26
Rochester Youth Development
    Study (New York), 157, 170
Rohypnol, 251
Roman law, 14, 282
Rome, ancient, 14, 29, 65, 282,
    368
Roper v. Simmons, 92–93
routine-activity approach, 209–
    210, 213, 216–217
Russia. *See also* Soviet Union,
    former
  Chechen rebels, 376
  child pornography and, 361
  self-reporting delinquencies
    in, 372
Rwanda, 198, 381

S
Safeway, *325*
same-sex marriage, 354, *355*
samples, 31
Sam's Club, 310
Sarbanes-Oxley Act of 2002,
    311–312, 336
satanic cults, 160
Saudi Arabia
  crime rates, 181
  economic terrorism and, 317,
    318

voting rights, denying
    convicted felons, 203–204

W

Wal-Mart Stores, *324*, 325
war crimes, 21, 198–199, 381,
    382
war on drugs, 5
War on Poverty, 122–123
Washington, D.C.
    assassination attempt on
        Ronald Reagan, 276–277
    ban on handguns, 275
    "beltway" snipers, 233, 236
    Pentagon terrorist attack
        (2001), 5, 8–9, 22–23, 216–217,
        262–264, 317, 376–378, 379
    Watergate debacle, 195
Washington Mutual Bank, 294,
    334
weapons of mass destruction, 7,
    268, 378–379
Wedtech Corporation, 318
whistle-blowers, 337

white-collar crime, 9–10, 37, 52,
    309–321. *See also* corporate
    crime
    classification of offenses, *313*
    classification of victims, *314*
    crimes committed by
        individuals, 312–314
    defining, 311–314
    examples of, 309–310
    future of, 336–337
    traditional image of criminals
        versus, 338
    types of, 314–321
    victims of, 314
White Collar Crime (Sutherland), 331
Witness for Peace, *202*
Witness Security Program
    (WitSec), 257–258
Women's Christian Temperance
    Union, 351–352
workers' compensation fraud,
    296–297
workplace homicide, 236–239
WorldCom, 336

World Crime Survey, 239–244
World Health Organization
    (WHO), 370
World Trade Center terrorist
    attacks (2001), 5, 8–9, 22–23,
    216–217, 262–264, 317,
    376–378, 379

X

X chromosomes, 82–83
XYY syndrome, 82–83, *105*

Y

Yale University, 70
Yanomami culture, 115
Y chromosomes, 82–83
Young Latino Organization, 153
Youth Crime Gun Interdiction
    Initiative, 275
Yugoslavia, 381

Z

Zamara v. State, *105*
zero-tolerance policies, 273